D0138936

To Martha

About the Author

Ron Powall

Jeremy Shapiro is professor of operations research and management in the Sloan School of Management at MIT. For 9 years he served as co-director of MIT's Operations Research Center. Previously, he was employed by Procter and Gamble, Hughes Aircraft Company, and the Port of New York Authority. He received B.M.E. and M.I.E. degrees from Cornell and a Ph.D. degree in Operations Research from Stanford. While an undergraduate at Cornell, he studied for 1 year at the University of Paris.

Dr. Shapiro has published over 50 papers in the areas of operations research, mathematical programming, logistics, supply chain management, finance, and marketing and is the author of *Mathematical Programming: Structures and Algorithms,* published by John Wiley in 1979. He is also president of SLIM Technologies, LLC, a Boston-based firm specializing in the implementation and application of modeling systems for supply chain management and other business problems. Outside interests include reading, traveling, biking, and playing tennis. He is married to Martha J. Heigham and has three children, Alexander, Lara, and Nicholas.

Contents

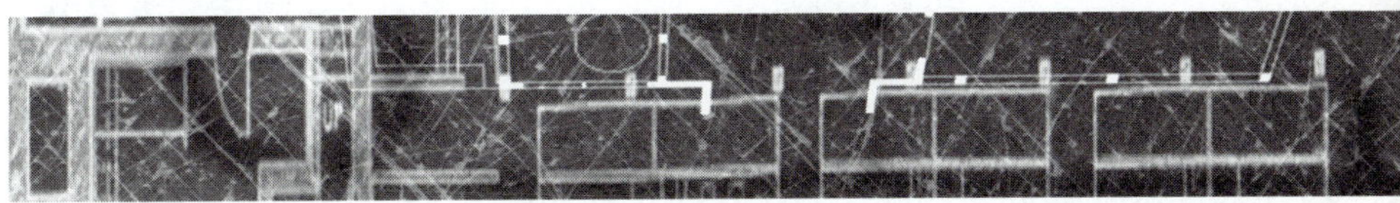

2

Information Technology 29

PART TWO Modeling and Solution Methods 61

3

Fundamentals of Optimization Models: Linear Programming 63

4

Fundamentals of Optimization Models: Mixed Integer Programming 125

5

Unified Optimization Methodology for Operational Planning Problems 177

6

Supply Chain Decision Databases 225

Preface

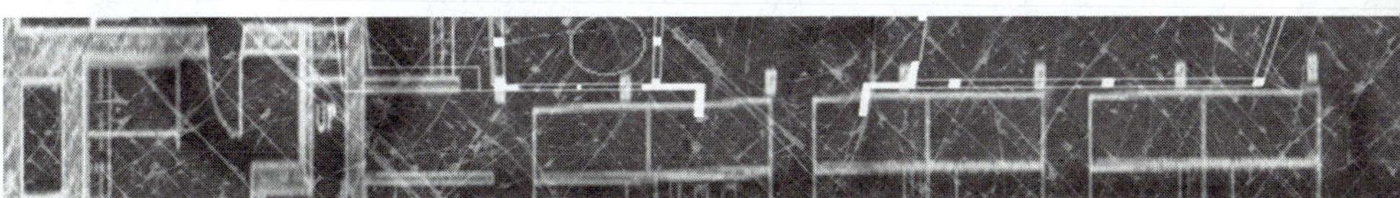

When I began writing this book 8 years ago, I was motivated by my consulting experiences applying mathematical programming (that is, optimization methods) to business planning problems. These experiences convinced me that data-driven models can and should play a central role in helping managers make decisions. As I waxed and waned in my efforts to articulate arguments supporting this viewpoint, developments in the business world and information technology put the issue in much sharper focus. These include:

- the emergence of supply chain management as a important concept underlying the strategy and operations of virtually all firms that manufacture and/or distribute products
- greater globalization in many companies of their supply chain activities
- the torrid pace of improvements and innovations in information technology, which make supply chain management possible and necessary—including faster computers, more flexible software for implementing interfaces and managing data, and the advent of enterprise resource planning systems and e-commerce
- the realization by managers that they must adapt their organizations to fully exploit information technology

As a result of these developments, many more managers today are actively seeking analytical tools to assist them in making effective supply chain decisions. Thus, the book's goal became to explain how models can be effectively constructed and applied to supply chain planning problems, rather than to argue why models must be considered for such purposes.

Although my studies and writing are still chasing the developments just cited, it is not premature to posit principles for exploiting data, models and modeling systems. In an era of dynamic change, such principles are needed to help managers identify coherent, long-term plans for acquiring systems and implementing processes that support data-driven decision making in their companies. Firms that succeed in such efforts will realize significant competitive advantage.

Harmonizing Qualitative and Quantitative Analysis

A story is told in Cambridge, Massachusetts:

> A young man, obviously a college student, is unloading his purchases at a supermarket checkout counter. A large sign above the counter indicates that it is for customers with eight items or less, but the young man has at least twenty. The clerk tells him, "You either go to MIT and you can't read, or you go to Harvard and you can't count."

The relevance of this story is: Managers and analysts need both qualitative (verbal) and quantitative (numerate) skills to achieve superior supply chain performance. On one hand, qualitative discussions about the importance of integrating decision making across the supply chain must be realized as new data collection and modeling systems and new decision processes if they are to have an impact. Conversely, despite the potential of modeling systems to reduce costs or increase profits, managers will be reluctant to use them if they have little understanding of how their decision problems are represented as models. Moreover, unless managers and analysts are given a vocabulary for describing insights into the qualitative goals of the company that models provide, modeling activities will be treated as sideshows of little importance.

Harmonization of qualitative and quantitative perspectives is also a central issue when we merge concepts from diverse management disciplines when constructing supply chain models. As we shall see, the following disciplines contribute important elements to such constructions: strategy formation, the theory of industrial organizations, operations management, logistics, transportation science, and managerial accounting. Furthermore, supply chain decisions should be integrated with marketing and financial decisions, especially when evaluating strategic plans. Quantitative models of marketing science and corporate finance, as well as qualitative concepts from these disciplines, can be used in extending supply chain models to the study of strategic planning questions from an enterprise-wide perspective.

Finally, research by organizational behaviorists into how individuals and companies actually make decisions helps managers and modeling practitioners understand the nature of barriers to fact-based decision making. These insights provide a good background for designing and implementing new business processes that overcome such barriers. In so doing, companies will better harness advances in information technology to achieve sustainable competitive advantage from the management of their supply chains.

Thus, an important goal of this book is to furnish students, managers, and analysts with discussions and examples that harmonize qualitative and quantitative thinking about supply chain planning problems and models. In so doing, we also attempt to integrate concepts and constructions from the disciplines discussed in the preceding paragraphs. Our approach relies heavily on optimization models, which provide frames or templates for such integration. Viewed another way, we will attempt to demonstrate that optimization models and methods provide comprehensive systems analysis approaches to integrated business planning, which is the essence of supply chain management.

Intended Audiences

The intended audiences for the book are as follows:

- managers who seek models and modeling systems to help them make better supply chain decisions
- information technologists who are responsible for developing and maintaining such systems, and for integrating them with enterprise resource planning and e-commerce systems
- consultants who conduct supply chain studies using models
- students who will become supply chain managers, information technologists or consultants

In other words, we intend the book to serve the needs of both initial and continuing education in the use of data and models to support supply chain decision making.

The initial objective of the book was to produce a guide for supply chain managers seeking modeling systems. In developing material supporting the merits of operations research models and methods, I examined papers and books written by academics and practitioners in the fields mentioned earlier that were concerned with issues of data, analysis, the role of information technology, and business process redesign in supporting managerial decision making. It seemed worthwhile to extend the book's scope to incorporate convergent ideas from these diverse disciplines. By adding such discussions, plus numerical examples and exercises, I believe I have created a textbook suitable for management students who wish to be educated about the form and function of practical analytical tools for supply chain management.

Overview of Content

The book is divided into four sections as follows:

Part I—Introduction to Supply Chain Management

Part II—Modeling and Solution Methods

Part III—Applications

Part IV—The Future

Part I, which comprises Chapters 1 and 2, discusses motivations for using models to analyze supply chain problems. Particular attention is paid to developments in information technology that have spawned an interest in and a need for integrated supply chain modeling and management. Part I also examines a hierarchy of linked supply chain modeling systems to support operational, tactical and strategic decision making.

Part II, which comprises Chapters 3, 4, 5, and 6, provides details of linear and mixed integer programming models for optimizing supply chain decisions. The discussion includes small examples of models for production, transportation, and inventory planning problems. Part II also explains algorithmic methods for solving these models and their economic interpretation, and provides illustrations of spreadsheet optimization formulations. Chapter 5 is devoted to the presentation of a unified optimization methodology for combining heuristic methods with mixed integer programming models to analyze operational planning problems. Finally, Chapter 6 examines in detail the supply chain decision database from which optimization models are generated.

Part III, which comprises Chapters 7, 8, 9, 10, and 11, discusses applications of modeling systems to strategic, tactical, and operational supply chain problems. Strategic and tactical planning models are examined in Chapters 7 and 8. The emphasis in Chapter 7 is on state-of-the-art applications in manufacturing and logistics. The chapter includes the presentation of several applications. It also includes a discussion of resource acquisition and allocation planning from the perspective of the resource-based view of the firm, a new paradigm for strategic planning.

The emphasis in Chapter 8 is on innovative applications to strategic and tactical planning of a supply chain. These are applications that may be beyond the current state-of-the-art, but have potential for practical applications in the future. Included are modeling approaches for integrating supply chain and demand management, for evaluating price competition among firms in an industry, and for explicit analysis of decision making under uncertainty using stochastic programming.

Chapter 9 presents modeling approaches for optimizing corporate financial planning decisions and for integrating them with models for optimizing supply chain decisions. This chapter also discusses integrated models for planning in multinational corporations that allow managers to blend decisions involving financial flows with those involving physical flows. The goal is to maximize after-tax profits that are repatriated to the parent company, subject to constraints on the performance of partially or wholly owned foreign subsidiaries.

Modeling systems for operational planning are examined in Chapter 10, including in-depth reviews of a vehicle routing system for an e-commerce company and a production planning and scheduling system for a semi-conductor company. The chapter also contains brief discussions of several other modeling applications to operational problems arising in production scheduling, vehicle routing and human resources planning.

Inventory management applications, which span all levels of planning, are discussed in Chapter 11. The chapter begins with a review of classical inventory theory, which is particularly appropriate for operational inventory decision making. We then examine methods for integrating inventory theory with optimization models for strategic and tactical supply chain planning. The chapter also includes several applications of models to inventory management in high tech and electronics firms.

Finally, Part IV, which consists of Chapter 12, discusses human and organizational issues surrounding a firm's efforts to exploit data and modeling systems when improving its supply chain management. The chapter discusses at length the conflict between a firm's desire to achieve fact-based supply chain management and the ecology of decision making that conspires to work against it. The chapter contains suggestions about business process re-design to meet the goals of fact-based decision making while overcoming organizational barriers. It also discusses factors that influence the role played by IT in providing the firm with superior supply chain management. The chapter and the book conclude with a forecast of developments in supply chain management over the next 10 years.

Exercises and Website

Except for Chapter 1, the printed book contains exercises at the end of every chapter. Some are modeling exercises while others are discussion questions. In addition, the book's Web site (www.scm-models.com) contains modeling exercises involving data files and discussion questions involving white papers. The Web site also contains hotlinks to other Web sites, organized by sections and chapters where they are relevant. The Web site is also accessible through www.duxbury.com.

Acknowledgments

My thinking and writing were influenced by that of many other academics and practitioners in supply chain modeling and related fields. In supply chain management, I would like to thank the following individuals for helpful ideas, models, and case studies: Corey Billington, Gabriel Bitran, Morris Cohen, Bill Copacino, Marshall Fisher, Arthur Geoffrion, Stephen Graves, Paul Kleindorfer, Rob Leachman, Hau Lee, Steve Klimczak, Mike Magazine, Tim Magee, Joyce Mehring, Kevin O'Laughlin, Don Rosenfield, Sridhar Tayur, Harvey Wagner, and Sean Willems. In other fields that I perused for insights into supply chain management and modeling, I would like to thank the following individuals: Jay Barney, Frank Bass, William Carleton, Arnoldo Hax, Robert Kaplan, Peter Keen, Donald Lessard, Gary Lilien, John D. C. Little, James March, Margaret Peteraf, Michael Porter, and Paul Schoemaker. I would also like to thank Linus Schrage and Wayne Winston for their interesting and comprehensive books on operations research modeling, which I found especially helpful in developing modeling examples and exercises.

For over 10 years, Vijay Singhal, Steve Wagner, and I have worked on many edifying and sometimes stressful consulting and modeling system development projects. My understanding of supply chain modeling, such as it is, is due in large part to these experiences. More recent experiences of a similar nature working with Kevin Jacobs, Francisco Jauffred, and Dan Sobbott have helped me crawl further up the never ending learning curve associated with putting theory into practice. Interactions with Fred Shepardson contributed significantly to my understanding of the practical aspects of modeling; he also provided valuable feedback on drafts of several chapters. John Bossert's careful reading of the final draft was also very helpful. Finally, Joan and Dexter Wingo displayed great skill and patience over the years in preparing the many drafts of this book.

The following reviewers provided helpful feedback on drafts of the manuscript: Hemant K. Bhargava, Pennsylvania State University; Armann Ingolfsson, University of Alberta; M. Eric Johnson, Vanderbilt University; Jerrold H. May, University of Pittsburgh; Sridhar Seshadri, New York University; Asoo J. Vakharia, University of Florida; and Wayne Winston, Indiana University.

Curt Hinrichs, my editor at Duxbury, provided unwavering enthusiasm for this project and, on several occasions, gently pushed me in valuable directions. Thanks are due to Sue Ewing of Duxbury for negotiating the scores of permissions needed to incorporate materials from other books and journals. Other individuals at Duxbury and in their production network were instrumental in transforming the manuscript to its final form: Tessa Avila and Melanie Field managed the overall production process; Nancy Young edited the manuscript; and Bill Turner created the production pages. Finally, thanks are due to Ankur Rohatgi and his colleagues at Cranomedia for developing the Web site.

Jeremy Shapiro

I Introduction to Supply Chain Management

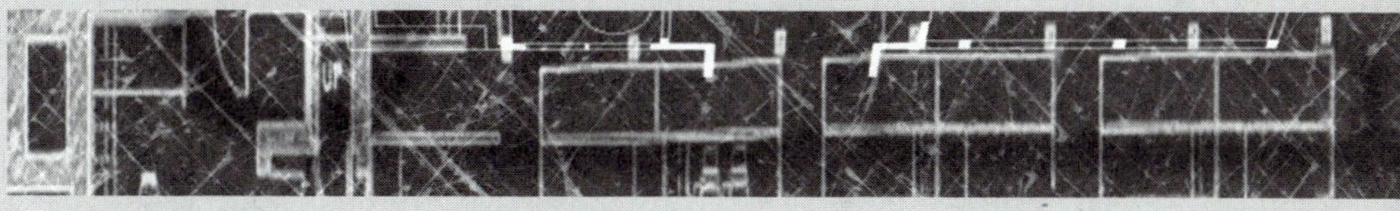

Supply Chain Management, Integrated Planning, and Models

Supply chain management is a relatively new term. It crystallizes concepts about integrated business planning that have been espoused by logistics experts, strategists, and operations research practitioners as far back as the 1950s.[1] Today, integrated planning is finally possible due to advances in information technology (IT), but most companies still have much to learn about implementing new analytical tools needed to achieve it. They must also learn about adapting their business processes to exploit insights provided by these tools.

The information revolution has accelerated significantly in recent years. Astonishing gains in personal computer (PC) computing speed, e-commerce, and the power and flexibility of data management software have promoted a range of applications. Widespread implementation of enterprise resource planning (ERP) systems offers the promise of homogeneous, transactional databases that will facilitate integration of supply chain activities. In many companies, however, the scope and flexibility of installed ERP systems have been less than expected or desired, and their contribution to integrated supply chain management has yet to be fully realized.

Moreover, competitive advantage in supply chain management is not gained simply through faster and cheaper communication of data. And, as many managers have come to realize, ready access to transactional data does not automatically lead to better decision making. A guiding principle is as follows:

> To effectively apply IT in managing its supply chain, a company must distinguish between the form and function of **Transactional IT** and **Analytical IT.**

Manufacturing and distribution companies in a wide range of industries have begun to appreciate this distinction. As a result, they are seeking to develop or acquire systems that analyze their corporate databases to identify plans for redesigning their supply chains and operating them more efficiently. An essential component of these systems are **optimization models**, which can unravel the complex interactions and ripple effects that make supply chain management difficult *and* important. They are the only analytical tools capable of fully evaluating large, numerical databases to identify optimal, or demonstrably good, plans. In addition to identifying cost minimizing or net revenue maximizing plans, optimization models can measure the trade-offs among these objectives and cost, service, quality, and time.

The application of an optimization model in a company requires the construction of an **optimization modeling system.** A key element in such a system is the **supply chain decision database,** which is derived from, but is significantly different from, the company's corporate databases. It is constructed from aggregate descriptions of the company's products, customers, and vendors. It contains the following:

- Direct and indirect cost relationships
- Submodels of production, transportation, warehousing, and inventory management
- Cost and capacity information about commodities, parts, and products offered by vendors
- Order information and forecasts of demand for finished products

Finally, it combines data inputs with outputs from model optimizations when creating graphical mapping representations of the company's current and future supply chain structure and activities.

The aim of this book is to examine in detail the roles of **data, models,** and **modeling systems** in helping companies improve the management of their supply chains. Principles of supply chain decision database and modeling system implementation will be illustrated by many successful applications. The applications will be concerned with analyzing business problems at strategic, tactical, and operational levels of planning. The ways in which companies must adapt their organizations to exploit modeling systems will also be examined.

In recent years, the number and scope of successful applications of models and modeling systems have grown significantly. Digital Equipment Corporation made extensive use of an optimization modeling system in developing downsizing strategies that produced documented net savings of over $100 million.[2] Cerestar, Europe's leading manufacturer of wheat- and corn-based starch products, implemented an optimization modeling system that increased average daily throughput by 20%, which lead to annual benefits in excess of $11 million.[3] Other companies have realized similar benefits from optimization modeling systems, although many have not publicized their successes because they believe secrecy enables them to better retain the competitive advantage provided by these systems.

Companies selling ERP systems have added modeling modules to their offerings to help customers determine effective supply chain plans based on transactional data collected and managed by their systems. SAP is completing implementation of an add-on called APO, which is made up of several modules for supply chain modeling. By acquiring CAPS Logistics, Baan added supply chain network optimization and vehicle routing modules to its suite of software packages. J. D. Edwards acquired Numetrix for similar reasons.

Despite these advances, most companies are still in the early stages of developing information technologies and implementing new business processes to promote effective supply chain management. In 1997, Boeing experienced a production foul-up that cost it billions of dollars; the company is only slowly developing new methods for lowering production costs.[4] Conagra, a $24 billion dollar agribusiness, has made a major commitment to tighter supply chain management to lower costs, in part by shutting down 15 production plants and 70 storage, distribution, and processing sites.[5] In short, in many companies, considerable room remains for improving supply chain management.

Our goal in this chapter is to set the stage for more detailed exploration of key concepts in later chapters. We will cover the following topics:

- Fundamentals of supply chain management
- Overview of supply chain models
- Supply chain modeling incorporates concepts from several disciplines
- Innovations in information technology support and require supply chain modeling
- Organizational adaptation to supply chain management and modeling

Throughout, we will use the term *optimization* to indicate that the company seeks to render its supply chain as efficient, flexible, and responsive as possible to achieve a competitive advantage. Improvements may be realized by making obvious changes in faulty business procedures, by strategic investment or divestment of assets, by better allocation of company resources, or by numerous other means. We shall argue that competitive advantage in supply chain management can be most fully realized by implementing and applying modeling systems to enhance managerial decision making.

1.1 Fundamentals of Supply Chain Management

A company's supply chain comprises geographically dispersed **facilities** where raw materials, intermediate products, or finished products are acquired, transformed, stored, or sold and **transportation links** that connect facilities along which products flow. The facilities may be operated by the company, or they may be operated by **vendors, customers,** third-party providers, or other firms with which the company has business arrangements. The company's goal is to add value to its products as they pass through its supply chain and transport them to geographically dispersed **markets** in the correct quantities, with the correct specifications, at the correct time, and at a competitive cost.

We distinguish between **plants,** which are manufacturing facilities where physical product transformations take place, and **distribution centers,** which are facilities where products are received, sorted, put away in inventory, picked from inventory, and dispatched but not physically transformed. Of course, we shall occasionally consider hybrid facilities, either plants with distribution capabilities or distribution centers with physical product transformation capabilities.

Supply Chain Networks

The supply chain is often represented as a network similar to the one displayed in Figure 1.1. The nodes in the network represent facilities, which are connected by links that represent direct transportation connections permitted by the company in managing its supply chain. Although networks are a useful device for depicting and discussing models, keep in mind that the one displayed in Figure 1.1 provides only a high-level view of a supply chain. Meaningful analysis requires the addition of considerable detail about transformation activities and processes, resources, and capacities and costs that describe facilities and transportation links.

The network of Figure 1.1 has four levels of facilities. Products flow downstream from vendors to plants, plants to distribution centers, and distribution centers to markets. In general, a supply chain network may have an arbitrary number of levels. Moreover, products may sometimes flow upstream when intermediate products are returned to plants for rework or reusable products are returned from markets to distribution centers for recycling.

We will restrict our attention to firms that manufacture or distribute physical products. The physical products may be unusual, such as electrical energy or industrial gases that are manufactured from air and electricity. Telecommunications networks could arguably be considered supply chains according to our definition. Moreover, optimization models have been successfully applied in analyzing their design and operations, although such models reflect operating characteristics that are peculiar to telecommunications.[6] Despite their importance, due to time and space limitations, we have omitted treatment of telecommunications networks in this book. Some service companies, such as banks or insurance companies, operate value chains of networks of facilities for which coordinated planning is required, although no physical products flow. We will not address analysis of such chains in this book.

Figure 1.1
Supply chain network

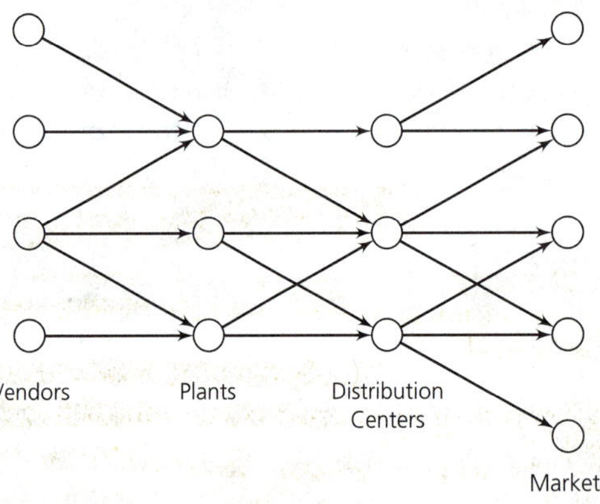

Integrated Supply Chain Planning

As we stated in the introduction, supply chain management refers to integrated planning. First, it is concerned with **functional integration** of purchasing, manufacturing, transportation, and warehousing activities. It also refers to **spatial integration** of these activities across geographically dispersed vendors, facilities, and markets. Finally, it refers to **intertemporal integration** of these activities over strategic, tactical, and operational planning horizons. Roughly speaking, strategic planning involves resource acquisition decisions to be taken over long-term planning horizons, tactical planning involves resource allocation decisions over medium-term planning horizons, and operational planning involves decisions affecting the short-term execution of the company's business.

Intertemporal integration, which also is called **hierarchical planning**, requires consistency and coherence among overlapping supply chain decisions at the various levels of planning. Although it is not yet widely appreciated, intertemporal integration is critical to the firm's sustained competitive advantage. Efficient operations will not lead to superior profits if the company's products are being manufactured in plants with outdated technologies that are poorly located relative to the company's vendors and its markets. Conversely, to evaluate a new or redesigned supply chain network, we must, at least approximately, optimize operations to be carried out under the design.

Another aspect of intertemporal planning is the need to optimize a product's supply chain over its life cycle through the stages of design, introduction, growth, maturity, and retirement. Like most areas of strategic planning, life-cycle planning requires **integration of supply chain and demand management.** For example, analysis of capital investment decisions in manufacturing equipment during the growth phase of a new product should take into account marketing decisions affecting product sales and gross revenues that may provide future returns sufficient to justify the investments.

Improved integration of activities across multiple companies sharing components of a supply chain is a concern of increasing interest and importance. Such integration is obviously relevant to the efficient operation of two companies after a merger or acquisition. It is also relevant to two companies that wish to tighten their working arrangements, such as a manufacturer of consumer durables and a major distributor of these durables or a manufacturer of food products and a wholesale grocery distributor. In such instances, integration is complicated because both companies have other vendors and customers; that is, their supply chains overlap significantly but are far from identical. Moreover, enhanced integration implies greater sharing of confidential information about costs and capacities as well as integrative management of business processes.

Developments in integrated supply chain planning have been both facilitated and required by advances in IT. Managers today have much faster access to much more complete databases than they did only 5 years ago. The challenge is to transform this capability into competitive advantage. IT developments are examined more fully in Section 1.4 and in greater detail throughout the book.

Objectives of Supply Chain Management

The traditional objective of supply chain management is to minimize total supply chain cost to meet fixed and given demand. This total cost may include a number of terms such as the following:

- Raw material and other acquisition costs
- Inbound transportation costs
- Facility investment costs
- Direct and indirect manufacturing costs
- Direct and indirect distribution center costs
- Inventory holding costs
- Interfacility transportation costs
- Outbound transportation costs

In building a model for specific planning problems, we might decide to examine only a portion of the company's entire supply chain and associated costs.

One can argue that total cost minimization is an inappropriate and timid objective for the firm to pursue when it analyzes its strategic and tactical supply chain plans. Instead, the firm should seek to maximize net revenues where

$$\text{Net revenues} = \text{gross revenues} - \text{total cost}$$

If demand is fixed and given, the implication is that gross revenues from meeting it are also fixed and given and, therefore, that the firm will maximize net revenues by minimizing total cost.

Our objection to focusing only on cost control when using an optimization model for strategic or tactical planning is that the model provides insights into product costs that should be exploited to increase net revenues by suitable adjustments in sales. For example, when planning for next year, information provided by a model about the marginal costs of products delivered to various markets could be used to change the projected sales plan. The company's sales force would be instructed to push products in markets with the highest margins, possibly at the expense of products in markets with low margins if total manufacturing capacity is limited.

The difficulty with trying to model decisions affecting demand management, even in the modest way we just described, is that it requires the commitment of marketing personnel, who generally feel uneasy with quantitative analysis. Moreover, once they agree to including marketing and sales decisions in a model, it is difficult to decide on the scope that can or should be considered. Nevertheless, integration of supply chain and demand management is an area of growing interest in many companies, although it has not yet been widely addressed.

Similarly, supply chain and demand management decisions are closely linked to corporate financial decisions, especially when planning the firm's strategy. Moreover, optimization models for exploring financial decisions linked to the corporate balance sheet, such as yearly changes in fixed assets and equity or dividends paid, have been proposed by academics for over 25 years, although they are not yet widely applied. Because these models can be seamlessly integrated with supply chain models, financial managers have recently become more interested in pursuing their implementation and use.

Of course, a company will also be concerned with nonmonetary objectives, such as customer service, product variety, quality, and time. Some authors even suggest that costs or revenues are relatively unimportant and that the company should focus instead on time, product variety, or other attributes of their business to achieve competitive advantage. Such recommendations are misleading because the company exists to earn profits. From an analytic perspective, it is not necessary to choose one objective over another. Instead, optimization models can assist management in evaluating the trade-offs among objectives.

As an example, consider the trade-off analysis depicted in Figure 1.2 between customer service, measured in days of delivery time, and supply chain cost. By days of delivery time, we mean the maximal number of days allowed for delivery to customers from sourcing locations across the supply chain; many customers will have shorter delivery times. Our analysis considers the trade-off of supply chain cost versus delivery times in the range of 1 to 4 days, which are the limits of interest to management. The curved line containing point A is called the **efficient frontier.** Any supply chain strategy on the efficient frontier is **undominated** in the sense that no achievable strategy exists that is at least as good as it is with respect to customer service and cost, and strictly better on one criteria. The efficient frontier in Figure 1.2 can be generated by iteratively solving an optimization model that minimizes supply cost subject to constraints on the maximal delivery time. Strategy A corresponds to a least-cost strategy with a maximal delivery time of 2 days.

Suppose that the company currently has a customer service policy guaranteeing delivery within 3 days and that the current supply chain cost corresponds to that of strategy B, which is off the efficient frontier. By using an optimization model, management has the opportunity to identify and implement strategy B^2 on the efficient frontier that lowers cost while maintaining the same customer service policy. Alternatively, the company could consider spending the same amount of money on supply chain management but using it more effectively to improve customer service by implementing the undominated strategy B^1. A third choice would be to reduce delivery time to 2 days and reduce cost to that of strategy A.

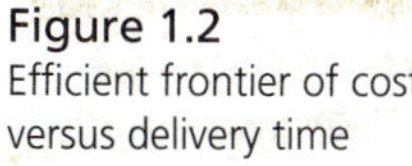

Figure 1.2
Efficient frontier of cost versus delivery time

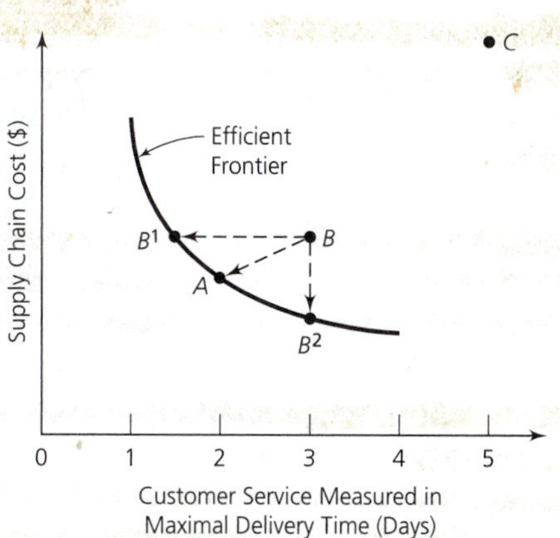

The selection of a specific strategy on the efficient frontier is left to managerial judgment, perhaps with the assistance of tools that help individual managers, or groups of managers, assess their preferences. Using a preference assessment tool becomes important when more than three objectives exist because the trade-offs cannot be easily depicted in graphical form. For such analyses, it may only be possible to sample efficient strategies, not to map out the entire frontier. In such a case, a preference assessment tool can be adapted to help managers search those areas of the efficient frontier of greatest interest.

Our assumption in promoting the use of models is that the company's supply chain is not grossly inefficient, and therefore global analysis is needed to make improvements. The strategy corresponding to B in Figure 1.2 represents such a situation in that we assume an optimization model is needed to identify the superior strategies corresponding to B^1, A, and B^2. By contrast, the strategy corresponding to C is so distant from the efficient frontier that significant improvements can be realized by obvious modifications of inefficient supply chain procedures.

For example, suppose that, due to sloppy management, cross-docking and dispatching at the company's distribution centers take much longer than industry norms. Suppose further that tightening these practices will eliminate the inefficiencies and allow maximal delivery time to be reduced to 4 days at little or no increase in cost. Such improvements are clearly important, but they can be identified without recourse to a supply chain model. Instead, they can be identified and implemented by pursuing supply chain best practices in a myopic manner.

1.2

Overview of Supply Chain Models and Modeling Systems

We have highlighted the need to augment Transactional IT with Analytical IT for the purposes of integrated supply chain planning. Analytical IT involves the implementation and application of two types of mathematical models. First, there are **descriptive models** that modeling practitioners develop to better understand functional relationships in the company and the outside world. Descriptive models include the following:

- **Forecasting models** that predict demand for the company's finished products, the cost of raw materials, or other factors, based on historical data
- **Cost relationships** that describe how direct and indirect costs vary as functions of cost drivers
- **Resource utilization relationships** that describe how manufacturing activities consume scarce resources
- **Simulation models** that describe how all or parts of the company's supply chain will operate over time as a function of parameters and policies

This list is representative of the wide range of descriptive models that the modeling practitioner might create to better understand a company's supply chain.

Second, there are **normative models** that modeling practitioners develop to help managers make better decisions. The term *normative* refers to processes for identifying norms that the company should strive to achieve. Our viewpoint is that *normative models* and *optimization models* are synonyms. Further, we view *optimization models* as a synonym for *mathematical programming models,* a venerable class of mathematical models that have been studied by researchers and practitioners in the field of operations research for over 50 years.[7] Henceforth, we will use the term *optimization models* to refer to models that might otherwise be termed *normative* or *mathematical programming.*

The construction of optimization models requires descriptive data and models as inputs. Clearly, the supply chain plan suggested by an optimization model will be no better than the inputs it receives, which is the familiar "garbage-in, garbage-out" problem. In many applications, however, the modeling practitioner is faced with the reality that although some data are not yet as accurate as they might be, using approximate data is better than abandoning the analysis. In other words, many model implementation projects pass through several stages of data and model validation until sufficient accuracy is achieved.

Supply chain managers should also realize that the development of accurate descriptive models is necessary but not sufficient for realizing effective decision making. For example, accurate demand forecasts must be combined with other data in constructing a global optimization model to determine which plants should make which products to serve which distribution centers and markets so that demand is met at minimal supply chain cost. Similarly, an accurate management accounting model of manufacturing process costs is necessary but not sufficient to identify an optimal production schedule.

Of course, to be applied, a model conceptualized on paper must be realized by programs for generating a computer readable representation of it from input data. In addition, this representation must be optimized using a numerical algorithm, and the results gleaned from the output of the algorithm must be reported in managerial terms. Programs for viewing and managing input data and reports must be implemented. Depending on the application, the modeling system must also be integrated with other systems that collect data, disseminate reports, or optimize other aspects of the company's supply chain. In short, an optimization model provides the inspiration for implementing, validating, and applying a modeling system, but the great bulk of the work is required by subsequent tasks.

Mathematical programming methods provide powerful and comprehensive tools for crunching large quantities of numerical data describing the supply chains of many companies. Experienced practitioners generally agree about what is, or is not, an accurate and complete model for a particular class of applications. Unfortunately, because most managers are not modeling experts, they can easily be taken in by systems that translate input data into supply chain plans using ad hoc, mediocre models and methods.

The opportunity loss incurred by applying a mediocre modeling system is not simply one of mathematical or scientific purity. Although a mediocre system may identify plans that improve a company's supply chain operations, a superior system will often identify much better plans, as measured by improvements to the company's bottom line. For a company with annual sales of hundreds of millions of dollars, rigorous analysis with a superior modeling system can add tens of millions of dollars to the company's net revenue, whereas analysis with a mediocre system may identify only a small portion of this amount. Such returns justify the time and effort required to develop and apply a superior system.

Thus, with the goal of converting nonexperts to more knowledgeable consumers of models and modeling systems, we provide in later chapters a detailed introduction to mathematical modeling of supply chain decision problems. We also provide a brief exposure to algorithms for optimizing these models. The mathematical development uses algebraic methods that are taught in high school, which should render it no more painful to readers than their experiences during a typical algebra class in years gone by.

A more subtle, related point is that good models and modeling systems expand the consciousness of managers and analysts regarding decision options and methods for improving supply chain design and operations. Their expanded consciousness relies on translations of qualitative and quantitative concepts from diverse management disciplines into modeling constructs employed by a modeling system. These disciplines and the relevant concepts are discussed briefly in the following section and in greater detail throughout the book.

Many of the ideas presented in this book stem from our experience in projects where optimization models were applied. Of particular relevance are applications of an off-the-shelf modeling system, called SLIM/2000, for analyzing strategic and tactical supply chain problems.[8] The principles used in constructing and applying this system and the connections between its optimization models and diverse management disciplines provided a cornerstone to our thinking.

1.3

Supply Chain Modeling Incorporates Concepts from Several Management Disciplines

At the end of the previous section, we asserted that good models and modeling systems provide the manager with a framework for representing concepts from various management disciplines, especially those concerned with improving supply chain management using data and analysis. To emphasize this point, we discuss briefly the following disciplines from the perspective of supply chain management and models:

- Strategy formation and the theory of the firm
- Logistics, production, and inventory management
- Management accounting

- Demand forecasting and marketing science
- Operations research

The relevance and application of each of these disciplines will be examined in more depth in the chapters that follow.

Strategy Formation and the Theory of the Firm

A number of important and useful concepts for analyzing supply chains from a strategic, top-down perspective are available from the field of strategy formation and related economic fields concerned with theories of the firm and how they compete. Most thinking in these fields has either been qualitative or theoretically quantitative in the sense that mathematical models are used to derive qualitative insights into the behavior of and competition among firms, not as templates for the collection and analysis of data and strategy. We can hope that strategic supply chain models to be discussed here will provide a mechanism for greater empirical testing of existing theories and that such applications will open up new areas of theoretical work.

The Value Chain. In his widely read book, Michael Porter espouses the concept of the value chain, which he describes as follows:[9]

> Every firm is a collection of activities that are performed to design, produce, market, deliver, and support its product. A firm's value chain and the way it performs individual activities are a reflection of its history, its strategy, its approach to implementing its strategy, and the underlying economics of the activities themselves.

The supply chain is a special case of the value chain for those companies that manufacture or distribute physical products. The value chain has also been called the *value added* chain to focus attention on the firm's ultimate objective of adding value to its products or services at each stage in the chain. By studying its value chain, a company acknowledges that successful implementation of high-level strategy requires careful coordination of its activities at a detailed, operational level. Competitive advantage will accrue to those companies that control value chain costs better than their competitors and/or differentiate their products by providing some combination of superior quality, customer service, product variety, unique market presence, and so on.

According to Porter, the generic value chain consists of nine activity types. We have reproduced it here in Figure 1.3 where we have added two new support activities, information technology and supply chain management.[10] Margin, or net revenue, is the difference between gross revenue and total cost, which are the costs associated with individual activities. Controlling these costs, and adding value to individual activities, is crucial to achieving and maintaining competitive advantage as measured by the firm's short- and long-term profits.

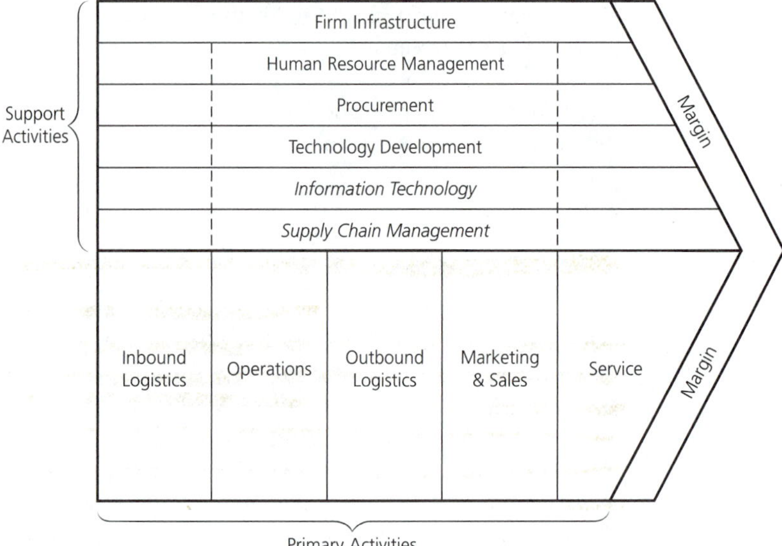

Figure 1.3
The Value Chain.
Source: M. E. Porter [1985]

Figure 1.3 shows that support activities, especially the two we have added, are becoming a larger portion of overall value chain activity, and pure primary activities are becoming a smaller portion. Moreover, people responsible for primary activities are participating more heavily in support activities, especially those relating to global supply chain management. Organizational structures to facilitate this matrix responsibility of supply chain managers are yet to be fully understood and implemented.

Porter emphasizes the importance of effective linkages among the activities in the value chain as follows:[11]

> Linkages can lead to competitive advantage in two ways: optimization and coordination. Linkages often reflect tradeoffs among activities to achieve the same overall result. . . . A firm must optimize such linkages reflecting its strategy in order to achieve competitive advantage. . . . The ability to coordinate linkages often reduces costs or enhances differentiation. . . . Linkages imply that a firm's cost or differentiation is not merely the result of efforts to reduce cost or improve performance in each value chain activity individually.

By optimize, Porter means "to make best" by whatever organizational or planning methods that the company can bring to bear on its value chain. The theme of this book is that, to be competitive, the firm can and must use data, models, and modeling systems to optimize and coordinate its value chain. This approach is obviously appropriate to the minimization of total cost. But, as we argued in the previous section, competitive advantage based on product differentiation also requires quantitative analysis to determine if the cost of differentiation is justified. If so, modeling systems can help identify cost-effective plans that sustain the company's superior level of customer service, quality, or some other differentiating factor.

The Theory of the Firm. The supply chain concept is, to a agerial interpretation of well-established **microeconomic mo** Microeconomics, or **industrial organization economics** as the recently named, is concerned with the construction and interp that describe in mathematical terms how firms operate, expand, n according to economic principles. It is also concerned with mod and how consumers demand a firm's products and how firms within an industry compete.[12]

Microeconomic models are highly relevant to the optimization models that we will be discussing because both types of models address supply chain decisions facing the firm. A major difference between them is their intention rather than their mathematical form. Optimization models are empirical; that is, they process numerical data describing a specific supply chain planning problem to identify optimal strategies for that problem. By contrast, microeconomic models, although they also employ mathematical constructions, are intended to provide qualitative insights into the economics of the firm and competition among firms in an industry. In Chapter 3, we reconcile the differences in objectives between the two disciplines by using microeconomic theory to explain and interpret optimal strategies computed by optimization models.

Subtle issues arise when the reality of a supply chain problem is not perfectly suited to microeconomic theory. Consider, for example, a company that establishes a policy restricting the acquisition of a critical raw material to at least two vendors with no vendor providing less than 20% of the total volume. Management has imposed the policy despite the fact that a particular vendor is offering to sell the raw material in unlimited quantities at significantly lower cost than other vendors.

This type of policy constraint is labeled an *externality* by economists, which means it is a planning factor that is not immediately justifiable by economic arguments. One might attempt to elicit management's reasoning for such an externality and to extend the theory of the firm to incorporate it. This is not practical because purchasing managers require immediate advice on how best to acquire the raw material. They do not have the time to analyze the rationality or irrationality of this, and many other, externalities.

By contrast, as we shall demonstrate, optimization models can readily incorporate policy constraints such as the one just described and many others. Moreover, they can provide information regarding the cost of imposing such constraints. Procedures are available to vary the effect of policy constraints if managers are somewhat unsure about how severe they wish to make them. In short, optimization models can perform policy analyses pragmatically and expeditiously.

Microeconomic theory is based on felicitous assumptions about the underlying structures of mathematical models that permit well-behaved results to be derived describing the firm's operations. Unfortunately, data from the real world do not always support these assumptions. For example, fixed costs and economies of scale associated with manufacturing or distribution activities wreak havoc with standard microeconomic theory. If such phenomena exist in an industry, there is no guarantee, from a theoretical viewpoint, that an equilibrium among competing firms will exist; that is, that each firm has geographical markets where it is dominant. Of course, disequilibrium may be a reality, but it is a messy concept that is more difficult to characterize.

Clearly, such phenomena are widespread. Mixed integer programming models, a special type of optimization model that we shall examine in later chapters, can readily capture a variety of complicating characteristics of real-life business planning environments. Thus, a difference between microeconomics and optimization models is that the latter can more readily accommodate real-world complications that may be poorly behaved from a mathematical or theoretical viewpoint.

Recently, research on strategy formation has turned to a new paradigm, called the **resource-based view** of the firm, with close ties to industrial organization economics.[13] Its philosophy is that a firm's sustainable competitive advantage depends heavily on the firm's resources and how they are used. In particular, the theory assumes that superior firms possess **heterogeneous** resources that differentiate them from other firms and permit them to earn rents; that is, the market price received by the superior firm for its product exceeds its average cost to supply the product. Roughly speaking, heterogeneous resources are not easily imitated, substituted for by other resources, or transferred.

The concept of a firm's **core competencies** is an important idea linked to the resource-based view of the firm.[14] Core competencies refer to the heterogeneous resources possessed by the superior firm that provide it with sustainable competitive advantage. Although the term enjoys widespread use, managers often cannot precisely identify their firm's core competencies or how they should be protected and enhanced.

The resource-based view of the firm is a new theory that has not yet produced empirical methods for identifying and measuring heterogeneous resources and core competencies. Clearly, some heterogeneous resources are qualitative and cannot be readily or easily measured; an example is the expertise of the company's design engineers. But many others can be measured; for example, costs and capacities associated with a product protected by patent. As we will argue in a later chapter, data-driven optimization models of the firm's supply chain can help management identify its heterogeneous resources and categorize them by their absolute and relative values. These models can also identify and categorize stranded resources that the firm should consider retiring or selling off.

Conversely, concepts from the resource-based view of the firm suggest directions for expanding the scope of optimization models for supply chain management in important ways. This is important because managers and practitioners remain tentative about extensions, although supply chain modeling applications are proliferating. Examples include the following:

- Models that explicitly analyze the company's resources in selecting plans to expand efficient resources while contracting inefficient resources
- Models that explicitly address strategic uncertainties in demand when determining resource acquisition plans for the firm's supply chain
- Models that analyze the firm's product line from a strategic perspective by simultaneously considering new product introductions, life cycle management, and product retirement

Logistics, Production, and Inventory Management

By contrast to the top-down, high-level strategic issues examined in the previous subsection, logistics, production, and inventory management are concerned with managing supply chain operations from the bottom up. Nevertheless, experts in these areas have long recognized the need for integrated planning.

Academic research and writing in these fields go back a long way, beginning with publication of the original paper on economic order quantity (EOQ).[15] Although motivated by real-world operational problems, many papers published in academic journals over the years have approached these problems in a theoretical manner, yielding results that have only a distant relevance to practical solutions. In the past, this phenomenon was the result of a lack of data and managerial interest in applying the theories. The situation has changed significantly in recent years as companies have begun to actively seek analytic tools to help them improve operations. Still, it will take time to overcome legacy thinking to create robust and powerful modeling approaches and modeling systems for operational problems.

Logistics. Logistics is concerned with managing transportation, warehousing, and inventory stocking activities. Transportation planning is a vast field unto itself that involves complex decisions about transportation modes, carriers, vehicle scheduling and routing, and many other activities that serve to move products through the company's supply chain. Optimization models and modeling systems have been successfully applied to these decision problems and applied research continues to seek faster and more powerful methods.

In the United States, deregulation of air freight, trucking, and railroads has generally led to more competitive prices while expanding the transportation options that the company must consider.[16] Advances in IT, such as the capability to select carriers over the Internet, have also expanded these options and will continue to do so for several years. The spot market in transportation will probably become much more sophisticated and spawn the need for new tools in selecting carriers.

About the same time that strategic thinkers like Michael Porter with top-down perspectives began to articulate the importance of integrated supply chain management, logistics experts with bottom-up perspectives came to the same conclusions. According to Stock and Lambert[17]

> The foundation of the integrated logistics management concept is total cost analysis, which we have defined as minimizing the cost of transportation, warehousing, inventory, order processing and information systems, and lot quantity cost, while achieving a desired customer service level.

Several conclusions can be drawn from this sentence.

First, Stock and Lambert correctly allude to the indirect costs, probably substantial, of IT needed to achieve integrated supply chain management. Second, they allude to the need to balance nonmonetary objectives, such as customer service, against cost minimization. Third, they offer the lot quantity cost as a surrogate for manufacturing costs. As such, it reflects the past and still current viewpoint of logistics managers that their responsibilities need not or cannot be integrated with those of manufacturing managers.

Expanding the scope of total cost analysis is important to future improvements in supply chain management practices. In the typical consumer products company, for example, sales strategies for next year are determined by marketing managers. Their plan is passed to manufacturing managers who are asked to develop an appropriate production strategy. The joint marketing and manufacturing strategy is then passed to logistics managers who are given the responsibility of developing appropriate transportation, warehousing, and inventory strategies to meet it. Thus, although the logistics managers may seek to minimize total logistics costs, larger issues of integrating strategies for logistics, manufacturing, and even marketing are not addressed. As a result, the overall supply chain strategy of the consumer products company may be significantly suboptimal.

Production Management. Production planning varies significantly across industries. Process manufacturing, which characterizes production in oil refineries or breweries, involves expensive capital equipment that is run continuously with infrequent changeovers. Discrete parts manufacturing, which characterizes the production of automobiles and their components or printed circuit boards, involves multiple-stage product lines with setups at each stage for intermediate products. Buffer stocks are maintained between stages to promote continuous production. Job-shop scheduling, which characterizes repair operations on aircraft engines or finishing operations in a paper mill, involves facilities with capital equipment that is used sporadically as individual jobs with different profiles of tasks to be completed are undertaken.

Thus, at the operational level, optimization models and modeling systems for production scheduling must be customized to the peculiarities of the production environment, particularly those associated with the timing of setups, changeovers, production run lengths, and so on.[18] Such models and modeling systems are needed to provide master schedule information to materials requirements planning (MRP) systems that produce detailed bill-of-materials instructions for managers charged with running operations. For some production environments, these modeling systems can also assist production managers in evaluating short-term make-or-buy decisions.

At the tactical and strategic planning levels where timing details are less important, the various classes of production planning problems can often be accurately modeled by general-purpose models and modeling systems that address multistage and multiperiod planning decisions. Still, intertemporal coordination of strategic, tactical, and operational production plans is very important, which presents the modeling practitioner with the challenge of coherently linking detailed operational models with more aggregate tactical models.

Production planning and scheduling models can play an important role in implementing new qualitative methods for improving production, such as **lean production** or **agile manufacturing.**[19] Lean production refers to the reduction of waste in the production line, including reduction of inventory, shortening of setup times, and improvement in quality. Although lean production rests heavily on the creation and use of interdisciplinary teams that foster better communication among production managers and workers, optimization models play an important role in identifying plans that squeeze out additional waste. Agile manufacturing refers to production environments that are more agile than in the past with respect to product customization and reengineering, product changeovers, changes in customer orders, and so on. Again, optimization models can be used to advantage in helping design and operate agile manufacturing lines.

Inventory Management. A company may hold inventories of raw materials, parts, work-in-process, or finished products for a variety of reasons. Inventories can serve to hedge against the uncertainties of supply and demand or to take advantage of economies of scale associated with manufacturing or acquiring products in large batches. Inventories are also essential to build up reserves for seasonal demands or promotional sales.

Recently, attention has been focused on creating business processes that reduce or eliminate inventories, mainly by reducing or eliminating the uncertainties that make them necessary. These efforts have been motivated in part by the recognition that metrics describing the performance of a company's inventory management practices can be important signals to shareholders regarding the efficiency of the company's operations and hence its profitability. Just-in-time inventory practices, which found widespread application in recent years, have been tempered by the realization that they may incur significant hidden costs in some situations, such as those realized by small suppliers to large companies in the automotive and aerospace industries.

Inventory management problems are characterized by holding costs, shortage costs, and demand distributions for products specified at a detailed stock keeping unit (SKU) level. Models for optimizing inventory policies for individual items use arguments and methods from statistics and applied probability theory. As such, they are structurally very different from deterministic optimization models, which broadly consider products, facilities, and transportation flows in analyzing resource acquisition and allocation decisions.

In this book, we study models for inventory management with an emphasis on approaches for integrating inventory decisions with other supply chain decisions. This perspective, which is sometimes overlooked by managers responsible for controlling inventories, is crucial because holding costs are only one element of total supply chain cost. As we shall see, incorporating inventory decisions in supply chain optimization models is difficult because they involve parameters and relationships, such as variances of market demands and delivery times and their impact on stock outages, which are not easily represented in optimization models. Nevertheless, depending on the scope of analysis, acceptable approximations of inventory costs can be developed. Improving these approximations is an important area of applied research.

Management Accounting

Management accounting is "the process of identifying, measuring, reporting and analyzing information about the economic events of organizations."[20] It is concerned with helping managers make better decisions and providing feedback and control on current performance. By contrast, **financial accounting** is responsible for reporting results about historical performance to the company's external constituencies, which includes stockholders, creditors, and tax authorities. Over the past century, developments in management accounting to support internal decision making and control were inhibited because government regulations imposed strict rules on financial accounting. Implementation of management accounting methods also requires information technologies that have only become available in recent years.

Management accounting methods for supply chain planning are closely linked to methods for creating and applying optimization models. In fact, the two disciplines overlap considerably in their approaches to analyzing business problems. Our discussion of the overlap will focus on the following two main tasks needed to create cost data for and from supply chain models:

- Develop causal cost relationships of direct and indirect costs
- Compute transfer, product, and customer costs from an optimal solution to a supply chain model

An optimization model requires inputs reflecting cost behavior as well as numbers, hence the emphasis on cost relationships. These are relationships between natural categories of direct and indirect costs discussed above and independent factors, called **cost drivers.** To provide managers with useful insights into costs and decisions, we seek causal cost relationships employing cost drivers that accurately and comprehensively reflect supply chain activities causing cost and value to be added to the firm's products and services. Cost behavior also refers to forecasts or projections about how costs will change as operations in the future differ in volume and mix from historical operations. Finally, it refers to costs and cost relationships involving new products, markets, vendors, facilities, and transportation activities that the company wishes to evaluate as part of its strategic and tactical planning exercises.

Selecting cost drivers for direct cost relationships is often straightforward because direct manufacturing and distribution activities usually depend on machines, people, and raw materials in obvious ways. Selecting cost drivers for indirect cost relationships is more difficult. It requires management account expertise plus knowledge of the company's business. Developments in **activity-based costing** methods, which is an important new area of management accounting, are aimed at identifying cost drivers for indirect costs.

Demand Forecasting and Marketing Science

Demand forecasting refers to quantitative methods for predicting future demand for products sold by the company.[21] Such forecasts are obviously essential for the construction of a supply chain model, either a total cost minimization model to meet a specific demand forecast or a net revenue maximization model incorporating functions relating demand to product prices, product sourcing locations, or other factors.

Uncertainties in the demand forecasts should be used in constructing multiple demand scenarios to be optimized by the supply chain model.

Demand forecasting techniques are primarily statistical methods. Analysts apply them to project future sales patterns from historical data about past sales and possibly other data about the company, its industry, the national economy, and the global economy. Time series analysis is a large class of methods for developing forecasts exclusively from historical databases. The well-known technique of exponential smoothing is a simple type of time series model.

In constructing a time series model, the practitioner attempts to find patterns in the historical data, such as seasonal effects or trends, that produce a good fit to the data as measured by the variance of the forecast. Sometimes patterns causing variability in the data are subtle. In such cases, considerable expertise by the modeling practitioner may be needed to produce a good model. In short, in addition to its mathematical underpinnings, demand forecasting has a decided artistic side, which may be difficult to document or explain to a nonexpert.

Time series models have a fatalistic aspect to them in that they assume the past will repeat itself without being influenced by external factors. Thus, the company may be well advised to combine statistical analysis with managerial judgment about the short-, medium-, and long-term outlooks for company sales to customers and markets. At the other extreme, supply chain planning based purely on intuitive, managerial judgments without recourse to formal predictive methods using data is not recommended.

Another large class of forecasting models, which includes regression and econometric methods, goes somewhat beyond the fatalism of time series techniques in seeking to provide insights into the product demand process through causal relationships, or at least explanatory factors, that link independent variables to demand forecasts. Examples are forecasting the increase in product demand as a function of the increase in gross domestic product (GDP) and the decrease in demand as a function of an increase in product price. But even causal models are susceptible to an overreliance on historical data, which again suggests the need to combine them with managerial judgments.

Once we open up our analysis of demand forecasts to causal modeling, a natural next step is to investigate marketing science models that relate forecasted sales to values of decision variables determined by the marketing department such as price, promotion, advertising, and sales force effort.[22] Because the cost of marketing strategies involving these decision variables will be significant, we must consider extended models that integrate supply chain management decisions with demand management decisions. Although such models have not yet been widely implemented, there is growing interest in them.

When a company faces the introduction of a new product, it has no historical data upon which to base its forecasts. In many instances, though, historical data is available for similar products. The challenge is to develop initial forecasts of the new product based on forecasting parameters extracted from historical data of these similar products. For example, the diffusion model for new products relates sales to parameters describing the rates at which two types of customers, innovators and imitators, decide to buy the product. This model has been used successfully to forecast new sales of new consumer durable electronic and high-tech products. Once a profile of the new product sales begins to emerge, the a priori parameters can be revised.

Operations Research

Operations research has been called the science and technology of decision making. The scientific component is concerned with ideas and processes for articulating and modeling decision problems by determining the decision maker's objectives and the constraints under which he or she must, or wishes to, operate. It is also concerned with mathematical methods, called **algorithms,** for optimizing the numerical systems that result when data is used to populate models. The technological component is concerned with software and hardware tools for collecting and communicating data, organizing these data, using them to generate and optimize models, and reporting results.

Operations research models and methods have demonstrated their relevance in a wide range of applications. This generality creates opportunities and challenges. A major opportunity is that many supply chain problems can be analyzed using optimization models and algorithms taken more or less off the shelf and quickly adapted for use. But the details of a given problem matter. A major challenge in any specific situation, therefore, is to precisely define an appropriate model. This book is devoted to an examination and elaboration of these opportunities and challenges.

Operations research was one of the disciplines that sprang to life at the start of the information revolution in the mid 1940s. The revolution began with the need for numerical computing in military operations during World War II. Despite these very early applications, subsequent advances of information technology in business were concerned with methods for data acquisition, communication, and management, as opposed to numerical computation. These concerns persisted until very recently. Now the interest in numerical computation in business has greatly increased as witnessed by the widespread use of electronic spreadsheet and sophisticated graphics programs as well as a renewed interest in operations research models.

Unfortunately, between 1970 and 1985, operations research drifted away from its origins because companies were more concerned with methods for acquiring data than methods for analyzing them. During that period, information technology to support practical implementations of operations research models lagged behind the theory. Often the data required for a realistic model were not readily available or could not be acquired in a timely manner. Without opportunities to work on real-world problems, academics and other researchers in the field kept busy by extending the theory, too often in directions with little practical relevance.

Despite the shortcomings of the past, the future of operations research is bright, especially for new and expanded applications. The growing interest by managers in supply chain management has opened up important opportunities for model building and analysis. At the same time, software packages for optimizing models have evolved to the point that they can be easily integrated with other system modules. Today's desktop computers have the power to optimize large-scale models in run times that are at least commensurate with those of mainframe computers of only a few years ago. For these reasons, operations research has become an important element in the methodologies of information technology.

1.4

Innovations in Information Technology Require and Support Supply Chain Modeling

In this section, we examine further the synergy between IT and supply chain modeling. As we observed earlier, recent developments in ERP systems provide the promise, and sometimes the reality, of transactional databases that are comprehensive and easily accessed. Such databases are the foundation from which we can construct and apply supply chain modeling systems. Conversely, supply chain modeling systems are critically needed to help management extract effective plans from these transactional databases.

To emphasize the need for modeling systems, we highlight two serious problems involving data currently faced by managers:

> **Data Problem One:** There is an overabundance of transactional data for the purposes of managerial decision making.

Managers have faced this problem for 20 years or more, although it has become more acute in recent years due to the advent of ERP, point-of-sales systems, and other systems focused on streamlining the collection and communication of transactional data.

Equally serious for the purposes of integrated supply chain management is

> **Data Problem Two:** Managers do not know what the data in the company's transactional databases imply about how to integrate their activities with the supply chain activities of other managers in the company and with those of the company's vendors and customers.

As we have discussed several times in this chapter, integrated supply chain planning will not occur magically once systems for managing transactional data are in place.

Solutions to these problems are the major theme of this book. At an abstract level, the solutions may be succinctly stated, but their execution requires technological development, learning, and business process redesign on the part of the company and its supply chain partners. The solution has two aspects. The first is as follows:

> **Technological Solution:** Develop and deploy modeling systems for analyzing strategic, tactical, and operational decisions affecting the company's supply chain.

We emphasize that the technological solution involves the construction and application of modeling systems for all levels of planning—strategic, tactical, and operational. Implicit is the need to implement supply chain decision databases feeding these modeling systems that are consistent and coherent in their descriptions of products, markets, vendors, facility activities, transportation activities, and a host of other factors. Moreover, supply chain decisions suggested by the various models must be consistent and coherent in their treatment of strategic, tactical, and operational plans.

Given the capabilities of today's software and hardware, achieving a technological solution to the analytical problems of interpreting transactional data is not a barrier. Instead, the barrier to integrated supply chain management is in realizing the following:

> **Organizational Solution:** Redesign company processes and revise managerial incentive schemes to promote and facilitate competitive strategies for supply chain management based on data, models, and modeling systems.

The process redesign requirements needed to exploit insights provided by modeling systems are not yet well understood or appreciated by most managers. Simply stated, the company must commit to routine application of modeling tools where the cycle time for their use depends on the type of analysis they perform. Strategic planning may be performed once a year, tactical planning once a quarter or once a month, and operational planning once a week or once a day. Business processes must be put in place to update the supply chain decision databases, to perform modeling analyses, to resolve conflicts among managers about proposed plans, and to disseminate the plans once they have been identified and agreed upon.

The execution of these tasks involves the creation of new types of jobs for individuals that combine skills in information technology with knowledge about business problems and analysis. Moreover, the company must revise its managerial incentive schemes so that plant managers, distribution managers, and other middle and upper-middle managers are encouraged to make decisions and pursue plans that serve to globally optimize the company's supply chain. Creating such incentive schemes is not easy because the success or failure of global supply chain optimization in a company may involve many aspects of the company's performance that are beyond the control of the individual manager. As a result, the manager may feel that his or her yearly bonus and prospects for promotion are unconnected with his or her job performance.

We are at a crossroad in the information revolution that is familiar to philosophers and historians who have studied human progress. The revolution began with the **thesis** that computers and communications networks must provide managers with timely and complete data about their company's operations, its suppliers, and the markets in which the company's products are sold. No one doubted the benefits to be gained by pursuing this thesis, which today is approaching realization. Still, the business community is now faced with an **antithesis** characterized by the two data problems stated above. History has shown that antitheses can and will be overcome by evolving technologies to form a **synthesis**, which becomes the new thesis and the process is repeated. Our contention is that the technical solution and the organizational solution characterize the synthesis sought by participants in the information revolution. Furthermore, we can hasten its arrival by articulating and promoting it.

1.5 Organizational Adaptation to Integrated Supply Chain Management and Modeling

In the previous section, we observed that the barriers to integrated supply chain management are organizational, not technical. Although myopic improvements in supply chain management can be achieved by elimination of obvious, inefficient, nonvalue adding activities, our interest here is in promoting the much larger improvements that can be realized when managers use modeling systems to achieve true integrated planning. Conveying the form and function of such systems is the goal of this book. Once a company's management understands them, it can begin to adapt its business processes to allow insights provided by modeling systems to be exploited.

Most companies are undergoing radical change due to a host of interconnected factors. It is difficult to separate cause and effect from among the following:

- Globalization
- E-commerce
- Enterprise resource planning systems
- Business process reengineering
- Organizational learning and change management
- Integrated supply chain management

A great deal has already been written about these phenomena, and even more will be written in the future. Our contention is that considerable discipline may be imposed on supply chain management by creating modeling systems, implementing their supporting decision databases, and then adapting the organization to exploit them. Although this contention may seem presumptuous, possibly even ludicrous, to someone unfamiliar with modeling technologies, we counter with the observation that an increasing number of managers in a wide range of companies are seeking to manage their supply chains based on facts, that is, data.

The application of modeling systems to enhance the rationality of supply chain management flies in the face of past research into human and organizational decision making, which has shown that timeless issues of ignorance, superstition, conflict, and self-seeking behavior still abound.[23] Business process reengineering is needed to assist humans and organizations to make better decisions in spite of themselves. Suggestions for achieving this goal are made in the final chapter of this book.

Notes

1. The publications by Hanssman [1959], Lalonde et al. [1970] and Porter [1985] discuss integrated planning from different perspectives. They illustrate how theory often precedes practice, sometimes by many years. The difficulty is to recognize when the world is ready for practical applications drawn from a theoretical base. In the case of supply chain management, the indications are strong that the time has arrived.
2. These applications are discussed in Arntzen et al. [1995].
3. See Rajaram et al. [1999].
4. Boeing's ongoing problems are discussed in Zuckerman [1999], who contrasts its supply chain with the more efficient one of Airbus.
5. Conagra's situation is discussed in Barboza [1999], who expressed the widely held view that the company is too large to operate its supply chains efficiently.
6. Cox et al. [1993] report on an optimization model to plan expansion of US West's fiber-optic telecommunication network.
7. Mathematical programming models and methods include linear programming, mixed integer programming, nonlinear programming, stochastic programming and other classes of models and methods. Schrage [1997] and Winston [1995] contain broad treatments of mathematical programming that assume the reader has an intermediate level of mathematical sophistication. Recent developments in heuristic optimization methods (see Reeves [1993]) are complementary to mathematical programming and extend their ability to extract useful plans from complex, mixed integer programming models.
8. An overview of an early version of SLIM/2000 and its application in a postmerger consolidation study is found in Shapiro, Singhal, and Wagner [1993]. Since then, the system has been applied to supply chain problems in more than two dozen companies. None of these companies has displayed serious interest in publishing details of their use of the system. In most instances, the system helped management identify savings in the millions, sometimes even tens of millions, of dollars.
9. See Porter [1985, 36].
10. The omission of information technology as an instrument of competitive advantage reflects the attitude about its importance held by many senior managers during the 1980s. Porter recognized this omission of his original concept of the value chain in the paper Porter and Millar [1985]. The perception that the company needs cross-cutting activities to support global supply chain management is still emerging.
11. See Porter [1985, 48].
12. The book by Cohen and Cyert [1965] was an important early contribution to the theory of the firm as it can be examined by mathematical models. More recent results are summarized in Holmstrom and Tirole [1988].
13. Wernerfelt [1984] coined the term *resource-based view* of the firm. Conner [1991] compares and contrasts the resource-based view of the firm with other theories from industrial organization. The resource-based view of the firm is discussed in more detail in Chapter 7.
14. The seminal paper on core competencies is Pralahad and Hamel [1990].
15. According to Sipper and Bulfin [1997], the original EOQ model was introduced by Harris [1915], although it was Wilson [1934] who widely promoted it.
16. Crum and Holcomb [1994] discuss improvements in the transportation industry since deregulation and the associated challenges.
17. See Stock and Lambert [1987, 39].
18. Shapiro [1993] provides an overview of models for different classes of production environments.
19. Lean production is a concept articulated by Womack et al. [1990] following their study of the automotive industries in Japan, the United States, and Europe. Agile manufacturing is a concept proposed by Goldman and Preis [1991].

20. See Atkinson et al. [1997, 3].
21. For an overview of forecasting methods, see Winston [1994, Chapter 24] or Makridakis and Wheelwright [1986].
22. Marketing science models and their integration with supply chain models are discussed in Section 8.2.
23. These issues are examined in detail by March [1994].

References

Arntzen, B. C., G. G. Brown, T. P. Harrison, and L. L. Traffton [1995], "Global Supply Chain Management at Digital Equipment Corporation," *Interfaces,* 25, 69–93.

Atkinson, A. A., R. D. Banker, R. S. Kaplan, and S. M. Young [1997], *Management Accounting,* 2d ed. Englewood Cliffs, NJ: Prentice-Hall.

Barboza, D., [1999], "Conagra Enlisting in the March Toward a Leaner Food Industry," *The New York Times,* May 13, C-19.

Cohen, K. J., and Cyert R. M. [1965], *Theory of the Firm: Resource Allocation in a Market Economy.* Englewood Cliffs, NJ: Prentice Hall.

Conner, K. R. [1991] "A Historical Comparison of Resource-Based Theory and Five Schools of Thought within Industrial Organizations Economics: Do We Have a New Theory of the Firm?" *Journal of Management,* 17, 121–154.

Cox, Jr., L. A., W. E. Kuehner, S. H. Parrish, and Y. Qiu [1993], "Optimal Expansion of Fiber-Optic Telecommunications Networks in Metropolitan Areas," *Interfaces,* 23, 35–50.

Crum, M. R., and M. C. Holcomb [1994], "Transportation Outlook and Evaluation," in *The Logistics Handbook,* edited by J. F. Robeson, W. C. Copacino and R. E. Howe. New York: The Free Press.

Goldman, S. L., and K. Preis [1991], *21st Century Manufacturing Enterprise Strategy,* Iacocca Institute Report. Bethlehem, PA: Lehigh University.

Hanssmann, F., [1959], "Optimal Inventory Location and Control in Production and Distribution Networks," *Operations Research,* 7, 483–498.

Harris, F., [1915], "Operations and Costs," *Factory Management Series,* 48–52. Chicago: Shaw.

Holmstrom, B. R., and J. Tirole [1988], "The Theory of the Firm," in *Handbook of Industrial Organization,* edited by R. Schmalensee and R. Willig. Amsterdam: North-Holland.

LaLonde, B. J., J. R. Grabner, and J. F. Robeson [1970], "Integrated Distribution Systems: A Management Perspective," *International Journal of Physical Distribution Management,* 40.

Makridakis, S., and S. Wheelwright [1986], *Forecasting: Methods and Applications.* Wiley.

March, J. G. [1994], *A Primer on Decision Making: How Decisions Happen.* New York: The Free Press.

*Porter, M. E., [1985], *Competitive Advantage: Creating and Sustaining Superior Performance.* New York: The Free Press, MacMillan.

Porter, M. E., and V. E. Millar [1985], "How Information Gives You Competitive Advantage," *Harvard Business Review,* 149–160.

Pralahad, C. K., and G. Hamel [1990], "The Core Competence of the Corporation," *Harvard Business Review,* May-June, 79–91.

Rajaram, K. R., Jaikumar, F. Behlau, F. van Esch, C. Heynen, R. Kaiser, A. Kuttner, and I. van de Wege [1999], "Robust Process Control at Cerestar's Refineries," *Interfaces,* 29, 30–48.

Reeves, C. R., [1993], *Modern Heuristic Techniques for Combinatorial Problems.* Oxford, Eng: Blackwell Scientific Publications.

Schrage, L., [1997], *Optimization Modeling with LINDO,* 5th ed. Pacific Grove, Calif.: Duxbury Press.

Shapiro, J. F., [1993], "Mathematical Programming Models and Methods for Production

Planning and Scheduling," in *Handbooks in OR & MS, Volume 4,* edited by S. C. Graves et al. Amsterdam: Elsevier.

Shapiro, J. F., V. M. Singhal, and S. N. Wagner [1993], "Optimizing the Value Chain," *Interfaces,* 25, 102–117.

Sipper, D., and R. L. Bulfin [1997], *Production: Planning, Control, Integration.* New York: McGraw-Hill.

Stock, J. R., and D. M. Lambert [1987], *Strategic Logistics Management,* 2d ed. Homewood, Ill: Richard D. Irwin and Company.

Wernerfelt, B., [1984], "A Resource Based View of the Firm," *Strategic Management Journal,* 5, 171–180.

Womack, J. P., D. T. Jones, and D. Roos [1990], *The Machine That Changed the World: The Story of Lean Production,* New York: Rawson Associates.

Wilson, R. H., [1934], "A Scientific Routine for Stock Control," *Harvard Business Review,* 13, 116–128.

Winston, W. L., [1994], *Operations Research: Applications and Algorithms,* 3d ed. Pacific Grove, Calif.: Duxbury Press.

Winston, W. L., 1995, *Introduction to Mathematical Programming,* 2d ed. Pacific Grove, Calif.: Duxbury Press.

Zuckerman, L. [1999], "Airbus's Stealth Advance," *International Herald Tribune,* July 10–11, 9.

*See the credits section at the end of this book for more information.

2 Information Technology

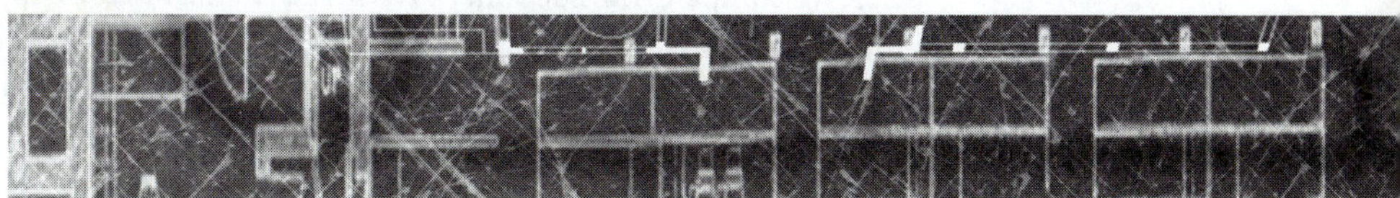

Rapid developments in IT, which is defined as both computing and telecommunications, have affected all aspects of business, not just supply chain management. During the 1990s, sales of IT grew to the extent that it has become the largest industry in the United States, exceeding construction, food products, and automotive manufacturing.[1] As shown in Figure 2.1, business investment in hardware and software in the United States has increased exponentially since the mid-1980s, reaching a torrid pace by the end of the 1990s, with no end in sight.[2] Moreover, these investments do not include sky-rocketing fees paid for IT consulting services.

The creation and management of corporate databases has been facilitated by widespread implementation of ERP systems. These systems offer the promise of transactional databases that are standardized across the company, thereby facilitating integration of supply chain activities. Models are playing an increasing role in helping managers extract effective supply chain plans from these databases. Nevertheless,

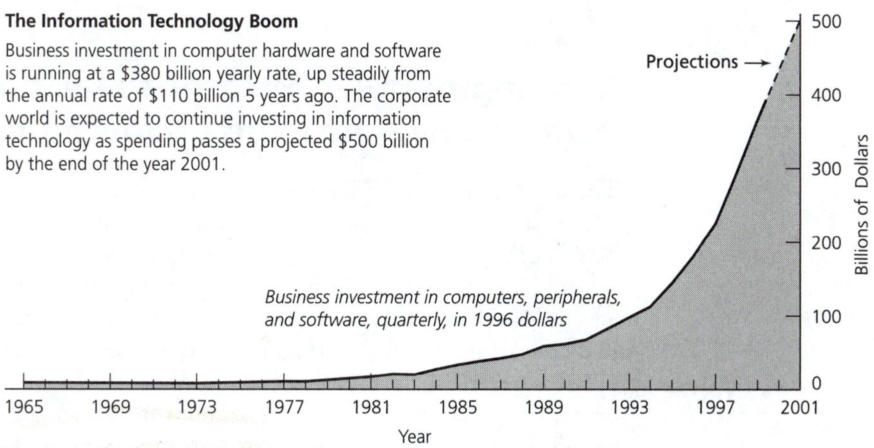

The Information Technology Boom
Business investment in computer hardware and software is running at a $380 billion yearly rate, up steadily from the annual rate of $110 billion 5 years ago. The corporate world is expected to continue investing in information technology as spending passes a projected $500 billion by the end of the year 2001.
Projections
Business investment in computers, peripherals, and software, quarterly, in 1996 dollars
Billions of Dollars
0
100
200
300
400
500
1965
1969
1973
1977
1981
1985
1989
1993
1997
2001
Year
SOURCE: Commerce Department; Macroeconomic Advisers (projections).

Figure 2.1
Business investment in computer hardware and software.
Source: Lohr [1999]

the purposes of such models, and their potential for improving a company's competitive advantage, are not yet fully understood by many supply chain managers.

In Section 2.1 we provide a brief overview of developments in ERP and e-commerce systems from the perspective of supply chain management. These systems are primarily Transactional IT, concerned with acquiring, processing, and communicating raw data about the company's supply chain and with the compilation and dissemination of reports summarizing these data. They also facilitate communication amond different companies in an extended or virtual supply chain. In Section 2.2, we compare Transactional IT with Analytical IT, which is created to assist managers in making supply chain decisions. Analytical IT employs models constructed from **supply chain decision databases** that are derived from the company's transactional databases. Analytical IT comprises these supply chain decision databases plus modeling systems and programs linking corporate databases to the supply chain decision databases.

In theory, the modeling systems in a company's Analytical IT and their decision databases should be organized in a suite of interconnected applications for strategic, tactical, and operational planning. This hierarchy of modeling systems is discussed in detail in Section 2.3. In practice, very few companies have yet come close to achieving a complete suite. Nevertheless, we believe there is value in laying out a comprehensive structure for these modeling systems and discussing linkages among the various components.

In Section 2.4, we discuss issues connected with enhancing legacy systems for and legacy thinking about supply chain modeling. These issues are a preview of behavioral research, which we discuss in Chapter 12, into barriers inhibiting rational decision making using models. The chapter concludes with Section 2.5 where we present final thoughts about the information revolution, especially as it relates to supply chain management.

2.1

Developments in Enterprise Resource Planning Systems and E-Commerce

The development of IT for managing and communicating transactional data has been a primary focus of computer scientists and information technologists for over 40 years. Figure 2.1 reveals the great expansion during the 1990s of managerial interest and investment in hardware and software for these purposes. Still, even with the advent of ERP systems and e-commerce, we would be naïve to suppose that companies have achieved permanent solutions to their data management problems.

It is beyond the aim of this book to discuss these software and hardware developments in great detail. Rather, we will be concerned in this chapter with the synergy between IT and supply chain management using modeling systems.[3] Today's IT enables the development of such systems, but paths to their successful implementation remain unclear in most companies. Although scholars and consultants often use expressions such as "the company must (can, should) optimize supply chain decisions," details about how such analysis can be performed are often missing. Moreover, managers do not yet fully realize how models can provide a comprehensive, high-level view of the tangled forest of their transactional supply chain data. Based on their growing interest in modeling systems, we expect that managers will soon become much better informed. By participating in processes to extract, aggregate, extrapolate, and otherwise transform transactional data into input data required by modeling systems to support decision making, managers will gain a fresh and important perspective on how to exploit IT advances.

In this section, we review recent developments in ERP systems and e-commerce. Our discussion of e-commerce is divided into separate examinations of business-to-consumer and business-to-business e-commerce. Business-to-business linkages via the Internet require extended or new ERP systems that facilitate communication among companies of diverse sizes and missions.

ERP Systems

An ERP system includes software and hardware that facilitate the flow of transactional data in a company relating to manufacturing, logistics, finance, sales, and human resources. In principle, all business applications of the company are integrated in a uniform system environment that accesses a centralized database residing on a common platform. Common and compatible data fields and formats are used across the entire enterprise. Moreover, data are entered once and only once, ensuring that all applications make consistent use of these data.

In 1997, worldwide sales of ERP systems and related services were estimated to exceed $10 billion. Of this total, approximately 50% was for software; 30% for installation, training, and customization; and 20% for maintenance and upgrades.[4] The large percentage and absolute amount spent on installation, training, and customization reflects the need for significant business process redesign to bring systems and practices across diverse functions into alignment. In addition to improving human data collection and communication processes, reengineering should, but does not always, include cleansing and tightening of data definitions; for example, a reduction in the number of SKUs to those that are truly distinct.

Implementing ERP systems has proven unexpectedly difficult in many companies. Numerous articles have appeared in magazines and journals offering guidelines for avoiding the worst headaches. Even when an implementation project is well managed, the result can be disappointing due to inherent limitations of current ERP systems. These include the following:[5]

- Imposed conformity—the ERP system imposes rigid requirements on data and processes that often inhibit the way the company can operate its business.
- Inability to employ software from multiple vendors—the company cannot integrate modules, including modeling systems, from multiple vendors with the monolithic ERP system acquired from the primary vendor.

- Incompatibility of ERP systems across the supply chain—the company cannot easily integrate supply chain databases with vendors and customers, especially those who are too small to afford a massive ERP implementation.

Current thinking is that these problems will be overcome by new ERP systems that are modular and Web enabled.[6] Individual modules for transactional data management and modeling analysis, often developed by third-party vendors, will be bolted onto ERP systems using middleware, which provides standard interfaces for the modules.

The rapid growth in e-commerce has magnified these deficiencies of ERP systems. The expectation is that Internet-driven reengineering will require integrating business processes across corporate boundaries. Modular, flexible ERP systems will be essential for implementing interenterprise information systems for supply chains made up of several companies of varying sizes and cultures. Moreover, because e-commerce is so new, Internet companies will need the capability to modify their ERP systems as new conditions emerge.

E-Commerce

Communication over the Internet is characterized by easy accessibility, low-cost usage, and speed. These features are the result of astonishing developments in recent years in computer networks, processing speed, data storage capabilities, software, display technology, and user interfaces. The linking of people and companies due to e-commerce has opened up exciting new marketing opportunities as well as new processes for improving supply chain management. Direct business-to-consumer marketing over the Internet of products such as clothes, groceries, and PCs is a red hot emerging concept. Business-to-business communication over the Internet is also expanding rapidly. We discuss these two new developments in the paragraphs that follow. We conclude by examining Internet systems and processes that facilitate the creation of supply and demand markets for commodities.

Business-to-Consumer E-Commerce. Business-to-consumer e-commerce is a new method of retailing that puts the consumer in direct contact with a grocery, clothing, or PC company offering products. These Internet companies face a host of new marketing and sales challenges including the following:

- Devising graphics to attractively display physical products on the Web site
- Pricing products to gain market share, reflect supply chain costs, or some other criteria that change radically with evolving markets
- Extrapolating sales patterns from initial markets to new markets
- Identifying demographics of Web site customers
- Devising acceptable and sustainable customer service criteria
- Devising strategies to retain customers
- Selecting the number and range of products to offer that the Web site and the supply chain can support

- Connecting Web site sales to physical inventory
- Providing security for payment by credit cards

Innovations of business-to-customer Internet companies occur largely on the demand side of their businesses, although changes to conventional thinking are also needed for supply chain management.

Despite the excitement of business-to-customer Internet companies, their sales are still only a small percentage of total retail sales. Moreover, they are not projected to make serious inroads in the near future in most industries. For example, the market for home delivery of groceries is forecast to reach $3.5 billion by 2002, which represents only 0.7% of total grocery sales projected for that year. Similarly, clothes and accessories acquired over the Internet are forecast to represent only 1.6% of total industry sales in 2002.[7]

The logistics of business-to-customer Internet companies is driven by the classic order fulfillment principle: deliver the correct product to the correct location at the correct time for a competitive price. These companies have only just begun to realize the full importance of this principle and how difficult it is to effectively link their Web-based marketing and sales activities to their order fulfillment activities. In simple terms, an Internet company has two choices. It can build its own warehouses and manage its own distribution systems or it can hire third-party logistics companies to handle distribution for it.

Either option can prove costly. An Internet company can expect to spend between $60 to $80 million constructing a 1 million square foot warehouse, a size that is required for a high volume company, especially during peak periods. In addition to needing access to large amounts of capital, the company obviously has to be confident that it will sustain a justifiable level of sales volume over the foreseeable future. Alternatively, it can employ a third-party distributor, who will charge roughly 10% of gross sales to fulfill orders.[8]

An additional problem for a business-to-consumer Internet company is the need to link its Web site to the system that manages its inventory. This connection is critical if customers are to receive real-time information about product availability. Again, if the Internet company has sufficient capital, in addition to building warehouses, it can develop customized integrated systems with seamless connections among the Web site, the inventory management system, and other systems needed to manage the company's supply chain. Such an integrated system is discussed in Section 10.4 where we examine supply chain management and modeling systems in a company making home deliveries of groceries. If, however, the Internet company decides to employ a third-party distributor, it runs the risk of trying to link its Web site and order entry system with the distributor's software for inventory management and tracking. Incompatibilities with the distributor's systems might cause headaches as large as those experienced in developing a customized integrated system.

Finally, an Internet company must anticipate escalating demands from customers for higher levels of service. For example, customers seeking home delivery of groceries will prefer companies offering same day delivery with tight time windows over those offering next day delivery with looser time windows. For manufactured products such as PCs, customers will prefer companies that offer to more fully customize their purchases over those offering little or no customization. To meet these increasing pressures, faster and more powerful data management and modeling systems are required.

In summary, supply chain management of business-to-consumer Internet companies is subject to serious economies of scale in paybacks from investments in warehouses, inventories, and integrated data management and modeling systems. Due to high and increasing customer service expectations, these economies of scale may be even more pronounced than those experienced by traditional retailers. It suggests that we may soon see a serious reduction in the number of Internet companies in a given industry as mergers and acquisitions allow companies to achieve volumes that justify capital investment in brick and mortar and integrated systems.

Business-to-Business E-Commerce. Although investors are enthralled with the promise of business-to-consumer e-commerce, the potential impact of business-to-business e-commerce on supply chain management is much larger. In principle, business-to-business systems can provide effective interenterprise communication of data and plans for manufacturing and distribution across virtual supply chains in many industries. This might allow companies to move work across corporate boundaries, reduce cycle times by direct interconnection, and develop collaborative forecasts. But many barriers must be overcome if the promise of virtual supply chains is to be realized.

First, multiple companies operating a virtual supply chain must have standardized definitions and meanings of data. A decision to shift production of a product from one company to a second in the virtual supply chain because the unit production cost is lower in the second company assumes that this cost is consistently defined and measured across the two companies. Moreover, systems must be in place for seamless integration of data. Such requirements are, of course, no different from those addressed and allegedly met by ERP systems. And, as we discussed above, ERP companies are currently active in developing modules and middleware that they believe will allow standardization and efficient communication to be achieved across virtual supply chains.

Second, virtual supply chains assume a level of intercompany coordination that is often not achieved today among business units of the same company. For example, we cannot presume that a manufacturer of consumer durables will be willing to share sensitive cost data with a major OEM distributor of these products, especially when the manufacturer sells to other distributors and to its own franchised stores. Another issue is how companies in a virtual supply chain will agree to split cost savings realized from improved business-to-business communication and supply chain management.

Third, faster communication of data does not automatically lead to better decision making. As we discuss in the following sections of this chapter, competitive supply chain management cannot be achieved merely by rapid and myopic response to today's supply chain needs. Optimization modeling systems are required to unravel the complex interactions and ripple effects that make supply chain management difficult *and* important.

Procurements over the Internet, Spot Markets, and Auctions. A variety of electronic markets have emerged over the past 5 years where commodities, collectibles, and other products are bought and sold. Our interest is primarily in business-to-business sales over the Internet, which could exceed $66 billion during the year 2000.[9] This development has been called Internet-based procurement (IBP). It is concerned with **direct procurement** of specific parts and components needed for production by buyers and **indirect procurement** of commodities and products not customized for production such as generic parts, office supplies, maintenance, and so on.

Electronic procurement is developing along the following three dimensions:[10]

- **Seller-side sites.** Suppliers place their catalogs and spec sheets on their Web sites. The functionality of the sites may be expanded to include search capabilities and electronic commerce functionality such as credit card sales. Boise Cascade and Office Depot have sites of this type.
- **Buyer-side sites.** Buyers have installed software, which is available from software providers, allowing them to read and standardize vendor catalogs. The software also allows the creation, routing, approval, and submission of orders.
- **Third-party sites.** These are neutral sites that serve as marketplaces where buyers and sellers can link up. They provide catalog information from several sellers and usually capabilities supporting direct sales between the buyer and the seller. These sites are usually specific to certain industries such as specialty chemicals or pharmaceuticals.

Most of the transactions performed on these sites are indirect procurements of commodity products. Market researchers have found that Internet purchasing has led to improved corporatewide purchasing strategies, lower transaction costs, and improved productivity among buyers.

Direct procurement over the Internet by manufacturing firms can be more complicated because the required parts and components may require some customization. Moreover, factors beyond cost, such as quality, on-time delivery, and supplier flexibility, may be very important. Richer, more flexible software solutions are needed, but they require customization and can be very expensive. For this reason, some industries are seeking to establish common standards for their suppliers. For example, a trade association in the automotive industry commissioned the implementation of a standards-based network, the Automotive Network eXchange (ANX). Recently, Ford and General Motors announced that their suppliers will soon be required to be connected to and use this network. The expectation is that communication over ANX with suppliers in the second, third, and fourth tiers will take hours rather than the weeks it takes using the current hodgepodge of systems.

A related development is electronic markets where buyers and sellers participate in auctions of goods and services. The intention of these auctions is to enhance economic efficiency through aggregation and matching.[11] Aggregation refers to the assembly of very large numbers of buyers and sellers. Matching refers to dynamic processes whereby buyers are able to link up with sellers offering products that best match their needs. These developments suggest the possible emergence of spot markets for industrial products and services, including contract manufacturing and shipping, that will seriously affect supply chain strategies in many industries.

2.2 Comparison of Transactional and Analytical IT

As we just discussed, widespread implementation of ERP and e-commerce systems offer the promise of homogeneous, transactional databases that will facilitate managerial decision making. In many companies, however, the scope and flexibility of installed ERP systems has been less than desired or expected. New ERP systems that are modular and Web enabled are scarcely past the drawing board stage, but we can expect to see significant improvements over the next 3 to 5 years.

In any event, competitive advantage cannot be gained simply through faster and cheaper communication of data. As many managers have come to realize, ready access to transactional data does not automatically lead to better decision making. In reality, ERP is a misnomer because it fails to provide insights into decisions affecting "resource planning." The guiding principle for overcoming these deficiencies is as follows:

> To effectively apply IT in managing its supply chain, a company must distinguish between the form and function of **Transactional IT** and **Analytical IT**.

Transactional IT is concerned with acquiring, processing, and communicating raw data about the company's supply chain and with the compilation and dissemination of reports summarizing these data. The data may originate from internal sources, such as a general ledger system or a manufacturing process control system, or it may originate from external sources, such as an order placed over the Internet or trucking rates of a common carrier accessed by electronic data exchange (EDI).

By contrast, Analytical IT evaluates supply chain planning problems using **descriptive and normative models.** Descriptive models, such as demand forecasting and managerial accounting models, describe how supply chain activities, costs, constraints, and requirements may vary in the future. Normative, or optimization, models, such as a linear programming model for capacity planning, describe the space of supply chain options over which supply chain managers wish to optimize their decisions. Normative models are constructed from **supply chain decision databases** using descriptive models and data aggregation methods. These decision databases are discussed in detail in Chapter 6.

Analytical IT is not very dissimilar in meaning from the term *decision support system* (DSS). We have avoided using this term because it has come to connote an unsystematic application of ad hoc methods to the analysis of business decision problems. The implication is that each new decision problem requires the design and implementation of a new model and a new DSS. We take an opposite viewpoint by arguing that optimization models provide a rigorous, rich, and coherent discipline for constructing and deploying general-purpose tools. These tools are the cornerstone of Analytical IT for integrated supply chain management. Optimization models are discussed in detail in Chapters 3, 4, and 5.

Differences between Transactional and Analytical IT can be contrasted across a number of aspects. In the subsections that follow, we discuss six contrasting aspects.

Time Frame Addressed

Transactional IT: *Past and present*

Analytical IT: *Future*

Transactional IT focuses on communicating, storing, and reporting on data describing the company's current supply chain operations. These data are added to historical databases. They may describe internal operations, such as the orders shipped today from a distribution center or the tons of product manufactured today by a machine in a plant. They may also describe the environment in which the firm does business, such as industry sales for the previous quarter. Analytical IT picks up where Transactional IT leaves off by extrapolating data into the future, and analyzing one or more scenarios to identify effective decisions.

Purpose

Transactional IT: *Communications*

Analytical IT: *Forecasting and decision making*

As we just discussed, Transactional IT communicates data describing the company's current and past supply chain activities, whereas Analytical IT seeks to forecast scenarios of the future and optimize decisions associated with these scenarios. Uncertainties about the future depend on the length of the decision problem's planning horizon and the nature of the industry in which the firm competes. The uncertainties may be slight for short-term decisions such as the selection of routes for shipping completed orders to customers over the next week. In such cases, operational plans may safely be developed from a single scenario of the future. At the other extreme, strategic plans stretching out 5 years or more may entail considerable uncertainty and require evaluation of many scenarios using a model.

Business Scope

Transactional IT: *Myopic*

Analytical IT: *Hierarchical*

By its nature, Transactional IT is myopically concerned with current transactions and the compilation of histories based on them. Analytical IT addresses future decisions through a hierarchy of decision problems at all levels of planning—operational, tactical, and strategic. Thus, in the short-term, it may address myopic operational decisions, whereas in the long-term, it may address global facility location and mission decisions that include aggregate descriptions of these same operational decisions to be made at a much later time.

Nature of Databases

Transactional IT: *Raw and lightly transformed objective data*

Analytical IT: *Raw moderately and heavily transformed data that is both objective and judgmental*

The databases created by Transactional IT are derived from raw data that are stored in formats that leave the data unchanged or "lightly transformed." We use this expression to define, admittedly in a vague way, the limits of Transactional IT. It refers to operations on data that are easy to understand although, for large data sets, the resulting transformations may require considerable processing time. An example of lightly transformed data is a report based on aggregate product categories of the cost and volume of SKUs acquired last quarter by a retailing company. Another example is the computation of average costs for shipping full truckloads last month from all company sourcing points to all market zones. By contrast, optimization models employed by Analytical IT require data inputs derived from raw data that may involve significant transformations. An example is the mapping of general ledger costs at each production plant into direct and indirect product and process costs and indirect plant costs, all of which may be fixed or variable, with variable costs that may be linear or nonlinear.

Databases created and used by Analytical IT tools will also contain judgmental data about the company's supply chain. An example might be constraints that mitigate production risk by limiting any plant to making no more than 75% of next year's forecasted demand of certain products. Another example is a constraint limiting to 400 miles the distance from each market to the distribution center that serves it.

These differences between transactional and analytical databases reflect the differences in business scope discussed above. From a bottom-up perspective, the handoff from Transactional to Analytical IT occurs when the company seeks to optimize operational plans for the short-term future. Data that are irrelevant to operational decision making, such as addresses to which invoices for customer orders should be mailed, are stripped from transactional databases, and the remaining data are fed to appropriate supply chain decision databases. Some modeling practitioners estimate that 80% or more of a transactional database is irrelevant to decision making and model construction.

As the planning horizon of decision problems to be evaluated by Analytical IT stretches further into the future, the link between Transactional and Analytical IT becomes more complex. The broader scope of longer-term decision problems requires aggregations of transactional data to provide the model and the decision makers with a better view of their "planning forest" rather than the "trees" representing details of the company's operations. The aggregations must be reversed when longer-term plans are translated into operational plans.

Response Time for Queries

Transactional IT: *Real-time*

Analytical IT: *Real-time and batch processing*

Computing speeds have reached a point where users expect instantaneous, or at least very fast, responses to data queries. This is especially true for Transactional IT, which is responsible for retrieving raw data from corporate databases. Of course, some applications involve databases that are so large that rapid response to queries requires a network of dedicated computers. For example, to support systemwide queries about inventory, large retailing companies stocking 50,000 SKUs across 500 stores and 10 distribution centers employ a data decomposition scheme in which multiple computers, each dedicated to a subset of the company's product line, are accessed through a server.

For certain types of Analytical IT, such as a system producing forecasts of demand for a single product by weeks over the coming year, the response may be nearly instantaneous. Although the underlying model may perform a nontrivial amount of number crunching in determining the forecast, computation is fast enough that the user does not perceive an appreciable delay. For other types of applications, such as the determination of a vehicle routing schedule for daily deliveries to 1000 customers, 15 minutes or longer may be required to generate and solve an optimization model on a high-end PC. Considerable number crunching in a batch mode is required for this application because it entails comprehensive evaluation of a complex system of customers and proposed routes rather than myopic analysis of data pertaining to a single customer or a single route.

The distinction between myopic analysis and comprehensive systems analysis of supply chain decision problems and their requirements for response time is not yet widely understood or appreciated. Many problems, such as the vehicle routing problem just cited, could be analyzed by myopic methods in real time or in no more than a few seconds. For complex problems, however, the plans identified by myopic methods will be markedly inferior to those determined by a global model and optimization method. The distribution manager would certainly be willing to wait several minutes to obtain a schedule produced by a batch run of an optimization model that delivers all orders using 10% fewer trucks. Moreover, considerable refinement by a human analyst may be needed to make the solution produced by a myopic method acceptable for implementation.

The importance of response time diminishes, but does not disappear, as the scope of the supply chain problems to be analyzed moves from daily operational concerns to tactical and strategic ones. Analysis of tactical decisions affecting activities over the next few days or months must still be made in a timely fashion. Strategic planning may require evaluation of many scenarios to complete a study within a tight time frame, thereby constraining the response time available for extracting useful answers from an optimization model describing a single scenario.

Implications for Business Process Redesign

Transactional IT: *Substitute for or eliminate inefficient human effort*
Analytical IT: *Coordinate overlapping managerial decisions*

The impact of IT on business process redesign is an immense subject that we discuss briefly here. We will return to it in Section 12.6. At this juncture, we simply point out that Transactional and Analytical IT have qualitatively different impacts on the organization and management of a company's supply chain. Transactional IT has allowed communication of data describing operational business processes to be automated and made more efficient. It has also provided managers with timely data to make better-informed intuitive decisions about short-term operations, although some decisions could be improved if they were based on model results.

Analytical IT allows supply chain decisions to be integrated across managerial responsibilities and across levels of planning, but to be fully exploited, it entails major organizational change. Although such changes are underway in many companies, their ultimate nature and extent depends on future IT and organizational developments about which we speculate in Chapter12. In summary, Analytical IT seeks to systematically identify opportunities for improving the management of the company's supply chain by functional and intertemporal integration of decisions, whereas Transactional IT addresses myopic opportunities for such improvement.

2.3

Hierarchy of Supply Chain Systems

In the previous section, we emphasized the importance of intertemporal integration of supply chain activities as well as their functional and geographical integration. Intertemporal integration can be fully achieved only by the application of a suite of modeling systems to the gamut of strategic, tactical, and operational planning decision problems faced by the company. These Analytical IT systems are linked to overlapping supply chain decision databases created from data provided by Transactional IT systems. Companies offering ERP software have realized this need. They are actively expanding their offerings to include modeling systems for all levels of planning, either by developing such systems themselves or by acquiring companies with modeling software. (Material in Section 2.3, through page 47, taken from Tayur, et al., 1999.)

Components of the Supply Chain System Hierarchy

In Figure 2.2, we display the Supply Chain System Hierarchy comprising six types of optimization modeling systems and four transactional systems responsible for intertemporal, functional, and geographical integration of supply chain activities in a manufacturing and distribution company that has multiple plants and distribution

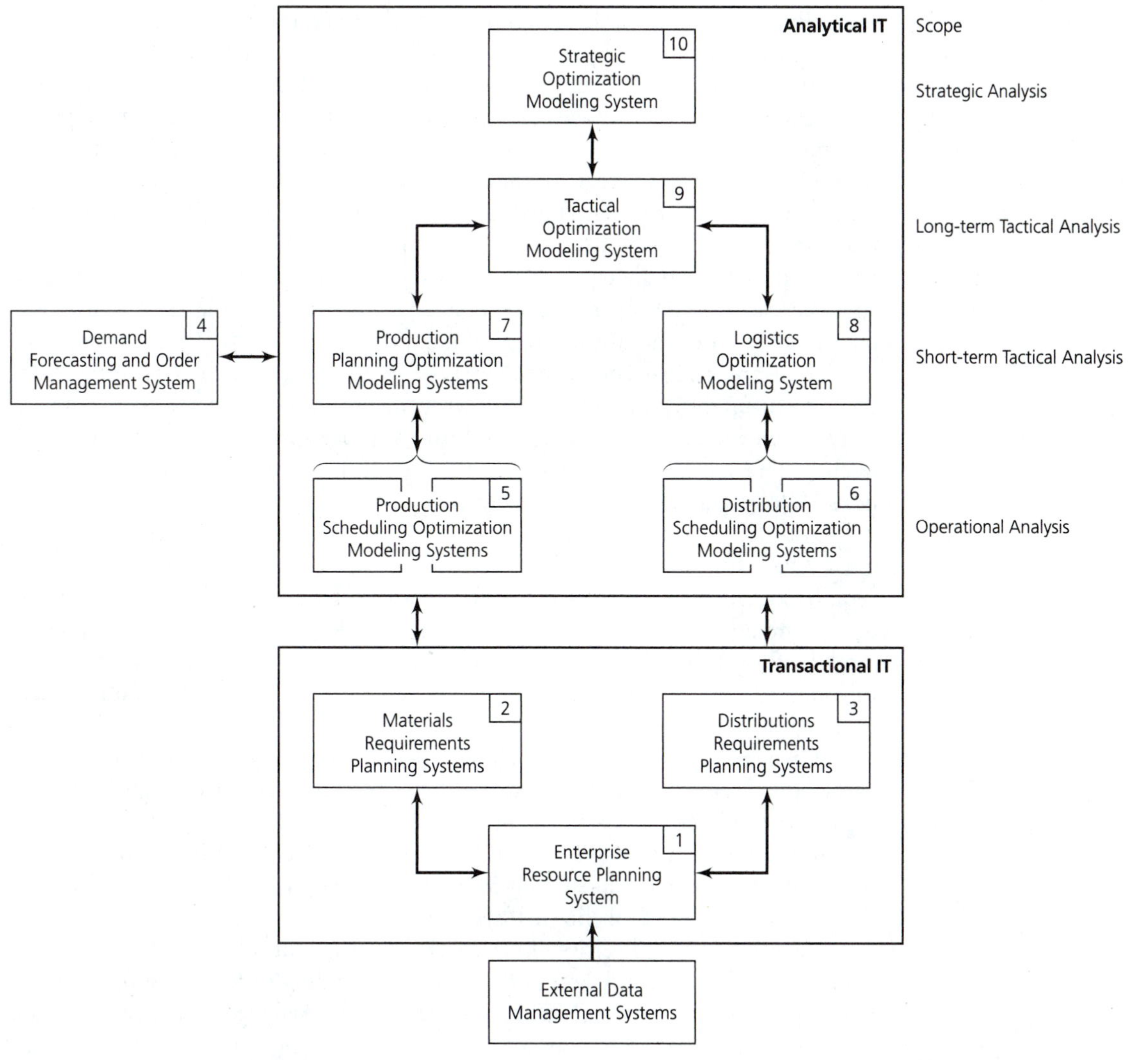

Figure 2.2
Supply chain system hierarchy. *Source:* Tayur, et al. [1999]

centers.[12] As shown in the figure, the six types of optimization modeling systems are Analytical IT, and the four other systems are Transactional IT. Strictly speaking, the demand forecasting and order management system is a hybrid with analytical capabilities for forecasting demand and transactional capabilities for handling customer orders.

We have also shown an important linkage between external data management systems maintained by the company's customers and suppliers and the company's enterprise transactional data. Recent advances in e-commerce offer the promise to streamline and enhance such communication. They also increase the need for modeling systems, especially to support operational decision making across multiple firms.

The Supply Chain System Hierarchy in Figure 2.2 is hypothetical. To the best of our knowledge, no company has implemented and integrated all nine types of systems, although many companies have implemented several of them. Moreover, the components and structure of the hierarchy may appear arbitrary, and we would expect that they might be modified for specific applications. Still, based on our participation in scores of projects in which supply chain modeling systems have been developed, the hierarchy represents the most likely configuration needed to analyze strategic, tactical, and operational supply chain planning problems in a firm that both manufactures and distributes products.

The transactional and scheduling systems in the system hierarchy represent the **bottom-up** thrust in supply chain management. IT developments are the driving force for innovations in this area, with business process redesign as a natural consequence. The area is red hot, with annual sales of software in the hundreds of millions of dollars, and it is growing rapidly.

Distinctions among the transactional and scheduling systems displayed in Figure 2.2 have become blurred. Software companies offering ERP systems have either acquired or entered into alliances with companies offering operational modeling systems. Similarly, some distribution requirements planning (DRP) systems include modules for vehicle scheduling and forecasting. For our purposes here, we choose to maintain separation between the form and function of the modeling and transactional systems.

When seeking to better manage its operations, a company must decide if it wishes to acquire **off-the-shelf systems** or to develop **customized systems** implemented by its internal IT staff, by outside system developers, or by some combination of the two. Customized systems, if they are implemented in an effective and timely manner, are more likely to provide the company with competitive advantage than the acquisition of off-the-shelf systems.

The number and diversity of off-the-shelf systems for operational supply chain management is increasing. Most off-the-shelf scheduling systems to support materials requirements planning (MRP) and DRP decision making use heuristics that are less formal, and less effective in identifying demonstrably good operational plans, than the optimization models we envision for the production scheduling and logistics optimization modeling systems. They rely heavily on graphical user interaction in developing scheduling solutions, often placing too high a burden on historical rules and the judgment of a **human scheduler** to extract a good operational plan from a complex data set. We believe the unified optimization methodology discussed and illustrated in Chapter 5 has the potential to provide modeling systems with superior performance.

Strategic optimization modeling systems in the system hierarchy reflect the **top-down** thrust in supply chain management. The driving force is senior management's need for strategic analysis in the face of globalization of the company's markets and supply chains and competition in cost and service. A typical strategic planning study is performed by consultants who employ an optimization modeling system. They exercise the system to provide management with quantitative insights into the evolution and redesign of their supply chains and answers to what-if questions about the long-term future.

The study mode for applying these systems is often very useful, but short sighted. Because the strategic supply chain problems evaluated by the modeling systems almost certainly will not disappear at the end of the study period, the company would profit greatly by making modeling analysis a permanent part of its strategic review processes. Nevertheless, senior management encounters several organizational barriers when it tries to use a strategic modeling system on a regular basis.

First, the company must commit to the design and implementation of IT procedures for collecting and updating the supply chain decision database. It must also commit to the creation and training of analysts who will devote a significant portion of their time to performing ongoing strategic evaluations. Second, training entails a complete transfer of the modeling system technology to the company from the modeling system developers and, in many cases, the external consultants who perform the study. Finally, the company must implement processes whereby senior management works with analysts and lower-level managers in performing modeling studies, reviewing results, and implementing plans that they suggest.

Long- and short-term tactical supply chain planning have thus far been mainly ignored by managers and consultants. They are the most difficult areas in which to develop better planning methods, based in part on optimization modeling systems. Despite the growing number of applications of strategic optimization modeling systems, we have seen few initiatives to move down the hierarchy to develop and use these systems for related tactical planning problems. The lack of interest by companies that have successfully used optimization modeling systems for strategic studies in extending them to tactical modeling applications is frustrating for modeling practitioners. From a technical perspective, such extensions are easy to accomplish because the model and the supply chain decision database will be validated during the study.

Still, this reluctance is not surprising because repetitive use of a tactical optimization modeling system requires considerable business process redesign. Tactical applications also require the development and upkeep of supply chain decision databases, which, as we already observed, are not yet well understood. Despite the difficulties, we are optimistic about the ultimate breakthrough of tactical modeling applications because the potential rewards are so great. Limited applications have demonstrated that a manufacturing or distribution company can expect to reduce its total supply chain costs by 5% or more by implementing plans identified by a modeling system. The tool is also valuable in helping management adjust to unexpected changes in its business environment, such as a fire at a company plant or a strike at a key vendor.

Starting from the bottom up, the following are synopses of the capabilities of each system type:

1. *Enterprise resource planning system:* The ERP system manages the company's transactional data on a continuous, real-time basis. This system standardizes

the company's data and information systems for order entry, financial accounting, purchasing, and many other functions across multiple facilities and business units. Despite the claim implied by the term *ERP,* effective "resource planning" across the "enterprise" can be identified only by optimization models created using data from the ERP System.[13]

2. *Materials requirement planning system:* Analysis with the MRP system begins with a **master production schedule** of finished products needed to meet demand in each period of a given planning horizon. Using these data, along with a **balance on hand** of inventories of raw materials, work-in-process and finished goods, a **bill of materials** description of the company's product structures, and **machine production data**, the MRP system develops **net requirements** by period of raw materials and intermediate products to be manufactured or ordered from vendors to meet demand for finished products. Products at all stages of manufacturing are analyzed by the MRP system at the SKU level.[14]
3. *Distribution requirements planning system:* Analysis with a DRP system begins with **forecasts** of finished products to be transported, a **balance on hand** of inventories of these products at plants and distribution centers, and **inventory management data** such as safety stock requirements, replenishment quantities, and replenishment times. In conjunction with the distribution scheduling optimization model systems, the DRP system then schedules inbound, interfacility, and outbound shipments through the company's logistics network, taking into account a wide range of **transportation factors** such as vehicle loading and routing, consolidations, modal choice, channel selection, and carrier selection. Products throughout the logistics network are analyzed by the DRP system at the SKU level.[15]
4. *Demand forecasting and order management system:* This system combines data about current orders with historical data to produce requirements for finished products to be met by the operational, tactical, and strategic plans. For operational and short-term tactical planning, an important challenge is to manage the transition from forecasts, which have a significant degree of uncertainty, to orders, which have much less uncertainty. Longer-term planning requires linkages to data on industry and economic factors that have a high degree of uncertainty.[16]
5. *Production scheduling optimization modeling systems:* These are modeling systems located at each plant in the company's supply chain that address operational decisions such as the sequencing of orders on a machine, the timing of major and minor changeovers, or the management of work-in-process inventories. The objective is to minimize avoidable short-term costs while satisfying the customer requirements. In some instances, the selection of orders to complete over the short term is a major decision. The models must fit the environment, which may be discrete parts manufacturing, process manufacturing, job-shop scheduling, or some hybrid.[17]
6. *Distribution scheduling optimization modeling systems:* The manufacturing and distribution company faces a variety of vehicle and other scheduling and oper-

ational planning problems. In addition to local delivery of products to customers, some companies must decide on a short-term basis which distribution center should serve each market based on inventory availability. As with production scheduling, distribution scheduling problems and models vary significantly across industries.[18]

7. *Production planning optimization modeling systems:* Each plant in the company's supply chain uses its version of this optimization modeling system to determine a master production plan for the next quarter for each stage of manufacturing, along with resource levels and resource allocations for each stage, that minimize avoidable manufacturing costs. As part of the optimization, the model also determines work-in-process inventories, major machine changeovers, and make-or-buy decisions. The models used by this system will cover multiperiods as well as multistages. Therefore, for reasons of computational necessity, products are aggregated into product families. These aggregations are reversed when the system hands off the master schedule to the plant's production scheduling and MRP systems. Although many papers have appeared in the academic literature discussing production planning models with this broad scope, few modeling systems based on them have yet been implemented.[19]
8. *Logistics optimization modeling system:* This system determines a logistics master plan for the entire supply chain that analyzes how demand for all finished products in all markets will be met over the next quarter. Specifically, it focuses on the assignment of markets to distribution centers and other facilities responsible for sourcing them. Its goal is to minimize avoidable transportation, handling, warehousing, and inventory costs across the entire logistics network of the company while meeting customer service requirements. Again, for reasons of computational necessity, finished products are aggregated into product families and markets are aggregated into market zones. These aggregations are reversed when the system hands off the master schedule to the plant's distribution scheduling and DRP systems. This type of optimization modeling system has also not yet been widely implemented.
9. *Tactical optimization modeling system:* This system determines an integrated supply/manufacturing/distribution/inventory plan for the company's entire supply chain over the next 12 months. Its goal may to be minimize total supply chain cost of meeting fixed demand or to maximize net revenues if the product mix is allowed to vary. Raw materials, intermediate products, and finished products are aggregated into product families. Similarly, markets are aggregated into market zones. This is another type of optimization modeling system that has not yet been widely implemented.[20]
10. *Strategic optimization modeling system:* This system is used to analyze resource acquisition and other strategic decisions faced by the company such as the construction of a new manufacturing facility, the break-even price for an acquisition, or the design of a supply chain for a new product. Its goal may be to maximize net revenues or return on investment. A number of off-the-shelf packages, with varying degrees of modeling capabilities, are available for this type of application.[21]

Frequency of Analysis, Cycle Times, and Run Times of Supply Chain Systems

In the following subsections, we discuss interactions among systems immediately adjacent to one another in the Supply Chain System Hierarchy depicted in Figure 2.2. Before delving into these details, we need to examine how and when these systems are applied. To this end, Table 2.1 reviews several timing features of each system:

- **Frequency of analysis.** The number of times each year, quarter, or month that managers and planners use the system
- **planning time.** How long it takes to complete analysis of the planning problems with the system each time it is used
- **run time.** Batch time required for each run of the system

The times shown in Table 2.1 are representative of the systems in the hierarchy. They may vary significantly from company to company. The frequency of analysis will be much longer than once a week for the tactical supply chain optimization modeling system and much shorter than once a quarter for the production scheduling optimization modeling system. The planning horizons of the optimization modeling systems, the MRP system, and the DRP system overlap. This facilitates coordination and communication among them.

The column labeled "Model Structure" refers to the number of periods incorporated in models generated by the modeling system. For example, a strategic optimization model will typically be a one period, or snapshot model, where the period is 1 year. A production planning optimization model might be a six-period model where the first four periods are weeks and the final two periods are months.

As we descend in Table 2.1 from strategic to operational systems, the planning horizon becomes shorter, and the description of time in the model structures, as measured by the number of periods in the models, becomes more detailed. In addition, the objective function shifts from net revenue maximization to avoidable cost minimization as we move from strategic to operational planning. Although, net revenue maximization should be sought at all planning levels, the company may have few options to affect revenue at the operational level.

One can expect or hope that, in the coming years, net revenue maximization will work its way down the hierarchy as the company's management improves its abilities to integrate supply chain and demand management decisions. For example, the production scheduling optimization modeling system could be employed to maximize short-term net revenues by identifying which customized orders to accept or reject or to determine prices for such orders to guarantee healthy margins. Such a change in using this system would require changes in business processes to support both the requisite analysis and negotiations with customers.

Communication Among Supply Chain Systems of Data and Decisions

In the subsections that follow, we discuss interactions among the systems in the Supply Chain System Hierarchy. In effecting these interactions, decisions determined

Table 2.1 Features of analytical and transactional systems

	Planning Horizon	Model Structure	Objective Function	Frequency of Analysis	Planning Time	Run Time
Strategic Optimization Modeling System	1–5 years	Yearly snapshots	Maximize net revenues or returns on assets	Once a year	1–2 months	10-60 minutes
Tactical Optimization Modeling System	12 months	3 months, 3 quarters	Minimize total cost of meeting forecasted demand or maximize net revenue by varying product mix	Once a month	1 week	60–120 minutes
Production Planning Optimization Modeling System	13 weeks	4 weeks, 2 months	Minimize avoidable production and inventory costs	Once a week	1 day	10–30 minutes
Logistics Optimization Modeling System	13 weeks	4 weeks, 2 months	Minimize avoidable logistics costs	Once a week	1 day	10–30 minutes
Production Scheduling Optimization Modeling Systems	7–28 days	7–28 days	Minimize myopic production costs	Once a day	30 minutes	10 minutes
Distribution Scheduling Optimization Modeling Systems	7–28 days	7–28 days	Minimize myopic distribution costs	Once a day	30 minutes	10 minutes
MRP Systems	7–28 days	7–28 days	Not applicable	Once a week	1–3 hours	60 minutes
DRP System	7–28 days	7–28 days	Not applicable	Once a week	1–3 hours	60 minutes
Forecasting and Order Management System	1 week–5 years	Varied	Not applicable	Varied	Varied	10 seconds–10 minutes
Enterprise Resource Planning System			Not applicable	Real time or continuous	Real time or continuous	Not applicable

Source: Tayur, et al., 1999.

by the modeling systems become input data to other systems with which they communicate.

ERP, MRP, DRP, and Forecasting and Order Management Systems. Figure 2.3 depicts interactions among the ERP, MRP, DRP, and forecasting and order management systems. Although we have shown them as separate systems, they could be viewed as a single ERP entity dedicated to acquiring, communicating, and managing transactional data requirements across the company. The MRP and DRP systems that are one level up from the ERP system develop and disseminate detailed production and distribution schedules. A separate MRP system is employed in each plant, whereas the DRP system addresses distribution operations across the entire company. These systems are mainly transactional programs that translate master production and distribution schedules into detailed schedules. The systems also keep track of actual production and distribution data. The typical planning horizon for these schedules is 7 to 28 days.

The ERP system provides the MRP and DRP systems with detailed data about costs, capacities, and equipment. It also passes data about orders to the forecasting and order management system, which in turn passes orders and forecasts to the MRP and DRP systems. The company's production and distribution managers use detailed schedules developed by these systems to execute the company's operational plans. These data, along with data about inventories, are also passed to the ERP system for tracking, accounting, and control purposes.

MRP and Production Scheduling Optimization Modeling Systems. Without the production scheduling optimization modeling system, users of the MRP system must determine master schedules and available capacities in an ad hoc way based on historical rules of thumb. Although the typical MRP system has rudimentary tools

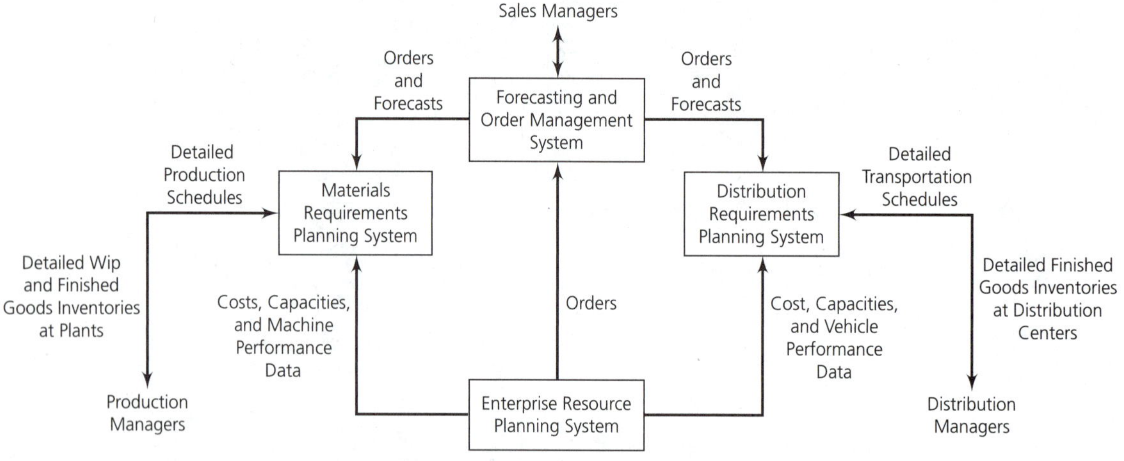

Figure 2.3
Supply chain transactional systems

intended to assist company planners in determining schedules, they leave much to be desired. For example, it might compute capacity loadings implied by the master schedule, but it cannot adjust the master schedule if the loadings exceed available capacity.

In short, the MRP system cannot identify a short-term schedule, required resource levels, and their allocations, which minimize total operational costs over the short-term planning horizon. Moreover, it cannot assist schedulers in determining a feasible schedule, or which orders to delay, when manufacturing capacity is tight. As a result, in using the MRP system without the production scheduling optimization modeling system, production managers can only muddle through the scheduling process by using trial-and-error methods. For this reason, the company needs a modeling system that employs optimization models and methods to determine an effective production schedule over a 13-week planning horizon, with particular attention paid to the next 4 weeks, which span the 28-day horizon of the MRP system. The typical model generated by this system looks out 13 weeks to ensure stability to the detailed plan for the next 28 days that ultimately will be executed according to the MRP system.

As shown in Figure 2.4, the optimization model determines production setups, production runs, discretionary resource levels, work-in-process, and finished goods inventories to minimize avoidable costs associated with attempting to meet customer orders. We say "attempting" to meet customer orders because the company may encounter order schedules that cannot be met. In such an event, based on implicit and explicit penalties associated with late deliveries, the production scheduling model assists production managers in determining which orders will be completed and shipped late.

The links between the production scheduling optimization modeling system and the MRP system involve aggregation when data are fed upward from the MRP

Figure 2.4
Linkages between short-term tactical and operational production planning systems in a plant

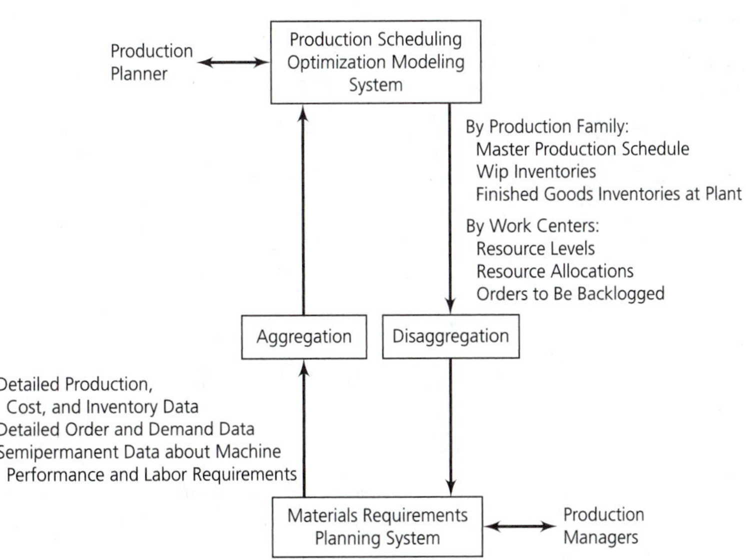

system to the modeling system and disaggregation when data are fed downward from the modeling system to the MRP system.[22] Upward aggregation entails aggregation of products into products families and detailed time-dependent data, such as scheduled maintenance or machine changeovers, into aggregate time-dependent data, such as the week in which these events will take place. Downward disaggregation entails translation of production schedules and inventories of product families into details regarding individual products. It also entails translation of the aggregate timing of time-sensitive decisions into more detailed timing. The disaggregation transformation is essentially an inversion of the aggregation transformation with rules of thumb applied to ensure that the resulting details are efficient and best satisfy downstream production and customer requirements. Thus, in designing the upward aggregation, care must be taken to ensure that the corresponding downward disaggregation can be easily and accurately carried out.

DRP and Logistics Optimization Modeling Systems. Figure 2.5 shows the relationship between the DRP system and the logistics optimization modeling system. Unlike the production systems just discussed that separately analyze each plant, these systems analyze decisions across the company's entire logistics network, which might include several plants and distribution centers and several hundred markets. They also coordinate company transportation activities with those of the vendors.

Otherwise, the company's motivation for implementing and deploying the logistics optimization modeling system is the same as that for the production scheduling optimization modeling system. Without such a system, distribution managers using the DRP system must muddle through the short-term scheduling of transportation movements and the operations of distribution centers to support them. For example, the DRP system has the capability to heuristically optimize daily vehicle loading and routing decisions, but it cannot determine which distribution cen-

Figure 2.5
Linkages between short-term tactical and operational distribution planning systems

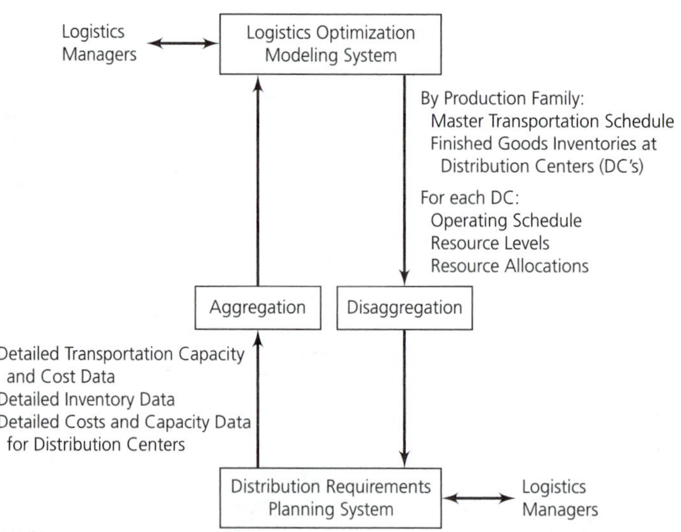

ters should serve each market and how operations at the distribution centers should be scheduled to minimize short-term costs.

The logistics optimization modeling system determines a master transportation schedule that includes inbound shipments of raw materials and parts to the plants, interplant shipments of intermediate and finished products, shipments of finished products to distribution centers, and outbound shipments to the markets of finished products. Decisions about the latter shipments fine tune the longer-term assignment of markets to distribution centers determined by the tactical optimization modeling system. In addition, the logistics optimization modeling system makes modal choices for large shipments based on timing considerations; for example, a choice between a single large rail shipment from a plant to a distribution center or many truck movements spread out over a month's time.

Production Scheduling, Logistics and Tactical Optimization Modeling Systems. The tactical optimization modeling system is the lowest-level system in the hierarchy that analyzes decisions across the company's entire supply chain. As shown in Figure 2.6, it passes aggregate details about the optimal supply chain plan for each of the 3 months of the immediate quarter to the production scheduling optimization modeling systems, one in each plant, and to the logistics optimization modeling system. The details of this plan are disaggregated to provide guidelines for the production scheduling optimization modeling system and the logistics optimization modeling system. Disaggregation may entail refinement of product families and the timing of

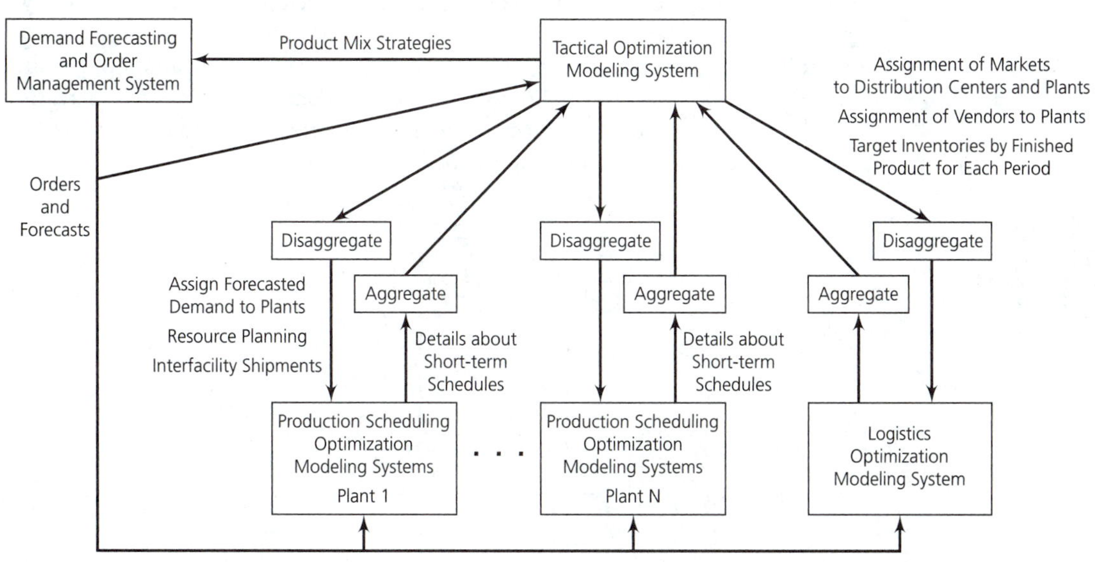

Figure 2.6
Linkages among tactical production scheduling, logistics, and optimization modeling systems and demand forecasting and order management systems

resource planning decisions. Schedules developed by the lower-level systems are fed back to the tactical optimization supply chain modeling system by reversing these disaggregations. These schedules reflect short-term commitments that the higher-level system treats as fixed and given.

Unlike the interactions discussed previously, we have shown linkages, which are two directional, between these modeling systems and the demand forecasting and order management system. In particular, the modeling systems receive order and forecasting information from this system, and the tactical optimization supply chain modeling system sends suggested product mix strategies to this system. Marketing and sales personnel can use these strategies in revising their plans to enhance the company's projected net revenues over the coming year.

Strategic and Tactical Optimization Modeling System. The strategic optimization modeling system assists senior management in determining the most effective long-term configuration of the company's supply chain network. Its models analyze decisions about major resource acquisitions and divestments and the manufacture and distribution of new and existing products over the coming years. The implications of these decisions to next year's tactical plans are passed to the tactical optimization modeling system, as depicted in Figure 2.7. Such data might include new facilities that will be available or products to be manufactured, distributed, and sold during that time frame. The tactical optimization modeling system provides detailed feedback to the strategic system about how these facilities will be used and how market demand will be met over the first year of a strategic planning horizon.

The demand forecasting and order management system provides medium- and long-term demand forecasts to the tactical and strategic optimization modeling systems. Conversely, the strategic optimization modeling system provides the demand forecasting system with feedback about the profitability of existing and new product lines. This information can be used to develop marketing strategies for increasing sales of profitable products. In fact, the demand forecasting system might well be extended to include marketing models to achieve this end.[23]

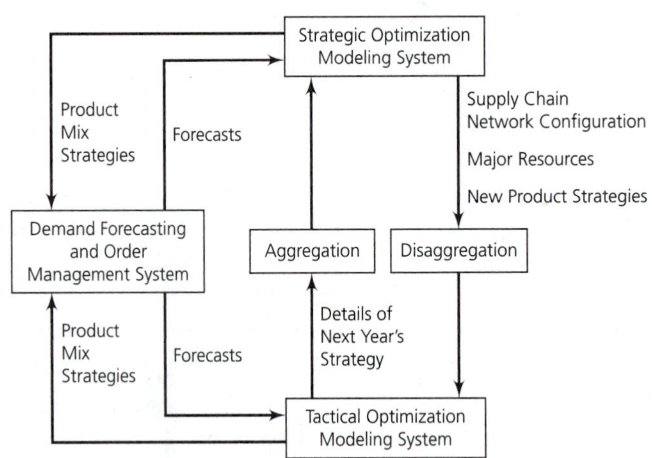

Figure 2.7
Linkages among strategic supply chain optimization modeling system, tactical optimization modeling system, and demand forecasting and order management systems

Balancing Centralized and Decentralized Decision Making

An important underlying purpose of the system hierarchy is to resolve management's conundrum of wishing to make supply chain decisions in both a centralized and a decentralized manner.[24] Centralized decision making is needed to realize efficiencies stemming from integration. Decentralized decision making is needed for rapid, detailed execution of operations. As we discussed extensively above, the conflict can be resolved by passing guidelines based on centralized planning using a modeling system to a lower-level modeling system.

For example, the supply chain manager uses the tactical optimization modeling system to determine short-term production targets for each plant. These targets are passed as inputs to the production planning optimization modeling systems, one for each plant, which product managers use to determine more detailed plans, including a master schedule and optimal capacity levels, for the plant to follow over the next quarter. These plans in turn are passed to the production scheduling and MRP systems, which lower-level managers use to determine a detailed implementation plan for the next month. In addition, the lower-level systems provide feedback to the high-level systems about adjustments to the centralized plans made necessary by the realities of more detailed operations.

2.4
Legacy Systems and Legacy Thinking

Legacy planning systems are outdated computer systems passed on to IT personnel and managers, who employ artistry in trying to apply them to planning problems that have changed, sometimes using awkward data linkages to new systems. ERP systems allow a company to replace inefficient legacy systems and to homogenize and integrate disparate corporate databases. Our interest here is to discuss issues connected with replacing legacy modeling systems and improving legacy thinking about how supply chain decisions should be made. Although the effort required to replace a legacy modeling system may be significant, overcoming the barriers due to legacy thinking about supply chain decision making is often a more difficult task.

In some instances, the legacy modeling system to be updated resides on a mainframe computer. The company wishes to replace it with a modeling system residing on a PC, which requires implementing programs that download data and upload plans identified by the system. Such was the case for a company that manufacturers and distributes food products that sought recently to replace a legacy system constructed in the 1970s. The system used mainframe modeling generation and optimization software that had been successfully applied for over 20 years. Nevertheless, the company wished to replace it because model generation time on the mainframe, due to inefficient data acquisition programs and the need to share CPU time with other users, was excessive.

Tests with several PC-based, off-the-shelf modeling systems indicated that the legacy system could easily be replaced by a better-performing system. The company, however, showed no interest in expanding the scope of analysis provided by the model, which, by 1970s standards was sophisticated, but by those of the 1990s, was simplistic. Specifically, the legacy model sought to minimize the total cost of meeting demand by assigning production to plants, making interplant shipments as needed, and by sole sourcing markets with shipments from a unique plant. Descriptions of production costs, capacities, and transformation activities in the legacy model were simplistically described by unit costs for each product at each plant and overall plant capacity. The legacy model did not address fixed costs, capacity planning, and economies of scale associated with each of several important stages of manufacturing at each plant. Moreover, it did not address decisions regarding the installation of additional capacity or the retirement of excess capacity at new or existing plants.

In short, over the course of 20 years, use of the legacy system induced legacy thinking in the company about integrated planning of its supply chain. For the reasons just indicated, the legacy model produced plans that were probably seriously suboptimal. No one in the company was motivated to question current processes or to spend time collecting data and making model runs to evaluate potentially better ways to manage its supply chain. It is telling that the legacy system had been designed and implemented by a corporate operations research group that gradually disappeared from the company, leaving operations personnel without internal resources for evaluating new decision processes and models. The operations managers could have sought outside help, but it was unclear which software vendors or consultants to trust. Moreover, an exercise to evaluate better models and modeling systems appeared expensive, although an improved model and modeling system would have paid for itself several times over in the first year of use.

As another example, a pharmaceutical company contacted a modeling practitioner because it wished to model a critical production planning step in the manufacture of a very successful product, with sales in the hundreds of millions of dollars, made from a natural ingredient of varying quality. The step involving blending the natural ingredient to produce the basic component used in subsequent manufacturing steps. Approximately 40 blends per year are made.

The company sought a modeling system that would automate and optimize a planning process that was previously performed manually by a key employee. According to legacy thinking about how to plan the blends, which we will describe very shortly, this employee did an excellent job. Nevertheless, the company wished to automate the process so that others could perform it; they also believed that it could be improved by computer-based optimization.

Because yearly planning of the blends of natural ingredient had been done manually, the goal in selecting them was to take the available pool of the natural ingredient and try to find the set of blends that yielded the most uniform product. This problem resembles blending of petroleum products, with the added qualitative concern that product quality would be closely scrutinized by the Federal Drug Administration. In addition, the blending constraints were defined relative to the composition of the pool, rather than absolute constraints, which are imposed on petroleum products.

Because the natural ingredient is expensive to acquire, the practitioners suggested that the company should expand the analysis to more carefully decide upon the amount of its yearly purchases and more carefully control its inventories. In addition, rather than select all 40 blends for the product at the beginning of each year, it was suggested that production plans for each month could be modified according to marketing requirements. Moreover, within limits, the optimization could select the pool of the natural ingredient to be used for a given year as well as to optimize the blends made from it. These suggestions fell on deaf ears. As a result, a model was designed and implemented that did no more than optimize the manual process. The company was very pleased with the resulting system and the blends it produced, which were superior to those produced by hand.

The examples just cited of a company's reluctance to go beyond legacy thinking in managing its supply chain are not exceptional. Although we could speculate further about the reasons for this reluctance, we must recognize that it is still early in the development and use of modeling systems. Many companies are still grappling with ERP system developments that they feel must proceed the development of analytical tools. Moreover, we must continue to educate students and managers about the value of rational decision making and the form, function, and benefits of models and modeling systems.

2.5 Final Thoughts

The growth in IT investment depicted in Figure 2.1 suggests that the information revolution accelerated significantly in the 1990s. Looking at the figure, one is also tempted to conclude that the revolution hardly began before 1980. Unfulfilled expectations about ERP systems and e-commerce indicate that developers and consultants are still struggling with advances in software and business process redesign needed to foster efficient and flexible systems for Transactional IT. At the same time, because managers have begun to recognize the need for Analytical IT, ERP system companies are actively seeking to add optimization modeling systems to their suite of offerings. Our discussion in this chapter is intended to set the stage for an indepth examination of optimization models and modeling systems that serve as the "brains" of Analytical IT systems for supply chain management.

Furthermore, we recommend that Transactional IT developers pay more attention to data requirements induced by modeling systems. New software is needed for creating and applying supply chain decision databases that sit between corporate databases and modeling systems. Transactional data that are irrelevant to decision making should be separated from transactional data that are relevant. Relevant data may require transformations before they can be used directly in an optimization model.

Despite 50 years of study in operations research models and methods, plus numerous examples of successful modeling system implementations, we are still in the early days of applying them in a pervasive and enduring manner to a range of supply chain applications. As we shall attempt to demonstrate, operations research academics and practitioners have filled their intellectual warehouse with models and methods that offer great promise. The opportunity to pick good ideas from this warehouse and apply them is exciting. At the same time, given the red hot pace of IT developments, modeling practitioners must strive to fend off and displace mediocre solutions that, in the confusion of the IT revolution, are being oversold to managers.

Exercises

In addition to the following exercises, modeling exercises involving data files and discussion exercises involving white papers may be found on the Web site (www.scm-models.com).

1. Inventory management is inherently an operational planning problem involving decisions about when to order replacement stock and how much to order when such decisions are made. Discuss reasons and situations in which inventory management is also a tactical or strategic planning problem. In addition, discuss ways that inventory decisions at the three levels of planning, operational, tactical, and strategic, are linked.
2. For a firm that manufactures industrial products, such as industrial chemicals or printed circuit boards, describe conditions under which it is appropriate to pursue *operational* plans that maximize net revenue. Your discussion should include reference to the operational time frame for such decision making and to processes for implementing plans that seek to maximize net revenues.
3. In their book, *Reengineering the Corporation,* Hammer and Champy state the following:[25]

   > To recognize the power inherent in modern information technology and to visualize its application requires that companies use a form of thinking that businesspeople usually don't learn and with which they may feel uncomfortable. Most executives and managers know how to think *deductively.* That is, they are good at defining a problem or problems, then seeking and evaluating different solutions to it. But applying information technology to business reengineering demands *inductive* thinking—the ability to first recognize a powerful solution and then seek the problems it might solve, problems the company probably doesn't even know it has.

   a. According to the dictionary, *deduction* is the process of reasoning in which a conclusion follows necessarily from the premises; reasoning from the general to the specific.[26] Moreover, *induction* is the process of deriving general principles from particular facts or instances.[27] Would you say that these terms were used correctly in the above statement? Support your answer.

   b. Provide arguments citing examples that support the intention of the statement that management must explore opportunities for reengineering the corporation to fully exploit new information technology.

c. Provide arguments citing examples where (so-called) inductive approaches have proven counterproductive.

d. Provide a summary describing the extent to which you agree or disagree with the statement.

4. In his book, *A Primer on Decision Making,* March describes rational decision making as based on answers to the following four questions:[28]

   i. The question of *alternatives:* What actions are possible?

   ii. The question of *expectations.* What future consequences might follow from each alternative? How likely is each possible consequence, assuming that alternative is chosen?

   iii. The question of *preferences:* How valuable (to the decision maker) are the consequences associated with each of the alternatives?

   iv. The question of the *decision rule:* How is a choice to be made from among the alternatives in terms of the values of their consequences?

   Proponents of rational decision making as a guiding force in managing companies and organizations have modified their original thinking to one of *bounded rationality.* They still believe that decision makers intend to be rational, but most decision makers are limited by their mental capacities and the accuracy and completeness of the information they have gathered. Specifically, they face serious limitations in attention, memory, comprehension, and communication.

   a. To what extent do models actualize and mechanize the theory of rational decision making?

   b. In your opinion, has the information revolution, including the advent of ERP systems and e-commerce, relieved or exacerbated the limitations on making rational decisions?

   c. How can descriptive and normative models be used to overcome human limitations of attention, memory, comprehension, and communication?

5. In Section 1.3, we discussed Porter's value chain and remarked that the intersection of primary and support activities displayed in Figure 1.3 suggest the need for a new type of matrix organization based on data and models. Elaborate on this observations with particular reference to the hierarchy of supply chain systems and the managers who use them that is discussed in Section 2.3.

Notes

1. Lohr [1997].

2. This figure is from Lohr [1999], who examines Internet developments through the end of 1999. He suggests that "... it is probably too early to judge whether an Internet revolution is truly under way. Historians say the Internet should be viewed mainly as the latest advance in communications, a successor to the telegraph and the telephone, more a technological step than a leap forward."

3. Robinson and Dilts [1999] give an overview of developments in ERP systems with an emphasis

on the role that operations research models can play in extending these systems to analyze supply chain decisions.

4. These figures are quoted in Deutsch [1998], who describes the pain that many companies have felt in trying to implement ERP systems.

5. Limitations as well as benefits of ERP systems are discussed in more detail by Robinson and Dilts [1999].

6. Latamore [1999] reports on developments in ERP systems, including extensions to Web-enabled versions.

7. Canedy [1998] reviews business-to-consumer developments, including projections of total Internet business in several markets by the year 2002, which are generally quite small relative to store sales. Of course, Internet developments far beyond 2002 are still shrouded in considerable mystery.

8. See Tedeschi [1999].

9. Foster [1999] quotes this figure, attributing it to Forrester Research in Cambridge, Massachusetts.

10. See Foster [1999, 20].

11. *Economist* [2000] contains a discussion of the pros and cons of achieving perfectly efficient markets over the Internet.

12. An early version of this subsection appeared in Shapiro [1999].

13. SAP, the leading ERP system company, has developed a suite of modeling modules to complement its ERP modules. Two other of the top five ERP companies, J. D. Edwards and Baan, acquired smaller companies with supply chain modeling systems.

14. For more information about MRP systems, see Baker [1993] and Sipper and Bulfin [1997, 337–363].

15. For more information about DRP systems, see Stegner [1994].

16. Demand forecasting is discussed in detail in Section 6.6.

17. Shapiro [1993] reviews a variety of optimization models for production scheduling. A production scheduling model and solution methodology is proposed in detail in Sections 5.2 and 5.4.

18. See Golden and Assad [1988] or Crainic and Laporte [1998] for a broad treatment of vehicle routing algorithms and applications and Hall and Partyka [1997] for a survey of off-the-shelf packages for vehicle routing. A vehicle routing model and solution methodology is proposed in detail in Sections 5.2 and 5.3.

19. Thomas and McClain [1993] provide a comprehensive literature survey of production planning models through the early 1990s. Two examples of implemented production planning optimization modeling systems are those developed at Harris Corporation (Leachman et al. [1996]) and Sadia (Taube-Netto [1996]). The applications at Harris Corporation are discussed in detail in Section 10.4.

20. Tactical supply chain models and modeling systems are discussed in Chapters 7 and 8.

21. Strategic supply chain models and modeling systems are discussed in Chapters 7 and 8.

22. Graves [1982] gives an example of an optimization model for which aggregation and disaggregation between short-term tactical and operational production scheduling are rigorously defined. For most applications, such rigor might be difficult to achieve. Nevertheless, practitioners would do well to push formal models and methods before resorting to ad hoc methods.

23. The integration of marketing and supply chain models is discussed in Chapter 8.

24. The notion that IT promotes schemes for simultaneous centralized and decentralized planning in the firm was suggested by Hammer and Champy [1993, 93]; however, they are vague about how it could actually be accomplished.

25. See Hammer and Champy [1993, 84].

26. See *The American Heritage College Dictionary* [1993, 362].

27. See *The American Heritage College Dictionary* [1993, 693].

28. See March [1994, 2–3].

References

The American Heritage Dictionary [1993]. Boston: Houghton Mifflin.

Baker, K. R. [1993], "Requirements Planning," in *Handbooks in Operations Research and Management Science: Logistics of Production and Inventory,* edited by S. C. Graves, A. H. G. Rinnoy Kan, and P. H. Zipkin. Amsterdam: North-Holland.

Canedy D. [1998], "Need Aspargus? Just Click It," *The New York Times,* C1, September 10.

Crainic, T. G., and G. Laporte, ed. [1998], *Fleet Management and Logistics.* Norwell, Mass.: Kluwer Academic.

Deutsch, C. H. [1998], "Software That Can Make a Grown Company Cry," *The New York Times,* November 18.

Economist [2000], "How to be Perfect," February 12, 82.

Foster, T. A. [1999], "Global eProcurement Solutions," *Supply Chain Management Review Global Supplement.* Spring, 19–22.

Golden, B. L., and A. A. Assad, eds., [1988], *Vehicle Routing: Methods and Studies.* Amsterdam: North-Holland.

Graves, S. C. [1982], "Using Lagrangean Techniques to Solve Hierarchical Production Planning Problems," *Management Science,* 28, 260–275.

Hall, R. W., and J. G. Partyka, "On the Road to Efficiency" [1997], *OR/MS Today,* 24, 3, 38–47.

Hammer, M., and J. Champy [1993], *Reengineering the Corporation,* New York: HarperBusiness.

Latamore, G. B. [1999], "ERP in the New Millennium," *APICS,* 9, 6, 28–32.

Leachman, R. C., R. F. Benson, C. Liu, and D. J. zRaar [1996], "IMPReSS: An Automated Production-Planning and Delivery-Quotation System at Harris Corporation-Semiconductor Sector," *Interfaces,* 26, 1, 6–37.

Lohr, S. [1997], "Information Technology Field Is Rated Largest U.S. Industry," *The New York Times,* November 18.

*Lohr, S. [1999], "The Economy Transformed, Bit by Bit," *The New York Times,* December 20.

March, J. G. [1994], *A Primer on Decision Making: How Decisions Happen.* New York: The Free Press.

Robinson, A. G., and D. M. Dilts [1999], "OR & ERP," *ORMS Today,* 26, 3, 30–35.

Shapiro, J. F. [1993], "Mathematical Programming Models and Methods for Production Planning and Scheduling," in *Handbook in Operations Research and Management Science: Logistics of Production and Inventory,* edited by S. C. Graves, A. H. G. Rinooy Kan, and P. H. Zipkin. Amsterdam: North-Holland.

Shapiro, J. F. [1999], "Bottom-up vs. Top-down Approaches to Supply Chain Modeling," in *Quantitative Models for Supply Chain Management,* edited by S. Tayur, R. Ganeshan, and M. Magazine. Norwell, Mass.: Kluwer Academic.

Sipper, D., and R. L. Bulfin, Jr. [1997], *Production: Planning, Control, Integration.* New York: McGraw-Hill.

Stenger, A. J. [1994], "Distribution Resource Planning," in *The Logistics Handbook,* edited by J. F. Robeson and W. C. Copacino. New York: The Free Press.

Taube-Netto, M. [1996], "Integrated Planning for Poultry Production at Sadia," *Interfaces,* 26, 38–53.

*Tayur, S., and R. Ganeshan, and M. Magazine, eds., [1999], *Quantitative Models for Supply Chain Management.* Norwell, Mass.: Kluwer Academic.

Tedeschi, R. [1999], "E-Commerce Report," *The New York Times,* C4, September 27, 1999.

Thomas, L. J. and J. O. McClain [1993], "An Overview of Production Planning," in *Handbooks in Operations Research and Management Science: Logistics of Production and Inventory,* edited by S. C. Graves, A. H. G. Rinnoy Kan, and P. H. Zipkin. Amsterdam: North-Holland.

*See the credits section at the end of this book for more information.

II

Modeling and Solution Methods

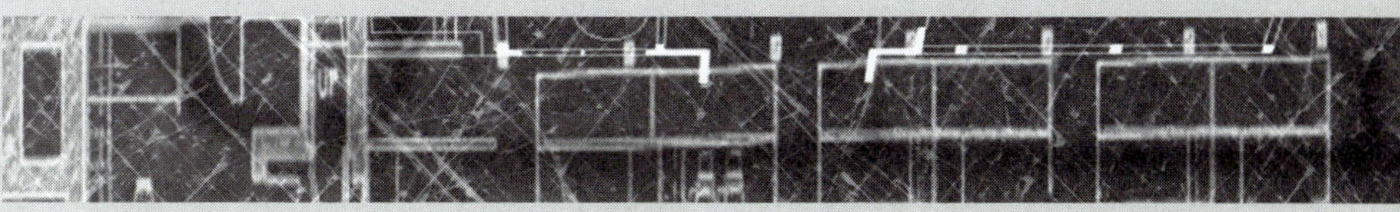

3 Fundamentals of Optimization Model
Linear Programmin

In the previous chapter, we discussed the central role of descriptive and normative, or optimization, models in supporting supply chain decision making. In this chapter and the next two, we provide details about how optimization models are constructed and solved. These models provide a rich and robust framework for combining data, relationships, and forecasts from descriptive models. They provide managers with broad and deep insights into effective plans, which are based on the company's decision options, goals, commitments, and resource constraints. In later chapters, we discuss descriptive models from managerial accounting, demand forecasting, inventory theory, and other disciplines used in identifying and validating the inputs to optimization models.

Technical knowledge about optimization models is critical if optimization modeling systems are to be used to their full advantage. Much of this book could have been written from the perspective that the analytical engines of such systems are "black boxes" that only specialists need to comprehend. We rejected such an approach because it fosters a dangerous lack of understanding on the part of managers and analysts. If they have little or no knowledge about how details of a model represent and analyze decision problems, managers might be unwilling to trust its results, or, equally unsatisfactory and dangerous, they might be too willing to blindly trust them.

Still, having committed us to study details of model construction and solution, we wish to reassure the reader that we are not about to embark on mathematical developments that require graduate training in operations research. Rather, we will employ only mathematical constructions taught in high school. Although this means that we will be restricted to small models that do not convey the richness of larger models for complex problems, we will be able to convey a comprehensive knowledge of the fundamentals.[1] Moreover, without going into excessive detail, we will describe in later chapters how large-scale models are constructed by synthesizing smaller, simpler submodels of the types discussed in this chapter and the next.

Examples of optimization models used in this and the following chapter address decision problems that arise in supply chain management. In particular, we will discuss the application of **linear programming models** and **mixed integer**

programming models to such problems. We also devote appendixes of these chapters to presentations of **algorithms** for numerically optimizing linear programming and mixed integer programming models. The appendixes are developed in the context of simple numerical examples intended to provide the reader with intuition about the number crunching that identifies optimal strategies from input data about a supply chain problem. In Chapter 5, we extend the scope of mixed integer programming models for operational planning by presenting a unified optimization methodology that combines model decomposition methods with heuristics. Finally, we note that the same modeling techniques and algorithms discussed here have been applied to decision problems arising in investment banking, engineering design, and many other areas.

In Section 3.1, we present simple examples of linear programming models, but they are sufficiently complicated to allow us to illustrate the underlying ideas. The examples are presented first in standard algebraic form and then in the format of two spreadsheet optimizers, Solver and What's Best. We discuss properties of linear programming models in Section 3.2, identifying weaknesses in their ability to represent some features of supply chain planning problems. This discussion serves as a prelude to richer, more comprehensive mixed integer programming models, extensions of linear programming models that are discussed in the next chapter.

In Section 3.3, we provide an economic interpretation of the conditions establishing optimality used by the simplex method of linear programming, which provides important insights into the optimization process. Moreover, the marginal costs implicitly computed by the simplex method have practical value to managers in resource and sales planning. Sensitivity and parametric analysis are also discussed in that section.

Linear programming methods can be adapted to measure trade-offs among conflicting objectives by tracing out the efficient frontier of solutions. These methods are discussed and illustrated in Section 3.4. The chapter continues with Section 3.5 where we discuss stochastic programming models which are generalizations of linear programming models that allow explicit treatment of planning uncertainties. Stochastic programming is illustrated by its application to decisions about production and inventory planning in the face of demand uncertainty. The chapter concludes with final thoughts in Section 3.6. In Appendix 3.A, we present the simplex method for optimizing linear programming models. The method is illustrated by its application to the simple model of Section 3.2.

3.1 Linear Programming Modeling Examples

Linear programming (LP) models, and methods for optimizing them, play a central role in all types of supply chain applications. The models and methods were originally devised to optimize the allocation of scarce resources to economic activities in a complex system.

Resource Allocation Model

In a manufacturing company or a supply chain network, many activities compete for resources, such as machine capacity at a plant or inventory of a finished product at a DC. The available quantities of some resources may be insufficient to accommodate all the demands placed on them. Moreover, some activities may consume several resources in producing desired outputs. Linear programming models allow resources to be allocated across the entire system being analyzed to determine how scarce resources can be optimally used.

Example 3.1

We consider a weekly resource allocation problem faced by the production manager of the Ajax Computer Company. Ajax sells three types of computers: the personal computer Alpha, the notebook computer Beta, and the workstation Gamma. The net profit of each Alpha sold is $350, of each Beta sold is $470, and of each Gamma sold is $610. Net profit equals the sales price of each computer minus the direct costs of purchasing components, producing computer cases, and assembling and testing the computer. For the moment we assume that all production during the week can and will be sold immediately. A little later we will consider an extension that addresses plans for several weeks in which some production goes into inventory and for which upper limits on sales exist.

This week, 120 hours are available on the A-line test equipment where assembled Alphas and Betas are tested, and 48 hours are available on the C-line test equipment where assembled Gammas are tested. The testing of each computer takes 1 hour. In addition, production is constrained by the availability of 2000 labor hours for product assembly; each Alpha requires 10 labor hours, each Beta requires 15 labor hours, and each Gamma requires 20 labor hours. Other activities at Ajax are involved in producing these computers, such as packaging computers for shipment, but the three just mentioned involving testing and assembly are the ones consuming scarce resources. The production manager wishes to allocate these resources to maximize net profits for the week.

She decides to construct an LP model of this week's problem. Her decision variables are as follows:

MA = number of Alphas to be assembled, tested, and sold during the week

MB = number of Betas to be assembled, tested, and sold during the week

MC = number of Gammas to be assembled, tested, and sold during the week

The total net profit from these decisions is 350MA + 470MB + 610MC. This sum is called the **objective function.** In our example the objective function is to be maximized. In other examples, the objective function may refer to costs or other quantities to be minimized.

The allocation of scarce resources can also be described by mathematical relationships. For example, the A-line test equipment utilization in hours is measured by MA + MB, and this quantity is constrained by MA + MB ≤ 120. Similar **constraints** must be written for C-line test capacity and labor capacity.

Combining the objective function and the constraints, an optimal strategy for the production manager can be found by solving the model shown in Figure 3.1.

Figure 3.1
One-week Ajax assembly model

$$\text{Maximize } Z = 350\text{MA} + 470\text{MB} + 610\text{MC}$$

$$\begin{array}{lrcrcrcrl}
\text{Subject to} & \text{MA} & + & \text{MB} & & & \leq & 120 & \text{(A-line test capacity)} \\
 & & & & & \text{MC} & \leq & 48 & \text{(C-line test capacity)} \\
 & 10\text{MA} & + & 15\text{MB} & + & 20\text{MC} & \leq & 2000 & \text{(labor availability)} \\
\end{array}$$

$$\text{MA} \geq 0,\ \text{MB} \geq 0,\ \text{MC} \geq 0$$

Note that we constrained the decision variables to take on nonnegative values. Negative values for them would have no meaning. Any solution MA, MB, MC satisfying the constraints is called a **feasible solution.**

In this model, the coefficients 120, 48, and 2000 are called the **right-hand sides.** Associated with each decision variable is an **activity** describing the rate at which the decision variable consumes resources and helps satisfy requirements. For example, the activity associated with the decision variable MA is

$$\begin{pmatrix} 1 \\ 0 \\ 10 \end{pmatrix}$$

The optimal solution to the model in Figure 3.1 is MA* = 120, MB* = 0, MC* = 40 with maximal net revenue *Z* * = $66,400. The asterisks on the decision variables indicate that they are taking on specific values. We compute this optimal solution using the simplex method presented in Appendix 3.A. Note that with this solution, the A-line test capacity constraint and the labor availability constraint are satisfied as equations. We say that these constraints are **binding.** Conversely, the C-line test capacity constraint is satisfied as a strict inequality. We say that such constraints are **nonbinding.**

The **theory of constraints** is in an approach to production planning and scheduling that has received wide attention since its formulation in the early 1990s.[2] It was originally proposed as a management philosophy for improving the performance of production systems by identifying system constraints. From a fact-based, decision-making perspective, it is an ad hoc approach to identifying the binding constraints in a linear programming model. As such, it may fail to identify an optimal plan.[3] Moreover, it fails to provide a rigorous context in which to define and evaluate decisions for acquiring and adjusting production resources, as well as allocating them.

To provide geometric insight into the solution of the model in Figure 3.1, we draw a picture in two dimensions corresponding to feasible values for the decision variables MA and MC. In so doing, we unfairly use omniscience to ignore the decision variable MB, which we know is zero in the optimal solution. This allows us to plot Figure 3.2 using the residual constraints MA ≤ 120, MC ≤ 48, 10MA + 20MC ≤ 2000, MA ≥ 0, and MC ≥ 0. The first two and the last two constraints limit the values of MA and MC to the rectangle shown in the figure. The constraint 10MA + 20MC ≤ 2000 cuts off the northeast corner of the rectangle. We can see this by plotting the constraint as the equality 10MA + 20MC = 2000, which intersects the axes at the points (MA = 200, MC = 0) and (MA = 0, MC = 100). Because labor usage must be less than or equal to 2000 hours, any feasible choice of MA and MC must lie to the southwest of this line where one or both of the variables have lower values. Thus, the shaded area in figure represents the **feasible region;** that is, the feasible values for MA and MC.

To graphically determine an optimal solution to this model, we try for an objective function value of 14,000 and display all feasible solutions yielding this value. These are the points in the shaded region that are also on the line labeled $Z = 14{,}000$. It is easy to see that other lines with constant values of Z are parallel to this line. Moreover, the objective function value they obtain increases as we move toward the northeast because that is the direction in which the values of MA and MC increase and add to the objective function value. If we carefully move a ruler to the northeast parallel to the line $Z = 14{,}000$, we find that the last feasible point we intersect before seeking an unattainable objective function value is the optimal

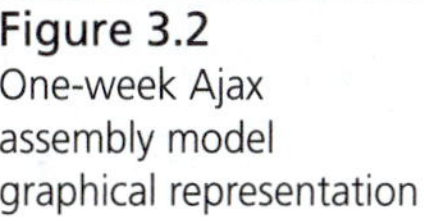
Figure 3.2
One-week Ajax assembly model graphical representation

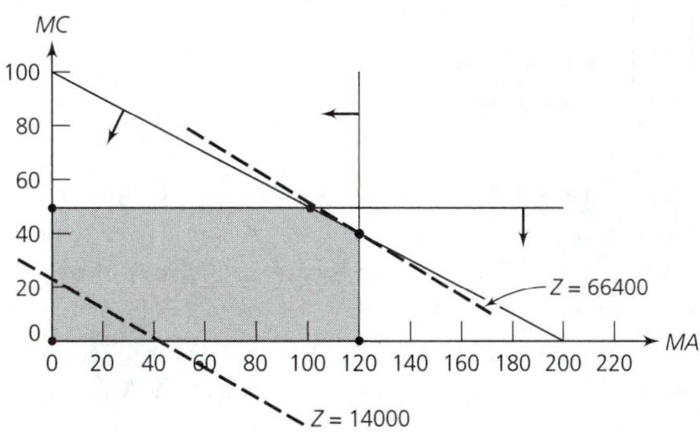

solution indicated in the figure with an objective function value of 66,400. Algebraically, we can compute the optimal solution by recognizing that the geometric optimal solution corresponds to a solution of the equations

$$\begin{aligned} \text{MA} \qquad\qquad &= 120 \\ 10\text{MA} + 20\text{MC} &= 2000 \end{aligned}$$

which is easy to determine (MA = 120, MC = 40).

Although the set of feasible solutions depicted in Figure 3.2 is infinite, it is intuitively clear from the above construction that, for any coefficients for MA and MC in the objective function, an optimal solution can always be found at one of the five heavy dots. The dots are called **extreme points** because they cannot be represented as combinations of two or more other distinct points in the feasible region. The algebra underlying the picture can be readily scaled to models involving an arbitrary (finite) number of decision variables. That is, for a well-behaved linear programming model, the feasible region has a finite number of extreme points, and one of them will always correspond to an optimal solution. The simplex method given in Appendix 3.A is a clever algorithm for systematically searching these extreme points to find a sequence of them with increasing objective function values (for a maximization model) until an optimal solution is found and proven to be optimal.

For future reference, we note that a linear programming activity may sometimes be viewed as a **recipe** describing how inputs of various resources yield outputs of products. A recipe includes both inputs and outputs. For example, the activity displayed above corresponds to the recipe

$$\begin{pmatrix} 1 \\ 0 \\ 10 \\ -1 \end{pmatrix} \begin{matrix} \text{A-line resource input} \\ \text{C-line resource input} \\ \text{labor resource input} \\ \text{assembled Alpha output} \end{matrix}$$

Suppose now there is a second recipe for producing Alphas indicating that

$$\begin{pmatrix} 0 \\ 1.5 \\ 10 \\ -1 \end{pmatrix} \begin{matrix} \text{A-line resource input} \\ \text{C-line resource input} \\ \text{labor resource input} \\ \text{assembled Alpha output} \end{matrix}$$

Alphas can also be tested on the C-line test equipment, whose full capacity is not used, but it takes 1.5 hours per unit. Letting MA1 denote the number of Alphas assembled according to the first recipe and MA2 denote those assembled by the second recipe, we expand the model in Figure 3.1 to that given in Figure 3.3. Note that we have added the equation MA – MA1 – MA2 = 0 to express the condition that recipes 1 and 2 provide the total output MA of Alphas. This model illustrates

Figure 3.3
Extended 1-week Ajax assembly model

$$
\begin{array}{lrrrrrl}
 & \text{Maximize } Z = 350\text{MA} + 470\text{ MB} + 610\text{ MC} & & & & & \\
\text{Subject to} & \text{MA1} + & & \text{MB} & & \leq & 120 \\
 & & 1.5\text{MA2} & & + \text{ MC} & \leq & 48 \\
 & 10\text{MA1} + & 10\text{MA2} + & 15\text{MB} & + 20\text{MC} & \leq & 2000 \\
\text{MA} - & \text{MA1} - & \text{MA2} & & & = & 0 \\
 & \multicolumn{6}{l}{\text{MA} \geq 0, \text{MA1} \geq 0, \text{MA2} \geq 0, \text{MB} \geq 0, \text{MC} \geq 0}
\end{array}
$$

how linear programming can be used to optimally select transformation activities (recipes) at the same time that it optimally allocates scarce resources.

The optimal solution to the model in Figure 3.3 takes advantage of the alternate recipe for Alphas. In particular, the optimal solution is MA* = 128, MA1* = 120, MA2* = 8, MB* = 0, MC* = 36 with Z* = $66,760. By using the new recipe to exploit unused capacity on the C-line test equipment, the production manager increased net revenue by $260.

Infeasible and Unbounded Models

The discovery of an optimal solution is the normal outcome of optimizing a well-posed linear programming model. However, two other outcomes are possible. One is that the model is **infeasible;** that is, there are no feasible solutions. This would occur in the Ajax assembly model, for example, if a constraint requiring at least 50 Gammas to be sold each week (MC ≥ 50) were imposed because the C-line testing capacity is 48 hours, or 48 Gammas.

The other outcome of optimizing the model is that the objective function is **unbounded.** For a maximization model, given any net profit amount, unboundedness means that some feasible strategy to the model exists that exceeds that amount. Such an outcome is mathematically possible but may be difficult to interpret physically and almost always indicates an erroneous model formulation.

Example 3.2

For the sake of illustration, suppose Ajax can outsource A-line testing equipment at $40/hour in unlimited quantities and can hire additional labor at $30/hour in unlimited quantities. Let

EA = quantity of outsourced A-line test hours

EL = quantity of rented labor hours

The model is shown in Figure 3.4.

Figure 3.4
Extended 1-week Ajax model; unbounded objective function

$$\text{Maximize } Z = 350\text{MA} + 470\text{MB} + 610\text{MC} - 40\text{EA} - 30\text{EL}$$

$$\begin{array}{lrcrcrcrcr} \text{Subject to} & -\text{EA} & + & \text{MA} & + & \text{MB} & & & \le & 120 \\ & & & & & & & \text{MC} & \le & 48 \\ & -\text{EL} & + & 10\text{MA} & + & 15\text{MB} & + & 20\text{MC} & \le & 2000 \end{array}$$

$$\text{MA} \ge 0,\ \text{MB} \ge 0,\ \text{MC} \ge 0,\ \text{EA} \ge 0,\ \text{EL} \ge 0$$

The first constraint states that A-line test capacity is constrained by

$$\text{MA} + \text{MB} \le 120 + \text{EA}$$

Similarly, the third constraint states that labor capacity is constrained by

$$10\text{MA} + 15\text{MB} + 20\text{MC} \le 2000 + \text{EL}$$

Because the net profit for each Alpha that is assembled, tested, and sold is $350, but would only cost $340 using the extra resources (1 hour outsourced A-line test @$40 + 10 hours labor @$30), Ajax can achieve an unbounded net revenue. If we optimized this model, we would find that *Z* was unbounded.

This situation of "buying low and selling high" to make an unbounded profit is called **arbitrage** by finance theorists. Occasional attempts have been made to use optimization models to uncover arbitrage opportunities in complex financial markets by identifying a series of trades that can be repeated infinitely, often to produce an infinite profit (unbounded objective function).[4] The reality of the situation at Ajax is that the marketing and sales department could not sell an unlimited number of Alphas, and even if the extra resource costs were accurate, the production manager would be limited in the extra A-line capacity she could rent and the qualified extra labor she could hire. Still, outsourcing A-line testing and renting labor are good deals and should be pursued.

Spreadsheet Optimization

For pedagogical reasons, we modeled Ajax' weekly resource allocation problem at the most elemental level in which constraints and the objective function combining input data with decision variables were explicitly written out. In practice, a modeling system will separate these data from the decision variables, which greatly simplifies the tasks of correcting data and preparing multiple scenarios. Spreadsheet optimizers are the simplest systems that allow such a separation, although they still require that the developer have knowledge about modeling.

In this subsection, we describe briefly the application of two spreadsheet optimizers, Solver and What's Best, to the generation and optimization of the 1-week

Ajax assembly model.[5] In addition to allowing data to be specified separately from the decision variables, spreadsheet optimization allows the user to employ the spreadsheet's functionality to check data, create reports and graphs, and to construct new models by copying objects from existing models. The simplex method underlying the optimization of models generated by Solver and What's Best is presented in Appendix 3.A.[6]

Table 3.1 depicts the model of Figure 3.1 in spreadsheet format. In columns B, C and D, we have the data pertaining, respectively, to the three products Alpha, Beta, and Gamma. On rows 5, 6, 7, and 8, we have the data pertaining, respectively, to utilization of the three resources, A-line test, C-line test, and labor, and the net profit per unit sold. The quantities in B9, C9, D9 are the **variable,** or **adjustable,** cells corresponding to decision variables to be determined by linear programming optimization. The resource usage in cells E5, E6, and E7 are computed as the sum of the data in rows 5, 6, and 7 multiplied by the decision variables in row 9. For example, the formula in the cell E7 is (E7) = B7 * B9 + C7 * C9 + D7 * D9. The total profit to be maximized is given by the formula located in B13, which is (B13) = B8 * B9 + C8 * C9 + D8 * D9.

Table 3.1 One-week Ajax assembly model; What's Best formulation

	A	B	C	D	E	F	G	H	I
1									
2									
3					resource		resource		
4	product	Alpha	Beta	Gamma	usage		available		
5		1	1		0	<=	120	A-line test	
6				1	0	<=	48	C-line test	
7		10	15	20	0	<=	2000	labor	
8	profit/unit	350	470	610					
9	quantity	0	0	0					
10									
11									
12									
13	total profit	0							

To access Solver, select the item Solver from the Tools menu. A dialog box labeled Solver Parameters appears and requires you to identify the cell to be maximized or minimized (designated by $B$13), the adjustable variable cells corresponding to the decision variables (designated by $B$9:$D$9), and the constraints (designated by $E$5 <= $G$5, $E$6 <= $G$6, and $E$7 <= $G$7). Note that the <= signs in the spreadsheet are a memory aid but do not serve a computational function in Solver.

You must also click on Options in the Solver dialog box to access a list of options. To indicate that you wish to solve a linear programming model, select Assume Linear Model. In addition, select Assume Non-Negative, which imposes nonnegativity on the decision variables. Then, making sure that you have selected Max or Min as the objective in the dialog box, click on the Solve button and the optimal solution given in Table 3.2 is computed. The optimal solution is displayed in the adjustable variable cells. The Solver Results dialog box also allows you to view reports pertaining to the solution. We will discuss the content and meaning of these reports in Section 3.3.

Using What's Best is not very different from using Solver. Again, after installation of the software, you select What's Best from the Add-Ins on the Tools menu. The WB! menu appears on the Excel toolbar. To create the model, choose Constraints from the menu, and then, in the Constraints dialog box, indicate that the Left Hand Side of the constraints is $E$5:$E$7, the Right Hand Side is $G$5:$G$7, and the <= Constraints may be stored in $F$5:$F$7. If we click on cell F5, we find the built-in What's Best macro =WB(E5,"<=",G5). Thus, unlike Solver, What's Best explicitly uses inequalities in identifying a model's constraints.

Finally, we specify that the sum of products given in cell B13 is the objective function. This sum is given as (B13) = B10 * B8 + C10 * C8 + D10 * D8. To indicate whether the objective is to be minimized or maximized, click on Best on the WB! menu, and select your choice in the dialog box that pops up. The 1-week Ajax assembly model is now completely specified and can be solved by clicking on the optimization icon (the bull's eye) in What's Best toolbar. The toolbar also contains icons that can be used as shortcuts for adding constraints, identifying decision variables, and identifying the objective function to be maximized or minimized. As with Solver, What's Best places the optimal solution it computes in the relevant cells in Table 3.2. Note that binding constraints are denoted by =<= whereas nonbinding constraints are denoted by <=. The toolbar also gives you the option to create reports, which we discuss in Section 3.3.

Multiperiod Resource Allocation Model

Supply chain planning is a dynamic process because decisions made in this period are linked to decisions that will be made in later periods. Resource allocation plans must account for the intertemporal nature of the decision making process. Inventories of raw materials, intermediate products, and finished goods play a central role in optimizing the impact of production and distribution resources decisions made within each period across the multiple period planning horizon.

Example 3.3

After reviewing the optimal assembly plan given in the spreadsheet of Table 3.2, Ajax' marketing manager doubts that his organization can sell 120 units of Alphas next week. Moreover, he is concerned that the plan does not call for the assembly of any Betas. Even if the profit margin from Betas is smaller relative to the other two products, the marketing manager feels strongly that it must be included in Ajax' product line.

Thus, he requests instead that the production manager develop a 4-week production strategy based on the sales forecasts shown in Table 3.3. The lower number in brackets

Table 3.2 One-week Ajax assembly model; optimal solution computed by What's Best

	A	B	C	D	E	F	G	H	I
1									
2									
3					resource		resource		
4	product	Alpha	Beta	Gamma	usage		available		
5		1	1		120	<=	120	A-line test	
6				1	40	<=	48	C-line test	
7		10	15	20	2000	=<=	2000	labor	
8	profit/unit	350	470	610					
9	quantity	120	0	40					
10									
11									
12									
13	total profit	66400							

represents the minimal amount that must be sold in the given week of the given product, whereas the upper number represents the maximal amount that can be sold. In effect, we view the upper bound on potential sales as a resource to be consumed in an optimal manner. In planning production and sales over the next 4 weeks, Ajax may elect to sell less than the market will absorb of a certain product to use its assembly facilities more profitably in producing other products.

Table 3.3 Sales forecasts

	Week 1	Week 2	Week 3	Week 4
Alphas	[20,60]	[20,80]	[20,120]	[20,140]
Betas	[20,40]	[20,40]	[20,40]	[20,40]
Gammas	[20,50]	[20,40]	[20,30]	[20,70]

The decisions in each week for each product are as follows:

1. How much to produce?
2. How much to sell?
3. How much to store in inventory?

Because Ajax has capital tied up in its products, carrying costs must be charged for items held in inventory. These carrying costs are \$9 per week for each Alpha, \$10 per week for each Beta, and \$18 per week for each Gamma. Initial inventory at the start of this week equals 22 Alphas, 42 Betas, and 36 Gammas.

To respond to this request, we develop the 4-period (week) planning model by replicating the decisions and constraints for each week and by adding inventory balance equations linking the weeks. For each product, these balance equations are of the form

$$\text{Ending inventory in week } t = \text{ending inventory in week } t-1 + \text{production in week } t - \text{sales in week } t$$

The result is a linear programming model with the following decision variables:

$Spt =$ sales of product p in week t

$Mpt =$ assembly and testing of product p in week t

$Ipt =$ inventory of product p at the end of week t (or inventory at the beginning of week $t + 1$)

where the inventory equations for product *p* and period *t* have the mathematical form

$$Ipt = Ip,t - 1 + Mpt - Spt$$

The initial inventories I*p0* are known and given.

We construct the 4-week model by expanding the 1-week model of Tables 3.1 and 3.2 and then using Excel's block and copy operations to extend it to 4 weeks. Expansion of the 1-week model entails addition of constraints involving the sales and inventory variables. The result is displayed in Table 3.4. The top portion of the spreadsheet has been copied from the spreadsheet of Table 3.1. To it, we add rows describing sales variables and constraints and rows describing inventory variables and constraints. Specifically, cells C9, C10, and C11 correspond to adjustable quantities (decision variables) of sales of Alphas, Betas, and Gammas. We constrain the sales of the three products in week 1 to lie

Table 3.4 Extended 1-week Ajax model

	A	B	C	D	E	F	G	H
1	Week 1							
2		product	Alpha	Beta	Gamma	resource usage		resource available
3		A-line test	1	1		120	=<=	120
4		C-line test			1	19.5	<=	48
5		labor	10	15	20	2000	=<=	2000
6		quantity assembled	38	82	19.5			
7								
8		net profit/unit	350	470	610			
9		sales	60	40	50			
10			>=	>=	>=			
11		lower bound sales	20	20	20			
12			=<=	=<=	=<=			
13		upper bound sales	60	40	50			
14								
15		beginning inventory	22	42	36			
16		holding cost/unit/week	9	10	18			
17		Ending inventory	0	84	5.5			
18			=>=	>=	>=			
19			0	0	0			
20								
21		Weekly net profit	69361					
22		Total net profit	69361					
23								

above the specified lower bounds (rows 10, 11) and below the specified upper bounds (rows 12, 13).

Finally, we model inventories on rows 15 through 19. First, we specify beginning inventory and inventory holding costs on rows 15 and 16, respectively. On row 17, we define adjustable cells equal to the left-hand side, or ending inventory, of the inventory balance equations for each of the three products. For example, cell C17 contains the equation (C17) = C15 + C6 – C9. We define constraints on rows 17 through 19 to limit the inventories to nonnegative values.

The objective function to be optimized is total net profit, which for the 1-week submodel equals weekly net profit. Weekly net profit is the sum of revenues from sales minus the cost of ending inventory for that week. For multiple weeks, the total net profit is the sum of weekly net profits.

Table 3.5 portrays Ajax' 4-week planning model, which was created by replicating the 1-week submodel. It also contains the optimal solution for this model. As we can see from this solution, the quantities assembled during the first 2 weeks when the upper bounds on sales are lower served to position inventories to exploit higher sales potential during the final 2 weeks. Nevertheless, the sales potential in week 4 cannot be fully realized due to Ajax' limited resources.

A technical issue with the optimal solution is the appearance of noninteger values in a few adjustable cells. Because the decision variables (quantities assembled, sales, ending inventories) all take on values of tens, if not hundreds, the practical approach to resolving fractions is to round them off. The result will be a solution that is feasible and optimal within the accuracy of the data. As we discuss below and in Chapter 4, however, in many other cases, rounding off fractions in a linear programming solution will not produce an acceptable plan.

The marketing manager does not like zero inventories for all products at the end of the planning horizon. Thus, to force and encourage the model to leave reasonable inventories at the end of the planning horizon, we extend it in two ways. First, we add lower-bound constraints of 10 on ending inventory of each product in week 4. These are the smallest lower bounds acceptable to the marketing manager. In addition, assuming items left in inventory will be sold within 2 weeks after the end of week 4, we credit each with a value equal to net profit minus 2 weeks inventory holding cost; these credits are \$332 for Alphas, \$450 for Betas, and \$574 for Gammas.

The result of this model change is a new 4-week plan that leaves 10 items of each product in inventory at the end of the 4 weeks. The credits were not high enough to induce higher inventories. The total net profit was \$645 less, a small price to pay for ensuring a smoother transition after the 4 weeks have ended. Equally

Table 3.5 Four-week Ajax model

	A	B	C	D	E	F	G	H
1	week 1							
2		product	Alpha	Beta	Gamma	resource usage		resource available
3		A-line test	1	1		120	=<=	120
4		C-line test			1	19.5	<=	48
5		labor	10	15	20	2000	=<=	2000
6		quantity assembled	38	82	19.5			
7								
8		net profit/unit	350	470	610			
9		sales	60	40	50			
10			>=	>=	>=			
11		lower bound sales	20	20	20			
12			=<=	=<=	=<=			
13		upper bound sales	60	40	50			
14								
15		beginning inventory	22	42	36			
16		holding cost/unit/week	9	10	18			
17		ending inventory	0	84	5.5			
18			=>=	>=	>=			
19			0	0	0			
20								
21		weekly net profit	69361					
22		total net profit	69361					
23								
24								
25	week 2							
26		product	Alpha	Beta	Gamma	resource usage		resource available
27		A-line test	1	1		120	=<=	120
28		C-line test			1	35	<=	48
29		labor	10	15	20	2000	=<=	2000
30		quantity assembled	100	20	35			
31								
32		net profit	350	470	610			
33		sales	80	40	40			
34			>=	>=	>=			
35		lower bound sales	20	20	20			
36			=<=	=<=	=<=			
37		upper bound sales	80	40	40			
38								
39		beginning inventory	0	84	5.5			
40		holding cost/unit/week	9	10	18			
41		ending inventory	20	64	0.5			
42			>=	>=	>=			
43			0	0	0			
44								
45		weekly net profit	70371					
46		total net profit	139732					

Table 3.5 *(continued)*

	A	B	C	D	E	F	G	H
47								
48	week 3							
49		product	Alpha	Beta	Gamma	resource usage		resource available
50		A-line test	1	1		120	=<=	120
51		C-line test			1	40	<=	48
52		labor	10	15	20	2000	=<=	2000
53		quantity assembled	120	0	40			
54								
55		net profit	350	470	610			
56		sales	120	40	30			
57			>=	>=	>=			
58		lower bound sales	20	20	20			
59			=<=	=<=	=<=			
60		upper bound sales	120	40	30			
61								
62		beginning inventory	20	64	0.5			
63		holding cost/unit/week	9	10	18			
64		ending inventory	20	24	10.5			
65			>=	>=	>=			
66			0	0	0			
67								
68		weekly net profit	78491					
69		total net profit	218223					
70								
71								
72	week 4							
73		product	Alpha	Beta	Gamma	resource usage		resource available
74		A-line test	1	1		120	=<=	120
75		C-line test			1	40	<=	48
76		labor	10	15	20	2000	=<=	2000
77		quantity assembled	120	0	40			
78								
79		net profit	350	470	610			
80		sales	140	24	50.5			
81			>=	>=	>=			
82		lower bound sales	20	20	20			
83			=<=	<=	<=			
84		upper bound sales	140	40	70			
85								
86		beginning inventory	20	24	10.5			
87		holding cost/unit/week	9	10	18			
88		ending inventory	0	0	0			
89			=>=	=>=	=>=			
90			0	0	0			
91								
92		weekly net profit	91085					
93		total net profit	309308					

important, the assembly/sales/inventory plan of week 1 was not affected by our imposition of terminal conditions at the end of week 4.

This plan is satisfactory for both the production manager and the marketing manager. Senior management, however, is worried that the marketing department is being overly optimist about potential sales. The danger is that sales will not match expectations and cause inventories to build up. The danger can be greatly reduced by employing the model on a **rolling horizon basis.**

To illustrate the concept, suppose that actual sales in week 1 turn out to be 50 (rather than 60) Alphas, 24 (rather than 40) Betas, 45 (rather than 50) Gammas. This implies, for example, that

Starting inventory of Alphas in week 2		Starting inventory of Alphas in week 1		Production of Alphas in week 1		Sales of Alphas in week 1
10	=	22	+	38	−	50

Then, at the beginning of next week, we would reoptimize the model with a new sales forecast for the next 4 weeks based on new starting inventories of Alphas equal to 10, of Betas equal to 100, and of Gammas equal to 11 (rounding production of Gammas in week 1 down to 19). Using these figures, plus new sales figures for week 5, which becomes week 4 in next week's model, we would reoptimize the model to determine the final plan for the new week 1, which was week 2 in the previous modeling analysis.

Network Models

A network is made up of nodes and directed arcs connecting pairs of nodes. Linear programming models with a mathematical structure corresponding to networks are called **network models.** Such models arise frequently as submodels in large-scale supply chain models. Recognizing that a model is a network model is useful for at least two reasons. One is that network models can be optimized very efficiently by tailored algorithms that exploit their special structure. More importantly, modeling practitioners find it very useful for communication purposes to display a supply chain model as a network, even when the underlying models are mathematically more complex than network models. We will often employ such depictions in later chapters.

Example 3.4

One type of network model is the **transportation model,** which we illustrate with the following example. As shown in Figure 3.5, the Ajax plant is located in Chicago. A company warehouse is located in St. Louis. Ajax sells its computers in the eight markets shown in the figure. To meet market demand for this week, the Ajax distribution manager must decide on a plan for shipping Alphas from its plant and its warehouse to its markets.

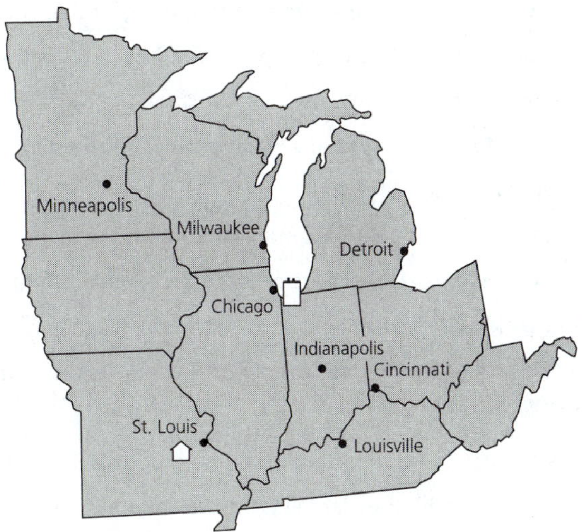

Figure 3.5
Ajax markets

Ajax has 100 Alphas available to be shipped from its plant and 45 Alphas available to be shipped from its warehouse. The market demands are given in Table 3.6 along with the cost per unit to ship Alphas from each source to each market. These transportation costs are the sum of handling costs at the facilities and at the markets and trucking (mileage) costs. The objective is to minimize the total transportation cost of shipping Alphas from the sources to the markets.

Table 3.6 Transportation cost data ($/Unit)

J = From/To	1 CHI	2 STL	3 DET	4 CIN	5 LOU	6 IND	7 MIL	8 MIN	Supply
Plant	14.00	24.00	21.00	20.00	21.50	19.00	17.00	30.00	100
Warehouse	24.00	15.00	28.00	20.00	18.50	19.50	24.00	28.00	45
Demand	22	14	18	17	15	13	15	20	

As a check on the feasibility of Ajax' transportation problem, we sum the demands and find that total demand equals 134 units, which is less than the total supply of 145 units. Thus, the problem is feasible. The general condition that supply must meet or exceed demand is simple to verify for this model. The condition is relevant for all supply chain problems and models, although it is more difficult to verify if the supply chain is complex.

Letting

$$XPJ = \text{flow of Alphas from the plant to market } J$$

$$XWJ = \text{flow of Alphas from the warehouse to market } J$$

We write the model for this problem as shown in Figure 3.6. The objective function is the total transportation cost. The two supply constraints state that the total amount shipped out of the plant and the warehouse cannot exceed the availabilities. The eight equations in the figure state that demand in each of the markets must be met exactly by shipments from the plant and the warehouse.

The model is called a network model because it can be represented schematically as the network in Figure 3.7. There are other forms of linear programming models in the class of network models. They all have the property that their algebraic statements as systems of equations can be transformed to network representations that are similar to Figure 3.7.

The optimal solution to this model is given in Table 3.7. Note that the Minneapolis market is served by both the plant and the warehouse in this solution. If Ajax has a sole sourcing policy—each market must be served by a single source—this solution will be infeasible. Mixed integer programming techniques, which we discuss in the next chapter, are needed to impose such a policy on the transportation model.

Figure 3.6
Alpha transportation model

$$\begin{aligned}\text{MIN} \quad & 14\,XP1 + 24\,XP2 + 21\,XP3 + 20\,XP4 + 21.5\,XP5 + 19\,XP6 \\ & + 17\,XP7 + 30\,XP8 + 24\,XW1 + 15\,XW2 + 28\,XW3 + 20\,XW4 \\ & + 18.5\,XW5 + 19.5\,XW6 + 24\,XW7 + 28\,XW8\end{aligned}$$

Subject to

$$\left.\begin{aligned} XP1 + XP2 + XP3 + XP4 + XP5 + XP6 + XP7 + XP8 &\le 100 \\ XW1 + XW2 + XW3 + XW4 + XW5 + XW6 + XW7 + XW8 &\le 45 \end{aligned}\right\} \text{Supply Constraints}$$

$$\left.\begin{aligned} XP1 + XW1 &= 22 \\ XP2 + XW2 &= 14 \\ XP3 + XW3 &= 18 \\ XP4 + XW4 &= 17 \\ XP5 + XW5 &= 15 \\ XP6 + XW6 &= 13 \\ XP7 + XW7 &= 15 \\ XP8 + XW8 &= 20 \end{aligned}\right\} \text{Demand Constraints}$$

All Variables Nonnegative

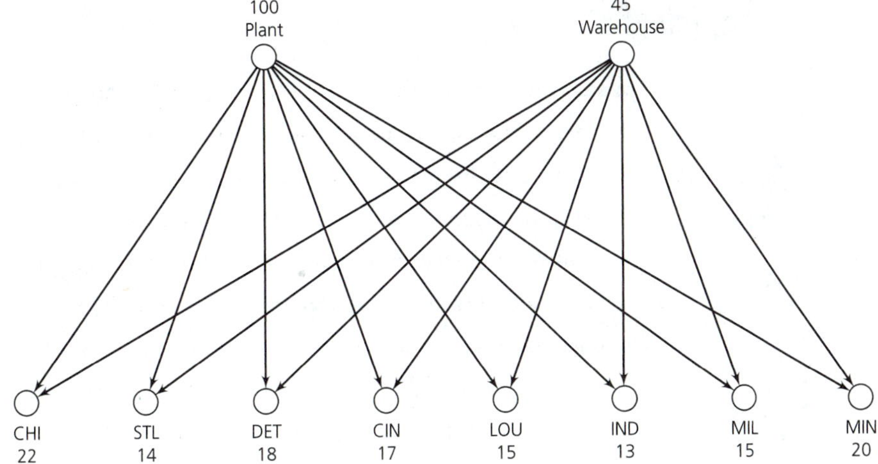

Figure 3.7
Alpha transportation network

Table 3.7 Optimal solution (units shipped) to Ajax transportation model

From	**To**	**CHI**	**STL**	**DET**	**CIN**	**LOU**	**IND**	**MIL**	**MIN**
Plant		22		18	17		13	15	4
Warehouse			14			15			16

COST = \$2583.50

The transportation model can be extended in several ways to accommodate complications arising in distribution planning. The model just reviewed involved the distribution of a single product. Multicommodity flow models generalize it to one for which multiple products are transported from sources to destinations and share capacities on directed arcs. Such models are used to describe flows in an express mail network where each origin/destination pair must be treated as a separate commodity, which shares transportation capacity with all other commodities using the same directed arcs.

Another generalization of the transportation model is to one involving a choice among modes of transportation, truck, air, rail, or barge, to be used on each directed arc. This generalization often requires the use of 0-1 decision variables to capture fixed costs and minimal flow requirements associated with certain modes. A mathematically related generalization is a transportation model with unit costs on flows that decrease with volume. Higher flows will allow greater utilization of full truckload shipments that are more economical than less-than-truckload shipments associated with lower flows.

Example 3.5

We extend the transportation example to a slightly more complex situation. The distribution manager at Ajax wishes to investigate the potential benefits of locating a crossdocking facility near the markets in Cincinnati, Louisville, and Indianapolis. This facility would receive products from the plant and the warehouse and immediately dispatch them to the three markets. It would have very little space for storing products. The possible advantage is that Ajax could achieve lower transportation rates to the cross-dock facility than those to the three markets due to product consolidation.

The situation is depicted in Figure 3.8 where we have extended the network of Figure 3.7 to include the cross-docking option. Table 3.8 contains the relevant new transportation data. In addition, there is a handling charge of \$2 for each Alpha transshipped through the cross-dock facility and a maximal capacity of 30 Alphas per week that can flow through there.

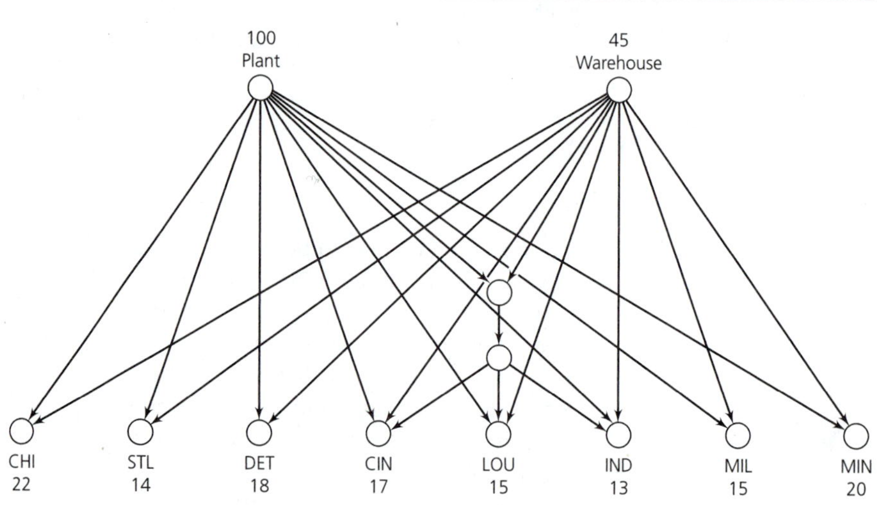

Figure 3.8 Extended Alpha transportation network

Table 3.8 Additional transportation cost data (\$/unit)

From	To	Cross-Dock Facility
Plant		11
Warehouse		10

From	To	CIN	LOU	IND
Cross-Dock Facility (XD)		6	5	5

To expand the transportation model to handle model this situation, we define the following new variables:

XPC = flow of Alphas from the plant to the cross-dock facility

XWC = flow of Alphas from the warehouse to the cross-dock facility

Z = throughput at the cross-dock facility

YCJ = flow from the cross-dock facility to market J ($J = 4, 5, 6$)

The new model is shown in Figure 3.9. The changes to the model in Figure 3.9 are the following. Six terms have been added to the objective function to describe the costs of shipping to the cross-dock facility, handling items there, and shipping these items to markets 4, 5, and 6. The variables XPC and XWC have been added to the supply constraint to reflect flows from the two sources to the cross-dock facility. The first two equations in the cross-dock constraint set are balance equations that require the flow into the facility to

Figure 3.9
Extended Alpha transportation model

$$\begin{aligned}\text{MIN}\quad & 14\,XP1 + 24\,XP2 + 21\,XP3 + 20\,XP4 + 21.5\,XP5 + 19\,XP6\\ & + 17\,XP7 + 30\,XP8 + 24\,XW1 + 15\,XW2 + 28\,XW3 + 20\,XW4\\ & + 18.5\,XW5 + 19.5\,XW6 + 24\,XW7 + 28\,XW8\\ & + 11\,XPC + 10\,XWC + 2\,Z + 6\,YC4 + 5\,YC5 + 5YC6\end{aligned}$$

Subject to

$$\left.\begin{aligned} XP1 + XP2 + XP3 + XP4 + XP5 + XP6 + XP7 + XP8 + XPC &\le 100\\ XW1 + XW2 + XW3 + XW4 + XW5 + XW6 + XW7 + XW8 + XWC &\le 45\end{aligned}\right\}\text{Supply Constraints}$$

$$\left.\begin{aligned} XPC + XWC - Z &= 0\\ Z - YC4 - YC5 - YC6 &= 0\\ Z &\le 30\end{aligned}\right\}\text{Cross-Dock Constraints}$$

$$\left.\begin{aligned} XP1 + XW1 &= 22\\ XP2 + XW2 &= 14\\ XP3 + XW3 &= 18\\ XP4 + XW4 + YC4 &= 17\\ XP5 + XW5 + YC5 &= 15\\ XP6 + XW6 + YC6 &= 13\\ XP7 + XW7 &= 15\\ XP8 + XW8 &= 20\end{aligned}\right\}\text{Demand Constraints}$$

All Variables Nonpositive

Table 3.9 Optimal solution (units shipped) to extended Ajax transportation model

From	To	1 CHI	2 STL	3 DET	4 CIN	5 LOU	6 IND	7 MIL	8 MIN	XD
Plant		22		18	2		13	15		19
Warehouse		14							20	11
From	**To**				**CIN**	**LOU**	**IND**			
Cross-Dock					15	15	0			

Minimal Cost = $2542

equal the flow out of the facility. The third constraint is the capacity limitation on throughput. Finally, we have added the variables YCJ for $J = 4, 5, 6$ to the demand equations, reflecting shipments sourced to those markets from the cross-dock facility.

The optimal solution to this model is displayed in Table 3.9. Using the cross-dock facility allows the minimal transportation cost to be reduced by $41.50 for the week. If the week can be viewed as a typical week, this implies an annual savings due to the cross-dock facility of $2158 for transporting Alphas to the market. Similar analyses could be carried out for Betas and Gammas, and the sum total of potential savings could be weighed against the cost of establishing the cross-dock facility.

3.2 Properties of Linear Programming Models

For several reasons, linear programming modeling techniques and algorithms are the mainstays of mathematical optimization. One reason is that linear programming models of significant size are usually surprisingly easy to optimize. Another is that most linear programming models can be solved by general-purpose optimizers without attention to special features that the models might have.

The efficiency of linear programming optimization is in large part a consequence of the model's relatively simple mathematical properties. We shall examine these properties shortly. They are sometimes too simple, and many real-world applications require models that are extensions of linear programming.

This does not, however, negate the importance of linear programming models and algorithms. A very high proportion of an extended linear programming model, measured in terms of the number of constraints and variables, may adhere to the pure linear programming form. Moreover, linear programming approximations, which are optimized by linear programming algorithms, serve a vital role in the algorithmic optimization of more complex models.

The five fundamental properties of a linear programming model are as follows:

- Linearity
- Separability and additivity
- Indivisibility and continuity
- Single objective function
- Data known with certainty

We examine each of these properties in the subsections that follow. Then, in later sections of this chapter and in later chapters in the book, we examine extensions that allow the over simplifications inherent in linear programming models to be overcome.

Linearity

As we saw in the Ajax Computer Company examples, all revenues, costs, and resource utilizations occur as linear functions of the associated decision variable levels. By linear we mean that the unit revenue, unit cost, and unit resource utilization are constant for all values of the associated decision variables. It is easy to imagine situations where revenues or costs are not linear. For example, suppose Ajax acquires microprocessors for the Gamma computers from the Riverfront Corporation, a high-quality and inexpensive vendor, under a long-term arrangement at a price of \$200/unit. Each Gamma requires one microprocessor. In the models of Figure 3.1 and its extensions, this cost was included in computing the net revenue of \$610/unit. Suppose now that Riverfront's future capacity to make this component for Ajax is limited to no more than 20 per week. With this restriction, Ajax' purchasing manager locates another vendor, the Glendale Company, who proposes to supply Ajax with as many of the microprocessors as needed per week, and with the same high quality, but at a cost of \$265/unit.

The component acquisition cost curve is depicted in Figure 3.10. We say it has a **diseconomy of scale** because the unit cost increases at higher volumes. We extend the linear programming model of Figure 3.1 to deal with the microprocessor supply decision. Let $V1$ = weekly microprocessor purchases from Riverfront and $V2$ =

Figure 3.10
Diseconomy of scale in purchasing microprocessors

weekly microprocessor purchases from the Glendale Company. First we change the objective function to

$$\text{Maximize } Z = 350\text{MA} + 470\text{MB} + 810\text{MC} - 200\text{V}1 - 265\text{V}2$$

where the net revenue of Gammas has been increased to \$810 from \$610 to correct for the microprocessor cost of \$200/unit that was formerly buried in the net revenue of \$610/unit. In addition, we add the constraints

$$\text{MC} = V1 + V2$$
$$20 \geq V1 \geq 0,\ V2 \geq 0$$

The equation captures the consumption of one microprocessor by each Gamma that is assembled and sold. The model is now ready to be reoptimized.

Suppose instead that The Riverfront Corporation proposes a new long-term arrangement with Acme that is more favorable to them and provides them with an incentive to add capacity to make microprocessors for the Gamma workstation. Riverfront will charge \$250/unit for microprocessors up to 30 per week and then drop the price to \$200/unit for any number of additional units. As shown in Figure 3.11, this option represents an **economy of scale** because the unit cost decreases at higher volume.

The purchasing manager decides to drop negotiations with Glendale, but he wishes to analyze Acme's optimal strategy for acquisitions from Riverfront. To this end, we extend the model of Figure 3.1 as follows. Let $W1$ = weekly purchases from Riverfront at \$250/unit and $W2$ = weekly purchases from Riverfront at \$200/unit. The proposed model extensions are to modify the objective function

$$\text{Maximize } Z = 350\text{MA} + 470\text{MB} + 810\text{MC} - 250W1 - 200W2$$

and add the constraints

$$\text{MC} = W1 + W2$$
$$30 \geq W1 \geq 0,\ W2 \geq 0$$

Unfortunately, unlike the diseconomy of scale case, the proposed extension will not yield the desired result. An optimization algorithm for the modified linear program-

Figure 3.11
Economy of scale in purchasing microprocessors

ming model will chose first to increase $W2$ from zero, rather than $W1$, because it is less expensive. But the price break is only available after Acme has acquired 30 units at the higher unit cost. As we discuss in the next chapter, cost economies of scale require mixed integer programming constructions.

Nonlinearities in resource consumption follow the same pattern as costs. For example, as stated in the model of Figure 3.1, each Gamma requires 20 units of labor, whether it is the first unit produced in a week or the fiftieth. This may be an accurate description to how labor is actually consumed in assembling Gammas. Alternatively, economies or diseconomies of scale might occur in utilizing labor utilization in their assembly. The case of diseconomies of scale is depicted in Figure 3.12. A reason for such a diseconomy may be the need to use workers who are less skilled in assembling Gammas.

This type of nonlinearity can be modeled directly by linear programming constructs. We define two new variables MC1 and MC2 corresponding to assembly of Gammas at the different rates, linked by the relationships

$$MC = MC1 + MC2$$
$$10 \geq MC1 \geq 0,\ MC2 \geq 0$$

In addition, the labor resource utilization constraint becomes

$$10\ MA = 15\ MB + 20\ MC1 + 24\ MC2 \leq 2000$$

The case of economies of scale is depicted in Figure 3.13. Economies of scale may be the result of short-term learning in each week that Gammas are produced.

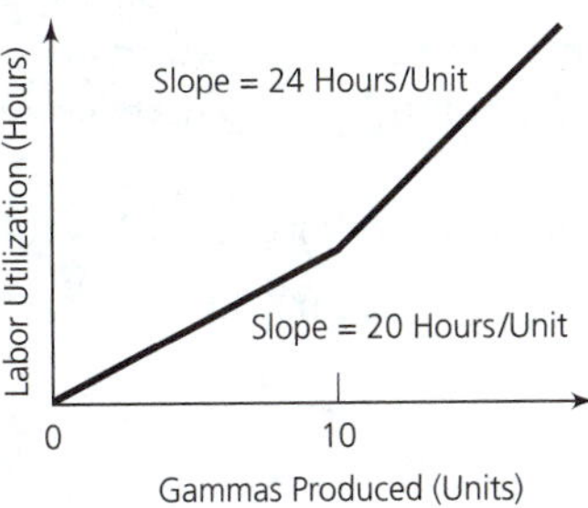

Figure 3.12 Diseconomy of scale in producing gammas

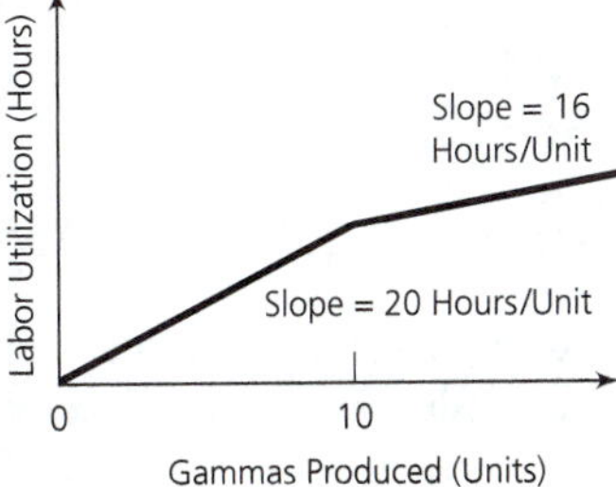

Figure 3.13 Economy of scale in producing gammas

As with the cost analysis, this case is subtly but seriously different from the diseconomy of scale case just discussed. To see why, suppose we were to make the same substitutions as in the diseconomy of scale case, with the result that the labor constraint becomes

$$10 \text{ MA} + 15 \text{ MB} + 20 \text{ MC1} + 16 \text{ MC2} \leq 2000$$

This reformulation would not produce the desired result because an optimization algorithm for the linear programming model will choose first to increase MC2 from zero, rather than MC1, because it is more efficient in its use of the labor resource. But such a result is counter to reality. The economy of scale can only be achieved after 10 units have been produced at the less-economical rate. Again, this type of nonlinearity requires mixed integer programming constructions.

Another type of nonlinearity that we might wish to capture in our optimization model is the dependency of the quantity of sales of Ajax' products on their sales prices. To take a simple example, suppose market analysis reveals that the quantity QA of Alphas that can be sold depends on the price PA according to the relationship

$$\text{QA} = 240 - 0.4 \text{ PA}$$

Thus, when PA = 300/unit, QA = 120 units, whereas when PA = 350/unit, QA = 100 units; that is, customers are sensitive to price and will demand more if the price is lower. Our interest is in revenues as a function of the quantity assembled and sold, which is our decision variable. Now

$$\text{Revenue} = \text{PA} * \text{QA} = 600 \text{ QA} - 2.5 \text{ QA}^2$$

where we solved for PA from the first equation, PA = 600 – 2.5 QA, and substituted in the revenue function. Because the revenue function is quadratic, we cannot incorporate it in the linear programming model. However, we can approximate it in the range of QA between 80 and 120 units by the **piecewise linear** relationship

$$\text{Revenue} = \begin{cases} 32000 + 150(\text{QA} - 80) \text{ for } 80 \leq \text{QA} \leq 100 \\ 35000 + 50(\text{QA} - 100) \text{ for } 100 \leq \text{QA} \leq 120 \end{cases}$$

With this approximation, revenue is exact at QA = 80, 100, and 120 and interpolated linearly between 80 and 100 and between 100 and 120. The approximation is depicted in Figure 3.14. We assume the marketing manager at Ajax imposes the given range on Alphas sales.

Recognizing that, in the linear programming model of Figure 3.1, all assembled Alphas are sold, we set QA = MA = MA1 + MA2 for $80 \leq \text{MA1} \leq 100$, $0 \leq \text{MA2} \leq 20$ and adjust the objective function to become

$$\text{Maximize } Z = 32{,}000 + 150 \text{ MA1} + 50\text{MA2} + 470 \text{ MB} + 610 \text{ MC}$$

Because the marginal revenue decreases from 150 to 50/unit as Ajax assembles and sells more Alphas, solving the extended model as a linear programming model will

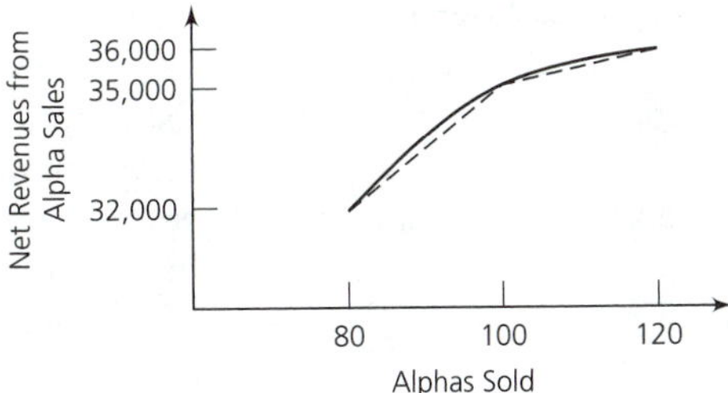

Figure 3.14
Piecewise linear approximation to nonlinear revenue curve

not introduce inconsistencies. The optimizer will make and sell all it can in the 80 to 100 range before it considers making and selling in the 100 to 120 range. Of course, we should also develop price-sensitive revenue functions for the sale of Betas and Gammas.

Separability and Additivity

In addition to the linearity assumption, we saw that our Ajax Computer models assumed that all effects were separable and additive. By separable, we mean that the net profit contribution of Alphas, and its resource utilization, is measured separately from, or independently of, the net profit contributions and resource utilizations of the other products (Betas and Gammas). By additive, we mean that these separate effects can be accumulated simply by adding them up.

Again, separability and additivity may produce a good first approximation in many cases. In others, it may be inaccurate. Continuing with the example just discussed, we might expect sales of all three products to be price sensitive with cross-price effects; for example, if the price of Alphas rises, the sales of Betas and Gammas will increase. If they were important, these effects could be modeled by advanced techniques.

Another example of a nonseparable effect is the following. Suppose testing of both Alphas and Betas on the A-line in a given week requires a major changeover that consumes 20 of the 120 hours available. This is partly a logical, rather than strictly numerical, relationship. Namely, if $MA \geq 0$ and $MB = 0$ or if $MA = 0$ and $MB \geq 0$ in a given week, 120 hours of testing are available; however, if $MA > 0$ and $MB > 0$, only 100 hours of testing are available. As we shall illustrate in the following chapter, this type of nonseparable effect can be handled by the introduction of 0-1 (integer) variables.

Indivisibility and Continuity

Optimizing a linear programming model produces decisions that can take on numerical values along the continuum of real numbers. This means that certain decisions, such as the number of Alphas assembled in week 2, can take on noninteger values. Mixed integer programming is a generalization of linear programming in which certain decision variables can be constrained to take on integer values (that is, 0, 1, 2, 3, . . .). As a practical matter, in most cases, it is necessary to explicitly constrain decision variables to equal integer, rather than continuous, values only when they are likely to take on small, important values; for example, a decision regarding how many jumbo jets to manufacture and deliver in a given month. By contrast, a decision in Table 3.5 to assemble 19.5 Gammas in week 1 can be rounded to 19 (or 20) without causing any noticeable damage to the feasibility or optimality of the solution.

Linear programming also does not allow us to model jumps in revenues, costs, utilization of resources, or meeting of requirements. For example, suppose space for inventory in Ajax' manufacturing facility is limited to a total of 60 units of any type of computer. To store more units in a given week, a lumpy (fixed) cost of $500 per week must be incurred to arrange for 50 more units of storage to be made available in a nearby public warehouse. Note that the common nomenclature "fixed cost" for this type of cost is misleading because it may not be incurred and therefore is not fixed. We shall demonstrate in Chapter 4 how to model such costs.

A frequent additional use of integer valued variables is to model nonnumeric conditions by using variables constrained to take on values of 0 or 1. For example, a decision regarding whether or not to construct a new manufacturing facility at a certain site would be captured by a 0-1 variable where a value of 1 indicates that the facility should be built there and 0 indicates that it should not be built. Similarly, a 0-1 variable would be used to model the decision whether or not Ajax should lease additional storage space in a given week.

Single Objective Function

In the Ajax Computer Company example, the planning environment appeared at first to be one dominated by a single objective; namely, to maximize net revenues over the 4-week planning horizon. Analysis of the optimal solution to the initial model revealed, however, that this objective was accomplished at the expense of ending inventories, which were driven to zero for the sake of short-term profit. We then discussed briefly how a second objective of the company—longer-term stability and profitability—might be achieved by specifying targets on ending inventory that would ensure a smooth transition from this month's operations to the next. More generally, many applications of optimization models involve trade-offs among multiple objectives. We discuss methods for evaluating such trade-offs in Section 3.4.

Data Known with Certainty

We assumed in developing linear programming models for the Ajax Computer Company that all data regarding the future—costs, capacities, sales, and so on—are known with certainty. This is an important assumption, one that could seriously limit the validity of any linear programming solution to a supply chain problem. Several approaches to analyzing and using a linear programming model can mitigate difficulties due to data uncertainties.

First, as we discuss in a later section, techniques are available for testing the sensitivity of a linear programming solution to the parameters of the model. Second, the analyst can construct multiple **scenarios** of an uncertain future and optimize a linear programming model for each scenario. In this way, the manager can investigate and understand the nature of major changes in the supply chain strategy proposed by a linear programming model that occur as the result of different scenarios. Moreover, if the model is embedded in an easy-to-use modeling system, the data can be updated and the model can be reoptimized on a timely basis. In this way, the strategies suggested by a model can be progressively adapted to changing data describing the company's operations.

Finally, if the uncertainties are sufficiently serious and well understood, a linear programming model can be extended to a **stochastic linear programming model** that explicitly considers multiple scenarios of the uncertain future. By considering multiple scenarios simultaneously, such a model is able to identify an immediate strategy that hedges against the uncertainties. The stochastic linear programming model is illustrated in Section 3.5.

In the final analysis, deterministic optimization of a model of a supply chain planning problem is often the most practical approach. In most planning situations, the development of point (that is, single) estimates of key parameters is difficult enough. For such problems, it is not realistic to attempt to develop extensive descriptions of how the parameters might vary in the future. Although the modeler may sometimes be forced to acknowledge that a deterministic model is imperfect in its description of the future, the benefits of using such a model are still substantial.

3.3 Interpreting an Optimal Linear Programming Solution

In Appendix 3.A, we provide a detailed description of the simplex method applied to the Ajax model in Figure 3.1. We placed the method in an appendix because it involves calculations that many find lugubrious, although familiarity with it can breed respect. Still, at first glance, it appears to be no more than a clever numerical scheme for finding an optimal solution to a linear programming model. It seems to offer little intuition about the economics of allocating resources or satisfying requirements that underlie the optimization process. However, an economic interpretation is available if we scrutinize the method in the correct way.[7]

The economic interpretation is important because it provides the following:

- Useful information for valuing resources and attributing costs to requirements and, in general, explaining why an optimal solution is optimal
- The underpinning for sensitivity and parametric analysis of model data
- The algorithmic basis for applying the simplex method and linear programming in a flexible manner to the optimization of large and complex models, including those that are not linear programming models.

Shadow Prices

A fundamental ingredient in the economic analysis of an LP model is the **shadow price** associated with each constraint, which is defined as the change in the optimal value of the objective function if the right-hand side of the constraint is increased by one unit. For reasons of symmetry, it is also defined as the change in the optimal value of the objective function if the right-hand side of the constraint is decreased by one unit.[8] The simplex method implicitly determines shadow prices when it optimizes a linear programming model.

We demonstrate this construction by reproducing two restatements of the Ajax model taken from Appendix 3.A. To apply the simplex method, the model is recast in canonical form, which refers to a restatement of the linear programming model, including its objective function, as a system of linear equations. For example, the Ajax model can be written in an initial canonical form as

$$\begin{array}{lllllllll}
Z - 350\text{MA} - 470\text{MB} - 610\text{MC} & & & & = & 0 & (3.1)\\
\quad\;\; \text{MA} + \text{MB} & + S1 & & & = & 120 & (3.2)\\
\quad\quad\quad\quad\quad\quad\quad \text{MC} & & + S2 & & = & 48 & (3.3)\\
\quad 10\text{MA} + 15\text{MB} + 20\text{MC} & & & + S3 & = & 2000 & (3.4)
\end{array}$$

where Z is the net profit to be maximized. The slack variables $S1$, $S2$, and $S3$ have been added to the resource inequalities to transform them into equations. Specifically, $S1$ measures unused A-line test capacity, $S2$ measures unused C-line test capacity, and $S3$ measures unused labor capacity.

In this and every subsequent canonical form, there are four decision variables (called the basic variables) with a value of +1 on some row and 0s elsewhere; in this form, these are the variables Z, $S1$, $S2$, and $S3$. A solution to the system of equations, and therefore a feasible solution to the model, can be found by setting the other variables (called the nonbasic variables) to 0. For this form we have the "do nothing" feasible solution given by $Z = 0$, $S1 = 120$, $S2 = 48$, $S3 = 2000$.

For future reference, we note that although slack variables are constrained to be nonnegative, increasing the right-hand side of the first constraint from 120 hours of A-line test capacity to 121 hours is notionally carried out by setting the slack variable $S1 = -1$. Similarly, the right-hand sides of the second and third constraints can be increased by one unit by setting $S2 = -1$ and $S3 = -1$, respectively.

The simplex method proceeds by a series of manipulation of the initial canonical form given above. The manipulations do not change the set of feasible solutions to the model but transform its mathematical representation to identify feasible solutions and test them for optimality. If the test fails, the representation is modified to identify a new feasible solution with a higher objective function value (in a maximization problem), and the test is repeated. Assuming that the model is well posed and does not allow the attainment of unbounded net revenues, the simplex method discovers, after a finite amount of computation, an optimal canonical form. For the Ajax model, this is the following:

$$
\begin{array}{llllll}
Z & + 32.5\text{MB} & + 45S1 & + 30.5S3 = & 66{,}400 & (3.1') \\
\text{MA} + & \text{MB} & + S1 & = & 120 & (3.2') \\
 & - 0.25\text{MB} & + 0.5S1 + S2 - & 0.05S3 = & 8 & (3.3') \\
 & 0.25\text{MB} + \text{MC} & - 0.5S1 & + 0.05S3 = & 40 & (3.4')
\end{array}
$$

To better interpret the canonical form, we rewrite it so that the (dependent) basic variables are written as follows as functions of the (independent) nonbasic variables:

$$
\begin{array}{lll}
Z & = 66{,}400 - 32.5\text{MB} - 45S1 - 30.5S3 & (3.1'') \\
\text{MA} & = 120 - \text{MB} - S1 & (3.2'') \\
S2 & = 8 + 0.25\text{MB} - 0.5S1 + 0.05S3 & (3.3'') \\
\text{MC} & = 40 - 0.25\text{MB} + 0.5S1 - 0.05S3 & (3.4'')
\end{array}
$$

All feasible solution to the Ajax model can be found by setting the nonbasic variables in this canonical form, MB, $S1$, $S3$, to any nonnegative values that make the basic variables (excepting Z) in this form, MA, $S2$, MC, nonnegative. The obvious one (called the basic feasible solution) is to set the nonbasics to zero and solve for the basics; this gives us $Z = 66{,}400$, $\text{MA} = 120$, $S2 = 8$, and $\text{MC} = 40$. Because the coefficients associated with the nonbasic variables in Equation 3.1″ are all nonpositive, any other feasible solution that has at least one nonbasic with a positive value will have lower objective function value then 66,400. Thus the basic feasible solution and the canonical form are optimal in the Ajax model. These equations are the point of departure for economic interpretation.

In the optimal solution, the slacks $S1$ and $S3$ are zero, indicating that the resources on these constraints, 120 hours of A-line capacity and 2000 hours of labor, are valuable and need to be allocated in an optimal manner. An additional unit of A-line capacity corresponding to setting $S1 = -1$ would cause the objective function to increase by \$45 because Equation 3.1″ tells us that

$$Z = 66{,}400 - 32.5\text{MB} - 45S1 - 30.5S3$$

Similarly, an additional hour of labor corresponding to $S3 = -1$ would cause the objective function to increase by \$30.50. On the other hand, because $S2 = 8$, we have an excess of C-line testing hours and therefore the addition of an hour would not cause the objective function to increase. In this last case, note that the slack variable $S2$ has a coefficient of zero in the final objective function, Equation 3.1″, because it is a basic variable.

Thus, for a linear programming model with an objective function to be maximized and all constraints written as ≤, we have illustrated the following principle:

> The coefficient associated with the slack variable on constraint i in the objective function row of the optimal table is the nonnegative shadow price for that constraint. If the slack variable is basic, the shadow price is zero.

A similar derivation and statement for an arbitrary linear programming model, one whose objective function may be maximized or minimized, and with constraints that are ≤, ≥, or =, could be derived. For the sake of brevity, we merely state the key properties. For a linear programming model with an objective function to be maximized, they are as shown in the following table:

Type of Constraint	Shadow Price Sign
≤	Nonnegative
≥	Nonpositive
=	Unconstrained in sign

As before, the shadow price is zero for ≤ or ≥ rows if there is slack or surplus on those rows. The intuition for a nonpositive shadow price on a ≥ constraint is that increasing a requirement by one unit can only cause the objective function to decrease. Similarly, we do not know if an = constraint should be viewed as a resource restriction or a requirement. Hence its sign may be either positive or negative.

For completeness, we list the properties for a minimization model. For a linear programming model with an objective function to be minimized, they are as shown in the following table:

Type of Constraint	Shadow Price Sign
≤	Nonpositive
≥	Nonnegative
=	Unconstrained in sign

The intuition here is that increasing resources in a ≤ constraint can only cause the minimal cost to be reduced. Hence the shadow price is nonpositive. Similarly, increasing a requirement can only cause the minimal cost to increase. And, as before, we cannot be sure of the impact of an = constraint and therefore the shadow price may have either sign.

Reduced Cost Coefficients

The simplex method implicitly uses the shadow prices to provide an additional economic interpretation of an optimal solution. Referring again to the optimal objective function row for the Ajax model, we see that the coefficient associated with the nonbasic variable MB (number of Beta computers to produce) is −32.5. Because MB is a nonbasic variable, it equals zero in the optimal solution. The interpretation is that the objective function would decrease by $32.50 for every Beta computer that Ajax would produce.

This coefficient, which is called the **reduced cost** of MB, can be derived by using the shadow prices to subtract a charge for the resources consumed by the manufacture of a single Beta from the net profit it would bring in. Numerically, this is expressed as

$$\text{Reduced cost of MB} = 470 - (45)(1) - (0)(0) - (30.5)(15) = -32.5$$

where the coefficients 45, 0, and 30.5 are the charges per unit (shadow prices) for the A-line test facility, C-line test facility, and labor, respectively, and the coefficients 1, 0, and 15 are the units consumed of these resources in producing one Beta, as stated by its activity. Because the resource charge exceeds the net profit, the simplex method holds production of Betas to zero. However, if we could increase the net revenue for each Beta by at least \$32.50 to an absolute value of at least \$502.50, the assembly of Betas would look attractive. The precise number to be assembled in this case would require additional algorithmic analysis and would depend on the actual numerical value of the net revenue associated with assembly and sale of each Beta.

The same calculation for Alphas and Gammas provides still further insight, as follows:

$$\begin{aligned}\text{Reduced cost of MA} &= 350 - (45)(1) - (0)(0) - (30.5)(10) = 0\\ \text{Reduced cost of MC} &= 610 - (45)(0) - (0)(1) - (30.5)(20) = 0\end{aligned}$$

The economic interpretation of this result is that the activities of producing Alphas and Gammas are **efficient** because their resource charges are perfectly balanced by their net profits. Moreover, the simplex method allows only efficient activities to be at positive levels (in the example, MA = 120, MC = 40) in an optimal solution because they are basic variables.

We can also compute reduced costs for the slack variables by the same calculation, as follows:

$$\begin{aligned}\text{Reduced cost of } S1 &= 0 - (45)(1) - (0)(0) - (30.5)(0) = -45\\ \text{Reduced cost of } S2 &= 0 - (45)(0) - (0)(1) - (30.5)(0) = 0\\ \text{Reduced cost of } S3 &= 0 - (45)(0) - (0)(0) - (30.5)(1) = -30.5\end{aligned}$$

The interpretation in this case is slightly different but consistent. For $S1$ and $S3$, the respective resources are in short supply, as indicated and measured by the positive shadow prices, which are the negatives of the slacks' relative costs. The slack variables take on zero values in an optimal solution because it would be inefficient to waste valuable resources. For example, increasing $S1$ to a value of 1 would cause the objective function to decrease by \$45. On the other hand, the reduced cost of the slack variable $S2$ is zero because the shadow price on row 2 is zero, indicating an excess supply of the corresponding resource. Therefore, it is efficient to have $S2 = 8$ in the optimal solution.

In summary, the reduced cost of an activity in a linear programming model is the difference between its objective function coefficient and an adjustment equaling a charge for resources consumed and a payback for requirements met. The adjustment is determined by computing the sum of the shadow prices on each resource or requirement multiplied by the resource or requirement level of the activity. These reduced costs identify the efficient activities in an LP model; namely, activities with zero reduced costs. Variables corresponding to inefficient activities in a maximization model have negative reduced costs, whereas in a minimization model, the inefficient activities have positive reduced costs. Variables corresponding to inefficient activities must have zero values in an optimal solution.

Dual Linear Programming Model

The existence and interpretation of shadow prices and reduced costs is based on optimization of a related linear programming model, which is known as the dual linear programming model, that the simplex method must also implicitly optimize when it optimizes a given model. In the ensuing discussion it will sometimes be called the **primal linear programming model.** We provide the following economic argument to intuitively motivate the form and meaning of the dual linear programming model for the Ajax model given in Figure 3.1. The reader should be aware, however, that a general mathematical theory of duality underlies these arguments, a theory that rigorously guarantees the types of results that we discuss informally here.

Example 3.6

The Immense Computer Co. is experiencing a rapid growth in sales. As a result, Immense has insufficient capacity for testing and assembling their computers, and the director of purchasing is looking to rent capacity from other smaller, companies. She is considering approaching Ajax to offer to rent its capacity on a weekly basis.

In particular, she wishes to determine nonnegative prices PA per hour of A-line test capacity, PC per hour of C-line test capacity, and PL per hour of labor capacity to offer Ajax that will induce Ajax into agreeing to rent its resources rather than to use them in the manufacture of its own products. At the same time, she wishes to pay the least amount for these resources. This example is not so far fetched. A number of large manufacturing firms are concerned with the economic viability of their small suppliers; in effect, the large firms need to know if they are paying enough, but not too much, to keep the smaller firms in business.

Because Ajax nets \$350 for the sale of each Alpha computer and uses one unit of A-line test capacity and 10 hours of labor in the process of assembling each unit, the prices PA and PL must satisfy $PA + 10\ PL \geq 350$ for Immense's offer to be attractive. In other words, this constraint describes the requirement that the income received by Ajax for renting the resources it intends to use to test and assemble one Alpha must be at least as great as the net revenues that Ajax would receive by using those resources itself. Similarly, by considering the net revenues of Betas and Gammas, we derive the following additional constraints:

$$\text{PA} + 15\ \text{PL} \geq 470$$

and

$$\text{PC} + 20\ \text{PL} \geq 610$$

Now, Immense's director of purchasing will pay a total of 120 PA + 48 PC + 2000 PL to acquire Ajax' weekly capacity of 120 hours of A-line test capacity, 48 hours of C-line test capacity, and 2000 labor hours. Because she wishes to minimize this quantity, we can summarize the pricing problem she faces as the **dual linear programming model** shown in Figure 3.15.

Note that the dual model involves the same data as the primal model except that it has been transposed. The objective function coefficients in the dual model are the right-hand side coefficients from the primal model. The right-hand sides in the dual model are the objective function coefficients from the primal model. Finally, there is a constraint in the dual model for each decision variable in the primal model, and the coefficients describing each constraint in the dual model are those associated with each decision variable in the primal model.

An optimal solution to the dual model in Figure 3.15 is PA* = 45, PC* = 0, PL* = 30.5. The weekly cost to the Immense Computer Co. of this solution is $66,400, or exactly the weekly net revenues that Ajax could achieve on its own by maximizing its resources in the assembly, testing, and sale of its computer. Equality of the optimal primal and dual objective function values has an intuitive explanation. Clearly, Immense can pay no less for Ajax' resources because Ajax could choose to retain them to achieve a net revenue higher than the offer. On the other hand, if Immense was considering to pay more than Ajax' maximal net revenue, it could pay less and its offer would still be attractive to Ajax.

Figure 3.15
Dual model to 1-week Ajax model

$$\text{Maximize } D = 120\text{PA} + 48\text{PC} + 2000\text{PL}$$

$$\begin{array}{llcrcr}
\text{Subject to} & \text{PA} & & + & 10\text{PL} & \geq & 350 \\
& \text{PA} & & + & 15\text{PL} & \geq & 470 \\
& & \text{PC} & + & 20\text{PL} & \geq & 610
\end{array}$$

$$\text{PA} \geq 0,\ \text{PC} \geq 0,\ \text{PL} \geq 0$$

Equality of the optimal primal and dual objective function values in this example is a general result: For any (primal) linear programming model that has a feasible and an optimal (bounded) solution, there is a dual linear programming model involving the same data in transposed form whose optimal objective function value equals the optimal objective function value of the primal model.

The discussion of dual linear programming models thus far was developed from the perspective of another company wanting to rent Ajax' resources. The perspective was mainly to provide the reader with an intuitive justification of duality. Now that we have examined the construction, we can drop the notion that Ajax is considering renting its resources and more directly discuss how the dual model provides Ajax management with insights into the optimal strategy suggested by the primal model. Alternatively, we could say that Ajax' senior management should be just as concerned with efficient utilization of its resources when these resources are used internally as the Immense Computer Co. would be when it considers renting them.

The optimal dual solution to Ajax' primal model is useful in several ways in interpreting the primal optimal solution. Letting Z^* equal the optimal primal objective function value and D^* equal the optimal dual objective function value, we know that

$$Z^* = D^* = 120 \text{ PA}^* + 48 \text{ PC}^* + 2000 \text{ PL}^*$$

Thus, if we were to increase the number of labor hours available by 1, Ajax' maximal net revenues would increase by PL* = \$30.50 Similarly, an increase of 1 hour of A-line test capacity would cause maximal net revenues by PA* = \$45, and an increase of 1 hour of C-line test capacity would leave maximal net revenues unchanged because PC* = 0. This marginal price interpretation shows that our previously defined shadow prices are precisely optimal dual variable values.

Parametric and Sensitivity Analysis

The shadow price of \$30.50 for each additional hour of labor is the measure of labor's contribution to net revenue maximization at the current levels of resource availability. It is not the hourly rate for assembly line labor, a quantity that is buried in the net revenue figure per unit for each product. If management is considering increasing production by working overtime, however, \$30.50 per hour is the breakeven rate for overtime work.

The shadow price on labor is valid only at the current levels of resource availability. To understand more fully labor's contribution to net revenues, we need to perform a **parametric analysis** of maximal net revenues as a function of labor hours available. This analysis is shown in Figure 3.16. The assumption underlying the construction of this figure is that all data in the Ajax model of Figure 3.1 are held constant except for labor availability. Then, we effectively optimize the linear programming model for all values of this parameter.

The linear aspect of the model facilitates the derivation of the curve in Figure 3.16. Each linear segment corresponds to a particular production strategy, as indi-

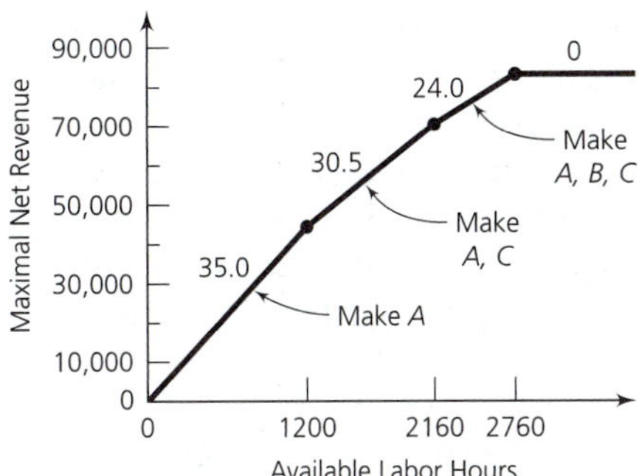

Figure 3.16 Maximal net revenue versus available labor hours

cated, with its associated shadow price. The decreasing value of labor is consistent with the economic theory of the firm that suggests that labor (and other) resources will be used first to support the most profitable activities, then to support the second most profitable, and so on. Thus, labor is worth \$35/hour up to 1200 hours, \$30.50/hour between 1200 and 2160 hours, \$24.00/hour between 2160 and 2760 hours, and \$0/hour for hours in excess of 2760. The microeconomic term for the plot in Figure 3.16 is a **production function.**[9]

By a similar argument, we can see that a shadow price equal to zero for the C-line test capacity does not mean that this resource is worthless. It simply means that relative to the availability of our resources, namely A-line test capacity and labor capacity, C-line test capacity is in excess, because only 40 out of 48 hours of capacity are used by the optimal solution. As with the analysis of the value of labor, we can best understand the value of C-line test capacity by performing a parametric analysis of maximal net revenues as a function of this capacity. This is shown in Figure 3.17. Thus, C-line test capacity is worth \$610 per hour up to 10 hours and \$130 per hour between 10 and 40 hours. Note also that the production function in this figure intercepts the maximal net revenue axis at \$54,600, which is the quantity that Ajax can achieve if C-line test capacity is zero.

In summary, shadow prices indicate how the optimal objective function value will change if an element of the right-hand side of an LP model is increased (or decreased) by a small amount. In our example, the small amount was one unit. For large increases, the shadow price may be overly optimistic about the change in objective function.

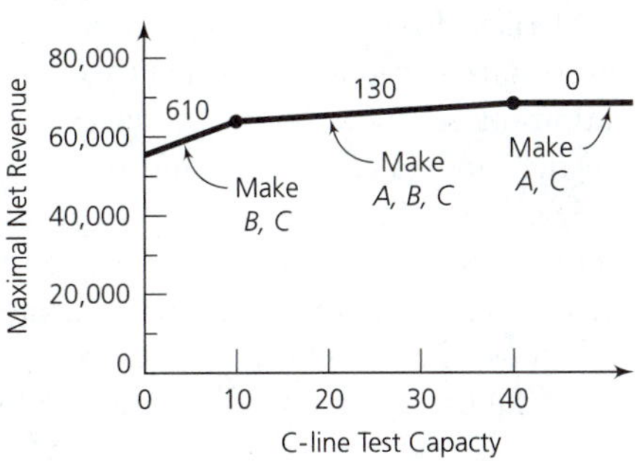

Figure 3.17 Maximal revenues versus C-line test capacity

For example, given the current level of 2000 labor hours in our Ajax model, the shadow price predicts that the objective function would increase by $30,500 as the result of an increase of 1000 hours. From Figure 3.16, however, we calculate an increase of $19,280; that is, the shadow price overestimated the increase. Similarly, the shadow price at 2000 labor hours predicts that the objective function would decrease by $30,500 as the result of a decrease of 1000 hours. Again from Figure 3.16, we calculate a decrease of $31,400; that is, the shadow price underestimated the decrease.

Of course, we cannot know precisely what is meant by "small" and "large" changes in right-hand side elements without performing parametric analysis such as the ones depicted in Figures 3.16 and 3.17. Thus, analysts must use judgment in interpreting this information. Some help is provided by **sensitivity analysis** of an optimal LP solution. Sensitivity analysis answers the question: What is the range on an individual parameter of an LP model in which an optimal solution remains optimal if all other parameters remain fixed at their given values?

We complete this section by reporting, as promised in an earlier section, the marginal net revenues on Alphas, Betas, and Gammas in the 4-week Ajax assembly model. In particular, Table 3.10 contains the shadow prices on the upper bounds on sales for the version of the model with lower bounds of 10 on ending inventory in week 4 of each of the products. This data tells us, for example, that net revenues would increase by $39.00 if another Alpha could be sold in week 1. The margins decrease over time, quite rapidly for Betas, due to the projected increase in sales potential by week 4.

Table 3.10 Marginal net revenues for Ajax Computer Company

Week	**1**	**2**	**3**	**4**
Alphas	39.00	33.50	24.50	15.50
Betas	20.00	10.00	0.00	0.00
Gammas	54.00	36.00	18.00	0.00

In effect, over the 4-week planning horizon, the projection indicates that Ajax' market position will be transformed from one characterized as having excess capacity to one characterized as sold out. Nevertheless, these results provide a clear priority for sales efforts when pushing Ajax' products over most of the planning horizon; namely Gammas get top priority for weeks 1 and 2, Alphas get top priority for weeks 3 and 4, and additional sales of Betas are less attractive.

The spreadsheet optimizers produce reports providing sensitivity analysis of an optimal linear programming solution. Solver produces a sensitivity report that lists the shadow prices on the model's constraints and the ranges in which the shadow prices are accurate in describing change in the objective function. For example, given labor resources of 2000 hours in the Ajax model, this report tells us that the shadow price of $30.50 remains accurate for increases no greater than 160 hours and decreases no greater than 800 hours. This information was used in constructing the production function of Figure 3.16, in which the shadow price of $30.50 was obtained for the range of labor hours from 1200 to 2160. Solver's sensitivity report also lists the reduced costs of the variables and gives ranges on changes in objective function coefficients such that the optimal solution remains optimal. What's Best produces a similar report.

3.4 Multiple Objective Optimization

Supply chain cost or net revenue may not be the only objective that the manager seeks to optimize. For example, in Section 1.2, we discussed the trade-off of minimal supply chain cost versus customer service measured by delivery time in studying how to redesign a company's distribution network. We remarked that an optimization model could be applied to map out the **efficient frontier** of undominated (efficient) solutions to such a multiobjective decision problem. An undominated solution on the efficient frontier has the property that no achievable other solution exists that is at least as good with respect to all the objectives and is strictly better on one of them. In this section, we present and illustrate methods for examining efficient frontiers. In particular, we review two methods, **goal programming** and **weighted objective function optimization,** show how they are related, and then present a third method that combines the features of both.

The methods will be developed in the context of a simple extension to the Ajax model that we analyzed in Section 3.1. Recall that the model, which was given in Figure 3.1, produced a net revenue maximizing strategy for the week. The marketing and sales manager objects to it because it entails much heavier sales of personal computers (120 Alphas) than workstations (40 Gammas). He fears this will have a detrimental affect on Ajax' longer-term market share.

To express his concern, the marketing manager proposes that the following type of constraint be imposed on the following net revenue maximizing strategy:

> The number of personal computers and notebooks sold can be no more than the number of workstations sold plus Q.

Mathematically, this can be expressed as the **goal constraint**

$$\text{MA} + \text{MB} - \text{MC} \leq Q$$

Upon further reflection, he suggests the value $Q = 20$. Note that his earlier concern that no Betas are manufactured is no longer an issue.

According to the method of goal programming, we create a **goal programming model** by adding this constraint to the original model. In general, we may add multiple goal constraints reflecting multiple objectives to the original model. Reoptimizing the Ajax model produces the new optimal solution, $\text{MA}^* = 0$, $\text{MB}^* = 68$,

MC* = 48, with a maximal net profit Z^* = \$61,240. Note that the goal constraint reduced maximal net revenue by \$4160.

The weighted objective function method for multiple objective optimization is distinctly different from the goal programming method. It leaves the feasible region unchanged from the original model but combines the original objective function to be maximized,

$$Z = 350\text{MA} + 470\text{MB} + 610\text{MC}$$

with the second objective function to be maximized,

$$W = \text{MC} - \text{MA} - \text{MB}$$

Intuitively, the second objective expresses the intent of the marketing manager, relative to the original optimal strategy, to try to sell more workstations and fewer personal computers. For the moment, we ignore the goal constraint on the relative level of personal computer and workstation sales.

The weighted objective function method combines the two objectives by weighting the second objective by the positive weight R and adding it to the first objective. The result is the following new objective:

$$Z(R) = (350 - R)\text{MA} + (470 - R)\text{MB} + (610 + R)\text{MC}$$

Clearly, R can be viewed as a reward for producing and selling workstations and a penalty for producing and selling personal computers and notebooks. If we take R= 50, for example, and optimize the original model, we obtain the new optimal solution, MA* = 104, MB* = 0, MC* = 48, with a maximal net revenue $Z^*(50)$ = \$62,880.

There are several comments to make about our analysis thus far. Both methods are flawed in that they each require an arbitrary selection of an important parameter. For the goal programming model, this was the parameter Q = 20 in the goal constraint. For the weighted objective function method, this was the reward/penalty R = 50 in the objective function. Unlike the other data in the Ajax model, which are objective, these parameters are subjective estimates intended to induce the net revenue maximizing strategy to reflect the second objective of balanced product mix. But the decision makers cannot be sure that they will have the desired or even a desirable effect.

Another issue is that we need to understand the meaning of $Z^*(50)$ = \$62,880 associated with the optimal solution to the weighted objective function model. In other words, we need to interpret the last solution obtained because we have corrupted the original net revenue figures by the penalty R = 50. It can be shown mathematically that the solution MA* = 104, MB* = 0, MC* = 48 with the original objective function value Z^* = \$65,680 is optimal in the original Ajax model with the following goal constraint:

$$MA + MB - MC \leq 56$$

That is, if we allow the number of personal computers and notebooks sold to exceed the number of workstations sold by 56, which is exactly the difference in the optimal solution to the weighted objective function model, this solution is optimal in the goal programming model with 56 as its right-hand side.

Thus, although they appear quite different, the two methods for analyzing linear programming models with multiple objectives are closely linked. Solution of the weighted objective function model for a given value of R yields an optimal solution to the goal programming model for some value of the parameter Q. Nevertheless, there is no apparent control over how the selection of R affects the induced value of Q.

The efficient frontier for the two objectives of the Ajax model is shown in Figure 3.18. It is easy to display because there are only two objective functions of interest. In effect, the efficient frontier in this case is determined by a parametric analysis of maximal net profit versus the parameter Q in the goal constraint. It allows us to present Ajax' management with a graphical display of the trade-off between short-term profit and balanced sales of its products.

At values of $Q = 80$ and above, the goal constraint does not affect net profit maximization. Moving down the curve from this value, we see that it has a mild effect until $Q = 56$ (\$30 reduction in profit for each unit reduction in Q), a stronger effect between $Q = 56$ and $Q = 21.33$ (\$110 reduction in profit for each unit reduction in Q), and a much stronger effect for $Q < 21.33$ (a \$470 reduction in profit for each unit reduction in Q). Given the marketing manager's concerns, the management committee decides to follow the strategy associated with $Q = 30$; namely, $MA^* = 26$, $MB^* = 52$, $MC^* = 48$, with a maximal net profit of $Z^* = \$62{,}820$.

For models with more than two objective functions to be optimized, it is more difficult to compute and display the efficient frontier. An alternate procedure is to sample points. This procedure, which we illustrate by its application to the Ajax model with two objectives, further reveals the hidden connections between the goal programming and weighted objective functions methods.

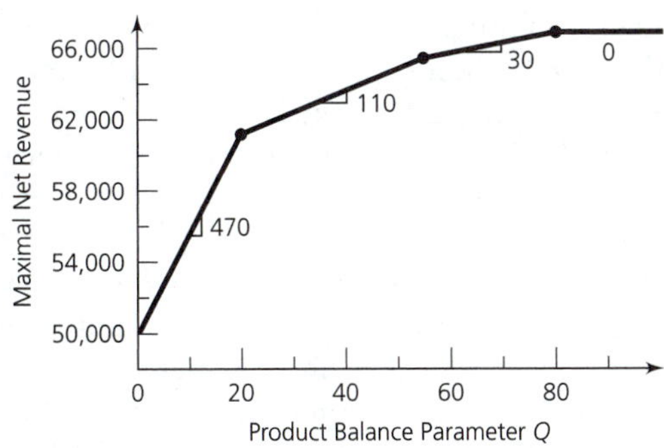

Figure 3.18
Efficient frontier for Ajax model; short-term profits versus balanced sales

The procedure begins with a target for Q in the goal programming model and a trial value for R in the weighted objective function method. In our case, we take $Q = 20$ and $R = 50$. As above, we solve the Ajax model with the weighted objective function $Z(R)$ and obtain the efficient solution MA* = 104, MB* = 0, MC* = 48, which yields the point (65,680, 56) on the efficient frontier in Figure 3.18.

Because the effective value of Q for this solution is higher than the target value of 20, we adjust the value of R to a new R' based on the following formula:

$$R' = R + t(56 - 20)$$

where t is an appropriately chosen positive number. (There is a mathematical theory for choosing t, but we omit details.) The underlying idea is that because $R = 50$ induced an optimal solution with a value of Q above the target, we must increase it to emphasize more fully the product balance constraint. Taking $t = 2$, we obtain $R' = 122$, which in turn produces the optimal solution in the weighted objective function model MA* = 0, MB* = 69.333, MC* = 48, which translates into the new point (61,866.65, 21.333) on the efficient frontier.

At this point, we might conclude from the effect it had on the objective function that the target $Q = 20$ was too stringent and adjust it to $Q = 40$. We would then adjust the value of R by the following formula:

$$R' = R + t(21.333 - 40)$$

for some suitable positive value of t and resolve the weighted objective function model. The procedure would continue until the decision makers believe that they have sufficiently explored the efficient frontier to choose a particular strategy.

3.5 Stochastic Programming

In Section 3.2, we discussed limitations of linear programming due to its deterministic treatment of the future. We argued that optimizing a model under multiple scenarios and timely reapplication of the model to reflect changes in internal and external data are often effective methods for dealing with uncertainties. Such arguments are weakest for long-term, strategic planning problems involving irreversible decisions such as the construction of a new manufacturing facility or the launching of a new product.

An extension of linear and mixed integer programming, called stochastic programming, is an attractive option for strategic planning because it allows the decision maker to explicitly analyze uncertainties and control risks.[10] The underlying idea is to simultaneously consider multiple scenarios of an uncertain future, each with an associated probability of occurrence. The model simultaneously determines an optimal contingency plan for each scenario and an optimal here-and-now plan that optimally hedges against these contingency plans. Optimization entails maximization (or minimization) of expected net profits (expected cost), where *expected* refers to multiplying net profits (costs) associated with each scenario by its probability of occurrence.

In this section, we present an example of stochastic linear programming applied to another problem faced by the Ajax Computer Company. The application addresses a short-term planning problem, rather than strategic planning, which would be more realistic. Nevertheless, the example illustrates the form and use of the stochastic programming model that suits our pedagogical needs. Other applications of stochastic programming are discussed in Chapter 8.

Example 3.7

Our example addresses assembly, inventory, and sales planning faced by Ajax over a 2-week planning horizon. Demand in the first week is known with certainty, but management is very uneasy about demand in the second week. In particular, it is unsure about the impact of a large advertising campaign on the quantities of Alphas, Betas, and Gammas that the company will be able to sell in the second week. Analysis of previous advertising campaigns and intuitive estimates by marketing personnel has identified three radically different scenarios, as shown in Table 3.11.

Table 3.12 displays a What's Best formulation of a stochastic programming model that we constructed to analyze this problem and its optimal solution. Note first that we

Table 3.11 Demand forecasts for Ajax stochastic programming model

Scenario	Maximal Sales	Probability
Low demand		0.25
Alphas	40	
Betas	30	
Gammas	30	
Medium demand		0.50
Alphas	80	
Betas	60	
Gammas	40	
High demand		0.25
Alphas	120	
Betas	100	
Gammas	100	

have incorporated a linear programming submodel for each of the three scenarios in week 2, as well as a single linear programming submodel for week 1. Thus, the model identifies a separate contingency plan for each of the three scenarios. Note also that we have added a contingency decision option, labor overtime, for each of the three scenarios (see rows 30, 53, 77). In mathematical form, the labor constraint looks like

$$10\text{MAS} + 15\text{MBS} + 20\text{MCS} - \text{OTS} \leq 2000$$

where MPS is the number of product *P* assembled and OTS is the number of overtime hours selected for the contingency plan for scenario *S*. Thus, the plan for scenario *S* has a labor resource of 2000 + OTS hours to allocate to assembly of Ajax' products. The objective function charge in scenario *S* net profit for each hour of overtime is $20. The total objective function is C22 + 0.25 * C46 + 0.50 * C69 + 0.25 * C92; that is, we add the first week net profit to the expected value of the second week net profit summed over the three scenarios.

A key construction in the stochastic programming model is the links between the here-and-now decision problem, which is the week 1 linear programming model, and the multiple scenario models in week 2. These links are the week 1 ending inventories of the three products that each scenario will use in developing its contingency plan. These are given as beginning inventories for each of the three scenarios (see rows 41, 64, 87). As such, they represent the optimal hedging strategy of week 1 in the face of great uncertainty in maximal sales during week 2.

A preliminary run of the model indicated that an unconstrained hedge could lead to very high inventories in unfavorable scenarios. Based on a cost per unit of $900 for Alphas, $1000 for Betas, and $1800 for Gammas, the total value of inventories at the end of week 2 in scenario 1 (low maximal sales) was close to $100,000. The CEO of Ajax saw this as a risk that she was unwilling to make. In addition to hurting the company's financial image, she was concerned that some items in inventory might become obsolete before they could be sold, either due to design changes or the emergence of new microprocessors. Thus, the constraint limiting ending inventory to a maximal value of $50,000 was added to scenario 1. A similar constraint was not required for the other two scenarios because scenario 1 was sure to be the scenario with the highest ending inventories.

Table 3.12 Ajax stochastic programming model

	A	B	C	D	E	F	G	H	I
1	Week 1								
2		product	Alpha	Beta	Gamma		resource usage		resource available
3		A-line test	1	1			92	<=	120
4		C-line test			1		33	<=	48
5		labor	10	15	20		1792	<=	2000
6		quantity assembled	50	42	33				
7									
8		net profit/unit	350	470	610				
9		sales	32	24	28				
10			=>=	=>=	=>=				
11		lower bound sales	32	24	28				
12			=<=	=<=	=<=				
13		upper bound sales	32	24	28				
14									
15		beginning inventory	22	42	36				
16		holding cost/unit/week	9	10	18				
17		cost/unit	900	1000	1800				
18		ending inventory	40	60	41				
19			>=	>=	>=				
20			0	0	0				
21									
22		weekly net profit	37860						
23		total net profit	37860						
24									
25									
26	week 2								
27	scenario 1	product	Alpha	Beta	Gamma	OT	resource usage		resource available
28		A-line test	1	1			0	<=	120
29		C-line test			1		0	<=	48
30		labor	10	15	20	-1	0	<=	2000
31		quantity assembled	0	0	0				
32		overtime				0			
33									
34		net profit	350	470	610				
35		sales	40	30	30				
36			>=	>=	>=				
37		lower bound sales	20	20	20				
38			=<=	=<=	=<=				
39		upper bound sales	40	30	30				
40									
41		beginning inventory	40	60	41		inventory value		max inventory value
42		ending inventory	0	30	11		50000	=<=	50000
43			=>=	>=	>=				
44			0	0	0				
45									
46		scenario 1 net profit	45900						
47									

Table 3.12 *(continued)*

	A	B	C	D	E	F	G	H	I
48									
49	Week 2								
50	scenario 2	product	Alpha	Beta	Gamma	OT	resource usage		resource available
51		A-line test	1	1			40	<=	120
52		C-line test			1		0	<=	48
53		labor	10	15	20	-1	400	<=	2000
54		quantity assembled	40	0	0				
55		overtime				0			
56									
57		net profit	350	470	610				
58		sales	80	60	40				
59			>=	>=	>=				
60		lower bound sales	20	20	20				
61			=<=	=<=	=<=				
62		upper bound sales	80	60	40				
63									
64		beginning inventory	40	60	41				
65		ending inventory	0	0	1				
66			=>=	=>=	>=				
67			0	0	0				
68									
69		scenario 2 net profit	80580						
70									
71									
72									
73	Week 2								
74	scenario 3	product	Alpha	Beta	Gamma	OT	resource usage		resource available
75		A-line test	1	1			120	=<=	120
76		C-line test			1		48	=<=	48
77		labor	10	15	20	-1	2000	=<=	2000
78		quantity assembled	80	40	48				
89		overtime				360			
80		net profit	350	470	610				
81		sales	120	100	89				
82			>=	>=	>=				
83		lower bound sales	20	20	20				
84			=<=	=<=	<=				
85		upper bound sales	120	100	100				
86									
87		beginning inventory	40	60	41				
88		ending inventory	0	0	0				
89			=>=	=>=	=>=				
90			0	0	0				
91									
92		scenario 3 net profit	136157.8						
93									
94									
95				total					
96				expected		123664.4			
97				net profit					

Generalizations

The preceding simple example allows us to briefly discuss several types of generalizations. First, uncertainties may evolve and be revealed over a greater number of time frames than two periods. In principle, a stochastic programming model may be extended to an arbitrary number of periods, although we must be concerned about controlling its size. Second, a stochastic programming model brings into clearer focus the need to identify and incorporate contingency options for different types of scenarios. In other words, the process of constructing a stochastic programming model encourages qualitative thinking about how to deal with unfavorable and favorable planning situations before they occur.

We also saw in the simple example that unconstrained hedging and contingency planning may place the company and/or the decision maker at risk with respect to measurable supply chain quantities such as inventories or net profits and losses. An important strength of stochastic programming is that it allows explicit constraints to be imposed on these quantities. Of course, such constraints may involve subjective parameters set by the decision maker, which might require an application of the multiobjective methods discussed in Section 3.6.

3.6 Final Thoughts

In this chapter, we demonstrated the application of linear programming models and solution algorithms to a central problem of supply chain management, the optimal allocation of resources in the firm. Resource planning also involves the acquisition, divestment, and adjustment of resources. Linear programming and its extensions to mixed integer programming, which we discuss in the following chapter, provide a rigorous approach for evaluating such decisions at all levels of planning.

We also discussed connections between the microeconomic theory of the firm and linear programming. We saw how linear programming algorithms can mechanize the theory by computing production functions describing the optimal allocation of resources to value adding activities. Further, linear programming provides an important link between this theory, which is largely abstract and not concerned with data, and empirical disciplines such as managerial accounting, demand forecasting, production management, and transportation science. The link is practical as well as conceptual. The supply chain decision database invoked by linear and mixed integer programming models can be represented by templates for assembling the data required to analyze supply chain planning problems faced by the firm.

Finally, we examined small, pedagogical models addressing production, inventory management, transportation, and purchasing decisions. In later chapters, we will discuss how such constructions have been employed in large-scale, practical applications. These modeling vignettes, and others we will discuss in the following chapter, serve as important elements in the practitioner's repertoire that he or she implicitly reviews each time he or she sets out to model a new supply chain planning problem.

Exercises

In addition to the following exercises, modeling exercises involving data files and discussion exercises involving white papers may be found on the Web site (www.scm-models.com).

1. A classical application is the **assignment problem:** The company must assign n individuals to n tasks to minimize total cost or maximize total benefit. An example arises in the assignment of drivers to daily routes. Suppose a company making home deliveries of groceries has selected 8 routes for today's deliveries. These routes are scheduled to depart at different times during the day. The company has 8 drivers who are also scheduled to arrive at different times during the day. Moreover, each driver has certain neighborhoods that he or she prefers for deliveries. Thus, for each route, the assignment of a specific driver will incur the following penalties:

   - Penalty = 0 if the driver arrives for work before the time the route is scheduled to leave and the route visits a preferred neighborhood of the driver.
   - Penalty = 5 if the driver arrives for work before the time the route is scheduled to leave but the route does not visit a preferred neighborhood of the driver.
   - Penalty = 25 if the driver arrives after the time the route is scheduled to leave, but within 1 hour of that time.
   - Penalty = 100 if the driver arrives more than 1 hour after the route is scheduled to leave.

The following table describes the possibilities for individual assignments:

Route	1	2	3	4	5	6	7	8
Sally	0	0	25	100	5	25	100	100
Jim	5	100	5	0	25	100	25	100
Bob	5	5	100	5	5	0	25	100
Carol	0	5	25	25	25	0	100	25
John	100	100	100	25	5	25	5	5
Bill	100	100	0	25	25	25	5	0
Frank	25	25	25	100	100	100	0	5
Harry	25	5	100	25	0	100	100	0

   a. Formulate this assignment problem as a spreadsheet optimization model and determine the optimal assignment.

   b. Suppose the cells with penalties of 100 were treated as illegal. This admits the possibility that some drivers and some routes may not be assigned. In such an event, the company will assign a supervisor to the route. How would you modify your formulation for this case?

c. Can you think of a better way to schedule routes and drivers?

2. Specific Motors manufactures three different car models, Model X, Model Y, and Model Z, with respective net revenues of \$1000, \$3000, and \$6000. Each Model X requires 40 person-hours of labor and 1 ton of steel to produce, each Model Y requires 65 person-hours and 1.50 tons of steel, and each Model Z requires 110 person-hours and 2 tons of steel. This month, Specific has available 16,000 person-hours of labor, 600 tons of steel, and ample supply of all other relevant resources.

   a. Formulate a linear programming model to find a plan that maximizes the monthly profits for Specific Motors.

   b. Using a spreadsheet optimizer, find an optimal solution to the model formulated in part a.

   c. Suppose an engineer develops the design for a Model Q yielding \$4000 profit and requiring 120 person-hours of labor and 1.25 tons of steel. Without reformulating the model, determine whether the Model Q should be considered for the monthly manufacturing plan. *Hint:* Use the shadow prices available in part b.

3. A grain cooperative with warehouses in Lincoln, Des Moines, and Pierre must meet market demands in Denver, Kansas City, Minneapolis, and St. Louis. The following table summarizes data relevant to this week's distribution problem. The numbers in the first three rows and the first four columns are the transportation costs per unit from each warehouse to each market.

From/To	Denver	Kansas City	Minneapolis	St. Louis	Supply
Lincoln	6	4	8	9	750
Des Moines	9	3	5	6	750
Pierre	9	11	6	14	500
demand	400	700	400	500	

   a. Construct a network representation of the problem of minimizing total transportation costs associated with shipping product from the warehouses to meet market demand.

   b. Formulate a linear programming model to solve this problem.

   c. Suppose the cooperative also has a warehouse in Omaha with a supply of 500 units and transportation costs to Denver, Kansas City, Minneapolis, and St. Louis of, respectively, 6, 5, 7, and 9. Extend the linear programming formulation of part b to include this option.

   d. Explain why the cost of meeting demand in part c cannot exceed the cost of meeting demand in part b.

   e. Solve the model given in part c using a spreadsheet optimization package.

4. Another classical application of linear programming is the **blending problem:** Minimize the cost of raw materials or maximize the revenues from finished products subject to constraints on raw material availability, finished product blending requirements, and finished product demands.

A pharmaceutical company faces such a problem in manufacturing a product made from a natural raw material whose ingredients vary. Specifically, the company's product planner has been provided with 10 drums of the raw material with the following characteristics:

Drum	Weight (kg)	Ingredient A (%)	Ingredient B (%)	Ingredient C (%)
1	80	0.60	0.20	0.20
2	78	0.59	0.18	0.23
3	76	0.57	0.19	0.24
4	81	0.56	0.20	0.24
5	82	0.54	0.21	0.25
6	80	0.53	0.20	0.27
7	77	0.51	0.19	0.30
8	79	0.50	0.20	0.30
9	81	0.49	0.19	0.32
10	79	0.48	0.20	0.32

The Food and Drug Administration (FDA) has set the following requirements on the product to be produced from these drums:

- Ingredient A percentage must lie within the range 54–56.
- Ingredient B percentage must lie within the range 19.5–20.5.
- Ingredient C percentage must lie within the range 24.2–25.8.

The production planner wishes to maximize the total kilograms of raw material that can be blended together that meets the FDA requirements. To this end, she constructs a linear programming model with the following decision variables:

xi = proportion of drum i to be used in the blend ($0 <= xi <= 1$)

The weighted sum of each of ingredients A, B, and C must be constrained to lie within the specified ranges. For example, the lower bound on the percentage of ingredient A in the blend can be expressed as the following **blending constraint:**

$$(.60)(80)x1 + (.59)(78)x2 + \cdots + (.48)(79)x10 \geq = .54(80x1 + 78x2 + \cdots + 79x10)$$

a. Using a spreadsheet optimizer, construct and optimize the production planner's linear programming blending model.

b. Suppose, in addition, that a drum can be included in the blend only if it is completely consumed (that is $xi = 1$). Extend your formulation of part a for this situation and reoptimize the model.

5. You are a currency trader faced with a 1-day currency exchange problem involving U.S. dollars, German DM, English pounds, and Japanese yen. At the start of the day, you have an inventory of 52,000 dollars, 163,000 DM,

97,000 pounds, and 111,000 yen. By the end of the day, you must have an inventory of at least 60,000 dollars, 140,000 DM, 99,000 pounds, and 108,000 yen. Today's exchange rates are given in the following table:

	Dollars	DM	Pounds	Yen
Dollars	1	2.12	0.61	1.11
DM	0.47	1	0.3	0.65
Pounds	1.6	3.37	1	1.82
Yen	0.88	1.49	0.55	1

The parameters *Rij* across each row *i* indicate the quantities of currency *j* that may be acquired by selling one unit of currency *i*. For example, you can exchange 1 yen for 1.49 DM.

Your problem is to exchange some starting inventories for different currencies to create the required ending inventories, while maximizing the surplus inventory of U.S. dollars. Using a spreadsheet optimizer, formulate this problem as a linear programming model and determine an optimal strategy.

Notes

1. Schrage [1997] and Winston [1995] offer more advanced but very readable presentations of optimization models and algorithms.
2. See Goldratt [1990].
3. Balakrishnan [1999] analyzes the relationship between linear programming and the theory of constraints including an example showing that the theory of constraints can fail to find an optimal solution. The paper also cites several earlier references to the theory.
4. For example, Christofides et al. [1979] propose an optimization model for determining the possible existence of arbitrage in real time among foreign currency exchange rates. An arbitrage opportunity has been identified if a cycle of currency exchanges causes the objective function to become unbounded.
5. Solver is an Excel add-in that comes with the Excel package. What's Best is an add-in that must be explicitly added to Excel; see LINDO Systems Inc. [1998]. A student version is available free from their Web site. Winston and Albright [1997] provide a detailed discussion of spreadsheet optimization and other spreadsheet modeling applications.
6. The simplex method has been successfully applied to industrial problems for almost 50 years. Over that time, computer scientists and operations researcher experts have employed and extended numerical analysis methods in developing robust commercial codes that can handle models with tens, even hundreds, of thousands of equations and variables. Dantzig [1963, Chapter 2] provides a brief history of developments in linear programming through 1960.
7. Koopmans [1957] pioneered research into the economic interpretation of linear programming. He received a Nobel prize for this work.
8. Strictly speaking, for occasional values of the right-hand sides, the two definitions of the shadow price may not provide the same value. In such a case, the shadow price is not well defined.
9. See Baumol [1977, Chapter 11] for a detailed discussion of production functions.
10. See Schrage [1997, 270] for further discussion of stochastic programming.

References

Balakrishnan, J. [1999], "Using the Theory of Constraints in Teaching Linear Programming and Vice Versa: Advantages and Caveats," *Production and Inventory Management Journal,* Second Quarter, 11–16.

Baumol, W. J. [1977], *Economic Theory and Operations Analysis,* 4th ed. Englewood Cliffs, NJ: Prentice-Hall.

Christofides, N., R. D. Hewins, and G. R. Salkin [1979], "Graph Theoretic Approaches to Foreign Exchange Operations," *J. of Financial and Quantitative Analysis,* 3, 481–500.

Dantzig, G. B., [1963], *Linear Programming and Extensions.* Princeton, NJ: Princeton University Press.

Goldratt, E. M., [1990], *What Is This Thing Called Theory of Constraints and How Should It Be Implemented.* New York: North River Press.

Koopmans, T. [1957], *Three Essays On the State of Economic Science.* New York: McGraw-Hill.

LINDO Systems Inc. [1998], *What's Best User's Manual.*

Schrage. L., [1997], *LINDO: An Optimization Modeling System,* 5th ed. Pacific Grove, Calif.: Duxbury Press.

Winston, W. L., [1995], *Introduction to Mathematical Programming,* 2d ed. Pacific Grove, Calif.: Duxbury Press.

Winston, W. L., and S. C. Albright [1997], *Practical Management Science: Spreadsheet Modeling and Applications.* Pacific Grove, Calif.: Duxbury Press.

Appendix 3.A

The Simplex Method of Linear Programming

In this appendix, we describe the simplex method for linear programming by applying it to the 1-week Ajax assembly model given in Figure 3.1. The development of this well-known and successful algorithm is the most mathematical subject in the book. We decided to include it because its development reveals the way in which mathematics can be used to unravel the complex interactions inherent in numerical data sets describing business problems. The robustness of the method is demonstrated by the fact that the main ideas underlying it can be illustrated by its operation on such a small problem. Although the construction below may at first appear arcane and arbitrary, we ask the reader to be patient and allow time for the method to sink in. Its procedures become more intuitive after their economic interpretation is revealed (see Section 3.4).

Perhaps the most important reason for digging into the details of the simplex method is that, empirically, it is an extremely efficient algorithm, much more so than we would believe from a theoretical analysis of its performance. One can expect to optimize a linear programming model in approximately m iterations, where m is the number of equations in the model. If the model also has n variables, where n is usually much larger than m, a theoretical upper bound on the number of iterations is

$$n!\,(n-m)!/m!$$

where $k! = k * k-1 * k-2 * \cdots *2*1$. This upper bound is astronomical for n much larger than m, and grows exponentially with n and m.

The efficient empirical behavior can be explained by two mathematical properties of the method. First, as we shall see shortly, the method limits its analysis to a certain class of solutions, called basic feasible solutions. These solutions correspond to $m \times m$ basis matrices made up of m columns of a linear programming model with the property that they are nonsingular or invertible. Geometrically, they correspond to the heavy dots in Figure 3.2. The upper bound cited in the previous paragraph assumes that any such $m \times m$ matrix might be nonsingular. Although, in theory, a random selection of m columns might yield a nonsingular matrix, in practice, many of them will not be nonsingular. Second, when maximizing an objective function, we shall see that the objective function montonically increases. With each increase, the number of nonsingular matrices made up of m columns of the model that might yield a still higher objective function value decreases, apparently significantly, thereby limiting the number of possible basis changes at the next iteration.

The simplex method adapts classical theory developed by nineteenth century mathematicians for characterizing solutions to systems of linear equations. In particular, the method extends the theory to take into account the following:

- The solutions must be nonnegative.
- An optimal solution must be chosen from among an infinite collection of feasible solutions.

Because we are applying the theory of linear equations, the first step in setting up the model of Figure 3.1 for solution by the simplex method is to convert the less-than-or-equal-to constraints to equations by adding **slack** variables. For example, the first constraint MA + MB ≤ 120 becomes the equation

$$\text{MA} + \text{MB} + S1 = 120$$

where the slack variable $S1$ is constrained to be nonnegative. For completeness, note that greater-than-or-equal-to constraints are converted to equality constraints by adding a **surplus** variable; namely,

$$X + Y \geq 10$$

becomes

$$X + Y - S2 = 0$$

where the surplus variable $S2$ is constrained to be nonnegative.

We rewrite the example of Figure 3.1 in equation form as follows:

$$\begin{array}{llllllll} Z - 350\text{MA} & - 470\text{MB} & - 610\text{MC} & & & & = & 0 \quad (3.A.1) \\ \text{MA} + & \text{MB} & & + S1 & & & = & 120 \quad (3.A.2) \\ & & \text{MC} & & + S2 & & = & 48 \quad (3.A.3) \\ 10\text{MA} + & 15\text{MB} + & 20\text{MC} & & & + S3 & = & 2000 \quad (3.A.4) \end{array}$$

where Z is the quantity we seek to maximize, and $S1$, $S2$, and $S3$ are slack variables.

The fundamental operation for analyzing a linear system is called **pivoting,** which we now define. A pivot consists of the following steps:

1. Select a nonzero coefficient called the **pivot element.** The pivot element is associated with a **pivot equation** and a **pivot activity.**
2. Replace the pivot equation with the same equation divided by the pivot element.

3. Eliminate each nonzero of the pivot activity in another equation by subtracting the appropriate multiple of the pivot equation from it.

Pivoting transforms the linear system to a more convenient equivalent form. By equivalent, we mean a form that has exactly the same set of solutions.

We illustrate these operations by pivoting on the coefficient 10 associated with the variable MA in Equation 3.A.4. The first step is to multiply the equation by 1/10, producing

$$\mathrm{MA} + 1.5\mathrm{MB} + 2\mathrm{MC} + 0.1\mathrm{S}3 = 200.$$

Then we subtract this equation multiplied by +1 from Equation 3.A.2 and subtract this equation multiplied by −350 from Equation 3.A.1. The result is

$$\begin{array}{llllllll} Z & + 55\mathrm{MB} & + 90\mathrm{MC} & & & + 35S3 & = 70{,}000 & (3.A.1') \\ & - 0.5\mathrm{MB} & - 2\mathrm{MC} & + S1 & & - 0.1S3 & = -80 & (3.A.2') \\ & & \mathrm{MC} & & + S2 & & = 48 & (3.A.3') \\ \mathrm{MA} & + 1.5\mathrm{MB} & + 2\mathrm{MC} & & & + 0.1S3 & = 200 & (3.A.4') \end{array}$$

In a similar fashion, we pivot on nonzero elements associated with the variables MC and $S2$. The result is

$$\begin{array}{llllllll} Z & + 32.5\mathrm{MB} & & + 45S1 & + 30.553 & & = 66{,}400 & (3.A.1'') \\ \mathrm{MA} & + \mathrm{MB} & & + S1 & & & = 120 & (3.A.2'') \\ & - 0.25\mathrm{MB} & & + 0.5S1 & + S2 & - 0.5S3 & = 8 & (3.A.3'') \\ & 0.25\mathrm{MB} & + \mathrm{MC} & - 0.5S1 & & + 0.5S3 & = 40 & (3.A.4'') \end{array}$$

In performing these three pivots, we have transformed the original system to a **canonical form** in which there is on each row a different variable with a +1 coefficient that has coefficients of zero on all other rows. These variables are called **basic** variables; the remaining variables are called **nonbasic** variables. This terminology is derived from the vocabulary of matrix algebra. We will not attempt to further explain it here. (The original system was also in canonical form, but not the one we wish to discuss first.)

The usefulness of the canonical form is that we can easily use it to calculate a solution to our system of equations and if it is feasible, check it for optimality. To do this, consider first Equations 3.A.2″, 3.A.3″, and 3.A.4″, which we rewrite expressing the basic variables MA, $S2$, and MC as functions of the nonbasic variables MB, $S1$, and $S3$. Thus, we view the basic variables as dependent on the nonbasic variables which we view as independent.

$$\begin{array}{llllll} \mathrm{MA} & = 120 & - \mathrm{MB} & - S1 & & (3.A.2'') \\ S2 & = 8 & + 0.25\mathrm{MB} & - 0.5S1 & + 0.5S3 & (3.A.3'') \\ \mathrm{MC} & = 40 & - 0.25\mathrm{MB} & + 0.5S1 & - 0.5S3 & (3.A.4'') \end{array}$$

All solutions to our original system of equations are characterized by selecting any values for the independent, nonbasic variables and solving for the basic variables. Naturally, we will choose nonnegative values for the nonbasics because we are only interested in feasible solutions. Note, however, that we can choose nonnegative values for the nonbasics that make the basics infeasible; for example, MB = 200, $S1 = 0$, $S3 = 0$ produces basic values of MA = −80, $S2 = 48$, and MC = −10.

The simplex method operates by examining a special class of solutions. These are **basic solutions** that we obtain by setting the nonbasics in a canonical form to zero and solving for the basics; in our example above, the basic solution is MB = $S1$ = $S3$ = 0, MA = 120, $S2 = 8$, and MC = 40. Note that this basic solution is also feasible. It is called a **basic feasible solution.** Not all basic solutions are feasible, but we have been lucky in our choice.

Given a basic feasible solution, the simplex method proceeds by testing it for optimality. Either the test establishes that the basic feasible solution is optimal, or it indicates how the solution can be improved. The test is derived by examining how the objective function value Z depends on values of the nonbasic variables. From Equation 3.A.1″ we see that

$$Z = 66{,}400 - 32.5\text{MB} - 45S1 - 30.5S3$$

From this equation, we see that an objective function value of 66,400 can be obtained by taking MB = $S1$ = $S3$ = 0, whereas any other nonnegative values of the nonbasics would cause Z to have a lower value. Thus, we can conclude that the given basic feasible solution is optimal. The optimality test (for a maximization problem) is as follows:

> Suppose we are given a canonical form corresponding to a basic feasible solution. If the coefficients of the nonbasic variables in the equation in which the objective function variable Z is expressed as a function of the nonbasics are all nonpositive, the basic feasible solution is optimal.

For a minimization problem, the optimality test is amended by replacing the word nonpositive with nonnegative. Then, the objective function can only increase from its current value by setting any of the independent nonbasic variables to positive values.

At this point, you probably have two nagging questions you would like to ask:

1. Suppose a basic feasible solution is not optimal?
2. How do we obtain a basic feasible solution in the first place?

We can provide satisfactory answers to these questions, but we must treat them one at a time. First, we will show how the simplex method proceeds from a basic feasible solution to an optimal basic feasible solution, or concludes that the objective function is unbounded. Then we will discuss how the method can be adapted to find an initial basic feasible solution.

For our sample problem an initial canonical form and basic feasible solution is readily available; namely, take the slack variables $S1$, $S2$, and $S3$ as the basic variables in our initial statement of the model in equation form. We illustrate the simplex method by proceeding from this basic feasible solution to the optimal basic feasible solution that we have already pulled out of the air and verified. To simplify notation, we rewrite the model in the **tableau** format in Tableau 3.A.1.

Tableau 3.A.1

Basics	Z	MA	MB	MC	S1	S2	S3	RHS
Z	1	−350	−470	−610				0
S1		1	1		1			120
S2				1		[1]		48
S3		10	15	20			1	2000

Note that we have treated the objective function variable Z as a basic variable in Tableau 3.A.1. The variable is a special one in that it will be treated as basic throughout the analysis. The abbreviation RHS stands for right-hand side. The basic feasible solution, of course, is $S1 = 120$, $S2 = 48$, $S3 = 2000$ with $Z = 0$.

If we examine the basic feasible solution of Tableau 3.A.1, we see that the coefficients of the nonbasic variables on the Z row, whose negative values are called the **reduced cost coefficients,** are all negative. That is, the reduced cost coefficients are all positive. This means that if we were to transpose the variables to the other side of the equation, the value of Z would increase if any or all of these variables were increased. Clearly, the optimality test has failed. The simplex method proceeds by selecting exactly one nonbasic to increase; the common rule of thumb is that the variable with the reduced cost coefficient that is the largest in magnitude. In Tableau 3.A.1, this is the variable MC.

The next step is to examine Tableau 3.A.1 to determine just how large we can make Z and retain feasibility. This is because as we increase MC, we not only cause Z to increase, but we cause some of the other basic variables to change. In particular, we see that

$$S2 = 48 - \text{MC}$$
$$S3 = 2000 - 20\text{MC}$$

The first equation implies that MC must be less than 48 to preserve feasibility, whereas the second equation implies MC must be less than 100. Thus, the first is the equation that blocks us from increasing MC any further, and the basic $S2$ is the blocking variable. This analysis to determine the blocking variable is called the **ratio test** because we computed the ratios 48/1 and 200/20.

We have just determined that the basic feasible solution of Tableau 3.A.1 can be improved to a new feasible solution by taking MC = 48, thereby implying that $S1 = 120$, $S2 = 0$, $S3 = 1040$, and $Z = 29{,}280$. This basic feasible solution is a substantial improvement and we naturally would like to test it for optimality. To do that, we need to recognize a very important fact. The new solution just produced corresponds to a different basic feasible solution from the one given in Tableau 3.A.1. Specifically, this is the basic feasible solution that results when we substitute MC for $S2$ as a basic variable (and $S2$ for MC as a nonbasic variable). Such a substitution appears reasonable because we associate positive values with basic variables and zero values with nonbasic variables.

Mathematically, the substitution of MC for $S2$ as a basic variable is carried out by pivoting on the nonzero coefficient that appears at the intersection of the $S2$ row and the MC column in Tableau 3.A.1. The result is shown in Tableau 3.A.2.

Tableau 3.A.2

Basics	***Z***	**MA**	**MB**	**MC**	***S*1**	***S*2**	***S*3**	**RHS**	**Ratio Test**
Z	1	–350	–470			610		29,280	
*S*1		1	1		1			120	120
MC				1		1		48	
*S*3		10	[15]			–20	1	1,040	69.33

The new basic feasible solution is $S1 = 120$, $\text{MC} = 48$, $S3 = 1040$, with $Z = 29{,}280$, which is what we had predicted before making the pivot transforming Tableau 3.A.1 to Tableau 3.A.2. The steps just executed to check the solution of Tableau 3.A.1 for optimality, perform the ratio test, and make a pivot is called an **iteration.** We see immediately that the new basic feasible solution is not optimal because the reduced cost coefficients of MA and MB are positive.

We decide therefore to bring MB into the basic set because it has the largest reduced cost coefficient. According to the ratio test, the variable $S3$ becomes nonbasic. The result is the new tableau, Tableau 3.A.3.

Tableau 3.A.3

Basics	***Z***	**MA**	**MB**	**MC**	***S*1**	***S*2**	***S*3**	**RHS**	**Ratio Test**
Z	1	–36.67				–6.67	31.33	61,866.5	
*S*1		0.333			1	1.333	–0.067	50.67	152
MC				1		1		48	
MA		[0.667]	1			–1.333	0.067	69.33	104.5

The new basic feasible solution $S1 = 50.67$, $\text{MC} = 48$, and $\text{MB} = 69.33$ is still not optimal because the cost coefficients of MA and $S2$ indicate that Z can be increased further ($Z = 61{,}866.5 + 36.67\text{MA} + 6.67S2 - 31.33S3$). We select MA as the new basic variable. According to the ratio test, MB is the basic variable that becomes nonbasic. We pivot on the indicated coefficient in Tableau 3.A.3 to obtain Tableau 3.A.4.

Tableau 3.A.4

Basics	Z	MA	MB	MC	S1	S2	S3	RHS	Ratio Test
Z	1	55				−80	35	65,680	
S1		0.5			1	[2]	−0.1	16	8
MC				1		1		48	48
MA		1	1.5			−2	0.1	104	

Tableau 3.A.4 is still not optimal because increasing the nonbasic $S2$ causes Z to increase. Bringing it into the basic set and taking $S1$ out results in the optimal Tableau 3.A.5. The simplex method has succeeded as promised in deriving an optimal basic feasible solution from an initial basic feasible solution.

Tableau 3.A.5

Basics	Z	MA	MB	MC	S1	S2	S3	RHS
Z	1		32.5		45		30.5	66,400
S2			−0.25		0.5	1	−0.05	8
MC			0.25	1	−0.05		0.05	40
MA		1	1		1			120

The simplex method worked for our sample model. We now give the argument why it will always find an optimal solution, if there is one. But first, we must deal with a pathological case. Suppose we had entered the wrong data for variable MC in Tableau 3.A.1 so that it looks like that in Tableau 3.A.1′.

Tableau 3.A.1′

Basics	Z	MA	MB	MC	S1	S2	S3	RHS
Z	1	−350	−470	−610				0
S1		1	1		1			120
S2				−1		[1]		48
S3		10	15	−20			1	2000

As before, we apply the usual rule in selecting the entering nonbasic variable MC. Then we try to apply the ratio test to see which basic variable it replaces. At this point, we discover that the ratio test is vacuous because increasing MC makes $S2$ and $S3$ larger and does not affect $S1$. When this happens, we conclude that Z is unbounded. Due to data input errors, we have effectively modeled a management decision problem where infinite profit is possible. We summarize the two possible outcomes for the simplex method at each iteration as follows:

> Given a nonoptimal basic feasible solution to a maximization problem, the simplex method will either find a different basic feasible solution with a higher

objective function value or will establish that the objective function is unbounded from above.

Given this result, a logical argument ensuring convergence of the simplex method is at hand. Starting with a basic feasible solution, the method will find a sequence of basic feasible solutions with strictly increasing objective function values. By their very nature, these basic solutions are unique; we set the nonbasic variables equal to zero and solve for the unique values of the basic variables. The implication is that the method will never repeat a basic feasible solution because that would mean repeating an objective function value, an impossible event because the objective function strictly increases from iteration to iteration. Because there are only a finite number of ways we can divide the variables of an LP into basic and nonbasic sets, the simplex method must terminate in a finite number of iterations. We summarize the convergence result as follows:

> Starting from a basic feasible solution to a maximization problem, the simplex method will, in a finite number of iterations, either find an optimal basic feasible solution or establish that the objective function is unbounded from above.

An important final point is that the simplex method always finds an optimal **basic** feasible solution, if an optimal solution exists. Supposing that the LP problem has m constraints, this means that m variables will be positive in an optimal solution. If the form of such a solution is undesirable for any reason, and you wish to control the number of positive variables in an optimal solution, you must modify the formulation, possibly using 0-1 variables, to force a greater or lesser number of variables to take on positive values.

Our final topic in this section is a brief discussion of the so-called phase one simplex method for finding an initial basic feasible solution. For the example model, this was not an issue because the "all slack" solution of Tableau 3.A.1 was a basic feasible solution. Such a solution may not always be available.

Suppose, for example, that Ajax' marketing sales manager wished to impose the additional constraint that combined sales of Alphas and Betas must equal at least 150; that is,

$$\text{MA} + \text{MB} \geq 150$$

In Tableau 3.A.1″ we convert this constraint to an equality using the surplus variable *S*4 and extend Tableau 3.A.1. The bottom row now corresponds to the equation

Tableau 3.A.1″

Basics	*Z*	MA	MB	MC	*S*1	*S*2	*S*3	*S*4	RHS
Z	1	−350	−470	−610					0
*S*1		1	1		1				120
*S*2				−1		[1]			48
*S*3		10	15	−20			1		2000
*S*4		−1	−1					1	−150

$$-\text{MA} - \text{MB} + S4 = -150$$

The basic solution $S1 = 120$, $S2 = 48$, $S3 = 2000$, $S4 = -150$ with $Z = 0$ is not feasible.

The idea of the phase 1 method is to add an artificial variable with an appropriate + 1 or −1 coefficient to any row where it is needed to achieve feasibility. In this example, we add the variable $W4$ to the new row with a −1 coefficient. The result is

$$-\text{MA} - \text{MB} + S4 - W4 = -150$$

Then we replace the original objective function with a new objective function that minimizes the sum of the artificial variables. In this case, the new objective function is

$$\min Q = W4$$

We apply the simplex method to the phase one problem with the artificial variables and the phase one objective function. By construction, we have an initial basic feasible solution to the phase 1 problem consisting of some basic variables that are artificial variables. In our example, the initial basic feasible solution to the phase 1 problem is $S1 = 120$, $S2 = 48$, $S3 = 2000$, and $W4 = 150$, with the phase 1 objective value $Q = 150$.

The simplex method always converges to an optimal solution to the phase 1 problem because an unbounded solution is not possible. Two outcomes are possible. First, if the minimal value of the sum of the artificial variables is 0, the artificial variables must all equal zero. In this case, we have effectively driven the artificial variables out of the problem. The result is a basic feasible solution involving the real (not artificial) variables, and we proceed as described above in computing an optimal basic feasible solution (this is called phase 2). Second, if the minimal phase 1 objective is greater than zero, we can conclude that the original model was infeasible because we are forced to use artificial (nonreal) variables at positive values.

4 Fundamentals of Optimization Models: Mixed Integer Programming

Mixed integer programming models are generalizations of linear programming models in which some variables, called **integer variables,** are constrained to take on nonnegative integer values, whereas the remaining variables, called **continuous variables,** are allowed to take on any nonnegative values. The most frequently occurring integer variables are **0-1,** or **binary, variables,** which are constrained to take on values of 0 or 1. Such variables are used to describe cost relationships, constraints, and logical conditions that cannot be captured by linear programming. As we shall demonstrate shortly, mixed integer programming constructions overcome many of the limitations of linear programming models discussed in the previous chapter.

Zero-one variables are employed in different ways in models that address operational, tactical, and strategic supply chain planning problems. For operational problems, they are used to model sequencing and routing decisions associated with the scheduling of machines, vehicles, or people. For tactical problems, they are used to model fixed costs, economies of scale, and a variety of nonnumeric, or logical, policy restrictions, such as sole sourcing of markets. For strategic problems, they are used to model the timing, sizing, phasing, and location of investment options.

Mixed integer programming models and methods provide a rigorous approach to supply chain analysis. The models accurately capture the important decision options, constraints, and objectives of a supply chain problem. The methods are capable of finding demonstrably good solutions to these models and can yield optimal solutions if the decision maker is willing to wait long enough for the algorithms to identify them.

The greater realism of mixed integer programming models is not achieved without a cost. In the appendix to this chapter, we discuss the **branch-and-bound** method for optimizing mixed integer programming as a sequence of linear programming approximations. The number of approximations that must be solved to optimize a given mixed integer programming model can grow exponentially with the number of integer variables in the model. Thus, the modeler must use mixed integer programming constructs sparingly in balancing the need and desire for realism against the burdens of computation.

Researchers are continuing to devise new and improved approaches for solving mixed integer programming models. In recent years, **heuristic methods** that generate trial solutions to these models, or the decision problems underlying them, have shown promise for some classes of models and problems. Heuristic methods use problem-specific or general-purpose procedures to search the discrete space of possible solutions. We believe heuristics have been oversold. A more accurate view of their merit is that heuristics play a complementary role to rigorous mixed integer programming modeling and optimization methods. In Chapter 5, we develop a unified optimization methodology for advanced planning and scheduling that exploits this complementarity.

Our discussion of mixed integer programming begins in Section 4.1 with modeling vignettes illustrating how 0-1 variables and constraints can capture phenomena such as fixed costs, economies of scale, and production changeovers. In Section 4.2, we use mixed integer programming to model and optimize the problem of locating distribution centers (DCs) in the supply chain network of a distribution company. In so doing, we describe how Solver and What's Best treat mixed integer programming variables and constraints. In Section 4.3, we use mixed integer programming to model and optimize a variety of strategic supply chain options faced by a manufacturing company.

We conclude the chapter with two sections in which we examine issues arising in the implementation of modeling systems based on linear and mixed integer programming. In Section 4.4, we discuss design principles for modeling systems to analyze strategic and tactical supply chain problems. Mixed integer programming models and modeling systems for vehicle routing, production scheduling, and other operational planning problems are presented in Chapter 5. The chapter concludes with a survey in Section 4.6 of off-the-shelf optimization software. The branch-and-bound method for mixed integer programming is presented in Appendix 4.A.

4.1 Mixed Integer Programming Modeling Vignettes

We illustrate several mixed integer programming model constructs for planning situations that arise in the management of Ajax' supply chain, which we discussed in Section 3.1. The reader is referred to that section for background on the model for which extensions are discussed here. Supply chain complications modeled in each subsection are not carried forward to later subsections. Zero-one variables and associated constraints can be employed to model a wide range of supply chain planning problems as well as many problems arising in financial planning, engineering, graph theory, and several other fields. Our constructions here illustrate some concepts, the interested reader is referred to specialist books for additional applications.[1]

Fixed Costs

In the formulation of Ajax' assembly model given in Figure 3.1, the A- and C-line test resources available for the week were given and their costs were netted out of the net revenue figures. Our decision problem was to optimally allocate these resources, along with labor resources, to the assembly and sale of Alphas, Betas, and Gammas. We extend that formulation to explicitly account for the costs associated with the test resources.

Graphical depictions of the cost versus resource functions are shown in Figures 4.1 and 4.2. Historically, before the implementation and use of a model, Ajax followed the weekly strategy of assembling and testing 64 Alphas, 48 Betas, and 32 Gammas. Under this strategy, the historical weekly utilization was 112 hours of the A-line test equipment and 32 hours of the C-line test equipment. As shown in Figure 4.1, based on these utilizations, the unit charge for A-line testing was $5600/112 = $50.00 per hour, or equivalently, per unit of Alpha or Beta tested because they each require 1 hour of testing. Similarly, the unit charge of C-line testing was $2432/32 = $76.00 per hour, or equivalently, per unit of Gamma tested. Now that we are explicitly modeling the costs of these resources, these quantities should be added to the net revenue figures, which become $400 for Alphas, $520 for Betas, and $686 for Gammas.

The next step is to replace the linear approximations ($50/hour for A-line usage, $76/hour for C-line usage) employed in the model of Figure 3.1 by the more

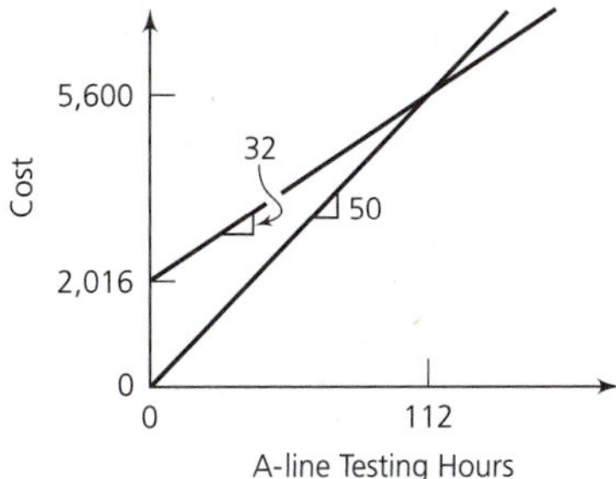

Figure 4.1
A-Line testing cost function

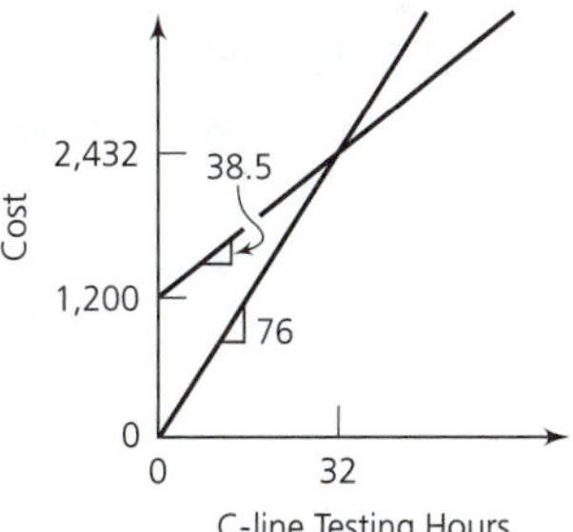

Figure 4.2
C-Line testing cost function

accurate cost functions involving the fixed and variable costs. For the A-line, the function involves a **fixed cost** of \$2016 if the A-line test equipment is used at all during the week and a variable cost of \$32 for each hour consumed. For the C-line, the function involves a fixed cost of \$1200 if the C-line test equipment is used at all during the week and a variable cost of \$38.50 for each hour consumed. These fixed costs equal the cost of supervisory and repair personnel who must be available full-time during the week if the test equipment is used.

The term *fixed cost* is misleading. From the viewpoint of the decision maker—the production manager—the fixed cost is not actually fixed because she might decide not to operate one of the two test lines, thereby avoiding all costs associated with it. Better terminology would be **lumpy, step,** or **discontinuous cost.** Nevertheless, we will continue to use the term *fixed cost* because it is widely accepted and understood.

Example 4.1

The function in Figure 4.1 is modeled as follows. We define a 0-1 decision variable FA by

$$\text{FA} = \begin{cases} 1 \text{ if the A-line test equipment is used during the week} \\ 0 \text{ if the A-line test equipment is not used during the week} \end{cases}$$

The approach taken by an optimization algorithm to impose this binary restriction on a decision variable is discussed in Appendix 4.A. We employ FA in the constraint

$$\text{MA} + \text{MB} - 120\ \text{FA} \leq 0$$

Recall that MA, MB, and MC are decision variables that indicate how many Alphas, Betas, and Gammas should be made during the week. Thus, if FA = 1, the constraint becomes MA + MB $\leq$ 120, whereas if FA = 0, the constraint becomes MA + MB $\leq$ 0, implying MA = MB = 0 because the variables must also be nonnegative.

Similarly, we define the 0-1 decision variable FC by

$$\text{FC} = \begin{cases} 1 \text{ if the C-line test equipment is used during the week} \\ 0 \text{ if the C-line test equipment is not used during the week} \end{cases}$$

and employ it in the constraint

$$\text{MC} - 48\ \text{FC} \leq 0$$

Finally, we extend the objective function to

$$\text{Maximize } Z = 410\text{ MA} + 520\text{ MB} + 686\text{ MC} - 2016\text{ FA} - 1200\text{ FC} - 32\text{ MA} - 32\text{ MB} - 38.50\text{ MC}$$

or, combining terms,

$$\text{Maximize } Z = 378\text{ MA} + 488\text{ MB} + 647.50\text{ MC} - 2016\text{FA} - 1200\text{ FC}$$

Reoptimizing the model using a mixed integer programming algorithm yields the same optimal solution as we obtained in the linear case, MA* = 120, MB* = 0, MC* = 40. Due to the more accurate descriptions of costs, however, we have determined that this solution has a net revenue of $68,044 rather than the $66,400 that we computed using the linear programming model of Figure 3.1. For the small Ajax model, the more accurate representation of some of the costs as fixed and variable did not change the optimal solution. Before the fact, we could not know this and should not regret generating and optimizing a more realistic model.

A constraint sometimes linked to a decision about whether or not to incur a fixed cost is the **conditional minimum.** This states that a continuous decision variable must either equal zero or be above a certain threshold. For example, Ajax' production manager might wish to impose the constraint that testing of Gammas in the week must either be 0 or at least 5. Using the previously defined 0-1 variable FC, this would be expressed as

$$\text{MC} - 5\text{ FC} \geq 0$$

Thus, if FC = 1, indicating that Gammas should be tested during the week, the constraint would impose the condition MC ≥ 5.

Note that this conditional minimum was satisfied by the latest optimal solution to the 1-week Ajax problem even though the constraint was not explicitly imposed. In most applications, many, if not all, conditional minima will be met without the imposition of formal constraints of the form just reviewed. You might well ask: When it is worth imposing such constraints?

One answer is that the constraints should be added if the strategy suggested by the model is intended to be implemented. The production manager does not want to waste time trying to decide which products with small suggested production levels should be dropped from the strategy and which should be bumped up to higher levels. By contrast, if the model run is one of many being made to study a company's supply chain in the aggregate, it may be that respecting conditional minima is not important and the constraints need not be written. The caveat in this case is that the impact of conditional minima on the optimal solution and the optimal objective function value should be small.

Economies of Scale

In Section 3.2, we stated without demonstration that a mixed integer programming construction is needed to correctly portray economies of scale in costs and resource utilization. One situation where this arises at the Ajax Computer Company is in the acquisition of microprocessors from The Riverfront Corporation for the Gamma workstation. Riverfront offers to sell microprocessors under a long-term arrangement for \$250/unit up to 30 per week and then drop the price to \$200/unit for any number of additional units delivered per week. As we demonstrate, a 0-1 variable is needed to enforce the condition that the lower price can be paid only after 30 units have been bought at the higher price.

Example 4.2

Let $W1$ = weekly purchases from Riverfront at \$250/unit and $W2$ = weekly purchases from Riverfront at \$200/unit. As before, we let MC denote the quantity of Gammas assembled in a given week, where MC = $W1 + W2$ because each Gamma requires one microprocessor. To impose the logical condition that $W2 > 0$ implies $W1 = 30$, we introduce a 0-1 variable D constrained to take on a value of 0 (economy of scale not achieved) or 1 (economy of scale achieved). Specifically, we impose this condition by the following constraints:

$$30 \geq W1 \geq 0,\ W2 \geq 0$$

$$-W1 + 30D \leq 0$$

$$W2 - 18D \leq 0$$

If $D = 1$, by the second constraint we have $W1 \geq 30$, which implies $W1 = 30$ by the first set of constraints stating that $W1 \leq 30$. By the third constraint, we have $W2 \leq 18$ because 48 is an upper bound on the number of microprocessors to be acquired for any given week, and 30 have been acquired at the higher price. Thus, $D = 1$ corresponds to the logical condition that $W1 = 30$ and $W2$ may take on any reasonable nonnegative value. On the other hand, if $D = 0$, the second constraint simply states (redundantly) that $W1 \geq 0$ and the second constraint states that $W2 \leq 0$, or $W2 = 0$ because $W2 \geq 0$ by the first set of constraints. Note that we could have $W1 = 30$, but $D = 0$ if the optimal solution does not entail assembling more than 30 Gammas. In other words, when $W1 = 30$, the model is free to choose $D = 0$ or 1, but it must choose $D = 1$ if lower-cost purchases are needed to achieve optimality.

Production Changeovers

In Section 3.2, we discussed setup resource utilization due to the changeover that occurs on the A-line in any week when both Alphas and Betas are tested. The 120 hours of available A-line test capacity is reduced to 100 hours if both Alphas and Betas are tested during a week because 20 hours is required to adjust the equipment for the changeover.

Example 4.3

Let TESTA denote a 0-1 variable that takes on a value of 1 if Alphas are tested in a given week or a value of 0 if Alphas are not tested in that week. Similarly, let TESTB denote a 0-1 variable that takes on a value of 1 if Betas are tested in a given week or a value of 0 if Betas are not tested in that week. Finally let TESTBOTH denote a 0-1 variable that takes on either a value of 1 if both Alphas and Betas are tested in a given week (TESTA = 1, TESTB = 1) or 0 if at most one of Alphas and Betas is tested that week.

The logical condition that TESTBOTH = 1 if both TESTA = 1 and TESTB = 1 is expressed mathematically by

$$\text{TESTBOTH} \geq \text{TESTA} + \text{TESTB} - 1$$

In interpreting this constraint, there are four cases to consider. If TESTA = 1 and TESTB = 1, we have TESTBOTH ≥ 1 by this constraint, implying TESTBOTH = 1 because TESTBOTH can take only values of 0 or 1. The other three cases are (1)TESTA = 1, TESTB = 0 implying TESTBOTH ≥ 0, (2) TESTA = 0, TESTB = 1 implying TESTBOTH ≥ 0, and (3) TESTA = 0, TESTB = 0 implying TESTBOTH ≥ −1. In these three cases, the optimizer can select TESTBOTH = 0 and avoid the changeover resource utilization; that is, it has the choice of setting TESTBOTH = 0 or 1 but would choose 0 if the A-line resource has value.

The changeover resource utilization is expressed by the constraint

$$\text{MA} + \text{MB} + 20\ \text{TESTBOTH} \leq 120.$$

Thus, if TESTBOTH is forced to take a value of 1 by the previous constraint, the net resources available for assembly of Alphas and Betas is 100 hours on the A-line. Finally, we link MA to TESTA and MB to TESTB by the constraints

$$\text{MA} - 120\ \text{TESTA} \leq 0$$

$$\text{MB} - 120\ \text{TESTB} \leq 0$$

These constraints express the condition that TESTA is forced to take on a value of 1 if any Alphas are tested in the week (that is, if MA > 0), and TESTB is forced to take on a value of 1 if any Betas are tested in the week (MB > 0). Under such conditions, MA or MB will not exceed 120, which is the capacity of the A-line.

Multiple Choice and Other Nonnumeric Constraints

Zero-one variables can be used to capture a variety of nonnumerical or logical constraints. A frequently occurring constraint of this type is the **multiple choice constraint,** which states that exactly one, or at most one, logical decision must be selected from among a set of possible logical decisions. An example is the sole sourcing constraint that we discussed in the context of the Alpha transportation model given in Figure 3.6. The optimal solution for that model had shipments to market 8 (MIN) from both the plant (XP8 = 4) and the warehouse (XW8 = 16). For reasons of customer service, the distribution manager at Ajax would like to investigate the consequences of limiting shipments to market 8 and all other markets to a single source.

Example 4.4

We illustrate how sole sourcing can be imposed on market 8 by using two 0-1 variables. Let DP8 = 1 if the plant serves market 8 and DP8 = 0 if the plant does not serve market 8. Similarly, let DW8 = 1 if the warehouse serves market 8 and DW8 = 0 if the warehouse does not serve market 8. We use these variables to rewrite the last equation in the demand constraints in Figure 3.6 as

$$20\text{DP8} + 20\text{DW8} = 20 \quad \text{or equivalently,} \quad \text{DP8} + \text{DW8} = 1$$

We must also adjust the supply constraints and the objective function to replace the flow variables XP8 and XW8 by the 0-1 variables DP8 and DW8, namely,

$$\text{XP1} + \text{XP2} + \text{XP3} + \text{XP4} + \text{XP5} + \text{XP6} + \text{XP7} + 20\ \text{DP8} \le 100$$

$$\text{XW1} + \text{XW2} + \text{XW3} + \text{XW4} + \text{XW5} + \text{XW6} + \text{XW7} + 20\ \text{DW8} \le 45$$

and

$$\text{Min } Z = 14\text{XP1} + \cdots + 17\text{XP7} + 600\ \text{DP8} + 24\text{XW1} + \cdots + 24\ \text{XW7} + 560\ \text{DW8}$$

Note that the transportation cost of supplying market 8 with 20 Alphas from the plant is $600 and from the warehouse it is $560.

Variations of multiple choice constraints are applicable to a range of planning situations. The number of variations is enormous and we illustrate only two in the following examples.

Example 4.5

Suppose that management policy requires that no more than three markets can be served by the warehouse. To capture this constraint, we define 0-1 variables DWJ for every one of the markets *J* where DWJ = 1 if market *J* is served by the warehouse and DWJ = 0 if market J is not served by the warehouse. In addition to the sole sourcing and other constraints described above, this policy would be expressed by the multiple choice constraint

$$\text{DW1} + \text{DW2} + \text{DW3} + \text{DW4} + \text{DW5} + \text{DW6} + \text{DW7} + \text{DW8} \leq 3$$

Finally, to illustrate a nonnumeric constraint with a different form than a multiple choice constraint, suppose management wishes to impose the policy that markets 4 and 6 must both be served either by the warehouse or the plant. This condition is expressed by

$$\text{DW4} - \text{DW6} = 0$$

It is easy to see that DW4 = 1 if and only if DW6 = 1 and that DW4 = 0 if and only if DW6 = 0. Letting DPJ = 1 if market *J* is served by plant *J* and DPJ = 0 otherwise, the sole sourcing constraints would tell us in the latter case that

$$\text{DP4} = 1 - \text{DW4} = 1$$

and

$$\text{DP6} = 1 - \text{DW6} = 1$$

or in other words, that markets 4 and 6 are served by the plant.

4.2 Distribution Center Location Models

Locating DCs is a classic application of mixed integer programming.[2] In a standard version of this problem, a distribution company must design or redesign the network of DCs from which to ship its products to its markets to meet forecasted demand for the coming year. The objective is to minimize the sum of warehousing and transportation costs while maintaining acceptable customer service. Although it is a strategic planning problem, next year's demand is assumed fixed and given. In many instances, the company's marketing managers determine the marketing and sales plan for the year without regard to the logistics consequences. The plan is passed to the logistics managers, who are responsible for ensuring that the products reach the markets at low cost and in a timely manner. In this section, we illustrate how to model a DC location problem. In the process, we will examine how spreadsheet optimizers can generate and optimize mixed integer programming models.

DC Location Model

The Electronica Corporation is a wholesale distributor of consumer electronic products to 20 markets in the midwestern states. The company is seeking a DC location strategy for next year that will minimize their total distribution costs. Table 4.1 contains the data for Electronica's DC location model, a statement of the model, and an optimal strategy.

Table 4.1 is divided into four sections. Eight potential locations for third-party warehouses and their distances to the 20 markets are listed in the **Distances** section. At each location, Electronica has the choice of selecting among no DC, a small DC, or a large DC. As shown in the section labeled **DC Options,** a fixed cost (FC) and a variable cost (VC) for outbound flows are associated with each DC. These flows are measured in truckloads for the year up to the stated capacity of the DC option. All costs are measured in thousands of dollars. The demands for full truckload shipments for next year, along with product flows from the DCs to meet them, are listed in the section labeled **Flows.** The costs of the DCs selected in the optimal solution are calculated in the **DC Capacities and Costs** section.

Before reviewing the details of Table 4.1, we discuss briefly how we use mixed integer programming to model the location decisions. The choices at each location are modeled by the introduction of two 0-1 variables. For example, we define

CHISM = 1 if a small DC is selected at Chicago location; 0 otherwise

CHILG = 1 if a large DC is selected at Chicago location; 0 otherwise

and impose the logical constraint CHISM + CHILG ≤ 1, which states that at most one of the two DC options at Chicago may be selected. If CHISM = 1, we see from the data under DC Options that the model will open the small DC at Chicago with a fixed cost of $175,000, a variable cost of $103 for each truckload shipped from the DC, and a capacity for next year of 2500 truckloads. If CHILG =1, the model will open the large DC at Chicago with a fixed cost of $300,000, a variable cost of $77 for each truckload shipped from the DC, and a capacity for next year of 7500 truckloads. If both CHISM = 0 and CHILG = 0, no DC will be opened in Chicago.

In the DC Options section, the adjustable cells B29 to I29 correspond to the SM 0-1 variables, whereas the cells B33 to I33 correspond to the LG 0-1 variables. The inequalities given in cells B34 to I34 pertain to the eight logical constraints, one for each location, similar to the one illustrated above for Chicago. These choices are translated into cost and capacity data in the DC Capacity and Cost section. Specifically, the constraints in the cells B65 to I65 and B70 to I70 constrain the

Table 4.1 Electronica distribution center location model

	A	B	C	D	E	F	G	H	I	J	K	L
1					**Distances**							
2	from DC's/to markets	Chicago	Indianapolis	Louisville	Memphis	St Louis	Cleveland	Nashville	Des Moines		**Total Cost**	2180.10
3	Detroit	277	292	368	726	530	101	546	643			
4	Cleveland	365	334	381	753	589	25	553	733			
5	Columbus	315	203	221	595	462	139	390	665			
6	Cincinnati	308	127	90	463	360	271	257	611			
7	Louisville	320	129	28	344	266	385	154	554			
8	Indianapolis	190	22	124	442	265	305	286	485			
9	Evansville	298	140	107	294	184	440	160	483			
10	Chicago	25	207	324	575	317	347	470	374			
11	Milwaukee	98	292	410	646	375	391	553	357			
12	Madison	146	336	449	769	352	476	573	274			
13	Peoria	126	223	320	474	196	463	420	267			
14	Springfield	212	213	277	368	91	504	337	292			
15	Dubuque	215	385	490	620	336	560	592	187			
16	Des Moines	363	491	577	598	341	716	635	28			
17	St Louis	309	261	284	271	19	570	286	333			
18	Kansas City	500	530	566	414	278	824	542	244			
19	Memphis	544	419	361	23	269	716	219	561			
20	Nashville	487	305	201	232	326	546	32	648			
21	Knoxville	540	344	291	398	464	482	186	775			
22	Little Rock	634	543	502	147	334	850	372	558			
23												
24					**DC Options**							
25		Chicago	Indianapolis	Louisville	Memphis	St Louis	Cleveland	Nashville	Des Moines			
26	FC - small DC	175	100	150	195	160	185	125	190			
27	VC - small DC	0.0103	0.011	0.0101	0.0096	0.012	0.0108	0.0104	0.0105			
28	capacity - small DC	2500	1750	2000	2000	2400	2000	1500	1200			
29	select - small DC	0	1	1	1	1	1	1	0			
30	FC - large DC	300	250	325	225	275	350	270	220			
31	VC - large DC	0.0077	0.008	0.0086	0.0075	0.0091	0.0082	0.0078	0.0085			
32	capacity - large DC	7500	6000	6500	8000	6800	7200	5500	4500			
33	select - large DC	1	0	0	0	0	0	0	0			
34		=<=	=<=	=<=	=<=	=<=	=<=	=<=	<=			
35		1	1	1	1	1	1	1	1			
36												

Table 4.1 *(continued)*

	A	B	C	D	E	F	G	H	I	J	K	L
37					**Flows**							
38	from/to	Chicago	Indianapolis	Louisville	Memphis	St Louis	Cleveland	Nashville	Des Moines	flow in		Demand
39	Detroit	0	0	0	0	0	894	0	0	894	=>=	894
40	Cleveland	0	0	0	0	0	773	0	0	773	=>=	773
41	Columbus	0	265	0	0	0	333	0	0	598	=>=	598
42	Cincinnati	0	144	562	0	0	0	0	0	706	=>=	706
43	Louisville	0	0	1334	0	0	0	0	0	1334	=>=	1334
44	Indianapolis	0	985	0	0	0	0	0	0	985	=>=	985
45	Evansville	0	356	0	0	0	0	0	0	356	=>=	356
46	Chicago	1670	0	0	0	0	0	0	0	1670	=>=	1670
47	Milwaukee	490	0	0	0	0	0	0	0	490	=>=	490
48	Madison	641	0	0	0	0	0	0	0	641	=>=	641
49	Peoria	378	0	0	0	0	0	0	0	378	=>=	378
50	Springfield	0	0	0	0	334	0	0	0	334	=>=	334
51	Dubuque	408	0	0	0	0	0	0	0	408	=>=	408
52	Des Moines	381	0	0	0	91	0	0	0	472	=>=	472
53	St Louis	0	0	0	0	1097	0	0	0	1097	=>=	1097
54	Kansas City	0	0	0	0	878	0	0	0	878	=>=	878
55	Memphis	0	0	0	1018	0	0	0	0	1018	=>=	1018
56	Nashville	0	0	0	70	0	0	1292	0	1362	=>=	1362
57	Knoxville	0	0	104	0	0	0	208	0	312	=>=	312
58	Little Rock	0	0	0	268	0	0	0	0	268	=>=	268
59	flow out	3968	1750	2000	1356	2400	2000	1500	0			14974
60	transp cost	274.20	86.16	70.92	47.43	195.81	93.54	48.02	0.00			
61												
62					**DC Capacity and Cost**							
63	flow - small DC	0	1750	2000	1356	2400	2000	1500	0			
64	cost - small DC	0	119.25	170.20	208.02	188.80	206.60	140.60	0			
65		=<=	=<=	=<=	<=	=<=	=<=	=<=	=<=			
66		0	1750	2000	2000	2400	2000	1500	0			
67												
68	flow - large DC	3968	0	0	0	0	0	0	0			
69	cost - large DC	330.55	0	0	0	0.00	0	0.00	0			
70		<=	=<=	=<=	=<=	=<=	=<=	=<=	=<=			
71		7500	0	0	0	0	0	0	0			
72												
73		3968	1750	2000	1356	2400	2000	1500	0			
74		=	=	=	=	=	=	=	=			
75	flow balance	3968	1750	2000	1356	2400	2000	1500	0			

output of each DC location to be less than or equal to the capacity implied by the selection of 0-1 variables in the DC Option section. For example, because the value in B33 is 1, or equivalently, because CHILG = 1, the outbound flow at the Chicago location is constrained by B70 to less than or equal to 7500 truckloads. Because the flow out of Chicago is from a large DC, its cost is computed in B69 using the fixed and variable costs for that large DC given in the DC Options section. Finally, this outbound flow must equal the outbound flow from Chicago given in B59 of the Flows section.

In Solver, we indicate that an adjustable cell is a 0-1 variable by referencing the cell in the Solver box Subject to Constraints, clicking on add, and then indicating on the pull-down menu in the middle of the Add Constraint box that the cell is bin (binary). In What's Best, we highlight the adjustable cells, click on the WB! menu and then select Integer. A dialog box labeled Integer appears, asking the user to name the highlighted cells and their integer type, which in this case is binary. We name the highlighted cells and click Add. Henceforth, these cells will be treated as 0-1 variables.

The section labeled **Flows** in Table 4.1 contains the adjustable cells corresponding to flows from DCs to markets. This submodel is an example of the transportation model discussed in Section 3.1. The cells in this section are treated as continuous variables. Looking across any row, we see how the market on that row is supplied. For example, row 49 corresponds to Peoria, which is supplied with 378 truckloads from a DC in Chicago. Looking down any column, we see the distribution of truckloads from the DC to the markets. For example, column G corresponds to Cleveland, which supplies 894 truckloads to Detroit, 773 truckloads to Cleveland (its local market), and 333 truckloads to Columbus.

At the bottom of the Flows section, we compute the transportation costs incurred for shipments out of each DC. For each DC location, we compute the sum of the products of the flows in the Flows section with the distances in the Distance section. This sumproduct gives us the projected total truckload-miles for shipments out of each DC next year, which we multiply by Electronica's cost per truckload-mile of \$0.60. Thus, the projected transportation cost out of the Indianapolis DC for next year is 0.0006 * (265 * 203 + 144 * 127 + 985 * 22 + 356 * 140) = 86.16 thousands of dollars.

The section **DC Capacity and Costs** is where we relate the choice of 0-1 variables at each location from DC Options to the costs incurred at those facilities. In these calculations, if there is positive flow out a DC in the Flows section, we force it to be priced by the cost function implicitly chosen in the DC Options section by the selection of a 0-1 variable to equal 1. For example, the equation specified in B74 states that for the Chicago location, B63 (flow through the small DC) + B68 (flow through the large DC) = B59 (flow from the Flows section) = 3968. In addition, the constraint in B65 specifies that B63 ≤ B28 * B29 = 0 because the 0-1 variable in cell B29 = 0. Thus, B63 = 0. However, the constraint in B70 specifies that B68 ≤ B32 * B33 = 7500, and therefore B68 can be positive and must equal 3968. The cost at the large DC is then given in cell B69 by the formula (B69) = B30 * B33 + B31 * B68 that adds the fixed cost of the large DC in Chicago to the variable cost associated with 3968 outbound truckload shipments.

Finally, the objective function to be minimized is the sum of the transportation costs in cells B60 to I60, the small DC costs in cells B64 to I64, and the large DC costs in cells B69 to I69. We apply the spreadsheet optimizer and find that the minimal cost solution involves the opening of a large DC in Chicago and six small DCs, one in every location except Chicago and Des Moines. The cost of the optimal solution is $2,180,100, of which $816,080 is transportation cost and $1,364,020 is distribution center cost.

Once the DC location model has been constructed and optimized, the director of logistics and other senior managers would undoubtedly want to make a number of other runs to evaluate what-if scenarios. For example, they might object to the optimal solution in Table 4.1 because it requires the opening of seven DCs and suggest that four DCs are the maximal number that they believe are needed to efficiently manage the distribution supply chain. We can test the impact of such a restriction by adding a constraint to the model, stating that the sum of the 16 0-1 variables in rows 29 and 33 may not exceed 4.

The optimal solution under this constraint is to open large DCs in Chicago and Nashville and small DCs in St. Louis and Cleveland. The minimal total cost becomes $2,293,260, a figure that is slightly more than 5% higher than the cost of the previous optimal solution. If senior management believes there are hidden costs associated with each additional DC that is opened, it might elect to implement the four-DC solution. Of course, a number of other what-if scenarios could be posed and evaluated. Space limitations prevent us from discussing them further.

Generalizations

The DC location model optimized in Table 4.1 was simple, although nontrivial. It could be generalized in a number of ways to create accurate and comprehensive models for specific distribution supply chain problems. Most applications would involve many products flowing from DCs to markets, and possibly multiple classes of customers in these markets. Some applications would also involve more than one level of DCs; for example, a distribution supply chain with large regional DCs that serve smaller warehouses closer to the markets. Such applications are discussed in Chapter 7.

Logistics managers frequently wish to impose **sole sourcing** constraints, similar to those discussed in Section 4.1, on the flows from DCs to markets. These constraints require that, for customer service reasons, each market receives all shipments from a single DC. Looking in the Flows section of Table 4.1, we see that 5 of the 20 markets are not sole sourced. This is a much higher percentage than we would expect to find in a realistic DC location model that might have perhaps 20 DC locations and 300 markets, where we might still find that no more than 5 or 10 markets are not sole sourced. Nevertheless, the logistics manager does not want to take on the burden of cleaning up an almost sole sourced solution. To explicitly model the requirement, we would define and use 0-1 variables and constraints that assign each market to a unique DC.

Another simple construction in the model of Table 4.1 was the treatment of transportation costs. Recall that the same cost per truckload-mile was used on all links connecting DCs to markets. If these shipments were being made by third-party carriers, we would need to employ a different cost per truckload-mile for each link in the network. The rate would be higher than average on links that are heavily traveled, and it would be lower than average on links experiencing frequent back-hauls (partially empty trucks returning to their depots).

A supply chain cost not captured by the model of Table 4.1 is inventory holding costs. This is a serious omission only if inventory holding costs are a significant percentage, say 5% or more, of total supply chain cost. Inventory holding costs are difficult, but not impossible, to model in a snapshot (one period) model such as the one in Table 4.1. In Section 11.2, we discuss empirical results for approximating inventory holding costs that allow them to be incorporated in a DC location model using mixed integer programming constructions.

4.3

Supply Chain Network Optimization Models

In the previous section, we examined a class of supply chain network optimization problems and models concerned only with distribution. Many important applications, such as the one we discuss in this section, involve manufacturing as well as distribution decisions. The model we develop also illustrates how diverse but related resource acquisition decisions can be evaluated together.

Strategic Planning at Ajax

We construct and optimize a mixed integer programming model to evaluate strategic planning options facing the Ajax Computer Company over the next 3 years. In particular, senior management at Ajax faces the following four interconnected sets of decisions:

- Should Ajax invest in a new assembly plant in Sunnyvale, California, and if so, in what year?
- Should Ajax invest in a major expansion of its existing assembly plant in Chicago and if so, in what year?
- Should Ajax invest in development of the new Delta workstation and if so, where should it be assembled?
- What quantity of each product should be assembled at each plant in each time period? Which plant should serve each market for each product in each time period?

Strategic planning at Ajax begins, as it does in many cases, with a forecast of potential sales for the company's products over the next 3 years. For expositional simplicity, we suppose that the strategic analysis is being performed 9 months in advance of next year and that this lead time is sufficient to introduce a new product

Table 4.2 Strategic analysis of Ajax supply chain network

	A	B	C	D	E	F	G	H	I	J	K	L	M	N	O	P	Q	R
1	**Base Case**									**Year One**								
2	**Global Objective**																	
3	**Max Disc Net Rev**				**Production at Existing Plant**			Capacity		Capacity	Capacity					**Investments at Existing Plant**		
4	13094212		Products	Alpha	Beta	Gamma	Delta	Used		W/O Exp	With Exp				Expand	Expand	Expand	Develop
5				1	1			5000	<=	6000	8000	A-line Test			Existing Pl	Existing PL	Existing PL	New Prod
6						1	1	1711	<=	2400	3200	C-line Test			Year 1	Year 2	Year 3	Existing PL
7	**Year One**			10	15	20	22	94222	<=	100000	133000	Labor		Invest Cost	834000	834000	834000	775000
8	**Net Revenues**		Unit Cost	1000	1175	2250	2100							Yes-No Var	0	1	0	0
9	4337656		Qty Made	3000	2000	1711	0	=<=	0		Delta FC Constraint			Invest Sum	1	=<=	1	
10														New Prod Sum	0	<=	1	
11																		
12					**Shipments from Existing Plant**						**Transportation Costs from Existing Plant to Markets**							
13			To	Alpha	Beta	Gamma	Delta		To	Alpha	Beta	Gamma	Delta					
14			Chicago	3000	2000	1711	0		Chicago	22	19	27	27					
15			North Calif	0	0	0	0		North Calif	52	48	58	58					
16			Seattle	0	0	0	0		Seattle	50	46	56	56					
17			Total	3000	2000	1711	0											
18				=<=	=<=	=<=	=<=											
19				3000	2000	1711	0											
20																		
21					**Production at New Plant**			Capacity								**Investments at New Plant**		
22			Products	Alpha	Beta	Gamma	Delta	Used		Capacity					Open	Open	Open	Develop
23				1	1			4700	<=	5000	A-line Test				New Plant	New Plant	New Plant	New Prod
24						1	1	1539	<=	2000	C-line Test				Year 1	Year 2	Year 3	New Plant
25				9	14	18	20	80000	=<=	80000	Labor			Invest Cost	2225000	2225000	2225000	775000
26			Unit Cost	925	1100	2125	1900							Yes-No Var	1	0	0	0
27			Qty Made	2700	2000	1539	0	=<=	0		Delta FC Constraint			Invest Sum	1	=<=	1	
28																		
29					**Shipments from New Plant**						**Transportation Costs from New Plant to Markets**							
30			To	Alpha	Beta	Gamma	Delta		To	Alpha	Beta	Gamma	Delta					
31			Chicago	0	0	289	0		Chicago	72	48	58	58					
32			North Calif	1500	1000	500	0		North Calif	20	17	25	25					
33			Seattle	1200	1000	750	0		Seattle	30	26	35	35					
34			Total	2700	2000	1539	0											
35				=<=	=<=	=<=	=<=											
36				2700	2000	1539	0											
37																		
38					**Sales**						**Forecasts of Maximal Sales**					**Sales Constraints**		
39				Alpha	Beta	Gamma	Delta		Alpha	Beta	Gamma	Delta						
40			Chicago	3000	2000	2000	0		3000	2000	2000	500		=<=	=<=	=<=	<=	
41			North Calif	1500	1000	500	0		1500	1000	500	300		=<=	=<=	=<=	<=	
42			Seattle	1200	1000	750	0		1200	1000	750	300		=<=	=<=	=<=	<=	
43			Total	5700	4000	3250	0											
44			Unit Rev	1350	1650	3000	2500											

Table 4.2 *(continued)*

	A	B	C	D	E	F	G	H	I	J	K	L	M	N	O	P	Q	R
45										Year Two								
46																		
47					Production at Existing Plant			capacity		capacity	capacity							
48			Products	Alpha	Beta	Gamma	Delta	used		w/o exp	with exp							
49				1	1			7300	<=	6000	8000	A-line Test						
50						1	1	2500	<=	2400	3200	C-line Test						
51				10	15	20	22	129500	<=	100000	133000	Labor						
52			Unit Cost	1000	1175	2250	2050											
53	Year Two		Qty Made	6000	1300	2500	0	=<=	0		Delta FC constraint							
54	Net Revenues																	
55	5078500				Shipments from Existing Plant				Transportation Costs from Existing Plant to Markets									
56			To	Alpha	Beta	Gamma	Delta		To	Alpha	Beta	Gamma	Delta					
57			Chicago	6000	1000	2000	0		Chicago	22	19	27	27					
58			North Calif	0	0	0	0		North Calif	52	48	58	58					
59			Seattle	0	300	500	0		Seattle	50	46	56	56					
60			Total	6000	1300	2500	0											
61				=<=	=<=	=<=	=<=											
62				6000	1300	2500	0											
63																		
64					Production at New Plant			Capacity										
65			Products	Alpha	Beta	Gamma	Delta	Used		Capacity								
66				1	1			4500	<=	5000	A-Line Test							
67						1	1	2000	=<=	2000	C-Line Test							
68				9	14	18	20	80000	=<=	80000	Labor							
69			Unit Cost	925	1100	2125	1850											
70			Qty Made	3800	700	2000	0	=<=	0		Delta FC constraint							
71																		
72					Shipments from New Plant				Transportation Costs from New Plant to Markets									
73			To	Alpha	Beta	Gamma	Delta		to	Alpha	Beta	Gamma	Delta					
74			Chicago	0	0	0	0		Chicago	72	48	58	58					
75			North Calif	2000	500	1000	0		North Calif	20	17	25	25					
76			Seattle	1800	200	1000	0		Seattle	30	26	35	35					
77			Total	3800	700	2000	0											
78				=<=	=<=	=<=	=<=											
79				3800	700	2000	0											
80																		
81					Sales						Forecasts of Maximal Sales					Sales Constraints		
82				Alpha	Beta	Gamma	Delta		Alpha	Beta	Gamma	Delta						
83			Chicago	6000	1000	2000	0		6000	1000	2000	1000		=<=	=<=	=<=	<=	
84			North Calif	2000	500	1000	0		2000	500	1000	600		=<=	=<=	=<=	<=	
85			Seattle	1800	500	1500	0		1800	500	1500	600		=<=	=<=	=<=	<=	
86			Total	9800	2000	4500	0											
87			Unit Rev	1350	1650	3000	2500											

Table 4.2 *(continued)*

	A	B	C	D	E	F	G	H	I	J	K	L	M	N	O	P	Q	R
88										**Year Three**								
89																		
90					**Production at Existing Plant**			Capacity		Capacity	Capacity							
91			Products	Alpha	Beta	Gamma	Delta	Used		W/O Exp	With Exp							
92				1	1			6343	<=	6000	8000	A-line Test						
93						1	1	2500	<=	2400	3200	C-line Test						
94				10	15	20	22	130143	<=	100000	133000	Labor						
95			Unit Cost	1000	1175	2250	2050											
96	**Year Three**		Qty Made	3000	3343	2500	0	=<=	0		Delta FC constraint							
97	**Net Revenue**																	
98	5167786				**Shipments from Existing Plant**						**Transportation Costs from Existing Plant to Markets**							
99			To	Alpha	Beta	Gamma	Delta		To	Alpha	Beta	Gamma	Delta					
100			Chicago	3000	2500	2000	0		Chicago	22	19	27	27					
101			North Calif	0	0	0	0		North Calif	52	48	58	58					
102			Seattle	0	843	500	0		Seattle	50	46	56	56					
103			Total	3000	3343	2500	0											
104				=<=	=<=	=<=	=<=											
105				3000	3343	2500	0											
106																		
107					**Production at New Plant**			Capacity										
108			Products	Alpha	Beta	Gamma	Delta	Used		Capacity								
109				1	1			3857	<=	5000	A-line Test							
110						1	1	2000	=<=	2000	C-line Test							
111				9	14	18	20	80000	=<=	80000	Labor							
112			Unit Cost	925	1100	2125	1850											
113			Qty Made	2000	1857	2000	0	=<=	0		Delta FC constraint							
114																		
115					**Shipments from New Plant**						**Transportation Costs from New Plant to Markets**							
116			To	Alpha	Beta	Gamma	Delta		To	Alpha	Beta	Gamma	Delta					
117			Chicago	0	0	0	0		Chicago	72	48	58	58					
118			North Calif	1000	1500	1000	0		North Calif	20	17	25	25					
119			Seattle	1000	357	1000	0		Seattle	30	26	35	35					
120			Total	2000	1857	2000	0											
121				=<=	=<=	=<=	=<=											
122				2000	1857	2000	0											
123																		
124					**Sales**						**Forecasts of Maximal Sales**					**Sales Constraints**		
125				Alpha	Beta	Gamma	Delta		Alpha	Beta	Gamma	Delta						
126			Chicago	3000	2500	2000	0		3000	2500	2000	2000		=<=	=<=	=<=	<=	
127			North Calif	1000	1500	1000	0		1000	1500	1000	1500		=<=	=<=	=<=	<=	
128			Seattle	1000	1200	1500	0		1000	1200	1500	1200		=<=	=<=	=<=	<=	
129			Total	5000	5200	4500	0											
130			Unit Rev	1350	1700	3000	2500											

or build a new plant for next year. The forecasts are given in Table 4.2 for Ajax' existing market in Chicago and for new markets opening up in Northern California and Seattle. Each of the 3 years is depicted in a separate section of the spreadsheet. The figures shown in the sections labeled **Forecasts of Maximal Sales** are the maximal quantities that Ajax can sell of each product in each market in each year. Ajax may choose to sell less than these amounts in seeking to maximize discounted net revenues over the 3-year planning horizon.

The forecast for the personal computer Alpha reflects a pattern based on introduction of a new version in year 2. The forecast for the notebook Beta reflects a pattern based on phasing out the current version and introducing a new one in year 3. The forecast for the workstation Gamma reflects a steady pattern over the 3 years for the current version, with higher sales in years 2 and 3 in the new markets. The forecast for the Delta server workstation, a new product, is based on the assumption that the product will be introduced in year1 (next year), with sales growth after that. Ajax still has the option to reject this product development.

Constructing an Integrated Supply Chain Model. Figure 4.3 is a high-level depiction of Ajax' supply chain network that we expand into a comprehensive model of the company's decision options, constraints, and objectives. Because it addresses many components of Ajax' supply chain, the resulting Ajax strategy model will be complex. It is created by assembling a number of submodels, as follows:

- For each year, a **production model** describing the capabilities of the existing assembly plant in Chicago with options to expand its capacities and to produce the new product Delta
- For each year, a **production model** describing the capabilities of the optional new plant in Sunnyvale with the additional option to produce there the new product Delta
- For each year and each product, a **transportation model** describing flows of the product from the plants to the markets

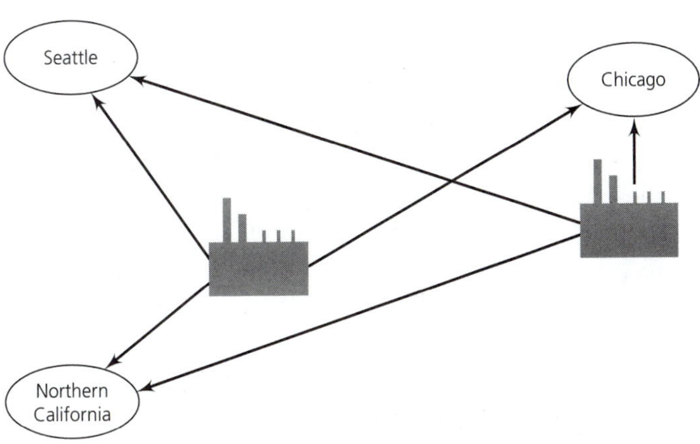

Figure 4.3
Strategic supply chain network for Ajax Computer Company

- For each year and each product, a **sales model** constraining sales in each market to be at or below its maximal limit
- **Multiple choice constraints** on sets of investment options stating that the option may be selected for at most a single starting year over the planning horizon
- **Net revenue functions** for each year and a **discounted net revenue function** summed over the entire planning horizon

The integration of these submodels is depicted in Figure 4.4. We use the spreadsheet in Table 4.2 and a spreadsheet optimizer to organize the data for the submodels, identify variables and constraints of the submodels, link connections among the submodels, calculate yearly and discounted net revenues, and perform strategic analyses.

We review the data and model sections of Table 4.2 beginning with year 1. The selection labeled **Production at Existing Plant** contains data that is similar to the data in the Ajax assembly model given in Figure 3.1. Here, the capacity data are much larger because they relate to yearly rather than weekly assembly operations. Because we have separated product assembly from transportation and sales, we have substituted unit costs in the production section for revenue figures.

Moreover, we have included options for expanding capacity and producing a new product. To describe analysis of these options, we define the following decision variables employed in the **Production at Existing Plant** and **Investments at Existing Plant** sections:

MAXPLt = number of Alphas assembled at the existing plant in year t (t= 1,2,3)

MBXPLt = number of Betas assembled at the existing plant in year t (t= 1,2,3)

MCXPLt = number of Gammas assembled at the existing plant in year t (t=1,2,3)

MDXPLt = number of Deltas assembled at the existing plant in year t (t=1,2,3)

$$\text{XPLt} = \begin{cases} 1 \text{ if existing plant is expanded in year 1} & (t = 1,2,3) \\ 0 \text{ otherwise} \end{cases}$$

$$\text{DELTAX} = \begin{cases} 1 \text{ if new product developed for assembly at existing plant} \\ 0 \text{ otherwise} \end{cases}$$

$$\text{DELTAN} = \begin{cases} 1 \text{ if new product developed for assembly at existing plant} \\ 0 \text{ otherwise} \end{cases}$$

The constraints needed to describe the investment options affecting the existing plant are

$$\text{XPL1} + \text{XPL2} + \text{XPL3} \leq 1$$

$$\text{DELTAX} + \text{DELTAN} \leq 1$$

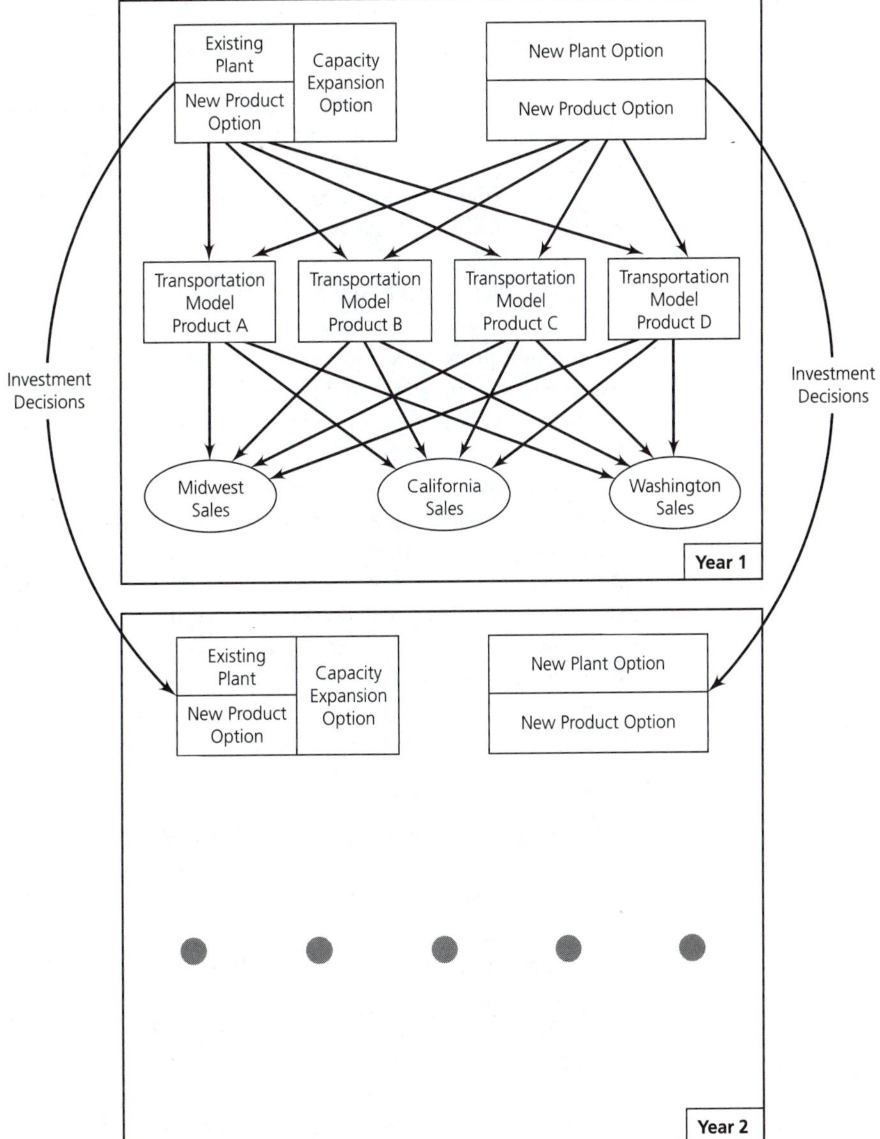

Figure 4.4
Modeling objects for Ajax strategy model

The first constraint (specified in cell P9) states that Ajax can elect to expand the existing plant for operations in at most 1 of the 3 years of the planning horizon. The second constraint states (specified in cell P10) that the new product may be developed for assembly at the existing plant, the new plant, or neither.

The 0-1 investment variables are also used to control production constraints at the existing plant as listed in the **Production at Existing Plant** section. For example, the assembly labor constraint of Figure 3.1 is extended (specified in cell I7) to

$$10\ \text{MAXPL1} + 15\ \text{MBXPL1} + 20\ \text{MCXPL1} + 22\ \text{MDXPL1} - 33000\ \text{XPL1} \leq 100000$$

According to this constraint, if XPL1 = 1, 133,000 labor hours will be available in year 1 for assembly at the existing plant. Conversely, if XPL1 = 0, 100,000 labor hours will be available. Similar constraints are written for available A-line and C-line test hours. Finally, production of the new product Delta is controlled by the fixed cost constraint (specified in cell H9)

$$\text{MDXPL1} - 1100\ \text{DELTAX} \leq 0$$

According to this constraint, positive production of Deltas (up to 1100 units) at the existing plant can occur only if DELTAX = 1. The limit of 1100 units is determined by the maximal number of Delta sales in all markets in year 1 as listed in the section Forecasts of Maximal Sales.

The constraints listed in cells D18 through G18 of **Shipments from Existing Plants** state that the quantity shipped out of each product cannot exceed the quantity assembled as computed in the Production at Existing Plant section. Because Ajax maintains very low inventories, we do not include them in the model. Thus, the quantity shipped will always equal the quantity assembled.

The section entitled **Production at New Plant** captures details similar to those of Production at Existing Plant. Letting

$$\text{NPLt} = \begin{cases} 1 \text{ if the new plant is opened in year } t & (t = 1, 2, 3) \\ 0 \text{ otherwise} \end{cases}$$

we write the logical constraint (specified in cell P27)

$$\text{NPL1} + \text{NPL2} + \text{NPL3} \leq 1$$

which states that the new plant may be opened at most once during the 3-year planning horizon.

These variables are used to turn on production in the new plant. For example, letting

MANPLt = number of Alphas assembled at the new plant in year t

MBNPLt = number of Betas assembled at the new plant in year t

MCNPLt = number of Gammas assembled at the new plant in year t

MDNPLt = number of Deltas assembled at the new plant in year t

the assembly labor constraint (specified in cell I25) is written as

$$9\ \text{MANPL1} + 14\ \text{MBXPL1} + 18\ \text{MCXPL1} + 20\ \text{MDXPL1} - 80000\ \text{NPL1} \leq 0$$

As before, if NPL1 = 1, the constraint is turned on and the new plant has 80,000 hours in year 1 for assembly of Ajax' computers. Conversely, if NPL1 = 0, the plant is not built and the new plant location cannot supply any products. Note that once the new plant has been paid for, its production is more efficient than the existing plant. Specifically, the labor assembly rates and the unit costs for all products are lower. Finally, the Delta fixed cost constraint (cell H27) at the new plant is the same as that for the existing plant, namely,

$$\text{MDNPL1} - 1100\ \text{DELTAN} \leq 0$$

The **Sales** section accumulates shipments from the two plants of each product to each market. These quantities are constrained by upper bounds in the **Forecasts of Maximal Sales** section and by the constraints listed in the **Sales Constraint** section. In the later section, =<= indicates that maximal sales of the product in the market is achieved by the optimal solution, whereas <= indicates that is has not.

This completes our discussion of the variables and constraints for year 1 of the strategic analysis of the Ajax supply chain network. The remaining construction to discuss is the objective function, which is to maximize

$$\text{Discounted sum of net revenues} = Z1 + 0.9\ Z2 + 0.81\ Z3$$

where Zt is the net revenue in year t given by

Zt = gross revenue from sales—production costs at the two plants
– transportation costs from the two plants to the markets
– investment costs in expanding the existing plant, constructing the new plant, and developing the new product
– production costs at two plants

These terms are computed by taking appropriate products and sumproducts in the spreadsheet. Note that the costs listed in the Investments sections for expanding the existing plant and constructing the new plant are annualized costs to be charged in the first year that the investment is active and every year after that. The new product cost is a one-time charge for year 1. Note that Ajax discounts cash flows at 10% per year.

The spreadsheets for years 2 and 3 are virtually identical to the spreadsheet for year 1. The only difference is the treatment of the available capacities at the existing and new plants. Specifically, expanded capacity at the existing plant and available capacity in the new plant in year t depends on whether or not an investment was made in year t or any earlier year. We omit further details about the construction of Table 4.2.

Base Case and Scenario Analyses. Table 4.3 summarizes the optimal investment decisions in Table 4.2 determined by the spreadsheet optimizer. The timing and

Table 4.3 Ajax supply chain model resolution of investment options (base case)

Option	Decision
Build new assembly plant in Sunnyvale	Build immediately for use in year 1
Expand existing Chicago assembly plant	Expand for use in year 2
Develop new product	Reject

sizing of the investments allow maximal sales to be made for Ajax' existing products in all years and all markets. We call this strategy the **base case.** It is the initial model run addressing the concerns of Ajax' senior management.

We should not expect that Ajax' senior management will accept the base case strategy without further analysis. Instead, they will seek to further refine their intuition about the company's strategic plans by making a number of additional runs with the model. The additional runs will be based on **scenario analyses** or **what if** questions about Ajax' strategic options and the internal and external business environments in which the company operates. We pose several scenarios in the following paragraphs and review the different optimal strategies associated with them in Table 4.4.

Some questions will require only small, narrowly focused model modifications. For example,

> **Scenario 1.** What if we delayed construction of the new plant in Sunnyvale to year 2 or year 3?

This scenario is evaluated by the model in Table 4.2 by setting the 0-1 variable in cell O26 = 0 and reoptimizing it.

Other questions involve more extensive modifications to the data feeding the model. For example,

> **Scenarios 2 and 3.** What is the impact on the optimal investment strategy if maximal potential sales in years 2 and 3 are 20% higher than forecast? What if they are 20% lower?

These scenarios are evaluated by appropriate changes in the Forecast of Maximal Sales sections for the 3 years.

Other what-if questions are motivated by details of the optimal solution to the base case. For example, close scrutiny of that solution indicates that the most important economic motivation for investing in expansion of the existing plant in year 2 is to increase labor capacity rather than testing capacity. This is evident by observing that labor capacity is much closer to binding in years 2 and 3, whereas the test line capacities are not significantly above their unexpanded capacities in those years.

This observation causes Ajax' CEO to suggest that a less costly option for increasing sales and revenues might be to use overtime labor capacity for product assembly at the existing plant. The VP for manufacturing makes a quick study of the option and concludes that Ajax could add up to 25,000 hours per year of overtime

Table 4.4 Summary of scenario results of the Ajax strategic supply chain model

Description	Base Case	Scenario 1. Delay construction of new plant until year 2 or 3.	Scenario 2. Forecasts of maximal sales in years 2 and 3 are increased by 20%.	Scenario 3. Forecasts of maximal sales in years 2 and 3 are decreased by 20%.	Scenario 4. Labor overtime option in existing plant.	Scenario 5 Force new product introduction.	Scenario 6. New product design.
Existing plant expansion	Year 2	Year 1	Year 2	Rejected	Year 2	Year 2	Year 2
New plant construction	Year 1	Year 2	Year 1	Year 1	Year 1	Year 1	Year 1
New product development	Rejected	Rejected	Rejected	Rejected	Rejected	Accepted at new plant	Accepted at new plant
Other options					Rejected		
Net revenues—yr. 1	4,337,656	3,609,900	4,337, 656	4,337,656	4,337,656	3,685,000	3,959,257
Net revenues—yr. 2	5,078,500	5,078,500	5,078,500	4,370,874	5,078,500	5,159,790	5,514,414
Net revenues—yr. 3	5,167,786	5,167,786	5,167,786	4,453,571	5,167,786	5,234,145	5,588,400
Max. discounted net revenues	13,094,212	12,366,456	13,094,212	11,878,835	13,094,212	12,568,469	13,448,834

to its labor capacity at an incremental cost of \$25/hour. The option would also involve a fixed cost of \$100,000 per year for supervisory personnel, increased insurance costs, and so on. We formally list this as follows:

> **Scenario 4.** What is the impact on the optimal strategy of adding a labor overtime option for the existing plant in each year?

This option requires the addition of three 0-1 variables, one for the fixed cost in each of the 3 years. It also requires three continuous variables, one for the quantity of overtime incurred in each of the 3 years up to the maximal number of overtime hours allowed. The fixed cost and continuous variables in each year are linked by a fixed cost constraint. The fixed and variable costs are subtracted from the net revenue function for each year.

Finally, the Ajax marketing manager and chief design engineer are disappointed that their new product, the Delta computer server workstation, is rejected by the base case optimization. They ask that we evaluate the following:

> **Scenario 5.** What is the impact on maximal net discounted revenues over the 3-year planning horizon if we force acceptance of the Delta computer?

This scenario is easy to test. We simply modify the <= constraint in cell P10 to a = constraint, thereby forcing the model to develop the new product and produce it either in the existing plant or the new plant. As we will review shortly, the optimal strategy for this scenario is decidedly less profitable than the base case optimal strategy.

Given this unpleasant news, the chief design engineer and the marketing manager decide to thoroughly review the new product design. After several weeks, they propose to add features to the Delta server workstation that will enhance its value and allow Ajax to sell it for \$3200 rather than \$2500 per unit. However, the redesigned version will cost \$200 more per unit to make and an extra 2 hours to assemble. They ask us to analyze the following:

> **Scenario 6.** How does the base case strategy change if the new Delta design is substituted for the old design?

Table 4.4 summarizes the results of the base case of Table 4.2 and reoptimizing the model under the six scenarios. The scenarios are not cumulative; for example, the restriction of scenario 1 was not imposed on later scenarios. Specifications for each of the other five scenarios are based only on changes to the base case.

Our scenario analysis thus far indicates that the base case strategy looks solid. Scenario 1 indicates that delaying construction of the new plant is costly. Scenario 2 indicates that the Ajax supply chain could easily become capacity constrained over the next 3 years. Similarly, scenario 3 indicates that lower demand also leads to capacity constraints because it becomes uneconomic to expand the existing plant. Scenario 4 indicates that half measures at capacity expansion are not attractive, assuming the sales forecasts of the base case are realistic. Scenarios 5 and 6 indicate that Ajax will be well served by redesigning the Delta server workstation before it is put on the market.

Ajax management will probably wish to run additional scenarios to further analyze their strategic plans. Thus far, however, the results of the base case and the six scenarios would indicate the following **cornerstones** to their strategic plans over the next 3 years:

- The new plant in Sunnyvale should be constructed immediately to be ready for use in year 1.
- The new product Delta should be redesigned to make it more competitive with Ajax' other products.
- Expansion of the existing plant should be delayed until year 2, with a final positive decision dependent on strong sales forecasts.
- Ajax management should prepare additional expansion options to deal with possible shortages in capacity to meet growth in product sales.

Generalizations

At least two areas of supply chain decision making at Ajax could be more fully represented in the model of Table 4.2. First, we could add cost and capacity details describing the acquisition of parts and components from Ajax' suppliers.[3] Second, as reviewed in Section 3.2, the Ajax marketing department could estimate price elasticities for the company's products and use them in implementing nonlinear revenue curves for each product in each market in each year.[4] Of course, industrial-strength models for analyzing manufacturing and distribution strategic plans in actual companies would be likely to address considerable more detail about plants and DCs. Typical applications are discussed in later chapters.

4.4 Designing and Implementing Optimization Modeling Systems for Strategic and Tactical Planning

Our examination of linear and mixed integer programming models in the first part of this chapter and the previous chapter provides us with details about how models represent supply chain planning problems. In this section, we discuss principles for constructing data-driven systems to support managerial decision making based on these models. In the following section, we discuss off-the-shelf packages for model generation and optimization.

Strategic and tactical supply chain planning problems share common features across many companies and industries, which allow practitioners to design and implement general-purpose optimization modeling systems for analyzing them.

Even when features of a company's business require model customization, it is often minor. Thus, model development can be rapidly achieved by employing off-the-shelf systems. This section is devoted to principles for designing and implementing such systems.

By contrast, operational problems arising in production, transportation, and other areas of supply chain management vary significantly from industry to industry and even company to company. As a result, scheduling systems often require considerable customization. Moreover, the form and content of the decision databases embedded in the modeling systems are specific to the industry and the company. These databases must be tightly linked with the company's transactional databases to provide accurate and timely analysis of operational problems.

Our exposition in this section is based on our experiences in designing and implementing SLIM, a general-purpose supply chain modeling system.[5] This system has been successfully applied to strategic and tactical supply chain problems in over two dozen companies, which supports our assertion that the application of general-purpose tools for such applications is realistic.

System Design

As in other areas of creative endeavor, the design of a supply chain modeling system begins with mental processes of analysis and abstraction. In Figure 4.5, we depict the practitioner's critical initial step in aligning his or her modeling **gestalt** with the class of real-world supply chain problems to be optimized. This gestalt is an integrated collection of mental elements whose functional whole is more comprehensive than the summation of insights provided by individual elements. It is formed by aca-

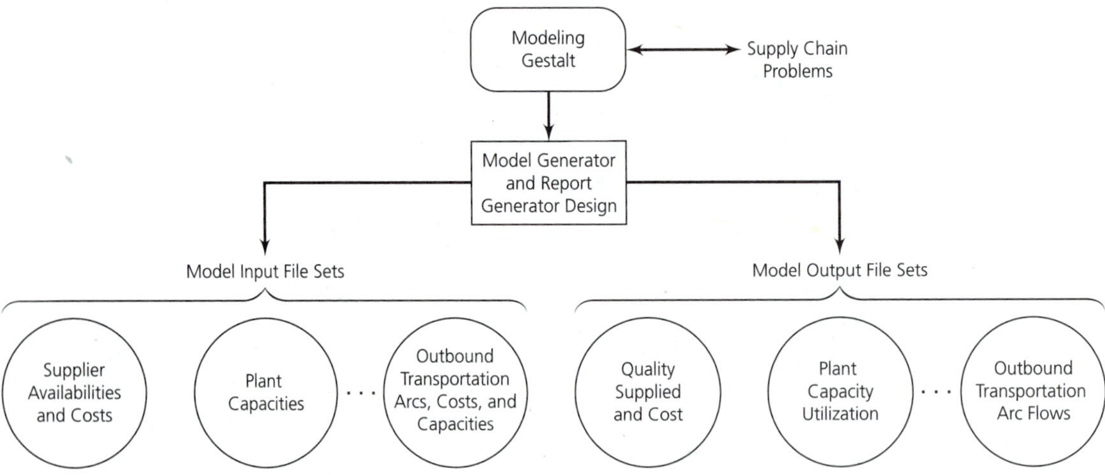

Figure 4.5
Designing a strategic or tactical supply chain modeling system

demic training and practical experience applying optimization models to supply chain problems. Although many paradigms are available for analyzing supply chain problems, this book emphasizes the application of optimization models to such problems.

After dialogue with decision makers and contemplation of the supply chain problems they face, the practitioner selects a specific optimization model for analyzing them. We wish to emphasize that the science and art of optimization modeling has progressed far beyond the stage where practitioners exhibited an attitude of "techniques looking for a problem." An accurate and comprehensive model can and should be chosen for each class of problems.

Once the practitioner's mental model has coalesced, his or her next step is to design the **model generator**, which accepts data from the supply chain decision database and correctly places them in the matrix representation of a model. Strictly speaking, the model generator will represent the problems as a class of models because model generation will be **data driven**; that is, depending on the data inputs, each run with the system will produce a different variation of the generic model.

The process followed by a practitioner in passing from contemplation of the supply chain problems to an implementation plan for the model generator depends on his or her style. Some practitioners may write out a mathematical statement of the model before they begin coding. Others may jump right into the coding, possibly using routines previously developed for similar applications as guidelines.

In any event, a critical step in constructing the model generator is a parsing of the data that will constitute the **supply chain decision database,** which we discuss briefly below and in detail in Chapter 6. Each of the **model input file sets** in this database will correspond to a self-contained and easily understood component of the supply chain being modeled. These file sets fall into two categories. First, the supply chain decision database contains file sets of **structural data** defining the supply chain. Included are the following:

- The names and locations of existing and potential suppliers, facilities and markets
- The names of products flowing through the supply chain network, which may be raw materials, intermediate products, or finished products
- The names of processes and transformation recipes utilized at the facilities
- The names of resources consumed by processes at the facilities
- The names of transportation links given by origin and destination pairs including those connecting suppliers to facilities and markets, connecting facilities to facilities, and connecting facilities to markets

Two points about the structural data require further discussion. The operations at each facility may include multiple processes or stages. Each process may correspond to multiple transformation recipes and may consume scarce resources that are shared among several processes. In addition, in describing the structure of the supply chain network, we have assumed that there are no flows from the markets back to the facilities or suppliers. Networks with this property are called **reverse logistics** networks.

Second, the supply chain decision database contains file sets of **numerical data** associated with these structures. Each numerical file set corresponds to a scenario. Included are the following:

- The quantities of raw materials available at suppliers and their acquisition costs
- Investment and indirect costs of acquiring and operating facilities
- Throughput capacities associated with facilities
- Quantities of input and output products associated with unit operations of transformation recipes
- Costs and capacities associated with processes and resources consumed by processes
- Costs and capacities associated with inventory management at facilities
- Logical data constraining locational and investment decisions
- Costs and capacities associated with all transportation arcs
- Exchange rate tables for multinational supply chains
- The quantities of finished products demanded at the markets (cost minimization) or revenue curves for finished products at the markets (net revenue maximization)

The practitioner also develops a report generator for summarizing the output from an optimization model in **model output file sets.** As with the input file sets, the output file sets represent a parsing of the output data into components that are easily understood. They correspond to optimal values for the decision variables associated with the above numerical data. Typical output data included are the following:

- Optimal quantities of raw materials acquired at each supplier
- Optimal locations and capacities of new facilities
- Optimal levels of inbound flows of raw materials from suppliers to facilities
- Optimal levels for transformation recipes and process activities at each facility
- Optimal levels of resource consumption at each facility
- Optimal interfacility flows of intermediate products
- Optimal outbound flows of finished products from facilities to markets

System Implementation

Developing a supply chain modeling system involves implementation of four major components: the analytical engine, the database management system, the user interfaces, and data transformation programs. The current dominance of Windows operating systems focuses and facilitates development of database management systems and user interfaces using Access and Visual Basic.

Analytical Engine. As shown in Figure 4.6, the analytical engine comprises the model generator, the optimizer, and the report generator. The model and report generators are assumed to be customized programs developed for the specific applications to be analyzed by the system. By contrast, we assume the optimizer is a com-

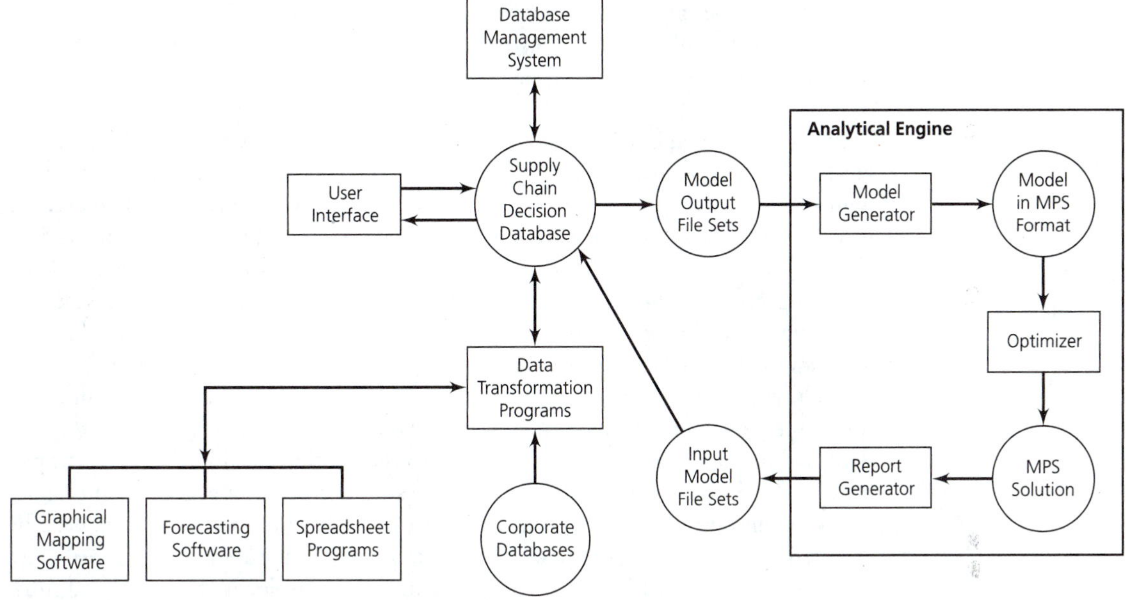

Figure 4.6
Optimization modeling system scheme

mercial package for optimizing linear and mixed integer programming models. These packages are discussed in detail in the next section of this chapter.

The model generator reads input data file sets when creating a matrix representation of the supply chain model to be optimized. In Figure 4.6, we assume this representation is given in MPS format, which is accepted by virtually all commercial optimizers of linear and mixed integer programming models.[6] By implication, these optimizers are interchangeable from a functional viewpoint, although some are considerably faster and more reliable than others. The practitioner's choice will depend on the effectiveness of the optimizer, its price, customer support, and his or her knowledge of the system.

Alternatively, the model generator may create a matrix representation of the model as an internal work file that is directly manipulated by the optimizer. By eliminating the steps of creating and then reading the MPS file, the process of model generation is made more efficient. The run time saved by this shortcut, although not trivial, will usually be small relative to the time required to optimize the resulting model. Thus, practitioners who choose this approach to using an optimization package face the possibility that the small computational gain will be offset by the need for considerable rework if and when they decide to employ a new and superior package.

The report generator organizes output from the optimizer. Output data is parsed in a way that is similar to the way in which it was parsed when creating the input data file sets. Although there is no standard format for output data from an optimizer, it does not vary greatly from package to package. Moreover, the structure of the input data file sets impose structure on output from the optimizer that facilitates construction of the output data file sets.

Database Management System. The input and output data file sets listed above are naturally presented as tables facilitating the application of relational database management tools to the supply chain decision database. These tools allow users to view and edit data from many perspectives, provide a flexible and extensible structure for organizing the data, and support the data processing requirements of the modeling system. The theory and practice of database management is a vast and changing topic.[7] We discuss it here only from the viewpoint of the unique features and requirements of the supply chain modeling system depicted in Figure 4.6.

The conversion of input data to output data by the intermediation of a linear or mixed integer programming model is a **nonstandard transformation,** which requires database management procedures peculiar to the application domain. For example, most of the decision variables in a large-scale supply chain model will assume values of zero in an optimal solution. Only the variables taking on positive values need be reported in the decision database. Moreover, other solution data, such as the values of 0-1 variables describing fixed costs or economies of scale, are technical and must either be suppressed or translated into recognizable supply chain elements. Finally, implicit solution data, such as shadow prices on plant capacities or scarce resources, need to be linked to the input data for which they are relevant.

A large-scale supply chain model can easily invoke a **large database** involving hundreds of thousands or even millions of data elements, which require careful handling to ensure efficient management. For example, a snapshot model involving 20 distribution centers that ship 100 product families to 500 markets will, in the worst case, contain 1 million outbound transportation arcs. These arcs constitute only one, although the largest, of many input data file sets for the model. Of course, not all distribution centers will or should be available as candidates for each market, implying that the number of outbound arcs could be reduced by a factor of 4 or more. On the other hand, for tactical planning purposes, a multiple period version of the model comprising 6 or 12 periods might be needed, implying that the number of arcs created by the model generator would reach several million. This set may not be prohibitively large for an optimizer because its mathematical structure is very simple.

Another peculiar feature of modeling analysis requiring special handling by data management routines is the generation and optimization of **multiple scenarios,** each of which is created by perturbing or modestly changing a base supply chain decision database. The practitioner must develop procedures to efficiently store and maintain data pertaining to each scenario. He or she must also develop tabular and graphical reporting procedures that allow the manager to compare, contrast, and display optimization results across scenarios.

Finally, the nature of supply chain modeling at the tactical level suggests that significant benefits would result from **distributing the supply chain decision database.** By this we mean that the decision database would be realized as a collection of interrelated databases residing on separate computers connected by a network.

Moreover, subject to data control and security considerations, access to all data would be transparent to all users. For example, cost, capacity, production transformation, and inventory data pertinent to individual plants and distribution centers would be maintained at those facilities. Each month, tactical planning across the entire supply chain would be carried out by the director of the supply chain, whose analysts would pull global facility data through the company's communication network. Optimal production and distribution plans for the month would then be sent back to managers at individual facilities via the network. A similar approach applies to virtual supply chains of separate companies connected via the Internet, assuming that software developments can support such an integration.

User Interfaces. The theory underlying the design and implementation of user interfaces is another vast topic that we will not review here.[8] The predominance of Microsoft software concentrates and limits, at least for the moment, the options available to the practitioner for implementing interfaces of a supply chain modeling system. Development tool kits, such as Visual Basic, facilitate the implementation of Windows interfaces with pull-down menus, toolbars, boxes, and point and click capabilities.

Data in the decision database may be viewed and modified within an optimization system using built-in spreadsheets, although the built-in functionality will not be as extensive as that found in comprehensive spreadsheet programs. The capabilities of such programs may be applied to the supply chain decision database by exporting and importing files between the modeling system and a spreadsheet package. Such a package may even be used as a primary tool for creating and editing the supply chain decision database by forming templates based on the structural data listed above. In using external spreadsheet programs, however, the practitioner must take care to avoid creating or editing files that may be too large for these programs, such as the set of outbound arcs with their costs and capacities.

Data Transformation Programs. In Figure 4.6, we display transformation programs needed to convert data from the corporate database in creating the supply chain decision database. These transformations include data aggregations that are discussed in Chapter 6. They include the mapping of raw cost data into a variety of direct and indirect costs, which we also discuss in Chapter 6. The current state of the art is to create transformation programs customized to the company's modeling and data needs. With the continuing development of enterprise resource planning systems, however, one can expect or hope that in the near future it will be possible to develop general-purpose transformation programs that will require at worst a moderate amount of customization.

Data transformation is also needed in the reverse direction. Some aggregations used in creating the decision database must be inverted to provide an appropriate level of detail for reports. Another useful transformation is the calculation of average product transfer costs at the plants and the markets based on the optimal solution. A related transformation is the calculation of performance metrics, such as machine utilization or transportation cost per mile, also based on the optimal solution.

Geographical Information System. A geographical information system (GIS) is another off-the-shelf package that can be usefully integrated with a modeling system for supply chain management. The typical GIS contains an extensive database of geographical and census information plus graphical capabilities for displaying maps with overlays pertaining to the company's supply chain activities. Geographical databases for many areas of the world have already been developed and can be employed by these systems. Some GIS packages also contain modeling capabilities for analyzing facility location and vehicle routing decisions.

For a company doing business in the continental United States, a GIS would be used to display the results of a logistics network design analysis. For example, the GIS could produce a map for each product showing the following:

- The optimal location of distribution centers supplying the product
- Color codes indicating which markets are served by each distribution center
- Links of variable thickness indicating the relative flows of product between distribution centers and markets

Graphical mapping displays of input and output model data do not add to a modeling system's inherent analytical capabilities. Still, they are very useful for communicating data, problems, and solutions, especially to managers who may be too busy to study detailed, tabular data.

4.5 Optimization Software

Commercial packages for optimizing linear and mixed integer programming have been available for decades. The first linear programming packages appeared during the late 1950s and the first mixed integer programming packages appeared during the early 1970s. Since then, their capabilities have evolved with advances in information technology. Optimization of linear and mixed integer programming models on today's PCs is significantly faster, measured in millions on instructions per second (MIPS), than it was on mainframes of 10 years ago, which cost several thousand times more in constant dollars. At the same time, the scope of optimization packages has expanded greatly to include algebraic languages for model generation and routines for managing data and implementing user interfaces. The growing interest in optimization of supply chain planning problems is due in no small part to these incredible technological advances.

Our discussion begins by differentiating among **optimizers, algebraic modeling language development kits,** and **spreadsheet optimization software.**[9] Optimizers are packages containing numerical algorithms that analyze a given matrix representation of a linear or mixed integer programming model to produce an optimal, or near optimal solution.[10] An optimizer is called as a subroutine in an optimization modeling system in the manner depicted in Figure 4.6.

Optimizers

In selecting an optimizer, the important features discussed in the following subsections should be considered.

Efficiency of Linear Programming Algorithms. Most commercial packages offer two distinct methods for optimizing linear programming models, the **simplex method** and the **interior point method.** Neither method dominates the other for all classes of linear programming models. Nevertheless, the efficiency of the package's simplex method is what matters for supply chain modeling because it is the preferred algorithm for solving linear programming approximations arising in the branch-and-bound method of mixed integer programming. These approximations are usually small perturbations of previously optimized models. The simplex method is very efficient at reoptimizing them. Because many supply models include mixed integer programming variables and constraints, applications of interior point methods to such models are very limited.

The efficiency of the simplex method in a commercial package depends on how well the method's procedures have been implemented. These include routines for inverting matrices, scaling data, resolving numerical degeneracy, and a variety of troublesome problems of numerical analysis. After more than 30 years of study, specialist of mathematical optimization have identified and largely solved these problems, with small differences in numerical routines found among different packages. Thus, the simplex algorithms available in the best commercial codes all perform very well, although some differences in performance will occur when optimizing large and difficult models.

Efficiency of Mixed Integer Programming Algorithms. As we discussed in earlier sections of this chapter, mixed integer programming models capture supply chain planning phenomena that cannot be captured by linear programming models. Their solution depends on the computational effort required by the branch-and-bound method (see Appendix 4.A), which searches the space of 0-1 (or integer) solutions using linear programming approximations to direct and limit the search. Relative to solving linear programming models, solving mixed integer programming models is less predictable in several ways:

1. *The practitioner must be prudent in his or her selection of planning issues to be modeled using mixed integer programming constructs.* Major decisions, such as whether or not to construct a new plant, clearly merit the use of 0-1 decision variables. By contrast, 0-1 variables should not be created to capture facility fixed costs that are relatively very small; for example, fixed costs that represent less than .001 of total facility cost. Instead, they should be averaged into the facility's variable costs. Similarly, small economies of scale in costs or resource utilization should not be explicitly modeled.
2. *The computational effort expended in optimizing a mixed integer programming model is intended to find a demonstrably good solution, rather than an optimal one.* Given sufficient computation time, a branch-and-bound search, which is

finite, will converge to an optimal mixed integer programming solution. As a practical manner, convergence often will require far too much time. Fortunately, as the search progresses, the method determines tighter and tighter bounds on how far the cost or value of the best known solution is from optimality. The search should therefore be terminated when a solution within an acceptable tolerance (e.g., 0.5%) or absolute difference (e.g., $10,000) from optimality is achieved. Note that a solution with such a positive tolerance may actually be optimal, but the search has not yet proven it so. In selecting the value of the bound to halt computation, the user should consider the nature of the run (e.g., exploratory or final), the accuracy of the data, the difficulty of the optimization, and the clock time available for obtaining a solution.

3. *For important and repetitive applications, the mixed integer programming algorithms should be tailored to exploit the particular structure of the model.* There are several types of tailoring. The most expedient is to customize the branch-and-bound search to the peculiarities of the application, including the use of branching priorities based on the relative importance of difference classes of 0-1 variables (e.g., plant location decisions are more important than those relating to economies of scale in a manufacturing process at the plant) or the use of a priori bounds on the cost or value of an optimal solution. Branching refers to the fixing of a 0-1 variable that is fractional in an optimal linear programming solution to values of 0 or 1. More ambitious customizations are discussed in Chapter 5.
4. *Commercial mixed integer programming codes vary significantly in the efficiency and flexibility of their branch-and-bound search methods.* Generally speaking, the practitioner should try to limit the number of 0-1 variables in a supply chain model to a few hundred. The better commercial codes will solve most models of this size in a time that is within a relatively small multiple, say 3 to 5, of the time to solve it as a linear programming model. Still, the codes do not perform uniformly well on moderately and very difficult models. Although a code may possess a fast simplex algorithm, to be effective, a branch-and-bound search also requires efficient handling of the data structures associated with hundreds or even thousands of linear programming approximations generated by the branch-and-bound method. Moreover, the search time can be significantly reduced by the use of priorities on 0-1 variables and other options directing the style of the search if such options are made available to the user.

Technical and Practical Limits on Model Size. Many commercial linear and mixed integer programming packages allow an unlimited number of variables and constraints. This is an important but dangerous feature. It is important because a supply chain model may naturally contain very large, but well-behaved submodels that do not require special attention. For example, an outbound transportation network submodel connecting 20 distribution centers to 500 markets for the distribution of 100 products will consist of approximately 50,000 constraints and 250,000 variables, assuming we allow approximately five distribution centers as potential sources for each market. Because the mathematical structure of such a network is simple, it does not cause serious computational difficulty. Thus, there may be no need to limit the dimensions of this network submodel. Nevertheless, the feature of unlimited size can be dangerous because it allows an inexperienced user to generate models of an arbitrary size without realizing the potential consequences to run times.

Availability of Callable Library. Some commercial codes allow individual routines within their suite of algorithms to be called from other programs. This capability is necessary for the implementation of specialized algorithmic approaches in a modeling system, such as customized branch-and bound or decomposition methods.

The view that an optimizer can and should be purchased off the shelf, rather than developed in-house, is not universally held. Some system implementers believe that their modeling system will have greater integrity and perform more efficiently using optimizers developed in-house. This is a false notion because the best commercial codes embody expertise based on many person-years of skilled implementation that is difficult to duplicate.

Algebraic Modeling Language Development Kits

An algebraic modeling language development kit has three major components:

- An algebraic modeling language interpreter
- Optimizers
- Database drivers

The algebraic modeling language permits the user to specify the mathematical form of a supply chain optimization model using an algebraic syntax similar to what he or she would use when writing out a model statement by hand. To test the consistency of the model statement, the user also specifies a data set describing a model instance. The system reads the model statement and the data set and attempts to interpret it as a well-defined linear or mixed integer programming model. If the interpretation is successful, it attempts to populate the matrix it has created with the given data. If the data set is consistent both internally and with the algebraic modeling specification, the interpreter creates a matrix representation of the model. The user must then check this matrix to ensure that it is a valid representation of the supply chain problem to be analyzed.

A development kit also contains one or more commercial optimizers that may be called to optimize the model once it has been successfully generated. Finally, the kit will contain database drivers that allow the user to organize and manipulate the model's database and to view and edit data. For some systems, these drivers may simply be programs linking input and output data to spreadsheet programs. For others, data management is achieved by using open database connectivity (ODBC) drivers that integrate the algebraic modeling language interpreter and the optimizers with Windows software components such as Excel and Access.

In principle, the entire analytical engine depicted in Figure 4.6 could be implemented using an algebraic modeling language and its optimizers. Moreover, if the database drivers of the development system were sufficiently elaborated, the entire modeling system could be implemented using it. In many situations, however, the resulting system would be inefficient, especially for large or complex models.

The broad capability of a modeling language to translate any algebraic statement into a linear or mixed integer programming model has a negative side. The interpretive programs cannot and will not produce models and matrix generation schemes that are as parsimonious and efficient as a well-executed, customized generator written in a programming language such as C++. Efficiency depends on the complexity of the model and its data sets. Thus, an algebraic modeling language development system is most appropriate for implementing prototype modeling systems. For a complex and important application, the prototype may need to be replaced by a more efficient system that employs a customized model generator, report generator, and database management routines.

In selecting an algebraic modeling language development system, the important features to consider are as follows:

1. *Intuitiveness and richness of the algebraic modeling language.* The syntaxes of modeling languages vary, although a competent programmer can readily master any of them. Nevertheless, all other factors being equal, the practitioner may find that one of the languages is more intuitive to use. Moreover, the development kits differ in their capabilities for implementing complex data management schemes or iterative modeling methods.
2. *Linkages to external data files and database management programs.* Today, most development kits are well integrated with Windows-based programs for database management and the creation of user interfaces. The richness of the user interfaces and programs for data acquisition needed for a modeling system prototype depends on the application. If the prototype will be used exclusively by the practitioner to study a company's supply chain problems, these programs and interfaces can be primitive. If the prototype will be used by supply chain managers and analysts, they must be more elaborated and user friendly.
3. *Imbedded optimizers.* Some development kits include several commercial optimizers. The user may select which optimizer he or she wishes to include in the development system. To achieve efficiency in the optimization step, the user must also have access to control parameters and special features of the optimizer. For mixed integer programming, these include branching priorities on 0-1 variables, bounds on the optimization error, and limits on the search. For repetitive modeling schemes, it is critical to restart optimization with advanced information about the likely optimal solution.
4. *Efficiency and reliability.* As we have discussed, the development kits are complex amalgamations of interpretive programs, third-party optimizers, and database drivers. Considerable effort is needed to integrate these elements in an efficient and error-free manner. Because the development kits are relatively new and the resources available for their implementation are limited, their performance can be volatile. As a result, in using them to develop a modeling system, the practitioner must be on guard against unexpected deficiencies and malfunctions that can inhibit rapid and complete demonstration of the value of a modeling approach.

5. ***Developer's commitment to system evolution.*** The practitioner must invest considerable time in learning to effectively use a development kit. The quid pro quo for such an investment is a commitment by the developers of the kit to evolve and improve the system in response to system deficiencies and the appearance of new computer systems for data management and user interfaces.

Spreadsheet Optimizers

Spreadsheet optimizers of the type discussed in Chapter 3 and earlier sections of this chapter allow the user to create and optimize a linear or mixed integer programming model from data in a spreadsheet by invoking a built-in optimization algorithm. In simplified form, these packages serve the same role as algebraic modeling language development systems. The application of spreadsheet optimizers to supply chain problems is limited to models that are small and simple relative to those that can be created by the algebraic modeling language development systems discussed above. Still, a practitioner may be able to rapidly develop and exercise a "proof-of-concept" model in a spreadsheet optimizer as the first step in a more serious examination of supply chain issues. These optimizers are easy to learn and available as a callable tool in a spreadsheet package.

4.6 Final Thoughts

We illustrated in this chapter how 0-1 decision variables can be employed to capture locational decisions, fixed costs, economies of scale, sole sourcing constraints, and other important supply chain planning phenomena that cannot be captured by linear programming models. These modeling vignettes are only a small sample of a vast number of modeling constructions that can be achieved using 0-1 variables.[11] A few more are given in chapter exercises.

We also illustrated the application of mixed integer programming models to two strategic planning problems; the location and sizing of DCs in a distribution network and the timing, phasing, and location of investment decisions in a manufacturing firm. These models are typical in form, although not size, of those being employed in an increasing number of supply chain studies being performed for medium- and large-sized companies. We will discuss several such studies in later chapters.

Using the design principles and tools discussed in Section 4.5, an experienced practitioner can, depending on the complexity of the supply chain problems to be addressed, implement a prototype or even permanent modeling system in just a few weeks or months. In this context, the term *experienced practitioner* refers to an individual with training in mathematical programming, experience in applying mathematical programming models to real-world problems, and competence in system design and computer programming. Such individuals are currently in short supply, although their value is becoming more obvious to software development firms and some supply chain and consulting companies. There are even signs that the short supply is creating demand for business and engineering students with these skills, which in turn is leading to wider course offerings in applications of mathematical programming models and the development of planning systems based on them.

Finally, research continues on better algorithmic methods for solving mixed integer programming models, although its connections so far to supply chain modeling has not been explicit. With the emergence of widely used supply chain modeling systems based on mixed integer programming, practitioners should focus on specializing recent research results to speed up the extraction of demonstrably good solutions. A tantalizing possibility is implementation and use of branch-and-bound methods on coarse-grained parallel computers. The idea is to distribute the solution of linear programming submodels that are solved as approximations by these methods to separate processors. Experimentation has indicated that near linear speedup can be achieved by such an approach; that is, if one processor requires 20 minutes to identify a demonstrably good solution, 10 processors will require not much more than two minutes to find such a solution.[12]

Exercises

In addition to the following exercises, modeling exercises involving data files and discussion exercises involving white papers may be found on the Web site (www.scm-models.com).

1. Ajax Computer Company must purchase 600 customized hard drives for its Alpha computer for next year. As shown in the following table, the company received quotes from three vendors for these drives:

Company	Fixed Cost	Unit Cost 1	Break Point	Unit Cost 2	Max. Available
Acme	15,000	240	200	200	500
Best	0	325	150	225	700
Champion	10,000	265	250	190	800

For example, Champion will require a fixed cost of $10,000 to tool up to make the drives. It will charge $265 per unit for the first 250 units and $190 per unit for additional units up to a maximum (supplied at both prices) of 800 units.

a. Formulate Ajax' vendor selection problem as a mixed integer programming model and optimize it using a spreadsheet optimizer.

b. Reformulate and reoptimize the model of part a under the additional constraint that no vendor is allowed to supply more than 75% of the total number of units required.

2. Regular-time assembly labor at Ajax Computer Company costs $20/hour, including benefits, up to a maximum of 2000 hours per week. Overtime costs $25/hour, including benefits, up to a maximum of 400 hours per week. There is also a fixed cost of $250 per week if any overtime is incurred. Extend

Example 4.1 to incorporate a direct accounting of Ajax' labor costs and to include the overtime option. Implement and optimize the revised model with a spreadsheet optimizer.

3. Home Grocery is a new company that makes same-day deliveries of groceries to people's homes. The company is launching its business in Metropolis, a large urban area. The marketing department has identified eight neighborhoods in Metropolis where the company should concentrate its business. The logistics manager has identified six locations where the company may locate grocery depots. The following table shows the average time (in minutes) required to travel from each of the six potential depot locations to the center of each of the eight neighborhoods. It also shows the target population (in thousands) for the company's service in each neighborhood.

	Depots						
Neighborhoods	**1**	**2**	**3**	**4**	**5**	**6**	**Population**
1	15	17	27	5	25	22	12
2	10	12	24	4	22	20	8
3	5	6	17	9	21	17	11
4	7	6	8	15	13	10	14
5	14	12	6	23	6	8	22
6	18	17	10	28	9	5	18
7	11	10	5	21	10	9	16
8	24	22	22	33	6	16	20

The company wishes to locate two depots so that they maximize the population served within 12 minutes of average travel time. Formulate and optimize a spreadsheet optimization model of this problem.

4. The manager of a job shop must schedule three jobs on four machines. Each job consists of three operations. The processing time (in minutes) for each operation on each machine is given in the following table where x indicates that a job does not have an operation on that machine:

	Machine			
	1	**2**	**3**	**4**
Job 1	23	x	17	18
Job 2	17	20	18	x
Job 3	19	24	x	19

For each job, processing on the machines must be done sequentially; that is, the operation on machine j can begin only after the operation on machine $j-1$ has been completed (or after the operation on machine $j-2$ has been completed if the job has no operation on machine $j-1$). In addition, only one job may be processed on a machine at a given time. The objective is to minimize the time required to complete all three jobs. Formulate a mixed integer programming model of this problem. Implement and optimize it on a spreadsheet optimizer. *Hint:* Define two types of constraints. For each job, an operation can be started on machine j only after the operation on machine $j-1$ has been completed. In addition, an operation can be started on machine j only if the operation scheduled immediately before that operation on the same machine, which is part of another job, has been completed.

5. A mail order company accepts telephone orders 7 days a week during the period 9 A.M. to 5 P.M. (local time). Based on analysis of historical data, the following number of people are needed each day in the call center to cover incoming orders:

Sun	Mon	Tue	Wed	Thu	Fri	Sat
12	17	8	9	10	11	8

The company hires staff to work 5 consecutive days a week. It pays these staffers \$100/day to work on Monday through Friday and \$150/day to work on the weekends.

a. Using a spreadsheet optimizer, develop and optimize a mixed integer programming model to minimize the cost of staffing the call center.

b. Suppose part-time staff working 3 consecutive days during Monday to Friday can be hired at a cost of \$110/day. The higher cost reflects higher training and turnover costs associated with part-time staff. The number of such staff cannot exceed 5. Extend the model of part a to incorporate this option, and determine a new optimal solution.

Notes

1. See Schrage [1997, Chapter 14] and Winston [1995, Chapter 9], including homework exercises, for a wide range of mixed integer programming applications.
2. Geoffrion and Graves [1974] provide a classic application of mixed integer programming to DC location problems. A recent overview of applications and systems can be found in Jiminez, Brown, and Jordan [1998].
3. See Bender et al. [1985] for a discussion of mixed integer programming models applied to purchases from vendors.
4. The construction in Section 3.2 ignored cross-price effects in examining Ajax product line; that is, the effect that price changes for a given product have on demand for other products. If cross-price elasticities can be measured, they can be incorporated in a quadratic programming model; see Schrage [1997, 285–286]. Further, the resulting cross-product terms appearing in the objective function of a quadratic programming model can be approximated by separable and additive relationships using a mixed integer programming trick; again, see Schrage [1997, 309].
5. See SLIM Technologies, LLC [2000].
6. The MPS format was employed by William Orchard-Hays, who was heavily involved in most, if not all, commercial implementations of the simplex method for linear programming between 1948 and the mid 1970s (see Orchard-Hays [1968]). Although this format is not particularly intuitive or easy to use, its existence facilitates comparative testing of linear and mixed integer programming packages.
7. See Vossen [1992].
8. See Jones [1992].

9. Sharda and Rampal [1995] discuss different types of optimization software. See also Tomlin and Welch [1992].
10. Nonlinear programming algorithms are another class of optimizers available in commercial packages. Nonlinear programming models contain nonlinear functions of vectors arguments; these models are optimized using constructions from calculus describing gradients and Hessians of such functions. We have chosen not to discuss nonlinear programming models and algorithms because they are infrequently applied to supply chain problems. Moreover, certain types of nonlinearities can be approximated by mixed integer programming constructs.
11. Winston [1995] discusses a range of mixed integer programming applications in Chapter 9, especially in the exercises on pages 560–564. Shapiro [1993] describes several mixed integer programming models for production planning and scheduling.
12. See Gendron and Crainic [1994].

References

Bender, P. S., R. W. Brown, M. H. Isaac, and J. F. Shapiro [1985], "Improving Purchasing Productivity at IBM with a Normative Decision Support System," *Interfaces,* 15, 106–115.

Gendron, B., and T. G. Crainic [1994], "Parallel Branch-and-Bound Algorithms: A Synthesis and Survey," *Operations Research,* 42, 1042–1066.

Geoffrion, A. M., and G. W. Graves [1974], "Multicommodity Distribution System Design by Benders Decomposition," *Management Science,* 20, 822–844.

Jiminez, S., T. Brown, and J. Jordan [1998], "Network-Modeling Tools: Enhancing Supply Chain Decision Making," in *Strategic Supply Chain Alignment,* edited by J. Gattorna. Adershot, Eng.: Gower.

Jones, C. V. [1992], "User Interfaces," in *Handbooks in Operations Research and Management Science—Volume 3: Computing,* edited by E. G. Coffman, Jr., J. K. Lenstra, and A. H. G. Rinooy Kan. Amsterdam: Elsevier Science.

Orchard-Hays, W. [1968], *Advanced Linear Programming Computing Techniques,* New York: McGraw-Hill.

Schrage, L., [1997], *LINDO: An Optimization Modeling System,* 5th ed. Pacific Grove, Calif.: Brooks/Cole.

SLIM Technologies, LLC. [2000], *SLIM System Overview,* Boston.

Shapiro, J. F. [1993], "Mathematical Programming Models and Methods for Production Planning and Scheduling," in *Handbooks in Operations Research and Management Science—Volume 4; Logistics of Production and Inventory,* edited by S. C. Graves, A. G. H. Rinooy Kan, and P. H. Zipkin. Amsterdam: Elsevier Science.

Sharda, R., and G. Rampal [1995], "Software Survey: AML," *OR/MS Today,* 22, 58–63.

Tomlin, J. A., and J. S. Welch [1992], "Mathematical Programming Systems," in *Handbooks in Operations Research and Management Science—Volume 3: Computing,* edited by E. G. Coffman, Jr., J. K. Lenstra, and A. H. G. Rinooy Kan. Amsterdam: Elsevier Science.

Vossen, G. [1992], "Databases and Database Management," in *Handbooks in Operations Research and Management Science—Volume 3: Computing,* edited by E. G. Coffman, Jr., J. K. Lenstra, and A. H. G. Rinooy Kan. Amsterdam: Elsevier Science.

Winston, W. L., [1995], *Introduction to Mathematical Programming: Applications and Algorithms,* 2nd ed. Pacific Grove, Calif.: Duxbury Press.

Appendix 4.A

The Branch-and-Bound Method for Mixed Integer Programming

We present the **branch-and-bound method** for optimizing mixed integer programming models specialized to models with only binary, integer variables. Extending the method to mixed integer programming models with general integer variables is straightforward. The method can also be adapted to systematically search the solution space of other combinatorial problems that have not been posed as mixed integer programming models.

We have chosen to include this introduction to the branch-and-bound method because mixed integer programming is important to accurate and comprehensive supply chain modeling. Supply chain managers are at risk if they treat the method as a black box of little consequence. Significant number crunching and batch processing time may be required in using it to extract an optimal or demonstrably good solution from a model. By understanding the logic underlying the branch-and-bound method, managers can more intelligently balance the computational effort they are willing to invest against the importance and complexity of the supply chain problems being analyzed.

The performance of the branch-and-bound method is less predictable than the simplex method, which it employs as a subroutine. Still, for strategic and tactical planning purposes, large-scale models involving hundreds of 0-1 variables can usually be solved in reasonable computation times. The scope and size of models that can be reliably optimized continues to expand as computing power grows. The increasing importance of mixed integer programming models to supply chain decision making is spurring research into new and improved algorithms. Large-scale models for operational planning can be challenging and require customized approaches; these models and methods are discussed in detail in the next chapter.

We illustrate the branch-and-bound method by examining its application to scenario 6 examined by the Ajax strategy model (see Table 4.4). Recall that the model involves eight 0-1 decision variables that determine the selection and timing of three investment options. We rewrite them here as follows:

$$\begin{aligned} XPLt = {} & 1 \text{ if the existing plant is expanded in year } t\ (t = 1,2,3), \\ & 0 \text{ otherwise} \end{aligned}$$

NPLt = 1 if the new plant is built to come on line in year t (t = 1,2,3), 0 otherwise

DELTAX = 1 if Delta is developed and assembled at the existing plant in year 1, 0 otherwise

DELTAN = 1 if Delta is developed and assembled at the new plant in year 1, 0 otherwise

To motivate the method, we discuss a simple but ineffective hunt-and-peck approach to optimizing the model. First, we enumerate all possible combinations of values of the eight 0-1 variables. Each combination corresponds to a fixed investment strategy; for example, the strategy given by XPL1 = 1, XPL2 = 0, XPL3 = 0, NPL1 = 0, NPL2 = 1, NPL3 = 0, DELTAX = 1, and DELTAN = 0. In words, this is the strategy in which the existing plant is expanded in period 1, the new plant is built to come on-line in year 2, and the new product is developed and will be assembled at the existing plant starting in year 1.

Because each 0-1 variable can take on one of two values, the number of such combinations is $2^8 = 256$. If we also consider constraints in the model that limit allowable combinations of the 0-1 variables, such as one stating that a new plant can be built to come on-line at most once in 1 of 3 years, the number of feasible combinations to be considered is 48. It is convenient to picture such combinations as generating a **search tree** where, starting from the null solution, we systematically pick values of 0 or 1 for the decision variables. A tree drawn only for the values of XPL1, XPL2, and XPL3 is depicted in Figure 4.A.1.

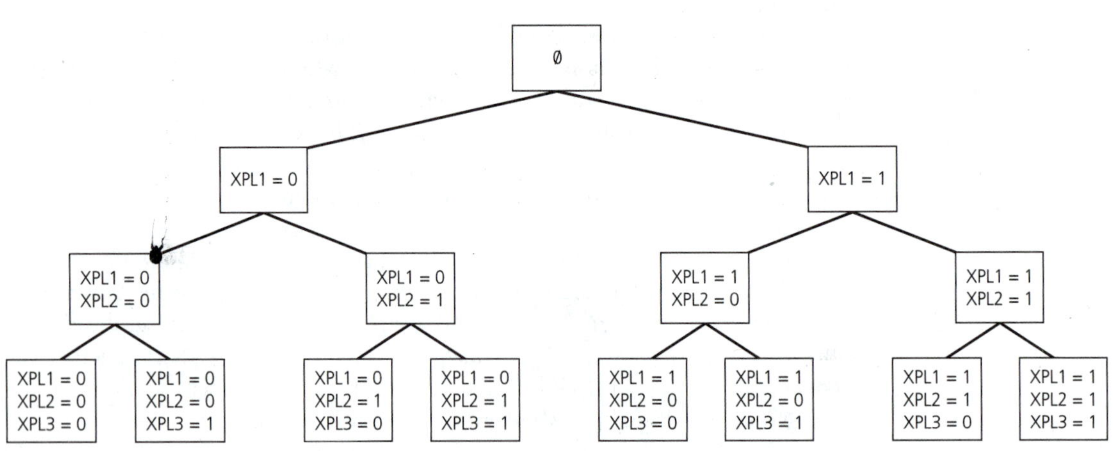

Figure 4.A.1
Search tree for three binary variables

For each of the 48 investment strategies, the hunt-and-peck method fixes the 0-1 variables at their indicated values and optimizes the residual linear programming model, which involves continuous variables for determining the optimal product assembly, transportation, and sales strategies. The 0-1 values of the variables plus the values of the continuous variables constitute a mixed integer programming solution. The hunt-and-peck method then exhaustively evaluates these solutions to find a feasible solution with a maximal objective function value.

The branch-and-bound method greatly improves on the hunt-and-peck method by using linear programming approximations to limit the search of the set of all 0-1 solutions. The entire set is still searched, but only implicitly. The number of linear programming approximations explicitly optimized will be far less than that required by total enumeration.

The linear programming approximation of a mixed integer programming model used by the branch-and-bound method is the obvious one. It is the model that results if the 0-1 variables are allowed to take on any values between 0 and 1, including 0 and 1. Such an approximation is called a **relaxation** because the set of feasible solutions to the mixed integer programming model is relaxed to include many other solutions that are not feasible in that model. Optimizing over the relaxation is an inexact approximation, but it has the advantage that it can be done much more efficiently.

The properties of linear programming relaxations that are exploited by the branch-and-bound method are as follows:

1. If the 0-1 variables in an optimal solution to the relaxation **fortuitously have values of 0 or 1,** the solution is an **optimal mixed integer programming solution.** This must be true because, if there were a better mixed integer programming solution, it would be a feasible solution in the relaxation, thereby contradicting the optimality of the original optimal solution for the relaxation.
2. For a model with an objective function to be maximized, the maximal objective function value of the relaxation is an **upper bound** on the maximal objective function value of the mixed integer programming model. This is because the relaxation maximizes the objective function over a larger set of feasible solutions than the mixed integer programming model. Hence the meaning of *bound* in the expression branch and bound.
3. Most relaxations encountered using the branch-and-bound method can be efficiently optimized. As we shall see when we discuss *branching,* relaxations are often perturbations of other, closely related relaxations. Therefore, they can be optimized quite rapidly by the simplex method.

Returning to the Ajax strategy model for scenario 6, the initial linear programming relaxation evaluated by the branch-and bound method is the one that results if we allow each of the eight 0-1 variables to take on any value between 0 and 1. Optimizing this relaxation, we obtain the solution for which the 0-1 variables take on the values given in Table 4.A.1. As stated above, if these values were all 0 or 1, the solution would be an optimal mixed integer programming solution.

Table 4.A.1 Branch-and-bound method for optimal linear programming relaxation of Ajax strategy model, Scenario 6

Linear Programming	Variable	Value
Relaxation	XPL1	0.4125
	XPL2	0.5875
	XPL3	0.0000
	NPL1	1.0000
	NPL2	0.0000
	NPL3	0.0000
	DELTAX	0.1400
	DELTAN	0.4000
Objective function value		$13,802,290

Unfortunately, four variables in Table 4.A.1 have fractional values and the branch-and-bound method must perform additional computation to find an optimal integer solution. The fractions indicate that the linear programming relaxation dithers about when to expand the existing plant and whether or not to develop the new product. It would like to commit to approximately 0.41 of the existing plant expansion in year1, with an additional 0.59 for year 2. In this way, the added assembly and testing capacity would be phased in so as to optimally spread the annualized fixed investment costs over the 2 years. Such a strategy is not realistic—Ajax must commit to the major expansion all at once or not at all. The linear programming relaxation does provide us with an **upper bound** = $13,802,290 on the maximal objective function value of the model.

The branch-and-bound method proceeds by selecting a 0-1 variable that is fractional in the linear programming relaxation and then by creating two new submodels from it, one with this variable **fixed** at (that is, set equal to) 1 and the other with this variable fixed at 0. This process is called **branching.** Each feasible mixed integer programming solution to the model will be a feasible solution in one of the two submodels, but not both.

The question now arises: Which 0-1 variable will the method branch on? In theory, the method will work regardless of the variable that is chosen. In practice, we try to choose a variable that will most effectively resolve the conflict about values for the 0-1 variable choices displayed by the optimal solution to the linear programming relaxation. Such a choice will never be more than an educated guess, but experience has shown that imposing human judgment on branching strategies can greatly speed up the method.

We choose the following **branching rule** because it will expeditiously eliminate fractional values in identifying an initial feasible solution to the mixed integer programming model:

> Branch on the 0-1 variable in a linear programming submodel with the largest fractional value

Our reasoning is that this is the fractional variable closest to being resolved by the linear programming optimization; it is likely, but far from certain, that it will turn out to equal 1 in an optimal 0-1 solution. We say that the new submodels created by branching from a given submodel are **continuations** of that submodel. These continuations serve to elaborate the branch-and-bound tree.

Thus, the rule leads the method to branch on the variable XPL2 in Table 4.A.1 to create the two submodels given in Table 4.A.2. Note that the new linear programming relaxations are not very different from the original one in that only one variable has been constrained to equal 0 or 1. By restarting the simplex method at the optimal solution to the original relaxation, the submodels can be optimized much more quickly than the original relaxation.

Table 4.A.2 Branch-and-bound method for initial submodels of Ajax strategy model, Scenario 6

Submodel 1	Variable	Value
	XPL1	0.0000
	XPL2*	1.0000
	XPL3	0.0000
	NPL1	1.0000
	NPL2	0.0000
	NPL3	0.0000
	DELTAX	0.3333
	DELTAN	0.4000
Objective function value		$13,752,564
Submodel 2	**Variable**	**Value**
	XPL1	1.0000
	XPL2*	0.0000
	XPL3	0.0000
	NPL1	0.8561
	NPL2	0.1459
	NPL3	0.0000
	DELTAX	0.3333
	DELTAN	0.4000
Objective function value		$13,716,569

*Fixed

The branch-and-bound method proceeds by reoptimizing the two submodels and checking to see if their solutions are feasible mixed integer programming solutions. Unfortunately, they are not. Submodel 1 is much closer to being integer than the original linear programming relaxation, but the optimizer is still dithering about whether or not to develop the new product. Submodel 2 is also fractional. Because all feasible mixed integer programming solutions are feasible in one of the two submodels, we can conclude that an upper bound on the maximal objective function value of the model is the maximum of the two objective function values to the submodels, or **upper bound** = $13,752,564.

We say that the two submodels are **unfathomed** because their linear programming solutions yielded fractional values for some 0-1 variables. Their unfathomed states connote that the method must branch further to try to achieve a linear programming solution with 0-1 values for the binary variables or to conclude that an optimal mixed integer programming solution will have different binary values for the fixed variables. Conversely, we say a submodel has been **fathomed** if the linear programming solution yields binary values for the 0-1 variables. It has also been fathomed if its optimal objective function solution does not exceed the **incumbent value,** which is the objective function value of the **incumbent,** or the best-known, feasible mixed integer programming solution. Because we have not yet discovered an incumbent, the second fathoming criterion cannot be invoked. Branching on a fathomed submodel is unnecessary, either because the method has found an optimal solution to the original model with the fixed variables at their assigned values or because the method has determined an incumbent value that eliminates the possibility that a continuation of the submodel will improve on the incumbent.

Thus, for our example, the branch-and-bound method continues by branching on one of the two unfathomed submodels. In general, the method will be faced with selecting the next submodel for branching from an indeterminate number of unfathomed submodels. To do this, we must specify a **search rule.** We call it a search rule because the selection of a submodel on which to branch determines the immediate extension of the branch-and-bound search. We employ the following two-phased rule:

1. Until an initial incumbent solution has been found, branch on the submodel with the smallest sum of fractions; that is, for each submodel, add up the values among all variables with fractional values, and select the submodel for which this sum is minimal.
2. If an incumbent solution has been found, branch on the submodel with the highest upper bound.

The efficacy of a branch-and-bound search is very dependent on finding a good incumbent quickly. Until an initial incumbent solution has been found, its goal is to eliminate fractions and achieve mixed integer feasibility as quickly as possible. Once an incumbent has been found, the method seeks a better incumbent to prove that the incumbent is optimal, or demonstrably good. The second rule serves both these purposes by branching on a submodel that could yield a better incumbent, while reducing the highest known upper bound on the objective function value of an optimal solution.

By a demonstrably good incumbent we mean one that is proven to be within a specified **tolerance** of an optimal solution as measured by its objective function value. Specifically,

tolerance = (upper bound – incumbent value) / incumbent value

In our example, we choose a tolerance = 0.01, or 1%.

Returning to the example, using the above search rule, the method elects to branch on submodel 1 because its sum of fractions is 0.4833, whereas submodel 2 has a sum of fractions equaling 1.7353. Using the stated branching rule, the method branches on DELTAN. The two resulting submodels are given in Table 4.A.3. Because the variables in the linear programming solution to submodel 3 have 0-1 values, we have discovered an **incumbent solution** with **incumbent value** = $13,448,834. Submodel 3 has therefore been fathomed, and branching from it will not be required.

Table 4.A.3 Branch-and-bound method for submodels 3 and 4 of Ajax strategy model, scenario 6

Submodel 3	**Variable**	**Value**
	XPL1	0.0000
	XPL2*	1.0000
	XPL3	0.0000
	NPL1	1.0000
	NPL2	0.0000
	NPL3	0.0000
	DELTAX	0.0000
	DELTAN*	1.0000
Objective function value		$13,448,834
Submodel 4	**Variable**	**Value**
	XPL1	0.0000
	XPL2*	1.0000
	XPL3	0.0000
	NPL1	1.0000
	NPL2	0.0000
	NPL3	0.0000
	DELTAX	0.4800
	DELTAN*	0.0000
Objective function value		$13,589,600

*Fixed

At this point, the branch-and-bound method is left with the unfathomed submodels 2 and 4. The upper bound on the optimal objective function value of the mixed integer programming model is the larger of these two, $13,716,569, a figure that is 2% above the incumbent value. Because the method has found an incumbent, the second search rule is invoked and the method selects submodel 2 on which it branches to create submodels 6 and 7. According to the branching rule, the method branches on the binary variable NPL1.

Computation thus far with the method is depicted in Figure 4.A.2. Each submodel is represented as a rectangle with the optimal linear programming objective function value indicated. Note that submodel 6 was fathomed by bound. The number in the upper right-hand corner indicates the order in which an unfathomed submodel was selected for branching. For the tree depicted in Figure 4.A.2, the upper bound has been reduced to $13,697,772, a value that is 1.85% above the incumbent value. The method now chooses submodel 5 as the one from which to branch.

The branch-and-bound method continues its analysis through the generation of a total of 10 submodels before establishing that the original incumbent is less than 1% lower in objective function value than an optimal solution (the tolerance actually jumps down to 0.3%). We omit a display of the complete search tree but

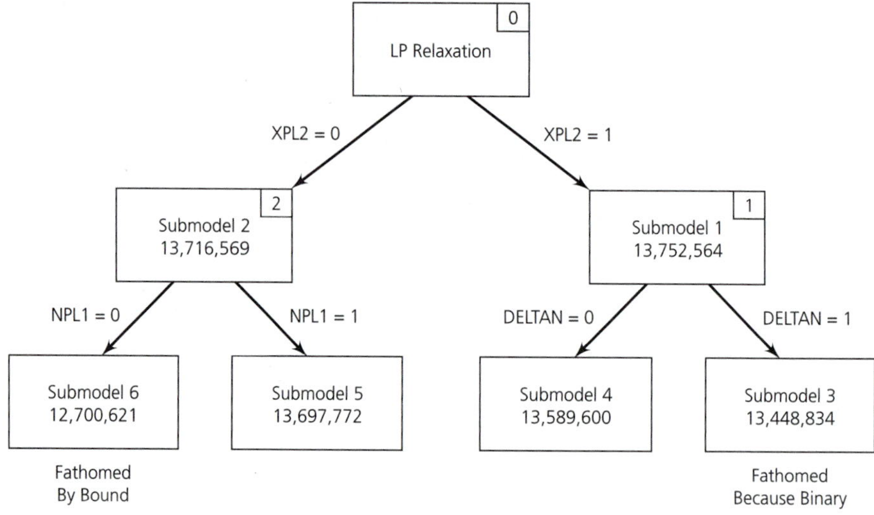

Figure 4.A.2 Intermediate branch-and-bound tree for Ajax strategy model, scenario 6

note that the branch-and-bound method successfully eliminated 38 of the 48 submodels that would be generated by an exhaustive search. Of course, for a mixed integer programming model with 100 0-1 variables, we would expect an efficient branch-and-bound implementation to search over a miniscule proportion of the number of submodels that could be generated by a hunt-and-peck search.

By another branch-and-bound run, we know that the incumbent is optimal, but the method using a positive tolerance cut off computation when the incumbent became demonstrably good. One of the 10 submodels yielded another feasible mixed integer programming solution at a value of $13,335,600. This solution is the same as the incumbent except that the new product is assembled in the existing plant rather than the new plant. If the branch-and-bound program allows it, the practitioner should output and report such near optimal solutions for management perusal.

In summary, the branch-and-bound method can be guaranteed to find an optimal mixed integer programming solution by an implicitly exhaustive search of the set of 0-1 solutions to a mixed integer programming model. It can also be programmed to find a demonstrably good solution if the computation time required to find an optimal solution and prove that it is optimal proves excessive. Finally, the method is very flexible and considerable artistry is required in selecting and implementing intelligent branching and search strategies.

5 Unified Optimization Methodology for Operational Planning Problems

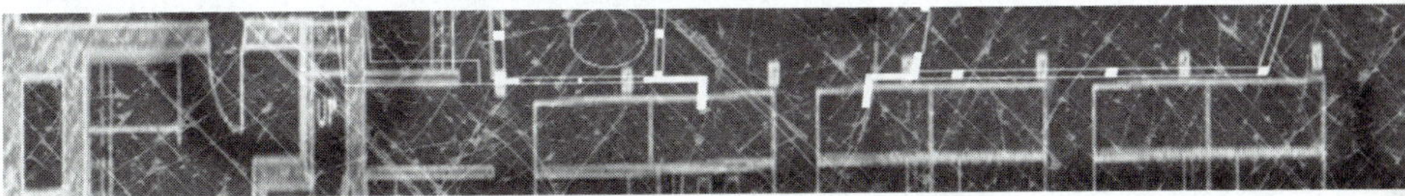

In the previous chapter, we examined mixed integer programming constructions that extend linear programming models to more realistic representations of supply chain problems at all levels of planning. Many large-scale mixed integer programming models have been successfully implemented and solved. Nevertheless, such models can be challenging to optimize, especially applications for operational planning that require considerable detail about the timing and sequencing of decisions.

This concern arose in a project in which we implemented a modeling system to support production scheduling at a paper mill. Major changeovers on paper machines over a planning horizon of 30 days were a key set of decisions. For four product families manufactured on a particular machine, the production manager wished to know the precise hour at which each changeover from one family to another should be started. A mixed integer programming model of this problem would have required 12 zero-one variables *for each hour of the planning horizon* to describe all possible changeovers from each product family to every other product family. Because there are 720 hours in the planning horizon, the model would have required 8640 zero-one variables to capture these decisions. However, it was unlikely that the model, or the company, would elect to make more than five major changeovers during the planning horizon; in other words, no more than 5 of the 8640 zero-one variables would equal 1 in an optimal solution. Needless to say, we designed and implemented a modeling approach that was less direct but much easier to optimize.

Vehicle routing problems invoke another class of models where brute force mixed integer programming needs to be tempered by more flexible methods. One example is the local delivery problem where a company dispatches trucks on a daily basis from a central depot to make deliveries to customers. Such problems can be modeled, but not easily solved, as monolithic mixed integer programming models. For a specific class of problems, which we will examine in Section 5.3, the models are made up of submodels that describe the routing of each vehicle plus constraints stating that each customer may be visited exactly once. The submodels are awkward to represent using mixed integer programming, but **heuristics** can find good solutions very quickly. Heuristics are ad hoc search methods customized to a specific decision problem based on rules gleaned by humans about the problem. The simplicity and effectiveness of heuristics applied to some supply chain problems has led to considerable applied mathematics research aimed at generalizing the methods and providing mathematical results characterizing their performance.

The implication of these stories, and others that we could relate, is as follows:

> It can be necessary and desirable, especially for an operational problem, to design and implement mixed integer programming models and solution methods that are customized to the problem. The customized methods should aim to determine a demonstrably good, rather than an optimal, solution to each numerical instance of the problem. Rigorous optimization methods should be combined with problem-specific and general-purpose heuristic methods to create schemes that rapidly compute these demonstrably good solutions.

In this chapter, we examine a general-purpose approach to such customization called the **unified optimization methodology** that combines **mathematical programming decomposition methods** with **heuristics.** By using the term **methodology,** which is a "body of practices, procedures, and rules used in a discipline," rather than the term **method,** which is as "an orderly arrangement of steps to accomplish an end," in describing this approach, we wish to convey that its implementation for a particular problem will entail a flexible specification and integration of various algorithms and methods appropriate to the problem.[1]

We are motivated to present the unified optimization methodology for several reasons. First, it has and can be successfully applied to a wide range of complex scheduling and other operational supply chain problems. Second, because it begins by posing a complete and accurate representation of a supply chain problem as a mixed integer programming model, we can be confident that our analysis of the problem will be comprehensive. Moreover, the generality of mixed integer programming permits model extensions to capture changing problem features.

Third, the united optimization methodology exploits the complementarity between heuristic methods and rigorous mathematical programming methods. Recently, heuristic methods have been oversold as all-powerful approaches for solving **advanced planning and scheduling** problems, a vague new term that includes complex planning problems arising in operational supply chain management. Heuristics do have an important role to play, but their effectiveness is primarily in analyzing certain types of homogeneous submodels embedded in larger, heterogeneous models. Moreover, heuristic methods are weak in analyzing resource allocation and other **cross-cutting** (that is, systemwide) constraints that are very well analyzed by linear programming. As we demonstrate in Section 5.2, decomposition methods isolate submodels that can be rapidly analyzed by heuristics and other fast algorithms.

Fourth, the unified optimization methodology includes procedures for systematically computing lower bounds on the cost of a minimal solution, thereby allowing computation to be terminated with a proven, demonstrably good solution. Although there is no guarantee that a tight bound will always be obtained within a fixed computation time, it provides the human scheduler with critical information about whether or not, or when, to terminate computation. Fifth, the unified optimization methodology facilitates the use of an advanced start for today's operational planning problem based on previous solutions of the problem and other problem-specific information.

In Section 5.1 we discuss problem-specific and general-purpose heuristics and illustrate them by analyzing submodels arising in and solutions to the local delivery problem. An overview of the unified optimization methodology is presented in Section 5.2 where we examine its application to a class of production scheduling problems. In Section 5.3, we return to the local delivery problem and illustrate a numerical application of the united optimization methodology to its solution. Similarly, in Section 5.4, we return to the production scheduling model and illustrate a numerical application of the unified optimization methodology to its solution. The chapter concludes with final thoughts in Section 5.5 about the unified optimization methodology.

5.1 Heuristic Methods for Combinatorial Optimization Problems

Heuristic methods are myopic search methods that attempt to quickly find a good solution to a decision problem. They may be **problem specific** or **general purpose.** Problem-specific heuristics use rules of thumb about a given decision problem in trying to determine a good, feasible solution. They are not guaranteed to find an optimal solution or even a feasible solution to the problem. General-purpose heuristics are methods for intelligently searching the space of feasible solutions; they may be combined with problem-specific heuristics to improve their effectiveness.

Heuristics are usually applied to **combinatorial optimization problems,** which involve the selection of an optimal combination of objects from a discrete set of possible objects.[2] Examples are a combination of approximately 20 customers that a vehicle should visit on its delivery route, which is selected from a set of 1000 customers, or a combination of approximately 50 routes in the delivery plan for all 1000 customers, which is selected from a set of 10^{10} possible routes. Another example is the combination of approximately 15 products to manufacture on a machine this week, which is selected from a set of 200 products or the selection of 200 production schedules over the planning horizon, one for each product, which is selected from a set of 10^{12} possible schedules. The fact that the set of possible objects is discrete (finite), although often astronomical in size, implies that we cannot use global search and optimization methods based on calculus, at least not directly.

Most, if not virtually all, combinatorial optimization problems can be formulated as mixed integer programming models, although some formulations are awkward and difficult to optimize by standard mixed integer programming methods. Fortunately, good heuristics are available for many combinatorial optimization

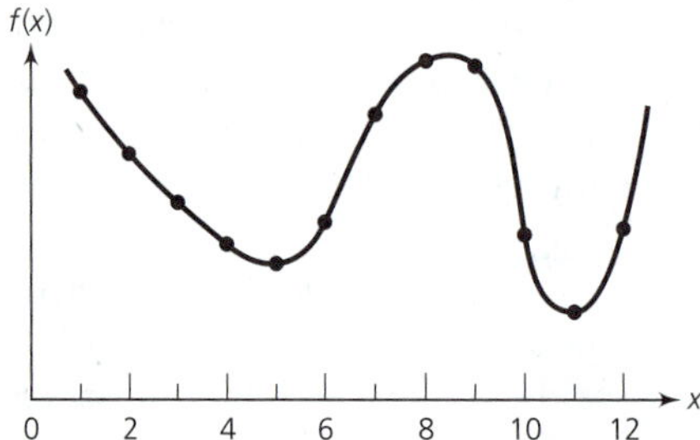

Figure 5.1
One-dimensional discrete optimization problem

problems that are poorly formulated as mixed integer programming models. Conversely, as we shall discuss when constructing the unified optimization methodology, linear and mixed integer programming methods can rigorously optimize constraints that are poorly handled by heuristic methods.

Unlike methods of mixed integer programming, the search methods of heuristics can become trapped at a local optimum. A simple, one-dimensional example is shown in Figure 5.1. The decision variable x is constrained to take on integer values between 2 and 12. If a search begins with $x = 5$, it will detect that this point is a (local) minimum of $f(x)$ because its value increases at both $x = 4$ and $x = 6$. Thus, the search has no local information for continuing its analysis. Nevertheless, the point $x = 11$ is a global minimum of $f(x)$; the only way to guarantee that it is found is to test $f(x)$ for all feasible values of x.

The discrete nature of combinatorial optimization problems illustrated by this example does not allow an application of properties based on calculus characterizing necessary and sufficient conditions for a global optimum. For the example of Figure 5.1, if a continuous value of x that minimizes $f(x)$ were being sought, it would suffice in seeking an optimal solution to check values of $f(x)$ where its derivative vanishes and at the end points of the interval $2 \leq x \leq 12$. Of course, we might well use this information about the continuous problem to initialize the search for an optimal solution to the integer problem.

Local Delivery Heuristics

Problem-specific and general-purpose heuristics are illustrated by examining a numerical example of the local delivery problem. In particular, we analyze the local delivery problem faced by Chemtech, a distribution company that acquires chemicals in bulk from manufacturers and sells them in small quantities to its customers. Chemtech has more than 50 depots located around the United States from which it makes its local deliveries.

Details of Chemtech's Local Delivery Problem. Figure 5.2 depicts the location of 13 customers requiring deliveries on a particular day and the depot that serves them. For future reference, Table 5.1 gives the distance from the depot to each customer and from each customer to every other customer. By company policy, trucks may not travel distances greater than 60 miles between successive customers. Because the

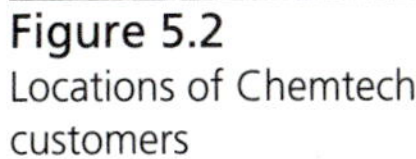

Figure 5.2
Locations of Chemtech customers

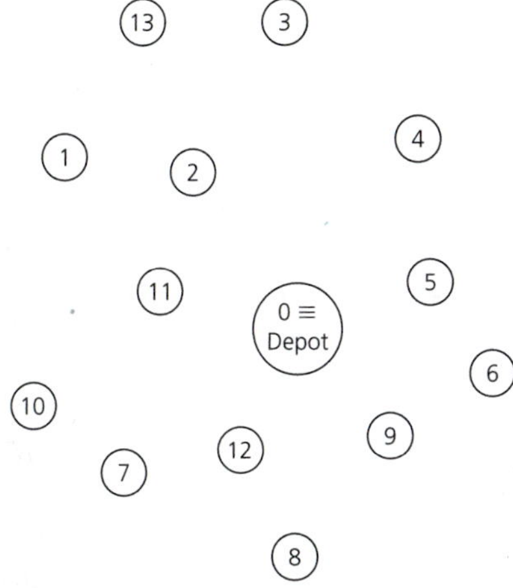

Table 5.1 Distance matrix for Chemtech local delivery problem

	1	**2**	**3**	**4**	**5**	**6**	**7**	**8**	**9**	**10**	**11**	**12**	**13**
0	45	31	47	34	19	30	32	35	20	42	16	19	50
1		21	43	55	58	x	49	x	x	35	24	54	23
2			27	29	38	56	48	x	50	44	21	45	21
3				33	50	x	x	x	x	x	52	x	22
4					19	36	x	x	45	x	47	56	45
5						18	56	50	25	x	41	40	56
6							59	44	17	x	55	41	x
7								30	41	18	43	18	x
8									25	50	48	17	x
9										56	42	23	x
10											24	35	56
11												29	38
12													x

x = greater than 60 miles; direct travel not allowed.

distances are symmetric, that is, the distance from customer i to customer j equals the distance from customer j to customer i, we provide only the distance d_{ij} between customer i and customer j for $i < j$.

The demand for product is given in Table 5.2; orders may not be split among two or more trucks. To make its deliveries, Chemtech has at its disposal an unlimited number of trucks with capacities of 10 tons. Each truck costs \$100 per day in overhead expense to put on the road (replacement cost, insurance, etc.). In addition, there is a direct cost of \$1 per mile (driver's wages and benefits, gasoline, etc.) to operate the truck. Chemtech seeks a set of routes such that all customer demands are met at minimal total cost.

Table 5.2 Customer demands

Customer	1	2	3	4	5	6	7	8	9	10	11	12	13
Tons	3	5	5	4	2	2	6	8	3	3	7	4	3

For this local delivery problem, a **feasible routing solution** comprises a collection of **feasible routes,** which are truck routes that leave the depot with 10 tons, or less, of product, make deliveries to one or more customers, do not visit consecutive customers who are more than 60 miles apart, and return to the depot. In a feasible routing solution every customer is visited exactly once by some feasible route. Like many operational planning problems, the local delivery problem faced by Chemtech is more complicated than it might appear at first glance.

In particular, it is an example of a combinatorial optimization problem involving the selection of combinations of customers to be visited by feasible routes and the selection of a combination of feasible routes in a feasible routing solution. The number of possible combinations grows exponentially as a function of the problem's dimensions. Even for the small Chemtech problem, there are approximately 750 feasible routes. As a result, models of industrial strength problems can be very complex. The practical application of optimization techniques to their analysis can seek only to find demonstrably good, rather than, optimal solutions.

Problem-Specific Heuristics. Our purpose in this section is to analyze Chemtech's local delivery problem using heuristics. In Section 5.3, we combine the heuristics with linear and mixed integer programming methods to more fully optimize the problem. Before stating the problem-specific heuristic we will use, we note that implicit in its analysis is the need to solve the following well-known combinatorial optimization problem:

> **The Traveling Salesperson Problem:** Starting at city 1, a traveling salesperson seeks a route that visits $K-1$ other cities exactly once and returns to city 1 while traveling a minimal distance.

The traveling salesperson problem has been well studied by researchers because it is so easy to state but difficult to optimize exactly when the number of cities exceeds 50.[3] It can be described in at least three distinct ways as a mixed integer programming model. It can also be optimized using dynamic programming, which is a clever, recursive computational method that bears a resemblance to some heuristic methods, except it is more rigid and designed to find an optimal route.[4]

Effective heuristics have been developed for quickly finding good solutions to the traveling salesperson problem. We encounter this problem in analyzing the local delivery problem when we select a combination of customers to be visited by a truck. The selection is constrained by the capacity of the truck. Assuming this constraint is satisfied, because the cost of the route in which the customers are visited depends on the total distance traveled, we solve a traveling salesperson problem in which the salesperson starts at the depot, visits the customers assigned to the route, and returns to the depot. This computation minimizes the total distance traveled, and therefore the cost.

For the stated vehicle routing problem, we apply the following:

> **Heuristic:** Send a truck from the depot to any unserved customer. Then send the truck to the nearest unserved neighbor such that the neighbor is within 60 miles, and the capacity of the truck is not violated.
>
> Continue until the truck has been completely filled or there are no unserved neighbors that the truck is allowed to visit. Return the truck to the depot. Record the resulting feasible route.
>
> Repeat for another truck until there are no unserved customers. For each feasible route in the resulting feasible routing solution, solve a traveling salesperson problem to determine the sequence for visiting customers assigned to the route that minimizes the total distance traveled. Exit with the indicated feasible routing solution.

Note that the postprocessing step of this heuristic in which we determine a traveling salesperson solution for each feasible route may itself involve a heuristic that quickly determines a good but not necessarily minimal distance route for visiting the assigned customers.

Note also that the heuristic can be modified to allow any unserved customer to be the first customer included in each new route. By repeating it with a different rule for selecting the first customer in a route, the heuristic may be used to generate multiple feasible routing solutions. In such a case, we would, of course, select the solution with the lowest total cost, which equals the sum of the costs of the individual routes. At any point during analysis of the problem, we refer to the best-known feasible routing solution as the **incumbent;** we refer to its cost as the **incumbent cost** and denote it by z_{INC}.

In general, we cannot guarantee that a heuristic will find a feasible solution or, indeed, if such a solution exists for the scheduling problem at hand. If, for example, we had imposed a constraint in the Chemtech problem that no more than five trucks may be used, we would be unable to find a feasible routing solution because the total capacity of the five trucks is 50 tons, whereas the total demand of all 13 orders is 55 tons. But, because we allowed the use of an unlimited number of trucks, we can be sure that a feasible routing solution exists and that such solutions may be easily identified.

Using only the heuristic, we have no information about the difference between z_{INC} and z_{MIN}, the cost of the minimal cost solution, which makes it difficult to assess the quality of the solutions. In fact, the search for z_{MIN} is ephemeral because, regardless of the techniques that we apply, we cannot expect to find an optimal solution to an industrial strength local delivery problem and prove that it is optimal. The number of possible routing solutions for such a problem is much too large, although it is finite. Nevertheless, because it incorporates a technique for computing lower bounds on z_{MIN}, the unified optimization methodology provides the means for terminating computation with a demonstrably good solution.

Example 5.1

We demonstrate the application of the heuristic given above to the generation of a feasible routing solution. The first customer of each route is the unserved one that is nearest the depot. Thus, we select customer 11 as the first customer on the first route. We then consider sending the truck to customer 2, the nearest neighbor of customer 11. This move is not allowed because the sum of demands of customers 11 and 2 is 12 tons, which violates the capacity of the truck. As a result, we consider sending the truck to customer 10, who is the next nearest neighbor of customer 11. This move is permissible because the sum of demands of customers 11 and 10 is 10 tons. This assignment of customers fills the truck to capacity and we send it back to the depot.

Thus, our first feasible route visits the nodes 0-11-10-0 with a cost = 100 + 16 + 24 + 42 = $182. (Because it visits only two customers, either of the two sequences is an optimal traveling salesperson route.) In this sum, 100 is the fixed cost, 16 is the mileage cost (16 miles * $1/mile) for the move from the depot 0 to customer 11, 24 is the mileage cost for the move from customer 11 to customer 10, and 42 is the mileage cost for the move from customer 10 to the depot 0. We continue applying the heuristic and obtain the following:

Feasible Routing Solution 1 from Heuristic

Route	Customers	Cost ($)
1	0-11-10-0	182
2	0-5-6-9-0	174
3	0-12-7-0	169
4	0-2-1-0	197
5	0-4-3-0	214
6	0-8-0	170
7	0-13-0	200
Total cost of feasible routing solution		1306

This solution is our first incumbent solution.

In selecting the first customer of each of the routes in feasible solution 1, we chose the unserved customer nearest the depot. We generate feasible solution 2 by choosing the first customer on each route to be the unserved customer that is farthest from the depot. To create an unambiguous labeling of the routes for further analysis, the first route of the heuristic on this second pass is called route 8. We continue to add new labels except when a route duplicates an earlier one, in which case we use the previous label. Thus, the second solution is as follows:

Feasible Routing Solution 2 from Heuristic

Route	Customers	Cost ($)
8	0-13-3-5-0	241
9	0-1-2-6-0	252
10	0-10-7-0	192
6	0-8-0	170
11	0-4-9-0	199
12	0-12-0	138
13	0-11-0	132
Total cost of feasible routing solution		1324

Feasible solution 2 does not replace the incumbent because it is more costly. The two feasible solutions are quite different except for repetition of the route 0-8-0. We could continue to generate feasible solutions based on other variations of the heuristic, but we choose for pedagogical reasons to omit further analysis.

Application of General-Purpose Heuristic. Theoretical and practical difficulties in optimizing combinatorial problems have fostered considerable research into heuristics that perform an intelligent search of the space of discrete solutions to a given problem. These methods begin with a solution, which may or may not be feasible, and attempt to improve it, either to find a new solution that is closer to being feasible if the given solution is infeasible or to find a new solution with lower cost if the given solution is feasible in a minimization problem. (We assume for convenience that all operational planning problems to be considered in this chapter have cost minimization as their objective.) Some methods are clever generalizations of neighborhood search methods that occasionally allow cost to increase when moving to a new solution to escape from a local, but not global, minimum. Although some general-purpose heuristics can theoretically extend their search until a global optimal solution is found, procedures based on these properties are difficult to apply in practice.[5]

It is beyond the scope of this book to review these general-purpose heuristics. Instead, we provide an example of a **genetic algorithm,** perhaps the most popular class of heuristics for analyzing combinatorial optimization problems arising in supply chain management. The term *genetic algorithm* connotes an analogy to selective breeding of plants or animals that seeks to create offspring with improved characteristics by controlling the way in which parents' chromosomes are combined.[6] The connection to a combinatorial optimization problem is to think of solutions to it as comprising chromosomes.

A genetic algorithm attempts to improve on a pair of solutions (the parents) by a *crossover* or exchange of chromosomes that, it is hoped, creates a new and improved solution (the offspring). Occasionally, the algorithm invokes a *mutation* of a chromosome in a given solution by randomly modifying it. Mutations are needed to escape from local optima. Both crossovers and mutations are invoked probabilistically because their value is uncertain. This allows variations in offsprings, with the fittest surviving to breed even better offspring. The likelihood that a chromosome is included in an offspring solution depends on its underlying *fitness value*, which is defined relative to the objective of the optimization. In this way, the general-purpose method reflects problem-specific goals.

Chromosomes are viewed as instances of underlying schemata, which can be thought of as defining subsets of similar chromosomes. For example, the route 0-13-3-5-0 from feasible solution 2 is an instance of the underlying scheme *-13-3-* where customers 3 and 13 are likely to be visited together because they are located near one another and their combined demand almost fills a truck. Theoretical properties of genetic algorithms are related to properties of schemata. A genetic algorithm will work best for a combinatorial optimization problem where short, low-order schemata are readily identified as building blocks and combined with each other to create steadily improving solutions.

We illustrate the spirit of a genetic algorithm by performing crossover operations on the two feasible solutions found above to Chemtech's local delivery problem. We have listed the two solutions at the top of Table 5.3 where the routes in each solution have been reordered by descending value of their dollar cost per delivered ton. This parameter is a good measure of the quality of each route; we use it as its fitness value.

In performing crossover analysis of the routes in the two solutions, we attach a probability of accepting each route based on its fitness value. Specifically, we compute this probability by

$$P(x) = \mathrm{K}e^{-\lambda x} \text{ for } x \geq 15$$

where $K = 1.953$ and $\lambda = 0.04463$. These parameters were chosen so that $P(15) = 1.0$, $P(x)$ decreases with increasing x, and $P(20) = 0.80$. The rationale behind these choices is the following. Experience with Chemtech's local delivery problem indicates that x will always be greater than 15. Any route with a fitness value approaching 15 should have a very high probability of being selected in a crossover solution. Similarly, routes with a fitness value of 20 are quite good and should be selected in a crossover solution with a fairly high probability, which we took to be 0.80. The parameters K and λ were chosen to fit the function to these two points.

We create a combined solution from the two feasible solutions by selecting routes according to P(select), their probability of selection. As shown at the top of Table 5.3, we have ordered the routes by their fitness value and computed P(select), their probabilities of selection according to the above formula. Specifically, a route is selected for potential inclusion in the crossover analysis if its P(select) value is at least as great as the random probability on the corresponding row in the spreadsheet. The random probabilities were drawn from a table of random numbers between 1 and 100. However, the route is not included in the combined solution if it visits a customer that has already been covered by an earlier route selected for the combined solution. For example, the route 0-11-0 overlaps with the route 0-11-10-0 selected earlier, and therefore it is not included in the combined solution.

Table 5.3 Genetic algorithm applied to local delivery problem

	A	B	C	D	E	F	G
1				**Routes Ordered by Fitness Value**			
2	Selection				Delivered	Cost/	
3	Order		Route	Cost	Tons	Delivery Ton	P(select)
4	1	route 3	0-12-7-0	169	10	16.90	0.92
5	2	route 1	0-11-10-0	182	10	18.20	0.87
6	3	route 13	0-11-0	132	7	18.86	0.84
7	4	route 6	0-8-0	170	8	21.25	0.76
8	5	route 10	0-10-7-0	192	9	21.33	0.75
9	6	route 5	0-4-3-0	214	9	23.78	0.68
10	7	route 8	0-13-3-5-0	241	10	24.10	0.67
11	8	route 4	0-2-1-0	197	8	24.63	0.65
12	9	route 2	0-5-6-9-0	174	7	24.86	0.64
13	10	route 9	0-1-2-6-0	252	10	25.20	0.63
14	11	route 11	0-4-9-0	199	7	28.43	0.55
15	12	route 12	0-12-0	138	4	34.50	0.42
16	13	route 7	0-13-0	200	3	66.67	0.10
17							
18							
19				**Crossover Analysis**			
20	Selection		Random			Overlap	Include
21	Order		Probability	Route	Cost	Earlier Route?	Route?
22	1	route 3	0.69	0-12-7-0	169	no	yes
23	2	route 1	0.56	0-11-10-0	182	no	yes
24	3	route 13	0.3	0-11-0	132	yes	no
25	4	route 6	0.32	0-8-0	170	no	yes
26	5	route 10	0.66	0-10-7-0	192	yes	no
27	6	route 5	0.79	0-4-3-0	x	x	no
28	7	route 8	0.55	0-13-3-5-0	241	no	yes
29	8	route 4	0.24	0-2-1-0	197	no	yes
30	9	route 2	0.80	0-5-6-9-0	x	x	no
31	10	route 9	0.35	0-1-2-6-0	252	yes	no
32	11	route 11	0.10	0-4-9-0	199	no	yes
33	12	route 12	0.98	0-12-0	x	x	no
34	13	route 7	0.92	0-13-0	x	x	no
35							
36					x = Rejected by Probability Test		
37							
38							
39		**New Feasible**					
40		**Solution**					
41				route 3	0-12-7-0	169	
42				route 1	0-11-10-0	182	
43				route 6	0-8-0	170	
44				route 8	0-13-3-5-0	241	
45				route 4	0-2-1-0	197	
46				augmented route 11*	0-4-6-9-0	207	
47					Total Cost	1166	
48							
49					*customer 6 was added to route 11 (0-4-9-0).		

Upon completion of the combined solution, we have selected six routes (routes 3, 1, 6, 8, 4, 11) that cover 12 of the 13 customers in the local delivery problem. The only orphan, or unassigned customer, is customer 6. We attempt to complete the solution by assigning the orphan(s) to selected routes. If any orphans are left after such assignments, we apply the heuristic to route them.

In this case, the orphan could be assigned to routes 6, 4, or 11. The most efficient assignment in terms of total cost is to assign customer 6 to route 11, creating the augmented route 11. This new route can be viewed as a mutation of the original chromosome route 11. The result is a new feasible solution with a total cost of \$1166, which is significantly better than the previous incumbent (feasible solution 1) with a cost of \$1306.

One numerical example does not validate a theory. Still, the example illustrates how blending crossovers from significantly different parents (feasible routing solutions) can yield an offspring (another feasible routing solution) of superior quality. Note also that subjective artistry was required in selecting *P*(select); at the same time, randomness worked in our favor in blending the crossovers. Because the computation is very simple, we can see that the crossover analysis could be applied hundreds of times a minute to a large-scale problem. Fortuitous blending of good solutions into better solutions need only occur a few times to obtain an apparently good solution.

5.2 Overview of the Unified Optimization Methodology

In this section, we provide an overview of a unified optimization methodology that combines mathematical decomposition methods with heuristics. A decomposition method breaks a large-scale, monolithic mixed integer programming model down into several submodels that are much easier to optimize. The method then iteratively reassembles subplans from these submodels in seeking an optimal, global plan; that is, an optimal solution to the original, monolithic model.[7]

By customizing the methodology to a supply chain problem and a model for analyzing it, the system developer is motivated to design and implement a modeling system that will reliably and quickly produce demonstrably good plans. The methodology is intended for those applications, arising especially in operational planning, for which the computational effort required to extract an optimal, or demonstrably good, solution from a monolithic mixed integer programming model would be prohibitive. Moreover, these are applications involving resource allocation decisions and other cross-cutting or, systemwide, constraints that cannot be effectively analyzed by heuristics alone.

Admittedly, the methodology is complicated and requires perseverance by the system developer to achieve success. Nevertheless, assuming the implementation project has sufficient resources and the commitment of the company's management, the likelihood of success should be very high. Notable applications in vehicle routing, personnel scheduling, and production planning have already been recorded.[8]

In the following subsection, we illustrate the application of a decomposition method to a production scheduling model. We generalize constructions from this method in presenting the unified optimization methodology in the subsection after that. In the following two sections, we apply the methodology to numerical problems arising in vehicle routing and production scheduling.

Production Scheduling Example of Decomposition

Because decomposition methods are intricate, we discuss a concrete application before presenting the general unified optimization methodology based on them. In particular, we apply a decomposition method to the monolithic, discrete parts production scheduling model depicted in Figure 5.3.[9] A numerical version of this model will be analyzed in Section 5.4. As shown, the model addresses production/inventory scheduling decisions for N items over a multiple-week planning horizon where the items must share, or compete for, scarce machine resources. Here items refer to specific products or SKUs. An individual item is produced intermittently with a setup preceding the manufacture of a variable number, called the **production lot size** of the item. Zero-one variables and fixed charge constraints of the type discussed in Section 4.1 are used to capture fixed costs and lumpy resource utilization due to setups. Balance equations of the type discussed in Section 3.1 are used to keep track of item inventories.

If an item is produced in a particular week, it uses machine resources that are a function of its setup time and its production rate. For each week, the sum of resource use across all items produced that week cannot exceed the available machine capacity. Such a model would be used to analyze discrete parts scheduling problems arising, for example, in the manufacture of tires, semiconductors, plastic products, or consumer durables.

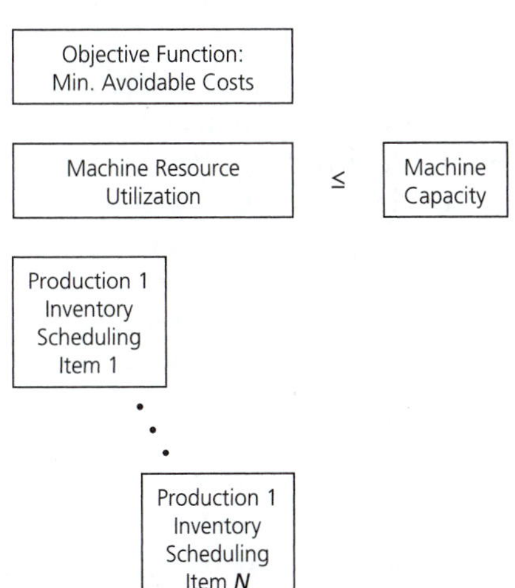

Figure 5.3
Discrete parts production scheduling problem as monolithic mixed integer programming model

For a 13-week planning horizon problem involving 500 items, the model would require 6500 zero-one setup variables. Other 0-1 variables and constraints might be needed to capture make-or-buy decisions or economies of scale in production. The number of constraint equations could easily exceed 20,000. In short, the mixed integer programming model would be large and probably difficult to optimize. Assuming that the production manager would want to exercise the model every week on a rolling-horizon basis, a decomposition approach could ensure that a demonstrably good plan would be quickly and reliably obtained.

Recall that a rolling horizon is a planning horizon of fixed length that is used in constructing the model each time it is exercised. Thus, period 2 from the previous model becomes period 1, period 3 becomes period 2, and so on. The final period of the new model is an addition to the old model.

A decomposition approach is motivated by the observation that the production/inventory scheduling submodels for individual items could be easily optimized if it were not for the machine resource constraints that link them. If we could accurately "price out" the machine resource constraints, we could optimize the schedule of each item separately from all others. By price out, we mean charge the production/inventory model of each item with a cost ($/hour) for machine resources consumed in each week, effectively converting constraints to objective function terms. The difficulty is that we have no idea what prices to charge for machine use. Arbitrary prices, or even educated guesses, can easily lead to production/inventory schedules for the items that, taken together, seriously violate capacity in some weeks and fall far short of capacity in other weeks.

The decomposition method depicted in Figure 5.4 resolves this difficulty. As shown, the method is initialized with input data to the master model extracted from several **feasible item schedules.** A feasible item schedule consists of weekly decisions regarding production and inventory such that demand for the item is met. Any constraints on production and inventory for that item, such as limits on the quantity that might be produced in a single run, are also met. A **feasible plan** is a collection of feasible item schedules with the property that the sum of the requirements each week on machine resources by feasible item schedules does not exceed machine capacity for that week.

For a significant proportion of operational planning problems, feasibility of the real-world problem and that of the optimization model representing it are serious concerns. Some companies find that they have committed to short-term orders beyond their capacity to produce, at least without the absorption of large avoidable costs for overtime or outsourcing. Because these companies will stay in business after the planning horizon has ended, at least for a while, their scheduling problems are not truly infeasible. They must therefore develop plans for late delivery of some orders or the expenditure of otherwise avoidable costs in trying to mitigate their poor performance. To simplify our discussion here, however, we assume model feasibility is attainable.

The trial feasible item schedules shown in Figure 5.4 might be constructed manually, by automated routines based on heuristics, or some combination of the two. For each schedule, the input data are the avoidable costs of the schedule, such as for setups and inventory, and its machine use by weeks over the planning horizon. The decision variable associated with the feasible item schedule is a nonnegative

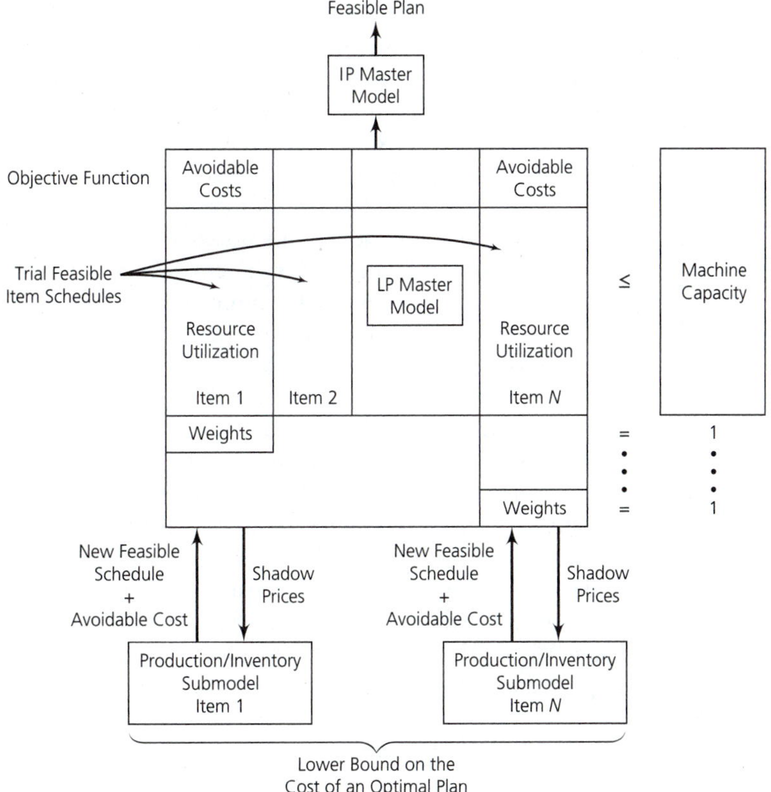

Figure 5.4
Decomposition scheme for the discrete parts production scheduling model

weight, which represents the fraction of that schedule that the model wishes to select. For each item, the sum of the weights over the schedules must equal 1.

The master model may be solved as a linear programming model (the LP master model), where the schedule weights are allowed to take on any values between and including 0 and 1. We say that a **pure plan** has been selected for an item if one feasible item schedule weight equals 1, and therefore all other weights are 0; otherwise, we say a **mixed plan** has been selected. A mixed plan cannot be implemented because it involves an illegal splitting of setups. For example, suppose the mixed plan for an item involves two schedules, each with a weight of 0.5, where schedule 1 has a setup in period 1 and not in period 2, whereas schedule 2 has a setup period in period 2 and not in period 1. The mixed plan suggests, in effect, that the production manager should make half a setup in each of periods 1 and 2. Such a conflict is the result of tight resources in periods 1 and 2.

Alternatively, the master model may be solved as a mixed integer programming model (the IP master model), where the schedule weights must take on values either of 0 or 1; that is, only pure, implementable plans are allowed for each item. The purpose of the LP master model is to select optimal combinations of the feasible item schedules and, in the process, to produce optimal shadow prices on machine resources and on the weight constraints, which will be used to generate new feasible schedules. The purpose of the IP master model is to determine the best feasible plan from the known feasible item schedules by selecting a pure plan for each item. This best feasible schedule may not be optimal because the IP master model has not considered all possible feasible item schedules for each item.

Assuming for expositional convenience that there is one machine capacity constraint for each week t, we let π_t denote the shadow price obtained by optimizing the LP master model. Similarly, for each item i, we let θ_i denote the shadow price on the equation constraining the weights for item i to equal 1. The decomposition method proceeds by passing these shadow prices to the production/inventory submodels. There is one such submodel for each item. Without the shadow prices, the objective function of each submodel is the minimization of avoidable direct production and inventory costs associated with the item. The shadow prices are used to add a resource cost, π_t* machines hours for machine hours consumed in week t in producing item i. For each feasible schedule, we call this augmented cost the **resource adjusted cost.** It can be demonstrated that θ_i equals the resource adjusted cost of the one or more feasible item schedules for item i in the LP master model that have minimal resource adjusted cost. These schedules include all schedules with positive weights in the optimal solution to the master LP model.

Each submodel is a simple mixed integer programming model that is easily and rapidly optimized to produce a feasible item schedule with minimal resource adjusted cost, which we consider adding to the LP master model. As described below, we test this new feasible item schedule to see if the LP master model could be improved by using it.

> **Test for a New Feasible Item Schedule:** For each item i, solve an optimization model to compute the minimal resource adjusted cost. Letting
>
> $$\Delta_i = \text{minimal resource adjusted cost} - \theta_i$$
>
> we add the new feasible schedule to the LP master model if $\Delta_i < 0$ because then the schedule is more cost effective than any of the current feasible schedules for item i in the model. When we reoptimize the LP master model with this new schedule, we can be sure that the optimal solution to the LP master model will change.
>
> Conversely, if $\Delta_i = 0$ (it can be shown that Δ_i can never be positive), we do not add the new feasible schedule for item $_i$ to the LP master model because it is not more cost effective than the feasible schedules already included in the master. Finally, if $\Delta_i = 0$ for all items i, decomposition between the LP master model and the submodels is terminated because analysis has determined that, for all items, no new feasible schedules exist that can improve the optimal solution to the LP master model.

In addition to suggesting new feasible item solutions for the LP master model, solution of the N submodels, one for each item, yields a lower bound on the cost of an optimal solution in the original mixed integer programming model. We use the notation LB_π to designate this lower bound, where the subscript indicates that the lower bound depends on the shadow prices π_t on the resource constraints.

Lower Bound Computation: Solution of the submodels yields a lower bound on z_{MIN}, which is the cost of an optimal solution to the discrete parts production scheduling model. This lower bound LB_π is

$$\text{Minimal objective function cost of LP master model} + \Delta_1 + \Delta_2 + \cdots + \Delta_N$$

Remember that all the Δ_i are nonpositive, and therefore the lower bound is less than or equal to the minimal objective function cost of the LP master model. Each time the LP master model and the N submodels are optimized, a new bound is determined. Because these bounds may not increase at each iteration, we must record the highest lower bound, which is the bound we use in deciding when to terminate computation with a demonstrably good plan.

An issue in applying this decomposition method is when to optimize the IP master model to determine a feasible plan for the production scheduling model. Ideally, we would like to optimize the IP master model once and then be able to terminate computation because the gap between its objective function cost and the highest lower bound is sufficiently small to declare the feasible plan demonstrably good. This fortuitous event might greatly reduce total computation time, but it may not occur very often. Thus, experimentation is needed for each implementation of the unified optimization methodology to determine the frequency of IP master model solutions.

The final important point to make about the decomposition method just outlined is that heuristics can and should be applied in several ways to speed up the computation. First, heuristics are needed to initialize the LP master model. The goal is to provide the LP master model with a range of good feasible schedules for each item. The intended effect of such an initialization is to produce an initial set of shadow prices that is not too far from a set providing the greatest lower bound. In Section 5.4, we present and discuss specific heuristics for this production scheduling problem. Second, heuristics may be developed to generate feasible schedules for the LP master model in addition to those identified by optimizing the production/inventory submodels. Such heuristics might entail refinements of feasible schedules from the submodels based on how well they performed in the iterative versions of the LP master model. Because linear programming computation times depend primarily on the number of equations in the model, and very weakly on the number of variables, the addition of heuristically derived feasible schedules would not seriously slow down computation. Finally, heuristics can and should be applied to optimizing the IP master model; we present one such heuristic in Section 5.4.

Unified Optimization Methodology

In this subsection, we generalize the discussion of the previous subsection in describing the unified optimization methodology for operational planning problems. The key elements of the methodology are depicted in Figure 5.5. We begin by decomposing a monolithic mixed integer programming model into an **LP master model** and a number of **Lagrangean submodels,** a term that we will explain in a moment.

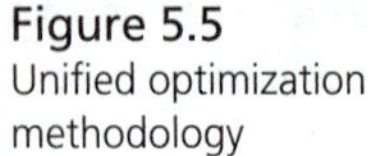

Figure 5.5
Unified optimization methodology

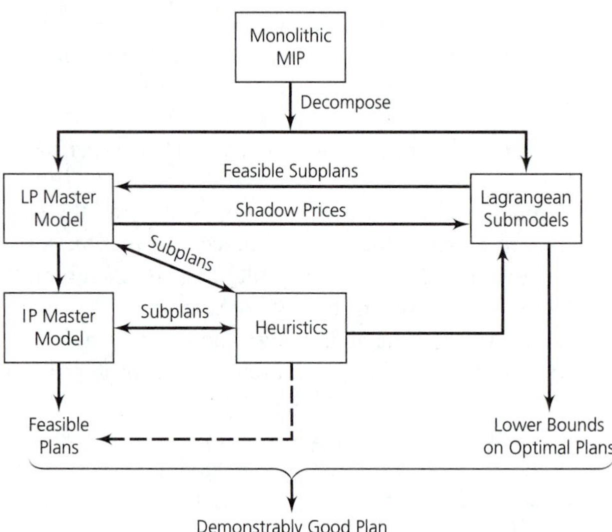

The assumption is that the monolithic mixed integer programming model is too large and complex to be optimized "as is" for operational planning under time-critical conditions. In any event, regardless of the model's complexity and our approach to extracting useful solutions from it, it is important that we begin analysis of an operational planning problem with an accurate and complete monolithic model. Such an approach requires and ensures that all important decision options, constraints, and objectives of the manager or managers responsible for the operational planning problem have been identified and incorporated.

The spirit of the decomposition is to place resource capacity and other **cross-cutting constraints**, those that pertain to large parts of the operational system, or all of it, in the LP master model. This allows the methodology to separately and independently optimize the Lagrangean submodels. Moreover, in most applications, very efficient algorithms or heuristic methods are available to optimize the smaller and mathematically simpler submodels. The production/inventory submodels discussed in the previous section are examples. We refer to the submodels as *Lagrangean* because the shadow prices used to convey information about charges for cross-cutting constraints are Lagrange multipliers, mathematical elements invented by the French mathematician Joseph Louis Lagrange in the early 19th century.[10]

The goal of the unified optimization methodology is to identify a demonstrably good **feasible plan** for the operational problem; that is, a feasible plan whose cost is within acceptable limits of the cost of an optimal solution to the original mixed integer programming model. Although, we will probably never know this minimal cost, the methodology develops lower bounds to it. A feasible plan comprises **feasible subplans** determined by optimizing the Lagrangean submodels. A feasible plan is a combination of feasible subplans that also satisfies the cross-cutting constraints. As in the previous subsection, we assume for expositional purposes that a feasible plan exists, while recognizing that feasibility may be difficult or impossible to achieve for some operational planning problems.

The LP master model and the Lagrangrean submodels are alternately solved many times. We refer to this method as the **subplan generation procedure.** Each cycle of the procedure, called an **iteration,** begins with the passing of shadow prices from the LP master model to each of the Lagrangean submodels. The Lagrangrean submodels are then optimized to produce new feasible subplans that are passed to the LP master model. For future reference, we note that an optimal solution to each submodel has a minimal reduced cost (see Section 3.4 for a discussion of linear programming reduced costs) among all feasible solutions to the submodel.

At each iteration and for each submodel, the LP master model finds an optimal combination of feasible subplans from among the subplans that have been passed to it. It does this by assigning nonnegative weights summing to 1 for the different subplans. If only one weight is positive, and therefore equal to 1, we say that we have a **pure subplan** for that submodel. If more than one weight is positive, we say that we have a **mixed subplan** for that submodel. In general, the LP master model will find mixed subplans for many of the submodels in the decomposition.

Mixed subplans cannot be implemented in practice. The production manager must select exactly one production schedule for a specific product and the dispatcher must select exactly one route for a specific vehicle. One reason we accept this deficiency of the subplan generation procedure is that, at each iteration, the LP master model produces shadow prices on the cross-cutting constraints that are used in generating useful new feasible subplans for each submodel. If we imposed a 0-1 restriction on the weights, which would guarantee the selection of pure subplans for all submodels, we would lose the ability to compute meaningful shadow prices.

The economic pricing underlying linear programming optimization allows us to test each new feasible subplan against all previously generated subplans for the submodel to determine if it can improve analysis by the LP master model. Specifically, if the reduced cost of the new feasible subplan is negative, it passes the test because when it is added to the LP master model, it can be used to improve the previously optimal solution. We add the subplan to the LP master model by incorporating data describing its impact on the cross-cutting constraints, along with its avoidable cost. The associated decision variable is the weight assigned to the new subplan. If the new subplan does not pass the test, we do not add it to the LP master model. If the test fails for all submodels, we say the subplan generation procedure has **converged,** which means that it can be terminated because, from the perspective of the procedure, there are no new feasible subplans worth computing.

In addition to identifying useful new subplans, each iteration among the LP master model and the submodels provides a lower bound on the cost of an optimal solution in the original, monolithic mixed integer programming model. It can be shown that the LP master model will generate a sequence of shadow prices, or Lagrange multipliers, that converge to an optimal set of multipliers in a so-called **Lagrangean dual problem.** They are optimal in the sense that when used in the submodels, they compute the **greatest lower bound** on the cost of an optimal solution in the monolithic mixed integer programming model.

The greatest lower bound may be strictly less than this optimal cost, in which case we say that there is a **duality gap.** As a practical matter for many applications, we can be optimistic that an optimal, or near optimal, set of multipliers will provide a reasonably tight upper bound. They also are effective in identifying the cross-cutting constraints that are binding in an optimal solution. Finally, they provide insight into the relative importance of the binding constraints based on the magnitude of the absolute value of their multipliers.

Occasionally, we will elect to impose 0-1 constraints on subplan weights, thereby creating the IP master model for which an optimal solution will correspond to a feasible plan. Typically, this will be done when the subplan generation procedure appears to be slowing down as indicated by changes in the optimal solution to the LP master model and the lower bounds. In creating the IP master model, we may elect to drop those subplans in the LP master model that have optimal LP reduced costs above a specified bound. The reasoning is that a subplan with a high LP reduced cost is unlikely to be selected as part of an optimal or demonstrably good plan computed by the IP master model. Moreover, dropping these subplans and their associated weights (variables) will enhance the efficiency of the branch-and-bound method applied to the IP master model. A feasible plan that is optimal in the IP master model may not be optimal in the original mixed integer programming model because the IP master model does not consider all feasible subplans for each submodel. It is hoped that the best known lower bound on the true minimal cost will allow us to terminate with this feasible plan because it is sufficiently good. If not, additional analysis by the subplan generation procedure and the heuristics will be required to create additional feasible subplans for the IP master model, which we would reoptimize.

As shown in Figure 5.5, heuristic methods play a central, complementary role in streamlining the methodology. As discussed in Section 5.1, these are both problem-specific and general-purpose heuristics. First, heuristics can be applied to the submodels to generate trial subplans for initializing the LP master model. The quality of this initialization, as measured by the initial shadow prices, is critical to the efficiency of the subplan generation procedure. If the LP master model is given initial subplans that are inefficient and too narrow in their coverage of the feasible regions of the submodels, the resulting shadow prices will inaccurately reflect the cross-cutting constraints. As a result, they will induce new feasible subplans that are misleading in their treatment of these constraints, and a vicious cycle will be initiated. Theoretically, the methodology will work its way out of this cycle, but, as a practical matter, it may require far too much computational effort.

Second, the heuristic methods may be extended to produce one or more feasible plans by combining feasible subplans. The difficulty of constructing a feasible plan will depend on the specific operational problem being analyzed and the tightness of the cross-cutting constraints. In some cases, a heuristic might produce a feasible plan that is subjectively judged to be sufficiently good and further computation deemed unnecessary, although a lower bound has not been computed. However, the ability of heuristic methods to assemble good feasible plans for operational planning problems with cross-cutting constraints has been oversold. Obviously, our premise in discussing the unified optimization methodology is that many operational planning problems require the analysis it can provide; that is, demonstrably good feasible solutions even when the cross-cutting constraints are tight.

A third potential use of heuristics is to quickly uncover good feasible subplans to the submodels. The choice between a heuristic and a rigorous mathematical programming approach to the submodel depends on the specific structure of the submodel. We will elaborate on this point when we discuss the illustrative applications in the following two sections. In any event, the subplan generation procedure requires only that analysis of the submodel produces a subplan that is better (lower reduced cost) than subplans considered by the LP master model, if one exists. The procedure does not require the identification of a minimal reduced cost subplan, although the lower its cost, the more likely it will have a significant effect on the LP master model. However, if the submodels are not optimized, we cannot compute lower bounds on the true minimal cost.

A fourth potential use of heuristics is to generate more subplans for the LP master model and the IP master model by extending subplans that these models have found attractive to other similar feasible subplans. In this context, attractive refers to their weights in optimal solutions to the master model. Because the computational effort to solve the LP master model is very insensitive to the number of subplans it evaluates, this use of heuristics is particularly attractive as a means to speed up the subplan generation procedure.

5.3 Unified Optimization Methodology Applied to Vehicle Routing

In this section, we illustrate the unified optimization methodology applied to Chemtech's local delivery vehicle routing problem, which was introduced in Section 5.1 where we applied heuristics to compute a feasible routing solution. Recall that we refer to the least cost known feasible solution as the incumbent. We extend that analysis following the logic of the methodology discussed in Section 5.2 and depicted in Figure 5.5.

We begin by describing the IP master model for the local delivery problem, which will find a feasible routing solution that is at least as good as the incumbent because we assume it considers all feasible routes generated by the heuristic. It will find a better solution if some combination of feasible routes not examined by the heuristic solves the routing problem at lower cost. Simply stated, given a collection of feasible routes, the IP master model seeks a minimal cost combination of some of them such that each customer is visited exactly once. We will shortly provide a mathematical statement of this model.

As we discussed in the previous section, the LP master model, which is a relaxation of the IP master model, also provides valuable information for generating new routes and computing lower bounds via a Lagrangean submodel. Specifically, we treat the linear programming shadow prices as rewards for visiting customers and solve a Lagrangean submodel to determine a route that maximizes its net reward, which equals the gross reward for customers visited minus the cost of the route. A lower bound on z_{MIN}, the (unknown) minimal cost of the local delivery problem, can be computed from the maximal net reward. Further details of the Lagrangean submodel and the lower bound calculation will be provided soon.

Statements of the Optimization Models

Our construction of the **local delivery IP master model** employs the following indexes and parameters.[11] Let M be the number of customers with orders to be delivered, which we index by i. Suppose we have somehow generated N feasible routes, which we index by j. We let c_j denote the cost of each route, and let

$$a_{ij} = 1 \quad \text{if route } j \text{ visits customer } i\text{; 0 otherwise}$$

Finally, we define the 0-1 decision variables by

$$x_j = 1 \quad \text{if route j is selected; 0 otherwise}$$

The **local delivery LP master model,** which is a relaxation of this integer programming model, is simply one where we replace the 0-1 definition of each decision variables by

$$0 \leq x_j \leq 1$$

Thus, statements of the local delivery LP and IP master models are shown in Figure 5.6. The objective function in this formulation is to minimize the total cost of the routes selected by the model, with z_{LPN} representing the minimal linear programming cost and z_{IPN} representing the minimal integer programming cost. The subscript N indicates the dependence of the minimal cost on the N routes being considered. Each of the M constraints state that each customer must be visited exactly once by some route. For the integer programming model, this restriction

Figure 5.6
Local delivery LP and IP master models

$$z_{LPN}, z_{IPN} = \min c_1x_1 + c_2x_2 + \cdots + c_Nx_N$$

Subject to

$$\begin{aligned}
a_{11}x_1 + a_{12}x_2 + \cdots + a_{1N}x_N &= 1 \\
a_{21}x_1 + a_{22}x_2 + \cdots + a_{2N}x_N &= 1 \\
&\cdots \\
a_{M1}x_1 + a_{M2}x_2 + \cdots + a_{MN}x_N &= 1
\end{aligned}$$

$$0 \leq x_j \leq 1 \text{ (linear programming)}$$

$$x_j = 0 \text{ or } 1 \text{ (integer programming)}$$

implies, for example, that among the routes j with the property that $a_{ij} = 1$ (routes visiting customer i), we must have exactly one $x_j = 1$. The same is true for all other customers.

The LP and IP (master) models are somewhat different in form from those displayed in Figure 5.4 for analyzing production scheduling problems. (To simplify exposition, we omit further reference to "master" model in this subsection.) Specifically, the local delivery models do not involve constraints summing weights to 1. We are able to construct and employ these simpler models for the local delivery problem because we are not seeking routes for individual trucks, but rather a number of routes for identical trucks.

Because the IP model does not consider all feasible routes, we cannot guarantee that the optimal solution to it will be optimal to the local delivery problem. In other words, all we know is that $z_{\mathrm{IPN}} \geq z_{\mathrm{MIN}}$. Also, because of the way we constructed the IP model, we know it provides us with an incumbent solution; that is $z_{\mathrm{INC}} = z_{\mathrm{IPN}}$. Each time that we solve it, we hope to obtain a new incumbent, but we might not because the routes added since the last time the IP model was solved do not combine well with each other and the previous routes.

In Figure 5.7, we specialize the logic of Figure 5.5 to the local delivery problem. We begin by applying the heuristics to generate one or most feasible routing solutions. The least cost of these solutions is designated the incumbent. We then pass feasible routes generated by the heuristic to the LP model and optimize it. This model seeks to minimize the total cost of routes required to make exactly one visit to each customer but allows unreal combinations such as "use 0.4 of route j and 0.6 of route k." Given such fractions, the unified optimization methodology must include rules deciding whether to proceed with optimization of the IP model or to use the Lagrangean submodel to create an additional route. If it elects to solve the IP model, the branch-and-bound method is employed to eliminate fractions in the linear programming solution. If it elects to create an additional route, it passes the shadow prices on the M constraints in the formulation in Figure 5.6 to the Lagrangean submodel, which we are about to describe.

Because optimizing the IP model will usually require much more computation time than that required to solve the Lagrangean submodel and reoptimize the LP model, we would most of the time direct the unified optimization methodology to create more routes. Conversely, repetitive optimization of the Lagrangean submodel will lead to diminishing returns as reflected by small, but still positive, net rewards of the routes it produces. When this occurs, we would elect to generate and optimize the IP model. We discuss the decision in Figure 5.7 about whether or not to terminate the unified optimization methodology after we discuss the Lagrangean submodel.

For this application, the Lagrangean submodel employs Lagrange multiplier π_i associated with each customer i as a reward for visiting the customer. In the unified optimization methodology, these multipliers are the shadow prices computed by optimizing the LP model. Specifically, we use a dynamic programming (list-processing) algorithm to solve the Lagrangean submodel by computing a feasible route that leaves the depot with 10 tons or less on board, makes deliveries to one

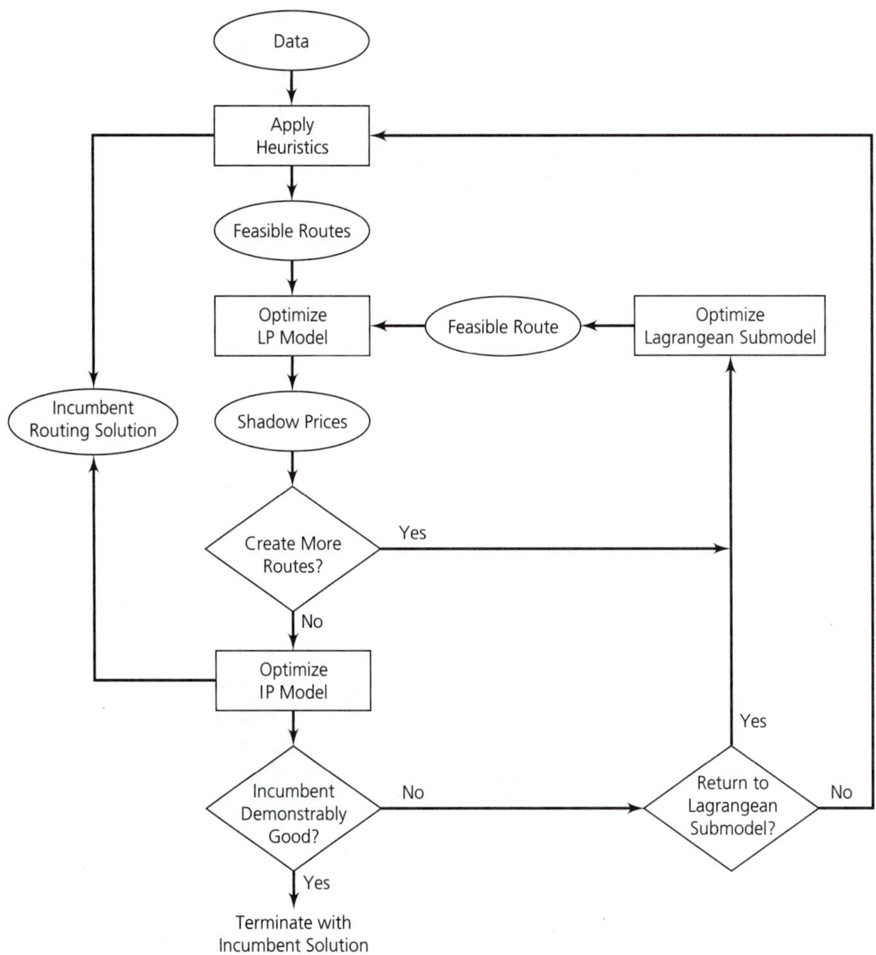

Figure 5.7 Unified optimization methodology for the local delivery problem

or more customers, and then returns empty to the depot. The objective is to maximize the net reward with respect to these multipliers, where net reward = gross reward – cost of the route. The algorithm also ensures that the distance traveled to visit the customers assigned to the route is minimal. The gross reward equals the sum of the multipliers for the customers receiving deliveries. If the net reward of this route is positive, we add the route to the LP model. Alternatively, if the net reward is zero (it will always be nonnegative), there are no improving routes to add to the LP model. We will return shortly to a discussion about how to proceed in this eventuality.

The theory of Lagrangean analysis tells us that the lower bound calculation of the local delivery problem is as follows:

$$z_{\text{MIN}} \geq \text{LB}_\pi = \pi_1 + \pi_2 + \cdots + \pi_M - (\text{maximal net reward}) * V$$

where V is an upper bound on the number of vehicles in an optimal solution. We let LB_π denote the lower bound computed by the Lagrangean submodel. We omit a proof or derivation of this calculation because it is beyond the scope of this book; it suffices to say, however, that the proof is simple but subtle.[12]

The interpretation of the shadow price π_i as a reward for visiting customer i is consistent with our discussion of shadow prices in Section 3.3. From a linear programming viewpoint, the shadow price measures the marginal benefit of lowering the requirement to visit customer i. Here, we make the optimistic approximation that, by delivering to customer i, a new route will reduce total cost by π_i. This is our motivation for using the shadow prices from the LP model as the multipliers in the Lagrangean model.

We let $LB_{\pi N}$ denote the lower bound computed by the Lagrangrean model using the shadow prices from the local delivery linear programming model with the first N routes. The maximal lower bound has been reached when the maximal net reward equals zero, indicating that the LP model cannot be further used to suggest a new route. For industrial strength applications, however, we will rarely attain the maximal lower bound because to do so will require the method to generate an excessive number of routes.

Unfortunately, Lagrangean analysis is imperfect in that the maximal lower bound LB_{MAX} may be strictly less than z_{MIN}. Figure 5.8 illustrates the information that we can obtain from the unified optimization methodology. We assume that the first time we pass feasible routes from the heuristics to the optimization models that all three models are optimized. This produces a linear programming solution, an incumbent with value INC1 computed from the IP model and a lower bound with value LB1 computed from the Lagrangean submodel. Note that INC1 is higher

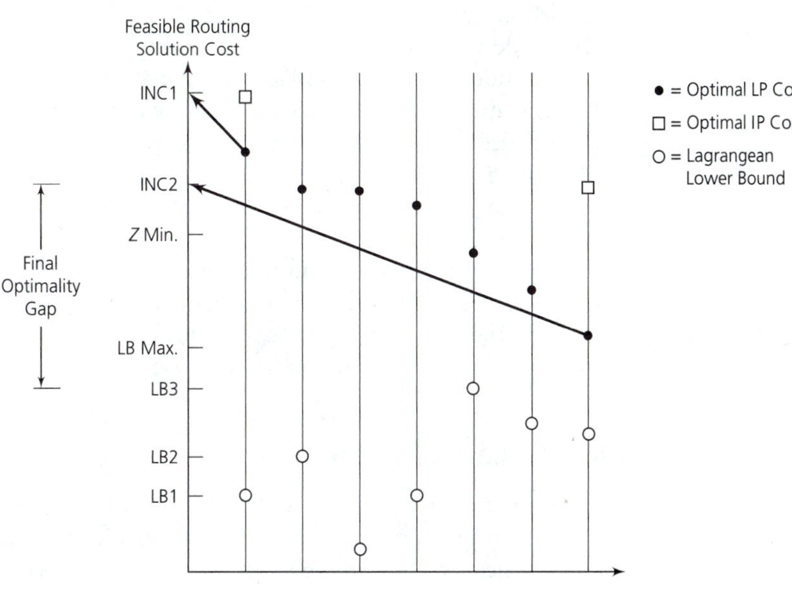

Figure 5.8
Upper and lower bounds produced by unified optimization methodology

than the cost of the linear programming relaxation from which it was derived by the branch-and-bound method. Assuming INC1 – LB1 is too large, we continue the route generation procedure linking the LP Model and the Lagrangean submodel.

Because we are adding routes to the LP model, its objective function cost cannot increase; it may occasionally remain at the same value because it cannot find a way to exploit an attractive new route. The addition of a new route with positive net reward to the LP model, however, always changes the shadow prices it produces because the simplex method will attempt to use the new route to further optimize the LP model. This means that the Lagrangean submodel will be able to find a new route with a positive net reward at the next iteration, if one exists. If no such route exists, $z_{LPN} = LB_{MAX}$ and there is no further use for the Lagrangean submodel.

As shown in Figure 5.8, the lower bounds computed by the Lagrangean submodel do not necessarily increase from one iteration to the next. Thus, we must record the highest known lower bound. Also as indicated by the arrow connecting an optimal LP cost to INC2, we decided after several iterations of the route generation procedure to optimize the IP model, which produces the new incumbent with value INC2. Because the computed optimality gap INC2 – LB3 is sufficiently small, say (INC2 – LB3) / INC2 < 0.10, we terminate with the demonstrably good feasible routing solution.

Although we have computed INC2 and LB3, the values z_{MIN} and LB_{MAX} shown in Figure 5.8 are shrouded in mystery. For most applications, they will never be known. Although we may believe z_{INC} is close to z_{MIN}, say less than 1%, we can only be sure of this if $(z_{INC} - LB_{MAX}) / z_{INC}$ is less than 1%. Conversely, $(z_{INC} - LB_{MAX}) / z_{INC}$ may be large, say 20%, but z_{INC} could actually be very close to z_{MIN}.

In many applications, we can expect that the computed optimality gap will be small or small enough to terminate computation within a reasonable length of time, say 5 to 30 minutes on a high-end PC, depending on the size and complexity of the local delivery problem. Nevertheless, the unified optimization methodology provides for additional analysis of the local delivery problem if the incumbent is deemed not good enough. As shown in Figure 5.7, one option is to return to the Lagrangean submodel and use it to continue finding new routes. Another option is to return to the heuristics and use them to generate new routes. This might entail extending analysis with problem-specific heuristics by incorporating new rules or extending analysis with general-purpose heuristics, like the genetic algorithm, to create new routes from attractive old ones. Alternatively, if we feel compelled to insist on a method that will ultimately find an optimal solution to the problem, we can embed the entire integrated solution methodology in a systematic search of the finite set of routes and routing solutions.[13] As a practical matter, there is little likelihood that a dispatcher would be able to wait for such a search to terminate.

Numerical Solution

We apply the unified optimization methodology to the numerical problem faced by Chemtech, beginning with the routes in the two feasible solutions found in Section 5.1 by the heuristic. According to the methodology, we continue analyzing the local delivery problem by constructing the LP and IP models based on the 13 distinct routes embedded in these feasible solutions. Our formulation is given in Table 5.4, an Excel spreadsheet to which we apply What's Best to optimize the choice of routes. In this spreadsheet, for example, the data for route 1 are entered in column B. The route cost is given in cell B2. The entries in column B on rows 3 through 15 are the values of the a_{1j} for $j = 1, 2, \ldots, 13$. The cells on the select route row correspond to the variables xj associated with selecting route j ($x_j = 1$), not selecting the route j ($x_j = 0$), or in the case of the linear programming model, a value at the two end points or somewhere in between ($0 \leq x_j \leq 1$).

The linear programming solution of the model in Table 5.4 is, by luck, an integer solution. In general, such a fortuitous outcome will occur only rarely. The objective function cost, \$1213, of this routing solution is found in the solution cost cell, which is significantly lower than the cost of either of the two feasible routing solutions determined by the heuristic. The new incumbent routing solution 2 from integer programming model follows:

Route	Customers	Cost (\$)
1	0-11-10-0	182
3	0-12-7-0	169
6	0-8-0	170
8	0-13-3-5-0	241
9	0-1-2-6-0	252
11	0-4-9-0	199
Total cost of feasible routing solution		1213

According to the unified optimization methodology, we use the shadow price information in Table 5.4 to determine a new route and, at the same time, compute a lower bound on z_{MIN}, the cost of the minimal (optimal) solution. As discussed above, we treat the shadow price associated with each customer as a reward for filling the order and compute a new route with maximal net reward, which equals the sum of the rewards for customers visited minus the cost of the route. The new route (route 14) is 0-1-4-5-0, with a cost of \$238 and a net reward of \$277. We add this route to the master models along with 0-11-1-0 (route 15) with a cost of \$185 and a net reward of \$144 and 0-5-6-7-0 (route 16) with a cost of \$228 and a reward of \$88. We heuristically added the additional two routes because they also had large net rewards.

The net reward associated with route 14 can also be applied to the computation of a lower bound on z_{MIN}, the cost of an optimal routing problem solution, according to the relationship given above. Unfortunately, because the net reward is so high, the bound is negative, or, in other words, we have gained no useful information because we already know that $z_{MIN} \geq 0$. The reason for the extremely weak lower bound is that computation with the integrated solution methodology has not yet produced a sufficiently good set of routes.

We continue to generate new routes using shadow prices from the LP master model. Table 5.5 displays our results after generating 13 additional routes, or 26

Table 5.4 Optimal linear and integer programming solution to Chemtech local delivery problem with 13 routes

	A	B	C	D	E	F	G	H	I	J	K	L	M	N	O	P	Q	R	S	T
1	Route	1	2	3	4	5	6	7	8	9	10	11	12	13					Order	Shadow
2	Route cost	182	174	169	197	214	170	200	241	252	192	199	138	132					(tons)	Price
3	Customer 1	0	0	0	1	0	0	0	0	1	0	0	0	0	1	=	1		3	197
4	Customer 2	0	0	0	1	0	0	0	0	1	0	0	0	0	1	=	1		5	0
5	Customer 3	0	0	0	0	1	0	0	1	0	0	0	0	0	1	=	1		5	15
6	Customer 4	0	0	0	0	1	0	0	0	0	0	1	0	0	1	=	1		4	199
7	Customer 5	0	1	0	0	0	0	0	1	0	0	0	0	0	1	=	1		2	119
8	Customer 6	0	1	0	0	0	0	0	0	1	0	0	0	0	1	=	1		2	55
9	Customer 7	0	0	1	0	0	0	0	0	0	1	0	0	0	1	=	1		6	142
10	Customer 8	0	0	0	0	0	1	0	0	0	0	0	0	0	1	=	1		8	170
11	Customer 9	0	1	0	0	0	0	0	0	0	0	1	0	0	1	=	1		3	0
12	Customer 10	1	0	0	0	0	0	0	0	0	1	0	0	0	1	=	1		3	50
13	Customer 11	1	0	0	0	0	0	0	0	0	0	0	0	1	1	=	1		7	132
14	Customer 12	0	0	1	0	0	0	0	0	0	0	0	1	0	1	=	1		4	27
15	Customer 13	0	0	0	0	0	0	1	1	0	0	0	0	0	1	=	1		3	107
16	Delivered tons	10	7	10	8	9	8	3	10	10	9	7	4	7						
17																				
18	Select route	1	0	1	0	0	1	0	1	1	0	1	0	0						
19																				
20	Solution cost	1213																		

routes in total. Specifically, we show optimal solutions for both the linear programming and integer programming models, where the latter model yields incumbent routing solution 3 from integer programming model, which follows:

Route	Customers	Cost ($)
1	0-11-10-0	182
3	0-12-7-0	169
4	0-1-2-0	197
18	0-3-13-0	219
21	0-6-8-0	170
26	0-4-5-9-0	198
Total cost of feasible routing solution		1135

Using the shadow prices from Table 5.5, we determine that 0-5-8-0 with a net reward of $6.77 has maximal net reward among all feasible routes in the Lagrangean submodel. Based on the safe assumption that the optimal local delivery solution employs six trucks, we use this result to compute a lower bound = 1094 – 6 * 6.77 = 1054 on z_{MIN}, the cost of an optimal solution to the local delivery problem. Thus, incumbent solution 3 is within 7.2% of optimality. Judging an error of such magnitude to be acceptable, at least for pedagogical purposes, we terminate computation with this solution.

Generalizations

Practitioners have modeled and analyzed many generalizations of the local delivery problem. An important generalization is to associate delivery windows with customers' orders. For the Chemtech example, customers might request that their orders be delivered within a 2-hour time window sometime between 9 A.M. and 5 P.M.

Another generalization is the selection of vehicles of different sizes for various routes. In addition, routes may be dispatched from more than one depot. Some routes may take a half day and others may take a full day. The time to move from one customer to the next include two components, a travel time and a delivery time that depends on the size of the order. Routing may also be constrained to obey laws relating to breaks; for example, a route longer than 4 hours must include a 30-minute break.

Despite these and many other complications, the unified optimization methodology remains a robust and rigorous approach. All its computational elements can be adapted to varying problem details and constraints. Moreover, the LP and IP master models can be extended to incorporate constraints that are difficult to incorporate in heuristics. Examples are limitations on the number of trucks, and therefore routes, that can be dispatched each hour from a depot and limitations on the number of trucks of a certain type available for the day's deliveries.

Even more broadly, there are generalizations of the local delivery problem to longer-haul delivery problems. Included are shipments lasting many days or weeks

Table 5.5 Optimal linear and integer programming solutions to Chemtech local delivery problem with 26 routes

	A	B	C	D	E	F	G	H	I	J	K	L	M	N	O	P
1	Route	1	2	3	4	5	6	7	8	9	10	11	12	13	14	15
2	Route cost	182	174	169	197	214	170	200	241	252	192	199	138	132	238	185
3	Customer 1	0	0	0	1	0	0	0	0	1	0	0	0	0	1	1
4	Customer 2	0	0	0	1	0	0	0	0	1	0	0	0	0	0	0
5	Customer 3	0	0	0	0	1	0	0	1	0	0	0	0	0	0	0
6	Customer 4	0	0	0	0	1	0	0	0	0	0	1	0	0	1	0
7	Customer 5	0	1	0	0	0	0	0	1	0	0	0	0	0	1	0
8	Customer 6	0	1	0	0	0	0	0	0	1	0	0	0	0	0	0
9	Customer 7	0	0	1	0	0	0	0	0	0	1	0	0	0	0	0
10	Customer 8	0	0	0	0	0	1	0	0	0	0	0	0	0	0	0
11	Customer 9	0	1	0	0	0	0	0	0	0	0	1	0	0	0	0
12	Customer 10	1	0	0	0	0	0	0	0	0	1	0	0	0	0	0
13	Customer 11	1	0	0	0	0	0	0	0	0	0	0	0	1	0	1
14	Customer 12	0	0	1	0	0	0	0	0	0	0	0	1	0	0	0
15	Customer 13	0	0	0	0	0	0	1	1	0	0	0	0	0	0	0
16	Delivered tons	10	7	10	8	9	8	3	10	10	9	7	4	7	9	10
17																
18	LP select route	0.67	0	0.78	0	0	0	0	0.33	0	0.11	0	0	0	0	0.33
19	LP solution cost	1094														
20																
21																
22	IP select route	1	0	1	1	0	0	0	0	0	0	0	0	0	0	0
23	IP solution cost	1135														
24																
25																
26																
27																
28																
29																
30																

	Q	R	S	T	U	V	W	X	Y	Z	AA	AB	AC	AD	AE	AF	AG	AH
1	16	17	18	19	20	21	22	23	24	25	26						Order	Shadow
2	228	227	219	247	224	170	214	217	205	193	198						tons	Price
3	0	0	0	1	0	0	0	0	0	0	0		1	=	1		3	82.67
4	0	1	0	0	1	0	1	0	1	0	0		1	=	1		5	92.56
5	0	0	1	0	0	0	0	0	1	0	0		1	=	1		5	112.44
6	0	0	0	1	0	0	0	0	0	0	1		1	=	1		4	76.56
7	1	1	0	0	0	0	1	0	0	0	1		1	=	1		2	40.78
8	1	0	0	0	1	1	0	0	0	0	0		1	=	1		2	50.78
9	1	0	0	0	0	0	0	0	0	1	0		1	=	1		6	112.33
10	0	0	0	0	0	1	0	0	0	0	0		1	=	1		8	119.22
11	0	0	0	0	1	0	1	1	0	1	1		1	=	1		3	80.67
12	0	0	0	0	0	0	0	1	0	0	0		1	=	1		3	79.67
13	0	0	0	0	0	0	0	0	0	0	0		1	=	1		7	102.33
14	0	0	0	0	0	0	0	1	0	0	0		1	=	1		4	56.67
15	0	1	1	1	0	0	0	0	0	0	0		1	=	1		3	87.78
16	10	10	8	10	10	10	10	10	10	9	9							
17																		
18	0	0	0	0.67	0	1	0.33	0.22	0.67	0.11	0.33							
19																		
20																		
21																		
22	0	0	1	0	0	1	0	0	0	0	1							
23																		
24																		
25																		
26																		
27																		
28																		
29																		
30																		

where products are picked up and delivered by trucks, barges, or container ships. Products may be cross-docked at an intermediate point from one long-haul vehicle, such as from a truck traveling from New York to Los Angeles stopping in St. Louis, to another long-haul vehicle, such as a truck traveling from Minneapolis to New Orleans also stopping in St. Louis. The long-haul routes may include multiple transportation modes; for example, container ships making ocean voyages, followed by trains making long-haul voyages across continents from ports where they pick up products to markets, and finally, trucks making local deliveries from train depots where they pick up products for delivery to customers. The spirit of the unified optimization methodology, which combines heuristics with more rigorous and comprehensive models, is attractive for analyzing such long haul problems.

5.4 Unified Optimization Methodology Applied to Production Scheduling

In this section, we return to the discrete parts production scheduling problem introduced in Section 5.2, and illustrate the unified optimization methodology applied to a numerical example. The example permits us to illustrate the structure of the LP and IP master models, the Lagrangean submodel, and problem-specific heuristic for this application. Similar realizations of the methodology are possible for other classes of production scheduling problems that are based on large models and their decompositions.[14]

In the paragraphs below, we provide background on the Goodstone Tire Company and numerical data about its operations. After that, we specialize the unified optimization methodology to Goodstone's production scheduling problem over the next 8 weeks and then apply it to the numerical data to determine a demonstrably good solution. The section concludes with a brief discussion of generalizations of the production scheduling problems and their optimization.

Company Background and Numerical Data

The Goodstone Tire Company manufactures six types of tires on a single machine in its Cincinnati plant. The machine is operated two shifts a day, 6 days a week, which is 96 hours per week. The machine is cleaned and maintained as needed on the seventh day (Sunday). Under conditions of heavy demand, a third shift may be run 4 days a week (Monday through Thursday), but at a high ($100) hourly cost to cover overtime and avoidable overhead costs. Thus, Goodstone has the option of scheduling up to 32 hours a week of overtime.

The production manager must decide on a production and inventory plan that meets the weekly demand for each type of tire over the next 8 weeks. The demands, which are given in Table 5.6, are based on a combination of customer orders and

Table 5.6 Demand for Goodstone tires

Week	1	2	3	4	5	6
1	254	359	303	412	501	622
2	306	388	283	428	484	702
3	339	416	276	465	437	645
4	328	447	258	488	463	717
5	340	470	206	358	497	677
6	315	505	208	334	552	745
7	284	533	222	516	589	728
8	327	562	236	477	640	576

forecasts. The manager's goal is to minimize the total avoidable cost, which includes setup, inventory holding, and overtime costs. Direct manufacturing costs, which are constant over the planning horizon, are unavoidable, and therefore they are not included in the total costs to be minimized.

Other data needed for production scheduling at Goodstone are given in Table 5.7. Note that scheduling involves both a setup cost and a setup time. The setup cost refers to direct labor and material costs that are required each time the machine is set up to make the indicated product. The material costs include the cost of cleaning solvents as well as lost raw materials. They do not include any imputed machine cost due to lost production time, which is impossible to determine without an optimization model. For example, no cost should be associated with lost production time in a week when Goodstone has excess capacity, but we cannot identify these weeks without optimizing the scheduling problem. However, as we know from discussions in Section 3.3, the LP master model will derive a marginal machine cost per hour depending on the optimal capacity loading for the week. Finally, note that the production manager has imposed a terminal inventory requirement for each tire to ensure that the transition to longer-term planning is smooth. A policy constraint not listed in Table 5.7 is that the number of units manufactured in any production run of any tire may make not exceed 50% of the total net demand for the 8-week planning horizon. This constraint is intended to promote manufacturing flexibility in the face of uncertain demand.

A **feasible item schedule** is a production/inventory plan for that item (tire), allowing demand for it to be met. A **feasible plan** is a collection of feasible item schedules, one for each item, with the property that machine capacity, including overtime, is not violated. The cross-cutting capacity constraints differentiate this production scheduling problem from the local delivery problem of Section 5.3, which was not constrained by scarce resources. It makes the production scheduling problem more difficult to analyze because if machine capacity constraints are tight, the construction of a feasible plan, using either heuristics or optimization models, can be arduous. Sometimes, a feasible plan might not exist because capacity is insufficient to meet the sum of demand for all tires. When this situation is possible, the

Table 5.7 Goodstone production data

Tire Type	**1**	**2**	**3**	**4**	**5**	**6**
Setup cost ($)	450	500	500	525	600	475
Holding cost ($/item/week)	0.33	0.38	0.35	0.41	0.48	0.34
Setup hours	2	2.5	3	4	3.6	2.8
Machine hours/tire	0.029	0.03	0.033	0.037	0.036	0.026
Initial inventory	301	578	446	667	355	678
Required terminal inventory	200	300	150	250	350	450

model should be extended to decision options for backlogging demand with associated penalties.

As with the vehicle routing problem, we could construct and optimize a monolithic mixed integer programming model of Goodstone's production scheduling problem. In practice, depending on the number of tires to be scheduled for production, it might be difficult to extract a demonstrably good schedule from such a model in a reasonable run time. The mixed integer programming model requires a 0-1 variable describing a potential setup for each tire and for each week of the planning horizon. Thus, for a problem involving 300 types of tires and 13 weeks, the monolithic model would need to optimize a model with 3900 zero-one variables, a formidable task, even with considerable customization of the branch-and-bound search. Moreover, a monolithic approach does not readily admit input from human schedulers regarding good, or possibly good, schedules for individual items. For these reasons, the more flexible, unified optimization methodology is attractive.

Unified Optimization Methodology Specialized to Goodstone's Production Scheduling Problem

We review briefly details of the unified optimization methodology as they relate to Goodstone's production scheduling problem; namely, we present and discuss heuristics, the LP and IP master models, and the Lagrangean submodels. The core of the methodology is the decomposition scheme for production scheduling developed in Section 5.2. We begin with a discussion of heuristics for identifying feasible item schedules.

An early result of operations research provides the basis of a useful heuristic for generating feasible item schedules.[15] This result follows:

> **Dynamic lot-size theorem:** Consider a production/inventory planning problem for a single item faced with variable demand over a planning horizon of T weeks. The objective is to minimize the sum over the planning horizon of setup

and inventory holding costs. Assuming initial inventory is zero, an optimal production/inventory plan is characterized as follows.

We set up in the first week to produce a lot size equal to the sum of demand over the first k weeks, where $1 \le k \le T$. (We do not know k, but we do know production should equal exactly k weeks demand for some k.) If $k \le T - 1$, we set up a second time in period $k+1$ to produce a lot size equal to the sum of demand over the next q weeks, where $1 \le q \le T - k - 1$. (Again, we do not know q.) We continue to develop an optimal plan in this way until demand for the entire planning horizon has been covered. In other words, the optimal plan has the property that production occurs only in weeks when inventory falls to zero.

Remark: The implication of the theorem is that the production/inventory planning problem can be optimized by a simple dynamic programming (list processing) computation that considers for each week t the following production decisions: 0 (no setup), d_t, $d_t + d_{t+1}$, . . . , $d_t + d_t + d_{t+1} + \ldots + d_T$, where d_s equals demand in week s. Thus, the number of decisions that must be considered by the computation is greatly reduced from the general case where any amount may be produced in any week.

We use the theorem to construct a heuristic that generates trial feasible item schedules, taking into account initial inventory and requirements on ending inventory, as follows:

Production scheduling heuristic: For a given item, wait until the last week before inventory runs out. Call this week t. Select an integer $k_1 \le T - t$ such that net demand (total demand – initial inventory in week t) over weeks t through $t+k_1$ does not exceed the allowed bound on production. Set up to produce a quantity of the item covering net demand for weeks t, $t+1$, . . . , $t+k_1$. Select an integer $k_2 \le T - t - k_1 - 1$ such that demand over weeks $t + k_1 + 1$, . . . , $t + k_1 + k_2 + 1$ does not exceed the allowed bound on production. Set up to produce items covering demand for weeks $t+k_1 + 1$, . . . , $t+k_1 + k_2 + 1$. Continue in this way until demand for the entire planning horizon has been covered. Requirements for ending inventory in week T should be added to demand in that week.

A drawback of this heuristic is that, with shared machine capacity constraints, it may be necessary to set up and make product in a week when inventory is positive. This suggests that we will need to apply a modified heuristic after we have identified weeks when capacity is tight by optimizing versions of the LP master model. We will return to this point later.

For completeness, we present detailed statements of the production scheduling LP and IP master models. We let I denote the number of items to be scheduled and K denote the number of trial feasible schedules produced by the heuristic for each item. We have assumed the same number of trial feasible schedules for each item merely for expositional convenience. From these trial feasible item schedules, we extract the following parameters:

C_{ik} = avoidable cost ($) of feasible item schedule k for item i

r_{ikt} = machine capacity (hours) used in week t by feasible item schedule k for item i

R_t = available machine capacity (hours) in week t without overtime

UB_t = upper bound (hours) on overtime available in week

P = cost ($/hour) for overtime

We also define the following decision variables:

w_{ik} = weight assigned to feasible item schedule k for item i

O_t = overtime (hours) in week t

The production scheduling LP and IP master models are displayed in Figure 5.9. The objective function terms z_{LPK}, z_{IPK} refer to the minimal cost of solving the LP and IP master models, respectively, when these models are constructed from a given set of K trial feasible item schedules for each item. As schedule generation progresses, these sets are augmented, which enables the master models to find better optimal solutions. The terms in the objective function are the avoidable production costs for each feasible item schedule multiplied by the weight (decision variable) associated with that schedule plus the cost of overtime. The constraints are of three types: resource, weight, and overtime. For each period t, the resource constraints restrict the machine capacity consumed by feasible item schedules for all items so that it does not exceed the available capacity $R_t + O_t$. The weight constraints state that the nonnegative weights (decision variables) for each item must sum to 1.

$$z_{\text{LPK}}, z_{\text{IPK}} = \min\; C_{11}w_{11} + \cdots + C_{1K}w_{1K} + \cdots + C_{N1}w_{N1} + \cdots + C_{NK}w_{NK} + \text{P} * (O_1 + O_2 + \cdots + O_T)$$

Subject to

$$\begin{aligned}
r_{111}w_{11} + \cdots + r_{1K1}w_{1K} + \cdots + r_{N11}w_{N1} + \cdots + r_{NK1}w_{NK} - O_1 &\le R_1 \\
r_{112}w_{11} + \cdots + r_{1K2}w_{1K} + \cdots + r_{N12}w_{N1} + \cdots + r_{NK2}w_{NK} - O_2 &\le R_2 \\
\cdots \\
r_{11T}w_{11} + \cdots + r_{1KT}w_{1K} + \cdots + r_{N1T}w_{N1} + \cdots + r_{NKT}w_{NK} - O_T &\le R_T
\end{aligned}
\quad \text{Resource Constraints}$$

$$\begin{aligned}
w_{11} + \cdots + w_{1K} &= 1 \\
\cdots \\
w_{N1} + \cdots + w_{NK} &= 1
\end{aligned}
\quad \text{Weight Constraints}$$

$$0 \le O_t \le \text{UB}_t \text{ for } t = 1, 2, \ldots, T \quad \text{Overtime Constraints}$$

$$0 \le w_{ik} \le 1 \quad \text{(Linear Programming)}$$

$$w_{ik} = 0 \text{ or } 1 \quad \text{(Integer Programming)}$$

Figure 5.9 Production scheduling LP and IP master models

As we discussed in Section 5.2, after solving the LP master model, the schedule generation procedure begins with the optimization of a Lagrangean submodel for each item. This submodel determines a production/inventory schedule that minimizes total resource adjusted costs, which equal total avoidable costs plus the sum of resource costs for each week. This resource cost equals the shadow price (π_t) multiplied by the resource usage of the schedule. The Lagranean submodels may either be solved by a dynamic programming algorithm derived from the dynamic lot size theorem or by representing and optimizing it as a simple mixed integer programming model.

If the cost of an optimal schedule for item i is less than the shadow price (θ_i) on the weight constraint for item i, we add the schedule to the LP master model. This means that we compute the cost and resource parameters for it as described above and assign a new weight variable to it. If the cost of an optimal solution equals the shadow price on the weight constraint for item i, we do not add it to the LP master model. If this latter condition holds for all items, the schedule generation procedure has run its course, and we do not reoptimize the LP master model.[16] Otherwise, the LP master model is reoptimized and the procedure is repeated.

Also as we discussed in Section 5.1, optimizing the submodels produces a lower bound on z_{MIN}, the cost of an optimal production scheduling plan. We rewrite this lower bound. For each item i, we define

$$\Delta_i = \text{minimal resource adjusted cost} - \theta_i$$

The lower bound is given by

$$\text{Minimal objective function cost of LP master model} + \Delta_1 + \Delta_2 + \cdots + \Delta_N$$

where all the $\Delta_i \leq 0$ by construction.

Occasional optimization of the IP master model yields a feasible plan. The least cost plan, the incumbent, with cost z_{INC}, is compared to the value of the greatest lower bound, and computation is terminated if the difference is deemed sufficiently small or, equivalently, if the incumbent is deemed demonstrably good. The logic of these cost and bounds is precisely the same as displayed in Figure 5.8.

Finally, we note again that feasible item schedules generated by the heuristic as initial inputs to the master models and later by the submodels will tend to obey exactly the property of the dynamic lot size theorem; namely, an item is produced only in a week when inventory falls to zero. With tight capacity constraints and/or expensive overtime, feasible item schedules with production in weeks when inventory is positive may be necessary and desirable for the construction of a demonstrably good plan by the IP master model.

This suggests the construction and application of additional heuristics to generate feasible item schedules with such a property. One approach would be to use shadow prices from the LP master model on the capacity constraints to decide on periods to violate the spirit of the dynamic lot size theorem. Specifically, a relatively high shadow price in a week t for which the shadow price in week $t-1$ was zero would suggest the construction of feasible item schedules with production in week $t - 1$ even though the week will end with positive inventory. Other heuristics are clearly possible.

Production Scheduling Solution

We apply the production scheduling heuristic with different timing of setups to produce three trial feasible item schedules for each of the six tires produced by Goodstone. A representative from among the 18 initial schedules is given in Table 5.8. This schedule meets demand for tire 1 by setting up in weeks 2, 5, and 8 and producing just enough at each setup so that inventory falls to zero by the week of the next setup. Letting this schedule be schedule 1 for tire 1, we see from the table that the total cost $C_{11} = \$2051.25$. Similarly, the machine capacity used in week 2 of this schedule is $r_{112} = 28.854$ hours. We compute this by multiplying 926 (production in week 2) by 0.029 (machine hours to make one tire of type 1 from Table 5.7) and adding 2 hours for setup (also from Table 5.7).

The LP master model constructed from data describing the 18 initial schedules and its optimal solution computed by What's Best is given in Table 5.9, where the column labeled "Sch *ik*" refers to schedule *k* for tire *i*. The data on rows 3 through 10 for columns B through S in the spreadsheet are machine utilization by week of the 18 schedules. The cost data on row 10 of the spreadsheet are the avoidable costs associated with the schedules. The total production hours by week required by a weighted LP solution to the model are given in column *T*. They are constrained in each week to be less than the capacity of 96 hours plus overtime by the constraints listed in column *V*. Overtime in each week is constrained to be less than 32 hours by the constraints listed in column *Y*. Finally, constraints forcing the sum of weights to

Table 5.8 Goodstone production scheduling problem—example of an initial feasible item schedule for tire 1

Week	Demand	Setup	Production	Ending Inventory	Cost ($)	Resource Utilization
0				301		
1	254	0	0	47	15.51	0
2	306	1	926	667	670.11	28.854
3	339	0	0	328	108.24	0
4	328	0	0	0	0	0
5	340	1	939	599	647.67	29.231
6	315	0	0	284	93.72	0
7	284	0	0	0	0	0
8	327	1	527	200	516	17.283
Net demand	2392			Total cost	2051.25	

Table 5.9 Goodstone production scheduling problem LP master model—initial solution

	A	B	C	D	E	F	G	H	I	J	K	L	M
1	resource												
2	used	sch 11	sch 12	sch 13	sch 21	sch 22	sch 23	sch 31	sch 32	sch 33	sch 41	sch 42	sch 43
3	period 1	0	28.85	19.34	0	33.46	20.05	16.73	10.92	0	0	0	0
4	period 2	28.85	0	0	33.46	0	0	0	0	30.98	10.40	60.65	43.92
5	period 3	0	0	0	0	0	0	0	30.98	0	52.51	0	0
6	period 4	0	0	30.51	0	0	45.16	25.18	0	0	0	0	33.08
7	period 5	29.23	29.23	0	47.74	47.74	0	0	0	30.98	0	0	0
8	period 6	0	0	0	0	0	0	0	0	0	35.45	60.61	48.25
9	period 7	0	0	25.52	0	0	44.35	23.06	23.06	0	0	0	0
10	period 8	17.28	17.28	0	28.36	28.36	0	0	0	0	30.90	0	0
11	cost	2051.25	2356.83	2234.73	2792	3184.16	2967.56	2197.55	2309.55	2195.95	3012.25	3172.98	3601.22
12	weight	1	0	0	0.512	0	0.488	1	0	0	0.808	0.192	0
13				=			=			=			=
14				1			1			1			1
15	total cost	17115											

	N	O	P	Q	R	S	T	U	V	W	X	Y	Z
1													
2	sch 51	sch 52	sch 53	sch 61	sch 62	sch 63	prod hours	overtime		capacity	shadow pr		ot limit
3	42.01	58.68	78.44	0	19.60	0	88.12	0	<=	96	0	<=	32
4	0	0	0	70.19	0	55.01	66.06	0	<=	96	0	<=	32
5	0	0	0	0	38.21	0	80.61	0	<=	96	0	<=	32
6	38.16	0	0	0	0	0	85.37	0	<=	96	0	<=	32
7	0	62.57	0	70.19	42.32	61.69	96	0	=<=	96	-3.20	<=	32
8	44.68	0	74.84	0	0	0	84.97	0	<=	96	0	<=	32
9	0	0	0	0	45.86	0	90.56	0	<=	96	0	<=	32
10	39.24	39.24	0	0	0	26.49	96	0	=<=	96	-5.20	<=	32
11	3741.12	4116.96	4398.72	4219.44	3204.24	3169.54							
12	1	0	0	0	1	0							
13			=			=							
14			1			1							
15													

equal 1 for trial schedules for each tire are provided on row 12. As we can see, the optimal solution to the LP master model is fractional with a total cost of \$17,114.99. No overtime is associated with this plan.

We choose, therefore, to impose 0-1 restrictions on the weights and optimize the IP master model. The optimal solution for this model found by What's Best is given in Table 5.10, which provides us with our first incumbent cost equaling \$17,599.39. The incumbent plan involves a small amount of overtime in periods 1 and 6. At this point, we have no information about how good the incumbent might be.

We digress briefly to mention that we could apply a simple heuristic to derive a feasible plan from the optimal solution to LP master model. Specifically, we could force a pure schedule for each tire that has a mixed schedule (tires 2 and 4) by selecting the trial schedule for each tire with the highest fractional value and making it 1. For the numerical example, this heuristic produces a feasible solution but one that is very unattractive compared to the incumbent. In particular, because it requires over 23 hours of overtime in week 5 and over 19 hours of overtime in week 8, the feasible plan produced by the heuristic costs \$21,305.71.

The heuristic just described would be much more effective in the more standard case when the number of items I is much greater than the number of periods T because it can be shown that an optimal solution to the LP master model will always have at least $I - T$ pure schedules. Thus, if $I = 200$ and $T = 13$, we would have at least 187 pure strategies in the LP master model solution, and rounding up the mixed strategies would have a much weaker effect. Of course, this heuristic can produce good plans only if the individual item strategies being considered by the LP master model are suitably economical and varied.

The indicated next step in the unified optimization methodology is to create and optimize Lagrangean submodels for each of the six types of tires using the shadow prices given in column *X* of Table 5.9 as resource charges. The shadow prices have negative signs, indicating that marginal decreases (increases) in the capacities in column *W* would cause the objective function to increase (decrease). The LP master model regards the 96 hours in any week as already paid for, and the shadow prices reflect better utilization of them. Positive additions beyond 96 hours in any week would cost \$100/hour, a figure that is much higher than the shadow prices. The submodels at this iteration of the schedule generation procedure will seek to adjust the utilization of the given capacities before paying for costly overtime.

We optimize the submodels as simple mixed integer programming models. The resulting feasible item schedules for each of the six tires do not set up and produce in periods when the shadow prices are positive. As shown in Table 5.11, each new schedule has a lower resource reduced cost than θ_i, which indicates that the schedule is better than any previously considered by the LP master model. These improvements are probably due more to the fact that we optimized individual item schedules using mixed integer programming than avoidance of resource charges in weeks 5 and 8 when capacity is tight. The lower bound on z_{MIN} computed in Table 5.11 equals the minimal master LP cost plus the sum of the (negative) Δ_i.

The results of applying the unified optimization methodology to the Goodstone production scheduling problem are given in Table 5.12. After five iterations between the master models and the submodels, the optimality gap between the cost of the

Table 5.10 Goodstone production scheduling problem IP master model—initial solution

	A	B	C	D	E	F	G	H	I	J	K	L	M
1	Resource												
2	Used	sch 11	sch 12	sch 13	sch 21	sch 22	sch 23	sch 31	sch 32	sch 33	sch 41	sch 42	sch 43
3	Period 1	0	28.85	19.34	0	33.46	20.05	16.73	10.92	0	0	0	0
4	Period 2	28.85	0	0	33.46	0	0	0	0	30.98	10.40	60.65	43.92
5	Period 3	0	0	0	0	0	0	0	30.98	0	52.51	0	0
6	Period 4	0	0	30.51	0	0	45.16	25.18	0	0	0	0	33.08
7	Period 5	29.23	29.23	0	47.74	47.74	0	0	0	30.98	0	0	0
8	Period 6	0	0	0	0	0	0	0	0	0	35.45	60.61	48.25
9	Period 7	0	0	25.52	0	0	44.35	23.06	23.06	0	0	0	0
10	Period 8	17.28	17.28	0	28.36	28.36	0	0	0	0	30.90	0	0
11	Cost	2051.25	2356.83	2234.73	2792	3184.16	2967.56	2197.55	2309.55	2195.95	3012.25	3172.98	3601.22
12	Weight	0	0	1	1	0	0	1	0	0	1	0	0
13				=			=			=			=
14				1			1			1			1
15	Total cost	17599											

	N	O	P	Q	R	S	T	U	V	W	X	Y	Z
1													
2	sch 51	sch 52	sch 53	sch 61	sch 62	sch 63	Prod Hours	Overtime		Capacity		Overtime Limit	
3	42.01	58.68	78.44	0	19.60	0	97.68	1.68	=<=	97.68	<=	32	
4	0	0	0	70.19	0	55.01	43.86	0	<=	96	<=	32	
5	0	0	0	0	38.21	0	90.72	0	<=	96	<=	32	
6	38.16	0	0	0	0	0	93.84	0	<=	96	<=	32	
7	0	62.57	0	70.19	42.32	61.69	90.06	0	<=	96	<=	32	
8	44.68	0	74.84	0	0	0	80.13	0	<=	96	<=	32	
9	0	0	0	0	45.86	0	94.44	0	<=	96	<=	32	
10	39.24	39.24	0	0	0	26.49	98.50	2.50	=<=	98.50	<=	32	
11	3741.12	4116.96	4398.72	4219.44	3204.24	3169.54							
12	1	0	0	0	1	0							
13			=			=							
14			1			1							
15													

incumbent and the greatest lower bound is 3.48%, which we consider to be sufficiently good to terminate analysis. Due to space limitations, we omit details of the final incumbent solution.

Note also that the iteration procedure between the master models and the submodels is converging as evidenced by the fact that the minimal LP cost, which always lies above the greatest lower bound, is approaching it; specifically, we know from these figures that the maximal lower bound must lie between 16,301 and 16,514. As a result, the sum of the Δ_i is going to zero, although small improvements in the schedules of four of the six items (types of tires) are still being found.

Convergence between the master models and the submodels could have yielded an incumbent for which the terminal optimality gap was larger. In such a case, we would apply additional heuristics to create additional feasible item schedules, concentrating on creating schedules with setups and production in weeks when inventory is positive. This should allow us to find a better incumbent but would not directly serve to appreciably increase the greatest lower bound and therefore decrease the optimality gap from both directions. To systematically increase the lower bound, we would need to embed the unified optimization methodology in a branch-bound search over the finite, but extremely large, set of possible combinations of setups for all items.

Table 5.11 Goodstone production scheduling problem—lower bound calculation

Tire	Shadow Price on Weight Constraints	Minimal Resource Reduced Cost	Δi (Difference)
$i = 1$	2234.73	2037.39	−197.34
$i = 2$	3092.35	2745.60	−346.75
$i = 3$	2197.55	2051.95	−145.60
$i = 4$	3172.98	2691.43	−481.55
$i = 5$	3945.24	3863.52	−81.72
$i = 6$	3339.72	2870.36	−469.36
		Min. master LP cost = 17,114.99	
		Lower bound = 15,392.67	

Table 5.12 Goodstone production scheduling problem—results of unified optimization methodology

Iteration	Min. LP Master Cost	Sum of Δi	Number of Improving Item Schedules	Lower Bound	Greatest Lower Bound	Incumbent Cost[a]	Optimality Gap
1	17,115	−1661	6	15,393	15,393	17,599	0.1253
2	16,740	−1479	6	15,261	15,393	17,599	0.1219
3	16,669	−729	6	15,940	15,940	17,599	0.0943
4	16,604	−303	4	16,301	16,301	16,903	0.0356
5	16,514	−236	4	16,278	16,301	16,889	0.0348

[a]IP master model not optimized for iterations 2 and 3.

Generalizations

The discrete parts manufacturing model examined in this section can be extended to more complex manufacturing environments, including those with multiple resources, multiple stages, buffer inventories, time lags in production, and manufacturing yield factors. It can also be extended to incorporate decision options about which orders to delay and for how long if short-term supply capacity cannot meet demand. Different classes of mathematical programming models can be developed for multiple-stage process manufacturing problems, and for job-shop scheduling problems. Decomposition methods have been studied, at least in the abstract, for virtually all these models. Thus, the unified optimization methodology could be specialized to many of these applications.

5.5 Final Thoughts

In this chapter, we developed a unified optimization methodology for optimizing operational planning problems and illustrated it with numerical examples in vehicle routing and production scheduling. Without "cooking the numbers," the examples demonstrated clearly how rigorous mathematical programming methods could be effectively combined with heuristic methods to identify demonstrably good plans for these applications. Specifically, the unified optimization methodology showed the following:

- Decomposition methods applied to large-scale mixed integer programming models can isolate submodels that can be efficiently analyzed by heuristics, dynamic programming, or small mixed integer programming models.
- LP and IP master models can capture resource and other cross-cutting constraints on plans such as machine capacities or single-stop customer deliveries.
- Heuristics can find good plans to the overall decision problems if the resource and cross-cutting constraints are not too tight.
- Heuristics can provide good subplans for initializing the LP and IP master models.
- Lagrangean submodels can provide attractive subplans for the LP and IP master models based on shadow prices on the resource and cross-cutting constraints.
- Heuristics can be used to modify and extend the subplans computed by the Lagrangean submodels.
- Lagrangean submodels provide lower bounds on the cost of an optimal plan.

Of course, the examples were illustrative and not of a realistic size, but references to realistic applications were provided.

The unified optimization methodology is admittedly not simple, but neither are the operational planning problems it is designed to address. Our goal in presenting it is to encourage modeling system developers and operational managers to design, implement, and use systems based on rigorous models and methods. By identifying demonstrably good solutions to operational decision problems, these systems can reduce operational costs by several percentages, thereby adding significantly higher percentages to a company's net profit.

Because analysis of operational planning problems is usually time critical, an area of research meriting attention is the implementation of the unified optimization methodology on coarse-grained parallel computers. By coarse-grained we mean distributed computation of the major blocks of a large-scale optimization model, which is precisely the approach afforded by the decomposition methods underlying the unified optimization methodology.[17] A coarse-grained machine has 2, 10, or 50 linked microprocessors that perform batch computations on the numerical problems assigned to them, with intermittent broadcasting of results and acquisition of new problems. Limited experimentation with decomposable problems has indicated that near linear speedup can be achieved by parallelization if the microprocessors can be kept busy throughout the computation; that is, if computation of a decomposable numerical problem takes 60 minutes on a single processor, we can expect it will take little more than 10 minutes on six processors.

Finally, the unified optimization methodology can provide the brains of a powerful operational planning system. It must be combined with a flexible user interface that allows the human scheduler or planner to control the logic of the analysis and manually adjust plans produced by batch algorithms. It must also be efficiently linked to data management systems from which input data are acquired and to which plans are sent once they have been determined. These topics are taken up again in Chapter 10 when we discuss operational problems and modeling systems.

Exercises

In addition to the following exercises, modeling exercises involving data files and discussion exercises involving white papers may be found on the Web site (www.scm-models.com).

1. Chemtech is faced with these new demands for local delivery:

Customer	1	2	3	4	5	6	7	8	9	10	11	12	13
Tons	5	4	2	7	3	5	4	4	6	5	3	2	6

   a. Apply the heuristic given in Section 5.1 to determine a feasible routing solution for the new demands; all other factors of the vehicle routing problem remain the same. In particular, apply the heuristic twice by changing the rule for selecting the first customer in a route. First, use the heuristic to select the first customer on each route to be the unserved customer that is nearest the depot. Second, use the heuristic to select the first customer on each route to be the unserved customer that is farthest from the depot.

   b. Apply the genetic programming algorithm outlined in Table 5.3 to perform crossover operations on the two feasible routing solutions found in part a using the probability function

Table 5.13 Random numbers

98	56	88	16	68	93	53	38	96	34	32	60
44	10	23	59	99	70	78	12	89	71	84	55
41	80	31	62	15	98	48	68	28	21	84	18
13	06	73	10	72	97	83	30	35	31	88	54
11	10	11	74	17	68	20	49	90	61	39	23
53	17	09	30	44	47	42	79	16	08	37	35
53	33	38	71	22	79	30	55	82	64	00	93
27	29	40	37	28	92	08	49	48	22	31	63
55	84	28	71	25	51	17	37	60	12	12	29
39	38	74	15	54	39	61	90	49	20	68	17
86	31	69	28	15	80	71	75	19	88	51	67
43	34	71	73	23	47	25	21	78	92	82	54

$$P(x) = 1.953e^{-0.04463x}$$

where x is the cost per delivered ton of x. Use random numbers drawn from Table 5.13 in applying the algorithm. Apply the heuristic to create routes for any customers not covered by the crossover analysis.

c. Use the routes from part a to construct and optimize in a spreadsheet optimizer the local delivery LP and IP master models discussed in Section 5.3. Use the LP shadow prices to find a new route with positive net reward as described in the discussion of the Lagrangean submodel. (You are not asked to solve the Lagrangean submodel in finding a new route with maximal net reward because such a computation is too complicated for our purposes here.) Add the new route to the LP and IP master models and reoptimize them.

2. Discuss how you would modify the unified optimization methodology for the local delivery problem given in Sections 5.1 and 5.3 if there were two depots from which to dispatch vehicles.

3. Mixed integer programming can be used to model the production/scheduling problems for individual items embedded in the multi-item model analyzed in Sections 5.2 and 5.4.

   a. Write out the mixed integer programming model that computes a minimal avoidable cost plan for tire 1 using the demand data in Table 5.6 and other data in Table 5.7. *Hint:* For each period, the decision variables correspond to setup, production, and inventory.

   b. Extend the model to include induced resource costs in each period based on the shadow prices in Table 5.9.

   c. Solve the model of part b using a spreadsheet optimizer.

4. Several weeks after the analysis performed in Section 5.4, the production manager at Goodstone Tire faces an oversold situation with respect to sales of tire 1. As described in the following spreadsheet, demand in weeks 1 and 2

equal to the sum of four orders in each week are well above average demand for the product. Current inventory (starting inventory for week 1) is 208. The sales department will treat the demand forecasted for weeks 3 through 8 as available to promise to customers. Given recent demand, the company can be confident that orders covering these sales will be made.

Week	Demand Tire 1	Order 1	Order 2	Order 3	Order 4	Order 5	Order 6	Order 7	Order 8
1	799	230	209	265	95				
2	427					115	108	79	125
3	239								
4	235								
5	195								
6	202								
7	184								
8	227								

The problem is compounded by the scarcity of an additive used in manufacturing tire 1. Over the next 2 weeks, additive is available to support manufacture of no more than 700 tires. Thus, some orders for weeks 1 and 2 will not be completed until week 3 or later. Only full orders may be shipped. The penalty for late shipment of an order is \$350 per week. A shipment of additive will arrive by the end of week 2, allowing production runs in week 3 and beyond to be as large as necessary.

Extend the mixed integer programming model of the previous exercise to decide on a production plan for this situation. Under the circumstances, we ignore issues associated with production of other types of tires. *Hint:* For each order, define 0-1 variables assigning completion of the order to weeks 1, 2, and 3. In addition, add a constraint that production over the first 2 weeks cannot exceed 700 items.

5. In Section 5.3, we presented the following local delivery IP master model for selecting the best routing solution from among N given routes:

$$z_{\text{IPN}} = \min\ c_1x_1 + c_2x_2 + \cdots + c_Nx_N$$

subject to

$$\begin{aligned} a_{11}x_1 + a_{12}x_2 + \cdots + a_{1N}x_N &= 1 \\ a_{21}x_1 + a_{22}x_2 + \cdots + a_{2N}x_N &= 1 \\ &\cdots \\ a_{M1}x_1 + a_{M2}x_2 + \cdots + a_{MN}x_N &= 1 \end{aligned}$$

$$x_j = 0 \text{ or } 1 \text{ (integer programming)}$$

Describe how you might use surplus and slack variables with associated penalties on each equation in constructing a related model that might be easier to optimize, especially in the case when it is unclear if a feasible routing solution can be extracted from the N given routes.

Notes

1. Definitions taken from *The American Heritage College Dictionary* [1993, 857–858].
2. A sample of combinatorial optimization problems and an introduction to heuristics is given by Reeves and Beastly [1993].
3. Lawler et al. [1985] devote an entire book to various formulations of the traveling salesperson problem and its generalizations. For example, Fisher [1994] provides a very large-scale formulation as a monolithic mixed integer programming that could only be solved by a decomposition approach.
4. Winston [1994] provides several approaches to solving the traveling salesperson problem, including mixed integer and dynamic programming formulations.
5. A comprehensive review of several general-purpose heuristics can be found in Reeves [1993a].
6. We follow the development of the genetic algorithm given in Reeves [1993b].
7. Decomposition methods fall into two main categories; price directed and resource directed. Both mechanize economic principles for achieving and computing equilibrium prices and quantities; that is, supply and demand prices and quantities in markets where the quantity supplied at the equilibrium price exactly equals the quantity demanded. With price-directed methods, the supply model broadcasts prices for scarce resources that it will supply to the demand model. The demand model responds by determining the quantities it wishes to acquire. This information is used by the supply model to adjust its resource prices, based not only on the immediate response from the demand model but also on all earlier responses. Under suitable mathematical conditions, the price adjustment process between the supply and demand models converge to an equilibrium. With resource-directed methods, the supply model broadcasts quantities of scarce resources that it will provide to the demand model, which responds with price information about how much it would pay to adjust the resources received. The mathematical theory of decomposition methods is presented in detail by Shapiro [1979, Chapter 6]. Price-directed methods are further explained and illustrated in Shapiro [1993, 384–397] and Winston [1994, 562–585].
8. Lasdon and Terjung [1971] report on an early, successful application in production scheduling. Barnhart et al. [1994] report on a successful application to airline crew scheduling. Desaulniers et al. [1998] describe a unified framework for optimizing vehicle routing that has considerable overlap with the unified optimization methodology; they provide several references to successful implementations of the approach.
9. A decomposition method for this class of production scheduling problems was originally devised by Dzielinski and Gomory [1965]; see also Lasdon and Terjung [1971].
10. The Lagrange multipliers are the prices in the price-directed decomposition method that we employ in the unified optimization methodology. The connection is explained in detail by Shapiro [1993, 384–397]. See also Graves [1982] for the use of Lagrange multipliers in hierarchical planning and Kohl and Madsen [1997] for their use in vehicle routing with time windows. The price-directed method is also called column generation because the Lagrangean submodels provide new columns for the master models; see Desrosiers, Sourmis, and Desrochers [1984] and Ribeiro and Soumis [1994] for applications in vehicle routing.

11. In the operations research literature, the local delivery IP master model is called a **set covering model.** For the vehicle routing problem, the set to be covered is the customers. They are covered by routes that visit subsets of customers. Schrage [1997, Chapter 6] discusses several other applications of set covering model.

12. An intuitive explanation of the lower bound is the following. The maximal net reward of the new route is a mathematically optimistic estimate of how much the cost of the LP master model could be reduced by using it. If we were able to use this route V times in constructing a feasible solution, we would have an optimistic (lower bound) estimate of the minimal cost of the LP master model that incorporated all feasible routes. Because the minimal cost of such an LP master would be lower bound on z_{MIN}, the term on the right, which is a lower bound on the lower bound, is itself a lower bound.

13. This approach is discussed in Desaulniers et al. [1998, 78–81].

14. Shapiro [1993] discusses decomposition approaches to process manufacturing and job-shop scheduling problems.

15. This is a classical result due to Wagner and Whitin [1958].

16. If the test concludes that no additional feasible schedules might be used to advantage in the LP master model, there may still be feasible item schedules of value to the IP master model. Unfortunately, the iterative procedure just described cannot discover them. Other procedures, including heuristics and branch and bound, could be applied to generate additional feasible item schedules.

17. Brown, Shapiro, and Waterman [1988] discuss how the decomposition scheme for the discrete parts production scheduling model could be exploited in a coarse-grained parallel computing environment.

References

The American Heritage College Dictionary [1993], 3d Ed. Boston: Houghton Mifflin Company.

Barnhart, C., E. L. Johnson, R. Anbil, and L. Hatay [1994], "A Column Generation Technique for the Long-Haul Crew Assignment Problem," pp. 7–22 in *Mathematical Programming and Modeling Techniques in Practice,* edited by T. A. Ciriani and R. Leachman. Chichester, Eng.: Wiley.

Brown, R. W., J. F. Shapiro, and P. J. Waterman [1988], "Parallel Computing for Production Scheduling," *Manufacturing Systems,* 6, 56–64.

Crainic, T. G., and G. Laporte, eds. [1998], *Fleet Management and Logistics.* Norwell, Mass.: Kluwer Academic Publishers.

Desaulniers, G., J. Desrosiers, I. Ioachim, M. M. Solomon, F. Soumis, and D. Villeneuve [1998], "A Unified Framework for Deterministic Time Constrained Vehicle Routing and Crew Scheduling Problems," Chapter 3 in Crainic and Laporte, eds. [1998].

Desrosiers, J., F. Soumis, and M. Desrochers [1984], 'Routing with Time Windows by Column Generation," *Networks,* 14, 545–565.

Dzielinski, B., and R. Gomory [1965], "Optimal Programming of Lot Size, Inventories, and Labor Allocations," *Management Science,* 11, 874–890.

Fisher, M. L. [1994], "Optimal Solution of Vehicle Routing Problems Using Minimum k-Trees," *Operations Research,* 37, 626–642.

Graves, S. C. [1982], "Using Lagrangean Techniques to Solve Hierarchical Production Planning Problems," *Management Science,* 28, 260–275.

Kohl, N., and O. B. G. Madsen [1997], "An Optimization Algorithm for the Vehicle Routing Problem with Time Windows Based on Lagrangean Relaxation," *Operations Research,* 45, 395–406.

Lawler, E. L., J. K. Lenstra, A. H. G. Rinooy Kan, and D. B. Shmoys, eds. [1985], *The Traveling*

Salesman Problem: A Guided Tour of Combinatorial Optimization. New York: Wiley.

Lasdon, L. S., and R. C. Terjung [1971], "An Efficient Algorithm for Multi-item Scheduling," *Operations Research,* 19, 946–969.

Reeves, C. R., ed. [1993a], *Modern Heuristic Techniques for Combinatorial Optimization Problems.* Oxford, Eng.: Blackwell Scientific.

Reeves, C. R., ed. [1993b], "Genetic Algorithms," Chapter 4 in Reeves [1993a].

Reeves, C. R., and J. E. Beasley [1993], "Introduction," Chapter 1 in Reeves [1993a].

Ribeiro, C., and F. Soumis [1994], "A Column Generation Approach to the Multiple Depot Vehicle Scheduling Problem," *Operations Research,* 42, 41–52.

Schrage, L. [1997], *Optimization Modeling with LINDO.* Pacific Grove, Calif.: Brooks/Cole.

Shapiro, J. F. [1979], *Mathematical Programming: Structures and Algorithms.* New York: Wiley.

Shapiro, J. F. [1993], "Mathematical Programming Models and Methods for Production Planning and Scheduling," in *Handbooks in Operations Research and Management Science, Volume 4: Logistics of Production and Inventory,* edited by S. C. Graves, A. H. G. Rinnooy Kan, and P. H. Zipkin. Amsterdam: North-Holland.

Wagner, H. M., and T. M. Whitin [1958], "Dynamic Version of the Economic Lot Size Model," *Management Science,* 5, 89–96.

Winston, W. L. [1994], *Operations Research: Applications and Algorithms,* 3d ed. Belmont, Calif.: Duxbury Press.

6 Supply Chain Decision Databases

Our major theme is that optimization models provide rigorous and comprehensive representations of supply chains for the purposes of determining effective plans. A model is the **inspiration** for uncovering new ways to improve the design or operations of a company's supply chain. By contrast, processes for collecting, organizing, validating, and updating the **supply chain decision database** used to generate the model are the **perspiration** of any system development project. These processes entail efforts that are much larger than those needed to design and implement the system's modeling engine. Still, the model is critical because it provides a framework for integrating data and decision making. The framework also induces a parsing of the data into intuitive subsets, each describing a coherent element of the supply chain.

The supply chain decision database is a new concept that may appear obvious to modeling practitioners and some supply chain managers. Still, many managers are only beginning to realize that easy access to transactional data assembled by enterprise resource planning (ERP) and Internet systems does not automatically lead to effective supply chain management. In most instances, more than 80% of the data in transactional databases are irrelevant to decision making. Data aggregations and other analyses are needed to transform the remaining 20%, or less, into useful information in the supply chain decision database.

Our discussion of the supply chain decision database and processes for creating it involves exploratory and problem-specific constructions that may require modeling expertise. We believe that more straightforward processes for generating decision databases will emerge as managers become familiar with the concept and expand their use of such databases and models. As an example, the SLIM/2000 modeling system has been applied in over 40 companies using the same decision database; the 30 file sets it uses are listed in the screen shot shown in Figure 6.1.[1]

In creating the supply chain decision database, we employ descriptive models from a range of disciplines. Managerial accounting is used to develop accurate costs and cost relationships. Forecasting methods are used to generate demand projections and to estimate other parameters for the optimization models involving statistically varying factors, such as commodity prices. Transportation science is used to estimate

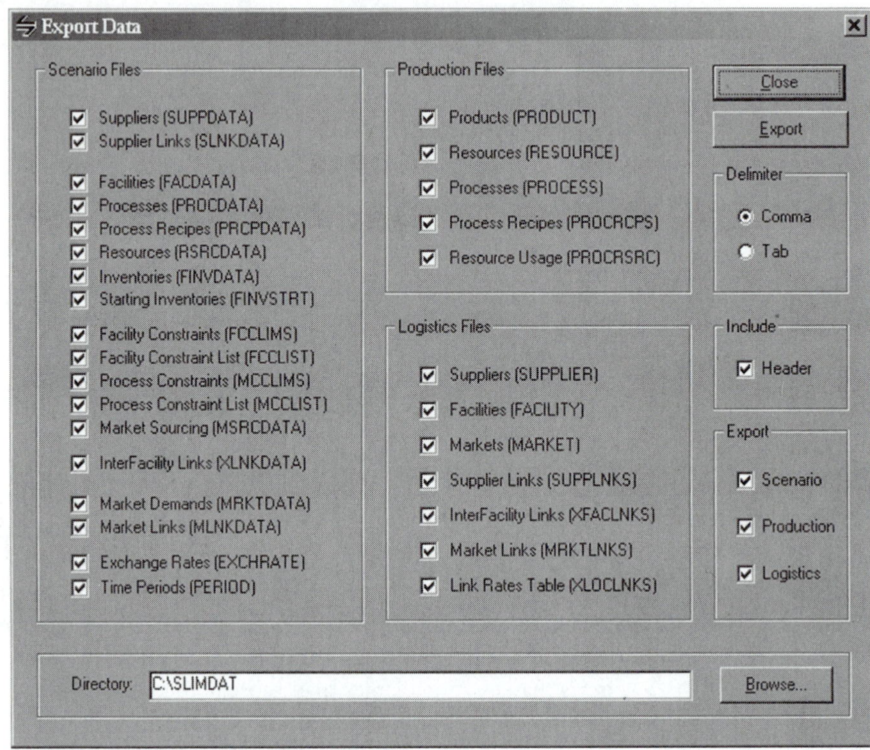

Figure 6.1
File sets in supply chain decision database generated and used by SLIM/2000

transportation rates, possibly for several modes, including those for new geographical links not previously employed by the company. Operations management concepts are used to compute inventory safety stocks and costs and to describe manufacturing rules and relationships. To the extent that the models generated by the system seek to maximize net revenues, marketing science is used to estimate parameters and relationships describing demand management options.

The funneling of descriptive data and models into templates provided by the optimization model are reviewed in this chapter. Obviously, we cannot furnish extensive details about the methodologies underlying descriptive models from each of the disciplines listed above. Instead, through notes, we refer the reader to articles and books containing discussions about such models.

To be specific in developing concepts and details about supply chain decision databases, we will employ a particular supply chain network representation. The network includes suppliers, facilities, and customers. Three types of products, labeled raw materials, intermediate products, and finished products, flow through the network Suppliers provide raw materials, which may actually be parts, components, or even products ready for sale, to facilities in the supply chain but do not receive raw materials from other suppliers or intermediate products from facilities. Customers receive finished products but do not send intermediate or finished products to other customers or facilities. Facilities receive raw materials from suppliers and intermediate products from other facilities and send intermediate products and finished products to other facilities and customers.

With these definitions, a product leaving a plant for a DC might physically be a finished product, but it is treated as an intermediate product. It does not become a finished product until it is shipped from a DC to a customer or market. Thus, the terminology reflects the logistics goal of delivering the correct product in the correct quantities at the correct time to each market.

Decision databases are distinctly different from the corporate transactional databases from which they are derived. They characterize supply chains at a level of aggregation appropriate to tactical and strategic planning, which is our focus in this chapter. Principles for aggregating products, customers and suppliers are examined in Section 5.1. Data aggregation is also relevant to the creation and use of optimization models for scheduling and other operational problems; we examine these models and their decision databases in Chapter 10.

We observed in Section 4.4 that the supply chain decision database is made up of structural elements, which define the supply chain network, and numerical elements linked to these structural elements, which describe costs, product transformations, transportation flows, resources constraints, and so on, for a particular planning scenario. It is these numerical elements that constitute the bulk of the supply chain decision database; they are organized according to the structural elements. In Sections 6.2, 6.3, and 6.4 we discuss, respectively, numerical elements in the supply chain decision database relating to facilities, transportation networks, and suppliers.

Costs and cost relationships are critical components of the supply chain decision database. Concepts and quantitative methods of management accounting are required to accurately develop them. The connections between management accounting and optimization modeling, which are important but thus far largely ignored by practitioners and academics, are examined in Section 6.5.

Customer demands for the company's products are the driving force for supply chain activities. Descriptive models for developing demand forecasts are reviewed in Section 6.6. More ambitious modeling efforts aimed at maximizing net revenues by integrating supply chain decisions with marketing and sales decisions are examined in Section 8.1.

Two final input elements in the supply chain decision database are data prescribing global constraints that apply to multiple facilities or otherwise cut across the entire supply chain and data describing management policies that may not be justified by the economics of cost minimization or revenue maximization. The latter are called **policy data.** Global and policy data are examined briefly in Section 6.7.

A supply chain decision database will also contain results from solutions obtained by an optimization model created from input data from the decision database. The output data are combined with input data to produce management reports and graphical displays of plans suggested by the model. Details of these output data and approaches for combining them with input data are presented in Section 6.8.

The company will require multiple supply chain decision databases developed for at least two important reasons. First, at a given level of strategic or tactical planning, due to uncertainties about the future, the model practitioner will need to create and optimize multiple scenarios to fully analyze the planning problems faced by the company. Second, integrated, intertemporal planning requires coherence among supply chain decision databases for strategic, tactical, and operational planning. These issues are discussed in Section 6.9.

To simplify the exposition, our discussion in this chapter will be limited mainly to decision databases and models that address tactical or strategic planning over a single period, or **snapshot,** of the company's supply chain operations. The length of the time period may be 1 month, 1 quarter, or 1 year. At first glance, it might seem that a multiple-period decision database of T periods could be easily constructed by combining T replicas of a single-period decision database. As a practical matter, however, we have found that multiple-period decision databases are challenging to construct because they require knowledge of dynamic phenomena that affect the data of different periods in different ways. Decision databases for models spanning multiple periods are also discussed in Section 6.9.

Graphical displays of input and output data in the supply chain decision database are important to engage decision makers in studying these data and to extend their intuition about supply chain problems and solutions. Many types of displays are possible, including geographical maps, schematics of facility operations, and multidimensional comparisons of multiple scenarios. Graphics are reviewed briefly in Section 6.10.

Although principles underlying the construction of supply chain decision databases are well understood, numerical methods for implementing them are, at least for now, more ad hoc than formal. In Section 6.13, we speculate about future developments for standardizing supply chain decision databases and methods for constructing them.

Finally, the traditional view of the company's supply chain is that the facilities are owned and operated by the firm, whereas suppliers and customers are outside the firm, is changing rapidly. Companies in many industries are entering into alliances with suppliers and customers aimed at operating their collective and sometimes virtual supply chains in a more integrated manner. We argue in Section 6.13 that the effectiveness of ERP and business-to-business Internet systems in managing virtual supply chains would be enhanced if system developers were to focus more attention on managers' needs for decision support at all levels of planning.

Many of the model entities that we discuss in the following sections were presented as small models and modeling vignettes in Chapters 3 and 4. These include resource constraints, recipes, fixed cost constraints, 0-1 location variables, transportation networks, and other elements. As they are arise in our discussion of the supply chain decision database, the reader can look in the index for references to them in earlier chapters.

6.1 Data Aggregations

The mapping of SKUs into product families, customers into markets, and suppliers into supplier groups is an important first step in conceptualizing and implementing a supply chain model for strategic and tactical planning. Such aggregations are necessary and desirable for management to achieve a global view of the company's supply chain.[2] As discussed in later sections, similar aggregation methods are important for computing indirect costs and for demand forecasting.

Aggregating Products

The practitioner begins model development by deciding how to **aggregate finished products** manufactured or sold by the company into product families. The goal is to define each family in such a way that the products it contains have similar manufacturing and distribution costs and activities throughout the supply chain, while restricting the number of such families to a manageable level. As a rule of thumb, the number of product families considered in a model should not exceed 200; for most applications, this number can and should be much lower. Guidelines for effective aggregations tend to be industry specific.

Aggregating Retailing Products. In retailing companies carrying 50,000 or more SKUs, products aggregated into the same family should have similar handling and transportation characteristics. The aggregation scheme should also reflect differences between fast-moving, high-volume items and slow-moving, low-volume items. The identities of high-volume items acquired from different suppliers, which are otherwise very similar, may need to be kept distinct to avoid unrealistic substitutions in the markets.

For example, consider the supply chain of a wholesaler who distributes sporting goods to retail stores that sell two major brands of sneakers. Suppose one sneaker manufacturer has its plant on the West Coast of the United States and the other has its plant on the East Coast. If sneakers were lumped together in a single family, the optimization model might supply all West Coast demand by shipments from the former manufacturer and all East Coast demands by shipments from the latter manufacturer to reduce transportation costs. This would, of course, violate demand patterns for the sneakers at individual stores. Instead, the model should maintain the two brands as separate products. Specific sizes and styles within each of these product lines, which correspond to many SKUs, could still be aggregated in forming these product families.

For retailers and other companies with many SKUs, the number of distinct product families that must be retained in constructing a model tends to limit itself by the 80/20 rule. Suppose we developed an aggregation scheme consisting of 1000 product families that we considered to be accurate in its groupings. If we ordered these product families by dollar volume of total forecasted sales, experience has shown that at least 80%, and probably even 90%, of total dollar sales for the entire product line would be reached by the total dollar volume of the top 200 families. This would allow us to collapse the bottom 800 product families into a small number of miscellaneous product families without introducing significant error. It might even be reasonable to omit entirely product families that have very low volume from strategic and tactical supply chain analysis.

Aggregating Manufacturing Products. For manufacturing firms, product aggregation is often much easier than it is for retailing companies because the number of

SKUs they produce is often smaller than those handled by distribution companies. The product lines of many manufacturing companies are also more homogeneous. For example, a food company will manufacture a product in several sizes that can be considered as one product, or a paper manufacture may produce a type of paper having 20 different weights that can be aggregated into families of heavy-, medium-, and light-weight paper.

In addition to aggregating finished products, it is sometimes necessary and desirable to create aggregate families of intermediate products and even raw materials. For example, the manufacture of consumer goods often entails packaging items of different sizes such as bottles, caps, boxes, and so on. Such materials can readily be aggregated into just a few categories, such as boxes, caps, and labels, without great loss of accuracy.

Product Aggregation Mappings. Mathematical procedures for implementing product aggregations correspond to mappings of index sets. In Figure 6.2, we display a scheme that allows for the creation of different aggregations for different applications of a modeling system. As shown, the set of unaggregated product indexes are mapped into a **fundamental aggregation** that the practitioner considers to be the finest that will ever be considered by the models. For a retailing company, this might entail a mapping of 50,000 products into 1000 product families, whereas for a manufacturing company, it might entail mapping 10,000 products into 100 product families.

The fundamental aggregation is used to create further aggregations for evaluating different scenarios. For example, 50 products (product families) might suffice for a strategic model addressing capital investment in new manufacturing facilities, whereas 150 products (product families) might be required for a tactical model addressing manufacturing plans across the company's supply chain for the upcom-

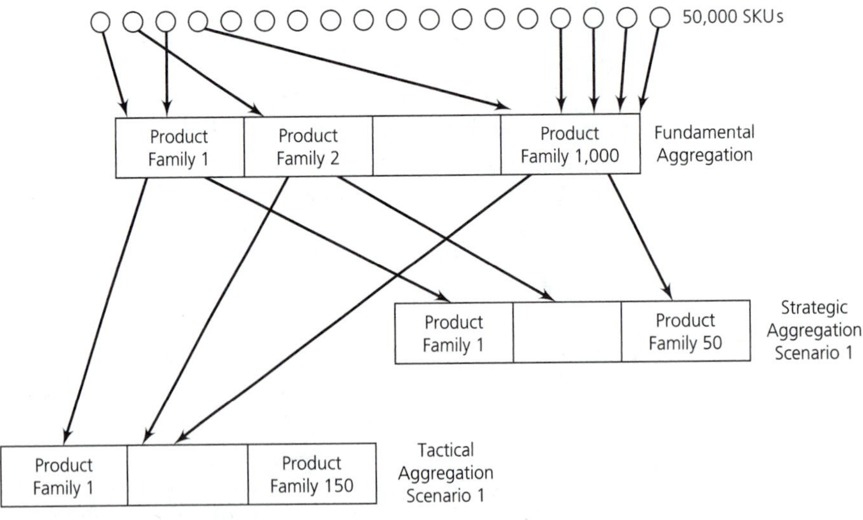

Figure 6.2
Product aggregation scheme

ing quarter. Even within the same time frame of planning and the same study, different aggregations might be required for different scenarios. For example, after plans for several scenarios have been optimized, management might decide to evaluate the construction of a new plant for some, but not all, products in a product family.

Our discussion has focused on aggregations of finished products because model size usually depends most heavily on the details of the subnetwork connecting distribution centers and other sourcing locations to the final markets. The size of the subnetwork is proportional to the number of possible links between sourcing locations and markets, which is a direct function of the number of markets multiplied by the number of finished products. Controlling the number of markets by aggregation is the next topic to be discussed.

Aggregating Customers and Markets

As with products, a company's customer base at the transactional level might be quite detailed, with thousands of customers receiving finished products each year. Methods that **aggregate customers into markets** consider grouping customers in a tight geographical region with similar demand characteristics into a market. It should be possible for most supply chain applications to constrain the number of markets included in a model to a few hundred, although models with as many as 1000 markets have been successfully generated and optimized.

Although customers within close proximity of one another are candidates for aggregation into a single market zone, their demand characteristics might require that they be kept separate. For example, in developing a model for a grocery wholesaler, it was necessary to preserve differences among several types of customers to accurately describe outbound transportation costs. The costs per hundredweight-mile of products delivered to large supermarkets receiving full truckload shipments were significantly different from those for small grocery stores receiving small deliveries from a truck that also visits several other small stores.

In addition, for reasons relating to customer service and perhaps even product requirements, it might be necessary to treat individual large customers as separate "markets" in a model. If a large customer requires better than average on-time delivery, the company might find that outbound transportation costs to that customer are higher due to a larger percentage of less-than-full truckload shipments. Similarly, if a large customer has contracted with a manufacturing firm for a customized version of one or more finished products, the customer and the products should be kept distinct and not aggregated with other customers and products.

The 80/20 rule also applies to customer aggregation; that is, if customers are ordered by sales volume, we can expect that more than 80% of the company's total sales volume is shipped to customers in the top 20% of the list. Even if the top 50 or 100 largest customers are preserved as separate entities for the reasons just cited, the total volume of the top 300 customers should be well over 90% of total sales volume. Very small customers may either be ignored in creating a strategic or tactical model or lumped in the market whose geographical center is closest to them.

Aggregating Suppliers

Finally, suppliers in close geographic proximity who provide parts or products in the same family may be aggregated into a supplier group. As with other types of aggregation, the form of supplier aggregation will depend on the application. When analyzing inbound logistics planning for suppliers to a large automotive manufacturer, the intended use of parts (e.g., chassis, engine, seats) is not relevant. Instead, suppliers are aggregated into groups based on their size, geographical location, and handling characteristics. For example, large suppliers that ship in full truckloads from the same three-digit zip code would be aggregated into a single group. Small suppliers that ship in less than full truckloads from the same three-digit zip code would be aggregated into a different group because their transportation costs per mile are higher.

6.2 Facility Data

In this section, we discuss data that specify a submodel of an individual facility in a company's supply chain. The facility might be a manufacturing plant where raw materials, parts, or components are physically transformed or assembled into intermediate or finished products. It might also be a distribution center (DC) where products are handled but not physically transformed. We model a distribution center using the same elements that we use to model a manufacturing facility because its activities add value to the company's products. DCs also incur costs, consume resources, and are subject to capacity constraints in a manner similar to manufacturing facilities.

Clearly, if we were to consider facilities in the broadest sense, we would need to describe an extremely large class of models and associated data. To focus our discussion, we propose instead a relatively simple modeling paradigm, which accurately addresses a surprisingly large class of facilities. In addition to illustrating the form and content of typical facility data in a supply chain decision database, the paradigm has proven valuable in practice. Details of the paradigm and the implied facility data are discussed in the next subsection. We discuss several applications in the subsection after that.

Recipes, Processes, Resources, and Costs

The modeling paradigm we propose is depicted in Figure 6.3. Products enter the facility, flow through multiple **processes** where they are transformed by **recipes,** and leave the facility as processed products. Remember that "products" might actually be product families. Also, products might be raw materials obtained from suppliers, intermediate products shipped between facilities, and finished products sold in the markets. Associated with each product is a unit of measure, which might change as

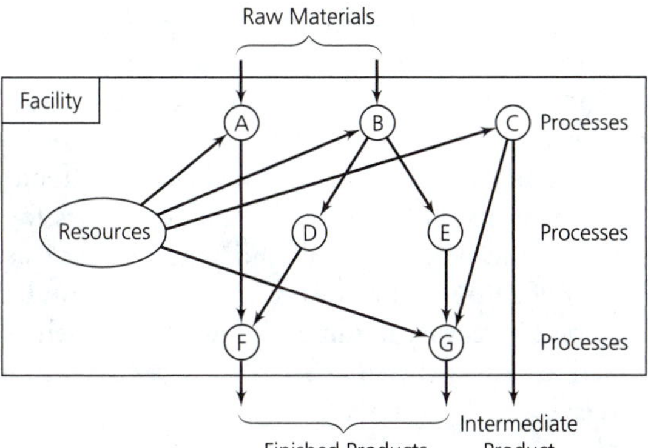

Figure 6.3
Faculty scheme

the result of a transformation. For example, for a packaging process at a brewery, beer inputs measured in hectoliters become packaged beer measured in 100 cases as outputs.

In general, multiple recipes will be available at each process, and each recipe may accept multiple input products and produce multiple output products. The processed products might be finished products that are then distributed to the markets or intermediate products that are transported to other facilities in the company's supply chain for further processing or downstream distribution. In addition, the facility contains **resources** that are consumed by recipes of multiple processes. Examples of such resources are labor hours spent on materials handling and space consumed by work-in-process inventory. As we describe shortly, process and resource capacities are linked to process and resource costs by the construction of cost relationships.

The recipes available at each process are the value adding activities of the facility. In fact, recipes are sometimes called **activities.** For example, a recipe at an oil refinery might be as follows:

$$\begin{matrix} -1 \\ b_1 \\ b_2 \\ b_3 \end{matrix}$$

where the -1 refers to input of a specific type of crude oil measured in 100 barrels to the distillation unit, and the b_j ($j = 1, 2, 3$) refer to intermediate products measured in 100 barrels passed to a catalytic cracker and other process units at the refinery. Associated with each recipe is an activity level that the model determines is optimal. For example, the above recipe might have an activity level of 100, indicating that 10,000 barrels of the crude oil are processed to yield 10,000 * b_j barrels of each intermediate product j. The activity level for each recipe for a given month selected by the optimization model would depend implicitly on demands for refined products to be met by the refinery and the mixture of crude oils available in the refinery's holding tanks. A recipe at a distribution center might have the same form, but the −1 refers to a consumer product measured in 100 cases from a supplier received at a cross-dock and the b_j (j = 1, 2, 3) refer to the number of 100 cases sorted for dispatching to retail store j.

Similarly, several product recipes may be used by food manufacturers to exploit differences in commodity prices. For example, recipes for a butter substitute may admit leeway in the percentages of different oils they use. The particular recipe selected to manufacture the product during a given month or quarter would depend on the company's inventory holdings of the oils and their relative commodity prices.

We describe costs incurred at a facility by a **cost taxonomy** that has the following four levels:

- **Product costs.** Direct recipe costs associated with manufacturing or handling a product (e.g., raw material costs, direct labor costs, setup costs)
- **Process costs.** Direct costs associated with physical processes used in manufacturing and distributing products (e.g., operating and replacement costs of crude oil distillation units, quality testing costs, and labor and equipment costs associated with cross-docking at a DC)
- **Facility resource costs.** Indirect costs associated with resources consumed by multiple processes (e.g., machine maintenance labor costs, materials handling costs for work in process, and inventory management system and associated human analyst costs)
- **Facility overhead costs.** Indirect costs associated with maintaining the facility (e.g., plant or DC manager's salary and benefits, energy costs, and labor and information technology costs for maintaining facility accounting systems)

For supply chain decision making, these costs must be represented by **cost relationships** that describe how costs will be incurred as a function of independent factors, called cost drivers or activities.

Cost relationships depict costs as a function of one or more cost drivers. Examples of cost drivers are processing machine hours for direct process costs and number of orders dispatched for indirect shipping costs. In Figure 6.4a, we depict a simple linear cost relationship characterized by the single parameter c. In Figure 6.4b, we depict a more complex cost relationship characterized by six parameters, F, c_1, M_1, G, c_2, M_2, which requires 0-1 decision variables. When describing process costs, the parameter M2 represents the hard capacity of the process for the time period of the model. Still more complex cost relationships involving nonadditive functions of multiple cost drivers are clearly possible; for example, a cost relationship that involves the drivers v_1 and v_2 and has a cost term of the form $g * v_1 * v_2$. For expositional convenience, we assume that all the cost relationships to be considered for the supply chain decision database do not exhibit this complication due to cross-products of decision variables, implying they can be modeled using mixed integer programming constructs.

The development of accurate and comprehensive cost relationships is a central and difficult task in the creation of a supply chain decision database. Principles for carrying out this task draw on recent work by management accounting academics

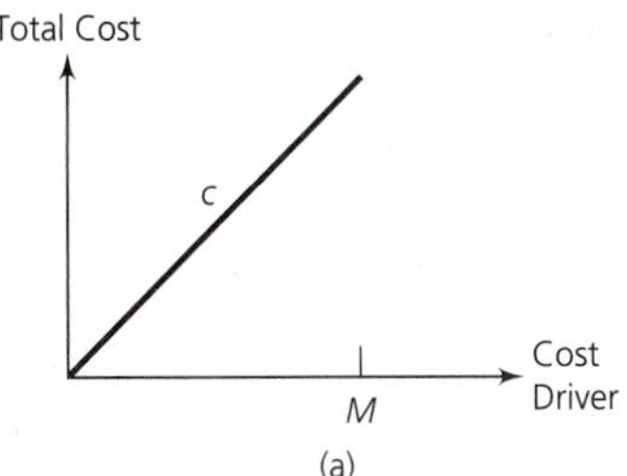

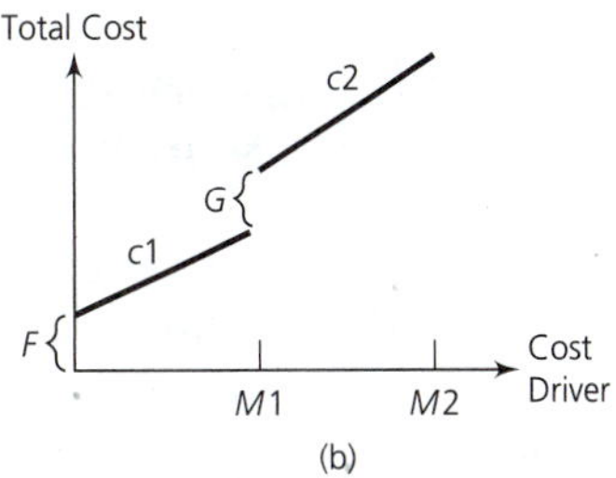

Figure 6.4
(a) Simple cost relationship; (b) complex cost relationship

and practitioners, especially those constructing and evolving **activity-based costing** methods. These developments are discussed in greater detail in Section 6.7; we defer further discussion of methods for estimating cost relationships until then.

Inventories. Decisions regarding inventories of raw materials and intermediate and finished products held at a facility are important to efficient supply chain planning. Moreover, inventory holding costs, which include capital costs, obsolescence, and out-of-stock costs, can be an important component of total supply chain cost. Unfortunately, classical inventory models, which pertain to operating policies for a single product, do not readily combine with snapshot optimization models for integrated supply chain management, which are concerned with total cost minimization at the strategic and tactical levels.

The difficulties are lessened if multiple-period optimization models are used because inventory costs can be computed on the basis of inventories at the end of each period. However, if the lengths of the periods are so large that considerable variation of inventory within periods is expected, serious modeling difficulties remain. Fortunately, theoretical and practical arguments support the construction of meaningful cost relationships for within-period inventory costs that use inventory throughput as the cost driver. These issues are discussed in detail in Section 11.2. Rather than repeat them here, we refer the reader to that section.

Applications. The following is a partial listing of different types of manufacturing and distribution facilities that can be effectively described by the modeling paradigm of the previous subsection:

- **Process plants.** Facilities where products flow through one or more stages in which raw materials are converted to intermediate and finished products (e.g., oil refineries, chemical plants, pharmaceutical plants, paper mills, food manufacturing plants, breweries)
- **Discrete parts manufacturing plants.** Facilities where parts and components are manufactured, assembled, and tested in several stages to produce discrete quantities of finished products (e.g., computer and electronics manufacturers, automobile manufacturers, manufacturers of consumer durables)
- **Packaging plants.** Facilities linked to process and discrete parts plants where consumer or industrial products are packaged for shipment to customers (e.g., distribution centers that package bulk chemicals for sale to medium and small

customers and distribution centers where some products are assembled before shipment to customers)

- **Distribution centers.** Facilities where products are received, sorted, sometimes stored, and shipped to customers (e.g., company-owned and third-party distribution centers of wholesale retailing and grocery companies, depots for reusuable containers managed by a third-party, reverse logistics company)

Figure 6.5 depicts a facility where potatoes and corn (measured in tons) are converted to potato chips and corns chips (measured in 100 cases). As shown, the facility has five processes and one resource. Figure 6.6 depicts a distribution center where products are received, sorted, and dispatched and some products are stored.

Job shops are a class of facility that the modeling paradigm does not easily describe. These are manufacturing plants where jobs comprising multiple tasks performed at different work stations are undertaken. The sequencing of tasks and the

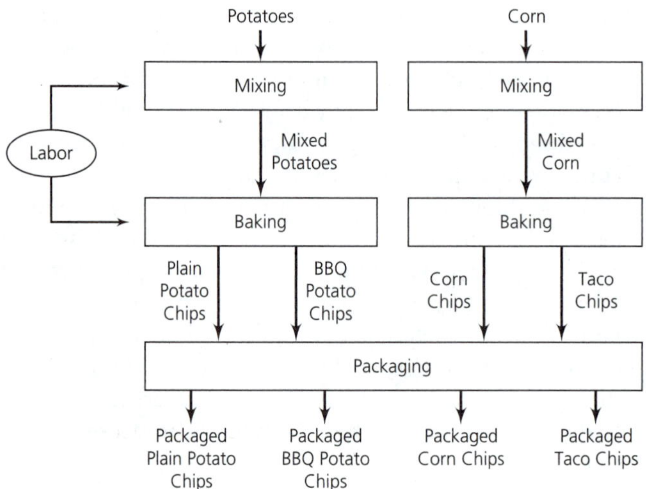

Figure 6.5
Process flow for a food manufacturer

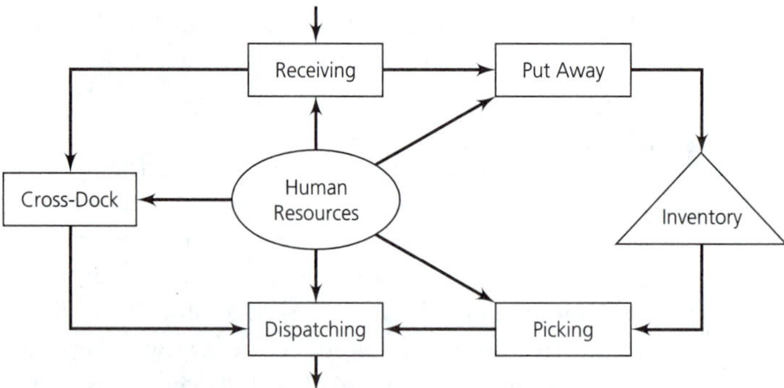

Figure 6.6
Process flow in a distribution center

times to complete them varies from job to job, and therefore it is difficult to track and control manufacture of intermediate and finished products. Job shops describe plants where trucks or aircraft engines are maintained and repaired, publishing shops, or plants that manufacture customized machine tools.

6.3 Transportation Network Data

In this section, we discuss structural and numerical data characterizing transportation network submodels connecting suppliers, facilities, and markets. The basic element in these networks is very simple. It is a (directed) link connecting an origin (supplier or facility) to a destination (facility or market) along which a product may flow. A relationship describing cost as a function of the volume of product flow is associated with the link. For many applications, the cost relationship is a simple linear function in which cost per unit of flow is multiplied by the volume. Implicit in the relationship is a capacity or maximal upper bound on the volume due to contractual commitments, company policy, or other reasons.

Despite the simplicity of data describing an individual link, generating and managing the data of a network submodel can be a demanding exercise because it may contain tens or even hundreds of thousands of links. Moreover, cost relationships might depend on large databases describing historical and current fleet operations, common carrier costs, and a host of other factors. The network description might also be complicated by modal choices and volume discounts. The growth of transportation science as a separate discipline has been stimulated by the need of logistics managers to understand and cope with these complexities.

Still, in discussing transportation networks, we should not lose sight of our focus on minimizing *total* supply chain cost over strategic and tactical planning horizons. The level of detail appropriate for network submodels depends on the relative importance of transportation costs in this total. For a company that manufactures paper in several mills and distributes it across the United States, transportation decisions are very important because transportation costs can be 20% or more of total delivered cost. In addition, a variety of distribution channels are available, including direct deliveries from mills to customers and truckload or rail deliveries to distributors at their warehouses. By contrast, because transportation costs of jewelry products will be less than 5% of a jewelry company's total delivered costs, the company can afford to pay far less attention to the details of transportation.

Transportation Network Submodels

The transportation components of a typical supply chain are as follows:

- The **inbound transportation network** linking the company's suppliers to its facilities

- The **interfacility transportation network** connecting its facilities to one another
- The **outbound transportation network** connecting the company's facilities to its customers and markets

As we discuss below, the extent to which one, two, or all three of these network submodels needs to be created and maintained in the same supply chain decision database depends on the mission and size of the company. In the following three subsections, we discuss modeling and data issues associated with each type of network.

Inbound Transportation Networks. For a specialty chemicals company seeking to optimize its worldwide production and distribution strategies, the inbound network describes feedstock shipments from sources on several continents to plants on several continents, some of which are quite distant from all feedstock sources. Thus, feedstock may travel thousands of miles by ship. The inbound network is small relative to others discussed below, but tactical planning is complicated by decisions about ship capacities, shipment sizes, and the timing of their arrivals. In making such decisions, the goal is to balance transportation costs against inventory costs.

For a manufacturer of mainframe computers with assembly plants in the United States, the inbound network describes shipments to a small number of plants of commodities, parts, and subsystems from a large number of suppliers located in the North America, Asia, and Europe. Some suppliers are other divisions of the company. For a U.S. automotive manufacturer, the network connecting suppliers to assembly plants is enormous, again with commodities, parts, and subsystems being shipped from several continents to plants located mainly in the midwestern region of the United States. An important set of decisions that determines the design of these networks is to locate and size warehousing and cross-docking facilities for consolidating inbound items from suppliers.

For a wholesale grocery company located in central Canada, the inbound network also involves a large number of geographically dispersed suppliers providing as many as 50,000 SKUs each year. These suppliers deliver to approximately six distribution centers located near the company's major markets. The network's configuration is shaped by Canada's geography, which restricts the number of distinct routes and directions from which supplies can enter the system. For many suppliers, the inbound cost of transportation is included in the delivered cost of their products. The company has undertaken a large supply chain study, in part to assess new pricing and inbound transportation strategies for reducing these costs.

Interfacility Transportation Networks. For a forest products company doing business only in the United States, each product line is manufactured in a small number of locations, and products are shipped directly to customers and retailers throughout the country. Thus, the company has no interfacility transportation network. Conversely, for a consumer paper products company seeking to consolidate its operations after a merger, interfacility shipments became an important part of its new production and distribution strategy. Under the new strategy, the company decided that each plant would produce only a portion of the company's entire product line. By cross-docking products from other plants at the plant's shipping facility, markets serviced by the plant would receive shipments of the company's full product line. Transshipments would also facilitate full truckload outbound deliveries from each plant.

Interfacility shipments are also very important for electronic firms like Hewlett Packard (HP) where products are manufactured in stages at geographically distinct locations to minimize total production and inventory costs. HP has had particular success in staging the manufacture of their inkjet printers to minimize the costs of specializing printers for markets in different countries. Because each country requires a somewhat differentiated product based on local power supply, power plugs, and the language used for documentation materials, HP designed generic versions of the printers that are manufactured and stored in inventory at facilities upstream in the supply chain. As needed, these units are shipped to facilities near the final markets where product differentiation is completed.

For the specialty chemicals company discussed above, intermediate products are shipped from manufacturing plants to smaller plants where the product is converted to final product and packaged. This arrangement allows the smaller, downstream plants to be located nearer the markets. Also, interfacility shipments made in bulk quantities are cheaper than shipments of finished product in packaged form.

For a company that distributes spare parts throughout Indonesia for a U.S.-based manufacturer of farm equipment, the distribution facilities are organized in a multiechelon network. Parts arrive in Singapore from the manufacturer, and a major portion of total system inventory is stored in a large distribution center there. Parts are then distributed and stored in smaller quantities through facilities at three lower levels. Due to Indonesia's island geography, spare parts are transported by ship and truck, with some emergency orders shipped by air. Normal and emergency shipments are made to customers from all levels of the network as well as to lower-level facilities. Inventory management of spare parts over a multiechelon network such as this one is a very complex problem. We will discuss it again in Chapter 11.

Outbound Transportation Networks. Efficient management of outbound transportation is a critical activity for many companies, especially distribution companies whose raison d'être is to deliver the correct product in the correct quantities at the correct time to its customers. For a company that distributes propane to more than 100,000 customers in a large metropolitan area, strategic supply chain analysis involves an economic rationalization of the number and location of depots. Propane arrives at the depots in large tanker trucks, it is then unloaded into small cylinders and tanks for delivery to customers in five major segments: residential, commercial, industrial, agricultural, and automotive. The goals are to achieve an appropriate balance between minimizing total cost and maximizing customer service. The total cost includes operating costs such as depot and transportation costs, and investment costs, which are based on capital tied up in real estate, delivery trucks, cylinders, tanks, and inventories.

Wholesaling and retailing companies typically have very large outbound transportation networks. For a wholesale grocery company with 6 distribution centers,

50 product families, and 500 customers of varying types, the network will have 75,000 links even when obviously uneconomic origin and destination combinations are eliminated. Fortunately, the structure of such a transportation submodel is mathematically simple, despite its size, allowing supply chain models for wholesaling companies to be optimized without undue difficulty.

Finally, we note that transportation flows are not always confined to the three types of networks just discussed. Many retailing companies are increasing the use of direct-to-store deliveries by qualified suppliers. Some manufacturing companies, especially those located in Germany and other European countries that have stiff environmental laws, must also consider transportation of products from their markets back to their plants for recycling. Our data and modeling constructions can be readily extended to deal with complications such as these and others.

Transportation Costs and Capacities

Transportation costs are those associated with the flow of products on links between facilities. They are the following two types of costs:

- **Flow costs.** Direct costs per unit associated with product flows between facilities (e.g., mileage costs for the company's trucking fleet, contract carrier costs, and pipeline inventory costs)
- **Transportation resource costs.** Indirect costs per unit associated with managing flows (e.g., routing system and human router costs, investment costs in spare parts for a trucking fleet, and legal and administrative costs associated with carrier contracts)

Product flow cost per unit on a link depends on the volume of flow and the choice of transportation mode, which we discussed at length above. It also depends, of course, on characteristics of the product, especially whether the cost of a truckload shipment of the product will depend on its volume or its weight. Unusual products, such as frozen foods or flammable liquids, will have costs reflecting special handling and investment in special equipment.

Most, if not all, transportation resource costs could be treated as resource costs at facilities where value added activities, such as vehicle routing, take place. The company, however, will face business decisions where it is important to use comprehensive transportation costs that include avoidable indirect costs. This would be the case, for example, when the company wishes to evaluate the economic benefits of a third-party transportation contract. If significant indirect transportation costs, such as routing and dispatching, were omitted from in-house fleet costs, the company might incorrectly reject the contract.

In discussing the major factors that determine product link costs, keep in mind that such costs must be computed for each link in the supply chain network along which the product *might* flow. Whether or not flow occurs on the link in an optimal solution to a supply chain model depends on considerations of global optimality. It is not uncommon to find that 80%, or more, of the links in a supply chain model have no flow on them in an optimal solution. Of course, it is difficult to know a priori which links will be used. Moreover, as we make several model runs to optimize different scenarios of the company's supply chain future, we can expect that different links will carry product flows. For supply chain scenarios involving new suppliers, facilities and markets and even new products, product link costs must be developed for links and perhaps products for which the company has little or no data. Fortunately, publicly available transportation databases can be acquired to help estimate new link costs.

In creating network submodels of appropriate and manageable sizes, remember that tactical and strategic supply chain planning models are based on products that are actually product families, each having many SKUs. Thus, the unit transportation cost of a product on any link will usually be a weighted average of the unit costs of the individual SKUs in the family. The assumption is that the unit costs of these SKUs do not vary greatly and therefore that averaging does not introduce significant errors.

Note also that the cost per unit of product flow might include components not directly associated with transportation operations such as in-transit inventory or duties. The in-transit inventory holding cost is computed by multiplying the number of days to travel between origin and destination by the daily cost of capital per unit of product. Additional in-transit costs might include losses due to evaporation or spillage. Obviously, such costs should be calculated and included in product flow cost only if they are significant. A duty cost per unit of flow can be included in the direct flow cost per unit when the origin and destination of the link lie in different countries and the origin country charges an export duty and/or the destination country charges an import duty.

Upper and lower bounds on the flow in links may reflect contractual commitments. They can also be used in the validation stage of a modeling project to constrain the solution of an optimization model to coincide with a historical solution. Finally, they may reflect policy constraints imposed by management on an optimal supply chain solution; for example, lower bounds on outbound product flows on certain links to promote full truckload shipments.

Modal Choice and Shipment Sizes

In the most general situation, a company will be faced with a **choice of transportation modes** for shipments along a link; they might include large truck, small truck, rail, air, and barge. Even if the shipment can only be made by one type of truck, the company may be faced with a choice of shipment size, which might be full truckload (FTL) or various sizes of less-than-truckload (LTL). Remember, we are concerned in this chapter with strategic and tactical planning. Therefore, these are not operational choices, but longer-term plans for which the company wishes to make a single choice of mode or shipment size. For strategic planning, modeling the choices needs only to accurately reflect transportation costs. For tactical planning, modeling the choices might also need to determine optimal choices for normal operating conditions.

From a modeling perspective, the choices regarding transportation mode and shipment size will require mixed integer programming constructs whenever there are volume discounts on product flow in a link, which, unfortunately, is the usual case (e.g., FTL shipments cost less per hundredweight than LTL shipments). A factor mitigating against this modeling complexity is that modal and size choices can often be resolved by simple rules prior to modeling that are approximately optimal: For example, if the link is more than 1000 miles, send the shipment by rail; otherwise, send the shipment by truck. The unit cost of the flow on these links would reflect the rule. Nevertheless, situations arise where modal choices can only be rigorously made using mixed integer programming.

Utilities for Generating Networks

To efficiently and flexibly generate large-scale transportation subnetworks for inclusion in tactical and strategic models, the company must acquire or develop software utilities that merge detailed data about the locations of suppliers, facilities and markets, distances among pairs of origin and destination locations, transportation rates, and possibly several other factors. Distances might be provided in tables reflecting road network distances, or they might be computed from geometric formulas. Similarly, rates might be computed from tables or, in the case of company fleets, formulas based on historical cost data.

An important consideration in generating transportation subnetworks is the specification of allowable origin-destination pairs. To ensure satisfactory customer service, the company might wish to limit outbound links from facilities to those markets within a specified maximal distance. These limits might be different for different classes of customers, which means the markets have to be appropriately defined. Even if customer service is not an issue, the modeling practitioner may limit the maximal distance for links in a subnetwork to control the size of the resulting optimization model. In most applications, this can be accomplished without fear of eliminating attractive options; for a distribution network with 20 distribution centers located across the United States, we can safely eliminate links from distribution centers in Atlanta or St. Louis to markets on the West Coast.

Finally, remember that strategic and even some tactical supply chain models will address decision options (e.g., DC locations, sourcing of new markets) involving transportation data that are not historical. The accuracy of these new data will affect the analysis. The company's analysts must employ different data acquisition methods to create and maintain transportation data about future options than they do for its historical options.

6.4 Supplier Data

Suppliers include vendors and other sources of raw materials, parts, components, or finished products. We assume that supplier data are used to populate modeling descriptions of costs, acquisition volumes, and maximal quantities. It is possible, of course, that the company will have more complex relationships with some suppliers.

For example, a large electronics manufacturing company might contract for production resources at a small contractor for the coming year and which the manufacturer will employ to make specific components as it sees fit on a monthly basis during the year. Such vendor relationships would be modeled as facilities in a supply chain model, and the data would be included in the facilities data. A company might also acquire third-party logistics services from vendors, such as transportation or warehousing. Data pertaining to them would be incorporated in data files describing transportation subnetworks or facilities.

Vendor Costs and Constraints

In the general case, a vendor of raw materials, parts, components, or finished products will offer the company **volume discounts,** which means the cost per unit will decrease as volume increases. The most straightforward volume discount is on the marginal price of the item; for example, the vendor will charge \$10 per unit up to 10,000 units, followed by a price break to \$8 per unit for purchases in excess of 10,000 units. As discussed in Section 4.1, mixed integer programming is well suited to modeling such economies of scale. Moreover, it can be applied to a vendor's price schedule involving several levels of volume discount based on marginal cost, although it might add to the model's complexity because we would need to employ a 0-1 decision variable for each price break. The complexity of the model becomes even greater if the company considers doing business with several vendors offering the same items, each with its own price schedule with volume discounts, possibly over different periods of time. Fortunately, the complexity is manageable, and effective mixed integer programming models have been implemented and successfully used for vendor selection problems with such characteristics.

A related construction arose in the implementation of models and modeling systems for an industrial gases company. The company produces liquid and gaseous oxygen, nitrogen, argon, and other elements in plants where the only variable production cost is the cost of electricity used to run compressors and liquefiers. In fact, 60% or more of total product costs may be money paid to the electric power company. A typical contract includes monthly charges for both energy consumption (kilowatt hour) and maximal power draw (kilowatt). Different plants in a geographical region might have significantly different contractual arrangements with their power company and equipment with different operating characteristics.

A regional planning model was implemented and applied to the problem of minimizing the sum of energy charges, power charges, and distribution costs to operate the plants in the region and transport products in meeting forecasted monthly demand. Using chemical engineering models, a collection of representative production slates was developed, each specifying a plant configuration, a production rate for each product, and its power draw. The production rates generally increased with increasing power draw.

The planning problem had the feature that if a particular slate at a plant was used and forced the power draw for the month to a level P^*, any other slates drawing less than P^* would effectively be free with respect to the power charge. The model determined the slates to be operated at each plant, the length of time they should be run during the month, the quantity of each product to be shipped to each market, and the maximal power demand at each plant. Optimizing over the vendors' contracts (that is, the power contracts) was the most important, and complicated, aspect of the planning problem.

A vendor might offer other terms requiring creative modeling to be evaluated according to the wishes of the decision makers. In implementing a vendor selection system for a computer manufacturer, we discovered that some vendors would offer a volume discount on average, rather than marginal, price. Figure 6.7 illustrates the situation where the average price per unit is \$10 for purchases up to 10,000 units within in a given year and then drops to \$8 per unit for purchases in excess of 10,000 units. Such a schedule has a glaring inconsistency. If the company had been considering an acquisition of 8000 units at a cost of \$80,000, it could acquire another 2000 units at no extra cost due to the volume discount. In effect the total cost curve has a flat portion between 8000 and 10,000 units.

Somewhat surprisingly, this anomaly was perceived as a problem by the buyers at the computer manufacturer. They did not want to give vendors offering such discounts the impression that they were exploiting them by acquiring units for no additional cost. Thus, the buyers requested that constraints be added to the vendor selection model that excluded volumes on the flat parts of the total cost curve as acceptable decisions. Again, mixed integer programming model constructs were employed to accommodate the request. Our suggestion that vendors always base their discounts on marginal rather than average cost was rejected out of hand. This is just one example of many real-world complications that cannot be ignored even when they might appear logically inconsistent to the modeling practitioner.

A range of constraints may be superimposed on the company's purchasing decisions by the vendors. For some chemical purchases, vendors may require that the company buy two or more chemicals produced by the same process in fixed ratios. These ratios reflect an efficient production configuration for the vendor. In the natural gas industry, a vendor may offer to sell gas at a set price in quantities between a yearly minimum and maximum. If the company elects to take less than the mini-

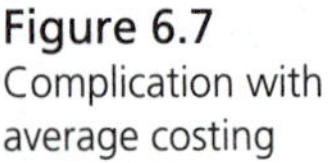
Figure 6.7
Complication with average costing

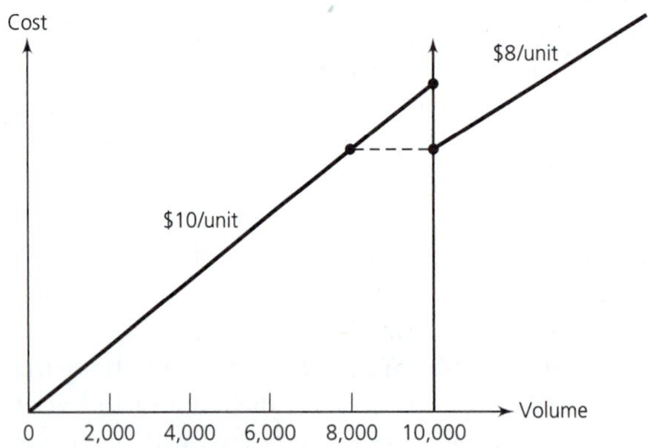

mum, it will still be obliged to pay for the minimum. This is a so-called take-or-pay policy. In later time years, the company has the option to acquire the quantity already paid for, but not taken, at no cost or at a greatly reduced cost. Again, these conditions can be accurately captured in a supply chain model.

The company might impose its own constraints on vendor purchasing strategies that reflect concerns about the **reliability** of supply. For example, for a critical raw material, part, or component, the company might require selection of two vendors for the coming year. This constraint as stated is imprecise because it fails to indicate the quantity to be supplied by the secondary vendor. If the company buys 1 million units per year, it would not be reasonable to acquire 999,999 from the primary vendor and 1 from the secondary one. The policy is fully articulated by indicating maximal and minimal quantities conditionally associated with each vendor; that is, the company either purchases nothing from each vendor or some quantity between a specified minimum and a maximum. The supply chain model can then be directed to select exactly two vendors that meet the company's needs.

Alternatively, the company may force redundancy by imposing the constraints that each vendor of a critical commodity can supply more than 75%, say, of the total volume needed for the year. Although such constraints are less complex because they do not require mixed integer programming, they may yield supply strategies that are difficult to implement. For example, a model with such a constraint might suggest a strategy where five vendors provide the commodity, but three of them provide less than 10% of the total volume. In short, this type of constraint might be useful for imposing redundancy during exploratory runs, whereas constraints of the type discussed in the previous paragraph would be needed to determine an implementable vendor selection strategy.

A large multinational company that manufactures commodities such as refined petroleum products or aluminum will sometimes enter into an **exchange agreement** with a competitor that manufactures similar or identical products. The agreement states that the company will acquire a certain volume of product from the competitor at a specified geographical location at a specified price during a specified time period. The company will reciprocate by supplying the competitor with the same volume of product at another location, possibly during a different time period. Supply chain models have proven very effective in evaluating the merits of proposed exchange agreements.

6.5 Role of Management Accounting

Management accounting is "the process of identifying, measuring, reporting and analyzing information about the economic events of organizations."[3] It is concerned with helping managers make better decisions and providing feedback and control on current performance. By contrast, **financial accounting** is responsible for reporting results about historical performance to the company's external constituencies of stockholders, creditors, and tax authorities. Over the past century, developments in management accounting to support internal decision making and control were inhibited because government regulations imposed strict rules on financial accounting. Implementation of management accounting methods also require information technologies that have become available only in recent years.[4]

Management accounting methods for supply chain planning are closely linked to methods for creating and applying optimization models. In fact, the two disciplines overlap considerably in their analysis of business problems. Rather than attempt to create a unified theory, which would be difficult, lengthy, and prosaic, we will adhere to our main theme by using optimization models as frames or templates for cost data developed by management accounting. By this we mean that optimization models provide data file sets, possibly in the form of structured spreadsheets or workbooks, to be filled in with cost data.

Our discussion will focus on the following two main tasks:

1. Develop causal cost relationships of direct and indirect costs
2. Compute transfer, product, and customer costs from an optimal solution to a supply chain model

Remember that we are concerned in this chapter with cost data for strategic and tactical planning of supply chains, which involves product, customer, and vendor aggregations. The cost data must be consistent with the aggregations. Cost data for operational planning will be discussed in Chapter 10.

The form, scope, and application of management accounting and optimization modeling methods for supply chain planning are still changing rapidly as ERP and e-commerce systems emerge and are adopted. Savings due to the application of modeling systems are not achieved free of cost. New methods are needed to define and estimate the costs of acquiring and maintaining information technologies and organizational processes for exploiting them.

As we discussed in Sections 6.1 and 6.2, supply chain models require facility and transportation costs and cost relationships using management accounting methods. For completeness, we restate them here. Facility costs are segmented as follows:

- **Product costs.** Direct costs associated with manufacturing or handling a product
- **Process costs.** Direct costs associated with physical processes used in manufacturing and distribution transformations of products
- **Facility resource costs.** Indirect costs associated with resources consumed by multiple processes such as maintenance labor or plant floor space used for inventory
- **Facility overhead costs.** Indirect costs associated with maintaining the facility such as plant manager's salary and benefits, real estate taxes

Thus, we have two levels of direct costs and two levels of indirect costs at a facility. The factors affecting direct costs are often more obvious, although the nonlinear dependence of costs on volumes may sometimes prove challenging to estimate.

A central concern of management accounting is the creation of better models of indirect costs at a facility, which have been increasing in recent years relative to direct costs due to increased customer demands, global competition, and the advent of new technologies. Of the two types of indirect costs, facility overhead costs are easier to estimate because they are unconnected with specific activities of the facility. Such costs are allocated on the basis of facility throughput.

Estimating resource costs, by contrast, requires the identification of meaningful categories of indirect value adding activities at the facility. Here we use the term *resource* in a general sense to connote physical, human, financial, information technology, marketing, organizational, and legal resources to be allocated to activities at the facility, while incurring indirect costs. Such resource costs can be difficult to identify, quantify, and validate. An important recent method of management accounting, **activity based costing,** was created to provide qualitative and quantitative insights into such indirect costs. We discuss this method in detail in the following subsection.

Transportation costs associated with the flow of products on links between facilities are segmented as follows:

- **Flow costs.** Direct costs associated with product flows between facilities
- **Transportation resource costs.** Indirect costs associated with managing flows

Product flow costs depend on the volume of flow and the choice of transportation mode. Transportation resource costs are indirect costs that should be incorporated to accurately describe and control total transportation costs.

Develop Causal Cost Relationships of Direct and Indirect Costs

An optimization model requires inputs reflecting cost behavior as well as numbers. Cost behavior is represented by **cost relationships** between natural categories of direct and indirect costs discussed above and independent factors, called **cost drivers.** Typical cost relationships are depicted in Figure 6.4. To provide managers with useful insights into costs and decisions, we seek **causal** cost relationships using cost drivers that reflect supply chain activities causing cost and value to be added to the firm's products and services. Cost behavior also refers to forecasts or projections about how costs will change as operations in the future differ in volume and mix from historical operations. Finally, it refers to new costs involving new products, markets, vendors, facilities, and transportation activities that the company wishes to evaluate as part of its strategic and tactical planning exercises.

Selecting cost drivers for direct cost relationships is often straightforward because direct manufacturing and distribution activities usually depend on machines, people, and raw materials in obvious ways. Selecting cost drivers for indirect cost relationships is more difficult. It requires management accounting expertise plus knowledge of the company's business. Developments in activity-based costing methods, which we discuss next, are aimed at identifying cost drivers for indirect costs.

Activity-Based Costing

Activity-based costing (ABC) is a "method of measuring the cost and performance of activities and cost objects. [It] assigns cost to activities based on their use of resources, and assigns cost to cost objects based on their use of activities. ABC recognizes the causal relationship of cost drivers to activities."[5] The following are involved in this description:

- **Activities** describe work performed in the organization that consume resources and cause cost to be incurred.
- **Resources** are economic objects that are consumed in the performance of activities.
- **Cost drivers** are factors affecting the cost of an activity and the resources it consumes.
- **Cost objects** are the output of activities and correspond to products, customers, and services.

ABC analysis of historical costs is intended to provide accurate and causal descriptions of indirect and support costs, which can be extended to forecasts of future costs. It also seeks to identify hidden, unneeded costs in the firm's supply chain, allowing management to take steps to reduce or eliminate them. Finally, it tries to calculate accurate costs reflecting diverse demands placed on the firm for customized goods and services.

ABC has been widely applied in manufacturing and distribution companies. Although it represents a large step forward in the calculation of meaningful costs of products and services for the purposes of planning and control, its impact on companies where it has been applied appears to be less than expected by its promoters. The method's poor showing in some companies may be partly due to its failure to explicitly analyze *supply chain decisions* that affect these costs. This suggests that integration of ABC with optimization models would greatly benefit both methods.

The logic of the ABC methodology is displayed in Figure 6.8. Analysis begins with a historical record of the raw costs of a company, or a company's facility, which are contained in a general ledger. Alternatively, analysis might begin with a budget of future costs. The costs in the general ledger or budget correspond to direct and indirect costs. Indirect costs are assigned to indirect cost pools called resources. Using resource cost drivers, these are allocated to activity cost pools, or activities. Direct costs based on general ledger data are also represented directly as activities without the intermediate step of assignment as indirect cost pools. The final step is to allocate costs for cost objects based on the activities and their cost drivers.

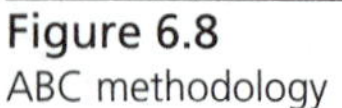
Figure 6.8
ABC methodology

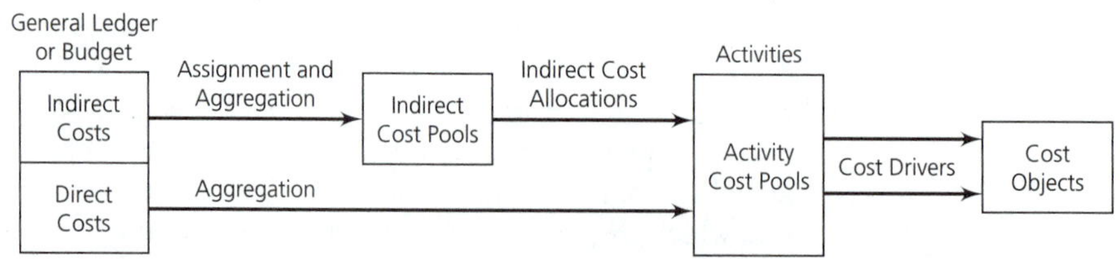

The design of an ABC model is viewed by management accounting practitioners as a flexible, even artistic, interpretation of principles rather than a well-programmed procedure. As with any modeling exercise, human judgment is needed to fit a model to the problems to be addressed. The practitioner must also strive to achieve a good balance between model simplicity, which facilitates its use, and model complexity, which is required to accurately describe cost relationships.

Curiously, ABC practitioners have so far largely ignored statistical data analysis problems that are relevant to the construction of ABC models. The problems are as follows:

- Segment and aggregate costs from the general ledger of the company or plant, which contains the universe of raw cost data, into appropriate resource cost pools
- Select statistically significant resource and activity cost drivers
- Estimate functional relationships and parameters linking cost drivers to activities

Note also that the usual assumption of a linear relationship between a volumetric cost driver and an activity cost may not be valid over the full range of possible values for the cost driver. The relationship may be nonlinear and even discontinuous, such as the cost relationship in Figure 6.4b. Moreover, the cost of an activity may depend on the values of multiple cost drivers, with some terms involving products of drivers.

ABC is a descriptive modeling methodology that could prove very valuable to companies where the communication and management of transactional, financial data has been streamlined through the implementation of ERP systems. Some ERP software companies have been more responsive than others in perceiving this opportunity and trying to exploit it.[6] In addition, ABC has the potential to assist multiple firms in a virtual supply chain to understand their individual and collective costs. Combined with analysis by optimization models, these firms could identify opportunities for shifting activities among partners to achieve cost savings and eliminate redundancy. Because such developments require improvements in interfirm IT and planning processes, they are still in the future.

We digress slightly to discuss briefly supply chain **performance metrics,** which are similar to budgets in that they set standards or incentives for superior managerial behavior with in the firm. They also serve as industry standards that spur middle-of-the-pack or inferior firms to improve their operations. However, rapidly changing IT and business processes in today's business world make it difficult to identify meaningful industry standards.

Metrics are concerned with the following:[7]

- **Utilization** (actual input/norm input); for example machine hours used/machine capacity
- **Productivity** (actual output/actual input); for example, ton-miles delivered/costs incurred
- **Effectiveness** (actual output/norm output); for example, on-time shipments/total shipments

Metrics may be based on historical or projected values, engineering standards, or values from an optimized model. If a modeling system is run on a repetitive basis to manage part or all of a company's supply chain, metrics may be employed as control devices to keep the supply chain running smoothly during the period between modeling analyses.

Connection of ABC to Optimization Models and the Taxonomy of Costs

The connections between ABC and optimization models have not yet been completely articulated. We take the admittedly simplistic view here that the primary role of ABC is to identify cost drivers for indirect cost relationships needed as inputs to supply chain optimization models; namely, the facility resource costs, facility overhead costs, and transportation resource costs discussed in the taxonomy description above. Implicit in this assumption is that cost drivers for direct costs are self-evident and do not require special attention, although considerable analysis may be needed to estimate accurate direct cost relationships. Managerial accounting expertise is required to aggregate data in the general ledger into meaningful pools of resources, which in turn are related to direct and especially indirect activities adding value to operations at the facility.

The process depicted in Figure 6.8 is used to identify and quantify cost drivers for facility and transportation resource costs based on a management accounting analysis of a general ledger or a budget. In so doing, we must distinguish between cost drivers corresponding to resources that may be scarce and those that are merely accounting devices for tracking indirect costs. We say the former cost drivers are the independent variables in **cost/resource relationships** and the latter are the independent variables in **cost/accounting relationships.** The cost/resource relationships are the facility and transportation cost relationships of our template, such as those shown in Figure 6.4. They will, or at least might, require resource allocation in an optimal solution and therefore must be represented by constraints in the optimization model. Their costs are also included in the model's objective function. The cost/accounting relationships do not require resource allocation and therefore need not be represented as constraints in the optimization model. The cost drivers in this case will appear only in the objective function of the optimization model.

Computation of Transfer Prices, Product and Customer Costs from an Optimal Solution to a Supply Chain Model

Transfer prices have different meanings and purposes depending on the context in which they are developed and the methods used to create them.[8] Our primary interest is in computing transfer prices on raw materials, parts, intermediate products, and finished products as they move through sequential stages of a supply chain located within one country. Such prices are often called **domestic transfer prices.** Multinational corporations employ and legally manipulate **international transfer**

prices for products transferred between tax jurisdictions in seeking to maximize after-tax income for the parent company. Sometimes companies or business units in a supply chain employ **market-based transfer prices** in trying to achieve equitable transfers; such prices are often difficult to determine because the markets may be imperfect and the products may be difficult to classify.

Although transfer prices can and have been computed using only managerial accounting procedures, our position is that they should be determined from an optimal, or demonstrably good, supply chain plan identified by an optimization model. Managerial accounting procedures are still needed to compute the transfer prices by interpreting the plan and incorporating costs and other factors that may not have been explicitly modeled. We illustrate the methodology by a numerical example in the following subsection. In the subsection after that, we discuss extensions for analyzing customer costs and value added services.

Transfer Prices for the Tasty Chips Supply Chain. We describe annual supply chain planning at the Tasty Chips Company, which manufactures and distributes four finished products: Plain Potato Chips (PChips), Barbecued Potato Chips (QChips), Corn Chips (CChips), and Taco Chips (TChips). The company has four plants located in Cincinnati, Nashville, Texarkana, and Peoria. The production flow at each plant is described in Figure 6.5. Corn and potatoes pass through mixing and baking stages to produce the four types of chips, which are then packaged and shipped to DCs. The DCs serve 41 markets in cities scattered across the central and southwestern United States. Corn and potatoes are bought from farm cooperatives in Idaho, Iowa, Kansas, and Maine.

The supply chain manager at Tasty Chips was asked to develop an annual plan for next year based on forecasts for the four products in the 41 markets. The objective is to minimize the total cost of meeting demand. Included among the major decisions were the following:

- What quantities of corn and potatoes should be bought from each of the four suppliers?
- How much of each product should be made at each plant?
- Which third-party DCs should be opened (selected) for operations next year from among the 15 locational choices?
- Which plants will source each open DC?
- Which DCs will source each market?

The supply chain manager acquired an off-the-shelf system to analyze the plan. He chose a modeling system that could generate and optimize mixed integer programming models to evaluate the strategic decisions listed above. After assembling the supply chain decision database, he made several runs to validate the model and the database and to evaluate assumptions by senior management about the outlook for next year.

The modeling system has now produced a demonstrably good solution (the objective function fell within 2% of optimality) that Tasty Chips management wishes to implement as the company's plan for next year. The plan involves purchases of corn and potatoes from three of the four suppliers (Iowa, Kansas, and Maine). All four products are made at all four plants. The plan chooses six open DCs (Chicago, Cleveland, Kansas City, Louisville, and Little Rock) to serve the markets. Before implementing the plan, the supply chain manager computed the transfer prices shown in Table 6.1 as a check that all the important options have been explored. Knowledge of the final transfer prices, which are the finished product prices, will also be useful to marketing and sales managers in making product pricing decisions for next year and in selecting markets with the highest margins as targets for aggressive sales efforts.

We explain details of the table's construction and interpretation. Starting at the beginning of the supply chain are the cost per ton of corn and potatoes leaving the suppliers. This is the cost per ton paid to the cooperatives. To these unit costs, we add transportation costs in computing the cost per ton of the raw ingredients arriving at the plants. These figures include weighted averages of delivered costs because some plants receive raw ingredients from more than one source.

Two sets of transfer prices for corn and potatoes arriving at the plants are given because products change units as they flow through the supply chain. Specifically, tons of corn and potatoes arriving at a plant become 100 cases of packaged products when they leave the plant. As shown in Figure 6.9, 10,000 tons of corn arriving at the Cincinnati plant (Cinpl) become 4391 hundred cases of corn products leaving the plant. Thus, because it takes 10,000 / 4391 = 2.277 tons of corn to produce 100 cases of packaged corn product, the cost of corn arriving at Cincinnati per 100 case of product output is 2.277 * 577.18 = $1314.96.

The transfer costs of the potatoes arriving at the plants vary significantly across plant because Tasty Chips encounters supply capacity constraints in Kansas and Iowa, which are located much closer to the plants than Maine and Idaho. The shadow prices on these constraints are $184.80 and $253.06 per ton, respectively, which indicate that additional potatoes from these suppliers would significantly reduce total cost. The high shadow prices reflect relatively large transportation costs for shipments from Maine and Idaho where additional potatoes are available. Before implementing the plan, Tasty Chips buyers should try to expand supply from the cooperatives in Kansas and Iowa for next year. They should certainly pursue a more aggressive acquisition plan from those vendors for the year after next. The capacity constraint on corn from Iowa is also reached, but because Kansas has unused capacity and is not that much farther from the plants, the shadow price is only $25.34 per ton.

The raw ingredients are transformed at the plants into packaged products to be shipped to the DCs by three direct activities (mixing, baking, and packaging) and two indirect activities (facility overhead, indirect labor), which, when added to the input transfer cost, give us the transfer prices leaving the plants. Table 6.2 provides a

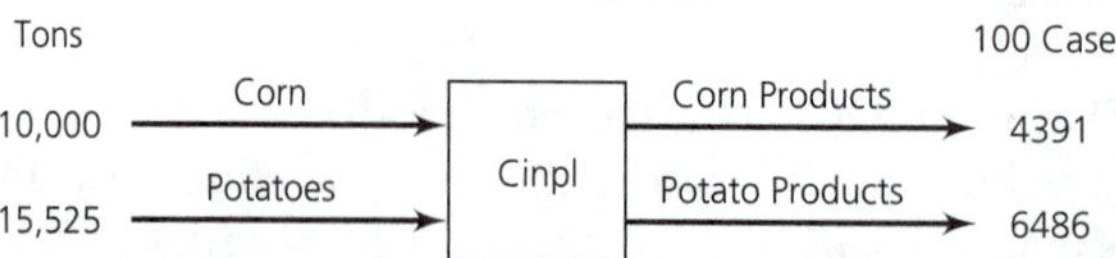

Figure 6.9 Accounting for changes of units at the Cincinnati plant

Table 6.1 Transfer prices for Tasty Chips' annual plan

	A	B	C	D	E	F	G	H	I	J	K	L	M	N	O	P
1							**Leaving Suppliers** (cost/ton)									
2							Iowa		Kansas	Maine						
3						Corn	Potatoes	Corn	Potatoes	Potatoes						
4						422	330	412	315	352						
5																
6							**Arriving at Plants** (cost/ton)									
7					Cinpl		Naspl		Texpl		Peopl					
8				Corn	Potatoes	Corn	Potatoes	Corn	Potatoes	Corn	Potatoes					
9				577.18	629.65	603.14	576.78	539.10	442.10	479.57	372.57					
10																
11							**Arriving at Plants** (cost/100 cases)									
12					Cinpl		Naspl		Texpl		Peopl					
13				Corn	Potatoes	Corn	Potatoes	Corn	Potatoes	Corn	Potatoes					
14				1314.46	1480.44	1419.09	1113.21	1338.67	1114.20	1187.38	918.04					
15																
16								**Leaving Plants** (cost/100 cases)								
17		Cinpl				Naspl				Texpl				Peopl		
18	PChipsP	QChipsP	CChipsP	TChipsP	PChipsP	QChipsP	CChipsP	TChipsP	PChipsP	QChipsP	CChipsP	TChipsP	PChipsP	QChipsP	CChipsP	TChipsP
19	2060.54	2080.54	1905.11	1935.11	1884.27	1904.27	2255.31	2285.31	2013.75	2033.75	2192.59	2222.59	1696.66	1716.66	1995.79	2025.79
20																
21								**Arriving at DC's** (cost/100 cases)								
22						Chic				Lou						
23					PChipsP	QChipsP	CChipsP	TChipsP	PChipsP	QChipsP	CChipsP	TChipsP				
24					2163.79	1853.98	2133.11	2163.11	2172.90	2192.90	2017.47	2047.47				
25																
26								**Leavings DC's** (cost/100 cases)								
27						Chic				Lou						
28					PChipsP	QChipsP	CChipsP	TChipsP	PChipsP	QChipsP	CChipsP	TChipsP				
29					2197.86	1888.40	2167.53	2197.65	2204.32	2224.66	2049.36	2079.32				
30																
31								**Arriving at Markets** (cost/100 cases)								
32						DsM				Cin						
33					PChips	QChips	CChips	TChips	PChips	QChips	CChips	TChips				
34					2423.11	2113.65	2392.78	2463.49	2386.34	2406.68	2231.38	2261.34				
35																
36			Shadow Prices		2688.17	2590.73	2446.00	2543.61	2581.33	2477.74	2323.89	2413.68				

detailed examination of the transfer prices on the four packaged products leaving the Peoria plant. The data in the upper left-hand corner of the table summarizes information about shipments out of the Peoria plant. The remainder of the table summarizes the calculations used in computing the transfer price of each product leaving the Peoria plant, which has the suffix P (packaged), indicating that it is an intermediate product leaving the plant headed toward the DCs. It does not become a finished product, and the suffix is not dropped, until it is delivered to the markets.

In Table 6.2, row 6 lists the transfer prices of potatoes and corn as they arrive at the plant. Row 7 allocates the facility overhead cost to the four products. The facility cost function at Peoria has a fixed cost, a variable cost, and a maximum throughput capacity measured by the output of 100 cases from the plant. We compute the overhead allocation cost/100 cases, which equals $133.31, by dividing the overhead cost by the total outbound cases. Similarly, the indirect labor cost function at Peoria has a fixed cost, a variable cost, and a maximal quantity of available labor, measured in shifts for the year. These shifts are consumed by maintenance activities linked to the mixing and baking stages of manufacturing. We compute the indirect labor allocation cost/100 cases, which equals $206.06, by dividing the indirect labor cost by the total outbound cases.

The next two rows (9 and 10) in Table 6.2 correspond to the direct costs of mixing and baking the corn and potato products. Again, each of these stages has a cost function comprising a fixed cost, a variable cost, and a maximum capacity measured in tons of corn and potatoes processed. We compute the corn and potato allocations as we did to obtain the rates $359.33 for corn products and $324.54 for potato products. These figures are adjusted slightly for the specific products to reflect small differences in cost. In particular, managerial accounting analysis of production recipes indicates that the Taco Chips cost approximately $30/100 case more to mix and bake than Corn Chips. Hence, the corn product processes cost allocation for CChips is reduced by $15 to $344.33 and the cost allocation for TChips is increased by $15 to $374.33. Similarly, the potato product processes allocation for PChips is reduced by $10 to $314.54 and the allocation for QChips is increased by $10 to $334.54.

Finally, the packaging cost function includes a fixed cost, a variable cost and a maximum capacity. The supply chain manager also imposed at each plant a conditional minimum on the number of 100 cases packed equaling one-half of the maximal capacity. Without this constraint, one of the plants tended to run at unrealistically low throughput. The packaging cost/100 cases was allocated as shown to yield a rate of $124.71. Thus, we have allocated all costs incurred at the Peoria plant to the four products, and on row 12 we compute the transfer prices leaving the Peoria plant by adding up the costs given on rows 6 through 11.

The transfer pricing computation after the products leave the plants continues in much the same manner. Due to space limitations, we show transfer prices into and out of only two of the six DCs open in the optimal plan and into only 2 of the 41 markets for finished products. The transfer prices arriving at the DCs equal those leaving the plants plus the appropriate unit costs of transportation. A weighted average is used to compute a product's transfer price arriving at a DC or a market if the DC or market receives product from more than one upstream source.

Table 6.2 Computation of transfer prices leaving the Peoria plant (Peopl)

	A	B	C	D	E	F	G	H
1	Corn chips out (100 cases)	3635						
2	Potato chips out (100 cases)	3146						
3	Total	6781						
4					PChipsP	QChipsP	CChipsP	TChipsP
5		Cost	Cost/100 cases		Cost/100 cases	Cost/100 cases	Cost/100 cases	Cost/100 cases
6	Transfer prices arriving at Peopl				918.04	918.04	1187.38	1187.38
7	Facility overhead	903970	133.31		133.31	133.31	133.31	133.31
8	Indirect labor	1397281	206.06		206.06	206.06	206.06	206.06
9	Corn product processes	1306179	359.33				344.33	374.33
10	Potato product processes	1021005	324.54		314.54	334.54		
11	Packaging	845642	124.71		124.71	124.71	124.71	124.71
12	Transfer prices leaving Peopl				1696.66	1716.66	1995.79	2025.79

The increase in transfer price for a product leaving a DC relative to the transfer price for the product arriving at the DC is due to three costs at the DC: DC throughput cost, cross-docking costs, and inventory holding costs. The computation is very similar to that of Table 6.2. As you can see, these costs are a small percentage of the total cost. The DCs were also subject to conditional minimal throughput constraints forcing the throughput of any open DC to equal one-half its capacity.

The transfer prices of the finished products arriving at the markets are the **product costs;** that is, the average delivered costs. When we multiply these costs by the product demands, we obtain the (nearly minimal) total cost of the supply chain plan. For comparison purposes, we listed the shadow prices associated with meeting demand in the two markets. The shadow prices are higher than the product prices because they reflect the marginal cost of meeting additional demand at these markets. Because more efficient options were consumed in meeting the given demand, marginal supply will employ less efficient options and therefore cost more.

Extensions to Customer Costs and the Costs of Valued Added Services. An important contribution of ABC to improved supply chain management is its focus on the calculation of a company's customer costs as well as its product costs. This is important for the following reason:

> Companies have been surprised with their customer profitability results. . . . (S)ome companies have discovered a 20-225 rule, where 20% of the customers generate 225% of the profits. A large number of customers (60%) huddle around breakeven profitability, and the least profitable 20% of the customers lose 125% of the profits.[9]

Transfer pricing and optimization modeling permit the company to identify and avoid the 20-225 rule. First, they can be employed to reveal customer profitability. Customers requiring unusual attention in the manufacture or distribution of their products should be treated as separate classes in the optimization model. Second, transfer pricing analysis can reveal the differences between product prices for these customer classes and other classes that are less demanding. Moreover, transfer prices can reveal how larger than standard product prices are the result of costly customer demands at all stages of the supply chain.

As an extreme example, we consider the cost of satisfying the demands of the Huge Supermarket Group, a customer of Tasty Chips. This customer requires a customized potato chip product that uses Idaho potatoes, a special blending recipe at the plant where the product is made, and delivery from a DC within 50 miles of its supermarkets. An optimization model is needed to identify the cost of meeting Huge Supermarket's needs. On the one hand, without their business, Tasty Chips' plan might still include the acquisition of Idaho potatoes and the location of a DC within 50 miles of Huge Supermarket's area. Thus, their requirements may not be very costly. On the other hand, a plan forced to meet their requirements when they would not otherwise be met might prove very costly. In the latter case, the transfer prices for raw materials and intermediate products would start diverging from standard values at the beginning of the supply chain.

Of course, one should probably view such demands for a customized product as a value added service, for which the customer pays extra, or a separate contract for a customized product. The combination of the model and the transfer pricing analysis would allow Tasty Chips to accurately price its business arrangement with Huge Supermarket. If the potential contract was sufficiently large, Tasty Chips could include resource expansion options in the planning model to support the new level of business.

6.6 Demand Forecasting

Like management accounting, the descriptive methodology of demand forecasting is central to the construction of accurate supply chain decision databases and optimization models. In this section, we view demand forecasting as concerned with the calculation of demand for finished products under the assumption that demand management decisions regarding price, advertising, promotion, and other factors are fixed and given. Thus, in this chapter, forecasting models provide inputs only for models that minimize the total supply chain cost of meeting forecasted demand over tactical and strategic planning horizons, which last from 1 month to several years. Modeling approaches for maximizing net revenues by optimizing demand management decisions as well as those concerned with supply chain management are examined in Sections 8.1, 8.2, and 8.3.

The scientific, technical, and artistic underpinnings of demand forecasting are as rich as those of mathematical programming. In this section, we present only a high-level overview of the methodology.[10] As with mathematical programming, successful applications to date of demand forecasting methods lag behind the theory, but we believe such applications will grow in number and scope as developments in IT make them possible and necessary. Perhaps even more than mathematical programming, the successful design, validation, and use of forecasting models requires practical experience as well as textbook knowledge. This suggests that company analysts using forecasting software are provided with adequate training in the artistry and science of forecasting. As we discuss below, many forecasting packages with a range of functionality are currently available to help analysts select the most appropriate model.

Background

Based on a combination of historical data, managerial judgment, and modeling practitioner expertise, forecasting models create demand data for multiple products (product families) in multiple geographical locations over multiple time periods and, when applicable, for multiple market segments in those locations. In constructing and employing forecasting models, we must keep in mind the following:[11]

1. *Good forecasts will still have significant errors.* The future will always remain uncertain and the further into the future we look, the larger the errors. Better forecasts will, of course, have smaller errors, but the forecasts will never be perfect. Appropriately frequent analysis with forecasting and optimization models at the tactical and strategic planning levels will allow management to take actions to correct mistakes due to forecasting errors, although some decisions, such as making a major acquisition, might be irreversible.
2. *Effective forecasting is often achieved by analyzing aggregate products and markets with results broken down into detailed components.* Thus, like optimization modeling, forecasting involves product and market aggregations. Applied research is needed to reconcile and integrate these different methods of aggregation.
3. *Forecast errors are correlated in time, across geographical regions, and among products.* An important aspect of the science and art of forecasting is to qualitatively and quantitatively identify these correlations and use such knowledge in the construction of good forecasting models.
4. *The science and art of forecasting follows predictable patterns, but exogenous or nonstatistical disruptions are difficult to anticipate and forecast.* Statistical methods are available to track forecasts to determine when and if exogenous disruptions have occurred, assuming they are not obvious. An issue for strategic decision making is the extent to which exogenous uncertainties can or should be anticipated, at least in a generic sense.

Types of Forecasting Models

A range of forecasting models and statistical techniques are available for demand forecasting. A brief review of several important ones follows.

Time series models. Time series models are exponential smoothing, moving average, and more sophisticated models that relate one or more (dependent) demand variables at a particular point in time to the values of the same (independent) demand variables at earlier, past points in time. Time series models may be applied to short-term forecasting, with planning horizons of 1 week to 3 months, or to medium-term forecasting, with planning horizons of 3 months to 1 year. Medium-term time series models must account for seasonal, cyclic, and trend factors in the time series data.

A time series model may be implemented and validated by splitting a historical data set into two portions: an **in-sample** portion that is used to estimate parameters for the model and an **out-of-sample** portion that is used to evaluate how well the model forecasts new data. This division of the data set must take into account seasonal, cyclic, and trend factors that the practitioner believes are present. The time series analysis might produce unexpected results indicating that the in-sample/out-of-sample partition must be modified. Of course, a good fit of the model to the out-of-sample data does not guarantee that true forecasts of the future will be as good, but such a result is reassuring when we use the demand forecast in a planning model.

For supply chain planning, an important but not widely recognized short-term demand forecasting problem, which requires time series analysis blended with order

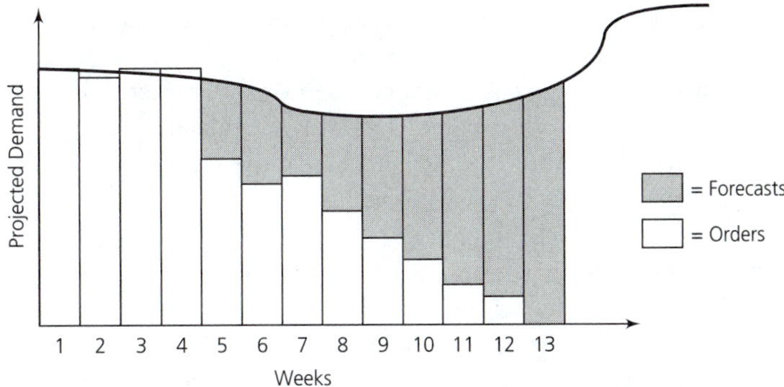

Figure 6.10
Transition of forecasts to orders

entry information, is depicted in Figure 6.10. As shown, the company has committed to firm orders for a given product over the next 4 weeks. After that, we see that a generally increasing component of projected demand corresponds to forecasted demand that has not yet become firm orders. Depending on the industry, these forecasts might correspond to demand from existing customers for which orders are expected but have not yet been placed or demand from more diffuse markets, rather than specific customers, for which forecasts are based on past sales data. Moreover, demand from new customers, or existing customers with changing patterns, will confuse the projections. The delicate point is to differentiate between these various classes of projections to avoid double counting or inadvertently omitting future demand.

Production planning based on the patterns in Figure 6.10 allows sales personnel to make accurate **available-to-promise** (ATP) decisions about promised delivery dates for incoming orders. For example, the production plan would schedule production to meet forecasts in each week as if they were firm orders. Sales personnel would then assign orders as they came in to the appropriate blocks. Moreover, the production plan for later weeks in the planning horizon could be updated on a weekly basis to provide timely response to new forecasts and order information.

Causal models. Causal models use statistical regression methods to relate dependent demand variables at a particular point in the future to independent variables that may include the same demand variables at earlier points but also include other variables whose values are believed to affect demand. A classic example is a model forecasting demand for automotive parts that depends on automotive sales and broad measures of economic activity. Causal models are important for long-term forecasting of 1 year or more because mere extrapolation of history to the long-term often produces poor forecasts.

New product models. The strategic design of a supply chain for a new product is an important area of decision making. For such a product, demand forecasting obviously cannot be related to historical data describing sales. Nevertheless, marketing scientists have developed models describing the anticipated form of growth of a new product; parameters for such models might be derived from histories of existing similar products. Such analysis provides management with a priori (no data) forecasts of new product sales upon which supply chain design decisions might be made using an optimization model. Then, as the markets for the new product reveal themselves, the a priori parameters can be updated to improve the forecasts, which, in turn, can be used to further analyze the supply chain strategy of the new product using the optimization model.

Judgmental models. Judgmental models are needed to forecast demand of new products for which no historical data is available or considered very relevant. Judgments of experts familiar with products and markets are systematically collected and integrated. The first step is to get the experts to agree on their judgments. One method for achieving this, called the Delphi process, uses anonymous responses from the experts and controlled feedback in an iterative scheme to achieve consensus. The group forecast is, by definition, the median of the individual forecasts obtained at the conclusion of the iterative process. The next step is to encode the forecasts as probability distributions using a priori parameters determined by the experts. These parameters are systematically updated as data about sales of the new products become available.[12]

Demand Data Specifications for Optimization Models

The **demand data set** for a single scenario needed by an optimization model is simply the quantities of products to be met in each market, possibly by each of several segments in that market. In addition, **shortfall costs** associated with not meeting demand for each product in each market (and market segment) should be included with the demand data set. Shortfall costs may be computed using marketing information about the long-term effects of lost sales. They are useful and important because they allow the optimization model to identify those products and markets that are least desirable to satisfy when the supply chain has insufficient capacity to meet total demand. In some instances, the presence of shortfalls may indicate that the delivered costs of some products to some markets are so high that the model elects to not meet demand despite the shortfall penalties. Finally, shortfalls may reflect data errors or inconsistencies; for example, a market that has inadvertently been left unconnected in a model to all sources of products.

Because forecasts are uncertain, for the purposes of strategic and tactical planning, management in the company will want to see the results of optimization runs with different scenarios of demand data sets. To accomplish this, the modeling practitioner must work with management in translating qualitative scenario descriptions, such as "high demand" or "low demand," into numerical demand data sets. Most of the forecasting models discussed above lend themselves to such quantification because they provide information about the variances of demand as well as their expected values.

Although the demand data set for a given scenario in the supply chain decision database might be simple, it will typically be derived from large historical databases.

As we discussed, efficient software routines for implementing aggregation schemes and carrying out statistical estimation methods are needed to link the historical databases to the supply chain decision database and therefore to the optimization model. Forecasting software is discussed briefly in the next subsection.

Forecasting Software

A recent software survey identified 40 software packages with a wide range of capabilities and prices.[13] The survey divided these software into the following three categories:

1. **Automatic.** The user enters data and asks the program to analyze it to select a forecasting model. Employing diagnostic tests, the software suggests a methodology that it judges to be the best fit. The user can agree with this recommendation or override it. The software then computes optimal parameters for the indicated forecasting model and produces forecasts along with statistics characterizing its accuracy, such as the mean-squared error of the estimates.
2. **Semiautomatic.** The user enters data and the software produces a list of suggested modeling method, but the user makes the selection. This mode might involve considerable user interaction, which can be tedious, in directing the search for optimal parameters and other computations.
3. **Manual.** The user must specify the method and the control parameters. This approach can easily involve many runs of a given data set and require the user to make judgments about improving the model.

The software packages were found to vary greatly in the ease and flexibility of inputting data, control of graphical output, and consistency of results.

6.7 Global and Policy Data

Most data in the supply chain decision database are objective data about entities in the supply chain, which are individual facilities, transportation subnetworks, vendors, and markets. In this section, we discuss briefly two additional types of data needed to construct an accurate and comprehensive optimization model. First, there are data describing **global resource constraints** that pertain to many or all facilities in the supply chain network. For example, the company might be considering the installation of a new technology, which requires significant capital outlay, in some of its manufacturing or distribution facilities. A global resource constraint might impose a capital spending limit across all facilities on investment in the new technology. Similarly, following a merger of two manufacturing firms, the combined companies might find that they have capital equipment in individual plants that needs to be moved to better meet their new mission. A global resource constraint would be imposed, limiting the number of pieces of capital equipment to be located and relocated in all plants to the number globally available. Any equipment not used in the global rearrangement could be sold.

Second, to achieve acceptable customer service or mitigate risk, management might wish to impose **policy constraints** on an optimal supply chain solution. For example, if the company follows a policy of 1-day delivery, which translates into a maximum trucking distance of 300 miles, from distribution centers to markets, this policy would be imposed on the links permitted in the outbound transportation subnetwork.

Another example is the imposition of a policy constraint for redundancy that no plant in the supply chain shall manufacture more than 75% of the total demand for any product. Although such a constraint may not be justified by pure economic considerations, management may feel it is needed to ensure the company against the catastrophic consequences that would occur if the product was made in a sole plant and that plant were forced to shut down for an extended period.

Although, for expositional reasons, we have deliberately kept away from supply chain decision databases and models for multiple-period strategic and tactical planning problems, such models may well require a greater range and number of global resource and policy constraints. Included are constraints affecting the timing and phasing of plant constructions, possibly due to capital investments constraints; for example, a new plant may be constructed in year 3 only if a potential acquisition for years 1 or 2 does not happen. At the tactical planning level, we might need to impose global constraints for smoothing production and distribution activities or for limiting patterns of opening and closing warehouses that deal with surges during peak periods.

6.8 Model Output Data

The supply chain decision database for each scenario contains output data that results from optimizing the model created from the scenario's input data. In effect, routines for creating management reports from these outputs invert the data processing performed by the model generator in integrating multiple data input files to create a model. These programs were reviewed in the context of optimization system design discussed in Section 4.5; see especially Figure 4.9. As we have in most of this chapter, we assume input and output data refer to a snapshot model for strategic or tactical planning.

Remember that output data may correspond to an optimal solution, or as often occurs when optimizing a mixed integer programming model, they may correspond instead to a demonstrably good solution. Typically, for a strategic or tactical planning model, we can expect a superior mixed integer programming package to identify a solution with objective function value within 1% or less of the optimal value. This solution might actually be optimal, but the algorithm has not yet proven it to be so. For convenience, we will hereafter refer to the solution produced by the optimization package as an "optimal solution," while recognizing that it might be suboptimal, but it is hoped, only slightly so.

Output from an optimization package provides a complete description of an optimal supply chain plan plus derived economic evaluations such as shadow prices giving the marginal return from each resource and the marginal cost of each requirement. The raw form of these outputs is monolithic, and therefore they must be parsed and reorganized to produce useful managerial reports. Some technical output data, such as the values of 0-1 variables used to model economies of scale, are suppressed in preparing the management reports.

In this section, we examine the form and content of management reports based on model output. We also examine implicit and derived measures based on the model output. Graphical displays of input and output data, which are important for communicating major results, trends, and comparisons are discussed in a later section.

Management Reports of Output Data

Management reports focus on activities associated with options actually employed in an optimal solution, which typically includes only a very small percentage of the possible options open to the model. These are the data to be reported. A distribution manager, for example, wishes to receive information only about those links connecting distribution centers to markets for which there is positive flow in an optimal solution. Still, as we discuss in the following subsection, model optimization provides sensitivity analysis information about how much the cost associated with each option not selected by the model would have to be reduced for the option to become attractive.

A list of typical output reports containing only supply chain activities and flows at positive levels follows:

- **Suppliers report.** For each supplier and product offered by the supplier, the quantity acquired, its cost, and the maximal quantity available from the supplier.
- **Inbound network flow report.** For each supplier, product, and facility considered by the model, the product flow, its cost, and where applicable, upper and lower bounds that might have been imposed on the flow.
- **Facilities report.** For each facility that might be in the supply chain network, the total throughput of all products, which may be zero, and the cost of this throughput, which might comprise the sum of a fixed or shutdown cost plus variable total throughput cost that depends on a volume-dependent cost relationship. The report also compares total throughput to the rated capacity of the facility. Total throughput is based on a formula weighting individual product throughputs.
- **Process report.** For each process in each facility, the total volume of activity of the process and its cost, which comprises a fixed cost, a variable process cost,

and a variable recipe cost. The report also compares total process activity to the rated capacity of the process.

- **Recipe report.** For each recipe associated with each process in each facility, the total volume of activity of the recipe and its cost, which comprises fixed and variable costs.
- **Resource report.** For each resource in each facility, the total volume of activity and its cost, which comprises one or more fixed costs and one or more variable costs. The report also compares total resource activity to the rated resource capacity at the facility.
- **Inventory report.** For each product in each facility, the total volume of inventory held during the period and its associated investment holding cost.
- **Interfacility network flow report.** For each link between facilities and product, the product flow, its cost and, where applicable, upper and lower bounds that might have been imposed on the flow.
- **Outbound network flow report.** For each market and each product, the product flow into the market from each facility and its associated cost and, where applicable, upper and lower bounds that might have been imposed on the flow. If demand cannot be met in a cost minimization model, this report will provide information about product shortfalls in specific markets.
- **Summary report.** A summary of the total cost, and if applicable, total net revenue, associated with the optimal solution. The summary report might also aggregate information found in the other reports listed above.

Assuming the form of the data used in these reports conform to a standard database format, an analyst can create customized reports by combining appropriate combinations of input and output data.

Shadow Prices and Reduced Costs

Optimization of a linear programming model implicitly involves optimization of a related dual model whose variables price out constraints in the primal. Specifically, these are the **shadow prices** that measure the marginal value of adding another unit of a potentially scarce resource or the marginal cost of meeting another unit of a potentially costly requirement. Strictly speaking, such shadow prices do not exist for mixed integer programming models. As a practical matter, if the 0-1 and other integer variables in a mixed integer programming model are fixed at their optimal values, the residual optimization model is a linear programming model for which we can compute the shadow prices. Most commercial optimization packages carry out this computation after solving mixed integer programming models.

Because shadow prices provide insights into markets, processes, and resources beyond those provided by an optimal solution, it may be beneficial to include them in management reports on a selective basis. For example, when minimizing the total supply chain cost of meeting fixed and given demand, the shadow price on each product/market combination reflects the marginal cost to the company of supplying another unit; an example was given in Table 6.1. Similarly, the shadow price on a plant process whose capacity has been totally consumed in an optimal solution reflects the marginal value to the company of squeezing out another unit of process capacity.

Shadow prices also serve to compute the **relative costs** of activities in a linear programming model by adjusting their given costs to reflect the implied costs and benefits accruing to the activities of using resources and meeting requirements. Thus, a transformation recipe might not be employed in an optimal solution because the implicit cost of its process and resource utilization, as measured by the shadow prices, outweighs its benefits. The relative cost measures this difference between real and implied costs and real and implied benefits. A production manager might well be able to take advantage of relative cost information when looking for ways to reduce real costs. For example, when looking to lower direct production costs, recipes with small positive reduced costs are much better candidates for improvement than those with high positive reduced costs.

Derived Output

Important information can be gleaned from the output data of a model for strategic or tactical planning by applying postprocessing procedures to them. Useful reports may, in some cases, be derived in a straightforward way by disaggregating details of the optimal solution. For example, when reporting the solution to a tactical planning model in which customers in close geographic proximity were aggregated into markets, the distribution manager might find it useful to receive a report that shows from which distribution centers each customer will be sourced. This information can be derived by a simple calculation that inverts the aggregation used in creating data describing the aggregate market in the optimization model.

A slightly more complicated example might involve detailed manufacturing plans for each product in a product family used by the model. If a tactical model indicated that 1000 tons of a product family should be made in a particular plant in a particular time period, a postprocessing algorithm might be used to specify the quantities of each product to be made and in what sequence. This algorithm might disaggregate the model results based on established production planning rules for the product family. For example, in the manufacture of paper, it is best to make lighter-weight products in the product family before heavier-weight products. If such rules are not known, additional research might yield rules that are fairly easy to implement; otherwise, the modeling practitioner might be forced to conclude that the aggregate model is an oversimplification that requires modification.

In Section 6.5, we presented a numerical example illustrating the computation of transfer, product, and customer costs from an optimal solution to a supply chain model. A transfer cost measures the average cost of an intermediate product as it leaves a facility in the supply chain network for another facility or as it leaves a process in a facility for another process. A product cost is simply a transfer price on a finished product reaching the market.

The computation of transfer and product costs usually assumes a one-way flow of products through the network; that is, intermediate and finished products do not return to earlier stages for rework, refunds, or other reasons. In such cases, the computation of transfer and product costs is straightforward. If such reverse flows exist, more complicated postprocessing routines are needed to compute transfer and product prices.

To exercise planning and control of customer and value added services, the company must compute added costs associated with servicing specific customers. Sometimes these added costs can be developed independently of the optimization model using managerial accounting methods. In other words, the complex interactions and ripple effects of the supply chain, which require analysis with an optimization model, may have a large effect on the cost of products delivered to geographical markets, but specific requirements of individual customers in a market and their implied costs can be determined by accounting analyses and added onto to the product cost.

Another reporting function that can be usefully derived from an optimal solution to a supply chain model is the construction of operating budgets for the planning horizon of the model. Typical operating budgets have the following six operating plans:[14]

1. Sales
2. Capital spending
3. Production
4. Materials purchasing
5. Labor hiring and training
6. Administrative and discretionary spending

In principle, all six operating budgets can be based largely on recipe, process, resource, and facility costs connected with activity levels in an optimal plan developed by a model.

The connections between optimal model solutions and operating budgets depend on the extent to which the models are comprehensive in their descriptions of costs and activities. If some activities were omitted from the model, their costs would need to be added to those identified by the model. A related concern is the extent to which the optimization model yields solutions that are viewed as practical and implementable or as standards that may not be achieved. In the latter case, management can expect only negative variances from the idealized standards.

6.9 Connections Among Supply Chain Decision Databases

In our discussion so far, we have concentrated on the form and content of a single supply chain decision database tied to a snapshot model for analyzing strategic and tactical plans. In this section, we discuss briefly connections among decision databases for alternate snapshot scenarios of a given supply chain problem, for multiperiod models, and among decision databases spanning strategic, tactical, and operational supply chain problems in a given firm.

Scenarios

In Figure 6.11 we depict the logic used to create multiple scenarios. At the top, the analyst defines data describing the structure of the supply chain to be studied for a given project. This structure includes the names of products (raw materials, intermediate products, and finished products), markets, and vendors. It also includes the names and locations of facilities that are currently part of the supply chain plus new facility options that the company wishes to evaluate. The names of processes, recipes, and resources at each of the existing and potential facilities must also be specified. Finally, the supply chain structure includes a specification of the links in the inbound, interfacility and outbound subnetworks.

Each scenario is created by extending the structural data of a project to include numerical data that characterize it. Included are costs of raw materials; costs and capacities associated with throughput, process, recipe, and resource at the facilities; costs and capacities associated with products flows on inbound, interfacility, and outbound links; product demands at the markets; and a host of other factors. The structural data combined with the scenario-specific numerical data constitute the input data of the supply chain decision database for that scenario.

Typically, the input data of a new scenario will be derived from that of an existing one, implying that data management of input data for most scenarios can be simplified by keeping track only of the changes. As shown in Figure 6.11, the

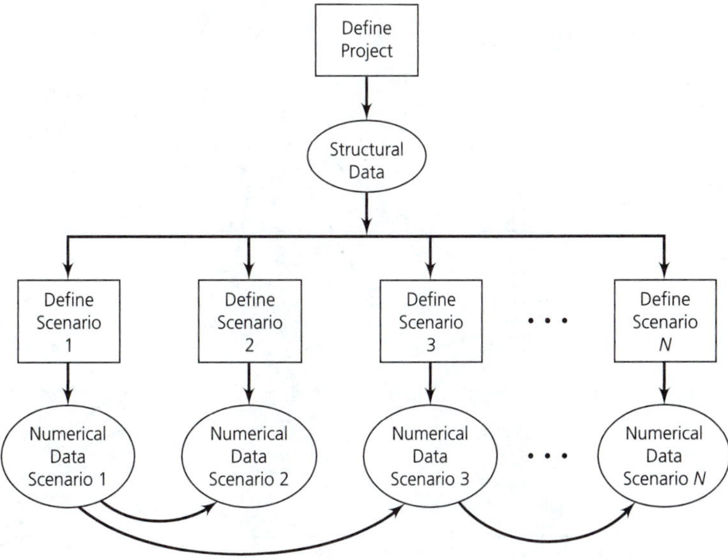

Figure 6.11
Project and scenario decision databases

numerical data of scenarios 2 and 3 are derived from the numerical data of scenario 1, whereas the numerical data of scenario *N* is derived from scenario 3. The output data (results of an optimization run) for each scenario will, in general, be completely different and must therefore be managed as an entirely separate entity. Of course, nothing prevents the analyst from changing structural data midway through a project; for example, by adding new distribution center locations as the result of initial scenario runs. Conceptually, though, we may assume that the *N* scenarios evaluated during a project were created from the same structural data because decision options not considered by a particular scenario can be easily labeled as not active during that scenario.

Multiperiod Decision Databases

The creation of a multiperiod decision database spanning *T* periods from a snapshot decision database is conceptually straightforward in many cases, although the resulting database will be roughly *T* times larger. As shown in Figure 6.12, the snapshot decision database is replicated *T* times, one for each period of the multiperiod model. Thus, managing the data describing multiple scenarios and optimizing the models can become significantly more difficult.

Moreover, the replication may require scaling of some data. This would be needed when creating a tactical planning model of 12 linked submodels, each of one month, from a strategic planning snapshot model of 1 year. Process capacities in each month, for example, would be approximately one-twelfth the level of those used in the yearly snapshot model. The replication may also require modification of structural and numerical data. For the example just cited, resource acquisition options in the strategic snapshot model, such as the possible establishment of new facilities and the manufacture of new products, would be treated as fixed and given in the multiperiod tactical model. At the same time, resource options might be

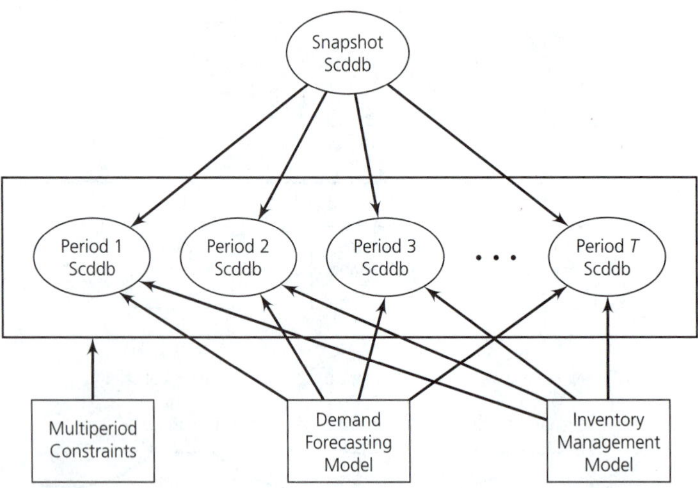

Figure 6.12
Multiperiod decision database

added to certain periods in the tactical model, such as extra warehouse space for periods with high seasonal demand. Similarly, numerical data describing production or transportation activities might vary with month or season, such as the imposition of higher transportation cost rates during the winter months in locations affected by the weather.

Figure 6.12 emphasizes that demand and inventory data are two critical categories that require differentiation in a multiperiod model. Most businesses exhibit some sort of seasonal or cyclic demand patterns for finished products that must be reflected in a multiperiod model. In a tactical planning model, forecasted demand must be blended with on-hand orders for early periods in the planning horizon. An inventory management model calculates several types of data for each of the periods. It provides data describing initial inventories for each product at the start of the first period. It also provides safety stock, holding cost, and inventory capacity information for each product at the end of each period. Finally, it provides targets for inventory at the end of the planning horizon.

Finally, we show in Figure 6.12 the presence of multiperiod constraints, which did not exist in the snapshot model, that cut across two or more periods. These might be smoothing constraints that place limits on changes from one period to the next in production plans at individual plants. They might be logical constraints such as the restriction that if a facility is closed in a given period, it must stay closed for the remainder of the planning horizon. They might be capital budgeting constraints on capital investment over the planning horizon on plant capacity expansions.

Hierarchies

In Section 2.2, we identified eight Transactional and Analytical IT systems in a Supply Chain System Hierarchy that are necessary and desirable for supporting strategic, tactical, and operational decision making in a firm that manufacturers and distributes products. We also discussed the types of data linkages required to achieve intertemporal integration of decisions at the various levels of planning. Now that we have examined supply chain decision databases from several perspectives in this chapter, we can examine briefly principles for achieving consistency among the decision databases tied to the system hierarchy. Our concerns at this point are speculative because, even for a single level of planning, the supply chain decision database is a new concept.

We expect that product, market, and vendor aggregations will become refined as we move from strategic planning toward operational planning. Similarly, we expect that the partitioning of time will become much more refined as we move from long-term tactical models, which might use time buckets of 1 month, to short-term tactical ones, which might use time buckets of 1 week, and finally to scheduling models, which may use time buckets of 1 hour. Significant thought must go into the design of disaggregation schemes facilitating communication among models at the different levels of planning.

The modeling of facilities in terms of the costs and capacities of processes, recipes, and resources would reflect these aggregations. Moreover, we would expect the structural descriptions of facilities to become more refined as we move from strategic to tactical planning. For example, in a strategic model for locating distribution centers, we might chose to describe the cost and capacity of each distribution center solely as a function of facility throughput. In a tactical model of the same company concerned with planning operations over the coming months, however, we might chose to describe each distribution center by the costs and capacities of several processes including receiving, flow-through, put-away, picking, dispatching. The refinement of manufacturing facility detail between a strategic model and an operational model would be even more pronounced.

Finally, demand forecasts used in strategic, tactical, and operational models must be consistent across products and time. For example, product demand forecasts used in a 1-month scheduling model to be met by manufacturing or inventory should be consistent with the product demand forecasts used in the first month of a 6-month tactical model. To achieve consistency, the demand forecasts used in the first month of the tactical model will need to coincide exactly with aggregations of daily demand at the SKU level into monthly figures for product families.

6.10 Graphical Displays of Data Inputs and Outputs

Our discussion thus far of the supply chain decision database has focused on numerical data, which are typically displayed in spreadsheets or some other tabular form. In this section, we discuss briefly graphical displays of these model inputs and outputs. Such displays are important because they serve to summarize key features of these data in formats that are appealing to human intuition.

For senior managers, graphical mapping of a product sourcing strategy acquaints them with the strategy's high points in a fraction of the time needed to plow through printed reports containing the same information. For operations personnel, graphical displays of manufacturing or vehicle schedules produced by optimization algorithms allows them to fine-tune the schedules to meet practical constraints not fully captured by the algorithms. For potential purchasers of an off-the-shelf modeling system, graphical displays of supply chain structures and data can have a significantly positive effect on their willingness to buy the system.

Despite the benefits, graphical displays of the supply chain decision database has its drawbacks. By examining only geographical depictions of a sourcing strategy, senior managers might not get beyond a superficial understanding of it. They might leave the details to supply chain coordinators, but this presumes the company has created such positions and adapted its organization to give coordinators the authority to implement integrated plans.

Similarly, fine-tuning of a proposed schedule by operations personnel might not always lead to a better operational plan. An open question for most operational scheduling applications is determining an "optimal" division of labor between computerized algorithms and manual intervention by human schedulers. Finally, esthetically pleasing graphics that help market a modeling system may serve to cover up serious deficiencies in the system's analytical capabilities.

Ultimately, it is the numerical details of tabular reports, not a map summarizing them, that specify a supply chain plan to be implemented. This is not to say that graphical displays are unimportant. Still, in designing or acquiring a modeling system, the wise manager will try to strike an effective balance between algorithmic number crunching and graphical displays, which should add value to the analytical capabilities of the system, not simply appeal to esthetic sensibilities.

For modeling systems that support strategic and tactical supply chain planning, at least four model elements require graphical display, as follows:

- Processes at a facility
- Geographical maps of product demand and supply chain plans
- Production planning and inventory management strategies
- On-line analytical processing and comparison of results from multiple scenarios

Space does not permit an examination of graphical displays that have been created by system developers for these model elements.

6.11 Final Thoughts

In this chapter, we have tried to demonstrate the ways in which the supply chain decision database is a critical element connecting transactional data to analytical tools supporting managerial decision making. Using the structure of mathematical programming models as a framework, the decision database integrates descriptive models from a variety of fields including managerial accounting, forecasting, operations management, and transportation science. Such analytical tools and their applications would be significantly improved if academics and practitioners working within these fields were to more actively embrace other disciplines.

For example, managerial accounting texts present myopic rules for computing product costs, allocating resource costs, or selecting product mix to maximize revenue that completely ignore the more powerful capabilities of linear and mixed integer programming to optimize such decisions across the entire supply chain. Similarly, logistics managers and transportation scientists concerned with the company's distribution plans often treat manufacturing plans made within the same company as distantly related decisions for which little coordination is needed. Practitioners with an expertise in inventory management tend to construct and apply supply chain models that focus on inventory decisions without systematic evaluation of other classes of supply chain decisions such as facility location and operations or transportation planning.

The decision database has value in its own right by providing managers with a high-level view of the forest of transactional data. Still, we must probably await the routine and repetitive use of modeling systems for tactical planning to achieve a clearer definition and wider acceptance of it. One can hope that ERP companies will eventually develop software for creating decision databases linked to modeling systems that truly analyze enterprise resource planning of the firm's supply chain or of virtual supply chains in which the firm participates.

An important challenge to integrated supply chain planning is the conceptualization and implementation of coherent decision databases and modeling systems for operational, tactical, and strategic planning. Although the theory of hierarchical planning has been rigorously pursued by academics, its application lags far behind. The most likely direction from which progress will be made is from top-down strategic planning exercises that lead to, again, routine and repetitive use of models systems for tactical planning. Once an enterprisewide framework has been established for tactical planning, it should be possible to extract and expand subsets of decision databases and planning problems for more focused operational problems such as production scheduling or vehicle routing.

An issue that we mentioned several times in this chapter, but which has not yet been widely explored, is the estimation of indirect information technology costs and their representation in supply chain planning models. These costs are important for traditional, brick-and-mortar companies that are investing large sums in ERP systems and beginning to acquire modeling systems to better manage their supply chains. The costs are even more important for companies planning to operate in the near future as members of virtual supply chains because, as we are about to discuss, their dependence on information technology to make them competitive is more pronounced.

The proliferation of data acquisition and warehousing in all areas of business has stimulated the emergence of **data mining**, which is a methodology for discovering patterns and relationships in large databases.[15] Data mining employs **exploratory data analysis** methods combined with **on-line analytical processing** (OLAP) techniques for constructing and visualizing multidimensional data structures.[16] The methodology relies heavily on graphical displays of multidimensional arrays that allow human analysts to interact with automated techniques for identifying and validating data patterns. Examples of data mining include analysis of historical response data to identify market segments for telephone solicitation and identification of hidden factors in process sensor data that predict machine failures.

Data mining is relevant to the supply decision database because the optimization model inducing it is constructed from descriptive submodels, many of which use relationships derived from large sets of raw data. Data mining would prove valuable, for example, in analyzing historical manufacturing cost data to identify cost drivers and cost relationships for plant submodels. Data mining and OLAP techniques are also attractive tools for analyzing and displaying output data from multiple scenario runs with the optimization model. Such analysis would seek to identify hidden trends in these output data.

Challenging issues face the modeling practitioner and system developer when creating decision databases and modeling system for virtual supply chains of several companies, presumably linked via the Internet. They include the following:

- To what extent do companies standardize and share descriptive data about costs, capacities, and forecasts, and what are processes for distributing such data?
- How can modeling tools be standardized across different companies?
- How and where will an integrated decision database for the entire supply chain be assembled?
- Who is responsible for performing integrated supply chain analyses?
- How will the resulting plans be disseminated and what incentives will be created to ensure that they will be followed?
- How are data sharing and integrated planning processes affected when individual companies participate in multiple supply chains?

These issues are not much different from those faced by large companies when they try to integrate planning among diverse business units.

Exercises

In addition to the following exercises, modeling exercises involving data files and discussion exercises involving white papers may be found on the Web site (www.scm-models.com).

1. Show how you would use 0-1 variables to model the restriction that the volume purchased in Figure 6.7 may not lie in the region between 8000 and 10,000 units.
2. Suppose the farm cooperative supplying Tasty Chips with corn and potatoes places the constraint that the ratio of tons of corn to tons of potatoes purchased from them must lie in the range 0.9 to 1.1. How would you model this restriction?
3. You are creating a model to analyze your company's supply chain plan for next year. Suppose the cost per ton shipped on a link from Chicago to Los Angeles is \$250 for a less-than-truckload shipment and \$150 for a full-truckload shipment. Suppose further that the logistics department estimates that: (a) shipments will be 100% less than truckload if the model chooses to ship up to 1000 tons for the year, (b) shipments will be 50% less than truckload and 50% full truckload if the model chooses to ship between 1000 and 5000 tons for the year, and (c) shipments will be 100% full truckload if the model chooses to ship more than 5000 tons for the year. Describe how you would use mixed integer programming to capture these costs in the model in determining the optimal flow between Chicago and Los Angeles for the next year. If similar costs pertain to all links in the model, should you be concerned? Why? Can you suggest an alternative modeling approach?
4. Suppose a supply chain cost is a multiplicative term of the form Kxy where K is a constant and x and y are decision variables. Define $z = x - y$. Show how you can use the relationship

$$(x - y)^2 = x^2 - 2xy - y^2$$

to construct a mixed integer programming approximation to the multiplicative term. *Hint:* You will need to use piecewise linear approximations of quadratic functions of a single variable.

5. In Table 6.1, the shadow prices reflecting Tasty Chips' marginal costs of supplying finished products to the markets were shown to be higher than the average or transfer prices for supplying the markets. Will this always be the case? Why?
6. In their paper, "A Review and Evaluation of Logistics Metrics," Caplice and Sheffi define the following eight metric evaluation criteria:[17]

   Validity. The metric accurately captures the events and activities being measured and controls for exogenous factors.

   Robustness. The metric is interpreted similarly by users, is comparable across time, location, and organizations and is repeatable.

   Usefulness. The metric is readily understandable by the decision maker and provides a guide for action to be taken.

   Integration. The metric includes all relevant aspects of the process and promotes coordination across functions and divisions.

   Economy. The benefits of using the metric outweigh the costs of data collection, analysis, and reporting.

   Compatibility. The metric is compatible with the existing information, material, and cash flows and systems in the organization.

   Level of detail. The metric provides a sufficient degree of granularity or aggregation for the user.

   Behavioral soundness. The metric minimizes incentives for counterproductive acts or game playing and is presented in a useful form.

   a. To what extent should metrics reflect the realistic capabilities of the company versus industry norms or best of breed?
   b. How can an ERP system contribute to the achievement of these criteria?
   c. Is the criterion of integration consistent with setting accountability and incentives for individual managers?
   d. What is the relationship between a valid metric and valid data for an optimization model?

Notes

1. See SLIM Technololgies LLC, [2000].
2. The relevance of product aggregation to effective modeling was recognized by researchers long before the importance of supply chain management became widely recognized; for example, see Geoffrion [1977], Zipkin [1982], and Axsater and Jonsson [1984]
3. Atkinson et al. [1997, 3].
4. Differences in the goals and methods of financial and management accounting are reviewed in Atkinson et al. [1997, 4–7]. They point out that major goals of management accounting were articulated in the late 19th century by Frederick Taylor and others. Thus, implementation of

"scientific management" concepts initially proposed at the height of the industrial revolution have had to await developments of the information revolution of the late 20th century. As a case in point, while working on a project at a large computer manufacturer in 1983, we were told by managers responsible for manufacturing planning that it would be impossible to unravel and then reassemble financial accounting data to create meaningful inputs for a production planning model. Today, the task would still be viewed as difficult but not impossible. With developments in enterprise resource planning data, the task might soon become straightforward.

5. This definition is taken from Turney [1992, Glossary].

6. Cokins [1999] reports on the interest of ERP vendors in incorporating ABC methods in their software.

7. Caplice and Sheffi [1994] provide an overview of properties of and principles for selecting logistics performance metrics, including a review of the literature up to 1994. They discuss eight criteria for evaluating metrics: validity, robustness, usefulness, integration, economy, compatibility, level of detail, behavioral soundness.

8. Transfer prices are discussed in Atkinson et al. [1997, 569–578].

9. See Cooper and Kaplan [1991, 472].

10. For further background on forecasting methods, see DeLurgio [1997], Diebold [1997], Rosenfield [1994], or Winston and Albright [1997].

11. We draw on Rosenfield [1994] in our discussion about features of forecasting models.

12. Bodily [1982] provides an overview of judgmental forecasting methods.

13. See Yurkiewicz [1998], who provides summary information for 40 major forecasting packages about operating systems, hardware requirements, data entry procedures, graphical capabilities, and available forecasting techniques.

14. See Atkinson et al. [1997, Chapter 9].

15. Useful references for data mining are Piatetsky-Shapiro and Frawley [1991] and Westphal and Blaxton [1998].

16. For more information about on-line analytical processing, see Bergson and Smith [1997] and Thomsen [1997].

17. See Caplice and Sheffi [1994, 14].

References

Atkinson, A. A., Banker, R. D., Kaplan, R.S., and Young, S. M. [1997], *Management Accounting,* 2d ed. Englewood Cliffs, N.J.: Prentice-Hall.

Axsater, S., and Jonsson, H., [1984] "Aggregation and Disaggregation in Hierarchical Production," *European Journal of Operational Research,* 17, 338–350.

Berson, A., and S. J. Smith (contributor) [1997], *Data Warehousing, Data Mining and OLAP.* Homewood, Ill.: McGraw-Hill.

Bodily, S. E. [1982], "Judgmental and Bayesian Forecasting," *The Handbook of Forecasting: A Manager's Guide,* edited by S. Makridakis and S. C. Wheelwright. New York: Wiley.

Caplice, C., and Sheffi, Y. [1994], "A Review and Evaluation of Logistics Metrics," *The International Journal of Logistics Management,* 5, 11–28.

Cokins, G. [1999], "Understanding Activity Based Costing and Supply Chain Management," pp. 142–149 in *Achieving Supply Chain Excellence Through Technology,* edited by D. L. Anderson. San Francisco: Montgomery Research.

Cooper, R., and R. S. Kaplan [1991], *The Design of Cost Management Systems: Text, Cases, and Readings.* Englewood Cliffs, N.J.: Prentice-Hall.

DeLurgio, S. A. [1997], *Forecasting Principles and Applications.* Homewood, Ill.: Irwin-McGraw Hill.

Diebold, F. X. [1997], *Elements of Forecasting.* Cincinnati, Ohio: South-Western College Publishing.

Geoffrion, A. M. [1977], "A Priori Error Bounds for Procurement Commodity Aggregation in Logistics Planning Models," *Naval Research Logistics Quarterly,* 24, 2, 201–212.

Piatetsky-Shapiro, G., and W. J. Frawley, eds. [1991], *Knowledge Discovery in Databases,* AAAI Press, co-published in London and Cambridge, Mass.: The MIT Press.

Rosenfield, D. B. [1994], "Demand Forecasting," in *The Logistics Handbook,* edited by J. F. Robeson, W. C. Copacino, and R. E. Howe. New York: The Free Press.

SLIM Technololgies LLC, [2000], *SLIM User's and Reference Manual.*

Thomsen, E. [1997], *OLAP Solutions: Building Multidimensional Information Systems,* New York: Wiley.

Turney, P. B. B., [1992], *Common Cents: The ABC Performance Breakthrough,* Portland Ore. Cost Technology.

Westphal, C., and T. Blaxton [1998], *Data Mining Solution: Methods and Tools for Solving Real-World Problems,* New York: Wiley.

Winston, W., and S. C. Albright [1997], *Practical Management Science, Spreadsheet Modeling and Applications.* Belmont, Calif.: Wadsworth Publishing.

Yurkiewicz, J. [1998], "Forecasting that Fits," *OR/MS Today,* February, 42–55.

Zipkin, P. [1982], "Exact and Approximate Cost Function for Product Aggregates," *Management Science,* 28, 1002–1012.

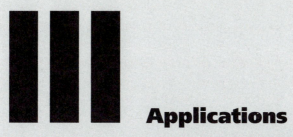

Applications

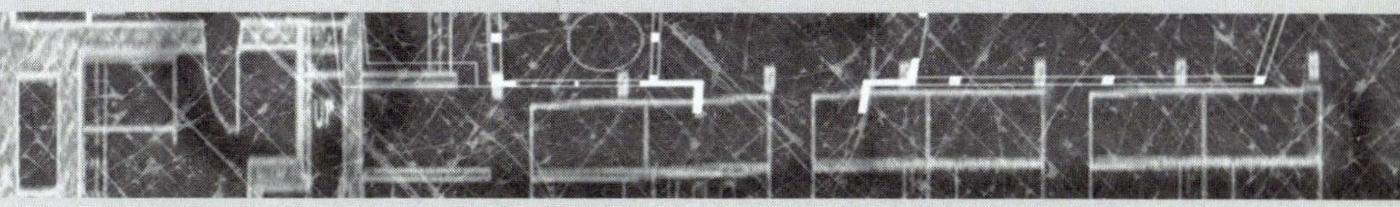

7 Strategic and Tactical Supply Chain Planning: State-of-the-Art Modeling Applications

Simply stated, the goal of strategic planning is to identify and evaluate **resource acquisition options** for sustaining and enhancing the company's competitive position over the long term. Because some of the company's product lines may be moribund, unprofitable, or otherwise undesirable, a complementary goal is to identify and evaluate **resource divestment options** leading to improved efficiency over the long term. For the moment, we are being deliberately vague about the nature of the resources to be acquired or divested but will return shortly to a detailed discussion of them.

Depending on the nature of the company's business, a long-term planning horizon may stretch 3 or 10 years into the future. For a wholesale grocery distributor, a 3-year planning horizon is appropriate for planning a major redesign of its distribution network. For a large oil company, a 10-year planning horizon is appropriate for evaluating mergers, acquisitions, oil and gas exploration plans, and the construction of new refineries or pipelines.

Because important resource acquisition and divestment decisions are often irreversible, management must carefully study their impact before committing to them. Optimization models provide a systematic and comprehensive approach to performing studies, especially in evaluating interactions among several options for resource acquisition and divestment. Moreover, by linking these options to aggregate descriptions of supply chain operations, models can measure the likely return on investments in strategic resources due to improved operations. The attractiveness of potential investments can only be fully measured by such models.

The number of strategic supply chain studies based on optimization models has greatly increased in recent years. Senior managers are more insistent about using data to understand dynamic changes in their companies and industries and more aware of the role that models can play in analyzing major decisions. In many cases, consultants are hired to implement the models using an off-the-shelf modeling system. They also assist management in evaluating and implementing strategic directions identified by the models. By installing the modeling system in-house and transferring the technology to an internal planning group, the consultants can provide the company with the capability to continue analyzing important, unresolved issues after the initial study has ended. Alternatively, the consultants may return periodically to review and extend the company's strategic supply chain plans.

Tactical planning is concerned with **resource adjustment and allocation** over planning horizons of a few months to a year. Within such a time span, the company cannot make major resource acquisitions or divestments, but it can and should adjust resources to its needs over the medium term. Tactical adjustments are best made in the context of optimal resource allocations to supply chain operations; whenever and wherever possible, tight resources should be expanded and underutilized resources should be reduced. Optimization models can assist managers in determining effective tactical plans that simultaneously adjust and allocate the company's resources.

We examine tactical planning models in this chapter and the next from a top-down perspective. Because it begins with a broad view of the company's supply chain, we think this direction is more natural than bottom-up constructions in which detailed operational models are combined. Nevertheless, when we discuss operational planning problems and models in Chapter 10, we will return briefly to methods for constructing tactical models from a bottom-up perspective.

In Section 7.1, we review the resource-based view of the firm, a new field of strategy analysis that we believe is helpful in conceptualizing and interpreting optimization models for strategic and tactical supply chain planning. In Section 7.2, we discuss a framework for logistics strategy analysis and relate it to the construction of optimization models. The framework is applied in Section 7.3 where we present the application of a mixed integer programming model to the location of distributions centers for an electronics distribution company.

We develop a framework for manufacturing analysis in Section 7.4, similar to the framework in Section 7.2, and relate it to the construction of optimization models. In Section 7.5, we discuss two modeling applications to the analysis of manufacturing strategy. One application evaluates global sourcing and manufacturing strategies for an industrial chemicals company. The second evaluates postmerger consolidation strategy for two consumer paper companies. The use of models for tactical supply chain planning is examined in Section 7.6. Tactical modeling applications in an industrial gases company and a beer manufacturer are presented in Section 7.7. The chapter concludes in Section 7.8 with our final thoughts about the state of the art for strategic supply chain modeling.

Strategic analysis of logistics and manufacturing supply chains does not constitute strategic analysis of the company as a whole. That would require integrating supply chain planning with demand planning, which we discuss in the next chapter. It would also require integrating supply chain planning with financial planning, which we discuss in Chapter 9.

7.1

Resources and the Resource-Based View of the Firm

We have emphasized the importance of resources to a company's strategic and tactical planning. The **resource-based view** of the firm is a new field of strategy analysis that provides important insights about a firm's resources and indirectly about the construction and use of optimization models for supply chain management.[1] It examines why companies with unique resources attain competitive advantage over other firms in the same industry. As we will argue, many concepts from the resource-based view of the firm can be captured or revealed by optimization models, at least to a good approximation.

Qualitative theories of strategy formation and analysis, such as the resource-based view, are important sources of ideas for elements to be incorporated in models for strategic planning. They also provide a useful vocabulary for interpreting solutions about competitive strategies suggested by models. The theories are audacious in scope, in large part because scholars proposing them are not inhibited by the ordeal of implementing and validating data-driven models. By contrast, modeling practitioners are much more cautious in selecting the scope of a strategic planning model. Practitioners and managers commissioning modeling studies can benefit by challenging themselves to devise quantitative descriptions that actualize abstract concepts about strategy and incorporating them in data-driven models. Conversely, strategy theorists can profit from "reality checks" provided by models and by refinements and extensions to their theories that will undoubtedly result.

Taxonomy of Resources

Strategy theorists developing the resource-based view of the firm have posited the following comprehensive **taxonomy of resources:**[2]

1. Physical resources (e.g., plants, distribution centers, inventories)
2. Human resources (e.g., machine operators, production managers, scientists)
3. Financial resources (e.g., cash flow, debt capacity, equity availability)
4. Information technology (IT) resources (e.g., inventory management system, communication network, supply chain modeling system)
5. Marketing resources (e.g., market share, brand recognition, goodwill)
6. Organizational resources (e.g., training systems, corporate culture, supplier relationships)
7. Legal resources (e.g., patents, copyrights, contracts)

Clearly, some resources, such as plants, machine operators, or cash flow, are **tangible** and possess measurable characteristics. Other resources, such as the skill of research scientists or corporate culture, are **intangible** and have characteristics that are difficult to measure, at least directly. A challenge for the modeling practitioner is to devise descriptive approaches for measuring the impact of intangible resources on the firm's strategy. An example is a decision tree created to describe and evaluate R&D scientists' assessments of the likely outcomes of their research and its market potential.

The academic literature has ignored legal resources as a distinct category. We included it because the existence of patents or contracts protecting the firm's valuable resources can have a large impact on its competitive position, especially in an era of rapid technological change. For example, a company may seek competitive advantage by hiring modeling system experts, working under a noncompete contract, to develop a customized system for managing its supply chain. The value of such legal resources may be an explanation, if not a justification, of the litigious nature of doing business in recent years in the United States.

Summary of the Resource-Based View of the Firm

The resource-based view of the firm seeks to explain why some companies attain and sustain competitive advantage over other firms in the same industry. According to the theory, a firm's superiority depends heavily on its resources and how they are used. It assumes that superior firms possess **heterogeneous** resources that differentiate it from other firms and allow it to earn rents; that is, the average and even marginal costs of their products are below, perhaps significantly below, the market prices they receive. The rents may be converted to sustainable profits if forces exist that limit competition for critical resources, once the industry has recognized their value.

Two factors limiting competition are **imperfect imitability** and **imperfect substitutability** of heterogeneous resources. Such factors exist when there are barriers due to patents, contracts, learning effects, or market preferences that make imitation and substitution by other firms difficult or impossible. Moreover, critical resources of the superior firm will be **perfectly immobile,** which means they are idiosyncratic and have no use in other firms, or **imperfectly mobile,** which means they can be moved or traded but have higher value within the firm. Finally, the theory states that a firm can establish heterogeneous new resources only if there are limits to competition prior to efforts on the part of the firm to create them. Otherwise, the rents that the superior firm can realize will be dissipated by excessive costs of initial competition.

Economists have identified four types of rents accruing to the superior firm. Ownership of scarce resources such as valuable land, production facilities near markets, or patents lead to **Ricardian rents.** As the result of collusion or government protection, the firm may achieve **monopoly rents.** Firms that undertake risky and entrepreneurial ventures in environments distinguished by instability and uncertainty may realize **Schumpeterian,** or **entrepreneurial, rents.** Firms with idiosyncratic resources that are scarce, but less scarce and less sustainable than Ricardian resources, may receive **quasi-rents.**

In considering **competitive sustainability**, several phenomena have been linked to characteristics of the process of accumulating heterogeneous resources.[3] Inefficiencies resulting from attempts to move too quickly in creating and exploiting heterogeneous resources are called **time compression diseconomies.** The phenomena of "success breeding success" in competitive endeavors leads to **asset mass efficiencies** and **learning effects;** they are forms of economies of scale and represent barriers to entry for late entrants in a market. When creation of a valuable asset does not necessarily lead to competitive advantage because complementary assets are absent, the firm has failed to recognize the **interconnectedness of stock assets.** Finally, **causal ambiguity** refers to the uncertainties and discontinuities associated with business success in creating a heterogeneous resource. If the causes of success are difficult to identify, the firm may find it difficult to sustain the ensuing advantage. Conversely, it may be difficult for competitors to replicate the resource.

When attempting to understand sustainability due to heterogeneous resources, management will be interested in the impact of strategic decisions on the duration of a competitive advantage as well as its existence. In all likelihood, the duration will be dependent on the scenario being analyzed. If an optimization model is being used to evaluate such scenarios, the modeling practitioner must devise schemes for extracting meaningful insights from the results of multiple scenario runs. The dependence of sustainability on scenarios also suggests the use of stochastic programming models to identify strategies for hedging against uncertain competitive or market developments that might erode the firm's advantage.

The concept of a firm's **core competencies** is an important idea linked to the resource-based view of the firm.[4] Core competencies refer to heterogeneous resources that provide the superior firm with sustainable competitive advantage. Often, managers in a firm do not clearly understand the precise nature of its core competencies, how they should be protected, and how new ones should be created. One of the objectives of an optimization model for strategic planning is to assist management in identifying, measuring, and tracking core competencies.

Connections with Optimization Models

Connections between the resource-based view of the firm and optimization models for strategic supply chain planning are both explicit and implicit. Optimization models accept explicit descriptions of many of the types of resources listed in the taxonomy and determine optimal levels for them in a strategic or tactical plan. Such descriptions include cost relationships describing investment, disposal, and fixed and variable costs as a function of the quantity of the resource made available, discarded, and/or consumed. The models also incorporate consumption rates for these resources as they are utilized by transformation and handling activities in manufacturing and distribution facilities.

Modeling Resources. Clearly, physical resources can be directly represented in a strategic or tactical model. Human resources as they relate to tangible supply chain activities, such as supervising a packaging line, maintaining machines, or dispatching, can also be directly represented, but at an aggregate level. By their very nature, financial resources readily admit objective, quantitative descriptions and can be explicitly incorporated in an optimization model. In fact, optimization models have long been proposed for corporate financial planning. Space has prevented us thus far from discussing such applications, but we will rectify the omission in Chapter 9.

Understanding and evaluating the role of IT resources in corporate strategy formation has proven difficult and ambiguous. Recent analysis, however, suggests that IT resources are necessary, but not sufficient, elements of a firm's competitive advantage. IT resources are different from other resources because they have make no explicit contribution in adding value to the firm's products and services but still benefit the firm by supporting better management of other resources.

Although IT resources have obvious importance to a company's strategic plan, they appear difficult to explicitly model, perhaps only because modeling practitioners have not yet made sufficient effort to do so. Investments in IT for improving manufacturing or distribution processes may be planning phenomena that are little different from investments in plants or production machines and should therefore be explicitly modeled. For example, this would be the case with investments in automatic flow-through equipment at a distribution center to streamline supplier-to-store shipments by a retailing company. The maximal throughput per year of such equipment could be incorporated in an optimization model as a hard resource constraint. By contrast, investment by a local delivery company with a rapidly growing business in a customized vehicle routing system may have significant, implicit benefits such as better on-time performance, but it would be difficult to forecast this performance and relate it to decision options in a supply chain model.

Marketing resources are both tangible and intangible and lie outside our standard frame of reference concerned with the supply side of the firm. Still, strategic planning should involve integration of supply chain and demand management. Although less prevalent than models for supply chain decision making, optimization models for acquiring and allocating marketing resources have been successfully implemented and applied. Such models should also reflect existing or potential conditions of Ricardian, monopoly, or entrepreneurial rents; for example, location of a manufacturing facility near an untapped, third-world market for its products may yield entrepreneurial rents. Examples of marketing models and their integration with supply chain models are discussed in Chapter 8.

Organizational and legal resources are intangible and therefore difficult to represent in a supply chain optimization model. Still, the modeling practitioner may find it possible and worthwhile to indirectly portray them in the structure of a model. For example, it may be important to represent suppliers in such a way that the model reflects their size and relationship with the company. A large impersonal supplier may be represented by a simple cost versus volume curve. By contrast, a small but important supplier who is capable of making several key parts may be represented by a more elaborated submodel that captures the supplier's costs and capacities and allows the model to determine the specific parts and volumes that the supplier will provide.

Heterogeneous, Homogeneous, and Stranded Resources. In building a supply chain optimization model, we must consider the cost and consumption of all the company's tangible resources, only a few of which may be heterogeneous. In general, we say that each resource falls into one of three resource classes: heterogeneous, homogeneous, or stranded. Heterogeneous resources are critical to the firm's competitive advantage, but the firm must appropriately acquire or divest, and allocate, all its resources. A resource is **homogeneous** if its availability can be increased or decreased at a cost that is at or near a well-established market cost. A resource is **stranded** if its value to the company is negative or well below market value. Because we probably do not know the category in which each resource lies, we must treat them as equals and try to deduce their category from the results of an optimal solution.

Model optimization provides insights indicating that certain resources may be heterogeneous and should be expanded, whereas other resources may be stranded and should be reduced. To illustrate, we consider a net revenue maximizing, snapshot model of next year's strategy for a manufacturing firm. A high shadow price on a resource at its maximal capacity in an optimal solution indicates that maximal net revenues could be significantly increased if more of that resource were available. Such a resource may be heterogeneous. Recall that the shadow price measures the marginal value of another unit of capacity.

In particular, suppose a snapshot model of next year's supply chain plan produced a shadow price of $100/ton on the yearly capacity of a specific type of production machine in a specific plant. Suppose further that a new machine of that type with a yearly capacity of 25,000 tons costs $500,000. The shadow price indicates that net revenues might increase as much as $2,500,000 if the new machine is acquired. The disparity between the potential value of the machine and its cost indicates that the physical resource of the machine and possibly related resources are heterogeneous. If it is not the machine itself, it may be that production personnel have learned how to use the machine in an extremely efficient manner. Alternatively, some or all of the products manufactured by the machine may be proprietary or even protected by patents. Or, it may be a combination of factors. In any event, causal ambiguity leading to resource heterogeneity could be unraveled by careful analysis of the input data and optimal solution to the optimization model.

We must be careful, however, in drawing conclusions from shadow prices because they measure only marginal values, which might decrease rapidly as more resources are made available. Thus, $2,500,000 is an upper bound on the contribution of a new machine to net revenue. It may be that increasing yearly capacity as much as 25,000 tons is actually much less attractive and may even lead to increased revenues that are far less than the machine's cost. The actual value can be determined by reoptimizing the model parametrically for capacities above current capacity to determine how many machines would be profitable to add, taking into account that the allowable payback period for machine investments is longer than 1 year.

Even if machine capacity is heterogeneous and investment in one or more machines would be highly attractive, we should analyze the sustainability of the resource as heterogeneous before we proceed with the investment. This would require extending the snapshot model of next year, which hinted at heterogeneity of the machine resource, to a multiple-year model. The decision options considered by the extended model should recognize the danger of time compression diseconomies in trying to too quickly exploit apparent heterogeneous resources. For example, is there sufficient time for human learning about using the additional machine capacity to take place? The extended model should also be optimized under a variety of demand scenarios to see if increased net revenues will be sustained under a reasonable selection of scenarios.

Similar arguments based on shadow prices may be developed for categorizing and further analyzing tangible resources as homogeneous or stranded. Homogeneous resources can be readily adjusted up or down to enhance profitably. Stranded resources are candidates for divestment as long as divestment costs are not too high. A large divestment, however, such as a plant shutdown or sale, may have an unfavorable effect on the capacity of the entire supply chain, which should be examined by an optimization model.

7.2 Strategic Analysis of Logistics Supply Chains

Logistics supply chain management is concerned with the flow of raw materials, parts, work-in-process, and finished products needed to ensure that the company's customers receive finished products at the correct time, in the correct location, and in the correct amounts. It is not concerned with plans regarding manufacturing processes, transformations, or resources, although manufacturing facilities might be treated as arms-length suppliers to the logistics network. Strategic analysis of manufacturing supply chains is discussed in the following section.

A logistics supply chain may describe a company that has no manufacturing activities, such as a retailer or a third-party logistics provider. It may also describe a division of a larger company with manufacturing divisions that is responsible for distributing the company's products, and possibly those of other companies, to the markets. A third possibility is a logistics supply chain describing logistics operations in a company with manufacturing plants, but management has separated the manufacturing and logistics functions. Such a separation would be suboptimal, but the company may not yet be organized to allow effective integration.

We begin this section with a review of the principles of logistics strategy formation. First, we present a qualitative framework for logistics strategy formation. Then we examine how optimization models can be constructed to analyze many of the issues addressed by the framework.

A Framework for Logistics Strategy Formation

It is only in the past 10 years that executives have come to realize the importance of logistics to their company's strategy. Improvements in logistics operations are undoubtedly due to advances in IT that have fostered better communication among distribution functions and the deployment of modeling systems. The potential to make such improvements has been realized by some companies, who have created competitive advantage from it. Wal-mart's success in the mass merchandising industry is an oft-cited example. The company achieved superior customer service, which resulted in impressive market share, by implementing innovative logistics operations coupled with well-managed replenishment inventory processes.[5]

An insightful framework for planning logistics strategy, which we review in this subsection, is depicted in Figure 7.1.[6] The driving force underlying the design and operation of a company's logistics supply chain is its **customer service strategy.** This will depend on the firm's products, markets, and customer service goals, which reflect expectations in the market. Many firms must implement complex customer service strategies because their markets fall into several segments that have different customer service needs and expectations. For example, a manufacturer of consumer products will serve bulk retail sellers differently from traditional retailers because they require shorter delivery times and 100% direct-to-store deliveries.

Superior customer service may be the key goal driving logistics strategy, but the firm must also consider cost, value added services, flexibility, and adaptability. Cost has become increasingly important, especially in industries with low margins. Value added services are services offered to specific customers at an added cost. These include, for example, bar-coding products for flow-through operations at customers' distribution centers, making drop shipments directly to stores, and vendor-managed

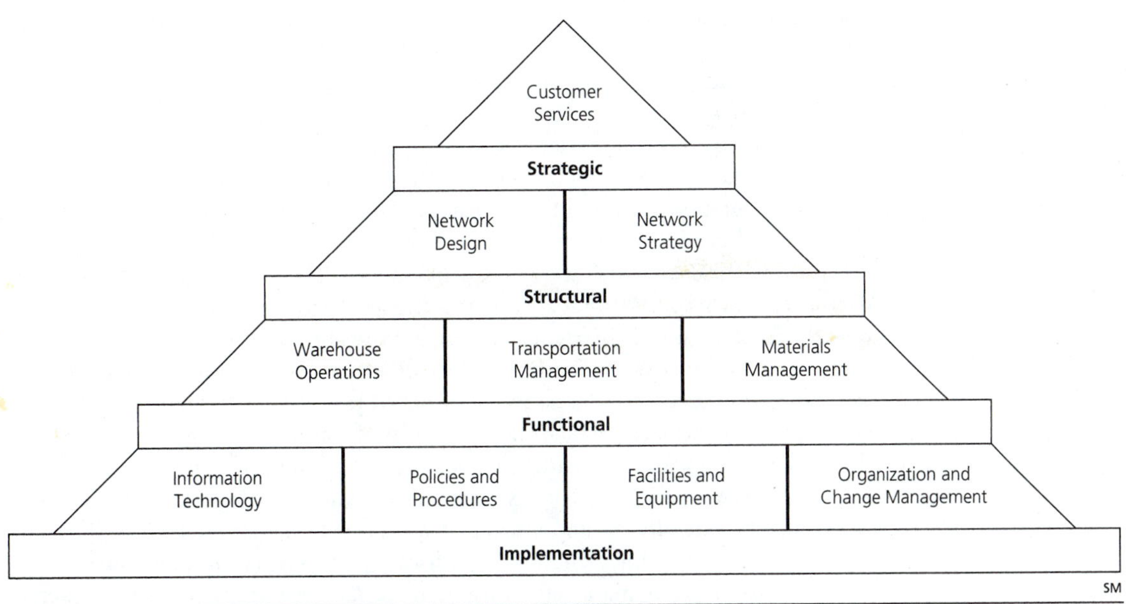

Figure 7.1 Elements of logistics strategy formation. *Source:* Service Mark by Andersen Consulting. © 1989 Andersen Consulting. All rights reserved. Found in O'Laughlin and Copacino [1994].

inventories at a customer's facilities. Flexibility refers to the firm's ability to rapidly design and implement new services for its customers. Adaptability refers to the firm's long-term ability to adjust its strategy to new conditions in its markets or advances in technology. It requires the firm to create and employ organizational and IT skills to identify trends and adapt to them. For example, a company may decide to implement new carrier selection processes to exploit imbalances in transportation spot rates that are broadcast by carriers over the Internet.

In laying out strategic logistics plans for the company, management must challenge itself to identify a broad range of options. A planning discipline based on scenario analysis to identify the company's strengths, weaknesses, opportunities, and threats, along with appropriate resource acquisition and divestment decisions, can prove effective in pushing management in this direction. The requisite planning processes should be institutionalized so that they are repeated on an annual, or some other periodic, basis.

Once its strategic goals have been articulated, the firm must identify structural elements for implementing its strategy, which are its **network design** and its **network strategy.** Network, or channel, design is concerned with activities and functions needed to achieve the customer service goals and how different participants in the supply chain carry them out. It involves decisions about the extent to which distributors will manage functions such as marketing, selling, delivery, and billing. Market share and size often determine the relative cost and value of direct distribution channels owned and operated by the company versus channels that are shared or run by third parties. Such decisions should also take into account expected long-term changes in the markets and the company's market share. If market share is expected to grow, it is important to consider investing in direct distribution channels, rather than working with third-parties, to accelerate the growth and to avoid future disruption and cost.

A distribution company may bring about major changes in its channel design by acquisitions of other distribution companies or even a merger. Acquisitions and mergers will obviously have a large impact on the company's strategic outlook, creating new markets as well as new opportunities for expanded and more efficient supply chain operations. Invariably, duplications in the company's logistics capabilities will arise and need to be eliminated.

The physical network strategy is concerned with decisions about the logistics network that can be fully evaluated in an integrated manner only by an optimization model. Key decisions include the location and mission of facilities and strategies for using these facilities to serve customers. Facilities refer to the company's national or regional distribution centers and warehouses, supplier plants or distribution centers, and customers' facilities, which may be plants, distribution centers, or stores. We discuss below these decisions and the construction of an optimization model.

As depicted in Figure 7.1, the structural elements in the logistics strategy framework must be extended to, and integrated with, functional elements to evaluate and fill out details regarding structural decisions. Decisions about **warehouse operations, transportation management,** and **materials management,** which refer to processes and systems for managing flows and inventories across the entire network, are linked to the structural decisions. This is another way of stating our principle that any strategic planning exercise must consider the interplay between strategy and functional operations.

The final level of the framework, implementation, involves people, business processes, and IT to support and execute the strategy. Of critical importance to the successful execution of a logistics strategy is the creation of order management and order replenishment processes and their integration. Implementation is perhaps the most difficult aspect of logistics strategy formation, in large part due to rapid changes in IT and the global markets, which require continual adaptation.

We conclude our discussion of the framework by briefly discussing its relationship to the resource-based view of the firm. A superior distribution company may owe its competitive advantage to heterogeneous physical and informational resources that allow it to provide **quick response** to its customers. Benetton, the Italian sportswear manufacturer, gained competitive advantage in the early 1990s by a quick response system that permitted retailers to place orders directly with the company's manufacturing facility.[7] A highly automated $30 million warehouse expedited these orders. Including manufacturing time, Benetton was able to ship completed orders in 4 weeks, which was a fraction of the time required by most of its competitors.

In the 1980s, Baxter Healthcare acquired American Hospital Supply Corporation to provide a large and direct distribution network for servicing its customers.[8] It also used the network to sell competitors' products to its customers. One major benefit of the acquisition was a significant increase in efficiency and lowering of costs. In the terminology of the resource-based view of the firm, the physical network and the people running it represented a resource that was heterogeneous because it achieved asset mass efficiency.

Constructing an Optimization Model for Strategic Logistics Planning

Constructing an optimization model to analyze a company's strategic logistics plans is a natural outgrowth of the conceptual framework just reviewed. Such a model, which we call the **logistics network model**, is intended to strengthen and extend managerial judgment about the company's markets, its products, its distribution channels, and a host of other factors. Moreover, by inducing a supply chain decision database for strategic analysis, the model highlights data collection and descriptive modeling activities that are prerequisites to management's realization of an informed and intelligent strategic plan.

Following the framework, we begin by discussing how to represent customer service requirements in the logistics network model. Requirements such as maximal delivery times for different market segments, direct-to-store deliveries, and sole sourcing can be explicitly represented within the transportation subnetworks of a supply chain model. Maximal delivery times are captured by limiting the maximal distance allowed for transportation arcs connecting a distribution center to the markets it serves. Direct-to-store deliveries correspond to links between the company's suppliers and its stores. The transportation costs of these links will largely determine whether or not they are selected for positive flows in an optimal solution. Sole sourcing is captured by 0-1 decision variables that determine whether or not each customer or market will be serviced by a particular distribution center.

Similarly, channel design options can be evaluated by the logistics network model. Their precise form depends on the nature of the options. As an example, consider a proposal offered by a third-party logistics provider to operate several warehouses and provide transportation from these warehouses to nearby markets. We assume for the purposes of illustration that this is a 1-year option and that the logistics network model depicts a 1-year snapshot view of the company's logistics network. The third-party warehouses and the appropriate transportation links would be included in the model's decision database.

The selection or rejection of the proposal would be represented in the logistics network model by a 0-1 decision variable that controls throughput at the third-party warehouses; that is, throughput at each of the warehouses would be allowed up to a contractual or practical maximum if the variable were chosen to be one by the model optimizer, whereas throughput would be forced to zero if the variable were chosen to be zero. In the latter case, outbound flows from the third-party warehouses would also be forced to zero because throughput there must be zero. The model would also incorporate cost details of the proposal, which might include warehousing and transportation costs, both of which might entail fixed and variable costs with volume discounts.

In general, the logistics network model would address a variety of no-yes (0-1) and related decisions about facilities and their functional operations. These would include the following:

- Which existing facilities should be left open or expanded? Which existing facilities should be shut down?
- Which new facilities should be opened with how much throughput capacity?
- What is the mission of each facility (e.g., which products does it handle and/or store in inventory)
- What equipment (e.g., flow-through sorters, conveyors, refrigerated storage areas) is needed at each facility to support its mission?
- Which facility or facilities will serve each customer or market?
- Which suppliers will replenish each facility?

A simple version of a logistics network model for addressing such decisions was constructed and optimized in Section 4.2.

The model might incorporate additional logical constraints based on 0-1 decision variables that reflect managerial judgment about flexibility and risk in shaping the firm's logistics strategy. For example, to prepare for possible surges in demand, we might add constraints forcing the total throughput capacity of all open facilities in each geographical region to be 25% greater than expected demand. Or, we might add constraints limiting the distance between any open facility and its nearest open neighbor to be less than 500 miles as a hedge against unexpected facility failure.

The decisions we just discussed are concerned with the structure of the logistics network. To evaluate strategy, we need to add decision variables and constraints that reflect activities, processes, resources, transportation flows, and costs involved in functional management of the network. Moreover, we must link them to decision variables and constraints describing structural options.

According to the framework of Figure 7.1, functional management of a logistics network falls into three categories: warehousing operations, transportation management, and materials management. All three lend themselves to comprehensive modeling. Warehousing operations at a distribution center are captured by a submodel of that facility comprising processes, transformation recipes, and resources describing the flow of products through the facility. An example is given in Figure 6.6, where we depict receiving, cross-dock, put-away, picking, and dispatching operations. The consumption of human resources by the five operations is also depicted in the figure. The optimization model determines human resources measured in thousands of labor hours needed to sustain the distribution center at its optimal level of activity, the allocation of these resources to the warehousing operations, and its cost. Finally, Figure 6.6 also depicts inventory holding costs associated with each product family as a function of throughput of the product at the facility.

The connections between structural decisions about the network and functional management are as before. At the structural, or design, level, we have a 0-1 decision variable that allows positive throughput at an optional facility if it equals 1 and constrains throughput to 0 if it equals 0. Thus, the processes, transformation recipes, and resources at a facility will be held at zero activity levels if the facility is not chosen to be part of the optimal logistics network.

As we discussed in Section 6.3, transportation management is represented in the logistics network model by the following three transportation submodels:

- The **inbound transportation submodel** connecting suppliers to supply chains facilities
- The **interfacility transportation submodel** connecting facilities to facilities
- The **outbound transportation submodel** connecting facilities to customers an markets

These logistics network models may also include options relating to transportation modal choice. The choice may be between truck and rail shipments connecting the company's distribution centers and its markets. Or, it may be a choice between full truckload and less-than-truckload shipments, where the latter incur a higher unit cost per hundred-weight-mile. The inclusion of modal choice decisions in an optimization model must be done cautiously because it can easily lead to a complex mixed integer programming model.

Finally, materials management functions relate to activities that cut across the entire supply chain. These might include decisions about allowable interfacility shipments or how many facilities will carry each product family. The development of data management and modeling systems for integrated supply chain management is the joint responsibility of the materials management and information technology functions.

7.3

Redesigning the Distribution Network of an Electronics Products Company

The following case is a classic application of optimization models to the problem of redesigning the logistics network of a distribution company.[9] It was performed in the mid-1980s by implementing a modeling system on a mainframe computer that was customized to the application. Today, the study could be performed much more quickly using off-the-shelf modeling software residing on a PC.

We were engaged as consultants by the director of logistics of the distribution division of a large electronics firm doing business throughout the continental United States. The division had originally been established to distribute company products to its customers. In recent years, however, it had expanded its business to include products manufactured by other companies. We were called in immediately after the division had acquired the customers and warehouses of a smaller distribution company. Our task was to develop an optimization model to help the director decide how to consolidate the combined, postacquisition logistics network.

This network had three levels: suppliers, distribution centers, and markets. Consolidation plans were to be based on total cost analysis of the following questions:

- For each product, which suppliers should replenish each distribution center?
- How should each demand market be served?
- Where should new distribution centers be opened? What size should they be? Which existing distribution centers should be shut down?
- What is the trade-off between customer service and cost?

Clearly, these questions are linked. For example, any decision about the location and size of distribution centers in the new network would influence the decision about which one would serve each market.

To answer these questions, we constructed a mixed integer programming model of the logistics network. Zero-one variables were used to describe the distribution center location options. They were also used to capture decisions about which product families would be handled by each distribution center that the model chose to open.

The first step in implementing the model was to define families of products, suppliers, and markets that captured the essence of the company's logistics activities. Eleven product families were defined on the basis of their physical shipping characteristics. Approximately 150 supplier zones were defined based on the product definitions and the suppliers' sizes and their geographical locations. Suppliers' capacities to source the products were also incorporated in the model, but not the sourcing costs, which were considered to be outside the scope of the study. Approximately 200 demand zones were defined based on size and location.

The next major task was to create data files of transportation links and their associated costs connecting suppliers to the distribution centers and connecting distribution centers to the markets. Included in the analysis were the 6 existing distribution centers and 17 potential new distribution centers. The latter set was provided by the director of logistics based on his knowledge on the division's business and likely costs associated with new facilities located in major population centers around the United States. To compute timely and accurate transportation costs, we acquired a transportation database with current interstate common carrier rates from a third-party company that specialized in collecting and disseminating such information.

Customer service was captured by specifying the permissible links from distribution centers to markets. For example, a customer service requirement of no more than 2-days' delivery to each demand market was translated into a maximal allowable distance for links from distribution centers to that market. The delivery time and hence the set of permissible links to each market were varied to measure the trade-off of service against total cost.

More than 30 major runs were made in studying possible new configurations for the division's logistics network. Table 7.1 shows a typical comparison of results for the coming year's operations obtained by the model. In moving from the current configuration to an optimal configuration, the model chose to shut down three of the six existing distribution centers and to open up six smaller distribution centers in new locations. The result was a reduction in total logistics cost of approximately 10%. As one would expect, some costs increased under the new network (facility variable, shut-down, and inventory holding costs), whereas others decreased (transportation and facility fixed costs). In summing up the net gains and losses, however, the new network configuration proved to be significantly less costly. Moreover, the potential savings of 10% identified by the optimization model is understated because distribution flows from suppliers to distribution centers and from distribution centers to demand markets for the current system were optimized by the model, although the distribution center locations were held fixed.

This level of cost savings stood up under a number of what-if scenarios about the division's operations. For example, the traffic manager objected to the distribution center location strategy of the optimal solution in Table 7.1 because it did not include a new distribution center in the Los Angeles area. He argued that intrastate rates in California, which were much lower than interstate rates in and out of the

Table 7.1 Logistics study results (costs in $1000s)

	Current	**Optimal**
Transportation costs	6226	5498
Facility fixed costs	1360	818
Facility variable costs	577	879
Facility shutdown costs	0	159
Inventory holding costs (safety stock)	281	319
Total	8444	7673

state, dictated the location there of a distribution center. We reran the model with the distribution center option in Los Angeles fixed as open and operating. The result was a different network configuration that was only $40,000 more expensive than the optimal one summarized in Table 7.1, or about 0.5% of the total cost. Given the accuracy of the data, the new configuration was, in effect, an alternative optima.

Despite the success of the study, extended evaluation of the division's operations was desirable. The total logistics cost analysis for the division was not total cost analysis because sourcing costs, a significant percentage of total delivered costs, were ignored. This omission represented a lost opportunity for the division to achieve greater cost savings by selecting suppliers and supplier contracts that were most economical from a higher-level, total cost viewpoint.

Today, a PC modeling system would be used to perform this study. The model and its database could be easily transferred to the company for continued use. At the time, transfer of the mainframe system was deemed by the distribution company to be too difficult. Its information systems department was unable, or unwilling, to deal with a modeling system comprising unfamiliar programs that they would have to install and maintain on a mainframe computer.

7.4 Strategic Analysis of Manufacturing Supply Chains

In this section, we consider strategic planning models for firms that manufacture physical products sold to other companies and/or end-use consumers. The range of possible products is very large and includes consumer products, consumer durables, industrial products, production machines, and aircraft, to name only a few. Moreover, the number of distinct production environments is very large and includes process manufacturing, discrete parts manufacturing, job shops, and many others. Although strategy formation in a particular firm will clearly depend on these factors, we find it possible and useful to develop a general framework for understanding it. Customization of the framework and associated model building may be required for a specific company and its product lines.

We begin by presenting our framework for manufacturing strategy formation. After that, we examine manufacturing supply chain models that mechanize the framework. In the following section, we discuss modeling system applications in an industrial chemicals company and in two consumer papers companies after a merger.

A Framework for Manufacturing Strategy Formation

We adapt the framework of Figure 7.1 for logistics strategy formation discussed in the previous section to one for manufacturing strategy formation.[10] As depicted in Figure 7.2, the driving force for a company's manufacturing strategy is the com-

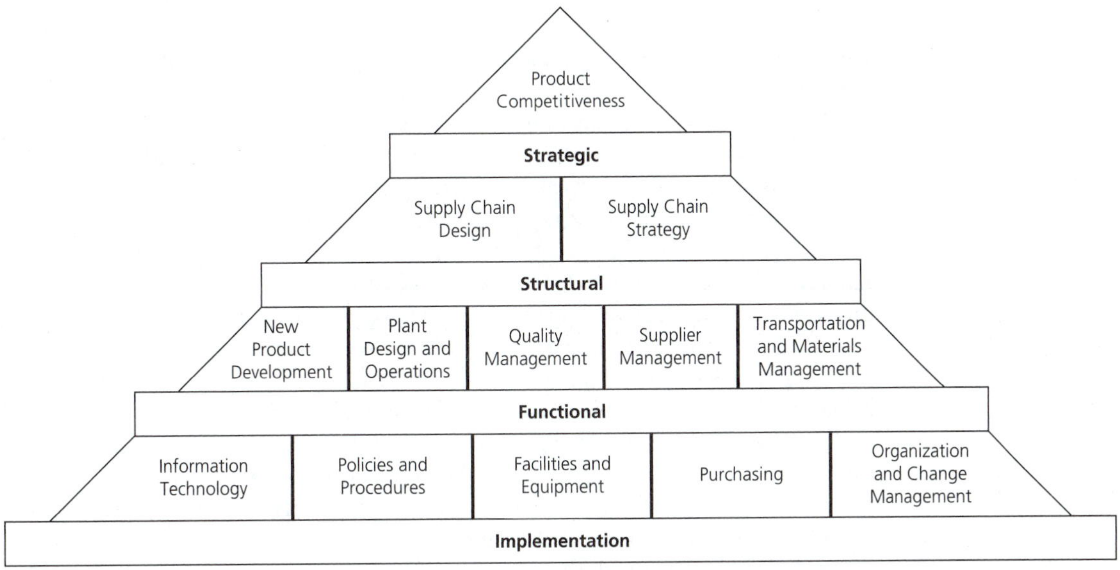

Figure 7.2 Elements of manufacturing strategy formation. *Source:* Adapted from Service Mark by Andersen Consulting. © 1989 Andersen Consulting.

pany's need and desire to manufacture competitive products. Product competitiveness depends on a number of factors including cost, differentiation, agility, quality, cycle time, and new product development.

It has long been recognized that **cost** and **differentiation** are two key dimensions along which firm's compete.[11] If the product is favorably differentiated from competitors' products in the eyes of the customers, a company may charge a higher price for it and possibly incur higher costs making it. Differentiation may result from the product's inherent superiority, brand awareness, or after-sales service. With growing demand for **make-to-order** (customized) products, differentiation may also be achieved by the company's **agility** in responding quickly and economically to such changes in product definition.[12]

Product **quality** may also be a source of differentiation and competitive advantage. The **cycle time** required to respond to changes in demand for **make-to-stock** (standard) products is another factor that can contribute significantly to the product's market share and hence its competitiveness.[13] Finally, because product life cycles are finite and may be decreasing in today's world of rapid technological change, sustained product competitiveness in most companies will depend on product innovation and **new product development.**

Given these factors affecting product competitiveness, management is concerned with structural elements for sustaining and enhancing them over the longer term. As shown in Figure 7.2, there are two classes of structural elements to be considered: supply chain design and supply chain strategy. **Supply chain design** refers to decisions regarding the facilities owned and operated by the company and the company's relationship with its suppliers. By contrast, we assume in addressing manufacturing strategy that we are less concerned with logistics strategy than with the distribution of the company's products downstream from manufacturing facilities to its customers.

Strategic issues of **vertical integration, acquisitions, mergers,** and **divestments** are important components of manufacturing supply chain design. Many medium and large manufacturing firms alter the structure of their supply chains on a frequent basis by acquiring and divesting business units or merging with other companies. Acquisitions cause vertical integration of the company's supply chain when the acquired companies are vendors of parts and components or distributors who sell the company's products. Acquisitions and mergers expand and diversify the company's product lines and markets and alter the structure of its supply chain.

A company's motivation in vertically integrating its supply chain may be to bring activities in-house whose value added components are, or could be, high relative to those of other activities in the supply chain. Thus, the company might decide to manufacture in-house a part that it had previously outsourced because management believes, possibly as the result of an accounting analysis, that the vendor's price included a hefty profit margin. Assuming that the company can produce the part at a cost that is near the vendor's cost, it can capture the margin previously realized by the vendor. Another reason to manufacture the part in-house might be to eliminate indirect transactions costs, such as those due to contract negotiations or higher inventories, that result from business arrangements between the company and the vendor.[14]

Of course, many other factors may enter into a company's decision to vertically integrate its business. The company may wish to acquire patents or specialized know-how possessed by its vendors. In addition to outsourcing a part, the company may decide that the part should be manufactured in-house in relatively low volumes to better understand the relevant processes, a step that could be essential to maintaining quality control and to estimating reasonable vendor costs. Moreover, if the part is critical to the company's business, such a strategy also mitigates the risk of interrupted or discontinued supply from the vendor. In such an event, the company would possess the in-house knowledge needed to manufacture the part in higher volumes.

Principles underlying vertical integration are changing rapidly with business-to-business developments on the Internet. The hope is that many manufacturing and distribution companies will be able to exploit the advantages of vertical integration without making important financial and organizational commitments. Still, companies in a virtual supply chain will need to make other commitments, such as sharing data, supply chain decisions, and profits, that are not yet well understood. Models offer the means for managing these new intercompany links in a rational and effective manner.

Supply chain design issues also become important when the company decides to **introduce new products** to its markets or to new markets. Depending on the industry, the decision to bring a new product to market may be the culmination of months or years of product development. The supply chain for a new product may be a new entity that is designed and implemented from scratch. More likely, it will share facilities and machines with supply chains of existing products, and it will involve existing facilities and equipment of the company' vendors and trading partners.

Once the options associated with supply chain design have been identified, the company must quantify and integrate them when analyzing its supply chain strategy. By quantifying options, we mean develop cost, performance, resource consumption, and other data allowing the options to be rationally evaluated. The integration of design options into a coherent effective supply chain strategy, one that enhances and sustains the competitiveness of the company's products, is a critical step in strategy formation.

As before, structural elements in the manufacturing strategy framework of Figure 7.2 must be extended to, and integrated with, functional activities to evaluate and fill out details regarding structural decisions. For our purposes, new product development affects supply chain design only when new products are ready to be manufactured. Plant design and operations must be viewed strategically to identify investments in new plants, expansion of existing plants, and new technologies, including IT.

Over the past 15 years, **quality management** has emerged as an important functional activity in virtually all manufacturing firms. The two major areas of management are design quality and conformance to quality standards. Processes for sustaining and improving quality involve organizational and human elements that cannot easily be quantified. Nevertheless, these processes are not free.

Many companies have attempted to justify the cost of quality by relating quality improvements to lower manufacturing costs; for example, lower assembly, rework, and final testing costs that result from the production of higher-quality parts that make up the product assembly. The drawback of such arguments is that they ignore market-share and price-premium effects due to higher-quality products. The manufacturing company may also enjoy positive market effects over the long term as the result of producing high-quality products.

A firm's **supplier relations** depend on the nature of its industry. At one extreme, automotive and aircraft manufacturers are supported by large networks of suppliers organized in several tiers. Within this network, medium-sized companies may be responsible for managing smaller suppliers under them. At the other extreme, manufacturing companies making industrial products, such as forest product or chemical companies, are often vertically integrated, at least to the product distributor level. Still, these companies buy chemicals and sometimes paper pulp from outside firms.

Some consumer and food products companies contract with third-party manufacturers to make their new products. This permits them to test the markets for the new products before investing in the capital equipment needed to manufacture them in-house. In addition to the direct costs of contract manufacturing, these companies can incur significant indirect costs associated with ensuring high-quality and timely production at the third-party manufacturers.

Management has only recently realized the strategic importance of **purchasing and supplier relations.** In managing these functions, the company is concerned not only with the cost of acquisitions but also with their quality and the responsiveness and flexibility of the supplier. Its priorities with respect to these criteria for specific items determine whether it seeks an **arms-length** or **alliance** relationship with suppliers of the items. With an arms-length relationship, the supplier enters into a short-term contract with the company based primarily on price without guarantees for follow-on work. The contract is usually quite explicit about the terms and conditions for acquisition of the items provided by the supplier. In many instances, the supplier is not the company's sole source for these items. Competition among suppliers to retain the company's business is intended to keep supplier costs down and allow the company to impose quality and delivery standards on supplier performance.

Alliances between the company and its suppliers were originally a Japanese practice that found favor in the United States during the early 1990s. In such a relationship, the supplier enters into a close working arrangement with the company under a flexible long-term contract. The supplier and the company agree to resolve to their mutual satisfaction any problems that arise in the manufacture or even redesign of the items provided by the supplier. Often, the supplier is the sole source of these items, although it is not considered good practice for the company to be the supplier's only or dominant customer. A typical rule of thumb is that the company should not provide a supplier with more than 30% of the supplier's gross revenue.

Alliances might be more expensive in terms of the direct costs of procurement. However, they allow the company to significantly reduce the overhead of maintaining a large supplier list and negotiating and monitoring contracts with multiple suppliers of specific items. Such relationships also allow the company to focus on product quality and more easily achieve integrated supply chain management with its suppliers, thereby reducing inventory costs.

Constructing an Optimization Model for Strategic Manufacturing Planning

We discuss the construction of a **manufacturing supply chain model** to analyze strategic options identified by applying the framework of Figure 7.2. Although many principles applied to the logistics network model that we discussed in Section 7.2 are relevant here, a manufacturing supply chain model will often be more complex due to the intricacy of the firm's production operations. For large firms with multistage process or discrete parts operations and with yearly sales exceeding several billion dollars, it may be impractical to try to capture the entire chain with a single model. Instead, models with selected planning elements should be constructed to analyze smaller business units or portions of the manufacturing supply chain.

We begin our discussion by considering submodels that describe manufacturing plants. In Figure 7.3, we depict the elements of an oil refinery submodel, which is one of the first applications of optimization models. For this refinery, crude oils C1 and C2 enter the distillation unit (DL). The output of the DL passes through the cracking units (TA and TB), whose output is mixed with intermediate products from the distillation unit in the blending units (B) to yield the finished products F1 and F2.

In a strategic planning model, such a submodel treats products and manufacturing stages in an aggregate manner to capture the essence of refinery operations, but without concern for details of an operational plan. This means some products are actually product families and some transformation units are actually an amalgam of several identical units. Obviously, we would enlarge the level of detail for a submodel that is to be used for tactical or operational planning. Similar submodels

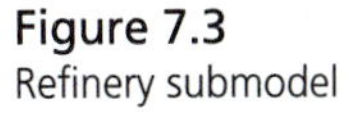

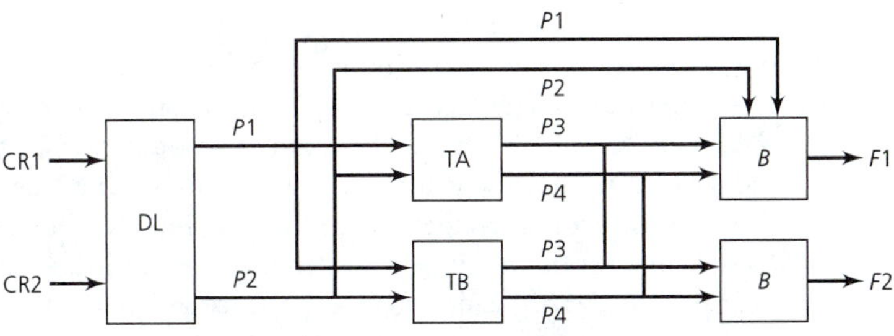

Figure 7.3
Refinery submodel

would be used to describe other process manufacturing environments such as petrochemicals, steel, and industrial chemicals.

A plant submodel is characterized by several interconnected processes or stages. Associated with each process are a number of recipes that describe how input products are transformed to output products. Associated with each recipe is a direct cost relationship that depends on product throughput. The process as a whole also has a cost relationship describing how cost is incurred as a function of total throughput of all products that are transformed there. In addition, the facility is characterized by resources that are shared among processes, such as maintenance labor, with associated cost relationships. Finally, the facility as a whole will have fixed and variable indirect costs as given by a cost relationship that is a function of total product throughput.[15]

Important decisions to be addressed by a strategic or tactical model are those describing **the mission of each plant.** The mission might be described by decisions about which products will be made at the plant and what technologies will be used to make them. To this end, we would define a 0-1 decision variable for each plant/product combination that would either allow the product to be made at the plant (the variable equals 1) or force the product to a 0-level there (the variable equals 0). Depending on the product, the 0-1 variable would be linked to recipes for making the product by a specific process that might make other products or it would be linked to a process dedicated to that product or it would be linked to a new technology requiring investment. The 0-1 decision variable would also be used to pick up the fixed cost associated with making a product at the corresponding plant and to impose a conditional minimum on the volume of the product produced at the plant.

In some industries, capital equipment needed for the manufacture of a product can be moved among plants to achieve a more effective strategic deployment. To determine this deployment, the manufacturing supply chain model would contain 0-1 decision variables for assigning each piece of equipment to at most one plant. A relocation cost can be associated with any assignment that involves transportation. Equipment that is not needed may be sold or discarded.

The plant's mission might also include choices of technologies for making one or more products. If multiple technologies were available, they would be selected by 0-1 decision variables in a multiple-choice constraint stating that exactly one, or at most one, technology could be chosen to make the product. For strategic planning, these decisions could be linked to capital budgeting constraints on investments for each plant, for the supply chain as a whole, or both. That is, if a 0-1 technology variable were chosen to be one in an optimal solution, it would turn on the technology and cause investment capital to be expended.

Large-scale manufacturing operations often involve **economies of scale** (decreasing marginal costs as a function of production volume). Given raw accounting data about direct and indirect manufacturing costs, determining economies of scale that depend on recipe volume, process volume, total facility volume, or some combination of them can be a challenging exercise in statistical analysis. Of course, a recipe, process, or facility might experience a diseconomy of scale (increasing marginal costs as a function of production volume) or both economies and diseconomies at different volume levels.

Short- and long-term **learning effects** associated with manufacturing a product or managing a process are a subtle type of economy of scale. In Figure 7.4a, we depict a typical learning cost curve that shows a decrease in the *unit cost* of manufacturing a product as a function of cumulative manufactured volume of the product. In Figure 7.4b, we display the *total cost* as a function of total product volume; this is the function that we would use in an optimization model. The initial items made have a very high relative cost. The unit cost of the 10,000th item may be 80% of the cost of the 1000th item; similarly, the unit cost of the 100,000th item might be 90% of the cost of the 10,000th item.

Assuming that the learning curve can be accurately forecasted before large-scale manufacture of the product begins, an important strategic decision faced by management is how quickly it wants to move down the learning curve. If the company has a lead over its competitors in the manufacture and sale of the product, it has an incentive to move down the learning curve sufficiently fast to create a barrier to entry for rivals firms that might wish to offer the same or a similar product at a later time.[16] Such a strategy has two benefits.

First, with no competition, the company can charge a higher price for the product depending, of course, on price sensitivity and its effect on evolving market size. Second, once competition arises, the company can afford to compete on price with new entrants because they have learned to make the product at a lower cost per unit. These planning issues clearly require a strategic planning model that has multiple

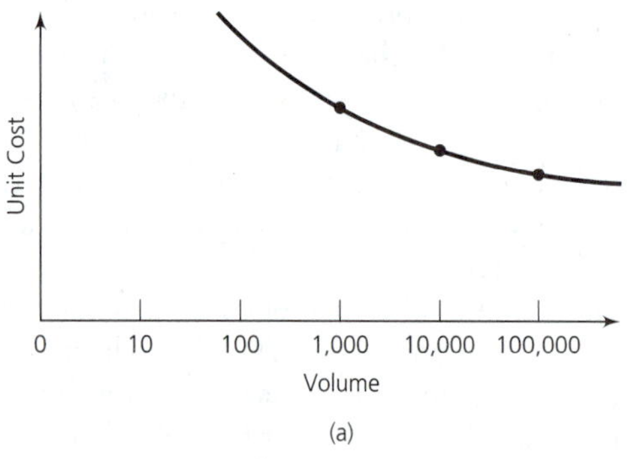

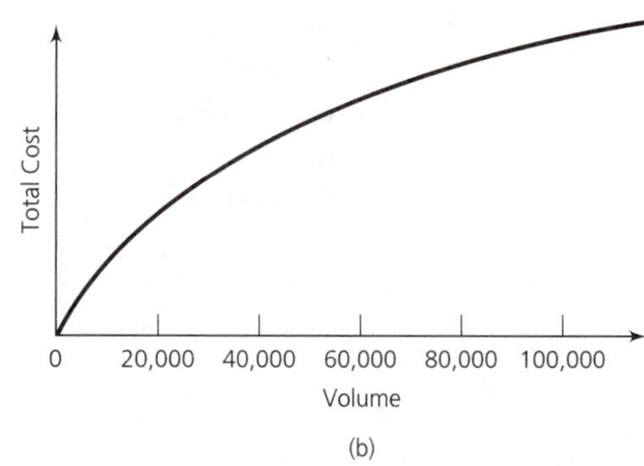

Figure 7.4 Learning curves for manufacturing costs

time periods. Moreover, similar to ordinary economies of scale, mixed integer programming constructs are needed to capture the condition that lower units costs can be achieved only after production volume at higher unit cost has been made. [17]

Another important factor to consider when designing the supply chain for a new product is the **cycle time** required to manufacture and distribute the product to meet unexpected surges in demand. This cycle time can be optimized by solving a **critical path model** that has been widely applied in project management.[18] Such a model considers a project comprising a collection of tasks, which in this context are activities needed to acquire raw materials or parts from suppliers, transport them to manufacturing plants, assemble or otherwise make the product, and transport it to the markets. Associated with each task is an execution time and a list of other tasks that must be completed before it may begin (the precedence relations). Model optimization determines a sequence of tasks whose collective execution times determine the minimal project completion time, which is the supply chain cycle time we seek. This sequence is determined by finding a path, called the **critical path,** through a network that describes the precedence relations. The tasks along the critical path are the bottleneck tasks that determine the cycle time.

An example of critical paths in a supply chain network is displayed in Figure 7.5. In this figure, we have included only those links showing the critical paths linking suppliers and plants to the markets. The cycle times to manufacture and transport parts and products to the markets are determined by the time length of these paths; for example, 20 days to M1, 22 days to M2, 18 days to M3, and 16 days to M4. As we have shown it, supplier S1 is the only critical supplier, and parts plants P1 and P2 are the critical parts manufacturers.

We assume multiobjective optimization methods were applied to the model to merge cost and cycle time objectives. Therefore, the cycle times to the four markets are undominated. In other words, no feasible supply chain plan exists that has the same or lower cost and cycle times to all markets with strictly lower cost or lower cycle time to at least one market. Research is underway to formally combine critical path models with manufacturing supply chain models.

We now consider supply chain optimization models for manufacturing companies that rely on extensive **supplier networks.** The suppliers may be vendors with an

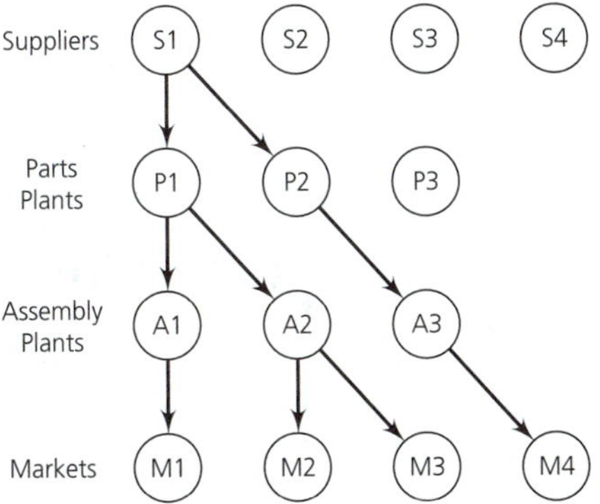

Figure 7.5
Critical paths through supply chain network

arms-length relationship to the company, trading partners engaged in alliances with the company, or other business units of the company. For arms-length relationships determined primarily by cost, optimization models are appropriate to the problem of supplier selection. Mixed integer programming constructs are very well suited to optimizing purchasing decisions involving volume discounts offered by the suppliers. They are also appropriate for contracts in which the company purchases supplier resources, such as machine and labor hours, to be assigned later to the production of specific items made by the supplier. Such an arrangement is, in fact, a melange of arms-length and alliance relationships.

The application of optimization models to alliance relationships is more ambiguous because such relationships entail intangible factors. An open issue is the extent to which the company and the vendor wish to share detailed supply chain data in the construction of an optimization model. If so, the company and the vendor should agree in advance of exchanging information about how savings due to greater supply chain integration will be shared.

Many manufacturing firms face a continuously evolving collection of make-or-buy decisions. In principle, a firm seeks to manufacture in-house those parts or components that are critical to its products and looks for economic outsourcing options for many of the others. However, the firm may not have the in-house expertise to manufacture all critical parts. It should then seek to establish and maintain long-term alliances with vendors of such parts. Another factor affecting make-or-buy decisions is the company's overall business volume and its effect on internal resources. If business volume is high, the company may be forced to engage in greater outsourcing due to internal resource shortages. Still, greater outsourcing may be economical even when business is not near overall capacity if vendors are available that can produce high-quality parts at lower cost than the company and if excess capacity can be sold off or otherwise retired.

Strategic outsourcing decisions require management to take a broad view of the options and their connections to internal resource planning. It can be very suboptimal to make strategic make-or-buy decisions based on myopic analysis of each option independent of all others. Optimization models can be developed and applied to rationalize decision making across the full range of make-or-buy options. In such models, each outsourcing option is linked to a 0-1 decision variable that determines whether to accept the option or not. These decision variables also are used to adjust demands on the company's internal resources, which are treated as variable quantities, and to record outsourcing costs.

7.5 Two Manufacturing Strategy Applications

We present two modeling applications in manufacturing firms that distribute their products. The first is analysis of worldwide sourcing strategies for Delta Industrial Chemicals. The second is a postmerger analysis of American Paper and Beacon Paper companies, two manufacturers of consumer papers. Details of these applications are based on actual studies; fictitious names have been used for the companies and data have been changed, but the overall depiction of the cases is accurate.

Worldwide Sourcing at Delta Industrial Chemicals

As an example of an optimization model developed to address strategic planning issues, we consider a successful application in Delta Industrial Chemicals (DIC). Annual sales of DIC have been growing from $500 million in 1994 to $800 million in 1998. DIC sells 200 products manufactured in approximately 20 plants to 3000 customers in a number of worldwide product markets: refractories, ceramics, abrasives and whitewear, polishing and surface finishing media, adsorbents and catalysts, papers, plastics, rubber, pigments, and flame retardants.

As shown in Figure 7.6, products in a given product line are manufactured in several stages from feedstock and then packaged and stored. Some facilities are full manufacturing sites, whereas others are process centers that receive intermediate products from manufacturing sites. Manufacturing sites are self-contained in that they can fully convert feedstock, package the finished products, and ship these products to distribution centers or customers around the world. The manufacturing sites may also ship intermediate product to process centers for additional processing and

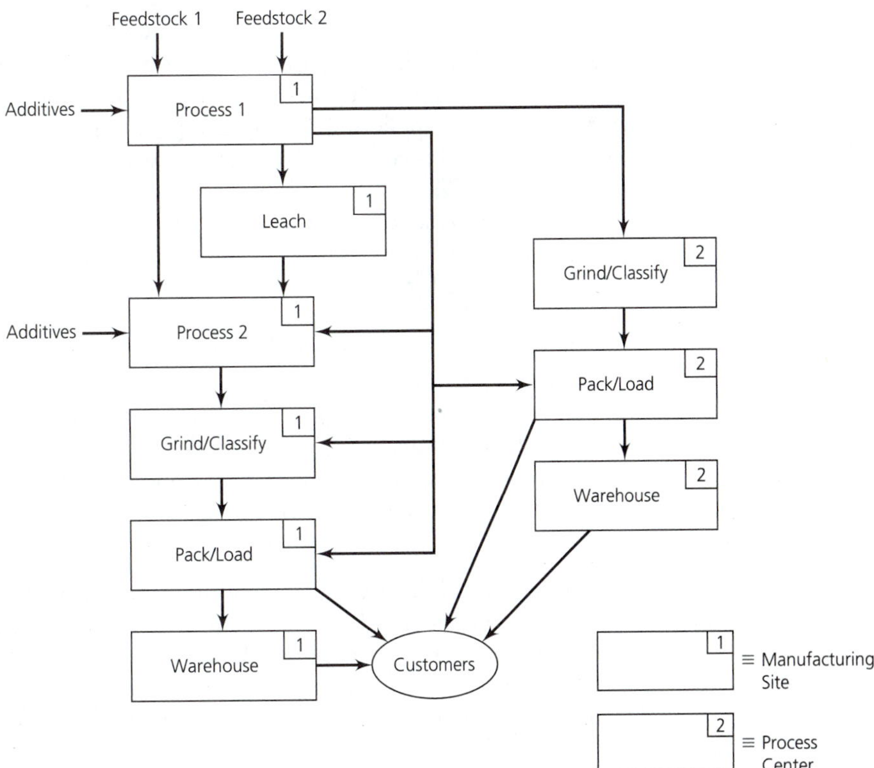

Figure 7.6
Generic manufacturing stages at DIC

packaging. These process centers lack equipment to perform one or more of the manufacturing transformations.

In general, DIC's supply chain has an inverted Y structure with a few feedstocks being transformed into a wide range of intermediate and finished products. For example, the manufacture of tabular products begins with one feedstock from which 30 coarse products and 10 fine products are produced. Of total supply chain costs, feedstock costs equal ~25%; logistics costs, ~20%; and manufacturing costs, ~55%.

Objectives of the Strategic Study. In 1994, DIC set out to double its business by the year 2000 through leverage of its competitive advantages. In particular, they intended to drive growth and profitability by the following:

1. Integrating and leveraging worldwide information and commercial and sourcing positions
2. Pursuing strategic alliances
3. Aggressively introducing new products, applications, and services
4. Developing and transferring technology

Although these objectives did not explicitly mention analysis with models, senior managers believed that modeling analysis could provide important insights. They recognized that the complexity of worldwide operations could be fathomed only by an integrative model rationalizing costs and capacities across the entire supply chain. Accordingly, a team of experts in manufacturing and logistics from the firm was assembled and charged with the responsibility of developing a modeling system for worldwide supply chain management. Once this was accomplished, the team would support its application throughout the company. Along with their other staff responsibilities, this **supply chain team** has worked on the modeling project since its inception.

The management goals listed above were translated into goals for the supply chain modeling project. Specifically, for each product line, a model would be developed to do the following:

- Determine optimal patterns for worldwide feedstock sourcing and manufacturing strategies
- Account for economies of scale in manufacturing
- Determine optimal patterns of interplant shipments of intermediate products
- Incorporate transportation costs for worldwide distribution of the products
- Evaluate the incremental cost of large and/or customized orders

Modeling Approach and Implementation. A mixed integer programming model was judged to be appropriate for the production/distribution planning problems discussed above. Mixed integer programming constructions were particularly needed to model fixed costs and economies of scale associated with the various manufacturing processes. Accordingly, an off-the-shelf mixed integer programming modeling system was selected as the tool to be used in the pilot study described below. Because the focus of the modeling effort was on manufacturing, outbound logistics was simplified by aggregating demands of individual customers into regional demand. Similarly, some details of the inbound logistics of feedstock supply, such as the sizes of the shipments to plants, were not captured by the model.

An expeditious, but effective, approach was taken to test the value of optimization modeling to DIC's supply chain problems. Data for a pilot model of part of the supply chain for refractory products were prepared over the course of approximately 4 weeks. The model was designed to accommodate manufacturing and transportation costs in local currencies. An exchange rate table converted the different currencies to U.S. dollars. These data were then used to generate and optimize a model.

Results. Results from optimizing the prototype model are given in Table 7.2. For the study year, the unconstrained optimization run of scenario 2 was over $9 million less in total supply chain cost than the base case run of scenario 1, reflecting the status quo. The projected savings were the result of shifting manufacturing to more efficient plants. A portion of these savings was lost due to higher interfacility and outbound transportation costs, but the net result was an impressive reduction in total cost of 8%.

Scenario 3 also produced an interesting result. With projected market growth of 50,000 metric tons, the worldwide system could increase total margin from a level of 22% for scenario 2 to a level of 29%, assuming that an optimal strategy would be implemented. The improvement in margin is again achieved by allocating demand to the most efficient plants.

Once the value of models was proven, DIC committed to a full-blown implementation of the modeling system and to validation of the data set for initial

Table 7.2 Worldwide refractory product analysis*

	Scenario 1	**Scenario 2**	**Scenario 3**
Total margin	$ 20,774,419	$ 29,947,381	$ 51,312,905
Total revenue	**$133,573,669**	**$133,573,669**	**$175,467,305**
Total costs	$112,799,250	$103,626,288	$124,154,400
Feedstock costs	$ 34,428,988	$ 33,358,175	$ 43,639,425
Inbound transportation costs	$ 75,551,950	$ 7,134,050	$ 9,409,050
Interfacility transportation costs	$ 657,470	$ 3,952,475	$ 5,760,330
Manufacturing costs	$ 61,375,848	$ 49,022,938	$ 51,566,913
Outbound transportation costs	$ 8,784,995	$ 10,158,649	$ 13,778,688
Volume, metric tons	159,420	159,420	209,420

*Scenario 1: Basecase: constrained to current supply chain flow; scenario 2: No constraints for supply; scenario 3: Projected market growth analysis.

product line. For each of the firm's product lines, decision making is complicated by differences among production costs at the various manufacturing and processing sites. The project team met with controllers to implement common costing standards across operations. In addition, production capacity at specific sites is sometimes strained to meet market demand that the division wishes to assign to them. Supply chain decision making is also complicated by costly and complex inbound and outbound transportation operations.

The modeling system has been used for several years on a range of scenarios for evaluating the following:

- Capital expansion and new equipment
- New products and new processes
- Options for transportation modes
- Acquisitions and joint ventures
- Benefit of reducing unit prices to boost revenues

In addition, shadow price information has been employed to measure the marginal cost of supplying additional tons to specific customers.

Conclusions. Despite the success of studies using the modeling system, the potential for integrated supply chain management at DIC has not yet been fully realized. Facility managers in Europe and the United States were reluctant to accept yearly manufacturing and distribution plans identified by the model that were radically different from historical plans, even if the model demonstrated that the new plans were much less costly. Their resistance was due in part to the lack of managerial incentives rewarding them for global, rather than local, supply chain optimization. As a result, supply chain planning with the modeling system has been restricted, for the moment, to North American operations where it is being actively applied.

Postmerger Consolidation of Consumer Paper Companies

This study analyzed options for consolidating operations in two companies that manufacture consumer papers, American Paper and Beacon Paper, after their merger.[19] The firms were approximately equal in size, each with annual sales of $175 million. They produced similar products for sale to customers throughout the United States, but had quite different customer bases. American Paper sold only to high-volume customers, and Beacon Paper sold only to distributors. Customers in both segments had high service expectations. As a result, at the time of the merger, American Paper's supply chain network had 3 plants and 25 distribution centers and Beacon Paper's supply chain network had 7 plants and 22 distribution centers. An additional plant was added to Beacon Paper's network after the merger.

Prior to the merger, the two companies had significantly different management philosophies and goals that reflected the differences in their customer bases. American Paper's three large plants were operated 7 days a week and had long production runs. Beacon Paper's seven smaller plants were operated 5 days a week and had shorter production runs. After the merger, the plants continued to produce only their original company brands, although all plants were capable of making both product lines, which, for many items, were identical.

The merged companies faced a number of internal and external issues and opportunities, as follows:

- Total production capacity available throughout the combined supply chain was excessive, with equipment overcapacity for 3 or 4 product types out of a total of approximately 20 product types.
- Space at most plants was underutilized.
- Fixed plant costs, variable labor costs, and energy costs varied significantly by location.
- Equipment availability and productivity varied greatly among plants.

Given these conditions, consolidation of the combined supply chain of the two companies was clearly indicated.

Nevertheless, any decisions to close down plants or to make major changes in production strategies needed to account for the following market conditions and customer service requirements across diverse product lines:

- The markets for the companies' products were mature and not expected to grow.
- Market demand for all products was very price sensitive, which resulted in low margins across the industry.
- Future growth opportunities were limited to acquisitions.
- Separate product identities were worth maintaining to retain market share based on brand image.
- Customer order cycle time was mainly 2 to 5 days.

Individual plants might continue to specialize in the manufacture of specific product lines. If so, significant interplant shipping would be required to support the sole sourcing expectations of the companies' customers.

In addition to closing down selected plants, consolidation options included the transfer of capital equipment between plants. In total, the production system had 63 machines. The larger plants were capable of holding 12 machines, whereas the smaller plants were capable of holding 2 to 9 machines. Usually, each machine could produce one of the four major product lines offered by the merged companies. Equipment transfers were easy to carry out, and this option was included in the strategic model.

Objectives of the Study. The complexity of the diverse consolidation options lead management to consider an optimization model to study them. Such a model would be used to optimize supply chain decisions under a variety of what-if scenarios about how the markets would be served. The motivation to make changes was great because each percentage point reduction in avoidable costs would add hundreds of thousands of dollars to the bottom line.

In particular, management sought to develop an optimization model that would simultaneously evaluate the following:

1. The number, size, mission, and locations of plants, considering existing and new sites and brand consolidation alternatives
2. Guidelines for interplant shipping
3. Assignments of markets to plants, with sole sourcing and multiple plant sourcing
4. The deployment of capital equipment among plants and their utilization
5. The impact of a 5-day workweek versus a 7-day workweek in all plants

Approaches to modeling the first three types of decisions were discussed in earlier sections of this chapter and in earlier chapters. Analysis of strategies for capital equipment deployment required a customized model construction involving a global resource—machines—to be deployed in integer quantities across the supply chain. The impact of the length of the workweek was analyzed by translating it into levels of production capacity available in the plants, which were represented in the model by appropriate changes in facility and process capacities.

Modeling Approach and Implementation. An off-the-shelf modeling system capable of generating the necessary mixed integer programming models was chosen as the tool for this study. The system employed snapshot models that captured costs, resources, and transformation processes describing manufacturing, interplant shipping, and plant-to-customer shipping. The objective function was to minimize total production and distribution costs associated with meeting forecasted demand.

For this study, products were aggregated into 18 product groups for strategic planning, which involved planning periods of 1 year, and 27 product groups for tactical planning, which involved planning periods of 1/4-year. Customers were aggregated into 81 demand zones. In addition, equipment was aggregated into 18 types for strategic planning that considered equipment moves among plants. Such moves were not included in the analysis of tactical plans.

The following manufacturing costs were associated with the product groups:

- Fixed production costs for operating a plant to its maximum capacity
- Indirect variable production costs based on total plant throughput
- Direct variable production costs, which differed among alternative transformation recipes on different machines

These data were developed from the general ledgers of the individual plants. In addition, annualized shutdown costs were developed for most plants based on contract obligations, severance pay, and other one-time costs.

Transportation costs and activities were modeled using the following assumptions:

- Interplant shipping

  Links connecting each plant to all other plants were defined.

  Transportation costs were based on full truckload rates.

- Plant to market shipping

  Each plant was connected only to those markets within 900 miles.

  Transportation costs were based on slightly less than full truckload rates to reflect occasional less than truckload shipments to some markets.

  Both sole sourcing and multiple sourcing of markets was analyzed.

The transportation cost data were developed from published data about carrier rates.

The model did not include costs and activities associated with purchasing raw materials, inventory management, and distribution center operations. Raw material costs were omitted because they are constant across the supply chain. Inventory management was not an important concern because large inventories are not a viable option for the companies' products due to their bulk. Finally, the distribution center activities were ignored because most products are shipped directly from the plants to the markets.

Results. Once the data were developed for the strategic model, the next step was to run a validation model with production plans and product flows set equal to their historical values in the previous year. After that, the model was optimized using the same data but allowing any plant to make any product to serve any market. Market demand in this optimization run was the same as that in the validation run. The model computed a total cost savings of $4 million as the result of closing 5 of the 11 plants. This figure represented a base against which changes in the supply chain could be measured.

The potential cost savings of $4 million computed by the model, and the associated strategy, were very important and useful information for management. Nevertheless, the potential savings due to consolidation was probably much larger. The costs included in the model were avoidable production and transportation costs that represented only a small fraction of the true total cost of running the merged companies. Additional indirect savings due to plant closings would have been realized by implementing the consolidation strategy found by the model.

Additional runs were made to measure the impact of closing some, but not all, of the five plants. After these initial runs, management decided to close only two plants for a projected annual savings of $1.4 million. The following reasons were given for leaving open the three plants that the model indicated should be shut down:

- One plant had only recently been constructed, but before the modeling study; closing this plant would have severely tarnished the company's image.
- One plant was located in the city where the merged companies have their home office; closing it would have been bad for morale.
- One plant would contribute only an insignificant savings if closed down.

Analysis continued with additional what-if scenarios run to evaluate the issues discussed in the subsection on objectives of the study. Sole sourcing was found to be $1 million more expensive than multiple sourcing, a figure that management felt was acceptable to provide superior customer service. Optimization runs to study capital equipment relocation indicated a potential savings of $1 million, but the strategy was never implemented.

The supply chain optimization model was exercised several times over a 2-year period as the consolidation unfolded. Over 120 scenarios were evaluated during that time. Gradually, all but one plant were converted to produce brands of both companies. Ultimately, the merged companies closed down 5 of the 11 plants that were running at the start of the modeling study.

Some of the lessons learned from this study include the following:

1. Validation is very important to gain management's trust. The immediate client for the study was the chief financial officer of the merged companies. He and his staff spent several days using independently constructed spreadsheets to verify the data used in the validation model and results of the initial optimization run.
2. It would have been desirable to have expanded the costs captured by the model to include a variety of indirect supply chain costs that would be affected by consolidation; for example, administrative costs at each plant, or economies of scale associated with long production runs.
3. Significant supply chain savings can sometimes be realized by myopic analysis of functional operations as well as by integrated analysis with a model. The merged companies were able to "cherry pick" substantial cost savings by changing their outbound distribution strategy from one focused on transfers through distribution centers to one comprising mainly direct deliveries from plants to customers.

Epilogue. This study was performed in the early 1990s. The merged companies continued their consolidation over several years to achieve more efficient operations and to deal with declining demand for their products. Around 1995, the merged companies were acquired by a third company, and consolidation entered a new stage.

7.6 Tactical Planning

Whereas the primary concern of manufacturing strategy is product competitiveness and the primary concern of logistics strategy is customer service, the primary concern of tactical supply chain planning is more direct: **maximization of net revenue.** In other words, assuming that product and service factors differentiating the company from its competitors at the strategic level are well established, at least for this year, the company seeks to execute its business over the medium term by maximizing profits. Some would argue that this principle is abused by firms overly focused on shorter-term profits. The implication for tactical planning models is that, while maximizing net revenues, they should incorporate constraints reflecting longer-term considerations such as sustaining market share by offering a diverse product line, sustaining customer service, or sustaining product quality by maintaining strong alliances with key suppliers.

Of course, if projected demand is treated as fixed and given, net revenue maximization is achieved by minimizing the total cost of meeting it. This approach to tactical planning is undesirable because most companies have flexibility over the medium term about how much of each product to sell. Because supply chain models provide meaningful product costs and margins, the company can benefit from insights they provide about adjusting sales plans to achieve greater profit. The issue to be addressed is describing how product mix options should be modeled. In the simplest case, they may be described by lower and/or upper bounds on sales of each product (product family), reflecting quantities that should or can be sold. The selling price per unit in such ranges may be constant or decreasing to reflect price elasticities.

Companies making products that may be customized, such as many industrial products and an increasing number of consumer products, face important net revenue maximizing decisions. They need to understand the impact of customizations on their product unit costs to ensure healthy profits. For companies with complex cost relationships involving resources shared across product lines, profit margins may be impossible to determine without the intervention of an optimization model to help select and allocate these resources. In some cases, the company might decide to decline business if it is unprofitable. When this happens, model results can be used to negotiate better prices with long-standing customers who seek unfavorable arrangements.

Tactical planning models can be derived from strategic planning models by fixing resource acquisition and divestment options according to the optimal or preferred configurations determined by the models and senior management. An important difference is that tactical models should be multiperiod to deal with seasonal and other time-dependent factors, instead of the snapshot models frequently employed in strategic planning studies. Dynamic effects to be captured by a tactical model include the following:

- Planning inventories to accommodate seasonal demand patterns or to achieve smooth adjustments to unexpected ebbs and flows in demand
- Adjusting operating shifts per week and other labor resources as the result of changing market conditions
- Scheduling yearly plant maintenance to minimize avoidable costs across the supply chain
- Exercising vendor contracts on a monthly basis to reduce inventory holding costs while avoiding contractual penalty costs for taking insufficient volumes

To extend a snapshot model to a multiple-period model, the practitioner must first reduce the time frame of the snapshot, which is usually 1 year, adjust the data accordingly, and then replicate it several times. The final step is to link the single period models by interperiod inventory flows, smoothing constraints, and other constraints and variables that cut across periods in describing dynamic effects. Such constructions can produce a very large tactical model. To control its dimensions, the practitioner must select product and market aggregations that balance the desire for accuracy against the need to compute plans in a timely manner. Similarly, because the number of periods represented in the model is a multiplicative factor in determining its dimensions, the practitioner must again select this number to balance the desire to evaluate longer-term effects of a tactical plan against the need to compute plans in a timely manner.

Organizationally, the use of tactical models is quite different from that of strategic models. Tactical models are meant to provide plans for managing the company's supply chain on a repetitive and routine basis. Strategic planning studies using models are easier to undertake because they are performed by an ad hoc team whose activities do not interfere with execution of the company's business. Thus far, few companies have implemented tactical planning processes driven by analysis with an optimization model, or any other tool for that matter. Given the top-down and bottom-up pressures to use data to improve supply chain management, it seems to be only a matter of time before the development and use of modeling system for tactical planning will proliferate.

7.7 Two Tactical Planning Applications

In this section, we report on two applications where mixed integer programming models were successfully implemented and applied to tactical planning. The first involves a snapshot, monthly planning model developed for an industrial gases company. The second involves a 12-month planning model developed for a beer manufacturer. Again, we use fictitious company names in reporting on these applications. A survey of journals and magazines finds very few examples of tactical planning applications, probably because most companies have not yet developed organizational processes for supporting such applications on a repetitive, routine basis. An exception is the scheduling and planning system developed for Harris' semiconductor business that we report on in Section 10.4.

Monthly Planning at an Industrial Gases Company

The Liquid Air Products (LAP) Company uses cyrogenic distillation methods to separate air into gaseous and liquid fractions. The company sells liquid oxygen to steel companies, liquid nitrogen to food processors, and other liquid fractions in smaller quantities to manufacturing firms in other industries. It operates approximately 50 plants located in the continental United States with tactical, monthly planning carried out on a regional basis. In particular, plants and customers are assigned to a region, and forecasted customer demand for the coming month is allocated to the region's plants, which number 3 to 10, depending on the region. Given sufficient demand, a plant operates 24 hours a day, 7 days a week.

The industrial gases business is a mature industry that has seen no significant technological breakthrough in almost a hundred years. Companies can compete only on price and customer service because the products are pure commodities. Operating costs are distribution costs, which are 35% of total cost, and production costs, which are 65% of total cost and consist largely of electricity costs paid to utilities.

Modeling Approach. Recognizing that a reduction of a few percentages in operating costs would significantly increase their narrow profit margins, LAP's management commissioned the development of a prototype modeling system to optimize regional planning on a monthly basis. The challenge was to integrate production and distribution planning for the region. The most difficult task was to develop a submodel of each plant's production capabilities and costs. Two complicated and overlapping elements needed to be captured by these submodels: electric power charges and plant configuration planning.

Each plant had a contract with its electric utility involving both energy and power charges, which were of the same magnitude, although energy charges were somewhat higher. The power cost was typically based on the maximal draw during the month. Thus, a spike in the power draw at a plant could invoke a significantly higher electricity bill at the end of the month. The energy charges were based on kilowatthours and were straightforward to model.

Prior to the prototype modeling system project, chemical and process engineers had developed a program to determine, for each plant, the plant configuration that would yield products at target rates while minimizing the power draw. Typical results of the program are depicted in Figure 7.7, where products P1 and P2 are jointly produced at rates measured in thousands of cubic feet per hour (mcf/hr). (The actual number of joint products was around five). The higher the rates within the region of feasible rates, the greater the power draw.

We refer to a point in the region of feasible rates as a **slate.** For a given slate, the program, which we call the slate optimization program, determined an optimal plant configuration and minimal power draw. It employed nonlinear programming methods to optimize configuration and electric power decisions over a system of chemical engineering equations describing the transformation of air by electricity into liquid and gaseous products.

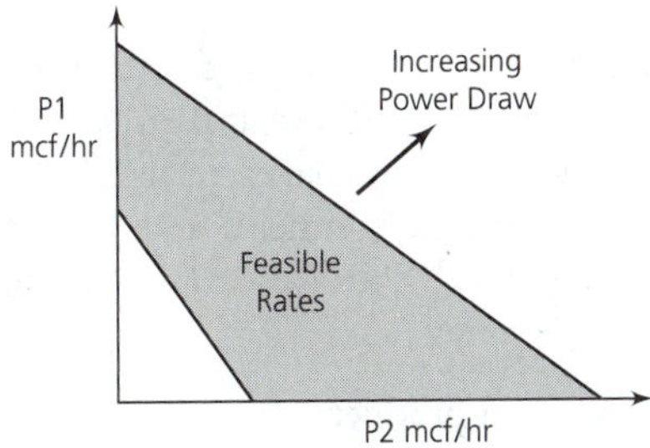

Figure 7.7
Feasible production slates

The optimization model was constructed by discretizing the region of feasible slates for each plant; that is, by using the slate optimization program to systematically generate a finite number of slates covering the region of feasible slates. The slates became, in effect, recipes at each plant that described the rates at which air could be transformed into products at a cost determined by the power draw. Due to setup times associated with each slate, a conditional minimum constraint was imposed on the use of each slate; that is, if a slate was used, it had to run for at least R hours. These data, along with demand data, transportation costs, and electric energy and power costs at each plant were used to construct the tactical planning model.

For some regions and some months, regional capacity exceeded regional demand, forcing LAP to shut down one or more plants for part of the month. This was handled by introducing a null slate at each plant corresponding to zero production of all products. The cost of the null slate was zero.

A 1-month snapshot model was constructed from these data. Because inventory of finished products was negligible, a multiple period was not needed. Given a planning horizon of T hours (e.g., $T = 720$), the decision variables were as follows:

t_{ij} = length of operating time that plant i uses slate j (hours)
W_i = maximal power draw at plant i (kilowatts)
x_{ij} = 1 if slate i used at plant j; 0 otherwise
y_{ikm} = quantity of product k shipped from plant i to customer m (mcf)

A description of the tactical planning model for each region is given below.

Results. The model and supporting system were implemented, validated, and initially applied to a region with three plants. It addressed distribution to around 1000 customers in that region. Aggregation of smaller customers into customer zones was possible and implemented for a later version of the model. The model identified supply chain plans with cost savings in excess of 3% of total cost, which convinced LAP to pursue widespread implementation of the approach.

Industrial Gases Tactical Planning Model

Minimize: The sum of energy and power charges over all plants in the region plus the sum of transportation costs of all product flows from plants to customers.
Subject to the following for each plant:

1. For each product, the total quantity shipped to customers is less than or equal to the quantity of the product produced at the plant.
2. The sum of times consumed by the slates equals T.
3. For each slate, its operating time is either 0 or at least R hours.
4. The power draw for the month equals the maximum of the power draws of the slates with positive usage times.

Subject to the following for each product:

5. For each market, the sum of product flows equals forecasted demand.

Extensions. In extending application of the basic tactical model, a complication arose because energy and power rates varied by time of day. In the simplest case, the energy and power charges fell into three categories; off-peak, midpeak, and peak. This led to a model extension in which slates were selected for each category at each plant. Slates with the highest yields and power draws were scheduled for the off-peak period each day, when power and energy rates were cheapest.

The success of the tactical model inspired follow-on projects. A scheduling model was implemented that addressed in more detail than the tactical model the slate selection during different times of the day, plant shutdowns, small inventories present at the start and end of the planning horizon, and a number of other factors. A strategic model was implemented that optimized over the entire supply chain to make decisions about plant replacements, permanent plant shutdowns, acquisitions, and pricing policies. Thus, modeling system innovation at LAP followed the unusual pattern of starting with the tactical level and then moving both up and down to models and modeling systems for strategic and operational problems.

Monthly Planning at a Beer Company

A large beer manufacturer, Hopkins Amalgamated Breweries (HAB), operating in a country outside the United States, developed a 12-month tactical planning model to optimize production and distribution planning. As shown in Figure 7.8, HAB's supply chain comprises 5 plants and 40 DCs. The DCs are organized in three levels: plant DCs, regional DCs, and local DCs. In addition, HAB has arrangements with third-party warehouses to handle surge inventory for peak demand during the summer season. Each surge warehouse is designated with an S in Figure 7.8. HAB sells approximately 100 products nationwide.

Our purpose in discussing this application is to confirm the feasibility, at least for this application, of a large-scale, multiperiod optimization model to analyze tactical supply chain planning problems. Specific results obtained by the model are

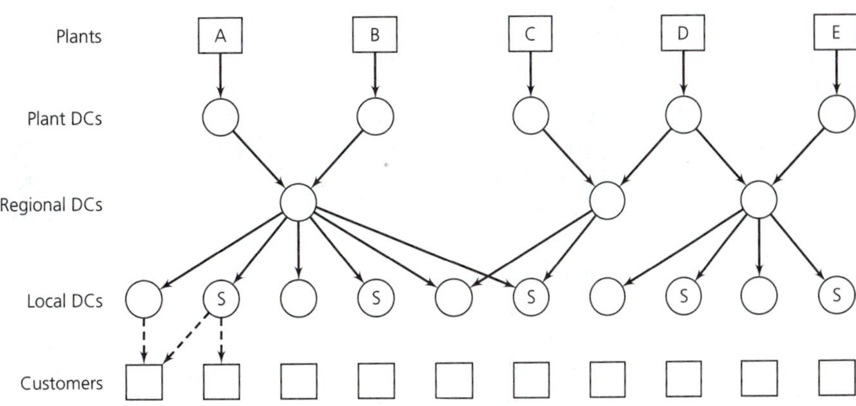

Figure 7.8
Supply chain network for a brewery company

proprietary and unavailable, but we can discuss characteristics of early versions of the model.

HAB's tactical planning model is large scale, with 12 monthly submodels linked by inventories of the company's 100 products. Specifically, the ending inventory of each product in a given month at each facility becomes the starting inventory for the product in the following month at the facility. The submodels for each month capture the manufacturing plans at the 5 plants and the distribution plans linking the 5 plants to 40 DCs and warehouses. Forecasted market demand is backed up to the 40 DCs. In other words, assuming that the customers to be served by each DC are known and given, we associate the sum total of their demand for each product with that DC. The result is a linear programming model with approximately 50,000 rows and 125,000 columns. It can be generated and optimized in about 30 minutes on a high-end PC. For over 1 year, HAB has successfully employed the model each month on a rolling horizon basis.

7.8 Final Thoughts

As we reported in this chapter, applications of optimization models to strategic planning studies of supply chains are proliferating. Still, senior managers who commission such studies and consultants performing them are only part way up the learning curve relative to the breadth and depth of the questions that can and should be examined by these models. We discussed qualitative theories regarding logistics strategy, manufacturing strategy, and the resource-based view of the firm to provide frameworks for stimulating more ambitious model creation and use. Such applications are discussed in detail in the following two chapters.

Many companies treat strategic planning studies as isolated activities for analyzing specific issues of current importance. This attitude is short sighted and reflects the sentiment exhibited by too many senior managers that data-driven studies are bitter medicine that should be taken sparingly. The companies would profit greatly by permanent and repetitive analysis of strategic supply chain plans centered about what-if runs made with optimization models created from timely data. Permanent and repetitive modeling analysis of tactical supply chain planning problems has thus far been even rarer, but its potential for improving a company's competitiveness is no less important. In Chapter 12, we discuss organizational barriers that inhibit adaptation to data-driven, global supply chain planning and provide suggestions for business process redesign to support the use of models on a systematic basis.

Although these barriers are largely organizational rather than technical, we can identify an area where new tools are needed to support ongoing strategic and tactical planning using models. As shown in Figure 7.9, new middleware is needed to link ERP databases to strategic and tactical supply chain decision databases. The middleware would promote flexibility and speed in creating the decision databases; for example, in defining product families and market zones or in computing representa-

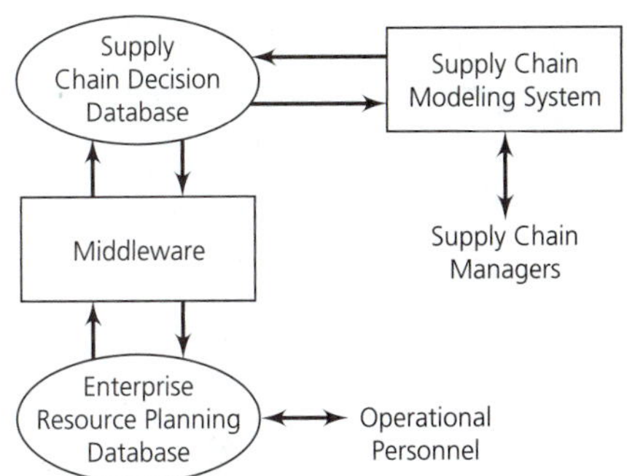

Figure 7.9
Middleware connecting ERP database to supply chain decision database

tions of inventory costs and safety stock requirements. The middleware would also allow tactical decisions suggested by a model and approved by middle managers to be broken down into details appropriate for execution by supply chain personnel at the plants and distribution centers. Over time, the central role played by the middleware and the modeling system would provide managers with a clearer perspective of the difference between effective supply chain decision making and the daily communication of transactional data.

Business-to-business (B2B) developments on the Internet have attracted considerable attention with the promise of enhanced communications and streamlined supply chains. Thus far, the focus has been almost exclusively on improving operations; namely, reducing short-term purchasing, inventory, and transportation costs. Supply chain decision making at the strategic and tactical levels, and models to support it, have been almost totally ignored. Given the torrid pace of B2B adoptions, it seems likely that, very soon, companies heavily involved in B2B commerce will encounter longer-term planning problems and begin seeking tools to help analyze them.

Exercises

In addition to the following exercises, modeling exercises involving data files and discussion exercises involving white papers may be found on the Web site (www.scm-models.com).

1. The DC location model employed in Section 7.3 incorporated an approximation of safety stock costs for each product family based on the number of the locations at which the product family is held. The cost is based on the square root law implied by safety stock formulas. Namely, if S is the safety stock cost of holding the product family in one location, the cost of holding it in K locations equals $K^{1/2}\ S$. Show how to use 0-1 variables to describe these costs.
2. The following is a simplified version of the tactical planning problem faced by Liquid Air Products (LAP) discussed in Section 7.7. Over the coming month, or a planning period of 720 hours, the production manager must select a combination of the five slates given in the table to produce at least enough liquid

nitrogen, oxygen, and argon to meet the given demands, which are measured in 1000s of liters. The production rates are given in 1000s of liters per hour.

	Slates					
	1	2	3	4	5	
Kilowatt draw	1000	1200	1250	1500	2000	Demand
Liquid nitrogen	4.05	4.20	4.39	4.81	4.79	3000
Liquid oxygen	1.01	1.29	1.72	1.19	1.63	795
Liquid argon	0.051	0.063	0.041	0.045	0.058	40

The objective is to minimize the sum of energy and power charges incurred. Energy is charged at a rate of \$0.05 per kilowatthour. Power is charged at a rate of \$10 per kilowatt for the maximal kilowatt drawn over the 720 hours. Thus, if slates 1 and 3 are used during the planning period, the power charge equals \$12,500 = \$10/kW * 1250 kW.

a. Using a spreadsheet optimizer, construct and solve a mixed integer programming model of this planning problem.

b. Indicate how you would modify the model to impose a conditional minimum on the use of any slate and a maximum on the quantity of surplus production of each product.

3. The Grasshopper Company manufactures electronic equipment. Its engineers have designed a new wireless laptop for accessing the Internet with a projected 3-year life. The product manager wishes to develop a plan for that time period, taking into account that there will be learning associated with production, limited markets in the first 2 years, and growing competition that will drive down prices over the 3 years.

   Specifically, the engineers have estimated the following unit manufacturing costs: \$500 for the first 100 units, \$400 for the next 600 units, and \$200 for any additional units. The marketing department has estimated that Grasshopper will be able to sell up to 675 units in year 1, up to 800 units in year 2, and an unlimited number in year 3. They further estimate that the market-selling price will be \$1000 in year one, \$500 in year 2, and \$400 in year 3. All revenues and costs will be discounted at 10% per year.

   The engineers have further estimated that they can acquire equipment to produce 500 units per year for a one-time fixed cost of \$40,000. This capacity may be expanded by an additional 500 units in any year, including year 1, at an additional one-time fixed cost of \$40,000. Management has imposed a constraint that no inventories will be carried over from 1 year to the next.

   Using a spreadsheet optimizer, construct and solve a mixed integer programming model to assist the product manager in developing her plans. In particular, for each of the 3 years, how much capacity is needed and what quantity of product should be manufactured and sold to maximize discounted net revenues? *Hint:* You must modify the construction in Section 4.1 used to model cost economies of scale due to volume during a period to the situation of economy of scale due to learning. For this application, an economy of scale can be realized if the sum of production from this year and earlier years is sufficiently great.

4. A health maintenance organization (HMO) operating in the state of Illinois wishes to contract with hospitals around the state to provide medical services for its members. From among the collection of possible hospitals with which to ally itself, the HMO must select specific hospitals and specific services within these hospitals in constructing a plan to provide adequate health care for its members who are distributed in cities and towns across the state. Discuss ways in which this planning problem resembles and does not resemble the DC location problems discussed in Sections 4.2, 7.2, and 7.3. Your discussion should include an examination of the objective(s) underlying the HMO's plan and modeling approaches for capturing facility mission, facility capacity, and customer service.

Notes

1. The formal origin of the resource-based view of the firm is the seminal paper by Wernerfelt [1984], although earlier publications anticipated it. Our review is based mainly on Mahoney and Pandian [1992] and Peteraf [1993], who provide extensive bibliographies. These papers and 20 others are collected in the compendium edited by Foss [1997]. The connections between the resource-based view of the firm and closely related disciplines, such as organization economics or the theory of industrial organizations, are well developed by Conner [1991] and Mahoney and Panadian [1992].
2. The taxonomy is due largely to Mahoney and Pandian, [1992, 364].
3. See Dierickx and Cool [1989] and Oliver [1997] for differing viewpoints regarding sustainability.
4. The term *core competency* was coined in the paper by Prahalad and Hamel [1990].
5. See Stalk, Evans, and Schulman [1992].
6. The framework and our discussion of it draws on O'Laughlin and Copacino [1994]. They also recognized the need for fact-based decision making using models.
7. See O'Laughlin and Copacino [1994, 59–60].
8. See O'Laughlin and Copacino [1994, 59].
9. See Shapiro [1992].
10. We also draw on concepts from Hax and Majluf [1991].
11. Methods for achieving competitive advantage based on cost and/or differentiation are discussed extensively by Porter [1980, 1985].
12. Christopher [1999] emphasizes the importance of supply chain agility in creating and sustaining competitiveness. Recent developments enhancing agility by postponement of product differentiation are discussed in Section 8.8.
13. Methods for achieving competitive advantage based on cycle time and other factors depending on time are discussed extensively by Stalk and Hout [1990].
14. Williamson [1989] discusses the microeconomic impact of transaction costs. Conner [1991] compares Williamson's approach to transaction economics to the resource-based view of the firm.
15. Surprisingly little applied research has been done, or at least reported, on the use of statistical methods to identify direct and indirect cost relationships underlying raw manufacturing data. Atkinson et al. [1997, Chapter 4] provide an introduction to some of the issues.

16. Learning effects are a good example of a strategic planning paradigm (Henderson [1984]) that can be quantified and analyzed by a model.
17. Hiller and Shapiro [1986] provide details of a mixed integer programming model to address capacity expansion in the face of learning effects.
18. Discussions of the critical path model can be found in Schrage [1997, Section 7.2] and Winston [1994, Section 8.4]
19. A shorter description of this application was given in Shapiro, Singhal, and Wagner [1993].

References

*Andersen Consulting. 161 N. Clark St., 11th Floor, Chicago, IL, 60601.

Atkinson, A.A., R. D. Banker, R. S. Kaplan, and S. M. Young [1997], *Management Accounting,* 2d ed. Englewood Cliffs, N.J.: Prentice-Hall.

Christopher, M. [1999], "Responding to the Global Supply Chain Challenge," *Supply Chain Management Review,* Global Supplement, 7–9, Winter.

Conner, K. R., [1991], "A Historical Comparison of Resource-Based Theory and Five Schools of Thought within Industrial Organization Economics: Do We Have a New Theory of the Firm?" *Journal of Management,* 17, 121–154.

Dierickx, I., and K. Cool [1989], "Asset Stock Accumulation and Sustainability of Competitive Advantage," *Management Science,* 35, 1504–1511.

Fine, C., and A. C. Hax [1985], "Manufacturing Strategy: A Methodology and an Illustration," *Interfaces,* 15, 28–46.

N. J. Foss ed. [1997], *Resources, Firms and Strategies: A Reader in the Resource-Based Perspective.* New York: Oxford University Press.

A.C. Hax, and N. S. Majluf [1991], *The Strategy Concept and Process: A Pragmatic Approach.* Englewood Cliffs, N.J.: Prentice-Hall.

Henderson, B. D. [1984], *The Logic of Business Strategy.* Cambridge, Mass.: Ballinger Division, Harper & Row.

Hiller, R. S., and J. F. Shapiro [1986], "Optimal Capacity Expansion Planning When There are Learning Effects," *Management Science,* 32, 1153–1163.

Mahoney, J. T., and J. R. Pandian [1992], "The Resource-based View within the Conversation of Strategic Management," *Strategic Management Journal,* 13, 363–380.

*O'Laughlin, K. A., and W. C. Copacino [1994], "Logistics Strategy," Chapter 4 in Robeson, Copacino and Howe [1994].

Oliver, C. [1997], "Sustainable Competitive Advantage: Combining Institutional and Resource-based Views," *Strategic Management Journal,* 18, 697–713.

Peteraf, M. A. [1993], "The Cornerstones of Competitive Advantage: A Resource-Based View," *Strategic Management Journal,* 14, 179–191.

Porter, M. E. [1980], *Competitive Strategy: Techniques for Analyzing Industries and Competitors.* New York: The Free Press, MacMillan.

Porter, M. E. [1985], *Competitive Advantage: Creating and Sustaining Superior Performance.* New York: The Free Press, MacMillan.

Prahalad, C. K., and G. Hamel [1990], "The Core Competence of the Corporation," *Harvard Business Review,* May-June, 79–91.

Robeson, J. F., W. C. Copacino, and R. E. Howe, eds. [1994], *The Logistics Handbook.* New York: The Free Press.

L. Schrage [1997], *Optimization Modeling with LINDO,* 5th ed. Pacific Grove, Calif.: Brooks/Cole.

J. F. Shapiro [1992], "Integrated Logistics Management, Total Cost Analysis and Optimization Modeling,"*Asia Pacific Journal of Logistics,* 5, 33–36.

J. F. Shapiro, V. M. Singhal, and S. M. Wagner [1993], "Optimizing the Value Chain," *Interfaces,* 23, 102–117.

Stalk, G., Jr., and T. M. Hout [1990], *Competing Against Time.* New York: The Free Press.

Stalk, G., Jr., P. Evans, and L. E. Schulman [1992], "Competing on Capabilities: The New Rules of Corporate Strategy," *Harvard Business Review,* March-April, 57.

B. Wernerfelt [1984], "A Resource Based View of the Firm," *Strategic Management Journal,* 5, 171–180.

O. E. Williamson [1989], "Transaction Cost Economics," pp. 136–182 in *Handbook of Industrial Economics,* edited by R. Schmalensee and R. D. Willig. Amsterdam: North-Holland.

W. L. Winston [1994], *Operations Research: Applications and Algorithms.* 3d ed. Belmont, Calif.: Duxbury Press.

*See the credits section at the end of this book for more information.

8 Strategic and Tactical Supply Chain Planning: Advanced Modeling Applications

In the previous chapter, we discussed recent applications of optimization models to strategic and tactical supply chain planning. Despite an increasing number of such applications, their scope has been modest. For example, most models minimize the cost of meeting projected demand rather than seeking to maximize net revenues, which is more appropriate for strategic and tactical planning. The limited focus on cost containment fails to provide managers with insights about competing for profits and market share based on price, delivery time, quality, and other factors that differentiate their products.

Similarly, planning uncertainties, such as those associated with demand, economic conditions, or initiatives by competitors, are typically examined by optimizing a deterministic model many times using different scenarios of the supply chain decision database. Each run of the deterministic model treats its scenario's description of the future as certain to occur. Stochastic programming models, which simultaneously consider multiple scenarios of the future to identify strategies that optimally hedge against major uncertainties and control risk, have yet to be widely employed. Such hedging strategies may be impossible to identify by scenario analysis with deterministic models.

There may be valid, historical reasons for this modeling timidity. Comprehensive databases and data management systems that serve as building blocks in constructing supply chain decision databases have only recently become widely available. Moreover, organizational reluctance to implementing data-driven decision processes inhibits the creation of imaginative modeling approaches. This reluctance is being overcome, but more slowly than proponents of models would prefer. Still, with recent developments in information technology, managers and modeling practitioners can and should be more audacious in choosing new approaches for analyzing strategic and tactical plans. For this reason, we examine applications in this chapter that are at the frontiers of practical modeling.

We begin with an overview in Section 8.1 of issues arising when the firm attempts to integrate supply chain and demand management. In Section 8.2, we discuss quantitative methods for modeling product prices and revenue curves that can be used to construct supply chain models seeking to maximize net revenues. A more ambitious marketing model that captures price, advertising, promotion, and sales efforts for consumer products is reviewed in Section 8.3, where we also outline its integration with a supply chain optimization model. We illustrate this integration by an extended numerical example. Models that forecast new product growth and their use in supply chain models are examined in Section 8.4.

The chapter continues in Section 8.5 with a discussion of the connections between supply chain optimization models and competitive analysis of markets. We present a tatonnement method for computing competitive equilibrics in commodity markets. An application of the computational scheme to the forest product industry is given in Section 8.6.

Explicit modeling of decision making under uncertainty is presented in Section 8.7. We illustrate the construction and application of decision trees and then extend them to stochastic programming models that also capture resource allocation and acquisition decisions. We illustrate the application of stochastic programming in determining inventories that hedge against uncertain demand during peak seasons. In Section 8.8, we expand on the use of stochastic programming and other methods for managing uncertain demand by focusing on strategies for postponing product customization. We also examine methods for managing production and sales of products with short life cycles.

The chapter continues with a brief introduction in Section 8.9 to the discipline of scenario planning. Scenario planning is important in its own right in assisting senior management to define scenarios of the long-term future that are consistent, plausible, and comprehensive. It also is useful for the construction of strategic supply chain models with the same properties. The chapter concludes in Section 8.10 with our final thoughts about the use of more audacious models for strategic supply chain planning.

Several times in this chapter we will refer to and discuss applications of mathematical programming decomposition methods to advanced supply chain models. Despite the term *decomposition,* the methods allow modeling practitioners to combine or synthesize disparate models that would otherwise be very difficult or impossible to integrate; for example, combining a supply chain and a marketing model for consumer products. The term was coined when the methods were originally devised over 30 years ago to overcome limitations due to computer memories that were too small to allow industrial strength models to be solved as large monolithic arrays. We employed the same methods in Chapter 5 to decompose large-scale models for operational planning into manageable easier-to-solve submodels.

8.1 Integrating Supply Chain and Demand Management

Integration of supply chain and demand management decisions should be a prime concern of any profit maximizing firm. But, in many companies, barriers inhibiting this integration have not yet been fully recognized. Changes in organizational behavior to overcome them lie in the future. By contrast, the barriers have been recognized for quite a while in the academic literature. Over the past 20 years, several authors have highlighted conflicts between the goals of supply chain managers and marketing managers.[1]

Table 8.1 contains a list of often-heard and complementary complaints from supply chain and marketing managers. Models can play an important role in resolving these conflicts by allowing managers on both sides of an argument to objectively evaluate and reconcile their differences. Without models or rational analysis, the conflicts are too easily decided by compromises or dictates that leave many managers feeling that they are being asked to support ineffective strategies.

The first step in using data and models to reconcile conflicts is to agree about quantitative methods for constructing **descriptive models** that forecast or otherwise project future demand for finished products, ideally as functions of marketing and sales decisions. Descriptive models of supply chain and marketing and sales costs are also needed, along with other descriptive data such as manufacturing capacities, transformation activities, and so on. Once this has been accomplished, the descriptive models should be embedded in **optimization models** that analyze how to link supply chain decisions with marketing and sales decisions. An effective integrated strategy will emerge only after many scenarios have been optimized and their results examined and interpreted. The exercise may also require refinements to descriptive models as insights into the likely form and structure of an optimal strategy reveal themselves.

Seemingly irreconcilable disputes between supply chain and marketing managers, even when models are used, might be resolved by adapting a standard method of data analysis, **in-sample versus out-of-sample validation.** Using a historical period, for example, data from the previous 2 years, descriptive and optimization models would be developed based on in-sample data drawn only from the first year. Then, the optimization model would be optimized for the second year based on forecasts for that year derived from the first year's data. The strategy suggested by

Table 8.1 Contrasting complaints of supply chain and marketing managers

Supply Chain Complaints	Marketing Complaints
Inaccurate long-term sales forecasts	Insufficient manufacturing capacity
Mercurial short-term forecasts	Excessive manufacturing and distribution lead time
Excessive inventory requirements for finished products	Insufficient inventory of finished products
Too broad a range of product offerings necessitating short, uneconomical production runs	Insufficient product variety
Unrealistic requirements for customer service, delivery time performance, quality	Excessive supply chain costs
Products should not be used in ways for which they were not designed	Excessive field service costs
Needless and/or costly product customizations and engineering changes	Resistance to and inefficient implementation of product customization and design changes that enhance competitiveness

the optimization model would then be compared with what actually occurred, which is the out-of-sample data. Serious discrepancies between the optimized and actual strategies might be due to errors in the demand forecasting model, which produced forecasts for the second year that were significantly different from what actually occurred. Alternatively, the discrepancies might be due to the structure of the optimization model, which led to an unrealistic strategy. Of course, it is likely that discrepancies between model results and reality were due to deficiencies in both types of models. Rational discussion of the cause and meaning of such discrepancies, and their elimination, would go a long way to resolving entrenched managerial positions.

Such an approach would clearly help marketing and supply chain managers reconcile the first conflict in Table 8.1 between opportunity losses due to insufficient capacity for meeting unexpectedly high demand and real losses due to excess capacity for meeting forecasted demand that is not realized. Similarly, the second conflict could be evaluated by applying a tactical 12-month model on a rolling horizon basis over the out-of-sample year, say once a month, to better understand the capabilities of the company's supply chain in responding to unexpected shifts in demand. Models would help reconcile most of the other conflicts in Table 8.1.

The key construction we seek is an integration of supply chain with **marketing science** models, which forecast the impact of price, promotion, advertising, and sales force efforts on market share and demand. Marketing science is a vast field that we can only sample in our discussions here.[2] Moreover, quantitative analyses of supply chain decisions involve costs, resources, and activities of physical products that are easier to measure and predict.[3] With this in mind, our approach to integrating supply chain and marketing science models will be biased toward constructions that extend supply chain models to marketing and sales decisions and constraints affecting demand and product mix. Such an approach can begin with a validated supply chain model that minimizes the total cost of meeting fixed and given demand. We can expect, or at least hope, that this perspective emphasizes the need for, and benefits of, a marketing science model, even if it proves difficult to validate.

8.2

Price and Location Sensitive Revenue Curves

An apparently simple extension of a model for minimizing the cost of meeting fixed and given demand is to one that maximizes net revenues by varying product mix. Specifically, we consider a model to maximize

$$\text{Net revenues} = \text{gross revenues} - \text{total supply chain cost}$$

where gross revenues are variable depending on how much of each product (product family) we sell. For the sake of discussion, we assume that the model addresses the company's supply chain and product mix strategies for next year, which would be reflected in targets set for the company's sales force.

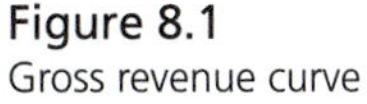

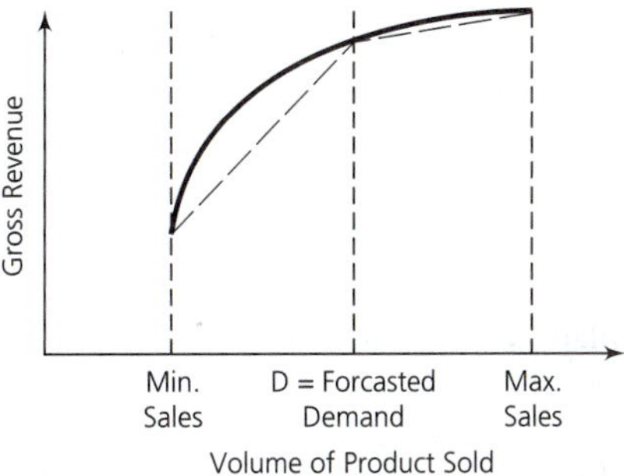

Figure 8.1
Gross revenue curve

As shown in Figure 8.1, we extend the cost minimization model by specifying a gross revenue curve (function) and allowing variations in the sales of each product in each market about its forecasted demand. We discussed a very similar figure and its construction in Section 3.2. We assume that the range on sales is relatively small, say ± 5% of forecasted demand. In constructing this function, the marketing and sales department believes sales of other products will not be affected if the company decides to reduce sales of a given product to the minimal sales level. It also believes it can attain a level of maximal sales without significant additional marketing and sales efforts. Thus, this modeling approach does not involve or address marketing and sales efforts such as large promotions, doubling the size of the sales force, or other initiatives that, depending on the industry, will significantly change the company's market share at a significant cost. Nevertheless, opening up the analysis to include product mix decisions could prove important. Even a variation of ± 5% of forecasted demand might lead to product mix strategies that yield a large increase in net revenues.

To incorporate the gross revenue function in Figure 8.1 in a supply chain model, we would approximate it by a piecewise linear function. A two-piece approximation is shown in the figure, but we could construct tighter approximations that employ more than two linear segments. Such an approximation allows us to use linear programming constructions to describe the function, rather than to require nonlinear programming methods if a mathematical representation of the function in Figure 8.1 were given. Note also that, unlike cost minimization of economies of scale functions, we do not need mixed integer programming constructions for the piecewise linear approximation because an optimization algorithm would naturally select sales at a higher price before selecting sales at a lower price.

Pricing Models. We began our discussion of product mix optimization by proposing the simple pricing model of Figure 8.1. Its construction may turn out to be more complex than we originally thought, for both technical and organizational reasons. Technically, the company must estimate the shape of the function in Figure 8.1. It is implicitly related to the **price elasticity of demand,** which describes how the rate of increase of the revenue function must decrease to achieve greater sales.[4] Roughly, at a level of sales d with revenue $R(d)$ as shown in the figure, the average price is given as $R(d)/d$, but the price must be decreasing to induce greater sales.

The elasticity of demand quantifies this relationship between price and its rate of change and implicitly describes the revenue function. Thus, the practical requirement for developing gross revenue functions is a statistical and/or judgmental method for estimating the price elasticity, or equivalently, the revenue function, for each product in each market over some interval containing the expected demand for the product.[5]

Moreover, when planning horizons are several months or longer, the firm may face both upward and downward pressures on price. Upward pressures include improvements in product features or company reputation and increases in supply chain and raw material costs. Downward pressures include the availability of substitutes, competitors' initiatives, or industrywide learning. Such dynamic effects would require the construction of a multiperiod supply chain model that incorporates a function such as that in Figure 8.1 for each product, market, *and* time period.

A further technical difficulty is that the pricing model constructions just discussed ignore demand relationships between pairs of products, which are called **cross-elasticities.** Specifically, demand for a given product in a company's product line may increase if the price of a second product, which could substitute for the first, is increased. The higher price for the second product would lead more customers to buy the first product at a fixed price. This would be the case, for example, for an automobile manufacturer offering a range of low-, medium-, and high-priced cars.

Practical demand forecasting is not sufficiently advanced to allow estimation of cross-elasticities in many situations where such effects are known, or at least suspected, to exist. Moreover, capturing them in an optimization model would require the application of quadratic programming constructions, which would make the models more difficult to optimize.[6] Despite these difficulties, descriptive and optimization modeling of product lines with important cross-elastic effects could be achieved if the company's management and modeling practitioners were determined enough to do so.[7]

Organizational barriers to net revenue maximization based on revenues functions may begin with lack of data; namely, the company's marketing department may not have data on which to estimate elasticities. The lack of data might be real, but it might also reflect the marketing department's reluctance to consider quantitative descriptions of future revenues. This attitude will depend, of course, on the types of products being sold.

For example, the product manager of an industrial product for which the majority of sales are made to large companies may believe that pure statistical forecasting is misleading. Instead, he may believe that his relationships with buyers at large client companies, plus his insights into trends in the industry, are more insightful than mere statistical projections. Nevertheless, the product manager would benefit from modeling analysis of his product line that incorporated revenue functions and supply chain costs and capacities because they would provide him with new insights into specific products and markets to push. The revenue functions would be based on some combination of historical data and judgment.

For a consumer package goods company, the manager of a product brand may be more focused on marketing initiatives such as advertising and promotion than on price adjustments. In such a case, the integration of supply chain and demand management, which may have begun with modest pricing and revenue decisions over a narrow range, can quickly escalate to consideration of a broader range of marketing decisions. Modeling this broader range of marketing decisions is discussed in the following section.

Location Sensitive Revenue Functions. In many industries, such as retailing or the sale of industrial commodities to customers in medium and small quantities, sales volumes may be sensitive to the proximity of the company's distribution centers to the markets. Delivery lead time for standard and emergency shipments, or the time delay for technical support, all depend on the distance between the customer and the distribution center that services them. Business-to-business sales over the Internet appear to obscure customers' perception of the impact of geographical location on service reliability, but its too early to assess the long-term impact. From an optimization perspective, the gross revenue function for sales of a product (family) in a particular market will depend on the facility sourcing that market.

By way of illustration, we consider a market k that can be sourced for product i from one of two distribution centers. As shown in Figure 8.2, the company has the choice between revenue functions 1 and 2 corresponding to distribution centers 1 and 2, where distribution center 2 is closer to the market. As shown, the price curves are constant, but they clearly could be modeled differently if the differences could be estimated. We model this option by using a 0-1 variable for which a value of 1 turns on the revenue function 1, whereas a value of 0 turns on the revenue function 2. In addition, the variable would constrain flows from the distribution center to the market to lie within exactly one of the two ranges indicated in the figure. In general, we would require a 0-1 variable for each realistic potential combination of distribution center, product, and market throughout the supply chain network.

The question remains: How do we estimate the revenue functions shown in Figure 8.2? One descriptive approach that has proven successful is the **logit model,** which is a function that translates the preferences of a consumer into probabilities that he or she will purchase a product or service.[8] In this context, the model can be used to estimate market share of each product as a function of service characteristics implied by the proximity of the sourcing location to the market. It was applied in a study of customer response to service factors offered by a national distributor of industrial chemical products and to study the redesign of its logistics network.[9] The logit model established that customers treated factors in the following descending

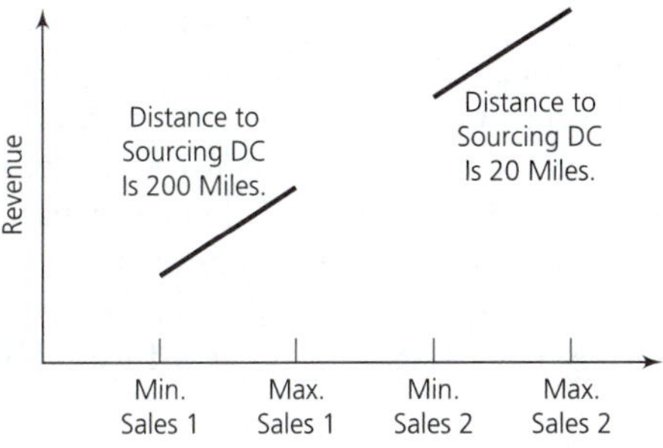

Figure 8.2
Location sensitive revenue functions

order: Price, dependable delivery lead times, short delivery lead-times, and distance to the sourcing facility. Ironically, explicit distance was a less important factor, but it proved more important as an implicit determinant of lead-time characteristics.

For the chemicals distribution company, the logit model was integrated with a mixed integer programming model that sought to relocate distribution centers to maximize net revenues. The net revenue maximizing strategy had 56 facilities compared to 76 facilities in the historical network and increased net revenues by over 6%. Overall product market share, and associated total supply chain volume and cost, were slightly lower in the net revenue maximizing strategy, indicating that the model chose to eliminate unprofitable sales along with some of the distribution centers.

8.3 Integrating Supply Chain and Marketing Models for Consumer Products

In this section, we consider models for integrating supply chain and demand management decisions in companies that **manufacture consumer products** such as personal products, soap products, food products, clothing, and books. The first three types of products are package goods that compete fiercely in retail stores for sales and market share. For these manufacturers, advertising, promotions, pricing, and the activities of its sales force are key factors affecting sales and revenues. Related marketing efforts by the retailing companies that they sell to also affects sales and revenues and complicates the construction of descriptive models. Again, e-commerce developments are disrupting traditional ideas about effective strategies for marketing consumer products, but it is too early to clearly identify new approaches. Moreover, except for a few products such as books and CDs, the volume of e-commerce sales of consumer products over the next few years are projected to be very small compared with the volume of in-store purchases.

Many consumer products companies are marketing driven in the sense that the company's strategy for next year is determined by senior marketing managers who devise plans intended to sustain or increase market share of the company's product lines. Given the demand projections, the manufacturing department is asked to devise plans for manufacturing finished products to meet them in a cost-effective way. Finally, given the manufacturing plans, the logistics department is asked to devise plans for distributing finished products to wholesalers and retailers in the correct quantities at the correct time in a cost-effective way.

In short, marketing, manufacturing, and logistics decisions in many consumer products companies are made in a sequential, uncoordinated manner. Our aim here is to discuss descriptive and optimization modeling approaches for integrating decisions across all three functions, which would serve to improve net revenues. In the process, many of the complaints listed in Table 8.1 would be reduced or eliminated.

Consumer Products Supply Chains

Supply chains for consumer products are complex arrangements among manufacturers, wholesalers, distributors, retail stores, and other organizations. Optimization models provide useful tools for defining and examining these arrangements, both qualitatively and quantitatively, as well as for identifying optimal strategies. The number of facilities in a consumer products supply chain and the products flowing through the network can be very large. For a multi-billion-dollar consumer products company, simply defining the supply chain network that connects the manufacturer to its markets for a major product category is a complicated and instructive exercise.

We report on a study performed for Proctor & Gamble. In the early 1990s, the company's North American supply chain included 60 plants, 15 distribution centers, and 50 major product categories, serving 1000 customers.[10] Since then, the company has undergone a major consolidation exercise, motivated by the following five factors:

- Deregulation of the trucking industry in the 1980s lowered rates.
- The trend toward product compactification allowed more product per truckload.
- Manufacturing quality improvements led to higher reliability and plant throughput.
- Shorter product life cycles (3 to 5 years reduced to 18 to 24 months) required plants to change equipment more frequently, implying a need for fewer plants.
- Excess manufacturing capacity due to acquisitions.

A supply chain study was performed using optimization models linked to a geographical information system, which facilitated the active participation of product-strategy teams, one for each major product category, in the study.

Two types of optimization models were employed in this study. The higher-level model was a simple facility-location mixed integer programming model that determined optimal distribution center locations and assigned each customer zone uniquely to an open distribution center. The lower-level model took optimal and near-optimal designs from the facility-location model to create a network optimization model that determined optimal product-sourcing decisions for each product category. In this product-sourcing model, link costs were the sum of manufacturing, warehousing, and transportation costs, all of which were approximated by constant, unit costs. Both distribution centers and customer zones were treated as locations with demand to be satisfied.

The product-sourcing model was linked to a geographical information system, allowing the product-strategy teams to interact with the model in real time. The graphical displays, rather than tables or spreadsheets, helped product-strategy teams better understand the connections among cost, capacity, and distribution network design. In several instances, the displays elicited important new options to be examined by the models. Upon its completion, the study had identified 12 facilities to shut down with a before tax annual savings of $250 million.

For the purposes of discussion, we have depicted in Figure 8.3 a supply chain from the perspective of a manufacturer who supplies **corporate wholesalers** and **distributors** with its products, who in turn replenish retail stores. We define a corporate wholesaler as a business unit of a company that owns and operates retail stores or has a close working relationship with franchised retail stores. The primary mission of the corporate wholesaler is to serve the company-owned or franchised retail stores so that overall corporate profits are maximized. The wholesaler may also serve third-party retail stores that are not part of a franchised chain. We define a distributor as a company that acquires products from many sources, possibly including manufacturing units of its parent company, and sells them to retailers and other customers. The primary mission of the distributor is to select products, customers, and a distribution system so as to maximize profits.

In Figure 8.3, we have shown the manufacturer making direct-to-store deliveries to retailers that are part of the corporate chain. Corporate wholesalers are actively seeking this type of cooperative arrangement with their vendors, when it makes economic sense, as a means for reducing the total cost of products delivered to the stores. Another method for expediting the distribution of products from the manufacturer to the stores, especially when efficient direct-to-store truckloads from the manufacturer cannot be easily scheduled, is **flow through.** This technology automatically sorts in-coming products that are bar coded by vendors into out-going truckload shipments to the stores.

A large manufacturer will have a variety of channels available for sale of its products. An important issue is how profit margins are allocated among the separate

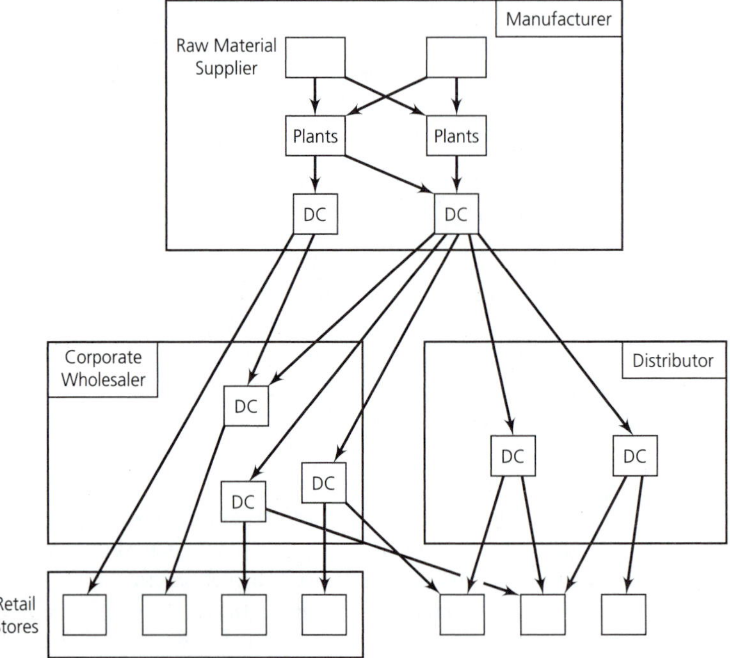

Figure 8.3
Supply chain of a manufacturer of consumer product

companies managing the manufacturing and distribution of the products. The issue becomes more explicit when these companies agree to cooperate more closely to reduce costs; to avoid later conflict, the companies should agree in advance about how the savings from such cooperation will be divided. Optimization models can be used to estimate the benefits of closer cooperation before serious commitments are made.

From the perspective of a corporate wholesaler or a distributor, the network of Figure 8.3 is, of course, quite different. For product sourcing, they may deal with hundreds, if not thousands, of vendors located in several continents from whom they acquire and distribute tens of thousands of SKUs on an annual basis. Cooperative relationships with vendors will have a major impact on the advantage they might hold over their competitors, who might also be seeking similar arrangements. Such developments will be an important driver of change in consumer products industries in the years to come.

Modeling the Effects of Marketing Decisions on Demand for Consumer Products

We consider the construction and application of descriptive models for measuring the impact of marketing initiatives by a manufacturer of consumer products. Decisions made by marketing managers regarding **advertising, promotions, price discounts**, and **sales force activities** strongly affect the company's market share and therefore its sales and gross revenues. In this subsection we examine a specific model that relates such decisions to sales and net marketing revenues.[11] In the following subsection, we discuss how it can be combined with a supply chain optimization model to integrate supply chain and demand management decisions.

Before delving into the details, we acknowledge that the model we will discuss, or a similar marketing strategy model, is an idealization of reality because the marketing decisions listed in the previous paragraph are not made in a coordinated manner in the typical company. Different groups are responsible for different categories of decisions, and each group often makes its decisions without knowledge of those made by other groups. In other words, marketing decision making is not done in an integrated manner. Moreover, as we stated earlier, quantitative analysis and modeling of marketing phenomena, which involves predicting the behavior of people, is difficult and open to skepticism.

Nevertheless, we suggest two important reasons for discussing the marketing model. First, its outputs are precisely the inputs required by an extended supply chain model that maximizes net revenues by integrating supply chain and marketing decisions faced by a consumer products company. These outputs could be developed by managerial judgment without a model and possibly even without much data, which brings us to the second point. The central theme of this book is the use of data, models, and modeling systems to improve managerial decision making. It is too early in the history of these developments to declare that marketing decisions based exclusively on managerial judgment could not be improved by the more formal use of data and models.

Statement of the Marketing Model. In the following paragraphs, we review the form and function of a descriptive model for a single product brand, such as mouthwash, bar soap, or baking mix, manufactured by a consumer products company. The brand manager for this product line is responsible for its profitability, and we assume that she manages a group that makes all marketing decisions in a coordinated manner. Although there may be ambiguity about the nature of the market segments in which her brand competes, and its size, she is very aware of and can easily cite an aggregate numerical market share held by her brand, which largely determines its competitive position. Marketing initiatives are aimed at sustaining and improving this market share, and it is the impact of these initiatives that we seek to model.

If S is the **market size** in units sold yearly by all companies of the product line, s is the **size of brand sales** in units sold yearly, and m is the **market share,** $m = s/S$. Letting g equal the gross contribution to profit per unit of the brand sold,

Net marketing profit $= g * s -$ marketing costs

These definitions of S, s, m, and g are overly simplistic in that such variables actually depend on time, location, and market segment. Furthermore, although the purpose of a marketing strategy is to sustain and increase market share over time, and perhaps to increase overall market size, the brand manager understands that it will decrease in certain periods, locations, and market segments, while increasing in others. To keep our discussion relatively simple, we assume throughout that the market size S is fixed and known.

The quantitative marketing model we seek describes how advertising, promotion, sales force, and pricing strategies affect s and m relative to **reference values,** which characterize their standard or nominal levels at the start of the planning horizon. For each period of the planning horizon, which we assume for convenience are the 12 months of next year, brand sales are expressed as the product of the reference value of brand sales multiplied by a number of marketing effect indexes that serve to increase or decrease brand sales. For example, if standard sales of the brand in the first month is 100,000 cases, and we forecast a 10% improvement due to each of two marketing effects, we forecast that brand sales in the first month will equal 100,000 * 1.1 * 1.1 = 121,000 cases.

The impact of marketing decisions and external factors on sales may be modeled by direct indexes (multiplicative factors) and response curves. A direct index is simply a number that describes the multiplicative effect on sales in a given period. For example, seasonality may be described as a set of numbers, one for each month, that forecast how sales will lie above or below its reference value. Direct indexes are useful for describing one-time events such as changes in the packaging or formulation of the brand. The actual values of these numbers will rely on a combination of statistical analysis and managerial judgment based on similar changes in the past. Response curves describe how marketing decisions and external facts affect sales over time.

The **advertising submodel** forecasts the effects of advertising on sales as a function of advertising control variables such as the number and timing of TV ads. This submodel employs a sales rate index due to advertising that is a function of the advertising rate, which we assume for simplicity expositional refers only to TV ads. This term is expressed as

Advertising rate = copy effectiveness * media efficiency * spending rate

Thus, the better the copy in the TV ad, the more efficient the TV programs are in reaching customers, and the greater the spending rate, the higher the advertising rate. The advertising rate is determined each month and its dynamic effect from month by month is captured by **exponential smoothing,** which describes how the advertising effect may grow or decay from month to month; namely,

Advertising effect in month $t = \alpha$ * advertising effect in month $t - 1 + (1 - \alpha)$ * response to advertising rate in month t

where α, which lies between 0 and 1, determines how quickly last month's advertising effect decays. If α is close to 1, last month's advertising effect decays very slowly; if α is close to 0, it decays very rapidly.

In-depth statistical analysis of the factors in the advertising rate, its response function, and the value of α produces the response curves shown in Figure 8.4. These curves represent how sales will respond to advertising rates that are above or below their reference values. If the advertising rate is consistently lower than its reference value, as computed by the advertising rate at its current reference values, the response functions show how sales (and market share) will decrease over time and level off at a lower value. Conversely, if the advertising rate is consistently higher than its reference value, the response function shows how sales (and market share) will increase over time and level off at a higher value.

The term **promotion** refers to a variety of sales stimulating devices including price reductions, coupons, samples, and premiums, such as free quantity add-ons. Some promotions can be modeled by direct indexes, where estimates are derived from market pretests or prior experience with similar promotions. Others are relatively fixed in their form but have an intensity depending on the money spent; these can best be modeled using response curves.

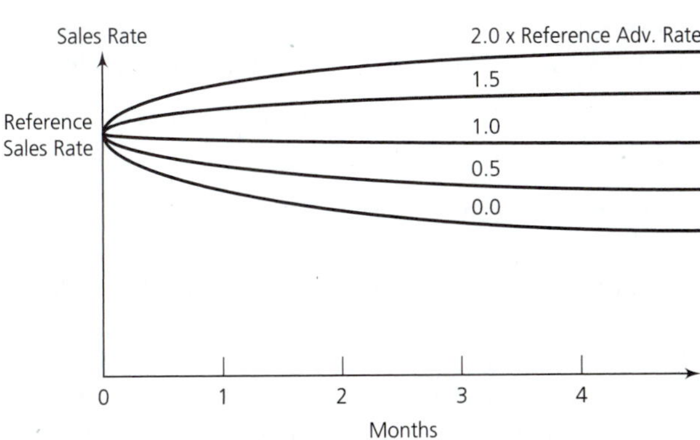

Figure 8.4
Sales response over time to different advertising rates. *Source:* Little [1975]

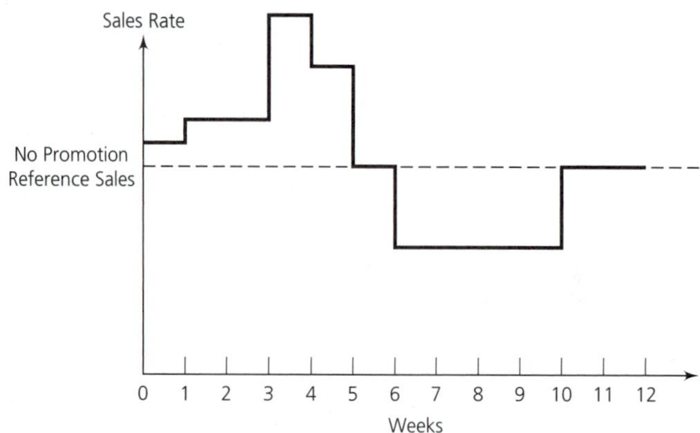

Figure 8.5 Time pattern of response to a reference promotion. *Source:* Little [1975]

The **promotion submodel** is constructed from a promotion time pattern and a promotion response function. A typical promotion time pattern for a 5-week promotion beginning in week 1 is shown in Figure 8.5. After the promotion is completed, the pattern predicts a cannibilization or sharp drop-off in sales for several weeks. The model predicts a scaling of the promotion time pattern based on a promotion response function that measures the promotional intensity, which describes the intensity of the given promotion relative to a reference or standard promotion.

Price is an important sales control variable; here we speak of the basic wholesale price, not temporary price reductions that are considered to be promotions. The basic wholesale price is not expected to change, or change significantly, during times of low inflation. Of course, anomalous factors might create the need for price increases such as the sudden increase in cost of product inputs. In any event, the brand manager must be careful when considering price increases because experience has shown that such increases are likely to provoke a competitive reaction. Although an established brand can realize large short-term increases in net revenues from price increases, over the long term, it is very likely that the brand will experience a loss in market share. If appropriate, a **pricing submodel** for forecasting long-term pricing effects similar to those discussed above can be developed.

Finally, the relative effort and effectiveness of the sales force can have a substantial impact on brand sales. Salespeople call on wholesalers and retailers to boost the company's products and deliver information about up-coming promotions, product changes, and so on. The effect of sales force activity on brand sales is similar to that of advertising; namely,

Sales force rate =
(effectiveness/call) * (calls/$) * ($ spent on salary and expenses)

The **sales force submodel** determines the effect for each month based on a response function mapping the above rate into a short-term marketing effect that is combined with last month's effect using exponential smoothing.

The four descriptive submodels (advertising, promotion, pricing, and sales force) can be combined, again calculating their overall effect on sales by multiplying

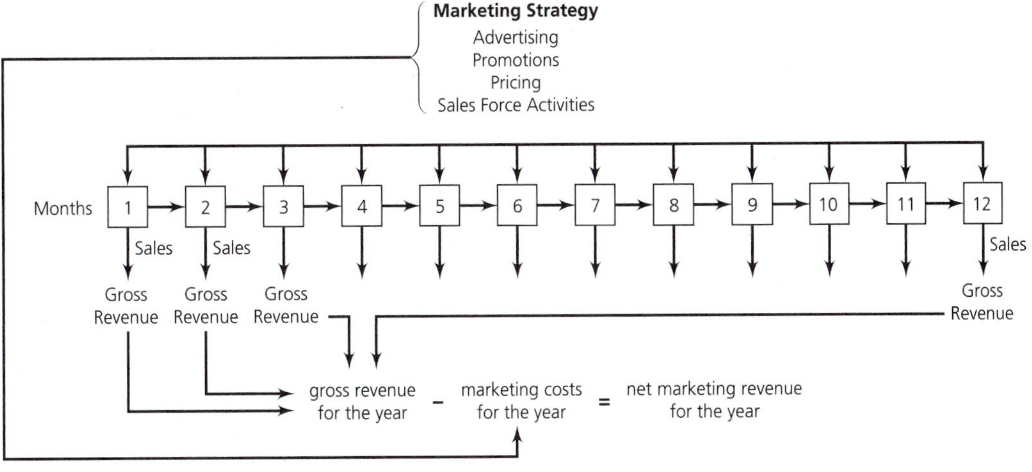

Figure 8.6 Forecasted sales and net marketing revenue determined by a marketing model

reference sales by a number of multiplicative factors, to produce sales forecasts for each month of next year. The logic is shown in Figure 8.6. The brand manager selects a **marketing strategy** for next year comprising decisions regarding advertising, promotions, pricing, and sales force activities on a monthly basis. Using the marketing model, this strategy determines brand sales, prices, and gross revenues for each month by location and market segment. The linkages between months shown in the figure refer to the dynamic effects of marketing control variables, which we have described by exponential smoothing relationships, on market share. The model also determines the associated cost for the year of such a strategy. The cost is subtracted from the gross revenues to yield the net marketing revenue for the year of the marketing strategy.

The logic of Figure 8.6 is clearly descriptive, rather than normative, because the brand manager has no analytical means for optimizing her marketing decisions by coordinating them with supply chain decisions to maximize net revenues, which equals net marketing revenue minus supply chain cost. Of course, she employs her best managerial judgment in choosing the marketing strategy. Nevertheless, if she is willing and able to quantify the impact of her decisions as required by the marketing model, the sales and cost quantities in Figure 8.6 will be more rationally determined and therefore can be better justified and, one would hope, will provide more accurate forecasts. The linkages to supply chain decisions are discussed in the following subsection.

Integrating Supply Chain and Marketing Models for Manufacturers of Consumer Products

In this subsection, we discuss how a manufacturer of consumer products can integrate supply chain and demand management decision making by combining the marketing model of Figure 8.6, which determines how marketing strategies induce demand and net marketing revenue, with a supply chain model, which minimizes the total cost of meeting fixed and given demand.[12] The objective of the combined models is to maximize net revenues, which equals net marketing revenues minus total supply chain cost. We assume that the market and supply chains models each have12 linked, monthly submodels. The integrated model might be employed on an annual basis to help determine next year's strategy. It might also be employed on a tactical, rolling horizon basis every 3 months to adjust the annual plan.

The integration scheme is depicted in Figure 8.7. The spirit of the method is similar to that employed by the unified optimization methodology described in Chapter 5. The difference is that here we are employing the decomposition method to integrate a supply chain optimization model and a market model with radically different mathematical forms. In developing the unified optimization methodology, we applied the decomposition method to large-scale operational models to overcome their size and exploit special structures of embedded submodels.

The integration scheme begins by exercising the marketing model under a number of settings for the market control variables to create a range of demand scenarios and associated net marketing revenues. Each demand scenario specifies a quantity of each product that will be demanded in each market in each month of the planning horizon. The marketing strategies are used to initialize the linear programming (LP) master model, which seeks to maximize net revenues by varying product mix among them.

To illustrate the concept of a mixed marketing strategy, we consider the case when the method begins with five initial strategies. As shown in Figure 8.8, the LP master model assigns nonnegative weights (decision variables), which sum to 1, to the five initial marketing strategies. We can imagine, but cannot depict, each strategy being represented by a point in the high-dimensional space describing demands for all products in all markets in all months. A net marketing revenue is associated with each such point. The space of all demands that can be spanned by the five initial

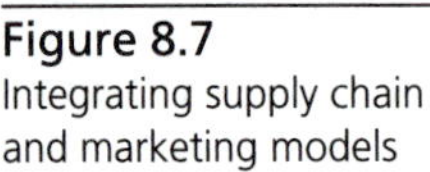
Figure 8.7
Integrating supply chain and marketing models

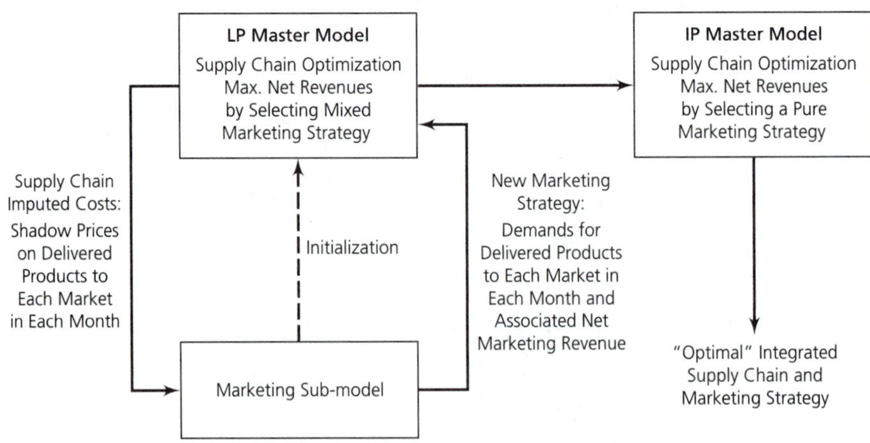

Figure 8.8
Mixed marketing strategy

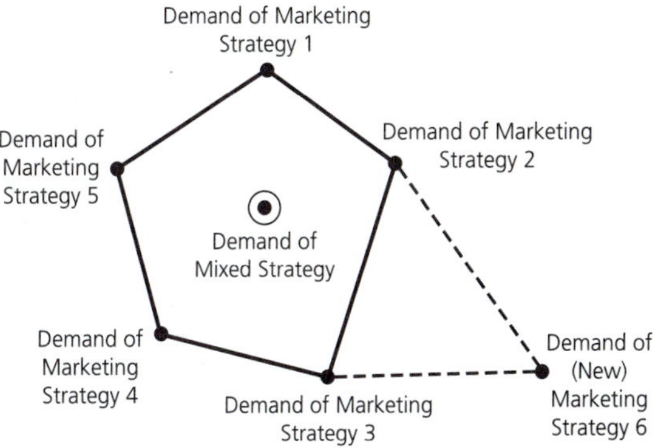

strategies multiplied by nonnegative weights summing to 1 is given by the irregular pentagon. Maximizing net revenues over that space indicates the optimal product mix strategy shown by the circled point, which corresponds to optimal weights of one-third for each of strategies 1, 2, and 4.

Clearly, the initial space of possible demands, and their net marketing revenues, may not include a product mix strategy that optimizes net revenues. The scheme in Figure 8.7 is intended to rectify this limitation by iteratively generating new marketing strategies. It does this by passing shadow prices (optimal marginal costs) on delivered products to each market in each month to the marketing submodel, which uses this information to generate a new marketing strategy.

Ideally, we would like the marketing submodel to select this new strategy by maximizing net revenues where delivered product cost in each market and each month is set equal to the shadow price. Given the form of the marketing model described in the previous subsection, this may be difficult to achieve. Alternatively, we can more safely assume that the marketing submodel can employ the shadow price information to identify a new strategy that is "good" in the sense that the new strategy, when it is added to the LP master model, will be given a positive weight in the new optimal solution. The determination of a good new strategy could be accomplished, for example, by selecting marketing control variables to increase demand for products in those markets and months that have relatively low shadow prices, which indicates that these products will have relatively high margins. As shown in Figure 8.8, the new marketing strategy expands the space of possible product mix decisions.

A complication, which forces us to use two versions of the supply chain master model, is that the space of mixed marketing strategies shown in Figure 8.8 may contain strategies that are not feasible in the marketing submodel, although all the pure strategies are feasible. The same complication arose in operational planning applications when we applied the unified optimization methodology. For example, TV ads must be purchased in integer quantities, and a mixed strategy that selects 2.3 ads in April could not be implemented. To overcome this difficulty, after a number of new strategies using the LP master model have been generated, we turn to the IP master model in which we impose the condition that a pure (that is, exactly one) marketing strategy must be selected from among those previously identified. Unfortunately, we cannot substitute the IP master model for the LP master model during the marketing strategy generation phase of the analysis because, by imposing pure (0-1) weights on the strategies, we lose the ability to compute meaningful shadow prices.

The result of optimizing the IP master model is an "optimal" integrated supply chain and marketing strategy, where we have put quotation marks around optimal because underlying technical difficulties would probably make it impossible for us to determine a truly optimal integrated strategy and prove that it has that property. This is not a serious practical drawback because the method lends itself to the computation of bounds on how far the best known solution is from optimality. Thus, the decomposition method "optimizes" in the sense that it finds an integrated strategy with a net revenue value that is within a known bound from the value of an optimal strategy; if this value is not good enough for the decision makers, the method can be continued until an acceptably profitable integrated strategy is found.

The synthesis of supply chain and marketing decision making depicted in Figures 8.6 and 8.7 was based on a marketing science model describing the impact of advertising, promotion, pricing, and sales force efforts on product sales. The resulting demand and gross marketing revenue data that we incorporated in the net revenue master models could have been developed by a less rigorous model; in the extreme, these data could have been determined solely by managerial judgment. From this perspective, it seems obvious that, to sustain and enhance its competitive position, the company must insist on the development of quantitative marketing data supported by rational analysis.

Illustrative Numerical Model

We illustrate the computational scheme depicted in Figure 8.7 with a modeling application for the Gold Beer Company. Gold Beer produces two types of beer, Gold Ale and Gold Lager, in its brewery located in Centerville. These products are distributed and sold in the Centerville and Douglas metropolitan areas. Gold Beer has a long-standing marketing campaign that is expected to maintain flat demand for the products over the foreseeable future. Roughly speaking, Gold Beer has a 15 to 20% market share for each product in each market.

The marketing department has created new TV ads, one for each product, that they believe could significantly increase Gold's market share over the next 6 months. Monthly demand for each product in each market is characterized by the following three parameters:

1. Current Gold sales (s). Monthly demand for Gold product without new TV ads
2. Maximal Gold sales (M). Highest attainable (maximal) demand for Gold Product
3. Total market sales (S). Total sales of Gold product and all competing products

Note that S minus M consumers are loyal to other brands and cannot be motivated to switch to Gold by TV ads. The values of these parameters are given in Table 8.2.

Table 8.2 Market sales in 1000s of six packs

	Current Gold Sales (s)	Maximal Gold Sales (M)	Total Market Sales (S)
Centerville, ale	1325	3000	9000
Douglas, ale	2250	5000	9800
Centerville, lager	1100	2500	7600
Douglas, lager	1800	4000	8750

Gold Beer has the options of running one to four ads each night for each type of beer in each market. Contracts with the TV stations in each city are on a monthly basis; that is, Gold Beer must contract to run the same number of ads each night in each city for a month. One ale ad each night for a month costs $625,000 in Centerville and $500,000 in Douglas. One lager ad each night for a month costs $400,000 in Centerville and $340,000 in Douglas. The cost of K ads in any month is K times the cost of one ad.

After analyzing historical data and performing market tests of the ads, the marketing department has developed a model describing the potential impact of an ad campaign. If x is the size of the market at the start of the month, the impact of a campaign depends on the number of ads run each night and the size of the untapped market $M - x$ for each product. Specifically, the marketing department has estimated the factors given in Table 8.3 that determine the percentage of consumers among the $M - x$ target segments that will switch from a competing beer to Gold. Thus, if Gold's market size for ale in Douglas at the start of the month is $x = 2700$, and the company elects to run one ad per night, the sales during the month are forecast to equal $2700 + 0.10(5000 - 2700) = 2930$, where 5000 is Gold's maximal market given in Table 8.2.

The effect of ads on market size decays in subsequent months if the ads are not repeated. Specifically, the residual effect of ads run last month on this month's market size is 0.75 relative to the base demand. Thus, for the example just cited, if no ads were run in Douglas for ale in the month after one ad was run, the market size would decline to $2250 + 0.75(2930 - 2250) = 2760$. For the second month without an ad, the residual factor is estimated to equal 0.35, for the third month without an ad it is 0.10, and for the fourth month it is 0.

Table 8.3 Marketing effects

Number of Ads	Marketing Effect Ale	Marketing Effect Lager
1	0.10	0.08
2	0.17	0.14
3	0.22	0.18
4	0.26	0.21

The marketing department has proposed the four ad campaigns displayed in Table 8.4. The first column with the quantities dpkt refers to demand for product p (*a*le, *l*ager) in city k (1 = Centerville, 2 = Douglas) during month t (t = 1, 2, 3, 4, 5, 6). We compute the corresponding demands using the data in Tables 8.2 and 8.3. For example, da11 under campaign 1 equals 1.10*1325 = 1457.5, where 1.10 is the multiplicative factor for one ale ad per night and 1325 is the base demand for ale in city 1. Similarly, demand da12 under campaign 1 equals 1325 + 0.75 * (1457.5–1325) = 1424.375, where 0.75 is the decay factor if 1 month has passed without an ale ad in city 1. The costs given at the bottom Table 8.4 are measured in thousands of dollars.

The ad campaign options of Table 8.4, plus the no-ad campaign 0, are combined with a model of Gold Beer's supply chain in a single integrated model, which is partially displayed in part in Table 8.5 and 8.6. As shown in Table 8.5, supply chain decisions each month are divided into the following four submodels:

- Production model
- Transportation model
- Inventory balance equations
- Sales cannot exceed demand inequalities

All volumes are measured in thousands of six packs, and all costs and revenues are measured in thousands of dollars.

We display only the first 2 months of the 6-month supply chain model in Table 8.5 to conserve space. The structure of the model for the other 4 months is identical. The production model has three constraints: a joint packaging constraint on the manufacture of ale and lager and two capacity constraints on the brewing of each product. The production model includes overtime (ot) on the packaging line. The transportation model ensures that the volumes of ale and lager shipped to the DCs at the two markets do not exceed production. The suffixes 1 and 2 refer to shipments to Centerville and Douglas, respectively. There is no inventory held at the plant.

For each product and each DC, the inventory balance equation states that ending inventory equals beginning inventory plus shipments received from the plant minus sales. The inventory at the start of month 1 is given. For each product at each DC, the sales cannot exceed demand as computed in the demand model given in Table 8.6. This model allows weighted combinations of the no-ad campaign and the four campaigns given in Table 8.4. As an example of the linkage of the demand model with the supply chain model, consider sales of ale in Centerville in month 1 (cell Q25), which equals demand there (cell S25) where the latter quantity equals the demand computed in the demand model (cell L132). The sales variable is also incorporated in the inventory balance equation for ale at Centerville on row 18. As usual, ending inventories for month 1 (cells I22, J22, K22, L22) become beginning inventories for month 2 (cells S39, S40, S41, S42).

The objective function for each month computes the net revenues of sales in that month, which equals gross revenues from sales minus production, transportation, and inventory costs. The global objective function equals the sum of the net

Table 8.4 Gold Beer marketing campaigns

Demand dpkt[a]	Ad Campaign 1	Demand	Ad Campaign 2	Demand	Ad Campaign 3	Demand	Ad Campaign 4	Demand
da10		1,325		1,325		1,325		1,325
da20		2,250		2,250		2,250		2,250
dl10		1,100		1,100		1,100		1,100
dl20		1,800		1,800		1,800		1,800
da11	1	1,458	2	1,550	1	1,458	0	1,325
da21	1	2,475	2	2,633	1	2,475	0	2,250
dl11	1	1,188	2	1,254	1	1,188	0	1,100
dl21	1	1,944	2	2,052	1	1,944	0	1,800
da12	0	1,424	2	1,797	1	1,612	1	1,493
da22	0	2,419	2	3,062	1	2,728	1	2,525
dl12	0	1,166	2	1,428	1	1,293	1	1,212
dl22	0	1,908	2	2,325	1	2,108	1	1,976
da13	1	1,582	2	2,001	1	1,751	0	1,400
da23	1	2,677	2	3,501	1	2,955	0	2,377
dl13	1	1,273	2	1,578	1	1,390	0	1,150
dl23	1	2,075	2	2,559	1	2,260	0	1,881
da14	0	1,518	2	2,171	1	1,876	1	1,560
da24	0	2,570	2	3,895	1	3,159	1	2,639
dl14	0	1,230	2	1,707	1	1,478	1	1,258
dl24	0	2,007	2	2,761	1	2,399	1	2,051
da15	1	1,666	2	2,312	1	1,988	0	1,501
da25	1	2,813	2	4,309	1	3,343	0	2,542
dl15	1	1,331	2	1,818	1	1,560	0	1,218
dl25	1	2,166	2	2,934	1	2,527	0	1,988
da16	0	1,581	2	2,429	1	2,089	1	1,651
da26	0	2,672	2	4,680	1	3,509	1	2,788
dl16	0	1,273	2	1,914	1	1,635	1	1,321
dl26	0	2,074	2	3,084	1	2,645	1	2,149
Cost		5,595		22,380		11,190		5,595

[a]dpkt = demand for product *p* in city *k* in month *t*.

revenues of the six months minus the cost of the ad campaign. It does not include unavoidable costs such as other marketing costs, capital replacement and depreciation costs, and administrative costs.

The model of Table 8.5 was optimized as a linear programming model. As we can see from Table 8.6, the model fortuitously chose a pure marketing strategy consisting of ad campaign 3, with a global objective function value of $177,195,000,

Table 8.5 Integrated supply chain and marketing model for Gold Beer with five ad campaigns

	A	B	C	D	E	F	G	H	I	J	K	L	M	N	O	P	Q	R	S	T	U	V	W
1	**Global Obj Fn**																						
2	177195		**Production**																				
3		ale	lager	ot																			
4	**Obj Fn**																						
5	**Month 1**	1	1	-1	6483		<=			7000		Packaging											
6	27644	1					=<=			4000		Ale Capacity											
7			1				<=			4800		Lager Capacity											
8	Dec Values	4000	2483	0																			
9	Unit Costs	2.75	2.28	0.12																			
10							**Transportation**																
11					ale1	ale2	lag1	lag2															
12					1	1			4000	=<=	4000	Ale Shipping Limits											
13							1	1	2483	=<=	2483	Lager Shipping Limits											
14	Dec Values				1869	2131	1139	1344															
15	Unit Costs				0.15	0.62	0.15	0.62											**Starting**				
16							**Shipments**				**Ending Inventory**				**Sales**				**Inventory**				
17					ale1	ale2	lager1	lager2	ale1	ale2	lager1	lager2	ale1	ale2	lager1	lager2							
18					-1				1				1				1200	=	1200				
19						-1				1				1			800	=	800			**Inventory**	
20							-1				1				1		1100	=	1100			**Balance**	
21								-1				1				1	600	=	600			**Equations**	
22	Dec Values								1612	456	1051	0	1458	2475	1188	1944							
23	Unit Costs/Revs								0.064	0.064	0.057	0.057	7	7	6.25	6.25							
24																	Sales		Demand				
25													1				1458	=<=	1458			**Sales**	
26														1			2475	=<=	2475			**Cannot**	
27															1		1188	=<=	1188			**Exceed**	
28																1	1944	=<=	1944			**Demand**	
29	**Obj Fn**																						
30	**Month 2**	1	1	-1	7000		=<=			7000													
31	29420	1					=<=			4000													
32			1				<=			4800													
33		4000	3000	0																			
34		2.75	2.28	0.12																			
35					1	1			4000	=<=	4000												
36							1	1	3000	=<=	3000												
37					0	4000	242	2758															
38					0.15	0.62	0.15	0.62															
39					-1				1				1				1612	=	1612				
40						-1				1				1			456	=	456				
41							-1				1				1		1051	=	1051				
42								-1				1				1	0	=	0				
43									0	1728	0	649	1612	2728	1293	2108							
44									0.064	0.064	0.057	0.057	7	7	6.25	6.25							
45													1				1612	=<=	1612				
46														1			2728	=<=	2728				
47															1		1293	=<=	1293				
48																1	2108	=<=	2108				

Table 8.6 Integrated supply chain and marketing model for Gold Beer with five ad campaigns

	A	B	C	D	E	F	G	H	I	J	K	L	M	N	O	P	Q	R	S	T	U	V	W
128																							
129						**Demand Model**																	
130																							
131						Campaigns						Weighted											
132				0	1	2	3	4				Sum											
133			da11	1325	1458	1550	1458	1325				1458											
134			da21	2250	2475	2633	2475	2250				2475											
135			dl11	1100	1188	1254	1188	1100				1188											
136			dl21	1800	1944	2052	1944	1800				1944											
137			da12	1325	1424	1797	1612	1493				1612											
138			da22	2250	2419	3062	2728	2525				2728											
139			dl12	1100	1166	1428	1293	1212				1293											
140			dl22	1800	1908	2325	2108	1976				2108											
141			da13	1325	1582	2001	1751	1400				1751											
142			da23	2250	2677	3501	2955	2377				2955											
143			dl13	1100	1273	1578	1390	1150				1390											
144			dl23	1800	2075	2559	2260	1881				2260											
145			da14	1325	1518	2171	1876	1560				1876											
146			da24	2250	2570	3895	3159	2639				3159											
147			dl14	1100	1230	1707	1478	1258				1478											
148			dl24	1800	2007	2761	2399	2051				2399											
149			da15	1325	1666	2312	1988	1501				1988											
150			da25	2250	2813	4309	3343	2542				3343											
151			dl15	1100	1331	1818	1560	1218				1560											
152			dl25	1800	2166	2934	2527	1988				2527											
153			da16	1325	1581	2429	2089	1651				2089											
154			da26	2250	2672	4680	3509	2788				3509											
155			dl16	1100	1273	1914	1635	1321				1635											
156			dl26	1800	2074	3084	2645	2149				2645											
157			costs	0	5595	22380	11190	5595				11190											
158		variable	weights	0	0	0	1	0					=	1									

which is shown in Table 8.5 under Global Obj Fn. This integrated supply chain and demand management plan is almost $25 million higher than the optimal value of a no-ad campaign.

The optimal shadow prices for this linear programming model indicated greater value to increasing demand for lager relative to that for ale; moreover, added demand in Centerville was more attractive than demand in Douglas. In addition, the optimal supply chain plan left unsatisfied demand for ale in Douglas in months 4, 5, and 6, indicating that ads promoting this demand should be cut back. After generating three more marketing campaigns, we identified a campaign yielding net revenue of $183,913,000. This campaign consists of one ad for ale every month in both markets, except no ads for ale in Douglas in months 3, 4, and 5, and two ads for lager every month in both markets.

From a rigorous viewpoint, of course, we have not verified that this solution is demonstrably good by computing an upper bound on the net revenue of an optimal strategy. Such a bound could be computed if we were to devise a method for finding a campaign with optimal "net reward" measured by the difference between the gross reward based on shadow prices minus the cost of the campaign. Such a method should be possible to construct, but we omit details here.

Analysis with the optimization models clearly indicated that the marketing cost of increasing demand for Gold Beer's products is significantly less than the supply chain cost of meeting such demand with current capabilities. It suggests that Gold Beer may wish to explore options for expanding these capabilities. Of course, capacity expansion might involve large, lumpy investment costs and require considerable time to implement.

8.4 Planning for New Product Introduction and Growth

The stages of a product's **life cycle** are design, development, introduction, growth, maturity, and decline. Planning for a new product begins at the design stage and lasts well into the growth stage. Our purpose here is to discuss briefly models for forecasting the demand for new products and their integration with supply chain models.

We consider that new product planning ends once the product's share and the size of its overall market settle down to somewhat predictable quantities. Still, the delineation between stages of a product's life cycle is not always clear. For some products, sales pass through a flat period before growth reoccurs. Similarly, for products with short life cycles, such as certain types of clothing or other style goods, the maturity and decline stages are brief or nonexistent. For these products, new product planning encompasses almost the entire life cycle.[13]

At the design stage of a new product, the motivation for considering supply chain decisions is to select not only those designs that are most attractive to consumers but also to identify those that will serve to maximize net revenues as the result of efficient manufacturing and distribution activities.[14] The new product's supply chain may require investments in equipment and possibly facilities. Alternatively, the new product may employ equipment and facilities currently used by other product lines.

This suggests that most companies would be well advised to implement supply chain models for new products very early in their life cycles, preferably during the design stage, even if hard data about demand and manufacturing costs are not available. Such a model should be multiple period and optimize net revenues. Initially, it will be used by the **new product team,** which includes representatives of the company's supply chain function as well as designers, engineers, and marketers, to assess the profitability of alternative designs.

The scarcity of hard data at the design stage should not be viewed as an insurmountable barrier. When no direct historical sales data are available, it may be possible to use surrogate data from similar products introduced in the past to make initial forecasts. These a priori forecasts can be systematically updated as initial sales are made. Approximate manufacturing costs and learning curves can usually be estimated from the development of similar products. Moreover, the new product team can and should create business processes and modeling analyses aimed at refining data and adapting plans to demand patterns as they are revealed. The model and its database should be updated and used on an appropriately frequent basis as the product moves into and through the stages of development, introduction, and growth.

The **diffusion model** has been frequently applied to forecast new product demand for consumer durables and high technology products.[15] A simple version of this model is based on the following relationship:

$$Q_t = p\,(Q^* - N_t) + r\,(N_t / Q^*)\,(Q^* - N_t)$$

where:

Q_t = nmber of adopters during period t.
Q^* = ultimate number of adopters.
N_t = cumulative number of adopters up to period t.
p = innovation rate.
r = imitation rate.

Adoptions refers to first-time buying of a new product. The model as stated assumes that the number of adopters in period t depends on the sum of two terms capturing adoption by innovators and imitators.

The innovator term $p\,(Q^* - N_t)$ is the product of the innovation rate times the number of ultimate adopters who have not yet done so. Thus, innovators are not influenced by other people's adoption. As time progresses, the innovators have a progressively diminishing influence on the rate of adoption because $Q^* - N_t$ gets smaller and smaller. The imitator term $r\,(N_t/Q^*)\,(Q^* - N_t)$ is the product of the imitator rate times the proportion of adopters to date times the number of ultimate adopters who have not yet done so. During the early stages of the new product introduction, the rate of imitator adoptions is very low because N_t is small and therefore the term N_t/Q^* is small. This term provides a progressively increasing contribution to the number of adopters until Nt exceeds $Q^*/2$ at which point the number of new imitators each period begins to drop off.

The combined **rate of adoption** by innovators and imitators is given by the term $p + r\,N_t/Q^*$ and increases over time because N_t increases over time. But this rate is multiplied by $Q^* - N_t$, which decreases over time. Thus, the shape of the sales curve of adopters depends on the relative values of these two tendencies, which turns out to be dependent on the relative values of r and p. Figure 8.9 shows the shape of new buyer (adopter) sales curves for the two cases $r > p$ and $r < p$. When $r > p$, the curve will rise and then fall; when $r < p$, the curve will fall continuously.

In the simple form stated above, the sales forecasts Q_t can be made once estimates of three parameters, r, p, and Q^*, have been made. Initially, these might be judgmentally determined from historical sales patterns of similar products. The a priori estimates would then be updated from actual sales data. Much applied research has been done on extensions of the basic model to describe new product diffusion and the ultimate number of adopters as functions of price and advertising.[16] Moreover, model extensions treat product sales of the product to multiple segments, perhaps those in geographically dispersed markets.

Our specific interest in the diffusion model is to use it to forecast sales for a new product that would provide inputs to a net revenue maximizing supply chain model. The model would be developed initially for strategic plans to accommodate the introduction and growth of the product. It would be used in a dynamic, rolling horizon fashion to plan yearly and then quarterly resource acquisition and allocation decisions to support the new product. The accuracy of the diffusion model would, of course, influence the quality of manufacturing, distribution, and sales decisions and, therefore, the realized net revenues. Marketing science modelers would have frequent opportunities to revise the parameters and even the form of the diffusion model to achieve greater accuracy. Even if initial estimates proved to be far off the mark, one can expect, or at least hope, that the forecasting model would improve significantly over time. In the final analysis, it is difficult to imagine that, when com-

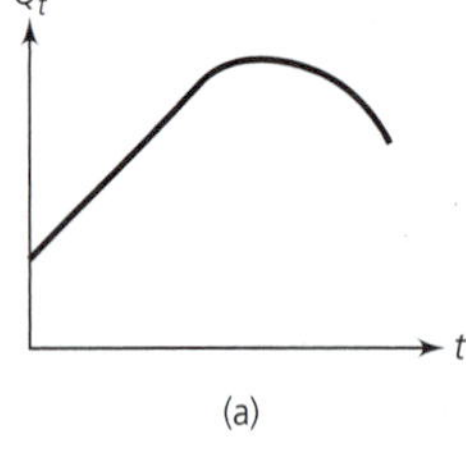

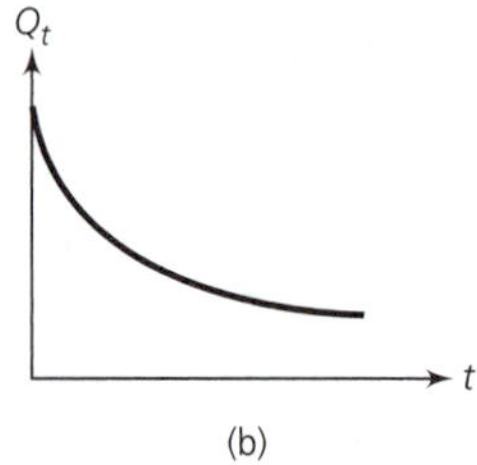

Figure 8.9
New buyer sales curves. (a) New buyer sales curve when the imitation rate exceeds innovation rate ($r > p$). (b) New buyer sales curve when the innovation rate exceeds imitation rate ($r < p$). *Source:* Bass [1969]

pared to a strictly subjective and qualitative approach, an integrated supply chain and demand management analysis based on models would lead to inferior net revenue performance.

8.5 Optimization Models for Competitive Analysis

The strategic planning models that we have studied thus far have not explicitly addressed competition among firms in an industry, although in the previous section, we introduced model structures implicitly linked to competition such as price elasticities and market share. In this section, we discuss models and solution methods for explicitly examining competition. Although these models and methods are currently beyond the frontier of practical applications, they are technically feasible and potentially very valuable. They have not yet been widely applied because they entail constructions that are not easily understood and require new types of data and descriptive models. Despite the barriers, we hope that our discussion will prompt interest in experimenting with competitive models.

We begin by reviewing a well-known qualitative theory of competition due to Michael Porter that relates competition among firms in an industry to five key forces. Porter's structural analysis of industries can be viewed as a managerial interpretation of the theory of industrial organization, a venerable and rich area of investigation within the field of economics. In large part, the theory derives its results from the construction, analysis, and optimization of theoretical mathematical models. There has been very little implementation of data-driven versions of these models.

Given the underlying theme of this book, we are challenged to translate the qualitative insights of structural industry models and the quantitative insights of models of industrial organization into decision support tools. Recognizing that a comprehensive response to this challenge would require an entire book unto itself, we compromise by providing an overview of important concepts, which we illustrate with a numerical example, and by presenting in the following section an application to industry analysis in the forest products industry. The application illustrates the value of focusing the vast theory of competitive analysis on pragmatic and data-driven decision problems faced by a specific firm in a specific industry.

Structural Analysis of Industries

Porter's structural analysis evaluates the impact of five competitive forces that determine industry attractiveness and the potential profitability of firms in that industry.[17] His subsequent study of the value chain (the supply chain) of an individual firm recognized that the firm's competitive position within an industry depends on how well the firm integrates its activities across the chain. We have followed an opposite course in this book by studying supply chains of individual firms in detail before considering how firms in an industry compete.

Porter's five forces are as follows:

- Rivalry among existing firms in the industry
- Bargaining power of suppliers
- Bargaining power of buyers
- Threat of substitute products or services
- Threat of new entrants

They are displayed in Figure 8.10 along with key factors that influence industry structure.

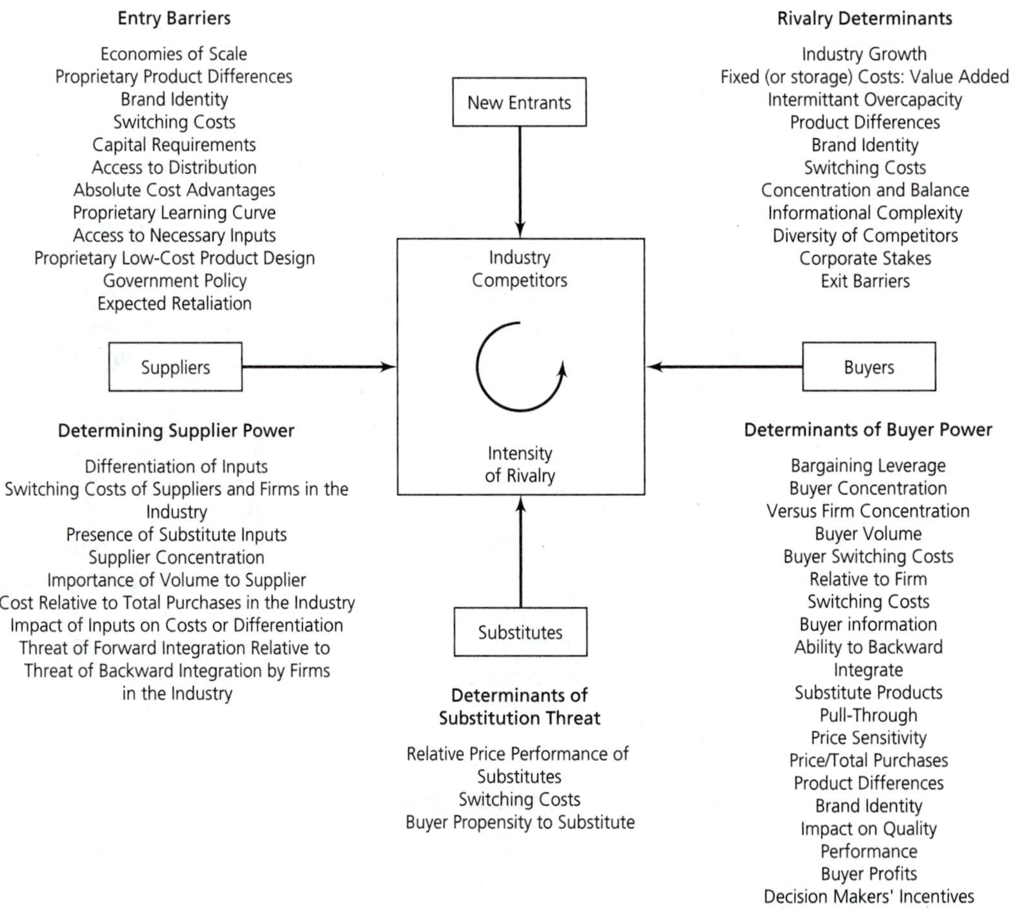

Figure 8.10 Elements of industry structure. *Source:* Porter [1985, 6]

The overall impact of the five forces determines the ability of individual firms in an industry to realize superior returns. Such returns will depend on the absolute and relative strength of each of the forces, which varies from industry to industry and can change over time. Profit potential is independent of the products manufactured by the firms in the industry, whether they are large or small or involve products that are new or old, high-tech or low-tech. For example, the pharmaceutical industry has traditionally allowed many competitors to earn attractive returns because many of the five forces are weak. Huge barriers to entry keep new firms out of the market. Pharmaceutical companies are vertically integrated, thereby eliminating the potential threat of suppliers that have strong bargaining power. Similarly, patented drugs may have no threat from substitutes; nonpatented drugs may be protected from damaging substitutions through advertising and sales activities that preserve market share. Finally, until recently, the bargaining power of buyers was low. This bargaining power has become more of a threat as HMOs and governments seek to control health care costs.

By contrast, returns in the forest products industry are less attractive because the rivalry among competitors is intense. The industry is not growing, industry capacity is intermittently in excess, and most products are treated as commodities, which does not promote brand loyalty or discourage switching. Moreover, large buyers have considerable bargaining power.

Limited space prevents us from discussing each of the elements listed in Figure 8.10. Many have been discussed in the context of supply chain models that we examined earlier in the book (e.g., economies of scale, buyer volume, price sensitivity). More generally, two issues arise when we attempt to develop data-driven models for decision support based on these elements and Porter's paradigm.

First, we must develop descriptive data and models of the elements of industry structure to serve as inputs to optimization models for supporting managerial decision making. For example, what is the switching cost of a supplier or buyer? Or, how do we represent substitute inputs in the descriptions of manufacturing recipes used by firms in an industry? The answers to these and other questions should be of considerable interest to senior managers in a firm, independent of their importance to the construction and optimization of normative models for industry analysis. Second, assuming that data and descriptive models of many of the elements in Figure 8.10 have been developed, we need a systems analysis framework for combining them. As we discuss below, this framework is provided by a synthesis of the theory of industrial organization with mathematical programming techniques for constructing optimization models and combining them using decomposition methods.

Theory of Industrial Organization

The field of **industrial organization** is concerned with the theory of the firm and how firms compete for profits.[18] Many scholars working in the field employ mathematical models and analysis to gain insights into strategic, competitive behavior.

These are theoretical, not data-driven, models and therefore they are not intended to assist managers in making specific strategic decisions. Nevertheless, the models provide a conceptual foundation for implementing data-driven models when they are combined with models and methods of mathematical programming.

Models for analyzing competition within an industry determine supply prices and quantities among the firms in the industry that balance demand quantities and prices among customers for the products offered by these firms. This balance is called a **competitive equilibrium.** An equilibrium solution generalizes the simple case in which a company increases its manufacture of a product to the level where its marginal cost equals the marginal price received for the product, at which point supply is balanced against demand. Equilibrium models play a central role in the theory of industrial organization as a method for characterizing stable patterns of interfirm competition.

Each firm in an industry equilibrium model seeks to maximize net revenues in the context of its industry's competitive structure, which might be price competition among many firms, or one where a monopolist sets prices without regard to its competitors' behavior. At the same time, buyers from the industry seek to maximize the utility they receive from their purchases.[19] From a supply chain perspective, competition has a distinct spatial aspect because manufacturing facilities and markets are geographically dispersed. An industry in which physical products are manufactured and transported to markets is characterized by a **spatial equilibrium.**[20]

The theory of economic equilibrium focuses primarily on price and spatial competition, implying that products are commodities, whether they are forest products or luxury automobiles in a certain price/performance category. Thus, the theory has relatively little to say about marketing, despite its obvious importance to the success of many physical products in the market place in the market place.[21] Unfortunately, space does not allow us to explore this ambiguity.

Decomposition methods of mathematical programming allow the computation of equilibria among data-driven models of competing firms and their markets. The relevance of these methods has remained unrecognized by economists, in part because their mathematical esthetic entails local characterizations of optimality based on arguments from calculus regarding differentiable functions, rather than global characterizations of optimality based on mathematical programming duality theory. Moreover, supply chain models based on mixed integer programming constructions, which we have argued are necessary in many cases to produce realistic models, violate mathematical assumptions underlying many of the central theoretical results obtained from models of industrial organization.

This does not destroy the practical value of data-driven equilibrium analysis using mixed integer programming models of the firm, especially when the number of firms in an industry is above two or three and when the number of manufacturing plants is above ten. In such a case, we can expect or hope that the minimal computed gap between supply prices and quantities and demand prices and quantities will be small. Conversely, a large gap is not merely a technical nuisance but represents market instability. New research is required to expand the theory of industrial organization to this realistic case.

A Model of Price Competition

We consider an industry of N firms that manufacture, distribute, and sell a single commodity to K markets. The firms' manufacturing facilities and the markets are spatially distributed. The firms compete for sales of the commodity solely on price. Industries with this characteristic include, at least to a first approximation, those manufacturing, distributing, and selling forest, petroleum, or chemical products.

In Figure 8.11, we describe an iterative computational scheme for analyzing the industry. We begin by letting p_k denote a trial price for the commodity in market k. Given this price, the market responds by demanding a quantity $Q_k(p_k)$. Note that we have assumed that the quantity demanded depends on the price according to a known mathematical relation called a **market demand function.** Such functions have the property that demand for the commodity decreases as price increases.

Let $p = (p_1, p_2, \ldots, p_K)$ denote the vector (array) of prices across the spatially distributed markets. Given these prices, each firm i responds by maximizing net revenues in determining the quantity $s_{ik}(p)$ to supply to each market k. The notation tells us that the supply to market k by firm i depend on product prices in *all* markets. The firm's net revenue maximization is performed by solving an **optimization model** of the type discussed in Section 8.1 and in earlier chapters. We let

$$S_k(p) = s_{1k}(p) + s_{2k}(p) + \cdots + s_{Nk}(p)$$

denote the total supply from all firms N to market k.

We say the industry for the commodity is in **equilibrium** at the price vector p if $Q_k(p_k) = S_k(p)$ for all markets k. In words, equilibrium is achieved at the price vector p if the quantity demanded in each market exactly equals the sum total of the

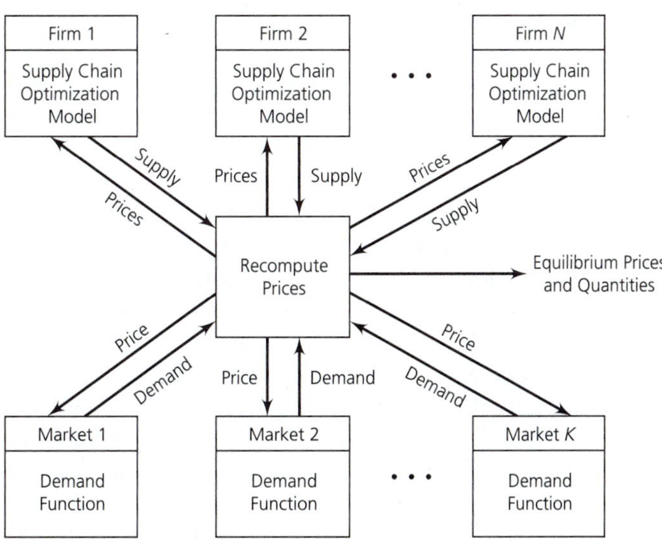

Figure 8.11 Computing a spatial equilibrium pure price competition

quantity provided to that market by the suppliers. For any firm in the industry, computation of an equilibrium can be useful in helping the firm develop its strategy or to evaluate an acquisition or a merger.

At this point, the reader might well ask the following three related questions:

- Under what conditions does an equilibrium exist?
- If it exists, is it unique?
- If it exists, how can we calculate it (them)?

Complete answers to the first two questions involve mathematical arguments based on properties of the market demand functions and the optimization models that are beyond the scope of this book. The properties have been thoroughly investigated by mathematical economists.[22] Roughly speaking, an equilibrium will exist if the optimization models characterizing the firm's net revenue maximization are linear programming models or well behaved nonlinear programming models and if the demand functions are strictly decreasing in price. Existence is an important property to establish before encoding a computational scheme, and uniqueness is a felicitous property that ensures no ambiguity in the outcome of the computation.

The scheme shown in Figure 8.11 implicitly assumes that an equilibrium can be computed. Let us suppose this to be the case and describe how to recompute the trial prices if they do not produce an equilibrium. For each market *k,* we compute the difference between the quantity of the commodity supplied and the quantity demanded; this is

$$\Delta_k(p) = Q_k(p_k) - S_k(p)$$

Because we are not at an equilibrium, at least one of the $\Delta_k(p)$ must be nonzero.

Selecting a weight $\theta > 0$, we adjust the prices for each market *k* according to the following formula:

$$p_k^{new} = \max\,(p_k + \theta * \Delta_k(p), 0)$$

By the definition of $\Delta_k(p)$, we see that p_k^{new} will be increased if demand exceeds supply in market *k* ($\Delta_k(p) > 0$), whereas it will be decreased if supply exceeds demand ($\Delta_k(p) < 0$). The formula says that p_k^{new} cannot be decreased below zero.

Thus, if demand exceeds supply when we resolve the firms' optimization models, they will be inclined to supply greater quantities of the commodity to market *k* because the price is higher. At the same time, when we recompute demand in market *k,* it will be lower because the price is higher. The opposite changes will take place if supply exceeds demand. By carefully selecting θ, we can expect to get closer to an equilibrium in that market. Assuming favorable mathematical properties of the supply models and the demand functions, this **tatonnement method** can be made to converge to an equilibrium by choosing an appropriate sequence of positive values for θ.[23]

The tatonnement method just described involves a myopic search for an equilibrium solution. A more powerful algorithm for recomputing trial equilibrium prices can be derived using a linear programming model that, at each iteration, takes into account the entire history of previously generated supply and demand strategies for all firms and all markets.[24] Thus, as these partial descriptions of the firms and the markets become more complete, the trial equilibrium prices will more closely approximate exact equilibrium prices.

Illustrative Numerical Model

We consider competition between two firms selling an industrial product in eight markets. Examples of such products include particleboard, chemicals, and plastic products. The first firm, the Wilson Company, has a plant located in Macon, Georgia, that has a yearly capacity of 22,000 tons and a plant in Tyler, Texas, that has a capacity of 15,000 tons. The second firm, the Richardson Company, has one plant located in Pine Bluffs, Arkansas, that has a yearly capacity of 26,000 units. The production cost function for each plant is made up of a fixed cost (FC), a unit cost c1 up to M1 tons, a lower unit cost c2 that obtains between M1 and M2 tons, and a higher unit cost c3 that obtains between M2 and M3, where M3 equals the maximal capacity of the plant. Values of these parameters are given in Table 8.7.

Differences in costs reflect the age of the plants and differences in raw materials, labor, and other factors at the three locations. Transportation costs play an important role in determining supply chain strategies because they equal approximately 20 to 25% of total cost. We assume both companies base their transportation costs on a rate of $0.175 per ton-mile. The distances between the markets and the plants are given in Table 8.8.

Table 8.7 Plant production cost functions (costs measured in $1000s)

Plant	FC	c1	M1	c2	M2	c3	M3
Macon	248	0.144	10,000	0.121	17,000	0.195	22,000
Tyler	175	0.128	6,500	0.103	12,000	0.137	15,000
Pine Bluffs	325	0.122	13,500	0.110	20,000	0.165	26,000

Table 8.8 Distance between plants and markets (miles)

	Macon	Tyler	Pine Bluffs
Chicago	725	856	648
St. Louis	608	598	389
Chattanooga	202	635	422
Greensboro	388	1078	811
Altoona	734	1203	994
Akron	637	1075	836
Jackson	421	366	198
Topeka	878	551	436

Table 8.9 Demand parameters (tons)

	a	*b*
Chicago	5,750	1,700
St. Louis	7,400	1,550
Chattanooga	7,500	2,200
Greensboro	12,000	1,300
Altoona	10,500	2,150
Akron	6,000	2,340
Jackson	6,500	1,660
Topeka	7,800	1,900

Demand for the commodity in each of the eight markets is price sensitive where q, the quantity demanded for next year, and p, the price per unit, are related by a linear function

$$q = a - b * p$$

Analysis of historical data has yielded the values in Table 8.9 for these demand parameters. Note that some markets are significantly more price sensitive than others.

Competition between the two firms for sales is based exclusively on price. As discussed in the previous subsection, given a vector of market prices for next year, each of the firms will pursue the supply strategy that maximizes net revenues. The supply and demand markets achieve an equilibrium when the quantities supplied at a given price equal the quantities demanded at that price.

Based on preliminary analysis of the equilibrium, we implement the tatonnement method displayed in Figure 8.10 starting with the initial price vector. This starting vector is based on cursory analysis of the problem. As we shall see, it is actually quite distant from the equilibrium solution.

As shown in Tables 8.11, 8.12, and 8.13, the Wilson and the Richardson companies use these prices to maximize their individual net revenues. Specifically, the market prices are used in cells G21 to G28 of Table 8.11, G35 to G42 of Table 8.12

Table 8.10 Initial market prices ($1,000/ton)

Chicago	0.390
St. Louis	0.348
Chattanooga	0.416
Greensboro	0.413
Altoona	0.453
Akron	0.480
Jackson	0.313
Topeka	0.355

Table 8.11 Net revenue maximization model for Wilson Company

	A	B	C	D	E	F	G	H	I	J	K	L
1				**Wilson Company**								
2												
3		FC	c1	M1	c2	M2	c3	M3	Prod'n cost			
4	Macon, GA	248	0.144	10000	0.121	17000	0.195	22000			**Production cost function**	
5								=<=				
6			10000		7000		5000	22000			**Production decisions**	
7		1		1					3510.00			
8			=<=	=<=	=<=		=<=				**Production constraints**	
9			10000	1	7000		5000					
10												
11		FC	c1	M1	c2	M2	c3	M3				
12	Tyler, TX	175	0.128	6500	0.103	12000	0.137	15000			**Production cost function**	
13								=<=				
14			6500		5500		3000	15000			**Production decisions**	
15		1		1					1984.50			
16			=<=	=<=	=<=		=<=				**Productions constraints**	
17			6500	1	5500		3000					
18												
19	from Macon plant	**Flow**			Transp		Market					
20	to	**decisions**		Distance	cost		price	Revenue				
21	Chicago	0		725	0.00		0.390	0				
22	St. Louis	0		608	0.00		0.348	0				
23	Chattanooga	4000		202	141.40		0.416	1663.58				
24	Greensboro	12000		388	814.80		0.413	4959.28				
25	Altoona	0		734	0.00		0.453	0.00				
26	Akron	6000		637	668.85		0.480	2878.23				
27	Jackson	0		421	0.00		0.313	0				
28	Topeka	0		878	0.00		0.355	0				
29	totals	22000			1625.05			9501.09				
30		=<=										
31	Production	22000										

Table 8.12 Net revenue maximization model for Wilson Company

	A	B	C	D	E	F	G	H	I	J	K	L
32												
33	from Tyler plant	**Flow**			Transportation		Market					
34	to	**decisions**		Distance	cost		price	Revenue				
35	Chicago	0		856	0.00		0.390	0				
36	St. Louis	0		598	0.00		0.348	0				
37	Chattanooga	3500		635	388.94		0.416	1455.63				
38	Greensboro	0		1078	0.00		0.413	0				
39	Altoona	0		1203	0.00		0.453	0				
40	Akron	0		1075	0.00		0.480	0				
41	Jackson	3700		366	236.99		0.313	1159.43				
42	Topeka	7800		551	752.12		0.355	2772.78				
43	totals	15000			1378.04			5387.84				
44		=<=										
45	Production	15000										
46												
47					**Market constraints**							
48		Total Wilson supply			Market capacity							
49	Chicago		0	<=	5750							
50	St. Louis		0	<=	7400							
51	Chattanooga		7500	=<=	7500							
52	Greensboro		12000	=<=	12000							
53	Altoona		0	<=	10500							
54	Akron		6000	=<=	6000							
55	Jackson		3700	<=	6500							
56	Topeka		7800	=<=	7800							
57												
58	Objective function	6391.34										

Table 8.13 Net revenue maximization model for Richardson Company

	A	B	C	D	E	F	G	H	I	J	K	L
1				**Richardson Company**								
2												
3		FC	c1	M1	c2	M2	c3	M3	Prod'n cost			
4	Pine Bluff, AK	325	0.122	13500	0.11	20000	0.165	26000			**Production cost function**	
5								=<=				
6			13500		6500		6000	26000			**Production decisions**	
7		1		1					3677.00			
8			=<=	=<=	=<=		=<=				**Production constraints**	
9			13500	1	6500		6000					
10												
11	From Pine Bluff	**Flow**			Transp		Market					
12	to	**decisions**		Distance	cost		price	Revenue				
13	Chicago	0		648	0.00		0.390	0				
14	St. Louis	7400		389	503.76		0.348	2573.27				
15	Chattanooga	7500		422	553.88		0.416	3119.21				
16	Greensboro	0		811	0		0.413	0				
17	Altoona	0		994	0.00		0.453	0				
18	Akron	6000		836	877.80		0.480	2878.23				
19	Jackson	0		198	0.00		0.313	0				
20	Topeka	5100		436	389.13		0.355	1812.969				
21	totals	26000			2324.56			10383.68				
22		=<=										
23	Production	26000										
24												
25					**Market constraints**							
26			Total Richardson supply		Market capacity							
27	Chicago		0	<=	5750							
28	St. Louis		7400	=<=	7400							
29	Chattanooga		7500	=<=	7500							
30	Greensboro		0	<=	12000							
31	Altoona		0	<=	10500							
32	Akron		6000	=<=	6000							
33	Jackson		0	<=	6500							
34	Topeka		5100	<=	7800							
35												
36	Objective function	4382.12										

and in cells G13 to G20 of Table 8.13 in computing revenues on flows from each of the three plants to the markets. Tables 8.11 and 8.12 represent the net revenue maximizing model for the Wilson Company, and Table 8.13 represents the net revenue maximizing model for the Richardson Company. Two 0-1 variables are needed to model each of the three production cost functions. These are the adjustable or variable cells B7 and D7 for the Macon plant, B15 and D15 for the Tyler plant, and B7 and D7 for the Pine Bluffs plant. One 0-1 variable forces the fixed cost to be incurred if the plant has any positive throughput. The other forces variable costs to be incurred at a rate of c1 up to M1 before the economy of scale associated with c2 can be achieved.

The outbound flow from each plant is constrained by two parameters. First, the flow from each plant to the markets may not exceed production at that plant. Second, the supply of each company to each market may not exceed the maximal possible demand in that market, which is the parameter a in Table 8.9. Given these capacities and constraints, each company maximizes net revenue, which equals gross revenue minus production costs minus transportation costs. For the Wilson Company, this objective function is given in cell B58 of Table 8.12. For the Richardson Company, it is given in cell B36 of Table 8.13.

The results of our supply and demand analysis at the initial prices of Table 8.10 are given in Table 8.14. The supply to each market is computed by adding the quantities that the two companies want to supply at the given prices. The cells in the delta column equal demand minus supply. As we can see, the supply and demand quantities are far from equilibrium; several markets are either doubly supplied or not supplied at all.

As discussed in the previous subsection, we initiate the tatonnment method using the delta quantities to adjust the prices. The new price vector shown in the right-hand column is computed by adding the delta vector multiplied by 0.00001 to the initial price vector. This parameter was chosen as appropriate for producing a reasonably large change in the prices. The theory underlying convergence of the tatonnement method is to choose a sequence of such parameters that monotonically decrease.

Table 8.14 Results of equilibrium analysis at the initial price vector

	Supply	Initial Price	Demand	Delta	New Price
Chicago	0	0.390	5,087	5087	0.441
St. Louis	7,400	0.348	6,861	–539	0.342
Chattanooga	15,000	0.416	6,585	–8415	0.332
Greensboro	12,000	0.413	11,463	–537	0.408
Altoona	0	0.453	9,527	9527	0.548
Akron	12,000	0.480	4,877	–7123	0.408
Jackson	3,700	0.313	5,980	2280	0.386
Topeka	12,900	0355	7,125	–5775	0.370
Totals	63,000		57,505		

After 13 iterations of the method, we attain a price vector with generally lower prices that still invokes 63,000 total units of supply but only 58,269.85 total units of demand. At this point in the computation, we switch to an ad hoc, manual procedure focused mainly on lowering prices in markets where supply exceeded demand, while making zero price changes in markets where demand exceeded supply. The underlying principle is to lower prices to the point where total industry supply approximately equals total industry demand. Of course, there is no guarantee that the two companies will split the markets perfectly when this occurs, but, at worst, it will provide us with a useful price vector for restarting the tatonnement method.

After approximately 15 additional trial price vectors, we obtain the results given in Table 8.15. In this solution, Greensboro, Altoona, Jackson, and Topeka were served by the Wilson Company, whereas Chicago, St. Louis, Chattanooga, and Akron were served by the Richardson Company. An exact balance of the quantities supplied and demanded in all markets was achieved by changes in the quantities supplied by the two companies to meet the given demands at the given prices. This produced a supply strategy for the Wilson Company that was 0.9% lower in net revenue than the optimal strategy at those prices. The supply strategy for the Richardson Company was 1.4% lower in net revenue than the optimal strategy at those prices. Additional manipulation of the prices might have led to a solution closer to an exact equilibrium, but this was deemed unnecessary for our purposes. In any event, given the structure of the production cost functions, namely, the fixed costs and economies of scale, there is no guarantee that an exact equilibrium exists.

Our computation analysis was fortuitous in that the two companies naturally divided the eight markets. The price equilibrium solution could and probably would be perturbed in that each company would consider raising prices in its dominant markets, thereby acting as a local monopolist in attempting to increase net revenues. A linear programming analysis of the equilibrium solutions for the two companies indicates the extent of the leeway for price manipulation open to each company in each of its dominant markets.

For example, the Wilson Company supplies 11,635 units to Greensboro at a price of $281 per unit. The optimal linear programming solution to the Richardson

Table 8.15 Approximate equilibrium solution

	Supply	Price	Demand	Delta
Chicago (Richardson)	5,750	0.285	5,266	–484
St. Louis (Richardson)	6,750	0.236	7,034	284
Chattanooga (Richardson)	7,500	0.243	6,965	–535
Greensboro (Wilson)	12,000	0.281	11,635	–365
Altoona (Wilson)	10,000	0.337	9,775	–225
Akron (Richardson)	6,000	0.319	5,254	–746
Jackson (Wilson)	6,500	0.201	6,166	–334
Topeka (Wilson)	5,500	0.233	7,357	1857
Totals	60,000		59,452	

Company model obtained by fixing the 0-1 variable at their optimal values indicates that the price on sales of the commodity in Greensboro would have to increase by $28.85 for that market to be attractive to the Richardson Company. This indicates that Wilson could safely increase its price per unit by $10 or $20 without losing sales to Richardson. Of course, price increase would cause decrease in demand. Thus, Wilson should maximize its net revenues with respect to price and quantity up to $309.85 in determining its supply strategy for Greensboro.

8.6

Application of Competitive Analysis in the Forest Products Industry

An approximate version of the method depicted in Figure 8.11 was developed and applied by a forest products company to better understand the markets for its products. We refer to the company as FPC to distinguish it from its competitors. The plants in the forest products industry are typically located near sources of wood and other raw materials. Transportation costs are roughly 25% of total delivered cost, which tends to give each company competitive advantage in markets near their plants.

Equilibrium analysis by FPC was used to divide its markets for each product line (e.g., particleboard, gypsum) into three categories. These categories reflect practical issues of industry price competition, which we cover in detail below, as well as insights gleaned from the equilibrium analysis. Category A referred to markets where FPC was a least-cost supplier; FPC could afford to compete strongly on price in these markets to keep other firms from gaining a larger market share. In addition, to an extent depending on the market and the competition, FPC could control prices offered to its customers in these markets because most or all other suppliers were less efficient in supplying the market. Thus, customers in these markets might be forced to pay a higher than purely competitive price because FPC was a quasi-monopolist supplier to them. More generally, the entire spatially distributed set of markets was supplied by an **oligopoly** of firms, each of which exercised control over its own subset of category A markets.[25]

Category B referred to markets where FPC was not the least-cost supplier, but its delivered cost to those markets was not much higher than that of the least-cost supplier; FPC could look for opportunities to be a secondary supplier to large customers in that market or even a primary supplier based on customer service or quality factors that the least-cost supplier failed to meet. Category C referred to markets where FPC's delivered cost was much higher than that of the least-cost supplier; FPC would not waste marketing and sales efforts in these markets.

Equilibrium analysis was also employed to evaluate the breakeven price for acquiring a new plant. The plant was owned by a small competitor. It was located in the midst of one of FPC's category A regions, about 50 miles from one of its plants.

When the new plant was added to FPC's supply chain model, the increase in net revenues in the equilibrium solution was relatively small because the existing plant had ample capacity for supplying nearby markets. This analysis indicated a low break-even and offer price for the new plant. However, when the new plant was added to the supply chain model of one of FPC's major competitors, the decrease in FPC's maximal net revenues was much larger in magnitude than the previous run. This indicated that FPC should offer a much higher price for the new plant to deny entry of the competitor into category A markets controlled by FPC.

Unfortunately, without a model, the competitor realized the potential benefit of acquiring the new plant, and snapped it up before FPC could translate its analysis into an offer. The equilibrium model was just being implemented when the new plant came onto the market. The failure to act should not be viewed as a deficiency of modeling, but rather, it illustrates the importance of having permanent analytical tools in place to evaluate strategic options as they present themselves.

Practical Issues of Price Competition

The application just reviewed of price competition in the forest products industry required resolution of several practical issues arising in the creation and solution of data-driven models. The theoretical equilibrium model of price competition described above that served as the analytical base for the study was an idealization of reality, much more so than supply chain optimization models of individual firms. In addition, the implemented model was constructed from an industry database that was less accurate than the supply chain decision database of FPC, the company performing the analysis. Using terms from economics, the application involved **externalities** that needed to be imposed on the equilibrium solution, and it used **imperfect information** in creating its descriptions of supplier and consumer behavior.

In the paragraphs that follow, we discuss four practical issues that affected FPC's equilibrium analysis. The issues merit discussion because they are relevant to any data-driven equilibrium analysis.

1. *Compilation of industry data.* To perform an equilibrium analysis for a line of forest products, FPC required data from which to construct supply chain models for each of approximately 10 other firms competing for sales of the given line. Although transportation rates were publicly available, manufacturing cost and capacity data for each plant operated by these firms were not. Such data were amassed by deducing details from published industry association reports, informal discussions with employees of competing firms, and information gleaned from former employees of the other firms, some of whom worked for FPC. Clearly, these data were somewhat inaccurate. But, FPC had no interest in industrial espionage, which seemed unnecessary as well as immoral and illegal. The analysts performing the study at FPC believed the data in-hand were good enough for their purposes, which were to qualitatively as well as quantitatively partition the markets into the three categories discussed above.

2. *Representations of market demand.* In developing the scheme of Figure 8.11, we assumed that market research would be performed to develop market response functions. This would have been a major undertaking that was beyond the resources of the equilibrium analysis study. Instead, for each product line, FPC treated price and demand in each market as fixed and given and computed an equilibrium in which the firms competed for this demand at the given prices. In economic parlance, demand was treated as inelastic. In addition, in each market, the price was imposed by the oligopolist firm (or firms) dominating that market.

3. *Treatment of imperfect markets.* With pure price competition, one would expect for some or many geographic markets that one firm would capture 100% of the market. There is because nothing in the pure model prevents a firm from fully exploiting its favorable position. In reality, it has been widely observed for markets of forest products that no firm can expect to capture more than 50% of the demand in any market. This externality of imperfect markets was explicitly imposed as constraints in the net revenue maximizing model for each firm. There are several explanations for the limit. First, many large customers will buy from two, three, or even four suppliers as a hedge against uncertainties, rather than buy 100% of their requirements from the least-cost supplier. In addition, nonprice factors such as quality, customer service, credit terms, and sales ability were known to have an impact, albeit a secondary one, on customer demand. These factors reflect the fact that the markets were not entirely homogeneous. Small product and service differences affected sales in specific segments; for example, particleboard sales to furniture manufacturers versus those to building construction companies.

4. *Use of mixed integer programming.* The supply chain models that described each firm's net revenue maximizing decisions were mixed integer programming models, which employed 0-1 variables to capture fixed costs and economies of scale associated with manufacturing. The mathematical properties of such models violate assumptions needed for the existence of equilibrium. To illustrate the difficulty, consider a situation where product prices in some markets are higher than marginal delivered costs but, due to plant fixed costs, not high enough to induce another nonoperating plant in some firm to become operational. The gap between supply and demand prices and quantities due to this imperfection might be small, however, especially in cases such as the markets for a forest product that is manufactured in 30 plants located across the United States and Canada. In other words, the nonexistence of an exact equilibrium would not be a serious practical deficiency of the competitive analysis.

8.7 Decision Trees and Stochastic Programming

During earlier discussions of models for strategic and tactical supply chain planning in this and earlier chapters, we underscored the need to optimize over multiple databases, each corresponding to a scenario describing a different realization of the company's uncertain future. Key uncertainties shaping the scenarios include demand for finished products, costs of raw materials, or the performance of new manufacturing technologies. Although reasons for considering diverse scenarios are intuitively clear, we have not yet discussed methods for systematically identifying and constructing them. Moreover, we have been vague about methods for formulating strategies from the results of multiple scenario optimizations, suggesting only that managerial judgment needed to be invoked.

Our goals in this section and the next two are to examine more rigorous methods for creating and analyzing models incorporating multiple scenarios and more explicit treatment of uncertainty. The methods involve two, overlapping disciplines: **stochastic programming** and a relatively new field of strategy analysis called **scenario planning.**[26] A high-level view of their connections is depicted in Figure 8.12. When employing a **deterministic model,** we address uncertainty by separately analyzing N different scenarios, each corresponding to a distinct database and data substantiated model. We presume scenario planning was employed in creating these scenarios. For each model run, these data are treated by the model as certain to occur, hence the term *deterministic.* By its nature, deterministic optimization cannot identify plans that hedge against risks.

As shown in Figure 8.12, a stochastic programming model, which more fully examines uncertainties and risks, may be constructed from a deterministic optimization model by expanding it to simultaneously consider multiple scenarios. In particular, the stochastic programming model computes an optimal contingency plan for each scenario and a here-and-now plan that optimally hedges against them. The probabilities of occurrence associated with each scenario are also taken into account by the optimization. Specifically, the model's objective function is the minimization of total *expected* supply chain costs or the maximization of total *expected* net revenues. For example, if net revenues of R_1, R_2, R_3 will be realized for each of three

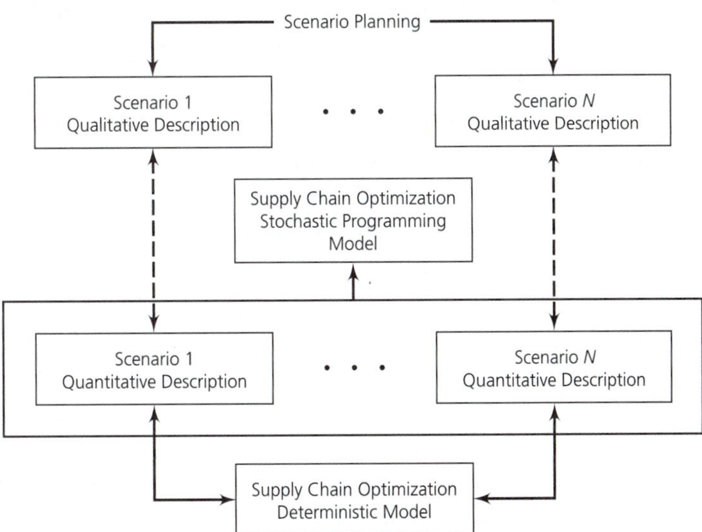

Figure 8.12
Stochastic programming and scenario planning

scenarios with probabilities p_1, p_2, p_3, the model seeks to maximize ($p_1 * R_1 + p_2 * R_2 + p_3 * R_3$).

Also as shown in Figure 8.12, there is a loose but important connection between stochastic programming and scenario planning. The aim of scenario planning is to assist senior management of a firm in defining scenarios of the firm's future that are consistent, plausible, and comprehensive. The methodology employs processes intended to expand its thinking about the future and to achieve consensus about which strategies to pursue. Scenario planning is discussed in Section 8.9.

From a methodological viewpoint, stochastic programming models combine decision trees describing an uncertain future with linear or mixed integer programming models describing resource acquisition and allocation decisions.[27] Decision trees were originally devised in the 1950s as an adjunct to utility theory, which provides an axiomatic framework characterizing decision making in the face of uncertainty. This theory formalizes a rational decision maker's attitudes toward the risks inherent in an uncertain future. It is not intended to provide pragmatic, data-driven models that managers can employ to enhance insights about important decisions. Nevertheless, modeling systems based on decision analysis have been developed and used in a number of important applications.

Stochastic programming was devised independently in the late 1950s as a natural extension of linear programming. At the most abstract level, its mathematical properties are very complex, requiring a rigorous integration of probability theory and mathematical programming. A central theoretical issue is how to transform uncertainties described by a multivariable continuous distribution into a finite number of scenarios, thereby permitting a finite mathematical programming model to be created and solved.

As a practical matter, stochastic programming models have not yet been widely applied. The time is ripe for such applications because an increasing number of deterministic models are being implemented and used. In considering such applications, we can sometimes ignore knotty theoretical complications, although combining complex statistical models with mathematical programming remains challenging.

Decision Trees

We begin by examining the decision tree depicted in Figure 8.13. For the purposes of discussion, we have chosen a tree that represents decisions and random occurrences associated with the development and marketing of a new product. The square nodes in the tree, which are called **states,** correspond to data characterizing the system at points in time just before decisions are made. For the moment, we treat decisions in a qualitative manner; we will use mathematical programming constructs to describe the decision space when we present stochastic programming in the following subsection. The round nodes, which are called **chance nodes,** correspond to points in time when random events occur.

The tree addresses immediate and future decisions regarding the new product. For the state at the top of the tree, management makes decisions about the development of the new product; for example, about the research strategy, budget, person-

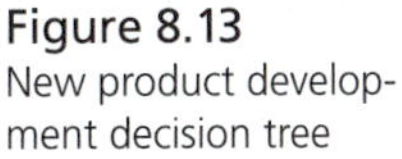
Figure 8.13
New product development decision tree

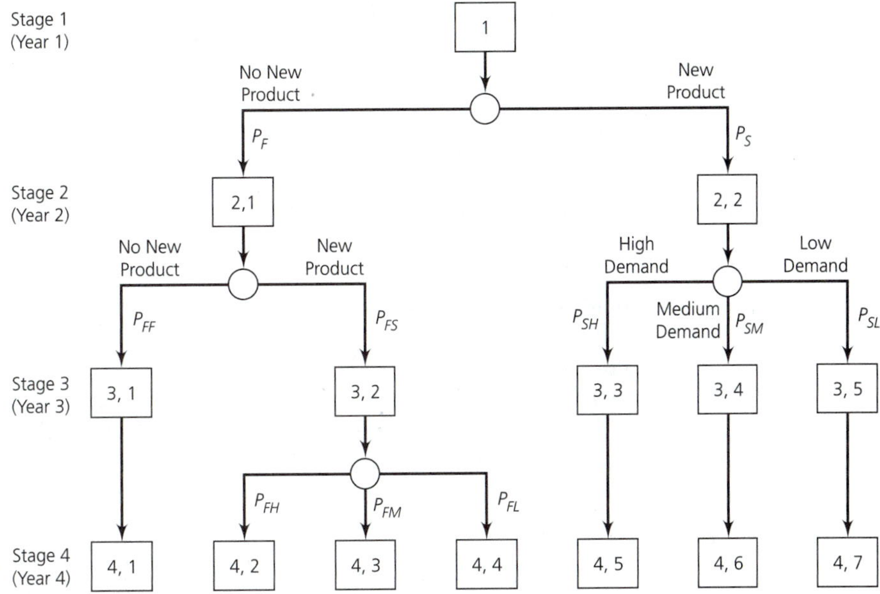

nel, equipment, and so on. These decisions are made at stage 1, the beginning of year 1. By the end of the year, one of two uncertain outcomes will be observed: No new product has been developed (failure), or the new product has been developed (success). As shown in the figure, analysis and managerial judgment has assessed the probabilities p_F and p_S of these two outcomes, where $p_F + p_S = 1$.

Moreover, the tree depicts two possible states at stage 2, the beginning of year 2. These are represented as decision nodes labeled 2,1 and 2,2, which are linked, respectively, to decisions regarding a renewed effort to develop the new product or decisions regarding manufacturing and marketing of the new product. As before, the uncertain outcomes are revealed at the end of the year.

For state 2,1, the outcomes revealed at the end of the year are that no new product has been developed, or the new product has been developed. The probabilities associated with these outcomes are p_{FF} and p_{FS} with the property $p_{FF} + p_{FS} = 1$. The probabilities of success and failure in the new product development are different than at the end of the first year because the company failed in its initial efforts. It may be that $p_{FF} > p_F$ because initial failure bodes poorly for ultimate success. Or, it may be that $p_{FF} < p_F$ because product developers have gained valuable insights from their research efforts during the first year. Finally, if may be that $p_{FF} = p_F$ if failure in the first year has no bearing on the probability of research success in the second year. For state 2,2, the uncertain outcomes at the end of the year are represented by high, medium, and low market demand for the new product with probabilities p_{SH}, p_{SM}, and p_{SL}, where $p_{SH} + p_{SM} + p_{SL} = 1$.

As a result of random occurrences observed at the end of stage 2, the company finds itself in one of the five states at stage 3, the beginning of year 3. The probabilities of being in the five states at stage 3 are multiplicative combinations of the first and second stage probabilities. For example, the probability that the company finds itself in state 3,1 at stage 3 is given by

$$p_{31} = p_F * p_{FF}$$

Similar calculations can be performed to compute $p_{32}, p_{33}, p_{34},$ and $p_{35}.$

As shown in Figure 8.13, we assume the company accepts ultimate failure in state 3,1 and makes no further effort to develop the new product. By contrast, for state 3,2, the company makes decisions about manufacturing and marketing the new product. The decision options and the decisions made may be different from those associated with state 2,2 because the product is being marketing 1 year later. Finally, the right-hand side of the tree depicts the assumption that once market demand is revealed at the end of year 2, no further uncertainties are involved. We terminate the tree at stage 4 (the start of year 4) because the major uncertainties have been totally revealed.

In making its decisions, the company seeks to maximize the expected, discounted value of its net revenues over the life of the product. Expected sales after stage 4 (the start of year 4) are discounted back to the seven possible states shown in Figure 8.13. Using the probabilities listed in Table 8.16, we illustrate the computations in Table 8.17.

In Table 8.17, we display a spreadsheet for computing the total expected discounted net present value (measured in millions of dollars) of an optimal strategy for the new product development. We assume that the decisions taken at each of the 15 states in the tree of Figure 8.13 were chosen to be optimal; namely, over all possible decision strategies from that state forward in time, they serve to maximize future expected discounted net value. For each state before stage 4, we show in the spreadsheet (1) the net revenue accruing to the company over the coming year as the result of being in that state and making optimal decisions, (2) the probability that the system finds itself in that state at the start of the coming year, (3) the factor discounting future revenues back to the start of year 1 according to a yearly rate of 0.80, and, in the final column, (4) the contribution of the firm's activities to the total discounted net revenue. For the states in stage 4, we have shown the discounted revenue stream over the remaining 3 years life of the product.

For example, the revenue of –8 (a cost of \$8 million) associated with state 1 is the cost of research on the new product in the first year. The revenue of –6 associated with state 2,1 is the cost of continuing research during the second year, whereas the revenue of –5 associated with state 2,2 is the cost of initiating manufacture and distribution of the new product. Finally, the net revenue of 20 associated with the state 3,3 is the payback in the third year from sales of the product under the high-demand scenario.

Table 8.16 Probabilities for decision tree new product analysis

Probability	p_F	p_S	p_{FF}	p_{FS}	p_{SH}	p_{SM}	p_{SL}	p_{FH}	p_{FM}	p_{FL}
Value	0.5	0.5	0.4	0.6	0.3	0.4	0.3	0.2	0.5	0.3

Table 8.17 Total expected discounted net value calculation in new product analysis

State	Net Revenue	Probability	Disc. Factor	Exp. Dis. NPV[a]
1	−8	1.00	1	−8.0000
2,1	−6	0.50	0.8	−2.4000
2,2	−5	0.50	0.8	−2.0000
3,1	0	0.20	0.64	0.0000
3,2	−5	0.30	0.64	−0.9600
3,3	20	0.15	0.64	1.9200
3,4	12	0.20	0.64	1.5360
3,5	8	0.15	0.64	0.7680
4,1	0	0.20	0.512	0.0000
4,2	48.8	0.06	0.512	1.4991
4,3	36.96	0.15	0.512	2.8385
4,4	24.64	0.09	0.512	1.1354
4,5	48.8	0.15	0.512	3.7478
4,6	36.96	0.20	0.512	3.7847
4,7	24.64	0.15	0.512	1.8924
Total				5.7620

[a]NPV = net present value.

According to Table 8.17, the optimal strategy yields an expected discounted net revenue of \$5.762 million. Our assumption was that the company set out to maximize this sum, despite the possibility that it might lose money in some scenarios. To put the risks in perspective, we have delineated in Table 8.18 the seven scenarios implicit in the decision tree, their discounted returns, and their probabilities of occurrence. Each scenario represents a realization of the random occurrences starting at state 1 and ending up at one of the seven possible states at stage 4.

We see from these data that the maximal expected discounted net revenue of the new product development is achieved by averaging over a collection of scenarios with a wide range of discounted net present values. For example, there is a 0.20 probability that the company will show a loss of \$12.8 million and a 0.29 overall probability

Table 8.18 Scenario payoffs in new product analysis

Number	Scenario	Disc. NPV	Probability
1	(1), (2,1), (3,1), (4,1)	−12.800	0.20
2	(1), (2,1), (3,2), (4,2)	8.990	0.06
3	(1), (2,1), (3,2), (4,3)	2.920	0.15
4	(1), (2,1), (3,2), (4,4)	−3.380	0.09
5	(1), (2,2), (3,3), (4,3)	25.790	0.15
6	(1), (2,2), (3,4), (4,4)	14.600	0.20
7	(1), (2,2), (3,5), (4,5)	5.740	0.15

that they will show some loss. Conversely, if all goes well, there is a 0.15 probability that the company will realize a gain of $25.79 million.

The dispersion, or variance, of the discounted NPVs of the seven scenario reflects the risks faced by management in undertaking the new product development. If the company is large and financially secure, with hundreds of millions of dollars in cash reserves, the risks of the new product development just discussed are very small. On the other hand, if the company is small and financially insecure, the new product development plan as structured in the decision tree may be unacceptable because the probability of being forced into bankruptcy by a failed project is too great. In such a case, we say the company is **risk averse.** It might then choose to restructure the plan by bringing in a cash-rich partner who could, in essence, insure the company against the worst-case scenarios in exchange for a hefty portion of the net revenues from the successful scenarios.

For a given application such as the one just reviewed, the decision tree may reflect a finite number of scenarios extracted from a statistical model. An example is a demand forecasting model that employs historical company sales, growth forecasts for the company's industry, and the national economies where it sells products. Or, it might be a model that forecasts learning effects (cost, manufacturing efficiency) for new products using historical data describing learning that occurred for similar products. We call these **objective uncertainties** because the probabilities associated with scenarios are derived from objective data.

The decision tree may also reflect uncertain events that are not readily forecast using statistical methods; for example, the passage of stringent, new product, environmental, or safety legislation that would cause significant increases in manufacturing costs. We call these **subjective uncertainties** because there is little or no historical data available to assess probabilities. Instead, human judgment, which should be that of experts in the areas of uncertainty, serves as the basis for forecasts of the future and assessments of scenario probabilities.[28]

Finally, although it may be a stretch, a decision tree may also roughly incorporate events that are unforeseen. Consider, for example, the likelihood of a prediction in 1985 by a defense aircraft company that the Soviet Union would suddenly collapse by 1991, which would obviously have a powerful effect on the company's strategy. Obviously, such a specific unforeseen event could not be articulated. Still, by brainstorming with management, the scenario planner might include generic unforeseen events in the decision tree; for the example just cited, the event might have been labeled "radical reduction in the cold war by 1995."

An Inventory Example of Stochastic Programming

We were deliberately vague in describing how decisions were made in the decision tree in Figure 8.13. We attempt to remedy this deficiency by considering a stochastic programming model for which the decision nodes in a decision tree are optimization models. As such, the model is a natural extension of deterministic supply chain optimization models studied previously that analyze manufacturing and distribution decisions for a family of products with seasonal demands.

For the purposes of discussion, we introduce stochastic programming by considering the tactical planning problem of managing a company's inventories in the face of seasonal demand uncertainty. In particular, we assume that finished product demands for the first three quarters of the coming year are known quite accurately but that demand during the peak fourth quarter is characterized by three distinct scenarios, high (H), medium (M), and low (L). The probabilities associated with these scenarios are, respectively, p_H, p_M, and p_L, where $p_H + p_M + p_L = 1$.

The company must decide at the start of the first quarter of the year how it will plan for the peak season. Although manufacturing capacity is not severely strained during any of the first three quarters, the company finds that it needs the entire 9 months to build up sufficient inventories for the fourth quarter surge. The supply chain manager wishes to create and apply a stochastic programming model at the start of the year to help determine **hedging plans** for inventory that will be made available at the end of the third quarter. At the same time, he will use the model to help devise **contingency plans** for exploiting these inventories and otherwise meeting demands associated with each of the three scenarios in the fourth quarter. The objective is to maximize expected net revenues over the four quarters. We emphasize that the hedging and contingency plans that accomplish this are optimized together by the model. A numerical version of this problem was presented in Section 3.5.

Note that analysis by stochastic programming provides a broad, systems analysis view of tactical inventory planning. It reflects linkages across the entire supply chain, such as production capacities, transportation distances and costs, raw material costs, and a host of other factors. In contrast is the classical inventory theory that we discuss in Chapter 11; it focuses on single-item operational inventory plans that ignore these supply chain complications.

The logic of the stochastic programming analysis is depicted in Figure 8.14 where the rectangular nodes represent data describing finished product inventories available at the end of each quarter and other data relevant to the quarter's plan. Recall that these ending inventories are also inventories available at the beginning of the ensuing period. The inventories describe the state of the supply chain system at those points in time. The triangles represent decisions regarding production and distribution available to the company during each period under each scenario. We assume these are represented by an optimization model.

As shown in the figure, the company faces three scenarios defined by the demand realized in stage 4. For the sake of discussion, we assume sales data and other information from late in the third quarter and early in the fourth quarter allow the marketing department to determine early in the fourth quarter which of the three demand patterns have occurred. We will return to further examine this assumption after we have discussed the example.

We elaborate on how optimal hedging and contingency plans are made by focusing on the inventory balance equations at the end of the fourth quarter. Again for the sake of discussion, we assume that markets are served directly from the plants. In addition, each market must be sole sourced for all products; that is, each market must receive all its volume for all products from exactly one plant. Thus, all products may be sold from any given plant, either by manufacturing the product there or by transshipping the product from another plant to the given plant.

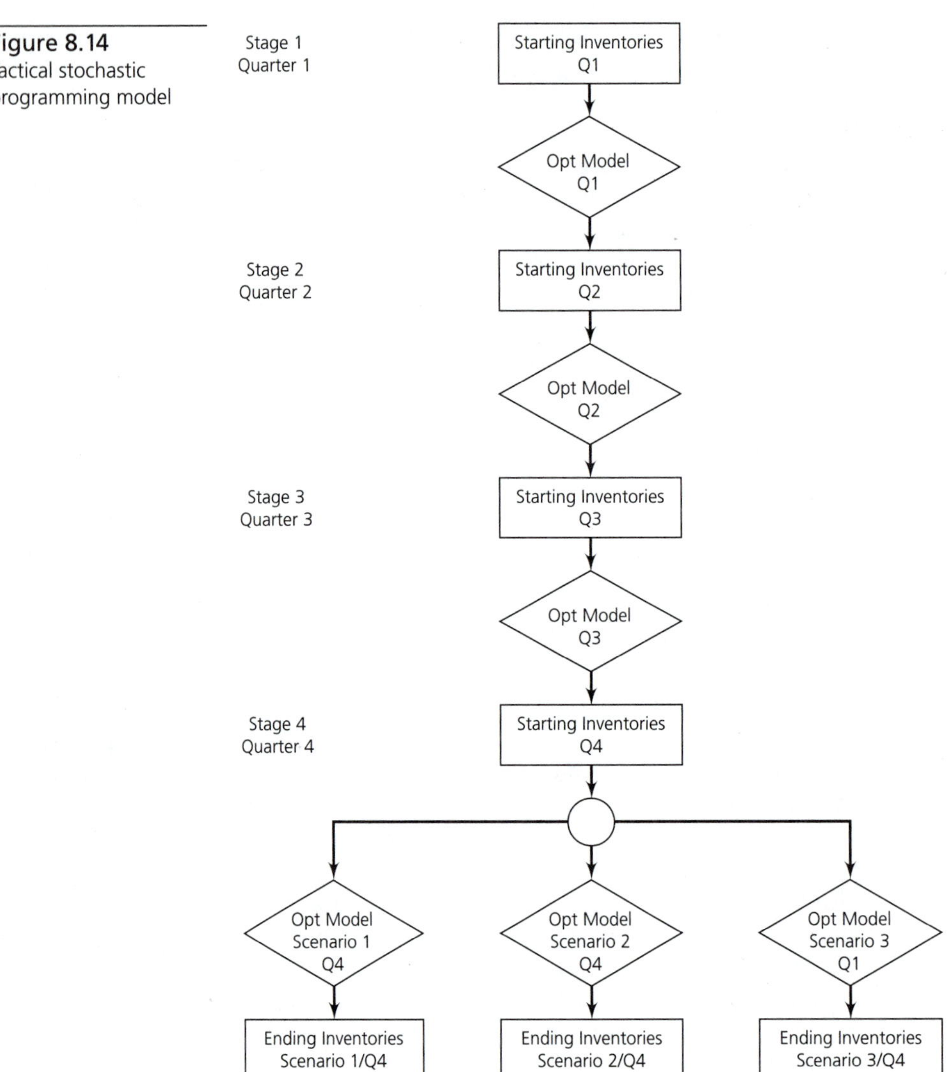

Figure 8.14
Tactical stochastic programming model

With this background, we define the following **hedging decision variables:**

I_{jk3} = inventory of product j on hand at plant k at the start of the fourth quarter

Similarly, for each scenario s, we define the following **contingency decision variables:**

M_{jk4s} = quantity of product j manufactured at plant k in the fourth quarter under scenario s

R_{jk4s} = quantity of product j received at plant k from other plants in the fourth quarter under scenario s

W_{jk4s} = quantity of product j manufactured at plant k sent to other plants in the fourth quarter under scenario s

Q_{jk4s} = quantity of product j sold from plant k in the fourth quarter under scenario s

D_{jk4s} = demand for product j assigned to plant k in the fourth quarter under scenario s (assignment determined by the stochastic programming model)

I_{jk4s} = inventory of product j on hand at plant k at the end of the fourth quarter under scenario s

For each product j, each plant k and each fourth quarter scenario s, the hedging variables and the contingency variables are linked by the following **inventory balance equations:**

$$I_{jk4s} = I_{jk3} + M_{jk4s} + R_{jk4s} - W_{jk4s} - Q_{jk4s}$$

This equation states that inventory at the end of the fourth quarter equals inventory at the end of the third quarter (beginning of the fourth quarter) plus production plus shipments from other plants minus shipments to other plants minus sales. It is important to note that the *same* quantities I_{jk3} of inventory of product j at plant k are available to *all* scenarios s at the end of the third quarter. The stochastic programming model determines the values of these variables as hedges against uncertain demand for the fourth quarter. If the sum of inventories for each product across all plants is too high, the company runs the risk of not being able to sell it all at full price. Conversely, if inventory is too low, the company runs the risk of losing profitable sales. Moreover, if deployment of the I_{jk3} across the plants is inefficient, the company will incur unnecessary transshipment costs due to numerous variables R_{jk4s} and W_{jk4s} at positive, high values.

To examine further how the hedging inventory decision variables I_{jk3} are complemented by the contingency decision variables, we use the fact that the inventory variables I_{jk4s} at the end of the fourth quarter for each scenario s must be nonnegative. In other words, the company cannot sell what it does not have. Again, for the sake of discussion, we assume excess product demand cannot be backlogged. This implies the following **supply chain sales constraint:**

$$Q_{jk4s} \leq I_{jk3} + M_{jk4s} + R_{jk4s} - W_{jk4s}$$

Thus, under scenario s, sales of product j out of plant k in the fourth quarter cannot exceed the sum of hedging inventory available at the start of the quarter plus the quantity manufactured at plant k or received there from other plants minus the quantity shipped to other plants. In addition, we have the following **marketing sales constraint:**

$$Q_{jk4s} \leq D_{jk4s}$$

This constraint says that sales of product j from plant k under scenario s cannot exceed the demand assigned to that plant.

In examining these two types of sales constraints on Q_{jk4_s}, the quantity of product j sold from plant k under scenario s, we see from the supply chain sales constraints that low values of the hedging inventory I_{jk3} at plant k and at other plants will cause those constraints to be binding for many products and plants under scenario s regardless of how we select values for the contingency decision variables. This implies that $Q_{jk4_s} < D_{jk4_s}$ in the marketing sales constraints for many products and plants for scenario s, which indicates lost sales.

Conversely, high values of the hedging inventory I_{jk3} at plant k and at other plants will cause the marketing sales constraints to be binding for many products and plants for scenario s regardless of how we select values for the contingency variables because they do not affect those constraints. Therefore, we will have $Q_{jk4_s} < I_{jk3} + M_{jk4_s} + R_{jk4_s} - W_{jk4_s}$ for many products and plants for scenario s, which indicates from the inventory balance equations that ending inventories I_{jk4_s}, which are the difference between the left- and right-hand sides of this inequality, will be too large for many products and plants. This situation can only be rectified by selling the product at a deep discount or by holding the product for an uneconomically long time.

The objective function driving the company's plan for the coming year is to maximize expected net revenues. Letting

R_t = net revenue for quarter t ($t = 1,2,3$)

R_{4_s} = net revenue for quarter 4 for scenario s ($s = H, M, L$)

the sum to be maximized is

$$R_1 + R_2 + R_3 + p_H * R_{4H} + p_M * R_{4M} + p_L * R_{4L}$$

The net revenue terms for each quarter may be discounted to reflect the time value of money.

We argued above that firms may be risk averse when planning in the face of uncertainty, especially if the uncertain returns may be large relative to the assets of the company. Thus, a strategy that maximizes net revenues may be deemed too risky if certain scenarios are particularly unattractive. An effective method for modeling such concerns is to add constraints to the stochastic programming model that reject overly risky plans. For example, we might add **risk constraint** for all s of the following form:

$$R_{4_s} \geq R_{4,\text{ target}}$$

which states that the return under any scenario s must be at least as great as $R_{4,\text{target}}$. Such constraint may only be binding for the low demand scenario ($s = L$), but even just one binding constraint will affect all scenarios by limiting feasible values on the hedging inventory variables I_{jk3}. This illustrates how we ensure performance in unfavorable scenarios by giving up potential gain in favorable scenarios.

The illustrative model just discussed had two major stages: a **here-and-now stage** encompassing the first three quarters during which demand was known with certainty and a **recourse stage** during which alternate contingency plans may be activated. In general, stochastic programming allows several recourse stages describing the iterative revelation of major uncertainties.

Such multiple-recourse stage models are conceptually richer than two-stage models because they allow plans to be formulated that entail the gathering of information about uncertainties as well as the evolution of hedging and contingency plans. For example, we might have incorporated two stages of recourse in the inventory model just discussed. The first recourse stage might have focused on supply chain and marketing activities during the tenth month of the year to better forecast and plan for the remainder of the peak selling season, which would be modeled as the final 2 months of the year.

A complication that was glossed over in the above example was the construction of the three scenarios and their associated probabilities. Stochastic demands are typically characterized by continuous and sometimes multivariate probability distributions. Procedures for extracting a finite set of consistent and meaningful scenarios from such distributions is a difficult and ongoing area of basic research. Finally, we point out that stochastic programming can be applied to other areas of supply chain planning under uncertainty including evaluations of new technologies and products, hedging against the cost of raw materials, and the growth of new markets in developing countries.

8.8

Supply Chain Strategies for Managing Product Variety

In the previous section, we discussed how inventories hedge against uncertain demand by balancing the risks of excessive ending inventories against the risks of backlogged or lost sales. We used stochastic programming to highlight the problems and decision options from the perspective of the complete supply chain. In this section, we specialize our analysis to the following three strategies involving uncertain demands as they affect and are affected by product variety:

- Exploit component commonality and postponement of product differentiation
- Assemble differentiated products from vanilla boxes
- Implement quick response to early sales

Applied research into stochastic programming modeling of all three strategies has been performed, although not yet decisively as part of a system for analyzing industrial strength problems.[29] Practically speaking, deterministic linear and mixed integer programming models can also provide very useful insights about these strategies while we await the maturation of more powerful stochastic programming methods.

Depending on the industry and the situation, other strategies might be appropriate for mitigating the risks of uncertain demand in other situations. New manufacturing technologies that reduce setup times can decrease the size of economic production runs and inventories and make it easier and less expensive for the company to respond quickly to unexpected shifts in demand. Integration of production scheduling and planning models with order-taking processes allows the company to promise shipping dates that can be met with greater reliability. At the same time, such integration provides production managers with early warnings that short- and medium-term demand has shifted significantly from its forecasted amounts.

Exploit Component Commonality and Postponement of Product Differentiation

Many durable industrial and consumer products, such as radar equipment and computers, are assembled and sold in product lines where individual products share many components, often in different ratios. Assembly may take place over several final stages but still constitute a small portion of the products' overall manufacturing cost and time. These can be distinct make-to-stock products or differentiated assemble-to-order products, although the differences may not be clear-cut. The perception by a customer or a consumer that two products are distinct or variations of one another depends on the extent of the commonality and the marketing of the products.

The use of common components reduces, but does not eliminate, difficulties in production planning due to demand uncertainty. At the start of each period of a rolling multiperiod planning horizon, the production manager must decide how to allocate her current inventory of common components to the assembly of finished products. The lengths of the planning periods are typically 1 week to 1 month. The manager must also decide when to order more of these components and the quantities to order. Assuming unmet demand is backlogged, the objective of production planning is to minimize the sum of inventory holding costs, backlogging costs, and avoidable assembly costs, such as overtime, over the multiperiod planning horizon.

The difficulty in resolving this planning problem depends on the length of lead times for obtaining components and the volatility and correlations of product demands. In the unfavorable case when lead times are long and product demands are highly volatile, the production manager can expect that when components finally arrive, her needs will be significantly different from the forecasted amounts. Moreover, if product demands have positive correlations, demand for all products in the product line will tend to shift up or down together. Thus, the shifts may not significantly cancel one another, which fosters either a serious shortage or overabundance of components. Stochastic programming models have been developed and tested to determine component replenishment and assembly strategies that optimally hedge against demand uncertainties reflected by a joint distribution of demands for finished products.[30]

Assemble Differentiated Products from Vanilla Boxes

A **vanilla box** is a semifinished product that is assembled into differentiated final products after customer orders for those final products have been received. Strategies for manufacturing vanilla boxes and assembling their differentiated products are a special case of strategies for exploiting component commonality, discussed in the previous subsection. In effect, the vanilla box is a single common component. As a well-defined special case, it promotes the invention of models for optimizing product design as well as for optimizing assembly strategies.

The vanilla box approach has been employed extensively in the computer industry. For example, manufacturers of mainframe computers and workstations produce vanilla boxes that are customized for each customer. Due to the cost of mainframe computers, one manufacturer allowed customers (companies) to modify their customization after the order had been placed, sometimes long after it had been placed. This caused considerable conflict among computer salespeople and production managers in trying to stabilize assembly operations. A vanilla box being customized for company B, with delivery in 4 weeks, might suddenly become suitable for company A, with delivery in 1 week, because company A changed its specifications. The original vanilla box being customized for company A might be suitable for another specific customer, or it might be held in inventory until another company requests the same or similar customization. Thus, it might pay to reassign the computer of company B to company A and customize another vanilla box for customer B.

As one can imagine, the number of possible combinations to be examined in assigning and reassigning vanilla boxes to customers were daunting. The biggest cost of reassignment was the testing of reconfigured computers. A computer customized and tested for company A might require only minor changes in its configuration to meet a change requested by company A, or be shipped instead to company B, but it would first need to undergo extensive retesting. To rationalize treatment of these complications, the computer manufacturer commissioned the implementation of an optimization modeling system called Order Assignment and Re-assignment System (OARS). As depicted in Figure 8.15, OARS would be used, for example, when company B decided to change its specifications. Assuming that the new specifications resembled those of company A, the system might reassign box 2 to company

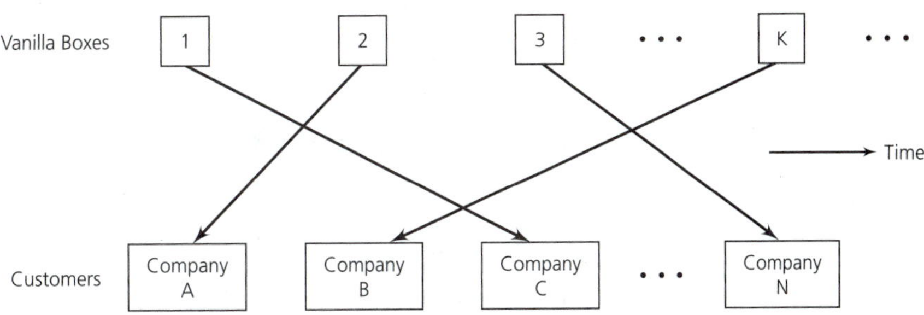

Figure 8.15
Order assignment and reassignment system

B, box 1 to company A, and box K to company C, while leaving all other assignments unchanged.

Once implemented and validated, OARS was exercised several times a week by an analyst at the mainframe assembly plant responsible for coordinating order reassignments among the salespeople and the production managers. Given a list of previous assignments, new boxes to be assigned, and customized order changes over a specified planning horizon, the system generated and optimized an assignment model that assigned or reassigned a unique vanilla or partially customized box to each customer to meet all promised delivery dates. The objective function was to minimize total avoidable retesting time associated with reassignments. A program was created for the application that computed the retest time required if a specific box, either a vanilla box or one that was already customized, was reassigned to customer J. By identifying the most costly reassignments, OARS provided the salespeople with information that could be used to ask companies to push back their delivery dates. Needless to say, these suggestions were not always made or accepted.

In general, a company selling a range of assemble-to-order products will manufacture more than one vanilla box. This flexibility is needed if different make-to-order products require different assembly sequences for combining components before reaching the final assembly stage. Models have been developed to analyze the design of vanilla boxes as well as their use in operational planning. Each design is specified by a bill-of-material listing the number of components in the given box. The designs must be evaluated in terms of their operational performance. Typical design and operational decisions include the following:

- How many vanilla box designs should be used and what are their bills-of-material?
- Given a forecast of demand for finished products over a finite planning horizon, how many of each type of vanilla boxes should we plan to assemble in each period?
- Given a forecast of demand for finished products over a finite planning horizon, how should vanilla boxes be allocated to finished products in each period?
- Given a forecast of demand for finished products over a finite planning horizon, what is an optimal schedule for manufacturing parts and components for the vanilla boxes or acquiring them from vendors?

We expect that research into deterministic optimization and stochastic programming models for this important class of manufacturing planning problems will continue and that successful applications will result from these efforts.

Implement Quick Response to Early Sales

For products with short life cycles, such as fashion apparel, personal computers, and automobiles, effective integration of production, inventory, and sales is arduous. Supply chain planning for a company in the fashion apparel industry is particularly challenging. Each year, the company introduces newly designed products that must be manufactured in time for sale during a short retailing season. Moreover, the difference in sales volumes and revenues between popular and unpopular items, which are difficult to identify before the season begins, are great. A further complication is that design, manufacturing, and sales activities are spread over countries on several continents. Thus, the company is faced with long lead times between the commitment to start production and the attainment of sufficient inventories for the retailing season.

In this subsection, we review processes and planning approaches called **quick response** that apparel companies have devised to deal with demand volatility over short, intensive periods. In modified form, these developments are appropriate for companies in other industries. Our discussion is focused on successful modeling analysis developed to support quick response at Sport Obermeyer, a skiwear designer and manufacturer.[31]

Company Background. Sport Obermeyer designs and manufacturers fashion skiwear that is sold in specialty ski shops throughout the United States. Their products include parkas, pants, suits, shells, jackets, sweaters, turtlenecks, and accessories. They redesign over 95% of their products each year, with changes in patterns, fabrics, and colors. Approximately 350 style/color combinations are manufactured each year. Production of components and garments is done outside the United States at supplier locations in Hong Kong, China, Korea, Jamaica, and Bangladesh. Completed garments are shipped to Seattle and then sent by truck to the company's warehouse in Denver. Shipments of individual orders are packaged and sent via carrier to the retail stores.

Supply chain and sales planning at Sport Obermeyer follow the yearly time line shown in Figure 8.16. The time line includes modifications to planning processes that were made to accommodate and exploit the modeling analysis discussed below. Starting at the left, the company makes initial commitments to about 40% of its projected production on November 1 of the previous year. This first stage of production begins around January 1. During the period between February 15 and May 31, the retailers preview the fall garments and place about 90% of their orders for the year. Many of the orders are received shortly after the annual fashion show in Las

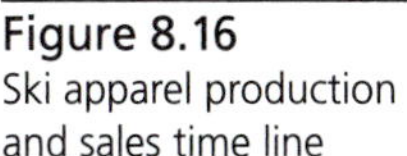
Figure 8.16
Ski apparel production and sales time line

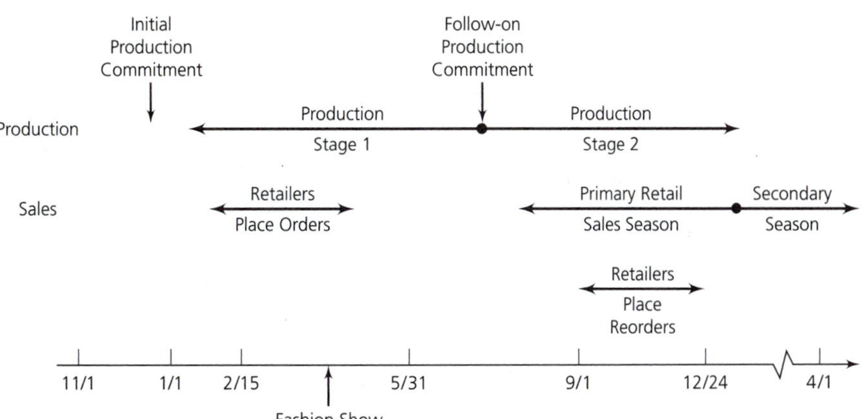

Vegas, held in the middle of March. As we discuss below, Obermeyer updates its forecasts based on orders received and then determines plans for the second stage of production, which constitutes about 50% of total production.

As shown in Figure 8.16, the primary retail sales seasons stretches from September 1 to December 24. About 10% of the goods sold for the year are sent to the retailers during the period October 1 through December 24 as reorders from inventory. Finally, during the period between December 24 and April 1 of the following year, surplus apparel are sold at discounts.

Descriptive and Normative Models. With the help of consultants, Obermeyer developed a two-stage stochastic programming analysis of their yearly production and sales planning. A key element in this analysis was a descriptive model that forecast demand based on the first 20% of demand for the new year's products received from the retailers during March. Previously, Obermeyer had developed initial forecasts based on historical data, which were largely irrelevant because the products change each year and the use of expert judgment regarding the new product line. The new forecasting model treated sales of each product in the first and second stages as a bivariate normal distribution with correlations between first and second stage demands. The correlation coefficients turned out to be quite high, around to 0.8 to 0.9 for most products, which indicated that first-stage demand information is valuable in predicting demand during the second stage.[32] The insights provided by the new forecasting model are displayed in Figure 8.17; the movement of points toward the 45° (perfect forecasts) line in the right-hand figure relative to the left-hand figure indicate the quality and importance of the forecasts.

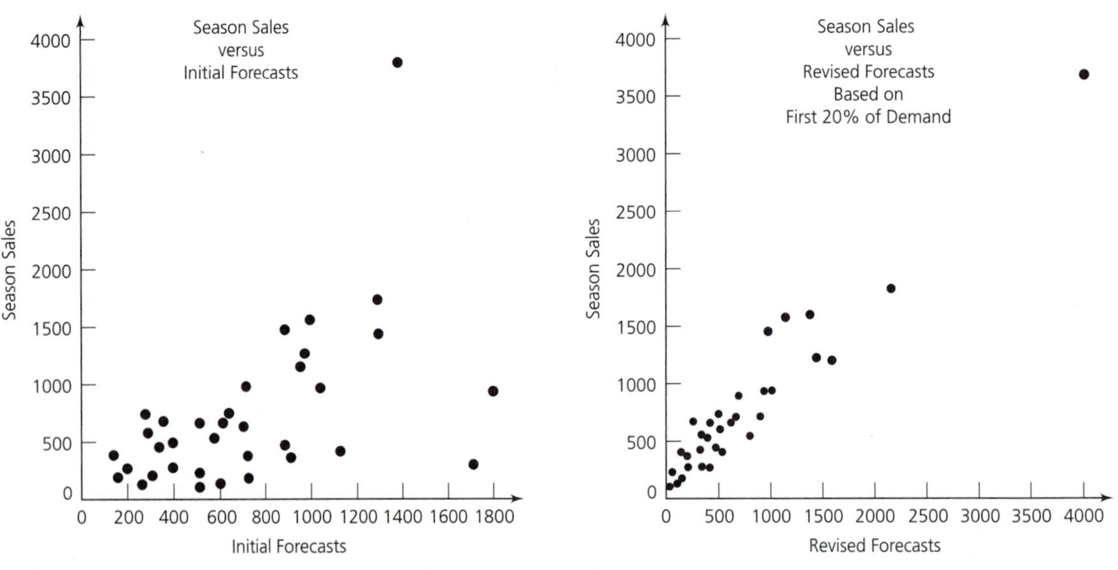

Figure 8.17 Observing a portion of demand improves forecast accuracy. *Source:* Fisher and Raman [1996]

The next step in the analysis was to construct a stochastic programming model to assist Obermeyer management in planning production and sales for each season by separating their production plans into the two stages shown in Figure 8.16. The initial forecast would be used to plan production for stage 1 and an initial plan for stage 2. The revised forecasts developed later would be used to revise the production plan for stage two.

The stochastic programming model employed the following variables and parameters:

x_{i1} = the number of units of product i to be produced in stage 1

x_{i2} = the number of units of product i to be produced in stage 2

D_{i1} = the units of product demand observed before the commitment to x_{i2} for the second stage (treated as an unknown random variable at the start of the first stage)

D_i = total units demanded for product i over the season

$f_i(D_{i1}, D_i)$ = bivariate normal density function for item i

O_i = the overproduction unit cost for product i

U_i = the underproduction cost per unit for product i

K = production capacity in stage 2

The construction of the bivariate density functions f_i for each item i was a challenging task in which the consultants artistically blended historical data from past products with expert judgment in estimating parameters.[33] The overproduction cost O_i was set equal to the variable cost of item i minus the expected markdown price. The underproduction cost U_i was set equal to the wholesale price of item i minus its variable cost. For most items U_i was 2 or 3 times greater than O_i, which promoted some production in excess of forecasted demand. Finally, decisions about production during the second stage were made subject to a capacity constraint because the time available during the stage was limited.

The two-stage stochastic programming model developed for this application involved a process whereby the first stage production variables x_{i1} were selected at the start of stage 1 using the initial demand forecasts for all items. The quantities D_{i1} were then observed and a revised forecast was developed. This forecast was used in revising the second stage production variables x_{i2}. The overall objective was to minimize the expected total cost of over- and underproduction of all items over the season. Some approximations were needed to make the necessary computations because of the complexity of the second-stage problem. We omit further details.[34]

Results. The descriptive and normative models were implemented for Obermeyer in parallel with previously standard planning procedures for the 1992 season. However, the second-stage forecast was used by Obermeyer to revise its actual production plans for that stage. The results are summarized in Table 8.19. The No Response case corresponds to the situation where Obermeyer makes a plan once and for all at the start of the season without updating its forecast based on stage 1 demands.

Table 8.19 Results for Obermeyer's 1992/1993 season

	Response Model		
	Model	**Actual**	**No Response**
Total Production	124,805	121,432	172,896
Overproduction	22,036	25,094	83,445
Underproduction	792	7,493	14,380
Overproduction Cost as % of Sales	1.30%	1.74%	6.80%
Underproduction Cost as % of Sales	0.18%	1.56%	3.58%
Total Cost as % of Sales	1.48%	3.30%	10.38%

Source: Fisher and Raman [1996]

As we can see, the model produced significantly better results than those actually implemented. In the skiwear industry, profits equal about 3% of sales. Therefore, a projected savings of 1.82% of sales due to analysis with the model represents a 60% increase in profit. Compared to the No Response case, the model represents a quadrupling of profits.

8.9 Scenario Planning

Scenario planning is a process intended to assist senior managers in defining scenarios of their firm's long-term future that are consistent, plausible, and comprehensive. Its goal is to organize, enhance, and demystify their individual and collective views of the future. It is qualitative and broad in nature and not primarily concerned with strategic decision making. We discuss scenario planning because the topic is important in its own right and because it is relevant to the creation and use of models for strategic supply chain planning.

Models, and even data, play a secondary role in scenario planning exercises, especially when the firm's senior managers face, or believe they face, an unstructured future. Thus, it might appear there is little overlap between scenario planning and our interests in applying data, models, and modeling systems to strategic analysis. Still, the quality of strategic planning based on models is dependent on the quality of the scenarios examined. Scenario planning provides a discipline that modeling practitioners can adapt to our somewhat different needs. Conversely, scenario planning exercises can benefit by collecting data and constructing models to evaluate qualitative scenarios once they have been articulated.

Methodology

Scenarios are defined as focused descriptions of fundamentally different futures presented in coherent narratives. A 10-step methodology of scenario planning is outlined in Table 8.20. It centers on learning and exploring interrelationships among strategic trends and key uncertainties.[35] It aims at overcoming human and organizational barriers to consistent and realistic assessment of the long-term future. In particular, scenario planning helps managers compensate for overconfidence and tunnel vision, which are frequent errors in strategic thinking. For example, many companies approach strategic planning by assuming only one scenario of the future and prepare only a single budget for the coming years.

The methodology is not intended primarily to predict the future, but rather to bound it and encourage consensus building among managers who have radically different views and expectations. Its discipline will help managers overcome psychological biases such as framing, anchoring, and availability. Framing refers to thinking that extrapolates the past without modification into the future; that is, a failure to think "outside the box" when describing the company's current situation. Even if some thinking outside the box occurs, managers are liable to fall prey to anchoring,

Table 8.20 Ten-step scenario methodology

1. *Define the scope and strategic issues to be analyzed.* Scope refers to the time frame for the strategic analysis, the products, suppliers, markets, geographic areas, technologies.
2. *Identify the major stakeholders.* Stakeholders are individuals or organizations with an interest in the strategic issues being addressed, including those who may be affected by strategic decisions and those who can influence them. The current roles, interests, and power positions of these stakeholders should be understood.
3. *Identify current trends.* This step involves the merging of perceptions of industry experts, managers, and knowledgeable outsiders. It is important to evaluate whether trends are mutually compatible during the time frame of analysis.
4. *Identify key uncertainties.* Uncertainties associated with the outcomes of key events must be identified, but at this point measurement of probabilities are not yet needed. Attention must also be paid to correlations among the uncertainties.
5. *Construct extreme scenarios.* Steps 1 to 4 set the stage for scenario construction. The initial step is to construct two, or a small number, of extreme scenarios. An example is one scenario of positive elements and the other of negative elements.
6. *Assess internal consistency and plausibility of extreme scenarios.* The extreme scenarios will very likely be internally inconsistent. First, it is possible that trends defining extreme scenarios are incompatible. Second, outcomes of uncertain events may be inconsistent. Finally, stakeholder inconsistency will result if the major actors in a scenario are placed in positions they dislike and can change.
7. *Create representative scenarios.* Using insights from step 6, create a variety of consistent scenarios that bracket a wide range of outcomes. Adjust scenarios to realistically reflect stakeholder behavior.
8. *Identify research needs.* Considering the scenarios identified in step 7, identify topics requiring further study to sharpen their definition and analysis.
9. *Develop and apply quantitative models.* These are descriptive and normative models for forecasting and optimizing decisions associated with the uncertain future. This step will probably lead to further scenario definition and refinement.
10. *Develop decision scenarios.* Use the results of step 9 combined with managerial judgment to describe decisions for different scenarios, keeping in mind that they may suggest alternate future equilibria for the company and its industry.

Source: Schoemaker [1993]

which refers to extrapolations of the past that are only small variations on the current situation. The availability bias refers to the human trait that situations that are difficult to imagine or remember are undervalued.

Connections to Optimization Modeling

The scenario methodology of Table 8.17 includes a step requiring analysis with quantitative models, but it shies away from the computation of probabilities on the occurrence of scenarios and the use of deterministic and stochastic programming models. This ambivalence toward the computation of scenario probabilities is related to an issue that arose in early sections when we discussed stochastic programming models and applications. Namely, what are rigorous yet practical methods for blending objective probabilities from a statistical forecasting model with subjective probabilities based on managerial judgment?

While admitting that sweeping analysis of a company's long-term strategy may well involve scenarios, probabilities, and other factors that are difficult to quantify and model, approaches can be devised that allow models, especially stochastic programming models, to play a more central role. First, mathematical programming methods can be used to compute ranges on probabilities within which optimal hedging and contingency plans remain optimal. The characterization of scenarios would then be extended to include these probabilities. For example, modeling analysis might suggest that if the probability of a successful merger by the end of year 2 is below 0.30, the company should start construction of a new plant immediately. If the probability is at least 0.30, the company should wait until year 3 and construct the new plant only if the merger fails. Managerial judgment could then be used to assess the value of this critical probability. If the decision remains highly ambiguous, managers on the strategic planning committee can take steps that will force the probability to move up or down, thereby clarifying their indicated course of action.

Second, quantitative analysis of strategic scenarios requires integration of supply chain models with marketing and sales models. Such integration was discussed in Section 8.1. We can hope that the scenario methodology would promote consensus among supply chain and marketing managers about using data and models to assess strategic options. The scenario methodology might also stimulate interest in the implementation and use of data-driven models for competitive analysis of the type discussed in Sections 8.5 and 8.6. Finally, analysis of strategic scenarios might well require integration of supply chain and marketing decisions with corporate financial decisions, a topic that we address in the following chapter.

8.10 Final Thoughts

While admitting that the number of successful supply chain modeling applications for strategic planning are increasing rapidly, we announced our intention at the start

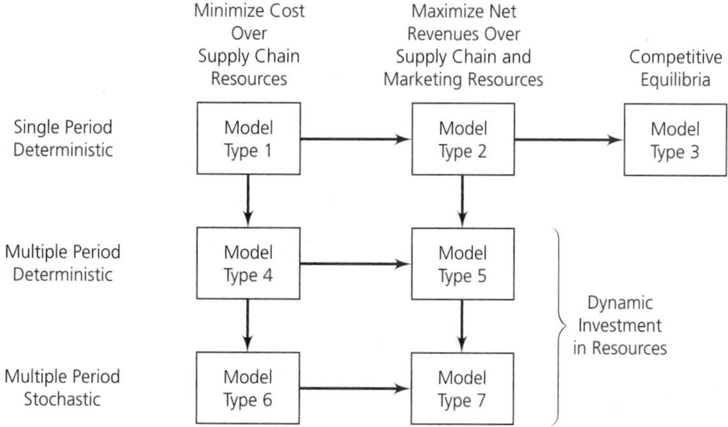

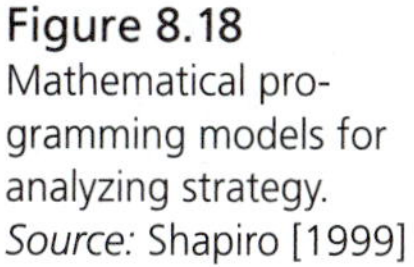
Figure 8.18 Mathematical programming models for analyzing strategy. *Source:* Shapiro [1999]

of this chapter to examine approaches for extending their scope. Our motivation was that state-of-the-art models ignore decisions involving revenues, marketing, competitive initiatives, and hedges against uncertainties. The extensions we discussed are depicted in Figure 8.18.

The state of the art in Figure 8.18 is represented by model type 1 (single-period, deterministic minimization of the total supply chain cost of meeting given demand). The arrows in the diagram reflect natural extensions of the models in a given box to those that are more ambitious. For example, extensions of model type 1 to model type 2 represent management's interest in varying product mix, probably in a cautious manner, to the maximization of net revenues. By cautious, we mean the model allows small deviations in product mix that entail little or no change in unit price. Methods for effecting this kind of extension were discussed in Section 8.2 when we reviewed the construction of price and location sensitive revenue curves.

Alternatively, extensions of model type 1 to model type 4 represent management's interest in the timing and phasing of capital investments (or divestments) in supply chain resources over multiple time periods, while still minimizing the total discounted costs of managing the supply chain to meet given demand. Traditionally, models of type 4 were applied to companies in capital intensive and regulated industries, such as electric power companies, that had little control over product prices and even gross revenues.

Extensions of model type 2 to model type 3 are ambitious exercises aimed at identifying company strategies that maximize net revenue in a competitive environment. Such models were discussed in Section 8.5. Of course, model type 3 could also be extended to multiple-period and stochastic versions. We have omitted such extensions in the figure because they would be stretching the state of the art beyond the bounds of likely implementation over the foreseeable future.

Extensions of model types 2 or 4 to model type 5 (multiple-period, deterministic maximization of discounted net revenues) are also ambitious. As we discussed in Sections 8.3 and 8.4, these models require the development of submodels relating marketing strategies for new and existing products, which are multiple-period in nature, and their integration with supply chain models. In other words, models of type 5 address product mix changes that are more audacious than those of model type 2. They must be multiperiod because time plays a central role in determining the effect of marketing decisions on market share and gross revenues.

Finally, we consider extensions of the deterministic model types 4 and 5 to the stochastic model types 6 and 7. A cautious approach to effecting the extensions in box 6 is to create a stochastic programming model by merging a small number of deterministic models of different scenarios. A willingness to pursue this approach is in the air. We recently discussed stochastic programming modeling projects with analysts in two large firms, a computer manufacturer and a pharmaceutical company. In both cases, the firms were seeking production strategies for making major components of finished products that optimally hedge against uncertain demand for these products.

Exercises

In addition to the following exercises, modeling exercises involving data files and discussion exercises involving white papers may be found on the Web site (www.scm-models.com).

1. Describe how you would use 0-1 variables to capture the production cost/capacity function for the Macon plant included in the model of Table 8.11.
2. In Section 8.2, we discussed briefly how data and models could be used to resolve the conflicts among supply chain and marketing managers listed in Table 8.1. Elaborate on this claim for each of the seven areas of conflict. For each area, your discussion should incorporate comments about the following:
   - Relevant data
   - Relevant descriptive models
   - The form of optimization models to support integrated decisions (length of the planning horizon, decision options, constraints, objective function)
   - Frequency of analysis with models

   Conversely, if you believe some of these conflicts cannot be well resolved using data and models, present your arguments.
3. In Section 8.5, we discussed briefly how data and models could be employed to analyze the elements of industry structure listed in Figure 8.10. Referring to the seven types of optimization models displayed in Figure 8.18, select five elements that you believe could be effectively analyzed by one or more of such models and discuss briefly how they would be employed to that end. In addition, select five elements that you believe would be difficult to model and present your reasons.
4. Grant Aerospace makes radar systems for commercial and military aircraft. Two of their systems, R100 and R101, are quite similar in that they differ in only two components, A and B. These components are added to vanilla

versions of the R100 and R101 systems at the final assembly step. The R100 requires two units of component A and one unit of component B. The R101 requires three units of component A and one unit of component B.

The production manager is worried about meeting orders for the two systems over the next 3 weeks. Orders for the R100 are 18 in the first week, 21 in the second week, and 18 in the third week. Orders for the R101 are 16 in the first week, 17 in the second week, and 12 in the third week. The production manager will receive shipments of 40 units of component A and 30 units of component B at the beginning of each week. Current inventory (at the start of week 1) is 104 units of component A and 86 units of components B.

Use a spreadsheet optimizer to construct and optimize a mixed integer programming model that attempts to schedule production of the two radar systems so that the number of backlogged orders for each system at the end of each of the 3 weeks does not exceed five. From among such solutions, the production manager seeks the schedule that minimizes the sum of the backlogs of both systems at the end of the three weeks. *Hint:* You will need to define production of each system in each period as a general integer variable; that is, one that can take on any nonnegative integer values.

Notes

1. Shapiro [1977] was perhaps the first to identify and categorize the conflicts of manufacturing and marketing managers. References to more recent articles may be found in Eliashberg and Steinberg [1993].
2. A extensive survey of many important topics in marketing science can be found in Eliashberg and Lilien [1993a].
3. In their introduction, Eliashberg and Lilien [1993b, 3] state, "Many see marketing processes as lacking the neat quantitative properties found in production and finance. In marketing, human factors play a large role, marketing expenditures affect demand and cost simultaneously and information to support truly systematic decisions is rarely available. A major force behind these [modeling] developments is the battle for markets that has been dictating organizational success and failure in recent years. Sales in many markets are flat or declining while competitors have been growing in number and becoming more desperate. Products are exhibiting shorter life-cycles, and leaner staff organizations have become buried in new types of data . . . , demanding rapid comprehension and sound decision making in dynamic and risky environments."
4. See Baumol [1977, 183–190] for a discussion of price elasticities.
5. Rao [1993, 543–545] discusses several approaches for measuring price elasticities. Surprisingly little empirical research has been reported on estimating parameters describing revenue functions.
6. See Schrage [1997, 285–286 and Problem 4, 295–296] for a discussion of quadratic programming models for maximizing net revenues of products with cross-price elasticities.
7. See Rao [1993, 534–538] for a review of multiple-product pricing models.
8. Thorough discussions of the construction and applications of the logit model can be found in Urban and Hauser [1980].
9. See Satterfield [1995].
10. See Camm et al. [1997].
11. The model we describe is Brandaid, developed by Little [1975]. Wind and Lilien [1993] provide a critique of Brandaid and other marketing strategy models. Also, see Cooper [1993] for

a review of market-share models with mathematical structure similar to the Brandaid model.

12. Covert [1987] implemented a prototype model using realistic data that integrated a supply chain model for personal products with a Brandaid marketing model that captures advertising, pricing, and promotion effects.

13. In Section 8.8, we discuss the successful application of stochastic modeling to products with short and uncertain life cycles.

14. The integration of new product design with supply chain design is a natural extension of earlier concerns about "design for engineering," which addressed the economics and efficiency of engineering realizations of new products.

15. The diffusion model is due in large part to Bass [1969]. See also Lilien [1992] and Mahajan, Miller, and Bass [1993].

16. These extensions are discussed in Lilien [1992] and Mahajan, Miller, and Bass [1993].

17. The characterization of competition in terms of the five forces is from Porter [1980]. It is also reviewed in Chapter 1 of Porter [1985].

18. Tirole [1988] provides a thorough introduction to the theory of industrial organization from a mathematical modeling viewpoint. Connors [1991] compares the resource-based view of the firm, which we discussed in Chapter 8, with five other models of industrial organization. Her paper also provides an extensive bibliography with accompanying comments.

19. Consumer's utility is measured by consumer's surplus, which is roughly the savings to consumers as higher demand induces lower prices; see Baumol [1977, 497–500] or Tirole [1988, 7–8].

20. Takayama and Judge [1971] provide extensive analysis of spatial equilibrium models.

21. Tirole [1988, Chapter 2] discusses product selection, quality, and advertising in the context of the theory of industrial organization. On page 115, he states "Advertising has long been perceived as wasteful and manipulative. One reason for this may be that advertising is one of the topics in the study of industrial organization for which traditional assumptions (especially those with regard to consumer behavior) are strained most. The advertising of a product has strong psychological and sociological aspects that go beyond optimal inferences about objective quality."

22. Arrow and Hahn [1971] furnish a rigorous and comprehensive mathematical treatment of competitive analysis.

23. See Varian [1978, Chapter 6] for a mathematical analysis of the tatonnement method and other features of equilibrium models. See also Miller et al. [1996] for an in-depth discussion of equilibrium analysis applied to facility location problems.

24. Mehring, Sarkar, and Shapiro [1983] elaborate on price- and resource-directed decomposition methods of mathematical programming for computing spatial equilibrium. With the price-directed method, market prices are broadcast to the suppliers and buyers; they respond with quantities that they wish to supply or buy. This is the method of Figure 8.11. With the resource-directed method, market quantities are broadcast to the suppliers and buyers; they respond with prices they wish to receive or pay. See also Schrage [1997, Chapter 11] for connections between mathematical programming and equilibrium analysis.

25. An oligopoly refers to a small number of large firms that produce and control the bulk of the supply in an industry. See Baumol [1977, Chapter 16] for further discussion of the economics of oligopolies.

26. See Schoemaker [1993] and Georgantzas and Acar [1995] for further discussion of the intentions and methods of scenario planning.

27. See Winston [1994, Chapter 13] for background on decision trees and decision analysis. See Bienstock and Shapiro [1988], Birge and Louveaux [1997], or Infanger [1994] for discussions of stochastic programming, including applications, from a mathematical perspective.

28. See Bodily [1982] for a review of methodologies for making judgmental forecasts.

29 See Swaminathan and Tayur [1999].

30. Swaminathan and Tayur [1999, 588–595] report on a stochastic programming model applied to the assembly of IBM's PS/2 workstations from common components. Ulrich and

Eppinger [1995] discuss product design principles for exploiting common components.

31. Our discussion summarizes results from the paper by Fisher and Raman [1996].

32. The correlation coefficient is defined as the ratio of the covariance of two random variables divided by the product of their standard deviations. This ratio is always less than or equal to 1. If it equals 1, the two variables move in a fixed ratio to one another. A value of 0.8 indicates that we can expect their movements to be closely linked.

33. This construction is discussed by Fisher and Raman [1996, 93–96].

34. See Fisher and Raman [1996, 90–91].

35. The scenario methodology is adapted from Schoemaker [1993, 197].

References

Arrow, K. J., and F. Hahn [1971], *General Competitive Analysis.* San Francisco: Holden-Day.

*Bass. F. M. [1969], "A New Growth Model for Consumer Durables," *Management Science,* 15, 215–27.

Baumol, W. J. [1977], *Economic Theory and Operations Analysis.* Englewood Cliffs, N.J.: Prentice-Hall.

Bienstock, D., and J. F. Shapiro [1988], "Optimizing Resource Acquisition Decisions by Stochastic Programming," *Management Science,* 34, 215–229.

Birge, J. R., and F. Louveaux [1997], *Introduction to Stochastic Programming.* New York: Springer.

Bodily, S. E. [1982], "Judgmental and Bayesian Forecasting," *The Handbook of Forecasting, A Manager's Guide,* edited by S. Makridakis and S. C. Wheelwright. New York: Wiley.

Camm, J. D., T. E. Chorman, F. A. Dill, J. R. Evans, D. J. Sweeney, and G. W. Wegryn [1997], "Blending OR/MS, Judgment, and GIS: Restructuring P&G's Supply Chain," *Interfaces,* 27, 128–142.

Connors, K. R. [1991], "A Historical Comparison of Resource-Based Theory and Five Schools of Thought within Industrial Organization Economics: Do We Have a New Theory of the Firm?," *Journal of Management,* 17, 121–154.

Cooper, L. G. [1993], "Market-Share Models," in J. Eliashberg and G. L. Lilien [1993a].

Covert, K. B. [1987], "An Optimization Model for Marketing and Production Planning," M. S. Thesis, Sloan School of Management, MIT.

Eliashberg, J., and G. L. Lilien, [1993a], eds. *Handbooks in Operations Research and Management Science, Volume 5: Marketing.* Amsterdam: Elsevier Science.

Eliashberg, J., and G. L. Lilien [1993b], "Mathematical Marketing Models: Some Historical Perspectives and Future Projections," Chapter 1 in J. Eliashberg and G. L. Lilien [1993a].

Eliashberg, J. and R. Steinberg [1993], "Marketing-Production Joint Decision-Making," in J. Eliashberg and G. L. Lilien [1993a].

*Fisher, M. L., and A. Raman [1996], "Reducing the Cost of Demand Uncertainty through Accurate Response to Early Sales," *Operations Research,* 44, 87–99.

Georgantzas, N. C., and W. Acar [1995], *Scenario-driven Planning: Learning to Manage Strategy Uncertainty.* Quorum Books.

Infanger, G. [1994], *Planning under Uncertainty: Solving Large-Scale Stochastic Linear Programs.* Danvers, Mass.: Boyd & Fraser.

Lilien, G. L., P. Kotler, and F. S. Moorthy [1992], *Marketing Models.* Englewood Cliffs, N.J.: Prentice Hall.

*Little, J. D. C. [1975], "Brandaid: A Marketing-Mix Model, Parts 1 and 2," *Operations Research,* 23, 628–673.

Mahajan, V., E. Miller, and F. M. Bass [1993], "New-Product Diffusion Models," Chapter 8 in J. Eliashberg and G. L. Lilien [1993a].

Mehring, J. S., D. Sarkar, and J. F. Shapiro [1983], "Decomposition Methods and the Computation of Spatial Equilibria: An Application to

Coal Supply and Demand Markets," 221–233 in *Energy Models and Studies,* edited by B. Lev. Amsterdam: North Holland.

Miller, T. C., T. L. Friesz, and R. L. Tobin [1996], *Equilibrium Facility Locations on Networks.* New York: Springer.

*Porter, M. E. [1980], *Competitive Strategy.* New York: The Free-Press-MacMillan.

*Porter, M. E. [1985], *Competitive Advantage.* New York: The Free Press-MacMillan.

Rao, V. R. [1993], "Pricing Models in Marketing," Chapter 11 in J. Eliashberg and G. L. Lilien [1993a].

Satterfield, R. L. [1995], *Profit-Maximizing Distribution System Design with Customer Service Dependent Demand,* Unpublished Ph.D. dissertation, Indiana University.

*Schoemaker, P. J. H. [1993], "Multiple Scenario Development: Its Conceptual and Behavioral Foundation," *Strategic Management Journal,* 14, 193–213.

Schrage, L [1997], *Optimization Modeling with LINDO,* 5th ed. Pacific Grove, Calif.: Brooks/Cole Publishing Company.

Shapiro, B. P. [1977], "Can Marketing and Manufacturing Coexist?" *Harvard Business Review,* 55, 104–114.

*Shapiro, J. F. [1999], "On the Connections Among Activity-Based Costing, Mathematical Programming Models for Analyzing Strategic Decisions, and the Resource-Based View of the Firm," *European Journal of Operational Research,* 118, 300.

Swaminathan, J. M., and S. R. Tayur [1999], "Stochastic Programming for Managing Product Variety," Chapter 19 in S. R. Tayur, R. Ganeshan, and M. J. Magazine [1999].

Takayama, T., and C. G. Judge [1971], *Spatial and Temporal Price and Allocation Models.* Amsterdam: North-Holland.

Tayur, S., R. Ganeshan, and M. J. Magazine [1999], *Quantitative Models for Supply Chain Management.* Norwell, Mass.: Kluwer Academic.

Tirole, J. [1988], *The Theory of Industrial Organization.* Cambridge, Mass.: MIT Press.

Ulrich, K., and S. D. Eppinger [1995], *Product Design and Development.* New York: McGraw-Hill.

Urban, G. L., and J. R. Hauser [1980], *Design and Marketing of New Products.* Englewood Cliffs, N.J.: Prentice Hall.

Varian, H. R. [1978], *Microeconomic Analysis.* New York: Norton.

Wind, Y., and Lilien, G. L. [1993], "Marketing Strategy Models," Chapter 17 in J. Eliashberg and G. L. Lilien [1993a].

Winston, W. L. [1994], *Operations Research: Applications and Algorithms,* 3d ed. Belmont, Calif.: Duxbury Press.

*See the credits section at the end of this book for more information.

Integration of Financial and Physical Supply Chains

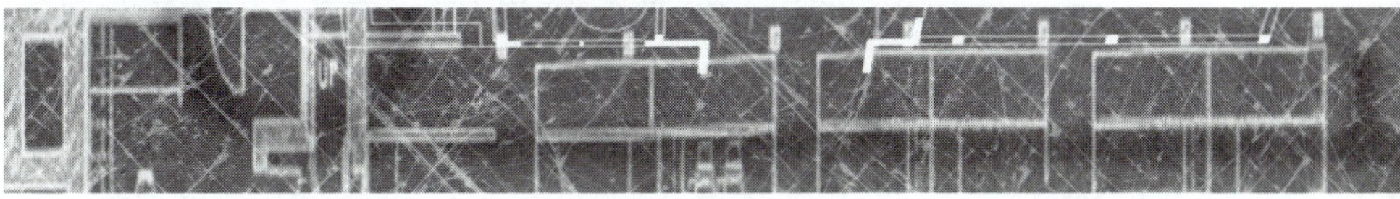

Physical supply chains are paralleled in all firms by financial supply chains involving decisions about capital investments, borrowing, dividends, and other factors under the control of the firms' financial managers. The two chains are inextricably linked, especially at the strategic level of planning. On the one hand, the purpose of integrated supply chain management is to improve the firm's financial performance as measured by its net and after-tax profits, return on investment, and other criteria. On the other hand, strategic supply chain planning involves capital investments in new plants, technologies, and products, implying that financial factors such as the cost of capital and borrowing constraints should be considered in the planning process.

This synergy between corporate financial and supply chain management is not widely appreciated by senior managers responsible for ensuring that the company's performance appeals to its stockholders.[1] These managers often view supply chain management as concerned only with operations, and therefore believe that it has little impact on financial performance metrics such as growth, profitability, and capital utilization. Conversely, supply chain managers often do not effectively articulate the importance of competitive supply chain management in enhancing financial performance metrics.

Optimization models offer an appealing framework for analyzing corporate financial decisions and constraints as well as for integrating them with supply chain decisions and constraints. Unfortunately, relatively few corporate financial models of this type have been implemented.[2] Instead, corporate financial managers have traditionally employed myopic methods for evaluating individual financial decisions rather than systems analysis methods for holistically optimizing the combined effects of many decisions. Still, optimization models for corporate financial planning have appeared in the literature, which we draw upon in presenting them here.

Coordination of physical and financial supply chains is especially complex for a multinational corporation (MNC) that has partially or wholly owned foreign subsidiaries. For a MNC, the financial supply chain will be complicated by legal structures connecting the parent corporation to its foreign subsidiaries, their business arrangements, tax laws in countries where the company makes or sells its products, the requirements of trade agreements on local content, and many other factors. The location of facilities and their operations can have a large impact on flows in the supply chain and therefore on how the multinational firm wishes to optimize its financial performance. A primary goal of this chapter is to examine optimization models for studying these interactions.

We present deterministic models for analyzing the integrated physical and supply chain planning problems just discussed. Deterministic models are the most practical for such applications. Uncertainties in key factors, such as demand, interest rates, foreign currency exchange, and economic conditions in countries where the company has plants and markets can be examined by optimizing over multiple scenarios. Of course deterministic models are not as insightful as stochastic programming models that identify hedging strategies and contingency plans for more directly dealing with uncertainty and risk. Although the practical application of stochastic programming methods to corporate and MNC planning is a reach, we conclude the chapter with an overview of their form and purposes. In addition to the possibility that such methods will be successfully applied in the near future, they provide qualitative insights into hedging using real supply chain options, as opposed to financial options, to mitigate risks associated with domestic and multinational operations.

We begin in Section 9.1 with an overview of optimization models for corporate financial planning. The section includes a numerical example set in a manufacturing firm for which a financial model based on the firm's funds flow equation is integrated with supply chain submodels. After that, in Section 9.2, we provide an overview of financial planning issues for a MNC. Connections between physical and financial supply chains for a MNC are discussed in Section 9.3 in the context of an integrating network. In Section 9.4, a case study in a pharmaceutical MNC, where the objective is to maximize repatriated after-tax net income, is presented. Methods for hedging or insuring against exchange rate risks are discussed in Section 9.5. This discussion is extended in Section 9.6 to methods allowing a MNC to employ supply chain strategies as real options for mitigating risks. The chapter concludes in Section 9.7 with final thoughts on optimization modeling of corporate financial decisions.

9.1 Optimization Models for Corporate Financial Planning

Like supply chain planning, corporate financial planning involves large quantities of objective numerical data, which suggests that analysis by optimization models is both possible and desirable. Typical financial decisions to be optimized include the following:

- Allocating capital to the development of new facilities, products, or markets
- Creating capital budgets from net revenues or borrowing or by issuing stock
- Managing short-term cash flows to balance receivables against payables
- Selecting capital depreciation schemes to exploit tax incentives

Also like supply chain planning, corporate financial decisions may be classified as strategic, tactical, and operational. Unlike supply chain planning, however, and despite long-standing academic research into their form and function, corporate financial planning models have not yet been widely applied.[3]

In companies that manufacture and/or distribute physical products, corporate financial planning decisions are closely linked to supply chain and demand management decisions. Because the raison d'etre of such companies is to fulfill the logistics and manufacturing missions discussed in Chapter 7, corporate financial planning models should be explicitly linked to supply chain models and reflect demand management options. We illustrate such modeling by a spreadsheet optimization example given below. Before that, we discuss how to model a firm's balance sheet, which contains summary information central to financial decision making in the firm.

Modeling the Balance Sheet

The decision options, constraints, and objectives of corporate financial planning can be explained by a simple example.[4] Specifically, we examine the sources and uses of funds for the XYZ Corporation, whose balance sheet follows:

Balance Sheet—XYZ Corporation

Current Assets (CA)	Current Liabilities (CL)
Fixed Assets (FA)	Long-Term Debt (L)
	Equity (E)

Current assets refer to liquid assets such as cash, inventories, or accounts receivable. Fixed assets refer to illiquid assets such as plants or equipment. In this analysis, we do not include intangible assets, such as customer good will or a cadre of superior design engineers, among the fixed or current assets. Current liabilities refer to short-term liabilities such as accounts payable or payroll. Long-term debt refers to long-term bank loans or bonds. Equity refers to the value of shareholder's interest in the firm.

The following five variables satisfy the equality:

$$\mathrm{CA} + \mathrm{FA} - \mathrm{CL} - \mathrm{L} - \mathrm{E} = 0$$

where shareholder's equity E is implicitly defined as the difference between assets (CA + FA) and liabilities (CL + L). Corporate financial planning is concerned with decisions made over time that improve the firm's balance sheet. Thus, letting Δ denote change during a year, differences in the balance sheet between the end of year $t-1$ and the end of year t satisfy

$$\Delta\mathrm{CA}(t) + \Delta\mathrm{FA}(t) - \Delta\mathrm{CL}(t) - \Delta\mathrm{L}(t) - \Delta\mathrm{E}(t) = 0$$

In words, the change in equity equals the net difference between the change in assets and the change in liabilities.

For expositional simplicity, we assume that the XYZ Corporation has a policy to never sell new equity issues. Therefore, the change in equity is given by

$$\Delta E(t) = PR(t) - D(t)$$

where $PR(t)$ = after-tax profits in year t and $D(t)$ = dividends paid to shareholders during year t. After-tax profits can also be described in terms of earnings before interest and taxes in year t ($EBIT(t)$) by

$$PR(t) = (1 - r)(EBIT(t) - iL(t))$$

where r is the corporate tax rate and i equals the interest rate that the corporation must pay on long-term debt. Again, for simplicity, we assume all long-term debt has the same cost. Substituting the last equation in the one above it, and substituting the resulting equation in the one above that, we obtain the following **funds-flow equation:**

$$\Delta CA(t) + \Delta FA(t) - \Delta CL(t) - \Delta L(t) - (1 - r)(EBIT(t) - iL(t)) + D(t) = 0$$

The funds-flow equation can be viewed as an accounting relationship used in creating the balance sheet for year t after all financial data for that year have been collected. It is also a cornerstone of corporate financial planning models because it identifies the major decision variables to be determined in planning for future years. Moreover, through the variables $EBIT(t)$ and $\Delta FA(t)$, it provides links among financial decisions, supply chain decisions, and marketing and sales decisions. Specifically, the quantity $EBIT(t)$ is the net result of marketing, sales, and supply chain activities for the year t. Investments in fixed assets intended to enhance the profitability of the firm correspond to increases in $\Delta FA(t)$.

We use the following three facts in rewriting the funds flow equation:

- $EBIT(t)$ and $\Delta FA(t)$ are determined by supply chain and demand analysis.
- $\Delta CL(t)$ is determined by current operational decisions.
- dividends $D(t)$ are set exogenously by management.

Placing these terms on the right, we obtain

$$\Delta CA(t) - \Delta L(t) + (1 - r)iL(t) = - \Delta FA(t) + \Delta CL(t) + (1 - r)EBIT(t) + D(t)$$

where the variables on the left are under control of financial planners whereas the variables on the right are outside their control. Finally, using the equation $L(t) = L(t - 1) + \Delta L(t)$, we have

$$\Delta CA(t) - [1 - (1 - r)i]\,\Delta L(t) = (1 - r)iL(t - 1) - \Delta FA(t) + \Delta CL(t) + (1 - r)EBIT(t) + D(t)$$

where, because the quantity $L(t - 1)$ is known at the start of year t, the variables on the left refer to financial planning decisions for year t; namely, decision options for $\Delta CA(t)$ and $\Delta L(t)$.

Before discussing objective functions that might be employed to optimally determine the financial and other decision variables, we review several types of policy constraints reflecting risk that might be imposed on the decision variables. First, the company's management and banks that might lend money to the XYZ Corporation might impose a **debt-to-equity constraint** of the form

$$\mathrm{L}(t) \le K\mathrm{E}(t)$$

where K is the maximal allowed debt-to equity ratio; that is, at the end of each year the company may incur long-term debt up to K times the equity at that point in time. Typically, K will be less than or equal to 1.

Second, management or the banks might impose a **debt service constraint** of the form

$$\mathrm{EBIT}(t) \ge Si\,\mathrm{L}(t)$$

This constraint states that EBIT in year t must be at least S times as large as the interest payments $i\,L(t)$ on long-term debt. A typical value for S is 5.

Third, management or the banks might impose a **minimum working capital constraint** of the form

$$\mathrm{CA}(t) \ge W\mathrm{CL}(t)$$

where W sets a minimum on the working capital available to the company during year t as a function of current liabilities. A typical value for W is 2. Four, management might impose policy constraints on after-tax profits $\mathrm{PR}(t)$ and dividends $\mathrm{D}(t)$ over several years of a strategic planning horizon to reassure stockholders of the company's market value.

Diverse performance measures are available as the objective function driving financial performance of the XYZ Corporation. The company may seek to maximize the discounted sum of after-tax profits, maximize equity at the end of a finite planning horizon, or maximize any one of a number of measures of financial performance. In other words, selecting a financial strategy is often an exercise in multi-objective optimization; we return to a discussion of this aspect of corporate financial planning at the end of this section.

Numerical Example of an Optimization Model for Corporate Financial Planning

We construct an example of a corporate financial planning model by extending a model of the Ajax Computer Company from Section 2.1. Although the example is simple, it allows us to concretely illustrate an application of the funds-flow equation and other relationships discussed above. Extensions to the model and its analysis are briefly discussed after that.

Ajax Financial Planning Model. In Section 2.1, we constructed a linear programming model to optimize decisions regarding the manufacture of three types of computers made by Ajax Computer Company: laptops (Alphas), desktops (Betas), and workstations (Gammas). The goal of the model was to maximize weekly revenues from sales of these computers, subject to capacity constraints on testing and assembling them. Here, we extend the model to analyze strategic investment decisions over a 3-year period associated with the development and sale of a new product, a lightweight laptop (Lambda). We also will analyze strategic expansion of manufacturing capacities, which might be needed to add Lambda to the product line.

Details of the investment options and constraints are as follows:

1. Ajax' hardware engineers and buyers will require 1 year, which we call year 1, to design the Lambda computer, to identify suppliers of parts and components, to build and thoroughly test prototypes, and to acquire new assembly equipment. The fixed cost of this new product development will be $1,100,000, which will be treated as an addition to the company's fixed asset base. The product will be ready for sale in years 2 and 3; it will not be sold after that because technological change will make it obsolete. Once full-scale production begins, each Lambda will consume 0.5 hours of A-line testing and 5 hours of assembly labor. When sold, it will yield net revenue of $250 per computer sold.
2. Ajax senior management also wishes to invest in expanding production capacity. An engineering study has shown that A-line test capacity can be expanded at an amortized equipment cost of $28.85 for each additional hour each week. Similarly, C-line test equipment capacity can be expanded at an amortized cost of $38.25 for each additional hour each week. Once these investments in equipment have been made, the equipment is available for 5 years. Due to personnel hiring and training constraints, these capacities may not be expanded more than 50% per year.
3. Equipment allowing expansion of assembly labor capacity can be added at an amortized cost of $1.54 for each additional hour of each week. In addition, an engineering study indicates that the assembly equipment wears out at a rate of 10% per year. Thus, some equipment replacements will be necessary merely to maintain the status quo in assembly capacity. For accounting purposes, however, the replaced equipment remains as a fixed asset on the books over the 3-year planning horizon. Assembly capacity may also not be expanded more than 50% per year.
4. At the start of year 1, Ajax' financial position is current assets (CA) of $300,000, fixed assets (FA) of $1,300,000, current liabilities (CL) of $200,000, long-term debt (L) of $600,000, and, equity (E) of $800,000, which is the difference between assets and liabilities. The company has a policy that projected long-term debt may not exceed projected equity at the end of any year. Moreover, no more than 50% of current assets at the start of any year may be invested in new fixed assets during that year. The corporate tax rate is 35% and the interest rate on long-term debt is 10%.
5. Earnings before interest and taxes in each year equal gross revenues from products sold in that year minus marketing and overhead costs not directly associ-

ated with product manufacture. These costs are projected to be $3 million in year 1 and $4 million in years 2 and 3.

6. Ajax management seeks a production, sales, and financial strategy that will maximize the company's equity at the end of 3 years.

A spreadsheet optimization model addressing Ajax' financial planning problem is displayed in Table 9.1. The financial variables from the balance sheet are displayed at the top of the spreadsheet with starting values listed at four points in time (years 1, 2, 3, 4) and with the delta, or change, values for each year listed on the appropriate rows. The column marked EBIT provides the earnings or net revenues from sale of Ajax' products as determined by the production submodels listed below the financial model. The after-tax profit is computed in the column marked PR using the formula given in the previous subsection relating PR to EBIT and L. The financial variables are not free to take on any values because they are connected through funds-flow equations.

Integration of the production submodels and the financial model for the Ajax Computer Company illustrates a major theme of this chapter. Net revenues from production are key variables allowing financial growth of the firm. Conversely, capital needed for developing the new product and for expanding production capacity in the production submodels is linked to the financial model; namely, long-term debt and current assets are available for financing these strategic options.

The spreadsheet in Table 9.1 displays the integrated financial and supply chain model for Ajax and an optimal solution to the base case scenario. All dollar figures are measured in thousands of dollars. Before discussing results, we provide further representative details of the model, mainly for year 1 because the constructions are repeated in a straightforward manner for years 2 and 3.

1. The data in cells 7C to 7G are fixed and given initial values at the start of year 1 for the financial variables.
2. The data in cells 8C to 8G are the delta (change) variables for year 1. Starting from the left, we have the following:
   a. C8 = G8 – D8 + E8 + F8; the change in current assets depends on changes in the other financial variables in the funds flow equation.
   b. D8 = K8 + F8; changes in long-term liabilities and investments from current assets determine changes in fixed assets.
   c. E8 = 50; the change in current liabilities is exogenously set.
   d. F8 is a nonnegative decision variable.
   e. G8 = I9 – J8; the change in equity equals after-tax profits minus dividends.
3. The other cells in the financial model for year 1 are linked by the following:
   a. H8 = C20 * C21 + D20 * D21 + E20 * E21 – 3000; earnings before interest and taxes equal gross revenues from sales minus fixed marketing and overhead costs.
   b. I9 = 0.65 * (H8 – 0.1 * F9); after-tax profits computed from earnings before taxes and interest on long-term debt.
   c. L9 = G9 – F9; when combined with the constraint in M9, enforces the constraint that long-term debt may not exceed equity.

Table 9.1 Integrated financial planning and supply chain model for Ajax Computer Company ($1,000)

	A	B	C	D	E	F	G	H	I	J	K	L	M	N
1	**Objective - Max**						**Financial Model**							
2	**Terminal Equity**													
3	6259							Earnings			Investment	Equity		
4			Current	Fixed	Current	Long-term		Before	After Tax		from	minus		
5			Assets	Assets	Liabilities	Debt	Equity	Int & Taxes	Profits	Dividends	Current Assets	Debt		
6			CA	FA	CL	L	E	EBIT	PR	D				
7		Start year 1	300	1300	200	600	800							
8		Delta	925	1281	50	1131	1025	2135		250	150			
9		Start year 2	1225	2581	250	1731	1825		1275			94	>=	0
10		Delta	1652	259	0	0	1910	3497		250	259			
11		Start year 3	2877	2840	250	1731	3736		2160			2005	>=	0
12		Delta	2426	97	0	0	2523	4439		250	97			
13		Start year 4	5303	2937	250	1731	6259		2773			4528	>=	0
14														
15	**Production**													
16	**and Sales**		Alpha	Beta	Gamma	Resource Use		Resource Available						
17	**Sub-Model**	A-line test	1	1		9360	=<=	9360						
18	**year 1**	C-line test			1	2780	=<=	2780						
19		Assembly	10	15	20	156000	=<=	156000						
20		Net Rev/Unit	0.35	0.47	0.61									
21		Sales	8000	1360	2780									
22			>=	>=	>=									
23		LB Sales	1000	1000	1000									
24			=<=	<=	<=									
25		UB Sales	8000	6000	6000									
26														
27							From	Long-term	Investment					
28		Investments	Expand A-line	Expand C-line	Labor	New Product	Current Assets	Debt	Balance					
29		Cost/Hr	0.02885	0.03825	0.00154									
30		Expansion	3120	284	52000	1100	150	1131	0	=<=	0			
31			=<=	<=	=<=		=<=							
32			3120	1232	52000		150							
33														

Table 9.1 *(continued)*

	A	B	C	D	E	F	G	H	I	J	K	L	M	N
34	**Production**													
35	**and Sales**		Alpha	Beta	Gamma	Lambda	Resource Use		Resource Available					
36	**Sub-Model**	A-line test	1	1		0.5	13700	<=	14040					
37	**year 2**	C-line test			1		2870	=<=	2870					
38		Assembly	10	15	20	5	218400	=<=	218400					
39		Net Rev/Unit	0.35	0.47	0.61	0.25								
40		Sales	6400	4800	2870	5000								
41			>=	>=	>=	>=								
42		LB Sales	1000	1000	1000	1000								
43			=<=	=<=	<=	=<=								
44		UB Sales	6400	4800	4800	5000								
45														
46						From	Long-term	Investment						
47		Investments	Expand A-line	Expand C-line	Labor	Current Assets	Debt	Balance						
48		Cost/Hr	0.02885	0.03825	0.00154									
49		Expansion	4680	90	78000	259	0	0	=<=	0				
50			=<=	<=	=<=	<=								
51			4680	1390	78000	613								
52														
53	**Production**													
54	**and Sales**		Alpha	Beta	Gamma	Lambda	Resource Use		Resource Available					
55	**Sub-Model**	A-line test	1	1		0.5	13960	<=	14040					
56	**year 3**	C-line test			1		3840	=<=	3840					
57		Assembly	10	15	20	5	235600	=<=	235600					
58		Net Rev/Unit	0.35	0.47	0.61	0.25								
59		Sales	5120	3840	3840	10000								
60			>=	>=	>=	>=								
61		LB Sales	1000	1000	1000	1000								
62			=<=	=<=	=<=	=<=								
63		UB Sales	5120	3840	3840	10000								
64														
65						From	Long-term	Investment						
66		Investments	Expand A-line	Expand C-line	Labor	Current Assets	Debt	Balance						
67		Cost/Hr	0.02885	0.03825	0.00154									
68		Expansion	0	970	39040	97	0	0	=<=	0				
69			<=	<=	<=	<=								
70			7020	1435	109200	1439								

4. The constraints in the production and sales submodel for year 1 are mainly straightforward and similar to those discussed in Section 2.1. Examples of exceptions are as follows:
   a. H17 = 6240 + C30; computes A-line capacity in year 1 where 6240 is the base and C30 is expansion financed by capital expenditure. The constraint C31 restricts expansion to 50% of capacity available at the start of year 1.
   b. I30 = C29 * C30 + D29 * D30 + E29 * E30 + F30 − G30 − H30; computes the net capital requirement for new product and capacity expansion in year 1 by subtracting from these needs the capital raised by long-term debt and transfers from current assets. The constraint J30 forces net capital requirement to be nonpositive; that is, capital made available from current assets and long-term debt covers capital expenditures.
5. Assembly capacity available in year 2 is given by the following:
   a. I38 = 0.9 * H18 + E49; reflects loss of 10% of assembly equipment capacity available in year 1.

With this background, we can examine the optimal solution computed by the spreadsheet optimizer. We see that heavy investment in year 1 is needed to develop the new product and expand production capacities. Even with expanded capacity, sales of Betas and Gammas fall far below their upper bounds. The investment budget in year 1 consists mainly of new long-term debt ($1,131,000) because initial current assets are relatively small ($300,000) and only half of that quantity is permitted for investment.

Fortunately, healthy after-tax profits in year 1 increase equity and current assets, facilitating capacity expansion in years 2 and 3. Expansion in year 2, plus the first year sales of Lambda, leads to an even larger increase in after-tax profits. This expansion does not permit maximal sales of Gammas, however, apparently because additional assembly capacity is used instead to make the other three products. Recall that capacity growth cannot exceed 50% in any year. Finally, in year 3, further expansion allows capacity to catch up to demand, and all four of Ajax' products attain maximal sales. At the end of 3 years, Ajax is positioned nicely for a major expansion, either by acquiring another firm or developing additional products.

We briefly review scenarios other than the base case scenario optimized in Table 9.1 that we analyzed with the model. In one scenario, we evaluated a plan put forward by the marketing department to spend $1 million in each of years 2 and 3 on additional advertising of the Lambda computer. The marketers were confident this plan would increase its demand (maximal sales) by 50% in those years. The resulting scenario indicated that the maximal equity attainable at the end of the 3 years would be over $300,000 less if this option were implemented. In another scenario, we reoptimized the base case with an objective function that maximized the discounted sum of after-tax profits over the 3 years. The discount rate was 0.80; that is, $1 earned 1 year in the future is worth $0.80 today. Not surprisingly, the reoptimized solution was almost identical to the base case solution. Finally, we constructed and optimized a scenario in which the Lambda computer development was dropped. This scenario produced poorer financial performance for Ajax. The precise difference from the base case depended on the savings in marketing and overhead that Ajax would realize by not developing and releasing the Lambda.

Model and Methodological Extensions

The simplicity of the model in Table 9.1 allowed us to illustrate the concepts underlying construction of a model for analyzing corporate financial decisions and how they are linked to supply chain decisions. Model extensions would be needed to fully describe and evaluate decisions faced by an actual company. First, the five categories of financial instruments would need to be refined to describe various subcategories. For example, for historical reasons, the company may have accumulated several categories of long-term debt or have several categories of capital assets that can be used in different ways to raise capital. The impact of depreciation of fixed assets on after-tax income should also be modeled. Policy and tax constraints would be written with respect to the refined categories of financial decision variables.

Second, the model might be extended to incorporate options for increasing equity by issuing new shares. Such a model could serve to evaluate the timing and sizing of these offerings, depending on the internal needs for additional equity and external conditions in the market. Third, the model might be extended to more explicitly incorporate marketing and sales options. These options might be simply described by a small number of scenarios with different market potentials and marketing and sales costs.

Methodological extensions might also be necessary or desirable. The linear programming construction of Table 9.1 would require mixed integer programming extensions to capture fixed and nonlinear costs associated with the capacity expansion decisions or to make a logical choice between two or more methods for depreciating equipment. Ambiguity about which financial goal to select as an objective function to drive the optimization, and which to employ as goal constraints with prespecified targets, would suggest the application of the multiobjective solution methodology presented in Section 3.4 for systematically searching the efficient frontier of financial and supply chain strategies. It would also suggest the implementation and application of a method that would assist senior managers in deciding on their ideal point on this frontier.

Financial and other uncertainties suggest the extension of our deterministic model to a stochastic programming model. For example, such a model could be used to evaluate contingency plans for selling fixed assets to raise capital under scenarios where equity fails to grow sufficiently rapidly to allow sufficient borrowing of long-term debt or where current assets fail to appreciate sufficiently to support needed capital investments. It could also be used to help identify strategies that hedge against external uncertainties such as interest rates or growth in the markets for finished goods.

In the final analysis, the application of a financial planning optimization model must be combined with managerial judgment and institutional knowledge about debt financing, dividend policy, issuing equity, and a host of other factors.[5] At the same time, an optimization model can provide a comprehensive and rational analysis of the complex interactions and ripple effects presented by a range of financial decisions and constraints. Decision making in corporate finance, which today relies on myopic rules and analyses, would profit greatly from the systems analysis perspective of these optimization models.

9.2

Financial Planning Issues Facing the Multinational Corporation

A MNC faces a host of complex planning issues when it seeks to optimize medium- and long-term financial performance.[6] Although the fundamental goal may be to maximize the sum of after-tax profits repatriated to the parent corporation over a suitably long-term planning horizon, the MNC must at the same time consider important secondary goals, which recognize a range of costs and constraints associated with cash flow and profits that are realized abroad by subsidiary companies. These may include the financial performance of such partially or wholly owned foreign subsidiaries as well as alternative goals for the MNC corporation itself on performance measures such as total tax expense, return on assets, and total repatriated income.

Constraints associated with cash repatriation are derived from legal and financial conditions extant in the countries where the MNC does business, and the tax laws in the home country of the parent. For MNCs based in the United States, the company's foreign tax credit position with the U.S. Internal Revenue Service is an important factor in optimizing multinational financial flows. Decisions regarding the source, timing, and amount of subsidiary earnings distributions, or other financial flows to the parent, often play a key role in generating or absorbing such credits. Strategies regarding product prices, transfer prices, license fees, royalties, and other interaffiliate flows may be employed to optimize the consolidated results of the MNC, taking into account the impact of local restrictions, incentives, or other conditions.

A MNC also faces a wider and deeper range of risks than a national corporation. Government regulations and tax laws may be subject to frequent and abrupt changes in some countries where the MNC has subsidiaries and affiliates. To protect itself against such risks, the MNC may impose operating restrictions intended to reduce exposure, such as tight limits on cash or equity earnings retained in foreign entities. In addition, changes in exchange rates may seriously affect the relative attractiveness of a country as a manufacturing site or as a market.

Optimization models can capture such financial planning constraints and opportunities and link them to physical supply chain decisions. Their application to problems of this sort has been suggested for more than 25 years.[7] Nevertheless, very few realistic model implementations have yet been made, in part because supply chain and financial data in subsidiaries around the world were not standardized for the purposes of global planning.[8] With the recent implementation of enterprise resource planning systems and business-to-business Internet communications in many MNCs, the modeling approaches we review here become possible and even desirable.

Of course, a MNC may face qualitative issues surrounding its business that are more difficult to capture in a supply chain model than those faced by a national corporation.[9] The knowledge base and skill level of employees in different subsidiaries, as well as their costs, may vary significantly. Similarly, the MNC faces issues surrounding the promotion of organizational learning across its subsidiaries. When introducing a new product, for example, the MNC must select the countries in which to initially manufacture and sell the product and decide when and how the experience gleaned there will be disseminated throughout the corporation.

Nevertheless, effective supply chain models of large portions of a MNC's business, both financial and physical, can be implemented. The complications just cited require that the models and data used to generate them reflect managerial judgment about realistic options and constraints. Analysts using such models can expect to perform extensive scenario analyses to fully evaluate the impact of risk factors on the corporation's strategies.

9.3 A Network Illustration

The network in Figure 9.1 illustrates the integration of the physical and financial supply chains of a MNC.[10] It depicts the interactions between two firms, a parent company in country A and a subsidiary in country B, over two time periods. The triangular nodes with links drawn out of a vertex are sources. The triangular nodes with links drawn to edges are sinks. As we are about to discuss, the links in this network may be partitioned into three sets corresponding to the types of decisions to be made by the MNC. Each set of links along with the nodes spanned by them constitute a subnetwork.

The subnetworks involving the nodes labeled cash balance, investment, bank loan, and bank repayment in *each firm* and the links connecting them are the **cash management networks.**[11] Each of these networks captures the management of cash, or liquid funds, in the country including cash needed to operate, construct, or expand facilities there and make local investments. The "bank" in each country may be viewed as a collection of various sources of debt capital available to the firm located there.

The subnetwork containing the nodes labeled cash balance, plant, market demand, dividend, royalty, management fee, internal equity, and direct loan in *both firms* and the links connecting them is the **intersubsidiary financial network.** This network captures decisions and constraints faced by the MNC in shifting cash (liquidity) between the subsidiary and the parent to meet the goals of the MNC. The payments of dividends and royalties from the subsidiary to the parent are limited by

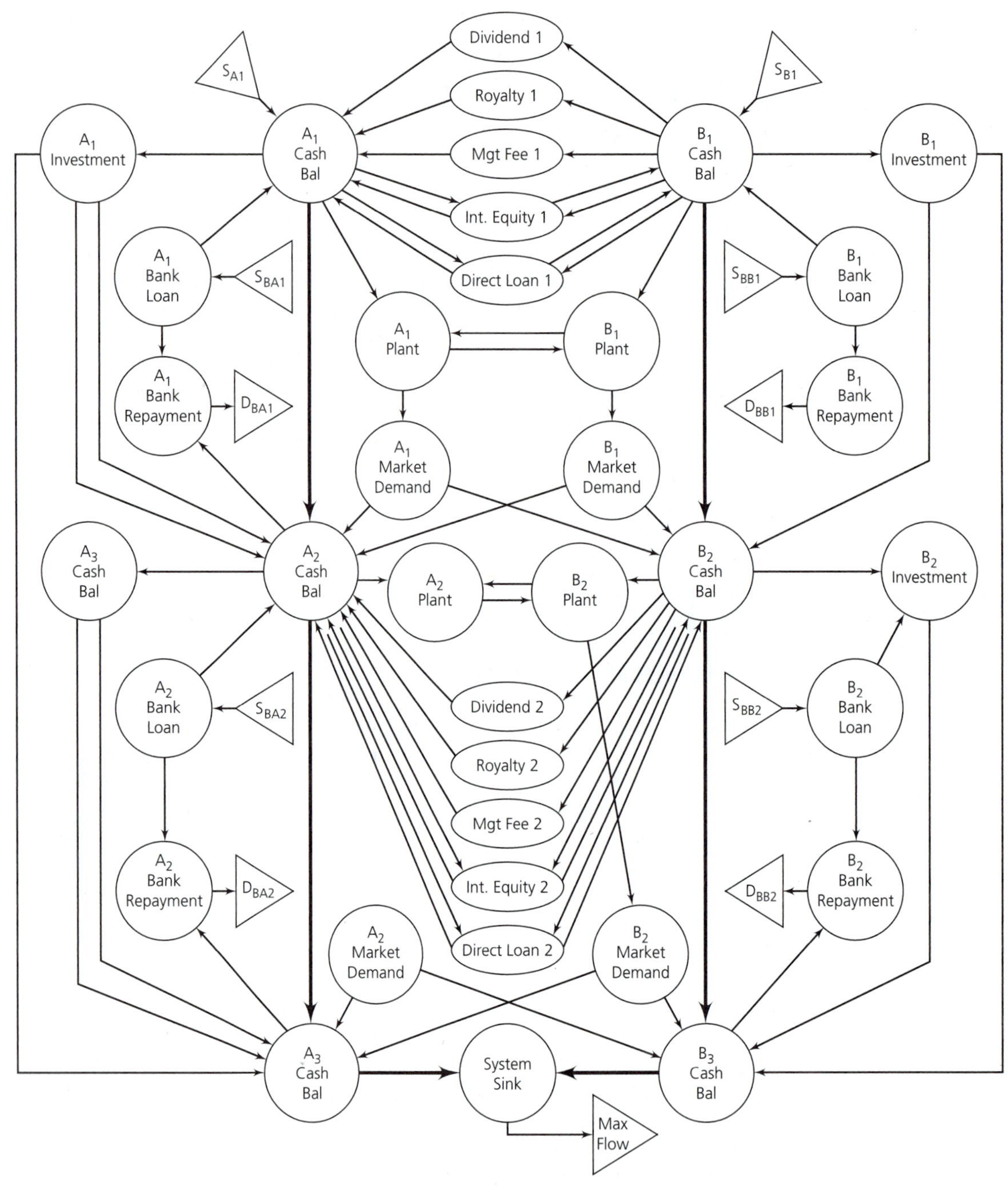

Figure 9.1 Physical and financial supply chain of a MNC Corporation. *Source:* Crum, Klingman, and Travis [1979]

the structure of the MNC. The management fee reflects the subsidiary's share of the cost of centralized management functions. Together, the cash management networks and the intersubsidiary financial network constitute the MNC's **financial supply chain network.**

Finally, the subnetwork involving the nodes labeled cash balance, plants, and market demand in *both firms* and the links connecting them is the **physical supply chain network.** This network is similar to the ones that we have discussed extensively in earlier chapters except that it connects plants and markets in the two countries. Capital requirements needed to run the firms in each country are also explicitly modeled. In addition, costs, processes, resources, and transformation recipes will vary between the countries, reflecting differences in markets and internal capabilities. The flows across national boundaries carry transfer prices that the receiving firm must pay the sending firm for the products.[12] These flows are subject to currency exchange, as well as taxes and duties, which are important factors in planning the MNC's overall strategy.

We elaborate briefly on the model structures. The node labeled A_1 Cash Bal is represented in a model by a balance equation for cash flow of the parent company in country A at the start of the first period. Note that this node is contained in three subnetworks with links to and from it contained in the cash management network for firm A, the supply chain network for the MNC, and the intersubsidiary financial network for the MNC.

The cash flow *into* A_1 Cash Bal is the sum of the following:

- Cash reserves from S_{A1}
- Bank loans with a line of credit S_{BA1}
- Dividends, royalty payments, management fees, internal equity payments, and direct loans received from the subsidiary in country B

The cash flow *out of* A_1 Cash Bal is the sum of the following:

- Investments made by the parent firm
- Cash retained for one period by the parent firm
- Cash needed to support physical supply chain activities in country A in period 1
- Internal equity payments and direct loans to the subsidiary in country B

Any cash flows between subsidiaries in a given period are converted from foreign to local currency at the rate of exchange prevalent in that period. Note also that dividends, royalty payments, and management fees are asymmetrical and flow only from subsidiary B to subsidiary A because A is the parent company.

Similarly, the node labeled A_2 Cash Bal represents a balance equation of cash flow of the subsidiary in country A at the start of the second period. In addition to the cash inflows of the type discussed for A_1, it has cash inflows from investments at the start of period 1 and from product sales in both countries A and B.

The node A_1 Plant has two inflows and two outflows. The inflows are raw materials or components acquired in country A in period 1 that are shipped to the plant and finished product produced in period 1 in country B and shipped to country A. In the latter case, the inflow may be subject to duties. The outflows from the plant are either to markets in period 1 in country A or to the plant in country B. They also may be subject to duties. The plants in countries A and B serve as transshipment points for imported finished products.

As implied by the system sink node in the figure, the objective function of the model is to maximize the discounted sum of net cash flows into the cash balance nodes of the parent and the subsidiary at the end of the two periods. Flows from the subsidiary are denominated in the home currency of the parent corporation. In general, optimization of supply chain strategies for MNCs is a complex, multiobjective process. On the one hand, the parent may seek to maximize the discounted sum of after-tax repatriated net revenues, denominated in the home currency. On the other hand, the performance of each individual subsidiary matters. Other criteria, such as return on assets, may also be important. Thus, methods of multiobjective optimization will be required to evaluate the trade-offs between the conflicting objectives.

Ultimately, Figure 9.1 is only a pedagogical tool. It does not reflect sufficient detail to be translated into a realistic model. Moreover, the network depiction is overly simplistic and does not capture, for example, the richness of processes, resources, and transformations at the plants. The model discussed in the following section captures such details.

9.4 Financial Flows Model

The financial flows model (FFM) was developed using realistic data describing strategic financial and supply chain issues faced by Worldwide Pharmaceuticals, a MNC that manufactures and sells pharmaceutical products.[13] Worldwide's parent company is located in the United States. The model to be described mechanizes many of the relationships depicted in Figure 9.1. In particular, it accepts three types of information for each legal entity in each country included in the model—product, financial, and tax information.

Product Information. FFM considers the production, distribution, and sale of a single product. For this product, production occurs in two stages: the initial manufacture of a primary component and the secondary "finishing" of the product for sale to customers. In FFM, we assumed that the primary component may be manufactured in three locations but that finishing must occur in the subsidiary (country) where the final customer sales are made.

A. Manufacturing cost of primary component
   1. Of customer sales
   2. Of affiliate sales
B. Distribution costs

    1. Of customer sales
    2. Of affiliate sales
C. Finishing costs
    1. On customer sales
D. Selling price
    1. Of customer sales
    2. Of primary component sales to affiliates
E. Annual demand
    1. Customer
    2. Affiliate
F. Marketing and sales costs
    1. Of customer sales

Financial Information

A. Working capital requirements and ratios
    1. Inventory (ratio to sales)
    2. Trade receivables (ratio to sales)
        a. Affiliate
        b. Third party
    Current liabilities (ratio to cost of goods manufactured)
    1. Payables to suppliers
        a. Affiliate
        b. Third party
        c. Other payables
B. Return on cash investments and cost of debt
    1. Cash and investments
    2. Cost of debt financing from
        a. Affiliates
        b. Third parties
C. Initial equity accounts
    1. Capital stock
    2. Retained earnings
D. Debt: Equity constraints
E. Cross-border financial flow constraints (government capital and exchange controls)
F. Initial financial position
    1. Cash and investment balances
    2. Debt obligations
G. Primary component supply price constraints
    1. Maximum
    2. Minimum

Remarks: Parameters and variables listed in Part A tend to vary from subsidiary (country) to subsidiary reflecting local norms for supplier credit, customer payment terms, local tax payment schedules, and so on. The parameters and variables associated with cash investments, debt, and equity accounts are dynamic quantities. In FFM, they are captured by balance equations and constraints associated with the beginning and end of each decision period.

Tax Information

A. Local income tax rate
B. Import taxes and duties
C. Export taxes and duties
D. Minimum entity profitability
E. Local withholding tax rates on dividends, royalties, and interest payments between pairs of entities

Remarks: The minimum entity profitability may reflect statutory, or alternatively, self-imposed constraints based on an assessment of the minimum taxable income that would be earned on similar transactions between independent parties.

Statement of the Financial Flows Model

For simplicity, the specific model presented here is a linear programming model. As we know from Chapter 4, mixed integer programming extensions would be required if there are fixed costs or nonlinearities in the product information. They would also be required if Worldwide Pharmaceuticals were faced with locational decisions such as which plants should manufacture a given product. Finally, they would be required if nonnumeric constraints reflecting company or governmental policy were present; for example, the restriction that a market be served by exactly one manufacturing source or the restriction that an entity may not borrow money from and lend money to other entities in a given year.

FFM incorporates financial and logistics constraints and variables over a multiperiod planning horizon. The constraints of the model are as follows:

- Demand constraints
- Manufacturing sourcing constraints
- Inventory balance equations
- Supply revenue constraints (min., max.)
- Royalty (trademark, patent and know-how) constraints (min., max.)
- Income equations
- Retained earnings balance equations
- Changes in working capital
- Interest rate constraints (min., max.)
- Debt/equity constraints
- Minimum dividend requirements
- Minimum earnings constraints
- Minimum taxes paid constraints
- Tax credit equations

The variables in FFM include those required to track financial performance in each period of the planning horizon. These include entity debt, cash, retained earnings, and so on. In addition, the model includes a host of variables describing supply chain activities such as quantities manufactured at a given source in a given year, inventories, product flows, and so on.

From the viewpoint of analyzing decisions, the key control variables are the following:

- Primary component transfer prices
- Royalty (trademark, patent and know-how) rates
- Dividends
- Loan quantities
- Loan interest rates
- Product flows

These control variables are allowed to range within a window of values centered about an average or nominal value. For example, interest rates on loans from entity A to entity B might be allowed in the model to vary between 7.2 and 8.8%. The range is intended to reflect leeway around the prevailing "market" rate of 8% that would produce income and expenses that tax authorities in the two countries would find acceptable.

The selection of an objective function to derive the optimization of FFM is complex. The typical U.S. MNC is faced with a range of conflicting objectives involving measurement of financial performance of the parent company and its subsidiaries. These may include earnings, net revenues, return on assets, or return on equity in every period of the planning horizon in every MNC entity. The time stream of a given type of variable in a given entity can, in principle, be collapsed into a net present value figure, but the choice of discount factor for the entity may not be obvious. This is especially true for entities in those countries where an assessment of sovereign risk suggests that cash or equity left undistributed from that country should be valued lower than an equivalent amount of cash in the United States.

In addition, the U.S. MNC needs to account for the levels of certain financial variables, such as existing but unutilized excess or latent tax credits, and certain supply chain variables, such as finished goods inventory, at the end of the planning horizon. Quantifying and constraining terminal effects are often a difficult and important issue in planning for our model because we are dealing with both financial and supply chain decisions associated with multiple entities.

We let WPC denote the entire or consolidated Worldwide Pharmaceuticals made up of the following 10 distinct legal and taxable entities:

- U.S. Consolidated Company (USC)
- U.S. Holding Company (USH)
- U.S. Domestic Company (USD)
- Country A (A)

- Country B (B)
- Country C (C)
- Country D (D)
- Country E (E)
- Country F (F)
- Country G (G)

Financial, tax, and physical logistics decisions for each of these entities, and WPC as a whole, over a 4-year period planning horizon, each period consisting of 1 year, are considered by the model. The primary component is manufactured in USD, A and B, and sold in USD, B, C, D, E, and F. The entity G serves as a capitalized, internal finance company occasionally receiving funds from the other entities, investing them, and lending money to the entities as needed.

The production/distribution network for WPC is depicted in Figure 9.2. The product's primary component is manufactured in three sites (A, USD, B) and distributed to the subsidiaries for finishing and sale as shown. Due to regulation by government officials abroad, WPC agreed not to distribute the primary component from the manufacturing site in A to any entity other than USD. The cost of this policy is examined in one of the optimization runs.

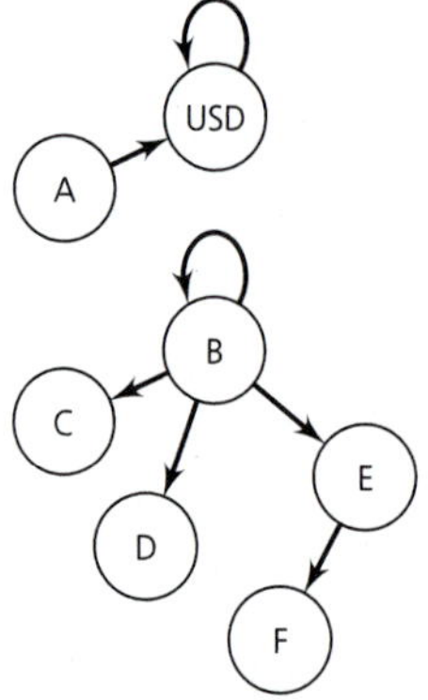

Figure 9.2
Production distribution network. *Source:* Klimczak, Magee, and Shapiro [1990]

Figure 9.3 describes the royalty network for WPC. Note that commercial considerations dictated that the patent and know-how license for manufacturing the primary component in B is through E. Country E was selected because its tax laws favor the receipt and management of such funds.

Figure 9.4 depicts the directions of possible flow in each period for dividends from subsidiaries to USH. In other MNCs the structure might be more complex, allowing, for example, dividends to be paid between any pair of entities. In such an event, the model would have greater flexibility in selecting these key control variables to the MNC's advantage.

During the implementation, we experimented with a number of numerical realizations of FFM. The experimentation led to changes in the form and magnitude of

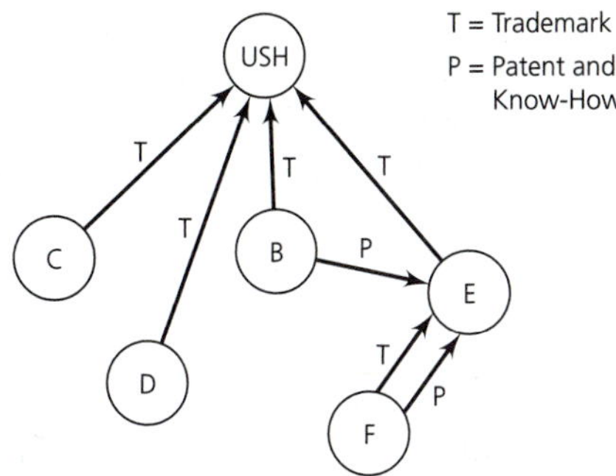

Figure 9.3
Royalty network.
Source: Klimczak, Magee, and Shapiro [1990]

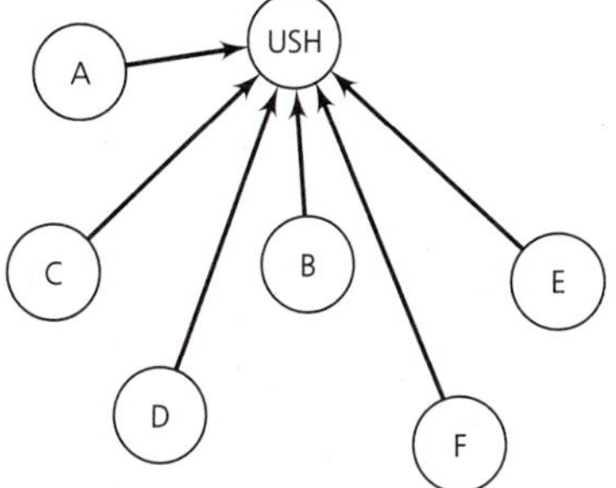

Figure 9.4
Dividend network.
Source: Klimczak, Magee, and Shapiro [1990]

constraints reflecting various company policies and in the selection of an objective function. Here we report on five closely related numerical models, and their optimal solutions, that indicate how financial planning problems faced by WPC can be realistically described. Features of these runs include the following:

- Minimum local tax payments equal to 10% of sales were required for B, E, A, and USD. Such minima were not imposed on D, C, or F because they degraded the performance of these entities to unacceptable levels. Taxes were paid in those countries, however, but at lower than the prescribed levels.
- Earlier runs indicated the need for smoothing constraints for each entity on retained earnings, equity, and cash distributions. These took the following forms:
  - Constant upper bounds on equity.
  - Lower bounds on equity equal to 7/8, 3/4, 5/8, and 1/2 of the equity at the end of year 0 at the end of years 1, 2, 3, 4, respectively.
  - The minimum cash flow distributed via dividends and royalties each year equaled 50% of net earnings.
  - Entities could be borrowers or lenders in a given period, but not both. This restriction was based on information from a first-run pass of the model, which induced certain high-tax countries in certain periods to borrow funds at the high end of the range of permissible interest rates and

relend at the lower end. Generally, tax rules do not allow entities to generate tax-deductible losses in this manner.

- Entities were not allowed to stockpile active ingredient beyond the amount required to meet current needs.

The objective function of FFM was to maximize the net present value of earnings in each period of the planning horizon in all entities. A yearly discount factor of 13% was used. This objective reflects the philosophy of financial planners at WPC that a dollar earned and held in any entity is the same as a dollar earned and held in any other entity. The philosophy is qualified by the imposition of constraints on the maximal amount of undistributed retained earnings that can be held by certain entities in any period. These upper bounds, expressed in thousands of U.S. dollars, are as follows:

B	*D*	*C*	*E*	*F*
74,885	22,950	20,750	None	828,000

As we shall discuss, optimal shadow prices for the constraints on retained earnings can be interpreted as sovereign risk factors. The financial manager can use this information to adjust the bounds to reflect his or her intuitive judgment about appropriate ranges and relative values for these factors.

Financial Flows Model Results

Table 9.2 contains a partial summary of the five runs. The first three runs indicate that somewhat tight and generally binding constraints on retained earnings in non-U.S. (overseas) entities do not have a large relative impact on the objective function of maximizing the discounted sum of retained earnings in all entities. In absolute terms, of course, the changes are large; for example, the objective function difference in absolute terms between run 1 and run 2 is $3.6 million.

The last column shows that the secondary objective of maximizing the discounted sum of earnings in the United States is more sensitive to the existence and severity of bounds on retained earnings overseas. The loss of $3.7 million in the primary objective function between runs 1 and 3 is balanced by an increase in secondary objective of $32.2 million. Thus, the models show that repatriation of earnings does not cost much in terms of more global objective function values, at least in the range of upper bounds on retained earnings of runs 1 through 3. Table 9.3 gives the breakdown of the present value of net earnings in all entities for run 3.

In run 4, we significantly reduced (from $50 million to $5 million) the initial inventory of excess tax credits. This had a pronounced effect on strategies selected by the model, particularly on the dividends paid by foreign entities to USH. For the most part, dividends increased in each entity in each period between runs 1 and 3 and between runs 3 and 4, but the pattern is far from uniform due to the complexity of the planning environment and the model.

Table 9.2 Summary of optimization runs for financial flows model

Model Run	Description	Objective Fn. Value (U.S.$ × 10^6)	Present Value U.S. Earnings over the Planning Horizon (U.S.$ × 10^6)
1	No upper bound on retained earnings.	1050.5	801.0
2	Upper bounds as stated above on retained earnings in B, D, C, F.	1046.9	831.9
3	Tighter upper bound on retained earnings in F ($414 million).	1046.8	833.2
4	Same as Run 3 except initial tax credits reduced from $50 million to $5 million.	1016.6	877.1
5	Multiple sourcing of primary component; upper bounds on retained earnings of run 3.	1088.2	944.5

Source: Klimczak, Magee, and Shapiro [1990].

Table 9.3 Breakdown of earnings from run 3

	Present Value of Net Earnings (U.S.$ × 10^6)
U.S.	833.16
A	83.31
B	19.52
C	17.09
D	–0.53
E	36.32
F	–67.80
G	125.48
Total	1046.80

Source: Klimczak, Magee, and Shapiro [1990].

In run 5, we allowed non-U.S. entities to receive primary component from the USD rather than B. This had a significant effect on the objective function, causing it to rise by $41.4 million, or 3.95%, due to less-expensive production and possibly to positive tax effects. The discounted sum of U.S. earnings increased from $833.2 million to $944.5 million, or 13.4%. Although an increase was expected, the model pinpoints the magnitude of the increase.

One of the goals for FFM was to assess the extent to which overseas subsidiaries borrow from USH to help pay dividends. Some borrowing did take place, but it was not highly significant. Table 9.4 depicts all borrowing by entities for run 4 and contrasts these amounts with the dividends paid.

Table 9.4 Borrowing and dividends (in U.S.$ × 10^6)

		Year 1	Year 2	Year 3	Year 4
B	Borrowed			8.08[a]	
	Dividends			42.13	
D	Borrowed			4.43[b]	7.30[b]
	Dividends			10.49	15.54
E	Borrowed			4.71[a]	6.81[a]
	Dividends			9.98	51.65

[a]From A.
[b]From USH.
Source: Klimczak, Magee, and Shapiro [1990].

Optimal shadow prices on the constraints on retained earnings in each period in the overseas subsidiaries reflect the objective function loss due to these constraints. By converting the shadow prices to common currency terms, combining the four shadow prices in a given entity for each of the 4 years, and taking into account the discount factors, we can translate the losses into sovereign risk factors for these entities (a score of 100 indicates no sovereign risk), (see Table 9.5). In effect, a sovereign risk factor in a foreign country of 70 indicates that WPC is willing to sacrifice 30 cents of each dollar earned in that country to restrict retained earnings at the current level.

The relative and absolute magnitude of some of these induced sovereign risk factors were inconsistent with those that the financial manager had in mind when he set the constraints on retained earnings. Changing them to precise values can be difficult due to the implicit and complex manner in which the simplex method for linear programming computes optimal shadow prices. A possible methodological extension that would eliminate the difficulty would be to set targets for the sovereign risk factors and use multiplier selection techniques to try to attain these factors while optimizing our stated objective function. With the new approach, the bounds on retained earnings would be implicitly derived from the sovereign risk targets.

Finally, FFM included a submodel to optimize the utilization of foreign tax credits by WPC in its U.S. tax returns. These tax credits refer to taxes paid in foreign countries during each year. The parent company may use them to reduce taxes paid in the United States during the given year or any other year starting 2 years before the given year and ending 4 years after the given year. We omit further details.

Table 9.5 Sovereign risk factors

Run	*B*	*D*	*C*	*F*
3	96.6	100.0	74.5	98.6
4	99.4	100.0	68.4	100.0

Source: Klimczak, Magee, and Shapiro [1990].

9.5

Modeling Exchange Rate Risks

In the previous three sections, we examined the application of deterministic optimization models in developing strategies that coordinate financial and supply chain modeling in a MNC. In this section and the next, we discuss areas of uncertainty and risk faced by MNCs and present modeling approaches that explicitly identify hedging strategies for mitigating risk. First, we examine in this section an approach based on financial options for hedging against exchange risks. Second, we examine global risks more widely in the next section and discuss how real supply chain options, instead of financial options, can be employed to mitigate them.

Risks due to exchange rate uncertainties play an important role in shaping a MNC's strategy. For example, a multinational manufacturing company pursuing a supply chain strategy that maximizes next year's after-tax net revenues measured in its home currency faces risks associated with exchange rates between this currency and that in foreign countries where it does business. If the currency in a country where the corporation has a manufacturing subsidiary becomes devalued with respect to the home currency, the cost of manufacturing the company's products there, measured in the home currency, will decrease. Revenues from sales in that country, however, will also decrease when measured in the currency of the home country. Thus, manufacturing products in the foreign subsidiary becomes more attractive with devaluation, but sales become less attractive. If the currency in the country of the subsidiary appreciates with respect to the MNC's home currency, the reverse is true. The implication is that, in forming its supply chain plans for the coming year, the MNC must develop manufacturing, distribution, pricing, and sales strategies that anticipate and exploit these uncertain movements in exchange rates.

One approach for controlling exchange rate risks is purely financial. It uses financial instruments, such as options and futures, to insure the MNC against such risks. The other approach is to adjust physical supply chain strategies to achieve similar effects. The two approaches are not mutually exclusive, although they use methods from separate disciplines, finance theory and operations research, which have not yet been fully integrated.

We illustrate financial hedging with an example involving options. At the simplest level, the corporation can insure itself against risk by using either a **call option** or a **put option.** A call option gives the corporation the right, but not the obligation, to buy an asset at a predetermined price, called the **strike price.** A put option gives the corporation the right, but not the obligation, to sell an asset at a predetermined strike price. An option may be a **European option,** which means it may be exercised at a given point in time in the future called the **maturity date.** Alternatively, the option may be an **American option,** which means it may be exercised any time up to and including the maturity date.

We consider a MNC that has a U.S. parent. The marketing department forecasts with confidence that, during the next accounting year, the corporation's after-tax net revenues in Germany will equal 100 million (M) deutsche marks (DM). These net revenues will be repatriated to the U.S. parent on October 31.

Management is less confident about its treasury department's exchange rate forecast for next October 31 of .66 U.S.$ per DM. Further analysis by the treasury department yields the **probability tree** shown in Figure 9.5 of possible states of the future with their associated exchange rates and probabilities of occurrence. According to the tree, the corporation can expect after-tax revenues repatriated from Germany to lie somewhere between U.S.$56M and U.S.$76M.

This situation would not require further attention if the corporation's senior management was willing to accept that changes in the exchange rate balance out over the long term. In this instance, the CEO is less sanguine. She believes strongly that the corporation must attain after-tax receipts from Germany next year of at least U.S.$60M to maintain confidence with the stockholders. In other words, the CEO wishes to insure the corporation against the **risk** that its after-tax receipts next year fall below U.S.$60M.

The request for insurance is passed to the corporation's treasury department. It arranges with a commercial bank to buy a European put option allowing the corporation to sell 100M DM next October 31 at the strike price of .606 U.S.$ per DM. The premium for this option is U.S.$0.6M. The effect of the option on U.S.$ revenues is displayed in Figure 9.6. The five points on the graph labeled "uninsured revenues" are the possible outcomes shown in Figure 9.5. The U.S.$56M outcome, which has probability .12 of occurring, is below $60M and therefore not acceptable.

On the other hand, the line labeled "insured revenues" in Figure 9.6 lies uniformly on or above U.S.$60M and is acceptable. The U.S.$56M outcome associated with the lowest exchange rate state is replaced by the U.S.$60M outcome by exercising the put option to sell the 100M DM for U.S.$60.6M. For this outcome, we say that the option **finished in the money.** The net amount accruing to the corporation, however, is only U.S.$60M because the corporation spent U.S.$0.6M to acquire the option.

For the other four exchange rate states shown in Figure 9.6, the net receipts accruing to the corporation lie below the uninsured revenues because the corporation has spent U.S.$0.6M on an option that has no value when the exchange rate is

Figure 9.5
Exchange rate probability tree

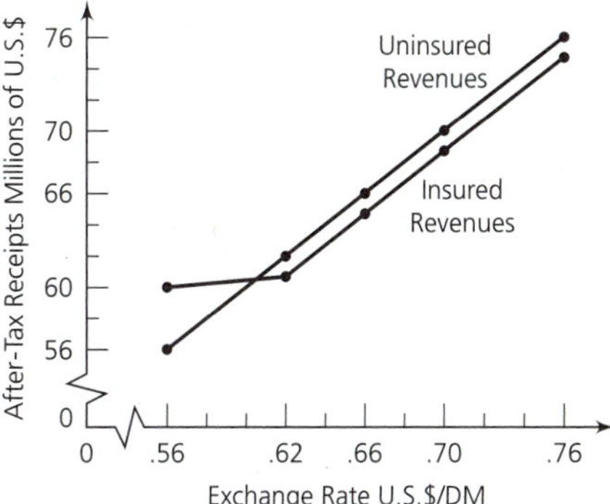

Figure 9.6
Insured vs. uninsured revenues

.606 U.S.$/DM or higher. We say the option **finished out of the money** for those states. The graph of the insured revenues illustrates how the corporation was willing to give up after-tax revenues associated with good states to insure acceptable performance in the bad state.

The example illustrates several other concepts about decision making in the face of uncertainty. If the CEO were indifferent to exchange rate uncertainties, assuming over the long term that up and down deviations would balance out, we would say that she is **risk neutral.** A risk-neutral decision maker is willing to maximize the expected return from an uncertain decision problem because, over the long term, such a strategy will yield the greatest average return per year. For the example, the expected return in millions of dollars is the sum of the probabilities times the payoffs or,

$$66 = (.12)(76) + (.20)(70) + (.36)(66) + (.20)(62) + (.12)(56)$$

Risk neutrality on the part of a decision maker is often associated with her company's great wealth relative to the gains and losses of the decisions she faces. This wealth allows her to be unthreatened by the downside chance of losing money.

We saw, however, that the CEO did feel threatened by the downside risk. In this case, we say that the decision maker is **risk averse.** She is willing to sacrifice upside benefits to insure herself against downside losses. For the example, the expected return in millions of dollars *using the option* is

$$65.952 = (.12)(76) + (.20)(70) + (.36)(66) + (.20)(62) + (.12)(60.6) - 0.6$$

By acquiring the put option and exercising it in the lowest U.S.$/DM state, the payoff from that state is U.S.$60M instead of U.S.$56M. Because the corporation paid U.S.$0.6M for the option, its expected return is reduced by U.S.$0.12M, which is the cost of the insurance policy. By contrast, the commercial bank that sold the option to the corporation has greater assets and is risk neutral, which enables the bank to make, on average, U.S.$0.048M from deals such as this. The bank is also involved in buying and selling a number of currency options whose payments tend to balance out.

The bank's fee for the option was based on its assessment of the uncertainties in the U.S.$/DM exchange rate over the coming year, which financiers call **volatility.** This information is used in formulas of options pricing theory to determine the breakeven price for such an option.[14] The bank's fee contains a mark-up from this breakeven price.

It is possible that the corporation and the commercial bank have different assessments of the exchange rate uncertainties. As a result, the expected payoff to the corporation using the option might be greater than U.S.$66M. This would occur, for example, if options pricing theory led the commercial bank to charge a premium of only U.S.$0.4M for the option. In such an event, the expected payoff using the option would be U.S.$66.152M. In other words, from the perspective of maximizing expected return, the CEO could have her cake and eat it too. She would be insured against the downside risk and could expect to make an additional U.S.$0.152M.

Such a situation is an **arbitrage** opportunity that admits an expectation of profits merely by **speculation.** If the CEO was convinced that its treasury department's assessment of the exchange rate uncertainties was correct, the corporation could buy put options for large quantities of DM at the same premium and at the same strike price and then plan to buy large quantities of DM on October 31 of next year if the rate falls to 0.56 U.S.$/DM. The expectation is that the corporation would earn U.S.$0.38 on every U.S.$1.00 spent on options, although the probability of finishing out of the money is 0.88. Chances are, however, that most corporations would consider pursuing such speculative opportunities as imprudent, leaving them to arbitrageurs on Wall Street.

In the future, we may well see the creation and use of new types of options on physical resources of a company's supply chain. As an example, we consider an uncertain and risky situation faced by a large paper company that manufactures publication papers for magazines. The company is plagued by large orders from long-standing customers that are not firm. A customer places an order several weeks or months in advance to ensure a place in the paper company's production schedule. Too often, the customer cancels the order just days before it is scheduled to be produced, with serious consequences to the efficiency of the production schedule. At other times, the customer may seek to place a large order on short notice after the production schedule has been set.

To mitigate the risks of canceled and last minute orders, the company could offer call options giving customers the right, but not the obligation, to buy specified quantities of paper. Associated with each option would be a price per ton for the paper (the strike price) and a date by which the option must be exercised. The assumption would be that the customer intends to exercise the option, and the premium on the option would reflect the disruption caused by not exercising it. This application of options is a form of **yield management**, similar to practices followed by the airlines in pricing seats on each flight, aimed at maximizing the return on capital invested in the paper company's production capacity.

The exchange rate risk just analyzed was significant in size, but isolated. Insurance against the risk used a method that focused myopically on one exchange rate transaction. The MNC will face a number of such situations that, in principle, should be evaluated together as a **portfolio problem** that could be analyzed using an optimization model. Moreover, the corporation should investigate methods for mitigating such risks and others associated with doing business in many countries by flexible management of their physical supply chain, as well as by using financial instruments. This topic is discussed in the next section.

9.6 Real Options for Hedging Risks in the Global Economy

The global economy is changing radically and will continue to do so for many years. Recent trends include the following:[15]

- Reduction of trade barriers
- Creation of regional economic zones
- Maturation of consumer markets in industrial countries
- Potential growth of consumer markets in emerging countries
- Increased expectations by consumers for product value, variety, and availability
- Increased environmental concerns with significant economic implications for manufacturing and distribution companies
- Increased volatility in financial and currency markets

These trends have simultaneously expanded the opportunities open to MNCs and increased their risks.

Major sources of uncertainty faced by a MNC include product prices, product demand, commodity prices, commodity supply, foreign exchange, new manufacturing and information technologies, competitor actions, and political changes. New tools of analysis and planning are needed to control risks associated with these uncertainties while guiding management toward enhanced profits and shareholder values. In this section, we discuss briefly current research aimed at developing such tools.

Financial and business risks associated with designing and operating global supply chains can best be mitigated by integrating tools of financial analysis with those of supply chain planning. Unfortunately, efforts to effect such an integration must overcome large cultural barriers within the firm. On the one hand, the firm's financial managers are accustomed to managing risk by applying options and other derivative instruments that they purchase from commercial banks. Financial engineers at these banks use options pricing theory to determine their cost based on probabilistic analysis of the uncertainties. The use of currency options to mitigate exchange rate risk that we presented in the previous section is a classic application of this type. Many supply chain risks do not lend themselves to insurance coverage using options; for example, the risk that consumer demand in a particular country will drop by 50% next year due to an economic or governmental crisis.

On the other hand, the firm's supply chain managers employ (deterministic) optimization models in trying to fathom the complex interactions and ripple effects that make supply chain planning difficult and important. These deterministic models do not identify contingency plans and hedging strategies for mitigating risk. Moreover, supply chain models have not yet been widely integrated with corporate financial planning models.

In short, options pricing models and mixed integer programming supply chain models are completely different in their derivation and mathematical form. Business processes for using them to support managerial decision making and control are also very different. However, scholars believe that the differences can be reconciled by the paradigm of stochastic programming because it offers a common starting point from which to control the risks of managing a global supply chain. Using the terminology of financial engineers, hedging strategies and contingency plans identified by a stochastic programming model are "real options" presented by facility location, production, inventory, and distribution decisions incorporated in the model. By contrast, financial options that are bought and sold by commercial banks to MNCs reflect the forecasts of global financial markets concerning currency exchange rates, interest rates, commodity costs, and other factors associated with tradeable goods. The challenge is to combine real and financial options in a stochastic programming framework.

We will not attempt to develop in any detail this important and unresolved area of basic and applied research. Instead, we briefly interpret stochastic programming from the viewpoint of identifying real options for mitigating global supply chain risk. Scholars have identified the following six generic types of real options:[16]

- Wait/postpone
- Expand
- Contract
- Exit
- Switch
- Improve

In earlier chapters, we discussed examples of all these types of real options in deterministic and stochastic supply chain models.

Postponement of final product assembly until uncertain demand is revealed or known with a higher degree of certainty is a new approach to supply chain management that has proven highly successful. Decisions to expand the company by the construction or acquisition of new facilities can be accurately described by deterministic mixed integer programming models; stochastic programming versions of these models in which expansion is viewed as a hedge or a contingency plan have also been developed.[17] For example, a stochastic programming model of a MNC supply chain might incorporate a contingency plan that shifts production from a plant in country A to a plant in country B in a scenario when the currency in country A becomes overvalued. In such a scenario, manufacturing costs in country A would reduce the profitability of products made there. Similar modeling constructions are available for the other types of real options.

Stochastic programming constraints on the company's performance in some or all scenarios of the future can insure the company against unacceptable downside risk in much the same way as financial options. An example is constraints stating that losses under all scenarios cannot exceed $10 million in any year of the planning horizon. Stochastic programming also allows the imposition of more subtle, probabilistic constraints; for example, constraints that limit the probability of losses in excess of $10 million in any year of the planning horizon to no more than 0.05.

The successful application of stochastic programming to such problems requires basic and applied research leading to practical solutions for a number of technical issues. First, probabilistic descriptions of important financial and supply chain uncertainties can be very complex because they involve diverse factors such as demand, exchange rates, and political unrest. Second, stochastic programming models can address only a finite number of scenarios of the future, but the relevant probabilistic distributions are often continuous multivariate functions, which implicitly describe an infinite number of scenarios. Thus, the multivariate distributions must either be discretized or sampled to accommodate the finite stochastic model programming structure. Rigorous and efficient methods for doing this have not yet been fully developed. Third, modeling practitioners need to devise new methods for incorporating financial options in stochastic programming models because certain risks, such as those due to exchange rates uncertainties, may be difficult to mitigate solely by real options. Despite these difficulties, the potential payback from an effective stochastic programming model is enormous. Moreover, without sacrificing too much rigor, knowledgeable practitioners should be able to fashion a pragmatic stochastic programming approach for specific MNCs with specific risks that is customized to the MNC's decision-making needs.

Finally, we emphasize that the application of stochastic programming to global supply chain planning must be embedded in managerial processes for gathering data, defining scenarios, performing analyses, and implementing plans. The discipline of scenario planning discussed in Section 8.8 is very relevant to establishing these processes. Senior management must also commit to ongoing and suitably repetitive strategic planning exercises in which its judgment is combined with data and analysis in refining existing strategies and devising new ones. These strategies should include real and financial options for mitigating risk.

9.7 Final Thoughts

We have demonstrated in this chapter that realistic optimization models for corporate financial planning, which include linkages to supply chain models, can be constructed. The reluctance of financial managers to consider such models may be due to a lack of knowledge about them coupled with legacy thinking about myopic approaches to financial decision making. In any event, we are hopeful that innovative financial managers are ready to consider broader, systems analysis approaches to the evaluation of their planning problems. On several occasions in recent years, while discussing supply chain modeling solutions in companies that manufacture and distribute physical products, financial managers present at the meetings have observed with enthusiasm that the models could also analyze the company's "financials" such as long-term debt, equity, retained earnings, and a host of other factors.

Models that link financial planning and supply chain networks for MNCs are particularly appealing because they allow the MNC to legally exploit a vast array of options for repatriating after-tax income in the company's local currency to the parent company. At the same time, using multiobjective optimization methods, these models allow senior managers to measure trade-offs among after-tax repatriated income and the performances of foreign subsidiaries. Finally, although they require more research, stochastic programming models to assist MNCs in selecting real and financial options are a tantalizing paradigm awaiting application in the near future. Due to uncertainties about interest rates, commodity prices, and other financial factors, stochastic programming is also very relevant to financial planning of a corporation doing business in only one country.

Finally, with the examples of this chapter and the previous one, we have demonstrated the capability of optimization models to holistically capture supply chain, marketing, and financial planning within the firm. This capability is a systems analysis projection of the **balanced scorecard** methodology that seeks to provide managers with a comprehensive range of internal and external measures and metrics describing the company's performance.[18] Specifically, the balanced scorecard links performance measures in four key areas: financial perspective, customer perspective (marketing), internal perspective (supply chain), and learning and growth (human resources). The balanced scorecard methodology has been translated into popular decision support systems that are sold off the shelf by several software companies. A comparison of the similarities and differences between holistic analysis with optimization models and the analytic tools in these decision support systems would be an interesting and worthwhile activity.

Exercises

In addition to the following exercises, modeling exercises involving data files and discussion exercises involving white papers may be found on the Web site (www.scm-models.com).

1. Timme and Timme-Williams discuss connections between supply chain management and the financial performance of the firm.[19] They assert the following:

   > A company must offer a competitive return in the financial markets to attract the funds it needs to maintain its existing business and provide for future growth. For a publicly traded company, a competitive return is measured by "total shareholder return" (dividends plus the change in stock price measured as a percentage of the price paid for the stock). . . . In the near term, it is not always clear what drives a company's stock price. Some speculate it is investors' emotions, while others claim its is animal spirits. However, over time, stock price tends to be driven by the financial performance of a company's operations, which is related to three key factors:

- *Growth*—How fast revenues are growing year-over-year.
- *Profitability*—How much is left over in profits per dollar of revenue after deducting operating expense (procurement, manufacturing, transportation, distribution, etc.). This is often called operating profit margin.
- *Capital Utilization*—How many dollars of revenue are generated for each dollar invested in capital (e.g., inventories and accounts receivable, warehouses, fleets, plant and equipment). We like to refer to capital utilization as "SPEED"—with the competing companies recording the highest average speed winning the race.

Thus, Timme and Timme-Williams suggest that the company seeks to maximize these three types of variables, which suggests the use of multiobjective optimization methods to analyze trade-offs among them. Discuss how the Ajax financial planning model in Section 9.1 analyzes these factors. Moreover, describe how you would extend the model to incorporate target performance constraints for each of these objectives. Your extensions should address measuring and constraining financial performance in each year of a multiyear planning horizon. Indicate how you would apply the methods of Section 3.4 to explore the efficient frontier. What additional modeling do you think is needed to relate solutions on the efficient frontier to stock price?

2. The 4R Company sells four consumer products: Cash Cow, Star, Question Mark, and Dog. The net revenues (millions of dollars) associated with each of the products under different strategies for each of the next three years are given in the following table:

	Cash Cow Strategy 1	Star Strategy 1	Star Strategy 2	Star Strategy 3	Question Mark Strategy 1	Question Mark Strategy 2	Question Mark Strategy 3	Dog Strategy 1	Dog Strategy 2
Year 1	2.5	–5.0	–3.0	–2.1	–2.0	–1.1	1.5	–0.5	–1.5
Year 2	2.5	2.1	1.0	0.9	–2.0	1.0	0.0	–0.5	0.25
Year 3	2.5	6.8	2.4	1.9	4.8	1.5	0.0	–0.5	0.0

The company wishes to use the positive cash flow from Cash Cow, plus debt financing, to promote development of Star and possibly Question Mark. Strategy 3 for Question Mark involves the sale of the product to another company in year 1. Strategy 2 for Dog involves an investment in year 1 so that 4R can sell the product to another company in year 2.

To cover possible cash requirements during years 1 and 2, the company can borrow up to \$1.0 million at a yearly interest rate of 8%, up to another \$1.0 million at a yearly interest rate of 10%, and up to another \$2.0 million at a yearly interest rate of 15%. Such borrowing is made at the start of each year and must be paid back at the start of the following year and new debt, if needed, issued. We assume that no debt will be needed or used in year 3. Excess cash generated at the end of year 2, if any, may be invested in year 3 at a 6% yearly return.

The company's chief financial officer wishes to select a pure (unique) strategy for each product, a debt financing plan and an excess cash investment plan, that maximizes net revenues for year 3. Use a spreadsheet optimizer to formulate and optimize a mixed integer programming model of this problem.

3. At the end of Section 9.4, we discussed briefly how a MNC whose parent company is based in the United States might apply tax credits that result from taxes paid in foreign countries to its taxes paid in the United States. Specifically, the credits may be applied to reduce taxes for the year in which they occur, retroactively to taxes paid in the 2 previous years or saved and applied to taxes to be paid over the next 4 years. The following table provides information (measured in millions of U.S. dollars) about the taxes that the company has paid and expects to pay over the relevant 7-year period:

Year	–2	–1	0	1	2	3	4
Taxes Paid	70	65	130	145	170	175	190
Tax Credits			60	70	80	90	80

It also contains the tax credit that may be applied for this year (year 0) and the anticipated tax credits for the next 4 years. The current inventory of unused credits is 50.

Construct a model for allocating the tax credits according to the following conditions:

- The net taxes paid in any year after the credits have been applied must be at least 60. This is the lower bound established by informal discussions with the internal revenue service.
- The inventory of unused credits at the end of year 4 must be at least100.
- The objective in selecting allocations of the tax credits is to maximize the net present value of the allocations where allocations for years –2, –1, and 0 are not discounted (take on full value), whereas allocations for years 1, 2, 3, and 4 are discounted at a rate of 10% per year. Thus, \$1 of credit spent to reduce taxes to be paid in year 1 is worth \$0.90, and in year 2 it is worth \$0.81, and so on.

Use a spreadsheet optimizer to formulate and optimize the allocation of tax credits.

4. The Major Electric Company, which has world headquarters in New York, sells electronic consumer products in Europe. The chief financial officer is worried about the impact of volatility in the exchange rate between French francs (FF) and the U.S. dollar on future cash flows. He anticipates a transfer of 500 million FF from the French subsidiary next March 31 but wishes to ensure against the exchange rate uncertainties given in the following table:

Exchange Rate (U.S.\$/FF)	0.180	0.175	0.170	0.165	0.160	0.155
Probability	0.08	0.21	0.25	0.23	0.15	0.08

Specifically, after the transfer has been converted to dollars, he wishes to ensure that Major Electric will receive at least U.S.$80 million under any scenario. Accordingly, he asks the Bronx Merchant Bank for a quote on a put option to sell 500 million FF at a strike price of 0.1625 (U.S.$/FF) on March 31 of next year. The Bank quotes a fee of $500,000 for this option.

a. Will the option satisfy the chief financial officer's needs?

b. If the chief financial officer were risk neutral, how much would acquiring this option cost him measured in expected value?

5. The Rugged Sports Shop experiences peak sales during the months of June, July, and August and then during the months of November and December.[20] Its projected cash flow (in thousands of dollars) for 2002 is given in the following table, where a negative inflow indicates that expenses exceeds receipts:

Month	Jan	Feb	Mar	Apr	May	Jun	Jul	Aug	Sep	Oct	Nov	Dec
Cash Inflow	−12	−10	−9	−6	−3	12	14	10	−2	−8	16	35

The store owner arranges with her bank to borrow money to cover expenses during the off-peak months. The bank offers her two options. First, she can take out a long-term loan for any amount up to $40,000 on January 1, 2002 to be paid back on January 1, 2003. No portion of this loan, including the entire loan, may be paid back early. Each month, the bank will charge interest of 1% on the loan. Second, at the start of each month she can borrow against a reserve credit line, not to exceed $40,000, with a monthly interest charge of 1.5% on the unpaid balance. Money borrowed against the reserve credit line can be paid back at the end of any month. It must be totally repaid by January 1, 2003. Finally, each month, the bank will pay interest of 0.3% on positive balances in her account.

Using a spreadsheet optimizer, formulate and optimize a model that maximizes the Rugged Shop's cash balance on January 1, 2003. *Hint:* Develop the model based on cash balance equations for each month that have the form:

Cash balance at
the end of month t = cash balance at the end of month $t-1$
+ interest paid on cash balance from month $t-1$
+ loans received at the start of month t
+ cash inflow at the start of month t
− Interest paid on the long-term loan at the end of month t
− Interest paid on reserve credit loan at the end of month t
− Long-term loan payback (only on January 1)
− Reserve credit loan payback from month $t-1$

Notes

1. Timme and Williams-Timme [2000] discuss the financial supply chain management connection and speculate on developments leading to supply chain management's transition from the backroom to the boardroom.
2. Informal or unreported optimization modeling of financial decisions and constraints may be more prevalent than it seems. Lucas [2000] reports that financial decision variables and constraints were incorporated in an optimization model employed by GM Europe to support facility and tooling utilization in their assembly and manufacturing operations.
3. Almost 30 years ago, Carleton, Dick, and Downes [1973] and Myers and Pogue [1974] proposed insightful and implementable mathematical programming models for analyzing corporate financial decisions. We speculate in Section 9.6 why these models have apparently not yet been widely applied.
4. We follow closely the development in Carelton, Dick, and Downes [1973].
5. See Brealy and Myers [2000].
6. The discussion in this subsection is based in large part on the Introduction in Klimczak, Magee, and Shapiro [1990].
7. See Rutenberg [1970] and Crum, Klingman, and Travis [1979].
8. See Cohen and Lee [1989] and Klimczak, Magee, and Shapiro [1990] for realistic model implementations.
9. These issues are discussed in MacCormack, Newman, and Rosenfield, [1994].
10. This figure is adapted from Crum, Klingman, and Travis [1979].
11. Cash management network optimization is an important financial planning paradigm in its own right for companies doing business in only one country; see Brealy and Myers [2000, Chapter 31].
12. Transfer pricing is an important mechanism for managing supply chains of companies operating in a single country where intermediate products are transferred among multiple plants. Their use in MNCs is even more important because the MNC can affect net revenues and cash flows from foreign subsidiaries by the legal manipulation of transfer prices. For this reason, internal revenue services are alert to abuses and may require careful justification of the corporation's determination of transfer prices for intermediate and finished products shipped between subsidiaries in different countries.
13. The material is this section is taken from Klimczak, Magee, and Shapiro [1990].
14. Options pricing theory is thoroughly developed in Cox and Rubinstein [1985].
15. Cohen and Hurchzermeier [1999] report on these global developments and their impact on global supply chain planning by MNCs.
16. See Cohen and Hurchzemeier [1999, 674]; also Copeland et al. [1995] and Trigeorgis [1996].
17. Bienstock and Shapiro [1988] discuss the modeling of resource acquisition decisions in stochastic programming models. They also present and demonstrate a decomposition method for optimizing the resulting stochastic mixed integer programming models. The decomposition approach involves a master model for here-and-now decisions and a submodel for contingency planning of each scenario.
18. The balanced scorecard methodology was originally proposed by Kaplan and Norton [1992] and elaborated upon in Kaplan and Norton [1999].
19. See Timme and Timme-Williams [2000, 34].
20. This exercise was adapted from Winston and Albright [1997, 115–119].

References

Bienstock, D., and J. F. Shapiro [1988] "Optimizing Resource Acquisition Decisions by Stochastic Programming," *Management Science,* 34, 215–229.

Brealy, R. A., and S. C. Myers [2000], *Principles of Corporate Finance,* 6th ed. New York: Irwin/McGraw-Hill.

Carleton, W. T., C. L. Dick, Jr., and D. H. Downes [1973], "Financial Policy Models: Theory and Practice," *J. of Financial and Quantitative Analysis,* 8, 691–709.

Cohen, M. A., and A. Huchzermeier [1999], "Global Supply Chain Management: A Survey of Research and Applications," Chapter 21 in *Quantitive Models for Supply Chain Management,* edited by S. Tayur, R. Ganeshar, and M. Magazine. Norwell, Mass.: Kluwer.

Cohen, M. A., and H. L. Lee [1989], "Resource Deployment Analysis of Global Manufacturing and Distribution Networks," *J. of Manufacturing and Operations Management,* 2, 81–104.

Copeland T., T. Koller, and J. Murrin [1995], "Using Option Pricing Methods to Evaluate Flexibility," 446-475 in *Valuation.* New York: Wiley.

Cox, J. C., and M. Rubinstein [1985], *Options Markets.* Englewood Cliffs, N.J.: Prentice-Hall.

*Crum, R. L., D. D. Klingman, and L. A. Travis [1979], "Strategic Management of Multinational Companies: Network-based Planning Systems," CSFM Research Report 9–79, The Center for Strategic Financial Management, U. of Florida, Gainesville.

Kaplan, R. S., and D. P. Norton [1992], "The Balanced Scorecard—Measures that Drive Performance," *Harvard Business Review,* January-February, 71–79.

Kaplan, R. S., and D. P. Norton [1999], *The Balanced Scorecard.* Cambridge, Mass.: Harvard Business School Press.

*Klimczak, S. R., T. M. Magee, and J. F. Shapiro [1990], "Optimizing Multi-national Financial Flows," Working Paper IFSRC No. 147-90, International Financial Services Research Center, MIT.

Lucas, J. [2000], personal communication.

MacCormack, A. D., L. J. Newman III, and D. B. Rosenfield [1994], "The New Dynamics of Global Manufacturing Site Location," *Sloan Management Review,* Summer, 69–80.

Myers, S. C., and G. A. Pogue [1974], "A Programming Approach to Corporate Financial Management," *J. of Finance,* 29, 579–599.

Rutenberg, D. P. [1970], "Maneuvering Liquid Assets in a Multi-national Company: Formulation and Deterministic Solution Procedures," *Management Science,* 16, B671–B684.

Timme, S. G., and C. Williams-Timme [2000], "The Financial—SCM Connection," *Supply Chain Management Review,* May/June, 33–40.

Trigeorgis, L. [1996], *Real Options: Managerial Flexibility and Strategy in Resource Allocation.* Cambridge, Mass.: MIT Press.

Winston, W. L., and S. C. Albright [1997], *Practical Management Science: Spreadsheet Modeling and Applications.* Belmont, Calif.: Duxbury Press.

*See the credits section at the end of this book for more information.

10 Operational Supply Chain Planning

In this chapter, we examine operational supply chain planning problems and modeling systems for analyzing them. Operational planning refers to short-term decision problems facing supply chain managers who execute the company's business. Such problems involve the timing and sequencing of decisions; for example, the routing of trucks making local deliveries, the sequencing of tasks on a printing machine, or the completion of orders for printed circuit boards to be shipped this week. They may also involve resource allocation, inventory management, and make-or-buy decisions. An important subclass of operational planning problems is **scheduling problems,** which are problems heavily focused on the timing and sequencing of decisions.

Optimization systems for operational planning problems employ linear programming and mixed integer programming models and methods that we discussed in Chapters 3 and 4. Furthermore, as we discussed in Chapter 5, many operational problems can best be analyzed by the unified optimization methodology, which combines these rigorous models and methods with problem-specific and general-purpose heuristics. For a particular application, the methodology is used to construct a customized modeling system. In general, models and modeling systems for operational planning require far more customization than those for tactical and strategic planning.

The operational modeling systems to be discussed in this chapter are a class of advanced planning and scheduling (APS) systems.[1] Our focus is on systems that employ optimization models to fully explore the space of operational options. By contrast, many APS systems available today are rule based; that is, they rely heavily on historical rules and therefore are limited in their exploration capabilities. In addition, APS includes tactical planning across multiple facilities as well as myopic operational planning for individual facilities, even for individual production lines. The links between tactical and operational planning problems, and modeling systems for analyzing them, were discussed in Section 2.3.

The breadth and depth of operational planning problems is enormous. For this reason, we provide an overview in Section10.1 of several types of production, distribution, and human resources planning problems, along with discussions of modeling approaches for optimizing them. In Section 10.2, we make general comments about data, information technology, and organizational issues surrounding the use of modeling systems for operational supply chain planning.

We provide in-depth discussions of two specific applications in the following two sections. In Section 10.3, we examine the implementation and use of a vehicle routing system for a company making daily home deliveries. In Section 10.4, we examine the implementation and use of a production scheduling system for a company that manufactures semiconductors.

A modeling system typically treats the physical configuration of an operational system as given and provides managers with suggestions about effective operating decisions. Other tools are needed to evaluate the robustness of a proposed operational system design when it is subjected to a range of performance factors. The company is particularly interested in the robustness of a design under stochastic performance and demand.

In Section 10.4, we discuss deterministic and stochastic simulation methods for analyzing operational configuration designs. Deterministic simulations serve to identify behavioral and physical rules linking operational decisions that affect performance. Deterministic simulations may also be used in constructing modeling systems to support supply chain decision making, although such systems are weak in their ability to optimize such decisions. Stochastic, or Monte Carlo, simulations are used to analyze proposed operational system designs for stability in the face of variability in key factors such as external demand, product yields, and product processing times. The chapter concludes in Section 10.6 with final thoughts about current and future developments in the application of optimization models to operational problems.

10.1

Taxonomies of Operational Planning Problems

Optimization models are needed to support operational decision making throughout the company's supply chain. Examples include the following:

- For a computer manufacturer, determining the timing and sizing of release orders sent to its vendors for parts
- For an automotive company, developing plans for consolidating orders of parts from small vendors located within a given geographical area for shipment in full truckloads to a company plant
- For a paper company, determining a schedule for the next 4 weeks of products by type and grade on the paper machines at a company mill
- For a company that manufactures semiconductors, developing a production plan over the next 3 months to support available-to-promise (ATP) delivery dates for new orders

- For a company that overhauls and repairs aircraft engines, planning the number of operating shifts by job category and week over the next 10 weeks
- For a retailing company, determining a daily schedule over the next 2 weeks for the arrival of products at each of its distribution centers for transshipment to 500 franchised stores
- For a pharmaceutical company, planning the routing and scheduling of company trucks making local deliveries to customers

An important characteristic of these problems, one distinguishing them from strategic and tactical planning problems, is that demand over the planning horizon is often known with a large degree of certainty. In this context, demand refers to orders from customers and reliable forecasts for finished products. It may also refer to internal requirements from downstream stages in the company's supply chain for the outputs of upstream stages. Examples are requirements at distribution centers for replenishment of products from a specific plant and the requirements at an assembly plant for parts from company plants that make components.

Another important characteristic of operational planning problems is that they are concerned with the detailed execution of activities within a single or a few contiguous segments of the supply chain rather than the entire supply chain. Integration of these activities with other activities in the supply chain and with longer-term plans is still important.

In summary, the characteristics of operational planning problems are as follows:

- Planning over a short-term horizon during which demand for finished products, work in process, receipt of raw materials and parts from vendors are reasonably well known
- Focused decision making among activities located within a single facility or a geographical region that is small relative to the area served by the company's entire supply chain
- Coordination of a number of time-dependent decisions associated with managing these activities

Production Planning and Scheduling

Many taxonomies have been suggested for production planning and scheduling problems. Here we use the following taxonomy that reflects differences in how the problems are modeled:[2]

- Discrete parts manufacturing
- Process manufacturing
- Job-shop scheduling

We also discuss briefly manufacturing environments that are hybrids of these three categories.

Discrete Parts Manufacturing. Discrete parts manufacturing refers to environments in which individual machines produce a number of similar items. The machines are intermittently set up to make lots of each item. Planning horizons vary from a few days to several weeks. Demands for the company's finished products are assumed to be known with certainty in each period of the planning horizon. These demands are satisfied from finished or semifinished goods inventory; that is, production is either **make-to-stock** of standard products, such as refrigerators or tires, or **assemble-to-stock** of products for which a small amount of customization is allowed, such as automobiles or printed circuit boards.

Discrete parts production planning is characterized by the following types of decisions:

- Minimization of avoidable short-term costs, especially machine setup costs, overtime, and inventory holding costs
- Capacity planning for the production of multiple products
- Inventory planning for work in process and finished products
- Integration of multiple stages of production with varying production lead times

Section 5.4 gives an example of a discrete parts production planning model and its analysis.

Materials requirements planning (MRP) systems are transactional programs that have been widely applied over the past 20 years to discrete parts planning problems. As shown in Figure 10.1, where we ignore for the moment the modeling system, a traditional MRP system requires a master production schedule (MPS) for finished products as input. In addition, it is given a bill-of-materials (BOM) description of the components and parts needed for making the finished products, along with lead times to make or acquire these components and parts. Finally, it is given inventories on hand or scheduled for delivery of finished products, intermediate products, and parts. Using this information, the MRP system develops a detailed plan by day or by week for in-house production and purchase orders of parts, components, and finished products.

A serious deficiency of a traditional MRP system is that it provides no assistance to the production manager in determining the MPS. He is left without tools that seek to minimize cost, achieve feasibility, or help him adjust production capacities to meet these goals. Recently, software companies have developed modeling systems

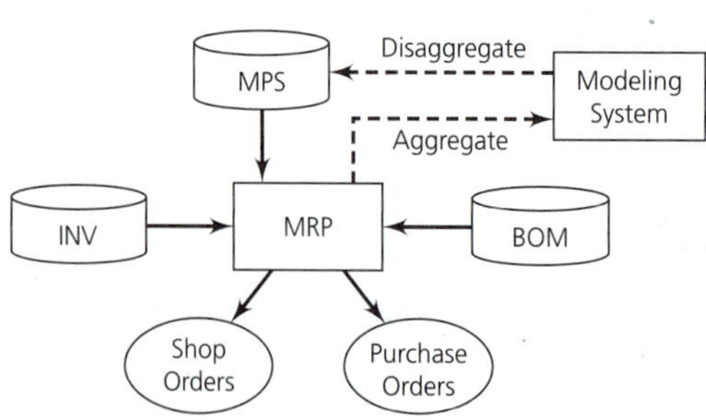

Figure 10.1
Materials requirements planning and modeling system to compute master production schedule

add-ons to MRP systems for these purposes. As shown, for many applications, it is necessary to aggregate SKUs when creating product families for the modeling system. This aggregation must then be reversed when creating the detailed MPS for the MRP system.

Process Manufacturing. Process planning and scheduling problems arise in capital intensive companies that manufacture products such as petroleum products, food products, paper, glass, industrial gases, and soap. These problems are characterized by the following features:

- Machines and plants must be operated continuously and near capacity to realize a profit on investment.
- Products flow continuously through several stages of processing.
- For each processing stage, product transformation activities can be smoothly adjusted as long as the equipment associated with the stage remains in the same major configuration.
- Intermittent changeovers in the major configuration of equipment, which are both time consuming and costly, are required to manufacture different classes of products.

The first successful optimization models, developed during the 1950s, were used for planning the operations of oil refineries.[3] These were single-period models, usually with a planning horizon of 1 month, for optimizing the production of a refinery. Starting about 1980, oil companies became concerned about scheduling production at a much finer level of detail. In the paragraphs that follow, we discuss a refinery scheduling optimization model, which exemplifies the general class of models for process manufacturing scheduling.[4]

The motivation of oil refining companies to develop and use modeling systems to schedule their refineries is due to several factors. First, worldwide competition has heightened and small improvements in margins translate into large increases in revenues. Second, the increased complexity of the world market for crude oils and their increased cost has greatly complicated the task of running refineries compared to 30 and 40 years ago when a refinery could be optimally configured to process a single type of crude oil (crude) for an entire month. Today, a refinery may receive each month several deliveries of crudes in tankers from more than one producing region with qualities, such as viscosity and sulfur content, that vary significantly. Major portions of the refinery will be reconfigured several times during the month to adjust distillation, production of intermediate products, and blending of final products to the properties of the crudes being processed. Thus, effective short-term scheduling of a refinery in today's environment requires an integration of crude supply decisions with production decisions. The final reason that oil companies are pursuing the development of scheduling systems is that computer technology has achieved a level of speed and flexibility that such systems are possible.

A high-level diagram of oil refinery process flow is depicted in Figure 10.2. Tankers arriving at the refinery and pipelines connected to the refinery fill crude tanks depicted at the top of the figure. Production scheduling is particularly difficult

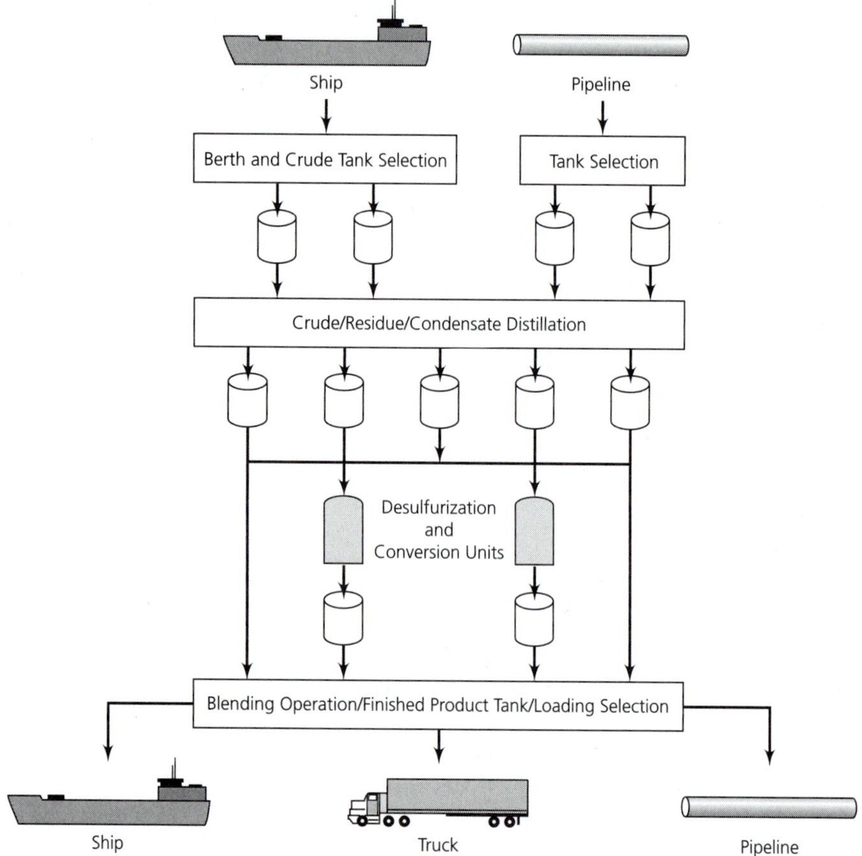

Figure 10.2
Oil refinery process flow. Adapted from Coxhead [1994, 189]

when the refinery relies exclusively on tanker deliveries of crudes from several producing regions. The refinery may have 20 such tanks and receive crude shipments from 10 tankers during a month. The tanks must have sufficient unused capacity to absorb the deliveries. In addition, available capacity should be distributed across the tanks in such a way that crude qualities in the tanks after delivery are favorable for optimizing the ensuing downstream refining operations. The properties of the crude in a tank after unloading will be a weighted average of the properties of the crude in the tank before unloading and the properties of the crude unloaded into it. A further complication is that a tanker ship may carry more than one type of crude.

As shown in the figure, crudes are distilled, processed further by intermediate desulfurization and conversion units, and then blended to make finished products. Buffer storage tanks allow production to be smoothed. A scheduling problem may be analyzed by a multiperiod mixed integer programming model, where the periods may be days and the planning horizon is 30 days. The refinery, or major portions of it, will be operated for a period of several hours to several days under a fixed configuration. A configuration is determined by the links of the crude tanks to the distillation units, the distillation units to the intermediate units, and the linkages of the intermediate units to the blenders. It is also determined by specific settings of temperature and pressure and other settings of equipment on the various units.

For each period of the planning horizon, the scheduling model addresses the following decisions and constraints:

- Assigning crudes from arriving tankers to specific tanks
- Selecting transformation recipes, which describe outputs and their qualities as functions of inputs and their qualities, that are associated with each unit and each configuration
- Determining values for continuous decision variables associated with production for each recipe
- Imposing production capacity constraints for each unit under each configuration
- Obeying inventory balance equations at the crude tanks and the buffer tanks with upper bounds on tank capacity
- Obeying pooling equations describing the quality of crudes and intermediate products in the tanks
- Obeying blending constraints by quality on finished products such as gasoline and heating oil
- Describing unit configurations and changeovers using 0-1 variables
- Obeying target production requirements for finished products

Some of these constructs are familiar from our discussion in earlier chapters. The ones associated with the last four listed items require further discussion.

The pooling equations are relationships that make refinery scheduling difficult. As a simple example, suppose the model decides to place a quantity $V2$ of crude or intermediate product with quality $Q2$ in a tank previously holding quantity $V1$ with quality $Q1$. The resulting volume $V1 + V2$ will have quality equal to

$$(Q1 * V1 + Q2 * V2)/V1 + V2.$$

This ratio is a nonlinear relationship of the decision variables $V1$, $V2$, which requires special treatment by methods for optimizing the model. Of course, the pooling equations in an actual scheduling model are more complex, involving the pooling of several flows. Moreover, the volume in a tank will be characterized by several qualities, each of which needs to be modeled and controlled.

The blending constraints in a scheduling model constrain the qualities of finished products, such as the octane rating of gasoline, to lie within product design specifications. Such constraints are standard in all process manufacturing models. For products such as pharmaceuticals, the blending constraints may be quite strict and sometimes difficult to meet.

Zero-one decision variables for each period are used to select the configurations for that period. These variables serve to turn on and turn off transformation activities associated with each configuration. The main effect of a change in configuration is the lost processing time. Changeovers in process manufacturing are more complicated than setups for discrete parts models because the time to change over, and therefore lost production time, depends not only on the configuration after the changeover but also on the configuration before the changeover. This phenomenon requires additional 0-1 variables that control before and after combinations of the changeovers.

The target requirements driving the schedule may be derived from longer-term models that reflect market demands for finished products and product margins. The objective function of the scheduling modeling may be simply to minimize a weighted combination of deviations from the requirements. Alternatively, the objective function might be to maximize the total value of the finished products made over the planning horizon subject to meeting specified target quantities of each product.

Job-Shop Scheduling. Job-shop scheduling refers to an environment in which a number of jobs, each having a variety of tasks, which may be processed on different machines in different sequences, are undertaken. Moreover, some tasks can be undertaken only if other tasks have been completed. Typical job shops include plants that overhaul and repair jet engines and foundries that manufacture customized castings. In general, **make-to-order** manufacturing involves elements of job-shop scheduling.

The objective of the basic job-shop scheduling model is to sequence tasks on the machines to which they have been assigned so as to minimize the total time required to complete all scheduled jobs. A variation of this model is to sequence tasks so that the sum of tardiness costs associated with completing the jobs is minimized. The tardiness cost for each job is a function that assigns penalties and rewards for late and early completion.

The constraints of the basic job-shop scheduling model fall into two categories. The first set describes precedence relationships among tasks associated with each job. These constraints determine the time when each task will begin and be completed. The time to complete each job is the completion time of the job's final task. The second set describes precedence relationships corresponding to sequencing tasks from different jobs on each machine. Zero-one variables are defined for each pair of tasks to be processed on the machine, say tasks A and B, where a value of 1 corresponds to processing A before B and a value of 0 corresponds to processing B before A.

The basic job-shop scheduling model can be extended to include constraints describing the assignment of tasks to machines if such assignments are not predetermined by the tasks, changeover times on the machines that depend on the task just completed and the new task to be performed, and constraints describing the time available for processing on each machine. These models, even the basic version, tend to be difficult combinatorial optimization problems. Like other classes of production scheduling models, they require analysis using a combination of mixed integer programming and heuristic methods.

Hybrid Manufacturing Environments. Some manufacturing environments include multiple stages that span several of the environments discussed above. Their hybrid nature makes them more difficult to control because diverse production planning activities and practices need to be integrated. An example is the manufacture of fine papers, such as stationery or paper for publications.

Multiple stages of manufacturing at a mill producing fine papers are shown in Figure 10.3. In this figure, the first two stages fit the process manufacturing paradigm. Raw materials, such as wood chips and paper waste, are fed to the pulp mill digestors that produce different types of pulps to feed to the paper machines. The pulp mill may consist of 20 digestors that are run continuously 24 hours a day, except for changeovers. The paper machines convert pulp taken from the pulp tanks along with other chemical inputs to "mother" rolls of paper, which may be 200 inches wide and weigh several hundred tons. A paper mill may have as many as six paper machines, each costing hundreds of millions of dollars. The paper machines also run continuously 24 hours a day, except for changeovers and maintenance.

The production stages that come after the paper machines fit the job-shop scheduling paradigm. First, the mother rolls must be trimmed, or slit, to produce rolls of much smaller widths corresponding to specific customer orders (e.g., 11-inch rolls to be converted to stationery). Trimming to minimize waste is a complex and important combinatorial problem, one that has been solved by sophisticated optimization techniques.[5] It is important because each percentage of waste in a large paper mill costs the paper company millions of dollars per year in lost raw material and valueless production.

The small rolls produced by the trim operations are passed to various finishing machines where the paper may be colored, coated, embossed, and so on. Each customer order is, in effect, a unique job comprising a number of tasks with associated precedence constraints. Scheduling when the paper for a particular order will be trimmed, passed through the necessary finishing operations, and then shipped to the customer is a classic job-shop problem.

Figure 10.3
Paper mill product flow

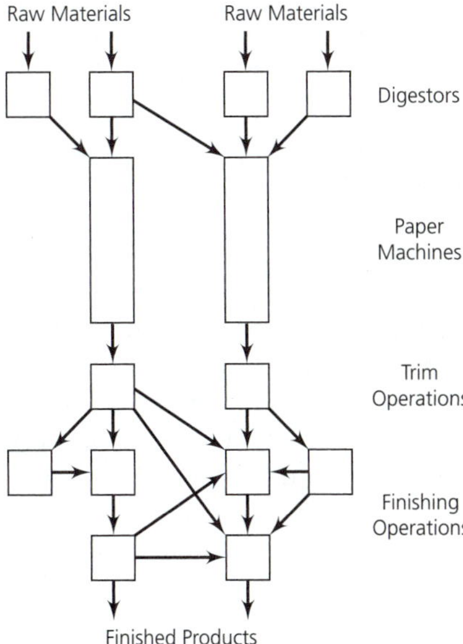

In summary, integrating upstream process manufacturing operations that produce paper with downstream operations that serve to meet specific orders for fine papers is difficult. Process manufacturing activities are organized to ensure continuous operation of capital intensive equipment. Job-shop activities are organized to manufacture unique products associated with individual customer orders, perhaps using equipment that is never more than 50% busy in any given month. Organizational cultures supporting the two types of work are radically different, which has led some paper companies to physically separate them.

Vehicle Routing and Scheduling

Over the past 20 years, a great number and wide variety of vehicle routing and scheduling problems have been successfully analyzed using optimization models.[6] Routing refers to the physical paths and sequence of stops visited by the vehicles. Scheduling refers to the timing of vehicle loading at distribution centers, plants, or ports and the timing of deliveries at customer locations. The vehicles may be trucks, trains, barges, ships, or airplanes. The planning horizons vary from 1 day for local truck deliveries to several weeks for oil tanker ships and container ships making pick ups and deliveries.

Operational planning of trucks alone involves a great variety of routing and scheduling problems. Examples include the following:

- Local delivery of retail products to stores from a distribution center where some stores impose time windows on deliveries
- Local delivery to and installation of propane cylinders at residential customers
- Tanker truck pick up of liquid nitrogen and oxygen at air products plants for short- and medium-haul delivery to industrial customers
- Long-haul shipment by truck with break bulk and local delivery at both ends of the haul

Problems such as these can be modeled and optimized, at least to a good approximation, using combinations of mixed integer programming and heuristic methods.

Local Delivery Problems. Local delivery problems encompass the delivery of mail and packages by the postal service or parcel delivery companies, groceries and other consumer products to residences, consumer products from distribution centers to convenience stores, and a range of other applications. Abstracting these problems slightly, they can all be modeled as the problem of selecting routes for individual vehicles that leave a depot, visit multiple customers (stops), and then return to the depot. In selecting the route, the capacity of each vehicle to carry products must not be violated. Often, a maximal time is imposed on the duration of the route. Usually, a delivery time window is associated with each customer, who may be visited only once. A feasible route is one that obeys the various constraints on capacity and time.

Long-Haul Problems. Long-haul routing problems involve trucks making transcontinental or other long trips and containerships, tankers, and other vehicles making trips of several days or weeks. As such, they may not immediately fit into the category of operational planning problems because the planning horizons are relatively long and the routes remain fixed over several months. Nevertheless, short-term opportunities arise that would allow a long-haul transportation company to reduce costs or increase revenues if it were to adjust routes in the short term.

We illustrate these issues by discussing a cargo containership routing problem. We approach it from a modeling viewpoint, although many containership companies have yet to fully exploit such models. In particular, we examine decisions faced by a containership company that moves containers among ports in North America and the Pacific Rim. It uses containerships of various sizes, each following a repetitive route to a subset of the ports. A typical route will require several weeks for the containership to visit all ports.

The planning problem of selecting routes is usually treated as a tactical planning problem to be resolved once a year. Even when the routes are fixed, the planning of shipments is difficult because, at each port, containers are both picked up and delivered. Containers that are picked up will be bound for several ports to be visited later by the containership. A related operational problem is simply to determine a placement in the ship of containers picked up at each port so that unloading them at the destination ports will be efficient.

Limitations on the number and destinations of the containers to be loaded at a given port are the capacity of the containership and the voyage time until it reaches other ports on its route. Because shipments have a guaranteed transit time, the containership might not reach some ports of call in time to deliver containers picked up at the given port. Obviously, the acceptability of travel time from port A to port B will depend on whether or not they are on the same side of the Pacific.

Even with fixed routes, the short-term planning objective should be to maximize net revenues, which are variable because the company has discretion about the business it will accept in each port. These options should be incorporated in a short-term model that treats the routes as fixed and given. Moreover, the worldwide cargo container market is often unstable with containers piling up in some locations and being in short supply in others. Thus, shipping charges in markets with scarce supply will be significantly higher than those in markets with a surplus supply. A containership company could exploit these imbalances by adjusting routes on a short-term basis, say once a month or even more frequently, to provide greater shipping capacity in markets with unsatisfied demand. To maintain adequate service for the long term, a model to maximize the benefits of such dynamic rerouting would need to incorporate constraints imposing an acceptable time frequency between visits to all ports where the company does business.

Integrated Manufacturing and Distribution Scheduling Decisions. An increasing number of companies are developing and deploying optimization modeling systems to improve the scheduling of specific manufacturing or distribution activities. Thus far, most systems have not addressed the need in many manufacturing firms to integrate these two sets of activities. For example, a refinery scheduling system such as the one discussed above should, in principle, integrate the timing of finished product production with distribution operations by tanker truck, pipeline, and ship.

This timing problem is particularly acute for a company like Methanex, which produces methanol at its plant in western Canada and other locations. Product manufactured at the plants is loaded onto tanker ships that carry it to customers around the world. The company hired a modeling software company to build a system for tactical planning that integrates production decisions with tanker route selection. The model combines a production planning submodel with submodels for routing the tankers to customers.

Human Resources Scheduling

Optimization models have been successfully applied in service industries in which skilled personnel are required to cover specific activities during specific time intervals. A prime example is airline crew scheduling. A large airline faces the problem of assigning flight crews to each of several hundred flights for each type of aircraft over a period of several days. Each crew is actually assigned to a sequence of flights, called a rotation, describing a circuit of flights that the crew follows in leaving and ultimately returning to its domicile airport. Due to the complexity of the airline route network and union rules regarding overtime and other features of a crew's schedule, the determination of a feasible, much less a good, schedule can be quite difficult. Fortunately for the airlines, optimization models have proven very successful in analyzing this class of problems. They are responsible for yearly cost savings totaling millions of dollars per year for individual airlines.[7]

We cite an example where human resources scheduling is relevant to supply chain management. First, it is often needed as a complement to vehicle routing. For example, a company making local deliveries each day from 8 A.M. to 10 P.M. may face several peak periods of demand. Drivers, moreover, may be constrained by law to routes with durations of 8 hours or less. Some drivers may be hired for half-day routes with durations of 4 hours or less. For these reasons, it may be difficult to coordinate the drivers' schedules with the route schedules. For example, the departure time of each route must coincide, at least approximately, with the start time for the driver assigned to that route. Conflicts can be avoided by integrating the daily routing model with a model describing driver availability. In this way the routing model will select routes that connect well with driver schedules.

The mathematical form of optimization models for vehicle routing is identical to that used in human resource scheduling.[8] This suggests that when the real-world problems overlap, an integrated model and solution can be readily implemented. An example of such a situation is a weekly delivery problem of manufactured products that keep drivers on the road for several days between returns to a factory. For such a problem, the routes must be linked to cost-effective and legal driver schedules for the week.

10.2

Modeling Systems for Operational Planning

In this section, we review principles for implementing and applying modeling systems for operational planning. In particular, we consider issues concerning data, models, the division of labor between model and analyst, system integration, training, learning, and system evolution. These are examined in the context of the following subsections:

- System Integration
- Steps to Follow in Using a System
- Real-Time Operational Planning
- Other Uses of a Modeling System
- Training, Learning, and System Evolution

The demands placed on operational modeling systems are different from those on tactical and strategic modeling systems because they are **repetitively employed** in a **time-critical** manner to support decisions that often will be **immediately carried out.** The use of tactical and strategic modeling systems may also be time critical, but to a far lesser extent. Moreover, business processes using the longer-term tools can be organized to ensure that sufficient time is available for analysts to exercise the systems and for managers to review and implement plans suggested by them. This may not be possible in operational planning environments.

The precise meaning of *time critical* depends, of course, on the operational environment. Many operational modeling systems are run at least once, if not several times, a day, with results obtained between 5 minutes and 1 hour depending on the complexity of the problem being analyzed. Recently, real-time optimization of an operational plan to support available-to-promise delivery dates for incoming orders has become an important system requirement. We discuss technical issues associated with real-time optimization in a separate subsection.

A company seeking an operational planning tool may develop a system customized to its needs or acquire an off-the-shelf package. Less risk is involved if a well-established, off-the-shelf system that meets the company's needs is available. Furthermore, most off-the-shelf systems allow modest customization of their interfaces and the logic of their algorithms. Still, a company with new or unusual operational planning features will achieve significant and sustainable competitive advantage if it successfully implements and continues to support a customized planning system.

System Integration

To be effective, an operational modeling system must be fully integrated with other analytical and transactional systems maintained by the company and, possibly, by

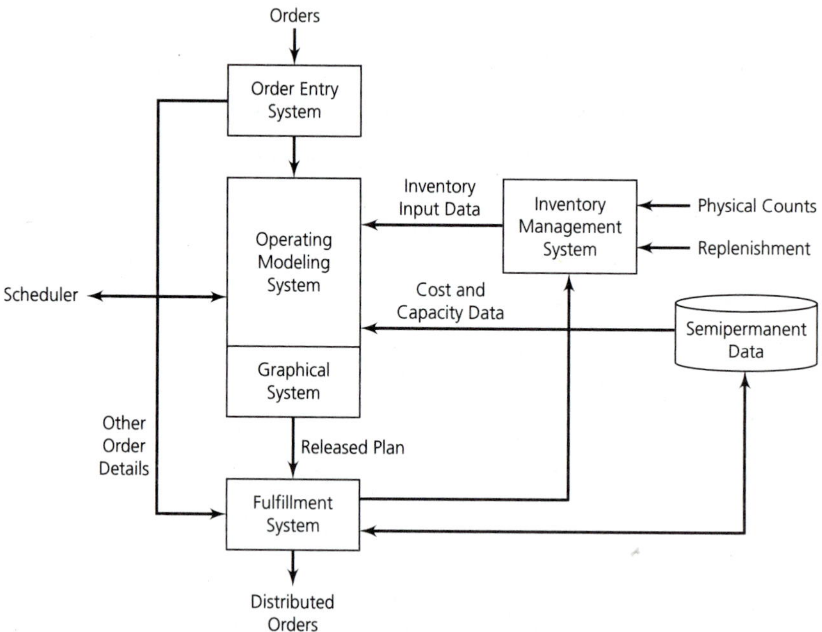

Figure 10.4
Operating modeling system integrated with other systems

the company's vendors and customers. For the purposes of discussion, a high-level example is depicted in Figure 10.4. Many other configurations are clearly possible, depending on the nature of the company's business.

We will use the following terminology. The purpose of the operational modeling system is to develop a **plan,** which the **scheduler** using the system releases to the fulfillment system. A plan will be made up of **subplans** for segments of the operational planning problem being addressed. For example, the set of cutting configurations for 50 mother rolls to be trimmed this week at a paper mill and their sequence is a plan, whereas each configuration is a subplan. The scheduler may be an operational planning manager, but more likely, she is an analyst who works under the direction of the manager.

As shown in the figure, orders are sent to the order entry system by telephone or fax, over the Internet, or by other means. When the scheduler makes a request, the order entry system passes relevant order input data to the modeling system. The order entry system also passes other details about the orders to the fulfillment system. As an example of the difference, for a local delivery routing problem, the modeling system requires only the vehicle capacity loading of each order, whereas the fulfillment system requires complete details about what has been ordered.

Of course, not all operational planning problems, and systems for analyzing them, involve the scheduling of external orders. A planning system might be needed to schedule production of a component needed in assembling a finished product at the next stage of production located in the same plant. These internal demands would be communicated to the scheduler over the company's internal network. Nevertheless, the logic of data flows and system integration is similar when demands are internal or external.

At the same time that she requests order input data, the scheduler requests updates on available inventory from the inventory management system. This information may be based on recent physical counts or deduced from product completions and shipments. Finally, the scheduler infrequently reviews semipermanent data about costs and capacities from the fulfillment system. Because some human interaction is likely, we have explicitly shown a graphical system module integrated with the modeling system that the scheduler employs in adjusting plans suggested by the optimization algorithms.

Once the two or three types of input data and been received and reviewed, the scheduler applies the modeling system when constructing an acceptable plan and then releases the plan to the fulfillment system. Depending on the company's business, the fulfillment system might be a MRP, DRP, or some other system that translates the released plan into detailed instructions for manufacturing and/or distributing finished products. Data generated by the fulfillment system about work-in-process and finished products is passed to the inventory management system.

Steps to Follow in Using a System

A scheduler uses the following steps to apply an operational modeling system:

- Retrieve input data
- Review and correct input data
- Review and adjust optimization model and control parameters
- Generate and optimize the model
- Review and manually adjust model results
- Release plan

The scheduler's goal in performing these steps is to identify and release the best possible operational plan in the available time. These steps are studied in detail in the subsections below.

Retrieve Input Data. As discussed above, we assume the modeling system is integrated with the company's order entry, MRP, DRP, or any other system from which the modeling system receives input data and to which it sends released plans. The company must strive to make this system integration as seamless and efficient as possible; otherwise, operational planning can easily become tortuous. Specific data received are internal or external orders to be filled today or over the next few days or weeks. Depending on the planning horizon and the industry, order data might be supplemented by short-term forecasts. Other input data include inventories of raw materials, parts, or finished goods and, if they vary over the short term, available capacities of machines and workers. In general, operational planning analysis will be based on real-time data, such as orders, and semipermanent data, such as the number of trucks or machine hours available and their capacities.

In retrieving input data, it is important to distinguish between operational planning problems that are analyzed by a snapshot (1 day or 1 week) model and those that are analyzed by a multiple-period model on a rolling horizon basis. In the former case, order entry and order fulfillment are accomplished fully each period independently of any other period. In the latter case, input data retrieved today describes updates to orders and other planning elements that were previously retrieved and new orders that were received since the last time the system was used. As we discuss below, rolling horizon analysis places additional burdens on the system and the scheduler.

Input data may be preprocessed or augmented in preparation for analysis by the modeling system. For a production scheduling system, demand data by SKU from the order entry system might be aggregated into demands by product family before it is passed to the planning system. Similarly, products with inventories near or below safety stock levels may be flagged for production no later than a certain date.

Review and Correct Input Data. Errorfree input data, or something close to it, is obviously critical to successful operational planning. The company's integrated suite of operational systems should have built-in routines for identifying errors and, in some cases, for correcting them automatically. Despite automatic error correction, the scheduler can expect that he may need to spend time reviewing these errors and, in some instances, correcting them. Error correction may be performed manually or semimanually using programs that suggest possible corrections. For the local delivery problem, orders from new customers may have incorrect addresses that cannot be automatically geocoded by the embedded geographical information system. They must be geocoded manually by the scheduler based on his knowledge of the geographical area being served. If this fails, the error can only be corrected by contacting the customer. For paper mill planning, the scheduler may know that a certain pulp digestor is down for repairs for the next 16 hours, although this information has not been recorded in the available capacity input file.

Review and Adjust Optimization Model and Control Parameters. The scheduler may elect to adjust parameters in the optimization model and parameters controlling the optimization algorithms. For a local delivery problem, an important parameter affecting the optimization model is the maximal number of travel and delivery hours allowed for a route. The ordinary maximum might be 8 hours, but the scheduler might increase that to 8.5 or 9 if the day's volume is particularly high or if bad weather is causing slow travel. Similarly, for a production scheduling problem, due to heavy demand, the scheduler might increase allowable overtime or the number of periods that orders may be backlogged.

The scheduler will also have access to parameters controlling the optimization algorithms. These might include those controlling the depth and breadth of a branch-and-bound search to solve an embedded mixed integer programming model or the acceptable optimality gap between the cost of the best known plan and the value of the greatest lower bound. The scheduler might elect to change these parameters depending on the nature of the specific optimization run. For example, if the modeling system is exercised several times each day, the goals for the first run and the final run may be quite different. Of course, the scheduler will probably have only an empirical, rather than conceptual, understanding of most of these parameters. In general, deciding which parameters to allow the scheduler to access can be difficult. It depends on the skill and education level of the scheduler and the extent of training that she will receive. These points are discussed again below.

For operational models spanning multiple days that are used on a rolling horizon basis, the scheduler has the added burden of reviewing past decisions to see if she wishes to hold them fixed at their previous decisions, or to rerelease some of them for analysis by the model. This issue arose in the use of a modeling system used by a reverse logistics company that rents containers to food manufacturers. The system assigns orders to depots over a 7-day rolling horizon basis. On a given day, the orders for that day and some orders for the following 2 days are treated as fixed and given based on previous optimizations. They are included in the model to keep track of inventories at the depots. The optimization model assists the scheduler in firming up the assignments for tomorrow (day 2) and the ensuing 2 days (days 3 and 4). Under certain circumstances, such as a physical inventory count at a depot that is much lower than expected, the scheduler might elect to unfix some fixed orders for day 2 that were assigned to that depot. The scheduler would make such a change only if she knew that the transportation arrangements for delivering the order could be changed.

Generate and Optimize the Model. In many instances, the optimization model is generated and solved in a batch mode without the scheduler's participation. Several options for involving the scheduler directly in the optimization process present themselves if the unified optimization methodology discussed in Chapter 5 (see Figure 5.5) is employed in designing and implementing the system. The methodology begins its analysis of an operational problem by specifying attractive subplans that the underlying optimization models will attempt to assemble into a demonstrably good plan. The initial subplans may be identified by automated heuristics, by review of recent subplans that remain feasible and attractive, or by the scheduler using a manual approach that has been computerized. The scheduler can and should be given control of this initialization procedure.

There are several opportunities during the optimization process for intervention by the scheduler. Given the initial subplans, the methodology continues to identify new subplans that complement the initial ones in seeking an optimal (demonstrably good) plan. Based on her understanding of the problems being addressed and previous performance of the methodology applied to them, the scheduler can decide when to terminate subplan generation and seek the best plan possible using the known subplans. However, if the methodology returns a plan that is not satisfactory because it is infeasible or not known to be sufficiently close to optimality, the scheduler should have the option to continue generation of new subplans. She may have several options for doing this based on automated heuristics or computerized manual procedures.

Review and Manually Adjust Model Results. Determining the most effective division of labor between the analytical capabilities of an optimization system and those of the human scheduler in developing an operational plan is a complicated and unresolved issue. At one extreme, some off-the-shelf packages perform very little analysis. Instead, the burden is placed heavily on the human scheduler to use a manual editor in searching through many possible subplans and plans until an apparently good plan has been constructed or time runs out. For the modeling system developer, heavy scheduler interaction requires the implementation of an easy-to-use, graphical manual editor with extensive built-in functionality to assist the scheduler with his search for an acceptable plan.

At the other extreme, the scheduler may be more than willing to let the modeling system determine the entire plan without any manual intervention. Unfortunately, this might not be a viable option due to real-world considerations that could not be, or were not, incorporated in the model. The extent to which models can capture all decision details perceived by a human scheduler is an unknown that will not be resolved very soon. A related issue is to distinguish between human judgments that are truly important to an effective plan and those that falsely perceived by the scheduler to be important or correct.

Thus, some balance between automatic plan optimization and human intervention is indicated for many applications. An important step in achieving this balance is to make myopic optimization of subplans available to the scheduler. The unified optimization methodology mechanizes such an approach by using rigorous optimization methods to integrate subplans into a demonstrably good plan.

Release Plan. Once the scheduler is satisfied with the plan that she has reviewed and adjusted, she will release all or part of it to the fulfillment system. She may release only part of the plan if subsequent modeling analysis will serve to optimize subplans to meet later orders. Data procedures for recording and managing released partial plans are critical to coherent operational planning. Otherwise, the scheduler can easily double plan the fulfillment of some orders and miss the fulfillment of others.

Real-Time Operational Planning

The discussion in the previous subsection described use of an operational planning system on an intermittent basis. Our assumption was that the system might be exercised once or a few times a day. For many planning situations, however, it would be desirable to reoptimize the plan each time a new order is being considered. This would enable details for scheduling the new order to be efficiently integrated with the plan for all other unscheduled orders. In some circumstances, it would also enable the salesperson taking the order to immediately quote a firm delivery date for the order.

This need for real-time response suggests that the system run the optimization model and methods on a continuous basis. New demands for products or deliveries would be incorporated in the model more or less instantaneously as they arrive. At that point, the model would seek to reoptimize the plan with the new order or orders. This model statement would prevail until the model received another input of new order(s). In addition, as time passes, some subplans for scheduling some orders would be fixed and effectively taken out of the model.

Many details of a continuous optimization scheme remain to be worked out. They will certainly depend on the nature of the operational planning problems being addressed; for example, number of orders that arrive per day or the nature of the resource constraints (vehicles, machines, people) on operational activities. We omit further discussion but signal the importance of this area of modeling research.

Other Uses of a Modeling System

An operational modeling system may be effectively applied to study potential or proposed changes in the company's operating environment. For example, using projected customer demand data, a local delivery vehicle routing system could be employed to study the impact of expanding delivery hours or adding new delivery territories. The system could help plan increases in the number of vehicles and drivers and anticipate changes in performance metrics. Similarly, using projected production and demand data, a production scheduling system could be employed to study the impact of new products on capacity loadings in the plant.

Although such applications might appear sensible and worthwhile, they can actually run counter to the culture of the organization. In many instances, schedulers are former operations personnel who have been trained in using the operational modeling system to support daily, or short-term, planning. They are not and usually have never been participants in longer-term planning activities and therefore may not have the mind-set needed to ask and analyze such planning questions.

Training, Learning, and System Evolution

To successfully apply a sophisticated and powerful operational modeling system, the scheduler must receive considerable training. Clearly, a balance is needed in the system design. It should not be too sophisticated for the scheduler; otherwise, effort will be wasted in developing the system, and the scheduler may misuse it through ignorance of its more subtle options. The company must also resist choosing a system that is too unsophisticated for the application, motivated in part by the conscious or unconscious desire to avoid the hard work of training schedulers.

There may also be a longer-term, learning aspect for both the scheduler and the company when the company elects to acquire and apply a modeling system to its operational planning problems. Given time to reflect about the impact of the system on the company's operations, the scheduler and his managers may find that previously held conceptions about good operating rules appear incorrect. Moreover, many businesses undergo changes due to improvements in technology, shifts in their markets, or a number of other reasons. The company should attempt to create processes for evolving the functionality of an operational modeling system to adapt to these changes. This assumes, of course, that the system allows customization to the extent needed by such changes.

10.3

Vehicle Routing System for an E-Commerce Company

In this section, we discuss the design, implementation, and use of a system to route vehicles making daily local deliveries. This system was developed for InterShop, a fictitiously named e-commerce company making home delivery of consumer products including groceries, pharmaceutical products, and other household items. A growing number of e-commerce companies making home deliveries of consumer products have arisen in the past few years. These companies have learned that effective supply chain management practices and the use of modeling systems are just as important to achieving competitive advantage as they are for traditional companies. The discussion that follows reflects experiences of the modeling practitioners and systems developers who implemented the InterShop Routing System (ISRS) and the routers who used it.

Although several off-the-shelf packages for local delivery routing were available shortly after InterShop began operations, the general manager chose to commission an outside company to develop a system customized to its business.[9] Moreover, the company sought a routing system that would be tightly integrated with its Web-based order entry system, order fulfillment system, and inventory management system. A high-level view of these integrated systems is displayed in Figure 10.5. Orders from the Web site, telephone, and fax are encoded in the Order Entry System, including the translation of each order into a delivery volume measured in number of totes required to deliver the customer's order. The order entry system also monitors out-of-stock inventory items. This information is conveyed to customers along with suggestions for substitute items whenever possible.

ISRS retrieves orders from the Order Entry System, and a routing solution is computed. This solution is translated into detailed reports of individual routes to be used by assigned drivers in making their deliveries. The routes along with their

Figure 10.5
Integrated operational systems

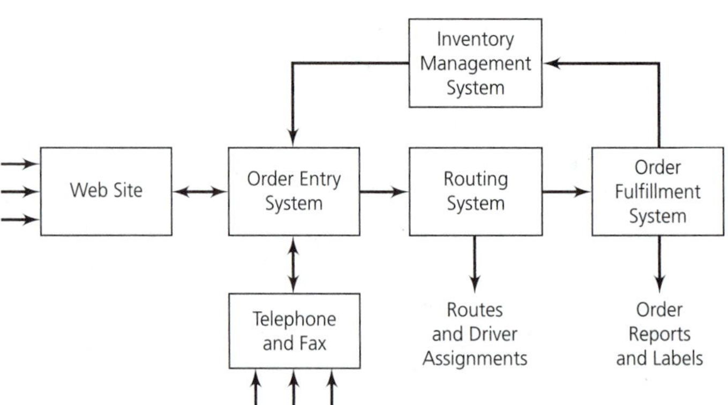

assigned orders are passed to the Order Fulfillment System, which produces order reports and labels to be used when picking the orders. The labels are attached to the orders and indicate the route and stop sequence of each order.

In the subsection that follows, we provide background on InterShop's business. After that, we examine in detail the functionality and use of ISRS. The section concludes with a brief discussion of driver assignments that complement the routing solution.

Company Background

InterShop currently operates in two medium-sized metropolitan areas and intends to expand its operations to several other cities over the next few years. Most of its orders are placed on its Web site; it also accepts orders by phone and fax, although the percentage of such orders has declined dramatically since the company's inception. Orders are placed for next-day delivery between the hours of 9 A.M. and 10 P.M. within delivery time windows of 2 hours. Time windows are constrained to begin with the hour. Limits are placed on the number of orders accepted for each time window. Orders are accepted up to midnight, although not for early time windows the next day. An order is delivered free of charge as long as the total cost of items purchased exceeds a minimum.

InterShop operates out of a single depot in each city. The depot serves as a warehouse organized to allow the efficient picking of orders from inventory and the loading of delivery vehicles. It is restocked by wholesalers with whom the company has established long-term relationships. InterShop currently stocks around 8,000 SKUs in each depot. The company intends to expand this number as its business in each city expands.

A typical day entails the delivery of around 1000 orders depending on the day of the week. The depots are capable of servicing 2000 orders per day, and it is likely that this number will be reached in the not too distant future. Due to volume and geographical distances, large metropolitan areas into which InterShop may expand will require two or more depots.

A few words about marketing and sales are appropriate before we delve into details about ISRS. When it began operations in the mid-1990s, InterShop did not expect Internet sales to grow as rapidly as they have. Fortunately, the company installed physical logistics facilities and processes adequate to the ensuing demand. Internet sales are particularly attractive because the cost of processing an Internet order is roughly 25% the cost of processing a telephone or fax order. Of course, this variable cost savings can only be achieved after considerable fixed cost is invested in the Web site.

A list of marketing and sales challenges facing InterShop include the following:

- Creating graphics to attractively display physical products on the Web site
- Pricing products so as to gain market share while still reflecting supply chain and marketing costs

- Forecasting sales patterns in new markets based on patterns in initial markets
- Devising strategies to retain customers
- Determining a number and range of products that the Web site and the supply chain can support

In summary, marketing InterShop's business expansion is an odd mixture of new product introduction and traditional retailing selling.

Routing System Description and Use

Every night ISRS is used to route orders for the following day. It has three major components. First, it contains interface and database management programs that allow the router to retrieve orders from the order entry system and to view and edit other data relevant to current operations such as vehicle and driver availability. Second, it contains components constructed from a geographical information system (GIS) tool kit for geocoding and other geographical analyses.[10] Finally, it contains routing engines that accept geocoded orders and produce a routing solution.

The customers placing orders vary from day to day, with a significant percentage of new customers each day (more than 3%) during the growth phase of the business, which has not yet ended. Therefore, each day's routing problem is unique and requires a tailored solution. This is in contrast to local delivery problems faced by wholesalers delivering products to retailers. For such problems, the wholesaler may repeat today's routes, or possibly this week's routes, indefinitely over the months to come.

We use terminology developed in Section 5.1 to describe the routing analysis performed by the system. The human **router** employs the system to determine an efficient, implementable **routing solution** for tomorrow's operations. A routing solution comprises **feasible routes**, which are routes that obey capacity, time window, and other constraints imposed on operations. A feasible route is generally judged to be a good route if it (almost) completely fills a vehicle and its order locations are in a tight cluster.

The sequential steps in the routing process are as follows:

- Order retrieval
- Order geocoding
- Travel time computations
- Routing solution optimization
- Manual editing of routing solution
- Routing solution release
- Driver assignment

In the paragraphs that follow, we review each of these steps.

Order Retrieval. Each evening, the router initiates the routing process by retrieving a Customer Order File from the order entry system. To ensure sufficient lead time for order fulfillment of the next morning's orders, the router initiates a **first wave** routing analysis at 9 P.M. from a partial Customer Order File; that is, a File generated before the midnight cutoff for accepting orders. Moreover, in analyzing the first wave, the router focuses on creating and then releasing a partial routing solution comprising several good routes that depart from the depot at the start of the day. Orders not placed on released routes are returned to the pool of unrouted orders to be routed later. The first wave is followed by one or two additional waves, and the final wave occurs after midnight when the router must, of course, place all remaining orders on some route.

Order Geocoding. A critical component of any vehicle routing and scheduling system is an integrated GIS that provides a **geocode** of customers, expressed as a pair of latitude/longitude coordinates. Moreover, for computing distances and travel times between pairs of customers, these coordinates must be located on a road map of the delivery area, which is represented as a **road network,** where the nodes are street intersections and the links are streets. Customers are located at the nearest node.

The Customer Order File for the day's orders is passed from the order entry system to ISRS. This file contains order data and customer data, including the customer's address, for the day's orders. It also computes the size of the customer order measured in delivery totes.

A batch program then attempts to geocode the locations of all orders. For previous customers who have not moved, the geocode is retrieved from a permanent file of customer addresses. The GIS is then used to generate a geocode for new customers and for old customers who have moved. Due to typographical errors, misnamed streets, or addresses on new streets not included in the road network, a few addresses may not be successfully geocoded. Resolution of these problems requires manual intervention and, occasionally, research by the router. Repetitive geographic errors can be documented and made available to the router through a pull-down list, thereby minimizing the manual geocoding effort. For a local delivery problem of 1000 orders with 50 new addresses, the router can expect that fewer than 10 customer addresses will not be automatically geocoded.

Once geocoding is completed, the router is ready to call the batch routines that compute travel times, travel distances, and a routing solution. Before doing so, he may review and edit parameters discussed below that shape the routing solution and control the routing algorithms.

Travel Time Computations. The GIS in ISRS contains an extensive database describing the speed and therefore the time to traverse each link in the road network. All links in the road network are partitioned into classes (for example, highways, major streets, local streets), which have standard speeds associated with them. The class speeds may be adjusted, but probably not during a routing session when time is very limited. The GIS also allows the speed on each link in the road network to be adjusted. This would be done, for example, for bottlenecks in the road network such as tunnels or bridges. The system also has a feature that allows the router to scale the speed on all links in the road network for each zip code by periods of 1 hour throughout the delivery day. This feature may be used to adjust travel times during peak periods. Thus, the router has a wide range of options open to him for adjusting speeds and travel times across the road network, either for a particular day when the weather is bad or more permanently. In general, extensive manipulation of these data is done during nonscheduling times by routers or other operations planning personnel who are knowledgeable about InterShop's business.

Travel times on individual links, or their distances, are the raw data for computing the shortest route from each customer location to every other customer location. The shortest routes may be computed on the basis of time or distance. When constructing feasible routes visiting multiple customers, the route followed between successive pairs of customers is assumed to be the shortest route.

Very efficient algorithms have been devised for shortest route computations. The GIS in ISRS contains one such an algorithm; the shortest route travel time matrix (or shortest route distance matrix) from each customer to all other customers for 1000 customer locations can be computed in less than 5 minutes on a high-end personal computer. Of course, the time to compute the shortest route matrices tends to increase exponentially with the number of customer locations. Moreover, for routing in a large metropolitan area, it is not necessary to determine the shortest route between customers who are several miles apart because they will never be visited successively by a route in the routing solution. Thus, for computational efficiency as InterShop's daily volume increases, it may become necessary to modify the shortest route algorithms to incorporate distance constraints on the shortest route computations.

Routing Solution Optimization. Once the travel times between all pairs of customers has been computed, ISRS undertakes the batch computation of an effective routing solution; that is, the creation of a set of feasible, low-cost routes such that every customer order is assigned. The programs that compute a routing solution use total cost of a routing solution as the objective function to be minimized. For each type of vehicle in InterShop's fleet, the operating cost includes a fixed cost for putting the vehicle on the road plus a variable cost per mile. The objective function also includes a cost per hour, including overtime, for the driver assigned to the vehicle.

In seeking a low-cost routing solution, ISRS incorporates a number of rules customizing routes to its business. Included among the rules are the following:

- **Time length of a route.** The maximal number of hours permitted between the time a vehicle leaves the depot and the time it returns.
- **Placement of rest and lunch breaks.** These breaks are dictated by law if the duration of the route is longer than 4 hours.
- **Maximal idle time.** The maximal allowable time during which a driver is not engaged in driving or delivering products.
- **Variable order delivery time.** Based on the size of the order and the difficulty of accessing the customer's location.
- **Delivery window dead time.** To ensure high-level customer service, orders must be scheduled to be delivered before a specified dead time at the end of the delivery window.

The system also incorporates algorithmic parameters controlled by the router that direct the algorithms and shape the solution. An important restriction imposed on the routing solution is that routes are constrained to lie within specified **territories** defined by zip codes. The constraint may be hard—each route must lie entirely in a territory—or, it may be soft—for example, at most two orders may lie in territories different from the remainder of the orders in a route. The imposition of territories allows drivers to be assigned to geographical areas that they know well. Moreover, the drivers will tend to deliver orders to frequent customers with whom they are acquainted.

Other parameters accessible to the router include those controlling the distance between successive stops, the minimal number of orders required for any route, the preferred vehicle type for specified zip codes, the number of vehicles available by vehicle type, and the extent of the search and therefore the time devoted to optimizing the solution. Because such parameters reflect modeling and algorithmic principles unknown to them, the routers require training and retraining in their use. An alternative approach is to hide all control parameters from the routers and to schedule regular sessions (for example, once a month) in which the system developers work with the routers to refine settings of the control parameters. In any event, an important, and often poorly appreciated, requirement for effective use of an operational planning system is the development of procedures for fine-tuning the routing algorithms as the company's business evolves.

The algorithms implemented and applied in ISRS are heuristics that begin the creation of each route from the pool of unrouted orders by selecting a single, seed order. Other orders in the geographical neighborhood of the order(s) are added in a myopic fashion to maintain feasibility with respect to the time windows, the capacity of the vehicle, and the customized rules. Myopic analysis is also performed to control the total cost of the route. For a 1000-order routing problem, the heuristics require approximately 10 minutes to determine a solution.

Although not implemented in ISRS, the developers experimented with linear and mixed integer programming of the type discussed in Section 5.3 to improve the routing solution by generating new routes based on optimal shadow prices. These optimization models begin with the routing solution generated by one or both of the heuristic algorithms. The experimentation was very promising, indicating that the unified optimization methodology merits further development for this class of applications.[11]

In addition to providing better routing solutions, the linear and mixed integer programming models can be extended to take into account portfolio constraints that shape the routing solution for each day's operations. (We use the word *portfolio* to emphasize constraints that affect the entire portfolio of routes selected for the day's operations.) Typical portfolio constraints follow:

- Upper bounds on the number of vehicles that may leave the depot each hour, which may reflect loading and dispatching capacity at the depot and/or driver availability
- Upper bounds on the number of each vehicle type employed daily

- Constraints and variables linking the routing solution to the driver assignment problem

Without the linear and mixed integer programming models, these constraints are imposed on a routing solution in an ad hoc manner, sometimes by manual intervention.

Manual Editing of Routing Solution. For several reasons, batch computation with the algorithms may produce an imperfect routing solution. First, some routes in the solution may be infeasible or unsatisfactory because they violate temporary or subtle rules not incorporated in the algorithms. Second, for a routing solution comprising 50 routes, it is possible or even likely that 5 routes, or more, will display inferior performance metrics. A related deficiency is the appearance of a small number of orphan orders that are not connected to any route. Orphans will tend to occur when the customized rules imposed on feasible routes become restrictive or even contradictory.

Thus, the human router must intervene to edit the routing solution produced by the algorithms. To accomplish this, he uses a **manual route editor** constructed from the GIS tool kit. The editor allows the router to view individual routes displayed on a map. It also allows him to make changes in a route by pointing and clicking at orders to be deleted or connected to one another or to a given route. The editor also contains a resequencer that accepts a set of orders on an adjusted or new route and determines the least-cost route that satisfies the customized rules and delivers to these orders without violating time windows. If the amended or new route is infeasible, the resequencer indicates the orders that must be deleted to achieve feasibility.

An open issue is understanding and then implementing an appropriate division of labor between the human router and the batch routing algorithms. In principle, the algorithms can produce a routing solution such that 80 or 90% of the routes require no, or very little, manipulation by the router. This degree of automation requires a constant commitment to fine-tuning and extending the routing algorithms as the company's business expands. Otherwise, the need to perform manual routing can increase, degenerating into an extended laborious activity as the human router attempts to overcome algorithmic deficiencies resulting from recent changes in the company's operational environment that have not been reflected in the algorithms.

Routing Solution Release. Upon conclusion of batch processing and manual editing of the routing solution, the router will release a certain number of orders to the fulfillment system. The purpose of the first wave release is to provide sufficient work for order fulfillment personnel to keep them busy until the next wave is analyzed and a new set of routes is released. In total, the router may analyze an entire day's routing problem by making two or three separate runs. The final wave to be analyzed, which is run after midnight, place all remaining orders on routes. The goal is to allow order fulfillment personnel to complete the assembly of all orders by 8 A.M., the beginning of the next delivery day.

Driver Assignment

The final analytical task of ISRS is assigning drivers to routes. Strictly speaking, this is a three-way decision problem in which routes, vehicles, and drivers are assigned together. The assignment of routes to vehicles is straightforward. Each route is assigned to a vehicle depending on the total size of the orders to be delivered. If smaller vehicles are in short supply, a larger vehicle may be assigned to a route for which it is not required. A few restrictions must also be obeyed that prohibit the assignment of large vehicles to certain zip codes. Because InterShop maintains a fleet of vehicles that is more than adequate for its business, the router can easily make the route to vehicle assignment using his judgment.

The assignment of drivers to route-vehicle combinations is more difficult. Each driver has a territory in which she usually makes deliveries, which should be the same as the territory of the route assigned to the driver. With a 12-hour daily delivery window, drivers are scheduled to arrive at the depot at various times during the day. The departure time of each route must therefore coincide, at least approximately, with the driver's arrival time.

Currently, driver assignments are computed in ISRS using a rule-based program that requires considerable manual adjustment. A linear programming model, which would optimize the assignment of drivers to route-vehicle combinations, could easily replace it. Specifically, the rule-based approach would be translated into an optimization model in which, for each route, a list of possible drivers is supplied. Some drivers in this list may be assigned without penalty, whereas others would have a penalty associated with them because such assignments are workable but should be avoided if possible. A much higher penalty would be charged if no driver is assigned to a particular route. The objective of the model is to minimize the sum of the penalties.

As we mentioned above, the developers have also experimented with extensions of ISRS in which linear and mixed integer programming models are employed to determine a routing solution. If this approach were implemented, a natural extension would be to incorporate the driver assignment model in these models. In this way, route selection for each day would be linked to driver schedules for that day.

10.4

Production Planning System for a Semiconductor Company

In this section, we report on a successful application from the mid-1990s at Harris Corporation's semiconductor sector of a production planning system based on large-scale optimization models.[12] Development of the system was begun in 1990 after the sector encountered serious difficulties consolidating operations following two large acquisitions in the 1980s. Prior to the acquisitions, the sector sold its finished products primarily to defense contractors and aerospace companies. The acquired companies sold products in the automotive and telecommunications industries where competition and customer service expectations were more demanding. The acquisitions tripled the size of the sector.

The expanded sector was selling more than 10,000 finished products manufactured across a supply chain of 30 manufacturing facilities located in the United States and Asia. On-time deliveries of 75% in 1989 were viewed unsatisfactorily by customers, causing sales and net revenues to decline. By 1991, the sector reported a net loss of $75 million on sales of approximately $500 million.

Around 1990, senior executives in the sector committed to the implementation of an automated sectorwide production-planning and delivery-quotation system, which they hoped would improve customer service and return the sector to profitability. This system, called Integrated Manufacturing Production Requirements Scheduling System (IMPReSS), based its supply chain analysis on an optimization engine, called the Berkeley Planning System (BPS). The BPS was originally developed under research contracts to the University of California, Berkeley, that were funded by the semiconductor industry. Its earlier applications were to production planning at individual facilities; the scaling up to IMPReSS represented an ambitious expansion of the earlier applied research project.

Manufacturing and Marketing Background

Semiconductors are manufactured in the following two major stages:

- **front-end stage.** Fabricating integrated circuits on silicon wafers and testing the circuits, which is called **wafer fab** and **wafer probe**
- **back-end stage.** Slicing wafers into individual chips, embedding chips in packaged devices, testing packaged devices, and creating finished products from packaged devices, which is called **device assembly** and **device testing**

Plants are called front-end and back-end plants. With only a few exceptions, front-end and back-end plants at Harris are geographically separate. In the course of a year, the 30 manufacturing facilities of the semiconductor sector would produce 2500 wafer types, 6000 packaged device types, and 10,000 finished goods types, based on 200 types of raw materials and using 200 types of processing equipment.

Manufacturing Process Flow. Semiconductor manufacturing is capital intensive, with plants operating 24 hours a day, 7 days a week. Demand can often outstrip capacity, especially for new products. Thus, in addition to supply chain management, production planning must address demand management by determining which orders to accept and their promised delivery dates.

Capacity planning is complex for several reasons. Products are routed through hundreds of operations and tests requiring cycle times (completion times) of 12 weeks or longer. The routings involve reentrant flows where a product may return several times to the same machine for additional work. Thus, work in process of different products at different stage of manufacture compete for the same resources.

A further complication is that semiconductor product families often include several quality grades, which expands assembly decisions to include alternative and substitutable source products. This phenomena is due to the probabilistic nature of wafer manufacturing processes, which yield products of several grades or qualities. These grades are separated into bins in a process called **binning.** The expected distribution of yields into each grade of product is called a **bin split.** If necessary, wafers with superior characteristics may be substituted for those with inferior characteristics. It is these substitution options, and related finished goods options, that require the development and use of optimization models to determine efficient allocations of parts to products.

Figure 10.6 depicts a typical process flow incorporating binning. In this diagram, the six rectangles are the major processes and the triangles are inventories of work-in-process and finished goods. A product moves from base wafer to wafer as the fab processes imprint the wafers with the patterns of an integrated circuit. A die is the circuit pattern on a wafer. In the probe stage, a completed wafer is subjected to electrical tests for each die. The probe stage is where the wafers are split into bins of varying quality. For example, a bin definition might be "speed between 30 and 40 megahertz and power consumption less than 100 milliamps."[13] The wafer bank consists of inventories of semiprocessed wafers, and the die bank consists of wafers that have completed the probe stage. These processes comprise the front-end stage.

In the back-end stage, the wafers are sliced up into individual chips that are assembled in packaged devices and tested. These devices are then labeled and packed into finished goods that are retested and shipped to customers. Note that packaged

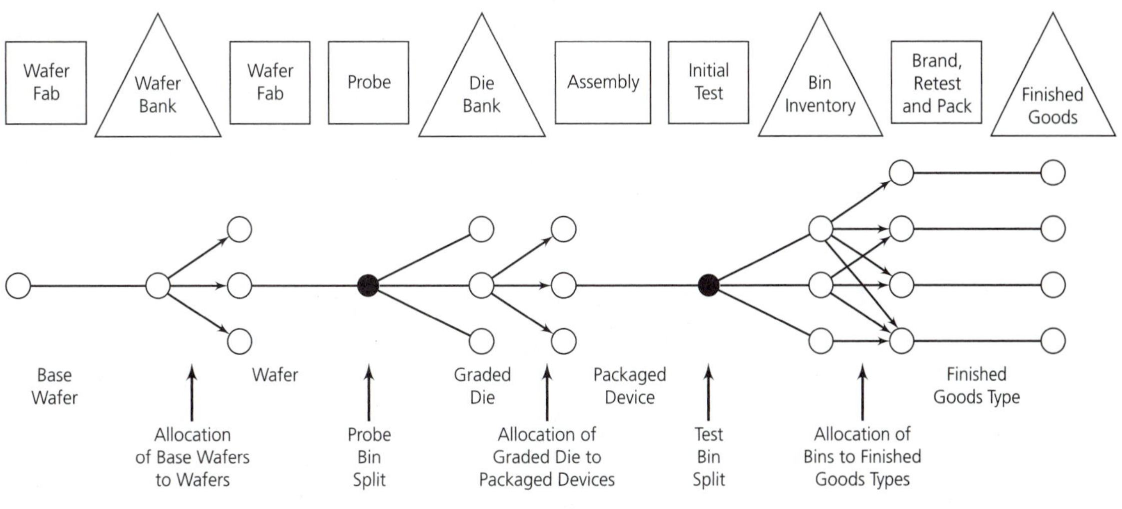

Figure 10.6 Semiconductor product flow. *Source:* Leachman et al. [1996]

devices are also separated into bins, and devices with superior performance characteristics may be used as a replacement for those with inferior characteristics if the latter type of device is not available. Again, finished products are related to the characteristics and quality of the wafer bins that went into them. Even after final testing during a burn-in period, finished products may be reclassed. Typical back-end manufacturing lots yield 500 to 2000 devices.

Marketing and Sales Priorities. Marketing and sales decisions for semiconductors ensuring competitive on-time deliveries and profits are difficult to make. Complications include lengthy production cycle times, dynamic work-in-process inventories by bins, tight production capacities, and varying product prices and margins. With these in mind, marketing and sales management divided the total forecast for each finished product in each planning period into the following three types of **priority classes:**

- **Order-board classes** comprising customer commitments and firm demands
- **Inventory replenishment classes** defined by safety stock requirements
- **Forecast classes** or projections of future customer demands

In this hierarchy, order-board demands had priority over inventory replenishment demands, which in turn had priority over forecasted demand. This logic allowed the sector to provide maximum service to its customers. Within a class, competition among products for capacity resources was reconciled by prices for finished goods.

Another marketing and sales policy to promote profits was the use of a **build-to-level code** for each finished product. Each level indicates the maximal quantity of finished product inventory allowed without firm orders on hand. Such a policy not only controls risk but also permits sales personnel to quote delivery quantities and dates based on the available slack in the build-to levels. Thus, order entry for finished products could be operated like an airline reservation system. Specific finished products could be promised to customers until their levels were exhausted. Of course, dynamic analysis with an optimization model on a rolling horizon basis is needed to determine realistic built-to levels. By providing this capability, IMPReSS anticipated later developments in available-to-promise (ATP) functionality of operational modeling systems.

Planning and Modeling Approaches

The discussion in the previous subsection is summarized in Figure 10.7. As shown, the planning cycle and the modeling analysis consists of the following three phases:

1. **Requirements planning,** in which inventory and work in process are subtracted from prioritized demands to determine net demands for new starts in back- and front-end production
2. **Capacity loading planning,** in which net demands are assigned to plants according to the priorities and subject to resource capacities

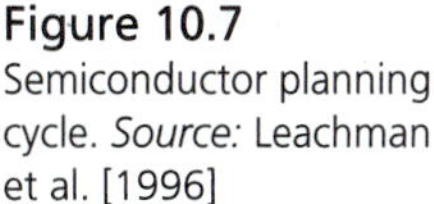
Figure 10.7
Semiconductor planning cycle. *Source:* Leachman et al. [1996]

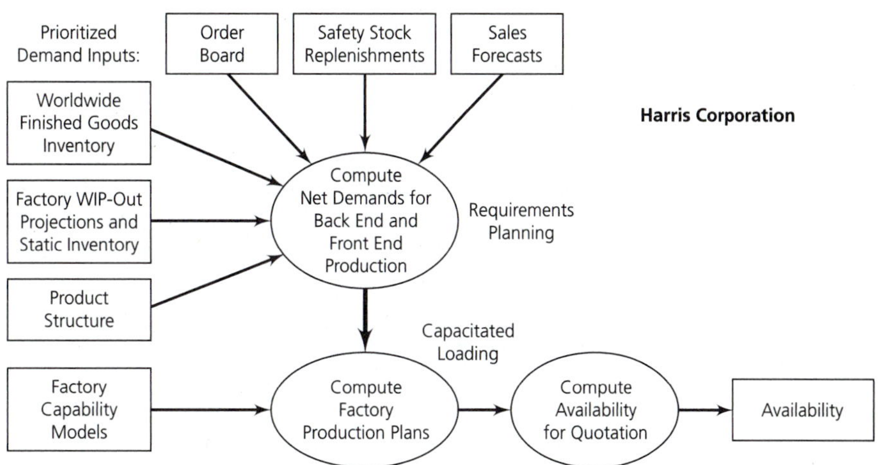

3. **Availability for quotation planning,** in which order-board demands are subtracted from the production plan to determine the quantity of finished products available for new quotations to customers

Requirements planning when there are no product choices due to binning is a straightforward calculation that can be performed by an MRP system; in other words, an optimization model is not required. However, if choices due to binning are present, optimization modeling is needed because the MRP system cannot compute requirements planning. These models, which employ inventory balance equations of the type studied in Section 3.1, are intended to capture the substitution choices afforded by binning. Allocating resource capacities also require optimization modeling.

We emphasize that models employed in this application addressed the multiobjective aspect of the production planning and scheduling problems. The conflict was between minimizing cost or maximizing revenues and customer service, which is a very important attribute by which companies in the semiconductor industry differentiate themselves. Thus, committed orders took precedence over forecasted orders, despite their potential margins, when optimizing the models. Further reconciliation of order fulfillment decisions was needed to deal with commitments that could not be met.

In the final analysis, it was not realistic to try to model all decisions and constraints in a single monolithic model. Moreover, the customer service considerations required that capacity loading decisions be made incrementally, working sequentially from the highest class demands to lowest class demands. Thus, the modeling practitioners sought a decomposition approach to optimize production planning.

Heuristic Decomposition Scheme. In the spirit of the unified optimization methodology discussed in Chapter 5, the developers of IMPReSS heuristically decomposed the planning problem and implied model of Figure 10.7 into a collection of manageable calculations and submodels that were linked together to provide a global planning strategy. Roughly, wafer and assembly requirements at all stages of the supply chain implied by orders, inventory requirements, and forecasts were determined independently of capacity loading decisions needed to meet these requirements. Moreover, capacity loading decisions for the front end of the supply chain were analyzed separately from capacity loading decisions for the back end.

A high-level view of the decomposition, which included five modules, is provided in Figure 10.8. In this figure, modules pointing to the left compute requirements plans, and modules pointing to the right compute capacity loading and availability plans. Given orders, inventory requirements, and forecasts, the following explains the purpose and form of these modules:

- **Test requirements planner (module 1).** Uses MRP calculations to determine worldwide net requirements for final test starts for each demand class by periods, netting out finished goods inventory and final test work in process.
- **Die requirements planner (module 2).** Uses MRP and linear programming calculations to determine net shipments to assembly areas from die bank by periods. Linear programming is needed because of the complexity of bin choices in finished goods. These calculations separate into many small linear programming models (fewer than 2000 rows) for planning requirements of individual finished goods families.

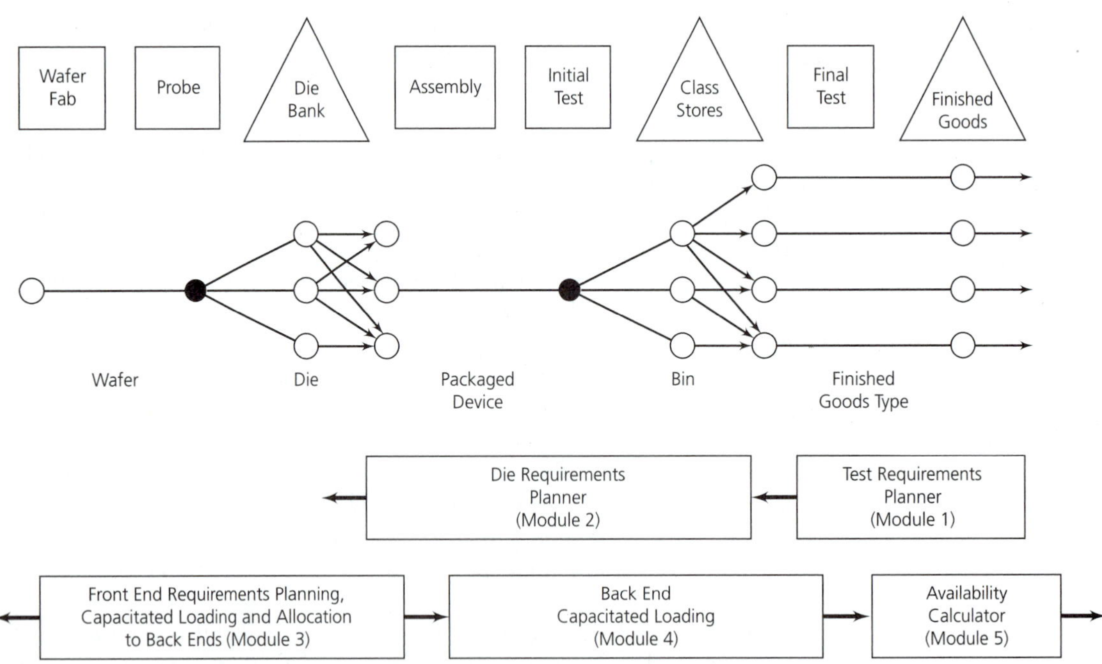

Figure 10.8 Decomposed modeling scheme. *Source:* Leachman et al. [1996]

- **Front-end capacity loading and back-end allocation planner (module 3).** Given requirements from module 2, computes front-end capacity loadings and allocation of planned die output to various back-end sites for each period. It uses two large linear programming models, where the largest had about 160,000 rows. These models were optimized in parallel. They also refine requirements planning decisions from module 2.
- **Back-end capacity loading planner (module 4).** For each back-end site, given available resources, raw materials, and dies, computes capacity loading for the site for each period. It uses large-scale linear programming models, where the largest had about 160,000 rows. These five models were optimized in parallel.
- **Availability planner (module 5).** The output from the five models of module 4 is used to calculate availability schedules by netting out all demand classes that are not forecasts.

The decomposition just described was heuristic in two important ways. First, it was based on reasonable assumptions about the approximate form of an optimal solution to the overall production planning problem. These included, for example, rules for preallocating demand to back-end sites and for rationalizing front-end capacity loading before back-end loading.[14] Second, no effort was made to rigorously integrate solutions to the submodels in a master model and to iterate through successive solutions of the master and the submodels to systematically improve the global solution. Given the complexity of the sector's planning environment and the quality of the results obtained from IMPReSS, this lack of rigor does not raise serious objections to the approach taken.

Implementation

Figure 10.9 depicts the modules and information flows that comprise IMPReSS, which took 2 years to complete and validate. Not surprisingly, the most difficult aspect of the implementation was standardizing data across the previously decentralized three companies that had recently merged. Managers and planners across the three companies held inconsistent conventions and intuitions about factory floor data, which they were reluctant to modify. Heavy and constant pressure from senior management was needed to overcome these barriers. In a real sense, data homogenization in the IMPReSS project anticipated enterprise resource planning developments for manufacturing firms that became widespread more than 5 years later.

As part of the project, the company acquired and installed a commercial demand forecasting software package, designed and implemented a bill-of-materials database, and upgraded the existing order entry system to provide on-line delivery quotation and reservation capabilities. Data management programs for converting old databases to new ones and to facilitate communication among factory floors and central computers were implemented. Initial tests about 1 year into the project indicated that data quality problems had not been totally solved. Considerable fortitude was needed during the ensuing year to improve the corporatewide database to the point where the system could be brought on-line.

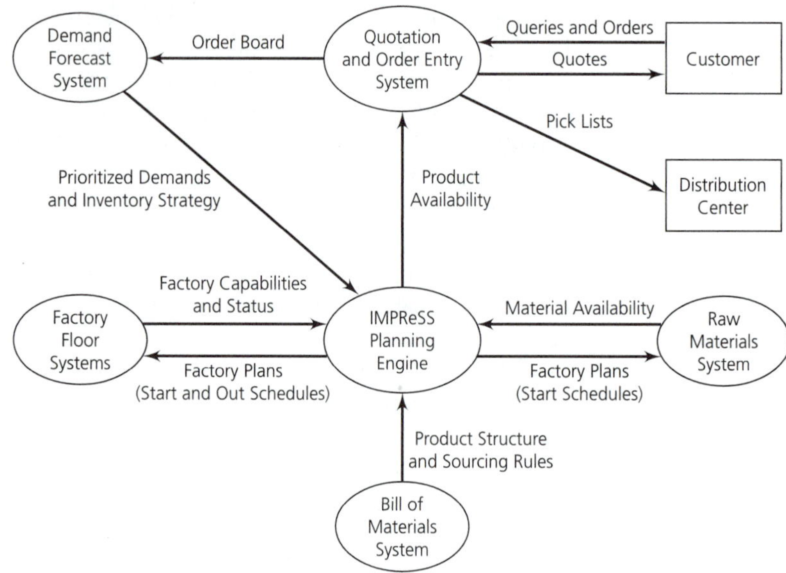

Figure 10.9
Information flows.
Source: Leachman et al. [1996]

Results

The system went on-line in May 1992. It was used each weekend to generate a production plan that revised availabilities in the quotation system. Specifically, the planning cycle began at midnight Saturday morning when all manufacturing sites in the United States and the Far East transferred factory and capacity data over the Internet to sector headquarters. The planning cycle ended by early Sunday afternoon, at which time the production schedules were sent out to all plants. By 1995, the turnaround time for the heuristic decomposition was 9 hours on an IBM RS-6000 workstation, Model 560.

In addition to providing more profitable production plans, IMPReSS significantly shortened the cycle time required in a decentralized environment to make plans and revise them. This allowed a much higher portion of a given plan to be based on customer orders rather than on forecasts that had significant variances. Moreover, the stability and the predictability of the plans were enhanced, and the number of planning personnel could be reduced.

Starting in 1993, use of IMPReSS caused on-time deliveries to attain a level of 94 to 95%, one of the best scores for a high-volume semiconductor manufacturer with a broad product line. Delinquent order line items fell from 5000 to less than 100 by late 1993. At the same time, sector inventories were held constant as a percentage of sales. The firm's reputation grew significantly as a consequence of these results, which led to large contracts with new customers. This confluence of improved performance permitted the company to begin showing a profit, which was $20 million in fiscal 1993, $30 million in fiscal 1994, and $42 million in fiscal 1995.

10.5

Simulation Models and Systems

In this section, we examine **simulation models,** which are defined as descriptive models that permit mangers or analysts to study the dynamic behavior of supply chain systems. The term *simulation* is sometimes used as a synonym for any type of model. This runs counter to our distinction between descriptive models, which include simulation models and normative or optimization models.

When discussing simulation models, an important distinction is between **deterministic simulation models,** which describe a system's dynamic behavior, assuming there are no random effects, and **stochastic simulation models,** which describe this behavior when there are random effects. Stochastic simulation models are often called **Monte Carlo simulation.** Monte Carlo is the casino where French mathematicians developed many of the early results of probability theory while trying to beat the gambling odds. In this section, we discuss both types, beginning with deterministic models. The discussion includes a brief overview of simulation software. We conclude by comparing and contrasting simulation and optimization models.

Deterministic Simulation

A deterministic simulation involves **state variables,** such as ending inventory or a machine's rate of production, describing a system at given points in time, and **equations** or other relationships describing how the state variables change over time as a function of decisions and external events. There is no uncertainty about these state changes. For example, based on 2 years of historical demand daily data for a product, we might simulate the impact of a specific inventory policy on inventory ordering and holding costs and on the product stock-out rate. An analyst would attempt to determine an effective inventory policy by experimenting with different parameter values.

In addition to analyzing decision policies, deterministic simulation models can assist managers in understanding complex interactions among system states, data, and decision variables. For example, due to lag and feedback effects in a manufacturing environment, work-in-process inventory may experience volatile and costly oscillations. A better qualitative understanding of the causes of these oscillations could lead to improved operations. A deterministic simulation model could indicate the extent to which stability of a manufacturing system depends on reducing the variance of delivery time between manufacturing stages, on improving the accuracy of demand forecasts for finished products, or on other means.

Monte Carlo Simulation

Monte Carlo simulation is a venerable and well-defined methodology of operations research. It refers to the implementation and application of computer programs that mimic the behavior of supply chain and other business systems in response to random variations in key parameters affecting them. Monte Carlo simulation provides insights about the operational performance of supply chain systems that are complementary to those provided by the optimization models discussed elsewhere.

Space does not permit us to develop in detail the elements of Monte Carlo simulation, although we present and discuss a simple example below. Clear and comprehensive discussions of the methodology can be found in a number of textbooks.[15] Simulation methods are intuitive to understand, more intuitive than the optimization models and methodologies. This is an important reason for their longtime and continuing application to supply chain problems.

Inventory Example. We illustrate key features of Monte Carlo simulation by a simple inventory example. The Outlet Store is open 7 days a week, 52 weeks a year, and it sells 10,000 consumer products at below normal retail prices. The store manager wishes to examine the inventory policy of one such product with average daily demand of about 20 units. Each product sale yields a net profit of $10/unit. If a customer requests the product but The Outlet Store is out of stock, he will try to purchase it at another store, and therefore the sale and its net profit are lost. Inventory holding cost equals $.05 per unit per day based on daily ending inventory. The manager seeks an inventory policy that maximizes average daily net profit from the product.

Analysis of product sales has led to the distribution given in Table 10.1 where, for the sake of simplicity, we have discretized daily demand into the four levels shown. The upper bound on the cumulative probability range for each possible level of demand refers to the probability that demand is less than or equal to that level; for example, the probability that demand on a given day is 20 units, or less is 0.85.

The manager wishes to analyze the following inventory policy: Whenever inventory falls to r units (the reorder point) or less, order q units (the reorder quantity) from the supplier. In selecting these values, she is concerned with maintaining a safety or buffer stock that hedges against uncertainties over the period during which an order has been placed but not yet received. In addition to demand uncertainties during the order period, inventory is subject to uncertainties in the delivery time of the q units. In particular, analysis of previous deliveries reveals that an order will be received in 2 days with probability equal to 0.10, in 3 days with probability, 0.70, and in 4 days with probability 0.20. An order cost of $50 is incurred each time an order for the product is placed.

Table 10.1 Product demand distribution

Demand	Probability	Cumulative Probability Range
10	0.05	0.01–0.05
15	0.30	0.06–0.35
20	0.50	0.36–0.85
25	0.15	0.86–1.00

We demonstrate how Monte Carlo simulation can be used to evaluate an inventory policy given by $r = 100$, $q = 250$. Analysis of 25 days of inventory, sales, and ordering is displayed in Table 10.2, where the beginning inventory is 125 units. Note that because expected daily demand is 18.9 units and the expected delivery time is 3.1 days, the expected demand over the order period is 58.59 units. Because we expect on average to place an order when ending inventory has fallen to approximately 95 units, the **safety stock** implied by this policy is approximately $95 - 58.59 = 46.41$ units.

The demand column displays simulated demand generated according to the distribution given in Table 10.1. Specifically, we selected random numbers from a table of previously generated random numbers that were uniformly distributed between 1 and 100, which means that any number between 1 and 100 has an equal probability of 1/100 of occurring. Each random number is translated into a random

Table 10.2 Inventory simulation

Day	Beginning Inventory	Demand	Sales	Ending Inventory	Order Placed	Order Received	Cumulative Net Profit ($)	Avg. Daily Net Profit ($)
1	125	15	15	110	0	0	144.50	144.50
2	110	20	20	90	250	0	340.00	170.00
3	90	15	15	75	0	0	486.25	162.08
4	75	25	25	50	0	0	733.75	183.44
5	50	25	25	275	0	250	920.00	184.00
6	275	15	15	260	0	0	1057.00	176.17
7	260	15	15	245	0	0	1194.75	170.68
8	245	20	20	225	0	0	1383.50	172.94
9	225	10	10	215	0	0	1472.75	163.64
10	215	15	15	200	0	0	1612.75	161.28
11	200	20	20	180	0	0	1803.75	163.98
12	180	25	25	155	0	0	2046.00	170.5
13	155	20	20	135	0	0	2239.25	172.25
14	135	25	25	110	0	0	2483.75	177.41
15	110	25	25	85	250	0	2729.50	181.97
16	85	15	15	70	0	0	2876.00	179.75
17	70	25	25	45	0	0	3123.75	183.75
18	45	20	20	25	0	0	3322.50	184.58
19	25	25	25	250	0	250	3510.00	184.74
20	250	20	20	230	0	0	3698.50	184.93
21	230	25	25	205	0	0	3938.25	187.54
22	205	15	15	190	0	0	4078.75	185.40
23	190	20	20	170	0	0	4270.25	185.66
24	170	20	20	150	0	0	4462.75	185.95
25	150	25	25	125	0	0	4706.50	188.26

demand by selecting the demand in Table 10.1 whose cumulative probability range contains the random number.

For example, the first random number was 06, which translated into a demand of 15 for day 1. The second random number was 47, which translated into a demand of 20 for day 2. Over the long term, the demands will distribute themselves according to the given probabilities because the random numbers fall equally likely among the numbers 1 to 100. Thus, for example, over the long term, half the random numbers will fall in the range 36 to 85 yielding a simulated demand of 20 units for the given day, which is consistent with the probability equal to 0.50 that demand will equal 20.

The sales in column in Table 10.2 are computed to equal demand, except in those periods when demand exceeds beginning inventory in which case sales are computed to equal beginning inventory. Lost sales did not occur during the 25 days simulated in the table, although we came very close in day 19. We assume orders are received late in the day and therefore not available for sale until the following day.

Ending inventory in Table 10.2 equals beginning inventory minus sales, except in those days when orders are received and added to ending inventory. Ending inventory falls to 90 units at the end of day 2, when we place an order for 250 units. We again selected random numbers uniformly distributed between 1 and 100 to simulate the delivery time distribution given above. A random number equaling 69 was translated into a delivery time of 3 days, and therefore, the first order was received during day 5.

The manager's performance metric for evaluating any r, q inventory policy is the average daily net profit associated with sales of the product. In Table 10.2, the average equals the cumulative net profit up to a given number of days divided by this number. The cumulative net profit each day equals the cumulative net profit from yesterday plus net profit from sales at $10 per unit minus the cost of ending inventory and minus the ordering cost of $50, which we assume is paid on the day the order is received. The given policy ($r = 100$, $q = 250$) appears to provide an average daily net profit around $185, but more analysis is clearly needed to be confident in this number. Moreover, to determine optimal values of r and q, we would need to run a number of Monte Carlo simulations to discover one that (approximately) minimizes average daily net profit.

We generalize from this simple example to briefly review major requirements of Monte Carlo simulation, as follows:

1. **Statistical analysis of properties of the system.** Monte Carlo simulation requires statistical analysis of key factors of uncertainty in the supply chain to be analyzed. Specifically, probability distribution functions describing these factors must be developed from historical data. These distributions may be multivariate; that is, they may involve multiple random factors if the factors are linked to one another such as sales of competing or complementary products.
2. **Discrete event simulation.** The example just examined was a discrete event simulation in which state variables (inventory, demand, orders) changed only at discrete points in time (each day). In general, a simulation is defined by its discrete time intervals, the states of the system to be observed in each of these periods, and the relationships describing how states change from one period to

the next. For some supply chain applications, a **continuous simulation** is required in which the state variables change continuous over time.

3. **Random number generation.** Random numbers play a central role in Monte Carlo simulation. Considerable mathematical research and computer system development has been performed to create tables of and functions for generating unbiased random numbers. In addition, efficient methods have been developed for using random numbers to extract random values for the system based on the statistical distributions of these factors.
4. **Statistical analysis of results.** A Monte Carlo simulation will easily generate large quantities of numerical data requiring considerable statistical analysis to understand and validate them. For the inventory example illustrated above, we could apply statistical methods to determine the number of days required by a simulation in order to be 99%, confident that the average daily net profit of the given inventory policy computed by the simulation lies within a bound of $1. A related issue is to understand the impact of the beginning inventory state on day 1 on our statistical analysis. We might also be concerned that trends in the random numbers affected our results, perhaps implying that we should make several simulation runs. The more complicated the real-world system, and therefore the Monte Carlo simulation, the more complicated the statistical requirements for specifying input data and for designing and executing experiments to extract validated results from the output data.

Advantages and Disadvantages of Monte Carlo Simulation. Monte Carlo simulation can be a useful tool for evaluating the design of a supply chain system faced with internal and external factors that vary randomly over time. It provides insights into the system's performance that cannot be obtained by deterministic optimization models, which treat all factors as known with certainty. It is particularly useful in evaluating interdependencies among random effects that may cause a serious degradation in performance even though the average performance characteristics of the system's components appear to be acceptable.

A **queuing system** is a well-known example of a system for which average performance characteristics do not reveal potential problems due to random effects. In one of its simplest forms, the queuing system consists of a server who serves customers at an average rate μ (number of customers served per unit of time when the server is busy) and customers for whom the average arrival rate is λ (number of customer arrivals per unit of time). Physically, the queuing system might correspond to a machine that intermittently processes identical jobs.

For example, if $\mu = 0.10$, $\lambda = 0.09$, and time is measured in minutes, we know that average service time $= 1/\mu = 10$ minutes, and the average time between customer arrivals $= 1/\lambda = 11.1$ minutes. Thus, $\lambda / \mu = 0.9 < 1$, or the server will process customers faster than they arrive. Assuming, however, that the service times and the interarrival times have random distributions, queuing theory results tell us that the average length of the queue of customers waiting for service will grow without bound as the ratio of λ to μ approaches 1. If a cost is associated with the time a customer spends in the queue, it might be necessary to design the system so that the service rate exceeds the interarrival rate by 20%, or more.

Applied mathematicians working in queuing theory have developed analytical results characterizing queuing systems with a wide range of properties. By analytical results, we mean formulas giving probability distributions for characteristics of the system such as the length of time a customer will spend in the system, the proportion of the time that a server will be busy, and so on. Consider, for example, a queuing problem involving one server with exponential service and interval arrival rates, which means that a customer is equally likely to arrive at any time and service is equally likely to be completed at any time, once it has begun. Letting $\rho = \lambda / \mu$, the probability that a customer who arrives at an arbitrary instant spends more than w time periods in the system (waiting in the queue and being served) is given by[16]

$$H(w) = e^{-\mu(1-\rho)w}$$

For the numerical example cited above, according to this formula, the probability that a customer will spend more than 20 minutes in the system is 0.8197. However, if we reduce the average service time to 8 minutes, or $\mu = 0.125$ and $\lambda / \mu = 0.72$, the probability that a customer will spend more than 20 minutes is reduced to 0.4975. If we were given the costs of customer waiting and the costs of speeding up service, we could quickly determine an optimal service speed by embedding this formula in a spreadsheet.

The example illustrates that the effort required to compute a service rate, balancing operating service costs against customer waiting costs, would be significantly less if queuing theory could be applied rather than Monte Carlo simulation. The general observation is that the modeling practitioner is always well advised to look first for analytical tools describing a supply chain system operating under uncertainty before electing to implement a Monte Carlo simulation. Still, Monte Carlo simulation might be required to analyze a queuing system or an inventory system if the system is so complex that analytical results cannot be obtained. This could be the case, for example, if we wanted to examine the performance of a multistage production line with multiple work-in-process buffer stocks, idle and unplanned downtime for machines, uncertain yields of certain manufacturing steps, and so on. Unfortunately, a Monte Carlo simulation might be developed to analyze such a system, but it would be viewed as a method of last resort because its implementation would require considerable resources.[17]

Thus, despite its popularity, Monte Carlo simulation has two serious deficiencies. First, considerable time and effort is required to construct and validate a Monte Carlo simulation of a complex system. Second, a Monte Carlo simulation provides no insights into how a system can be optimized, from the perspective of either operating the system and designing it. For these reasons, it cannot be used to support operational decision making.

Simulation Software

Systems dynamics is a well-elaborated methodology for deterministic simulation.[18] Several software packages for creating and running systems dynamics models are available on the market. These packages use causal feedback loops (e.g., describing the synergy between sales and perceived service quality), flow diagrams (e.g., describing the impact of word of mouth and advertising of customer awareness and therefore on the rate of acquiring new customers), and other types of diagrams to describe connections between factors affecting the performance of a dynamic system. The diagrams may be turned into equation-based models to run deterministic simulations. Most systems have built-in facilities for creating graphs and tables of inputs and outputs, and utilities for extracting causal explanations of observed dynamic behavior.

Off-the-shelf packages for Monte Carlo simulation have been available for over 30 years, although today's offerings are obviously more sophisticated. A recent software survey listed 54 packages intended for manufacturing and other supply chain design problems as well as a range of applications in health services, engineering design, and many other areas.[19] Packages range from Excel add-ons costing $395 to stand-alone systems costing $30,000 or more. They offer a range of features, including graphical model construction, templates, animation, curve fitting, and run-time debugging.

Simulation versus Optimization

Although the distinction between simulation and optimization may be clear from a formal, methodological viewpoint, it is much less clear from a managerial or application viewpoint. For example, a deterministic simulation package may include routines for creating a decision support system by allowing a developer to easily wrap the simulation models in a user-friendly interface. Although such a system might permit a manager to make better decisions, he must evaluate them either in a myopic, hunt-and-peck manner or using hard coded decision rules that may be suboptimal.

Such an approach may have the advantage that the decision logic employed by the model is easier for the manager to understand than that of a mathematical programming model. Nevertheless, the deterministic simulation can too easily lead to decisions that are much worse than they need be. Moreover, the myopic search for good decisions can inhibit the manager's view of how different classes of decisions interact in affecting the overall system under his control. The conflicting goals of the two modeling approaches can be reconciled by agreeing that a deterministic simulation model should, at some point in its application, be extended to an optimization model in which key decisions are treated as decision variables subject to system and resource constraints. Then, by selecting one or more objective functions, a more formal and effective optimization may be carried out.

The situation is more complicated when comparing Monte Carlo simulation models with mathematical programming models. Monte Carlo simulation may be the only method capable of providing insights into the performance under random behavior of complex manufacturing and other supply chain systems. As such, it may be the method of last resort, but well worth the effort in studying an investment in which the company will invest millions of dollars. The open issue is how to integrate optimization modeling methodologies with Monte Carlo simulation to optimize, at least approximately, a complex design. This is an area of current needing considerable basic and applied research.

10.6 Final Thoughts

The growing interest in advanced planning and scheduling (APS) systems indicates that supply chain managers have recognized the importance of analytical tools to support operational decision making. At the same time, many managers and system developers are confused about the capabilities appropriate for APS systems. This confusion is due to a lack of focus about the planning problems to be addressed and to ignorance about the role that can and should be played by optimization models for planning and scheduling.

First, supply chain managers must distinguish between tactical planning and operational scheduling of supply chain decisions. Both areas are considered part of APS. Tactical planning involves planning horizons of a few weeks to 12 months, broken down into periods of 1 week or 1 month. Operational scheduling involves planning horizons of 1 day to a few weeks broken down into planning periods of 1 hour or 1 day. Tactical planning involves broad, perhaps global, evaluation of the company's supply chain options. Operational planning focuses on scheduling activities for a given facility or even for a particular production line or stage.

In addition, tactical and operational decisions should be coordinated. A tactical plan for a manufacturing company's supply chain establishes targets for the quantity of each product to be made at each plant. The aggregate cost and capacity data used in the tactical model that helped identify these targets must be sufficiently accurate that the production manager at each plant can develop detailed operational plans that are consistent with them. Moreover, the tactical model must be exercised sufficiently often on a rolling horizon basis to allow for timely revision of the targets as new data about demand, inventories, and so on, become available. In short, formal or informal hierarchical planning methods should be employed to coordinate tactical planning and scheduling decisions.

A second source of confusion is the extent to which operational decisions suggested by an analytical system should be based on historical rules or the results of optimization models. Rule-based systems are more comprehensible to supply chain managers because the embedded rules reflect their intuitions about how to run their supply chains. Some rules may be effective, whereas others may be counterproductive, but, using only a rule-based system, a manager has no way of testing the quality of the solutions it identifies. At the other extreme, rigorous optimization models allow a much wider and deeper exploration of the company's supply chain decision problems. Carried to an extreme, though, a rigorous optimization model might be difficult or impossible to solve, even to a rough approximation, especially under time-critical conditions.

The distinction between tactical and operational planning is reflected in the form of optimization models to support decision making in the two areas. Optimization models for tactical planning do not address detailed timing factors associated with supply chain activities. For example, tactical models are not usually concerned with the time it takes to ship a product by truck from a specific plant to a specific distribution center or the start and end times of a production run specified in hours on certain days. By contrast, optimization models for operational planning are very much concerned with such timing details, which, because the details can be complex, is a primary reason that the scope of such models must be much smaller.

The unified optimization methodology discussed in Chapter 5 resolves the conflict between rule-based methods and optimization models by harmonizing them. The methodology treats rule-based methods as problem-specific heuristics that can be seamlessly blended with optimization models. Heuristics are generally effective in solving myopic subproblems (e.g., production/inventory planning for a single item), whereas optimization models are generally effective in optimizing across an entire operational system (e.g., production/inventory planning for many items under capacity constraints). Using decomposition methods, the unified optimization methodology combines solutions to subproblems in a rigorous manner while seeking demonstrably good global solutions to operational planning problems. In summary, to create systems that are truly effective in analyzing complex APS problems, additional basic and applied research is needed into the unified optimization methodology.

Exercises

In addition to the following exercises, modeling exercises involving data files and discussion exercises involving white papers may be found on the Web site (www.scm-models.com).

1. Rerun the Monte Carlo inventory simulation discussed in Section 10.5 with results displayed in Table 10.2. Begin with the same starting inventory (125 units) but select a new sequence of random numbers from Table 5.13 to determine daily sales and the number of days for delivery when orders are placed. Compare your results with those of Table 10.2.

2. The Texarkana Paper Company faces the classical **cutting stock problem** when seeking to complete orders for paper produced at its single paper mill. Its paper machines produce mother rolls of paper that must be cut into rolls of smaller widths to meet given demand for those widths. The goal is to determine a collection of cutting patterns that minimizes waste or, equivalently, minimizes the total number of mother rolls that must be cut to meet demand.

   As an example of this problem, we consider mother rolls 50 inches wide to be cut to fill orders for rolls that have the following widths: $w_1 = 5$ inches, $w_2 = 8$ inches, $w_3 = 11.5$ inches, and $w_4 = 13$ inches. Letting (a_1, a_2, a_3, a_4) denote a vector (array) corresponding to a cutting pattern where a_i = number of rolls of width w_i in the pattern, we require

   $$5 * a_1 + 8 * a_2 + 11.5 * a_3 + 13 * a_4 \leq 50$$

   for the cutting pattern to be feasible. For example, (10,0,0,0), (0,6,0,0), (0,0,4,0), (0,0,0,3), and (1,1,2,1) are all feasible cutting patterns. The last pattern produces one roll 5 inches wide, one roll 8 inches wide, two rolls 11.5 inches wide, and one roll 13 inches wide for a total of 49 inches used out of the 50 inches available on the mother roll.

a. Suppose the company is faced with cutting mother rolls to meet the following orders: 40 rolls w_1 wide, 47 rolls w_2 wide, 75 rolls w_3 wide, and 80 rolls w_4 wide. Using a spreadsheet optimizer, formulate and optimize a linear programming model to minimize the number of rolls needed to fill these orders using the five patterns given above. *Hint:* The decision variables are the number of times each pattern should be used. A demand constraint is needed for orders of each width.

b. Your solution in part a should involve fractional numbers of mother rolls for some patterns. Re-solve the model with the decision variables constrained to be general integers.

c. Let π_i denote the shadow price on the demand equation for width i in the linear programming model of part a. We know from Section 3.3 that a new feasible pattern (a_1, a_2, a_3, a_4) will look attractive in the linear programming model if its reduced cost is negative; namely if

$$1 - \pi_1 * a_1 - \pi_2 * a_2 - \pi_3 * a_3 - \pi_4 * a_4 < 0$$

To discover if such a pattern exists, we solve the **knapsack model**[20] as follows:

$$\text{Max } \pi_1 * a_1 + \pi_2 * a_2 + \pi_3 * a_3 + \pi_4 * a_4$$

Subject to

$$5 * a_1 + 8 * a_2 + 11.5 * a_3 + 13 * a_4 \leq 50$$
$$a_1, a_2, a_3, a_4 \text{ nonnegative integer}$$

d. Using the results of Section 3.3, argue that the value of the optimal solution in this knapsack model must be at least 1.

e. If the maximum value in the knapsack model is greater than 1, the corresponding pattern has a negative reduced cost and we add it to the linear programming model and reoptimize it. Use the shadow prices from the model of part a in constructing and optimizing the indicated knapsack model. Add the new cutting pattern, which should yield a negative reduced cost, to the linear programming model and reoptimize it.

f. If, at some iteration between the linear programming model and the knapsack model, no new pattern improving the linear programming solution can be found, we resolve the model as a general integer programming model and use the resulting cutting stock plan. Can we be sure that this plan is optimal? Why?

g. The cutting stock problem as described above is static in that the orders to be filled were given without reference to time. Suppose, instead, that the company is given orders of specific widths that need to be shipped in a given week and must decide which orders to cut and then ship on each day of the week. Discuss briefly how you would extend the model to capture these additional decisions.

3. The Vermont Clothing Company manufactures and sells men's and woman's clothing to catalog customers over the telephone. Each month it must schedule

personnel to take orders. The phones are covered 7 days a week from 9 A.M. to 5 P.M. (company local time). For planning purposes, each day is divided into a morning (A.M.) session (9 A.M. to 1 P.M.) and an afternoon (P.M.) session (1 P.M. to 5 P.M.). According to statistical analysis of past business, the following number of order takers will be required to ensure that 95% of the time, a customer will wait 5 minutes or less before making contact with an order taker:

Day of the Week	Mon	Tue	Wed	Thu	Fri	Sat	Sun
Number of Order Takers, A.M.	24	17	22	15	20	27	16
Number of Order Takers, P.M.	22	17	25	15	15	24	20

Full-time order takers work 5 consecutive days and cost the company $600 per week in salary and benefits. Part-time order takers are available for 3 consecutive half-days and work exclusively in either morning or afternoon sessions for the 3 days. Each part-time order taker costs the company $200 per week in salary and benefits.

Using a spreadsheet optimizer, construct and optimize a linear programming model that minimizes the company's weekly personnel costs. If the optimal solution to your linear programming model is fractional, resolve the model as a general integer programming model. *Hint:* The decision variables are the number of full-time order takers starting each day of the week and the number of part-time order takers starting during the morning or afternoon of each day of the week.

4. The Franklin Ice Cream Company faces the following production scheduling problem for the coming week. It produces four flavors of ice cream, chocolate, vanilla, strawberry and mocha, using a single ice cream machine. The machine operates continuously 168 hours per week. As shown in the following table, the net revenue per hour of production for each flavor varies significantly:

Ice Cream Flavors	Chocolate	Vanilla	Strawberry	Mocha
Net Revenue per Hour of Production ($)	280	350	295	330
Weekly Production Upper Limit (hours)	60	40	50	50

Due to demand limitations, marketing has placed upper limits on weekly production, which translates into upper limits on the weekly production hours for each flavor. It has also imposed a uniform lower bound of 20 hours per week for each flavor.

Production scheduling for the week is further complicated by flavor changeovers that require considerable time for cleaning and testing the quality of the new product. As shown in the following table, the changeover time depends on both the flavor being made before the changeover and the flavor to be made after the changeover:

Changeover Hours (from/to)	Chocolate	Vanilla	Strawberry	Mocha
Chocolate		6	3.5	2
Vanilla	1		1.45	1.25
Strawberry	2	4		2.5
Mocha	1.75	3	2.5	

For example, the changeover from chocolate to vanilla requires 6 hours, whereas the changeover from vanilla to chocolate requires only 1 hour. At the start of the week, the machine is set up to make strawberry. Three additional changeovers will be made to produce the other flavors.

Using a spreadsheet optimizer, construct and optimize a mixed integer programming model that determines a production sequence and a production plan that maximizes Franklin's net revenues for the week.

Notes

1. APS systems are reviewed in Layden [1998].
2. See Shapiro [1993] or Sipper and Bulfin [1997, Chapters 7–9].
3. Bodington and Baker [1990] provide a history of mathematical programming applications in the petroleum industry starting in the 1950s. The history mirrors the evolution of information technology, especially in the application of scientific computing methods and their impact on organizational decision making. The models also mirror increasing complications in the world refining market due to global competition for crude oil and refined products.
4. Coxhead [1994] addresses recent planning issues associated with integrating short-term scheduling, which is linked to crude-oil trading rather than long-term contracts, with medium-term planning. These real-world complications have created a need for more complex models.
5. The problem of minimizing waste in cutting mother rolls of paper is called the cutting-stock problem. A recent discussion of an effective decomposition approach for solving it can be found in Winston [1994, 562–568]. A variety of other material waste problems, including those spanning two dimensions, such as cutting cloth to make clothes, and those spanning three dimensions, such as packing trucks or containerships, have been successfully modeled.
6. The books by Golden and Assad [1988] and Crainic and Laporte [1998] contain collections of papers describing many vehicle routing applications and addressing technical issues connected with modeling and optimization.
7. Barnhart, Hatay, and Johnson [1995] provide a recent application of the unified optimization methodology to airline crew scheduling that was ambitious and successful.
8. Desaulniers et al. [1998] provide an extensive discussion of the overlap in vehicle routing and crew scheduling models as well as versions of the unified optimization methodology for optimizing them.
9. An overview of technical issues in developing vehicle routing systems is given by Hall and Partyka [1997]. *OR/MS Today* [1997] is a survey of 20 vehicle routing packages.

10. See Burroughs and McDonnell [1998] and Koch [1999] for discussions of GIS state-of-the-art and speculations about future developments.
11. Desaulniers et al. [1998] report on successful implementation of a version of the unified optimization methodology for vehicle routing problems with time windows.
12. This section is based on the paper by Leachman et al. [1996] that won the 24th annual Franz Edelman Award for management Science Achievement, a competition sponsored by INFORMS and the College of the Practice of Management Sciences.
13. Leachman et al. [1996, 14].
14. Additional details about the heuristics and the decomposition approach can be found in Leachman et al. [1996, 26–29].
15. Wagner [1969, Chapter 16] provides a clear and thorough introduction to Monte Carlo simulation, which speaks to the venerability of the method. See also Winston [1994, Chapter 13] and Winston and Albright [1997, Chapter 12], which contains spreadsheet realizations of Monte Carlo simulations.
16. Wagner [1969, 857].
17. Wagner [1969, 890] makes the point that Monte Carlo simulation becomes the method of last resort when the problems to be evaluated are too complicated for analytical methods such as queuing theory.
18. See Sterman [2000] for a comprehensive overview of systems dynamics and its applications, including those in the management of supply chains.
19. See *OR/MS Today* [1999].
20. The knapsack problem is the decision problem faced by a hiker who needs to decide how many of each of n items to take on a hike. The knapsack can be filled with a combination of items not exceeding W pounds. Each item i has a value v_i per unit and a weight w_i per unit. The hiker's decisions can be optimized by solving a simple integer programming model consisting of one constraint involving positive integer coefficients and decision variables that can take on any nonnegative integer values. Despite its simplicity, the knapsack problem has provided important insights into general mixed integer programming models.

References

Barnhart, C., L. Hatay, and E. L. Johnson [1995], "Deadhead Selection for the Long-Haul Crew Pairing Problem," *Operations Research,* 43, 491–499.

Bodington, C. E., and T. E. Baker [1990], "A History of Mathematical Programming in the Petroleum Industry," *Interfaces,* 20, 117–127.

Burrough, P. A., and R. A. McDonnell [1998], *Principles of Geographical Information Systems.* Oxford, Eng.: Oxford University Press.

*Coxhead, R. E. [1994], "Integrated Planning and Scheduling Systems for the Refining Industry," in *Optimization in Industry 2,* edited by T. A. Ciriani and R. E. Leachman. New York: Wiley.

Crainic, T. G. and G. Laporte, ed. [1998], *Fleet Management and Logistics.* Norwell, Mass.: Kluwer.

Desaulniers, G., J. Desrosiers, I. Ioachim, M. M. Solomon, F. Soumis, and D. Villenueve [1998], "A Unified Framework for Deterministic Time Constrained Vehicle Routing and Crew Scheduling Problems," Chapter 3 in Crainic and G. Laporte [1998]

Golden, B. L., and A. A. Assad [1988], *Vehicle Routing: Methods and Studies.* Amsterdam: North-Holland.

Hall, R. W., and J. G. Partyka [1997], "On the Road to Efficiency," *OR/MS Today,* 24, 3, 38–41.

Koch, T. [1999], "GIS: Mapping the OR/MS World," *OR/MS Today,* 26, 4, 26–31.

Layden, J. [1998], "The Reality of APS Systems," *APICS,* September, 50–52.

*Leachman, R. C., R. F. Benson, C. Liu, and D. J. Raar [1996], "IMPReSS: An Automated production Planning and Delivery Quotation System at Harris Corporation—Semiconductor Sector," *Interfaces,* 26, 6–37.

OR/MS Today [1997], "'97 Vehicle Routing Survey," 24, 3, 42–47.

OR/MS Today [1999], "Simulation Software Survey," 26, 42–51.

Shapiro, J. F. [1993], "Mathematical Programming Models and Methods for Production Planning and Scheduling," in *Handbooks in Operations Research and Management Science: Vol. 4, Logistics of Production and Inventory,* edited by Graves, S. C., A. H. G. Rinooy Kan, and P. H. Zipkin. Amsterdam: North-Holland.

Sipper, D., and R. L. Buffin, Jr. [1997], *Production: Planning, Control and Integration.* New York: McGraw-Hill.

Sterman, J. [2000], *Business Dynamics: Systems Thinking and Modeling for a Complex World.* Boston: Irwin/McGraw-Hill.

Wagner, H. M. [1969], *Principles of Operations Research,* 1st ed. Englewood Cliffs, N.J.: Prentice-Hall.

Winston, W. L. [1994], *Operations Research: Applications and Algorithms,* 3d ed. Pacific Grove, Calif.: Duxbury Press.

Winston, W. L., and S. C. Albright [1997], *Practical Modeling and Applications: Spreadsheet Modeling and Applications.* Pacific Grove, Calif.: Duxbury Press.

*See the credits section at the end of this book for more information.

11 Inventory Management

A company may hold inventories of raw materials, parts, work in process, or finished products for a variety of reasons, such as the following:

- To create buffers against the uncertainties of supply and demand
- To take advantage of lower purchasing and transportation costs associated with high volumes
- To take advantage of economies of scale associated with manufacturing products in batches
- To build up reserves for seasonal demands or promotional sales
- To accommodate products flowing from one location to another (work in process or in transit)
- To exploit speculative opportunities for buying and selling commodities and other products

Models for optimizing inventory management decisions that take these factors into account have been proposed and applied for over 60 years.[1] Recently, attention has focused on creating business processes that reduce or eliminate inventories, mainly by reducing or eliminating the uncertainties that make them necessary.

Metrics describing the performance of a company's inventory management practices can be important signals to shareholders regarding the efficiency of the company's operations and hence its profitability. Figure 11.1 illustrates this point. The ratio of sales to inventory for Ford and General Mills improved almost threefold between 1975 and 1994, conveying the notion that supply chain management in these companies improved significantly over that period.[2]

Recently, attention has focused on creating business processes that reduce or eliminate inventories, mainly by reducing or eliminating uncertainties that make them necessary. Better communication between and coordination of activities across company functions and between the company and its vendors and customers can greatly reduce uncertainties. Specific measures include the following:

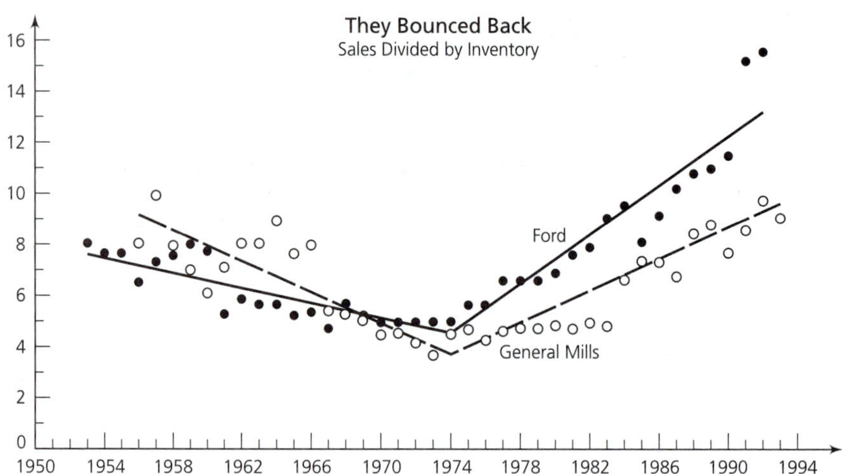

Figure 11.1
The Economist,
June 20–26, 1998

- Improving the accuracy of forecasts by developing better forecasting models and by promoting better communication between supply chain managers and marketing and sales personnel
- Sharing supply chain information with vendors, third-party transportation providers, and other suppliers
- Consolidating the number of locations where products are held and reducing product variety
- Postponing product customization to downstream stages of the supply chain

Of course, despite such efforts, significant uncertainty may remain between stages of a supply chain, implying that inventories will still be needed to ensure effective operations. Inventory management problems are characterized by holding costs, shortage costs, replenishment delays, and probabilistic demand distributions for products specified at a detailed SKU level. Models for optimizing inventory policies for individual items use methods from statistics and applied probability theory. As such, they are very different in form from deterministic optimization models, which broadly consider products, facilities, and transportation flows in analyzing resource acquisition and allocation decisions. Inventory models involve parameters and relationships, such as variances of market demands and delivery times and their impact on stock outages, which are not easily represented in optimization models. For this reason, incorporating inventory decisions in supply chain optimization models is difficult. Nevertheless, depending on the scope of the analysis, acceptable approximations of inventory costs can be developed. Improving these approximations is an important area of current applied research.

In this chapter, we study models for inventory management with an emphasis on approaches for integrating inventory decisions with other supply chain decisions. This perspective, which is sometimes overlooked by managers responsible for controlling inventories, is crucial because holding costs are only one element of total supply chain cost. In some industries, such as consumer products that have rapid turnover, inventory costs may be less than 5% of total supply chain cost. In other industries, such as electronics products made of expensive components with long manufacturing times, inventory costs may exceed 20%. Moreover, inventory costs, and the extent of management's concern for inventory control, will depend on the cost of capital, which will continue to vary over economic cycles.

Classical inventory is reviewed in Section 11.1. We examine modeling approaches in Section 11.2 for incorporating inventory management decision in supply chain optimization models for strategic and tactical planning. In Sections 11.3 and 11.4, we discuss models that were successfully developed and applied to inventory management problems in distribution and manufacturing. The chapter concludes with final thoughts in Section 11.5.

11.1 Inventory Theory Models

The number of published papers on inventory theory is vast, with numerous books dedicated to the subject.[3] In this section, we discuss briefly only a few such models. Our goal is to provide key insights into concepts of inventory modeling in preparation for subsequent discussions about how to incorporate inventory decisions in supply chain optimization models.

Starting at least as far back as the 1950s, the focus of models was on inventory policies for finished products sold to customers. We review such models in this section. Inventory management of work in process or raw materials held in manufacturing firms is more complicated because demand for such items is internal to the company and may be subject to capacity constraints and unpredictable delays. We discuss such problems in a later section of this chapter.

Deterministic Models

The simplest and most venerable of inventory models is the **economic order quantity** (EOQ) model.[4] This model addresses inventory management of a single item. Its assumptions follow:

- Demand is known with certainty and occurs at a constant rate totaling D units per year.
- Whenever a replenishment order of any size, say q, is placed, a fixed ordering or setup cost K is incurred.
- Each order is delivered immediately; that is, the lead time is zero.
- Shortages are not allowed.
- The cost per unit-year of holding inventory is h.

The unit holding cost h is a key parameter in the EOQ and all other inventory models. Its value will depend on the company's cost of capital and other risk factors such as the possibility that the products will spoil or become obsolete. For global corporations, the cost of capital will depend on interest rates prevailing in the countries where inventories are held and the sovereign risks of doing business there.

Let $I(t)$ denote the amount of inventory on hand at time t. Figure 11.2 depicts $I(t)$ as a function of q, the size of an order. The EOQ model determines a value of q that minimizes the sum of setup and holding costs; namely, the optimal order quantity

$$q^* = \left(\frac{2KD}{h}\right)^{1/2}$$

Note that the **number of turns per year** equals D/q^*. The EOQ model has been extended to incorporate deterministic lead-time delays and to allow for backlogging or losing demand with a cost penalty.

Figure 11.2
Deterministic EOQ model

The EOQ model has found widespread application over the past 50 years, clearly because its form and interpretation are simple. Still, in today's complex world of integrated supply chain management, it seems difficult to derive a meaningful ordering or setup cost K for each item held in inventory. Instead, inventory ordering policy is often set by deciding on turns per year to meet anticipated yearly volume, which in turn is based on a manager's intuition about effective stocking policies.

Example 11.1

Consider an auto retail outlet that sells 3000 units per year of a popular make and size of tire. Suppose further that the fixed cost of an order is \$300 and that the yearly holding cost of a tire is \$5. Plugging into the EOQ formula, we obtain $q^* = 600$. Thus, in following the optimal policy, the retail outlet receives five shipments per year (i.e., has five turns per year) of 600 tires per shipment.

A number of simple, deterministic models have been proposed and studied that extend the EOQ model by combining manufacturing with inventory decisions. One such model, which we examined in detail in Chapter 5, is the **dynamic lot size**

model. In this model, demand for a single item over a number of time periods is known with certainty. A fixed cost K is incurred every time a machine is set up to make the product. Once this cost has been incurred, there is an incentive to produce many items. The countervailing force, however, is inventory holding cost. Unlike the basic EOQ model, which is optimized by a formula, the reconciliation between manufacturing setup and inventory costs can be effected only by solving a dynamic programming or mixed integer programming model.

Probabilistic Models

The EOQ model just discussed and its generalizations are limited because they treat all parameters relating to future operations as deterministic. The primary concern of inventory management models and systems is to determine strategies for holding excess products, called **safety stocks,** that hedge against uncertainties while minimizing avoidable expected costs.[5] The major sources of uncertainty include the following:

- Demand over the delivery lead time
- The length of the lead time

Demand uncertainties are a reality that most companies must accommodate in managing their supply chains. Supply chain processes that have been well designed and well executed can reduce, but not eliminate, lead-time uncertainties. Similarly, uncertainties associated with product quality, completeness of orders, product spoilage, and so on, can be greatly reduced by careful management. Thus, in the discussion that follows, we will concentrate on methods for hedging against demand uncertainties.

The deterministic EOQ model can be extended to consider the impact of uncertain demand for an item over the positive lead time between placing an order and its delivery. The extended models employ concepts and constructs from probability theory. A **random variable** X can assume more than one value with an associated probability. We write $P(X = x)$ to denote the probability that X assumes the specific numerical value x. Such probabilities lie between 0 and 1. A **probability density function** describes the values of X where it takes on positive probabilities and the values of these probabilities.

In the simple case when the probability density function for the random variable X takes on a finite number of values, say $X = x_1$ with probability p_1, $X = x_2$ with probability p_2, and so on until $X = x_n$ with probability p_n, its **expected value,** denoted by $E(X)$ is given as

$$E(X) = p_1{}^* x_1 + p_2{}^* x_2 + \cdots + p_n{}^* x_n$$

We also have

$$p_1 + p_2 + \cdots + p_n = 1$$

Its **variance,** denoted by $\sigma(X)$, is a measure of probabilistic dispersion. It is given as

$$\text{Var}(X) = p_1{}^* (x_1 - E(X))^2 + p_2{}^* (x_2 - E(X))^2 + \cdots + p_n{}^* (x_n - E(X))^2$$

The **standard deviation** is the square root of the variance. The underlying concepts become more complicated when the probability density function assumes positive values along a continuum and may involve more than one random variable. We assume the reader is familiar with these concepts and do not elaborate further.[6]

A commonly used construction in inventory theory is the normal density function, which has the well-known bell-shaped form that is centered at the expected value of the random variable it describes. Its dispersion is proportional to the variance of that random variable. If the expected value of the normal random variable is denoted by μ and the variance by σ^2, we denote the density function by $N(\mu, \sigma^2)$. The normal distribution is standardized by transforming it to the new random variable $(X - \mu)/\sigma$, which has an expected value of 0 and a variance equal to 1. This allows the distribution to be described by a standard table of probabilities; these probabilities can be related to those describing an arbitrary normal random variable by inverting the transformation. The normal distribution is used to describe fast-moving items that have frequent demand. Other distributions, such as the Poisson density function, which is skewed to the left, may be used to describe slow-moving items that have infrequent demand.

A direct extension of the deterministic EOQ model is the **(r, q) model:** When inventory falls to the **reorder point r**, order the **replenishment quantity q.** The result of following this strategy is depicted in Figure 11.3. A time τ is associated with delivery of q items during which a random amount of demand occurs. Note that in some reordering cycles demand becomes negative before the order is received. The probability that this occurs is controlled by the quantity of safety stock held. As we have shown it, negative demand is treated as a backlog that must be filled once replenishment occurs.

Hedging against the uncertainty in inventory levels over the delivery time τ is the essence of inventory theory. For consumer products, inventory stockouts may lead to customer dissatisfaction or lost sales. For inventories of critical parts for a machine tool, mainframe computer, or commercial aircraft, inventory stockouts may cause costly equipment downtime. Managerial judgment must be used to decide how much to spend on safety stock to avoid, but not eliminate, these costs or to ensure that stockouts occur only with a sufficiently low probability.

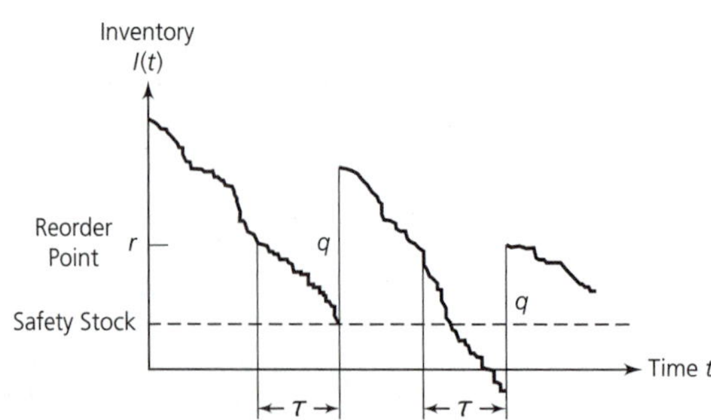

Figure 11.3
Inventory subject to uncertain demand

An optimal strategy for the (r, q) model is a natural extension of the optimal strategy for the EOQ model. The extended model seeks to minimize the expected total cost of maintaining inventory, which is the sum of expected inventory holding and stockout costs. In particular, if we now let D denote random demand, $E(D)$ denote the expected annual demand for the item, and c_B denote the cost incurred for each unit of the item that is short (backlogged), the optimal values r^* and q^* must satisfy

$$q^* = \left(\frac{2KE(D)}{h}\right)^{1/2}$$

$$\text{Probability (demand during lead time} \geq r^*) = \frac{hq^*}{c_B\,E(D)}$$

The probability describes the event that a stockout will occur during a lead time. Thus, it allows a reconciliation of the backorder cost with the company's desired **order fulfillment rate,** which equals 1 – probability (demand during lead time $\geq r^*$). For this item

Safety stock = $r^* - E$ (demand over the lead time)

Figure 11.4 depicts the density function of demand, which we have assumed to be normal. The value of the reorder point r^* is determined implicitly by the above probability requirement. For fixed expected demand, it is an increasing function of σ^2_D, the variance of demand, because a larger variance implies a larger value of r^* and a larger value for the safety stock. **Replenishment stock** is defined as the difference between actual inventory $I(t)$ and safety stock.

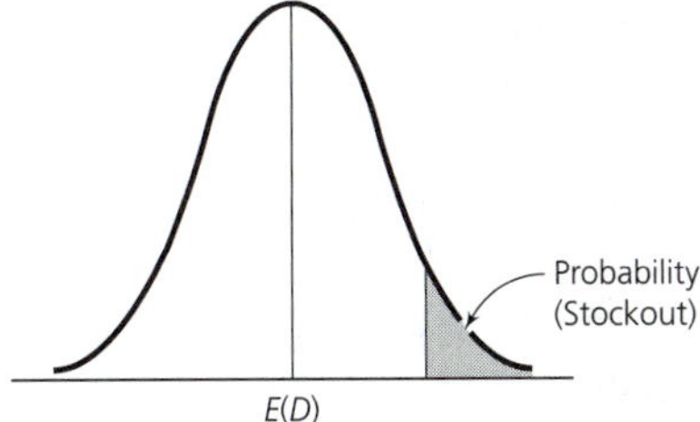

Figure 11.4
Normal density function of demand

Example 11.2

Consider Example 11.1 with the following complications. Demand for the tire over the year is normally distributed with expected demand equal to 3000 units, which was the certain demand in Example 11.1, and standard deviation $\sigma_D = 500$. Moreover, orders require a lead time of 2 weeks for delivery, and a marketing analyst has determined that the cost of a backlogged order is \$50. Plugging into the formulas above, we still have an order quantity $q^* = 600$ because the formula is effectively the same. The probability statement defining the reorder point is

$$P(\text{demand during 2 week delivery lead time exceeds reorder delivery level}) = \frac{5 * 600}{50 * 3000} = 0.02$$

In other words, given the unit cost of backlogging, the auto retail store will tolerate a 2% out-of-stock probability, or a 98% order fulfillment rate, on each replenishment cycle. The expected demand during the 2 weeks (1/26th of a year) is 3000/26 = 115.38, and the standard deviation is $500/\sqrt{26} = 98.06$. Using normal distribution tables, we determine that the optimal reorder point $r^* = 115.38 + 2.054 * 98.06 = 278$, where 2.054 is the number of standard deviations above the mean that corresponds to a 2% stockout rate. The safety stock = 2.054 * 98.06 = 201, which is the quantity above expected demand needed to ensure only a 2% stockout rate.

The (r, q) model just analyzed requires an accurate estimate of the backlogging unit cost c_B. If such a cost is difficult to determine, an alternate approach to computing r^* is to determine safety stock by specifying the out-of-stock rate or, equivalently, the order fulfillment rate.

For this construction, by appeal to Figure 11.4, the larger the value of the variance of demand, the larger the value of r^*, the reorder point and, therefore, the larger the value of the safety stock. If the lead time is also a random variable, probability theory tells us that the variance of demand over the uncertain lead time will increase by a positive quantity equal to the variance of the lead time multiplied by the square of the expected yearly demand. Thus, as we would expect, the reorder point and the safety stock will increase relative to the case when there is no uncertainty in the lead time.

Finally, the (r, q) model can also be modified for the case when inventory shortage leads to lost sales rather than backlogging. We let c_{LS} denote the unit cost of a lost sale. The optimal order quantity q^* in this case is the same, but the reorder point r^* is determined by using the normal distribution tables to find r^* that satisfies

$$\text{Probability (demand during lead time} \geq r^*) = \frac{hq^*}{hq^* + c_{LS}E(D)}$$

Assuming that $c_{LS} > c_B$, a comparison of the two probability statements shows us that the reorder point and the safety stock will be larger in the lost sales case.

The (r, q) model assumes that an order can be placed at exactly the moment inventory falls to the reorder point r. This assumption is reasonable for systems handling many orders of relatively small size, such as large retail networks where each distribution center may replenish 50 or 100 stores. In other situations, such as in the management of spare parts networks, an order may be received simultaneously for several items of demand, thereby causing net inventory to suddenly fall way below the reorder point. For these problems, we apply the following:

> **(s, S) model:** Whenever inventory falls below s, say to the level z, place an order for $S - z$ items.

The (r, q) and (s, S) models require continuous monitoring of inventory levels. An alternative is to use a periodic review base stock policy, as follows:

> **(R, S) model:** Every R periods of time, check the inventory level. If it is below S, place an order to bring it up to S.

This type of policy will lead to higher inventory holding costs than an (r, q) or (s, S) policy, but it is easier to manage. Periodic review of multiple items also facilitates coordination of orders for these items, especially for those items supplied from the same source.

ABC Classification

The models just reviewed can provide useful inventory management plans described by reorder points, order quantities, safety stocks, and order fulfillment rates. Nevertheless, they are simplistic because inventory management involves real-world considerations that are difficult to capture. Examples include the following:

- The timing of delivery orders of an item to a stocking point may depend on when a full truckload from the supplier can be assembled and dispatched.
- Many items may be ordered together and shipped together in full truckload shipments.
- Capacity constraints at a supplier may limit the size of item lots that can be manufactured to replenish the item.
- Demand from other stocking locations for an item might force a supplier to allocate his limited supply among these locations.

In addition, for companies with thousands of SKUs, it can be very difficult, if not impossible, to estimate the parameters required by the models.

A practical solution to these difficulties, which is recommended by inventory management experts, is to apply the **ABC classification method** to the company's product lines. This method recognizes that a small percentage of SKUs account for the majority of sales, whereas the majority of SKUs account for only a small percentage of sales. A typical breakdown is displayed in Figure 11.5. As shown, 20% of the items account for 60% of the sales; these are the type A items. Another 20% of sales account for an additional 20% of sales; these are the type B items. The remaining 60% of the items account for only 20% of sales; these are the type C items.

Different inventory management methods and models are suggested for each of the three categories. For type A items, the order fulfillment rate should be set relatively low, say in the 80% range, because the holding cost of maintaining higher

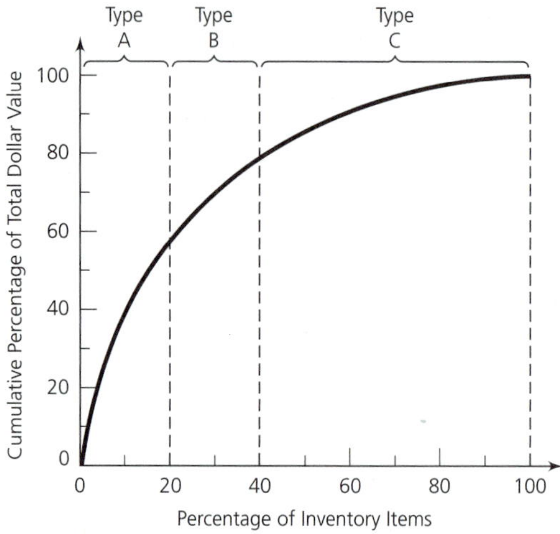

Figure 11.5
ABC classification method. *Source:* Winston [1994, 934]

inventories to achieve higher rates would be prohibitive. Individual forecasts should be made for these items with frequent review of key model parameters such as demand forecasts, their variances, and lead-time length. The company should also work closely with its suppliers to reduce lead times. In so doing, uncertainties and therefore safety stocks will be reduced, and backlogging will be cleared more rapidly.

For type B items, higher order fulfillment rates should be set, and model parameters may be reviewed less often. For type C items, still higher order fulfillment rates may be employed because total investment in inventory is relatively low. Moreover, items may be grouped into families and the parameters for these families may be reviewed relatively infrequently, such as once or twice a year.

Finally, we point out that there is an indirect management cost associated with each SKU held in stock. This cost comprises physical and human resources needed to administer, store, count, and order the item. For retailing companies, aircraft manufacturers, and other companies with tens of thousands of items in stock, such indirect inventory costs can be quite large. This suggests that such companies should frequently review their product lines with an aim to retiring or consolidating items.

11.2

Incorporating Inventory Management Decisions in Strategic and Tactical Supply Chain Models

In this section, we examine modeling approaches for incorporating inventory management decisions in supply chain optimization models that analyze broad resource acquisition and allocation decisions. For strategic planning problems where we use models to evaluate options for designing, expanding, modifying, or contracting the company's supply chain, the role of inventory management submodels is to approximate inventory deployment plans and their implied costs across the supply chain. For tactical planning problems where we use models to determine cost minimizing supply chain plans for satisfying product demands, which fluctuate by time and market, the role of inventory management submodels is to identify inventory decisions that smooth the effects of such fluctuations. As in other parts of the book where we discuss strategic and tactical supply chain planning problems and models, we use the term *product* to denote actual products or families of similar products. The ABC classification method discussed at the end of the previous section should be one of the criteria used in constructing these families.

Incorporating Inventory Management Decisions in Strategic Supply Chain Models

The strategic supply chain models we will consider are snapshot, or one-period, models. Such models require modeling artistry to capture inventory planning phenomena because the dynamic effects of inventory decisions cannot be explicitly modeled. Even if we were to employ a multiple-period strategic model, the length of the periods would be too great, probably 1 year or longer, to ignore within-period variations in inventory. This point is discussed below in more detail when we examine inventory decision making in the context of multiple-period tactical planning.

The key inventory planning phenomena to be captured in a strategic model are as follows:

- Pipeline inventories
- Safety stock inventories
- Replenishment inventories

Pipeline inventory costs may be readily incorporated in a supply chain optimization model. For a product flowing along a transportation arc, we add a pipeline inventory unit cost to the transportation unit cost. This cost is determined by multiplying the value of an average unit of product times the average number of days in transit on the arc times the daily cost of capital. Of course, there are many situations where pipeline inventory costs on transportation arcs are negligible because the product values and/or the number of days in transit are small. By contrast, pipeline inventory costs for products moving from one continent to another by ship can easily be large enough to warrant inclusion in a supply chain model.

Similar constructions can be used to model pipeline inventory costs associated with delays at distribution centers due, for example, to cross-docking or customs inspection. These costs may be added to product handling costs at the distribution centers. If, in addition, the distribution company is not paid for product delivered to a customer's site until the product is sold, the outbound pipeline inventory cost can include a holding charge based on the average time the product remains unsold.

Modeling Safety Stock Inventory. In this subsection, we discuss several modeling approaches for capturing safety stock and replenishment inventory decisions and

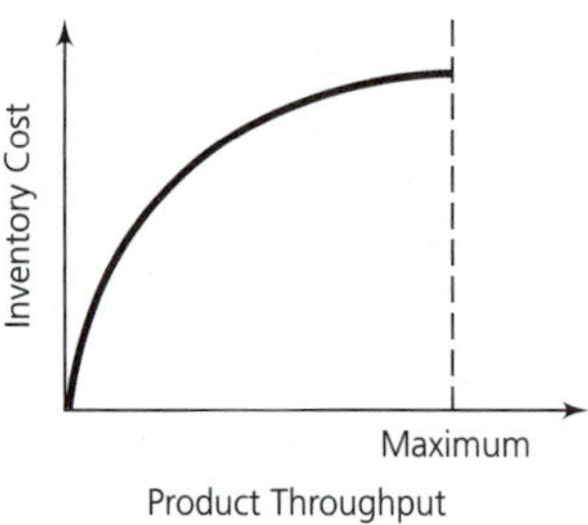

Figure 11.6
Inventory cost as a function of throughput

costs in strategic supply chain models. The common result of these approaches, and others suggested in the literature, is that inventory costs for a product at a facility can be represented by a function of the form shown in Figure 11.6. The key property of this function is that marginal inventory cost decreases as throughput of the product at the facility increases. In other words, there is an economy of scale associated with inventory costs of each product at each facility.

In the paragraphs that follow, we discuss constructions that can provide us with parameters specifying the inventory cost curves of Figures 11.5 and 11.6. Ultimately, they might be based purely on empirical statistical evidence.[7] One suggestion from the literature is that inventory of a product held at a facility, and therefore inventory cost, can be expressed as the exponential function KV^b, where V is the product throughput there.[8] The parameters K and b can be estimated from historical data; experience has shown that b is usually between 0.5 and 0.8, implying that the cost function has the form shown in Figure 11.6.

As we discussed in Chapter 3, cost curves such as the one in Figure 11.6 can be approximated by piecewise linear functions as depicted in Figure 11.7. The simpler approximation in Figure 11.7a would require only one 0-1 variable to capture the economy of scale. Of course, we might decide to approximate the curve using more than two linear segments, in which case we would require an additional 0-1 variable for each additional price break.

In addition to the economy of scale, the approximation in Figure 11.7b would incorporate a fixed cost for holding the product at the distribution center and a conditional minimum on throughput of the product at the distribution center. This construction would serve to tighten the approximation and also to impose a sensible

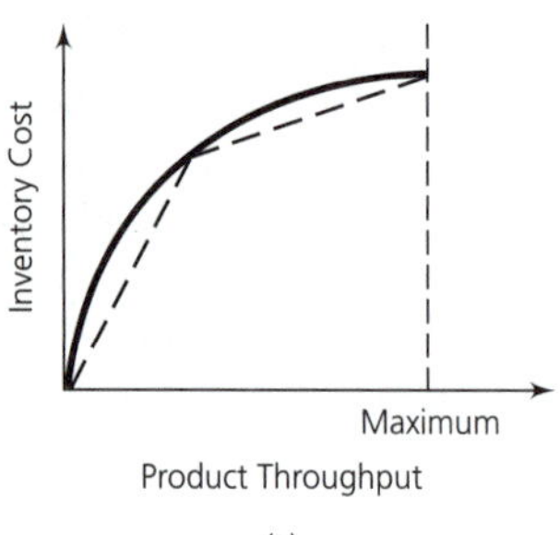

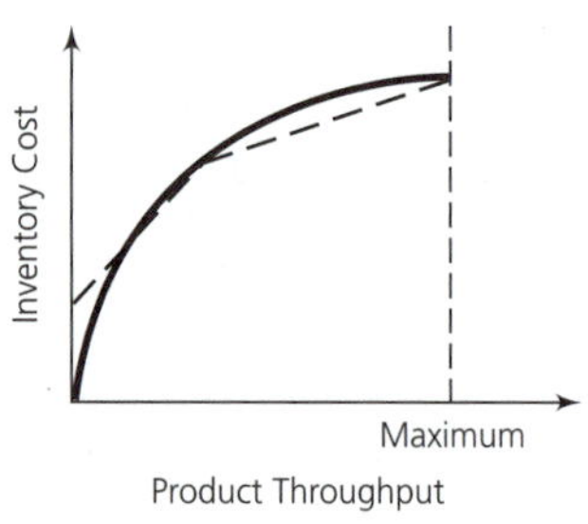

Figure 11.7
(a) Mixed integer programming approximation requiring one 0-1 variable;
(b) mixed integer programming approximation requiring two 0-1 variables

policy constraint on minimal volume that is needed to justify having the distribution center carry the product. The fixed cost could include other lumpy cost elements associated with handling the product at the distribution center such as special handling or storage requirements. It has the drawback that it requires two 0-1 variables. Thus, for a model considering 25 products each of which might be shipped through 10 distribution centers, 500 zero-one variables would be required to model inventory costs using Figure 11.7b, a large but not unmanageable number.

An alternative to the construction of Figure 11.7 is to treat safety stock costs as the only avoidable inventory costs. Modeling safety stocks in a snapshot supply chain optimization model is challenging. We illustrate the issues by considering a simple example involving a distribution center with three markets that might be assigned to it. For convenience, we assume the single period equals 1 year.

The safety stock for a single product k held at distribution center i would depend on the following parameters:

$E(D_{jk})$ = expected demand for product k per year at market j ($j = 1,2,3$)

σ^2_{jk} = variance of demand for product k per year at market j ($j = 1,2,3$)

We assume, at least for the moment, that the variability of lead time is small and does not enter into the analysis, although expected lead time itself does, as discussed above in Example 11.2. We also assume for convenience that each market will be sole-sourced from a single distribution center for each product.

If we let the decision variable

$$x_{ijk} = \begin{cases} 1 \text{ if market } j \text{ is served by DC } i \text{ for the product } k \\ 0 \text{ otherwise} \end{cases}$$

the safety stock for product k at DC i would be computed as a function of

Total expected yearly demand for product k shipped through DC $i = E(D_{1k})* x_{11k} + E(D_{2k}) * x_{12k} + E(D_{3k}) * x_{13k}$

and

Total variance of yearly demand for product k shipped through DC $i = \sigma^2_{1k} * x_{11k} + \sigma^2_{2k} * x_{12k} + \sigma^2_{3k} * x_{13k}$

Because the relationships developed in the previous section between these quantities and optimal safety stocks for product k at DC i are nonlinear, implicit functions of probability distributions and, moreover, because we would have similar relationships for every product and every distribution center, it would be a very difficult exercise in optimization modeling to explicitly model safety stock decisions and costs based on such equations.

We develop two approximation methods for circumventing this modeling dilemma. Figure 11.8 displays one approximation that has been suggested in the literature.[9] It may be implemented by computing the safety stock cost SS_{1k} that would

Figure 11.8
Safety stock cost relationship

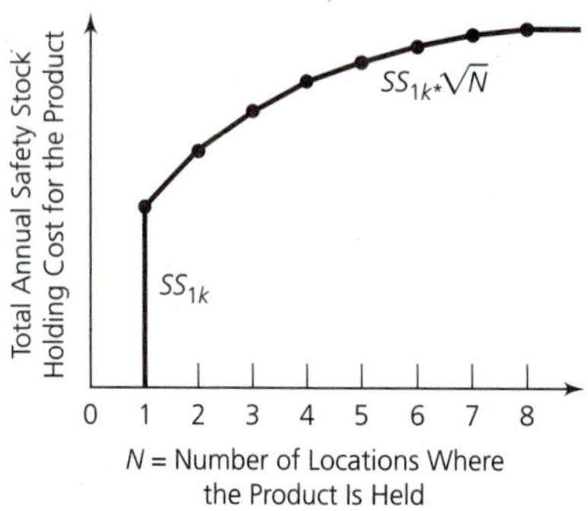

occur if one distribution center were to source all markets for the given product k and then projecting the cost to multiple DCs N using the multiplier $\sqrt{N}$. The approximation assumes that, as the optimization model assigns market demand for product k to various combinations of distribution centers, the statistical characteristics of uncertain demand handled by each is identical or at least very similar. This is a large assumption because some distribution centers will handle significantly larger demands than others.

A second approximation method is to model safety stock cost for each product k at each distribution center as a cost relationship with decreasing marginal cost, as shown in Figure 11.6. The assumption underlying this curve is that all markets for a given product experience a constant rate of demand variability as characterized by

σ^2 = variance per unit of expected yearly demand for product k

This implies that if market j has expected demand $E(D_j)$ for the product, the variance of demand is $\sigma^2 * E(D_j)$. For example, if we combined two markets with identical normal demand distributions $N(E(D), \sigma^2)$ and no correlation between demands, the variance of demand for product k in the combined markets would be 2 σ^2, which is consistent with our assumption. This construction suggests that product families be assembled with similar demand variance (as well as other) characteristics.

For the purposes of supply chain modeling, if we let

w_{ik} = outbound flow of product k from DC i

the variance of demand seen by distribution center i is $\sigma^2{}_k * w_{ik}$. Because the safety stock cost depends on the standard deviation $\sigma_k * \sqrt{w_{ik}}$, we obtain the curve shown in Figure 11.6.

Example 11.3

We consider a 1-year snapshot model for analyzing the supply chain strategy for a food products company for the coming year. The company's supply chain has four levels: suppliers of raw materials and packaging, manufacturing plants, distribution centers, and markets. The model helps management decide which plants will make each product and in what quantities, how these plants will source the DCs, and how the DCs will source the markets to maximize net revenues.

We illustrate the construction of a safety stock cost relationship for a given product *k* at a given DC *i*. For convenience, we assume the product is not perishable and has a shelf life of over 1 year. The unit of measurement for the product is 100 cases. The holding cost per year per unit of product *k* is $120. Demand in all markets is normally distributed with a variance of demand per unit for the product for 1 year of $\sigma^2{}_k = 3$. Thus, in a market with an expected demand of 5000 units, the variance of demand is 15,000, which implies that we can be 95% certain that demand for the year in that market will lie between 4760 and 5240 units.

Assuming the lead time for delivery is 3 days, we develop a safety stock cost relationship for product *k* at DC *i* based on a 99% order fulfillment rate. In particular, we compute the safety stock cost as a function of outflow at DC *i* for three levels of yearly outflow as follows:

Yearly Flow	Flow over Delivery Time	Variance over Delivery Time	Safety Stock (99% Order Fulfillment Rate)	Safety Stock Annual Cost ($)
10,000	82.2	246.6	36.54	4,385
50,000	311	1233	81.71	9,805
100,000	822	2466	115.56	13,867

To illustrate the calculations, consider the case when yearly flow of the product out of the DC is 10,000 units. On average, the flow over the 3-day delivery time = (10,000/365) * 3 = 82.2 units with a variance = 3 * 82.2 = 246.6, or standard deviation = 15.70. To ensure a 99% order fulfillment rate, the safety stock must equal 2.327 standard deviations of demand, or 36.54 units. The yearly cost of this safety stock is $4385.

We fit a curve of the type given in Figure 11.6 from the three points listed above to create the safety stock cost relationship for product *k* as a function of outflow of the product from DC *i*. The relationship may be approximated by one of the piecewise linear functions shown in Figure 11.7.

Modeling Replenishment Inventory. Modeling holding costs on replenishment inventory at a distribution center depends on the company's replenishment policies, which may be complex and based only partly on analysis with inventory models. Moreover, holding costs on replenishment inventory may be largely unavoidable, which suggests they could be omitted from an optimization model. Nevertheless, we discuss briefly modeling approaches for approximating holding costs on replenishment inventory. As we shall see, these approximations are similar in form to those developed for safety stock inventories.

We can expect that yearly holding costs on replenishment inventory to exhibit economies of scale because higher volumes of throughput would allow a greater number of turns per year, thereby reducing average inventory levels. Of course, some factors might serve to counterbalance these economies, such as greater delivery or demand uncertainty associated with higher volumes. Example 11.4 illustrates how we might develop the necessary cost relationship.

Example 11.4

We consider the same company, supply chain model, product, and DC as Example 11.3. Suppose management policy is to seek 5 turns per year for the product if the volume handled by the DC is 10,000 units and 10 turns per year if the volume is 50,000 units. This implies an average replenishment inventory of 1000 units with an annual cost of $120,000 in the former case and 2500 units with an annual cost of $300,000 in the latter case. The annual inventory cost per unit of product handled is $12 in the former case and $6 in the latter case. This illustrates the decreasing marginal cost associated with holding this product. One of the approximations in Figure 11.7 could be used to describe the replenishment inventory cost relationship.

Thus, our analysis of safety stock and replenishment costs at a DC resulted in cost relationships based on product outflow of an identical form. This suggests that the cost relationships could be combined to produce a single relationship, such as that shown in Figure 11.6, between the sum of total inventory cost (safety stock and replenishment cost) for each product and product outflow at the DC.

Finally, we emphasize again that the modeling artistry presented above is required to describe inventory holding costs in a single-period, snapshot model. The purpose of these constructions is to approximately capture inventory holding costs as they are linked to other strategic supply chain decisions and to identify broad plans for inventory deployment. The constructions are not intended to assist in inventory management strategies at tactical and operational levels of planning.

Incorporating Inventory Management Decisions in Tactical Supply Chain Models

We assume that a multiple-period model will be used to analyze tactical supply chain problems. Such a model is necessary to analyze supply chain decisions in a dynamic, or time-dependent, planning environment spanning several months. Typical deci-

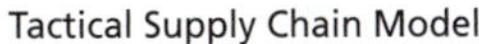

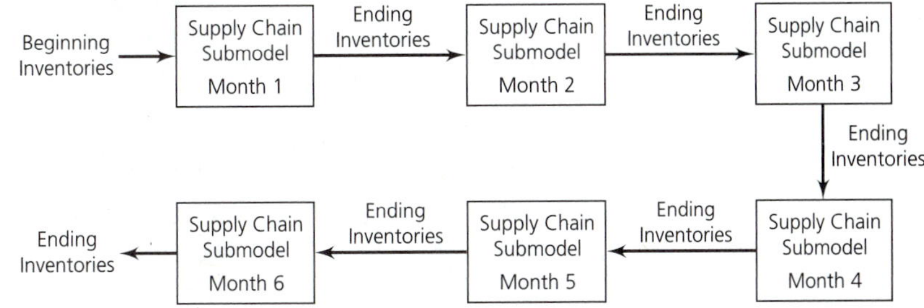

Figure 11.9 Multi-period tactical supply chain model

sions with a dynamic aspect include those involving raw material acquisitions where cost and availability vary by period and there are planned shutdowns for plant maintenance or seasonalities in demand.

As shown in Figure 11.9, at the end of each period in a multiple-period model, a holding cost per unit of product is charged on *ending* inventory at each distribution center. The holding cost reflects the company's cost of capital for the length of the period and possible other costs such as spoilage. A simple analysis shows that this calculation captures the average inventory holding cost, at least to a first approximation. For the purposes of discussion, we assume all periods are of even length. Let

$$Y_{kt} = \text{inventory of product } k \text{ at the end of period } t$$
$$= \text{inventory of product } k \text{ at the beginning of period } t+1$$

If h_k is the holding cost per unit per period,

$$h_k * (Y_{k1} + \cdots + Y_{kT}) = \text{total inventory holding cost over } T \text{ period planning horizon}$$

The final inventory Y_{kT} will typically be driven to zero unless the model is constrained or given an incentive to do otherwise. This is because the objective function of the model, whether it is minimizing cost or maximizing net revenue, does not account for benefits from inventories that will be realized after the multiple-period planning horizon has ended. Because most or all product lines will be continued after the horizon has ended, it is incorrect to let inventories fall to zero. There are two approaches to overcoming this difficulty. One is to impose targets on the Y_{kT} that must be met or exceeded by the supply chain optimal plan. The other is to reward the model for producing positive values of the product by crediting the objective function with revenue R_k for each unit of positive inventory at the end of the planning horizon. These two methods may be combined.

Further insight into this method of modeling inventories is achieved by rearranging the above inventory holding cost expression as follows:

$$h_k * (\tfrac{1}{2}Y_{k1} + \tfrac{1}{2}Y_{k0}) + h_k * (\tfrac{1}{2}Y_{k2} + \tfrac{1}{2}Y_{k1}) + \cdots + h_k * (\tfrac{1}{2}Y_{kT} + \tfrac{1}{2}Y_{k,T-1}) + h_k * (\tfrac{1}{2}Y_{kT} - \tfrac{1}{2}Y_{k0})$$

where Y_{k0} is starting inventory. Each of the terms in this expansion, except the final one, is of the form $h_k * (\frac{1}{2}Y_{kt} + \frac{1}{2}Y_{k,t-1})$. This represents a charge on inventory over period t based on the average of ending inventory and beginning inventory. The final term, $hk * (\frac{1}{2}Y_{kT} - \frac{1}{2}Y_{k0})$, will not introduce a significant error if we expect inventories at the end of the planning horizon determined by the model to approximately equal inventories at the beginning of the planning horizon.

Of course, inventories at the end of the planning horizon may be higher than inventories at the beginning of the planning horizon for some products, but lower for others. Without seasonal trends, we can expect, or hope, that the sum of the differences across products will introduce only a small error. On the other hand, if seasonal trends enter into the analysis, the unit cost per period h for inventory at the end of the planning horizon may be suitably adjusted; for example, if inventory of product z is constrained to be abnormally high at the end of the planning horizon, we could charge a unit cost h_{zT} for it that is larger than h_z for other periods to reflect the larger, expected length of time until the product is sold and revenue received.

Safety stock requirements on products may be reflected through lower bounds on the quantities Y_{kt}. They would be computed prior to construction of the supply chain optimization model and provided as input data. In making these calculations, we must keep in mind that each product is actually a product family, albeit one composed of products with similar characteristics. Thus, the lower bound representing safety stock refers to the weighed sum of safety stocks for the product in the family.

Two situations revealing the accuracy of the approximation to average inventory are shown in Figure 11.10. In Figure 11.10a, actual inventory varies evenly and moderately about the straight line connecting $Y_{k,t-1}$ and Y_{kt}, reflecting a constant increase in inventory over the period as implied by the approximation. In this case, the approximation is quite accurate. In Figure 11.10b, actual inventory lies uniformly and significantly below this straight line until the end of the period when, due to an inflow of product at the facility, there is a rapid rise in inventory. In this case, the approximation is inaccurate. If the situation of Figure 11.10b, and other similar inaccuracies, are common to many products and many periods, it indicates that the periods of the model are too long to describe inventory holding costs. The modeler should then consider subdividing the periods to better capture inventory movements.

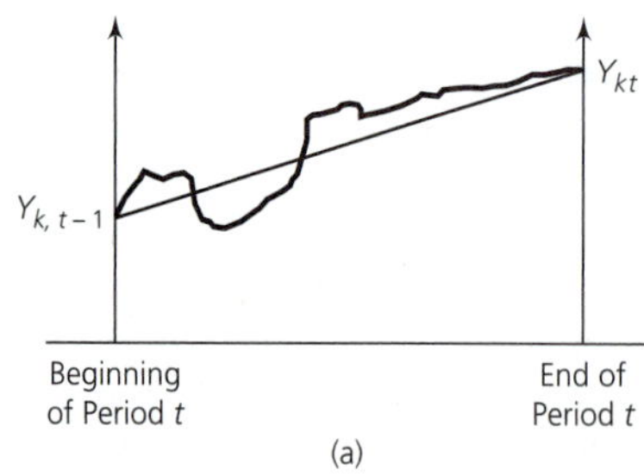

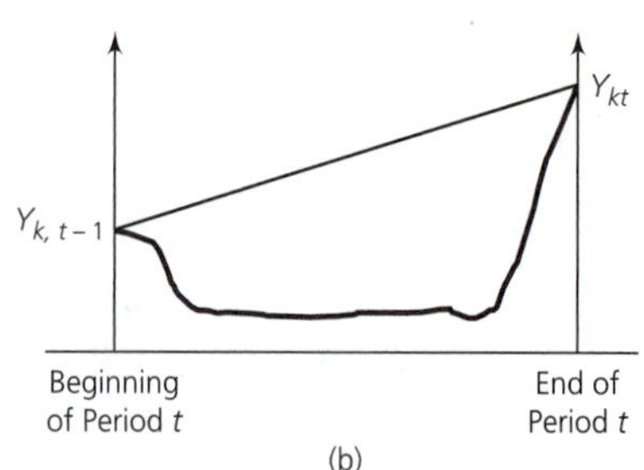

Figure 11.10 (a) Accurate approximation; (b) inaccurate approximation inventory patterns

Still, increasing the number of periods in a supply chain model comes at a price. The size of the model, and hence the computational effort required to optimize it, is directly proportional to the number of periods. A yearly planning model of four 3-month periods may be preferred to one of 12 1-month periods, even if inventory holding costs are less accurately captured. This is especially true if inventory holding costs are a small percentage of total supply chain costs.

The multiple-period supply chain model implied by Figure 11.9 is deterministic in the sense that demand forecasts for all products are assumed to be known without error. Uncertainties in these forecasts may be analyzed by optimizing multiple scenarios with varying market demands. An alternate modeling approach, which we presented in Section 3.5, and discussed again in Section 8.7, is to construct and optimize a stochastic programming model that explicitly considers multiple demand scenarios in a single optimization. Such a model provides an inventory plan that optimally hedges against multiple demand scenarios. The plan is superior in its expected benefits to any plan produced by a deterministic model.

The stochastic programming modeling paradigm for managing inventories and other supply chain decisions is at the frontier of practical modeling developments. It has already been applied in a small number of companies. If used judiciously, it can provide valuable insights that are not available from multiple scenario runs with deterministic models.

11.3 Inventory Management in Distribution Supply Chains

In this section, we discuss two successful applications of models to the optimization of supply chains plans in distribution networks where inventory decisions were explicitly modeled. The first case describes a modeling system used by a reverse logistics company to manage a pool of containers that it rents to its customers. The second case describes a modeling system used by a computer manufacturer to manage its multiechelon network of spare parts inventory. Our discussion permits us to examine further the interplay between optimization models for global supply chain analysis and inventory theory models.

Distribution Scheduling in a Reverse Logistics Company

Reverse logistics refers to supply chain networks where products distributed by a company to its customers are subsequently returned to the company.[10] The products may be reusable containers, equipment on short-term rental or long-term lease, warranty returns, or product upgrades, recalls, and trade-ins. Items received at a reverse

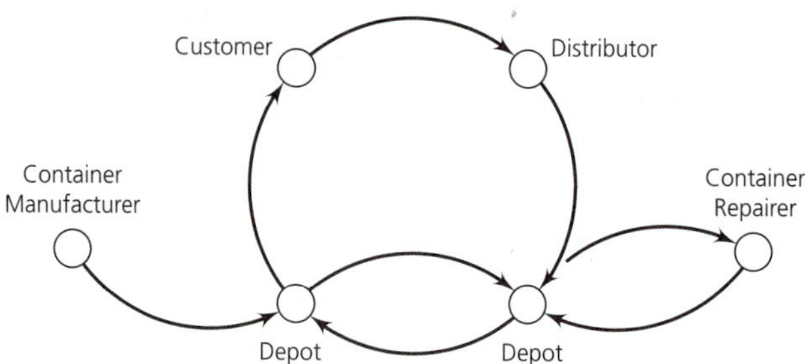

Figure 11.11
Container pool reverse logistics network

logistics facility are inspected and then differentiated as ready for reissue, repair, or discard. A reverse logistics supply chain may stand alone, such as that of a company that rents reusable containers or automobiles, or it may be linked to a standard supply chain, such as that of a consumer electronics company with a facility dedicated to warranty returns and repairs. For companies with stand-alone reverse supply chains, the pricing of products and services is nonstandard due to the complex relationship among capital costs, operational costs, and customer service.

Company Background. As shown in Figure 11.11, we consider the supply chain network of a reverse logistics company that maintains a pool of containers, which are rented to customers who are manufacturers of consumer products. The manufacturers use them to transport goods to distributors. After a certain length of time, the distributors return the containers to a company depot. Containers are periodically relocated among depots to balance inventories. In addition, damaged containers are either discarded or sent to repair facilities, which may be owned and operated by the company or by third-party companies. Finally, the company receives new containers from container manufacturers to replace discarded containers and to increase the pool as the business grows.

The company maintains more than 100 depots across the United States, which, for the most part, are located near the distributors. Inventory and transportation costs are avoidable operational costs, but they are in conflict. If each depot were able to maintain large inventories, each customer could be served by the nearest depot. Such a strategy would be very suboptimal because it would require an enormous capital investment in an enormous container pool. Thus, the company must incur higher transportation costs to accommodate a pool size that is tight but, in principle, optimal.

IT Systems. At an early stage of its business, the company decided to implement an operational scheduling system, called the order assignment system (OAS), that would generate and optimize a model assigning orders to depots to minimize short-term inventory and transportation costs across the entire national distribution system. A simple prototype developed in-house using a spreadsheet optimization package clearly demonstrated the potential value of such a system. The company

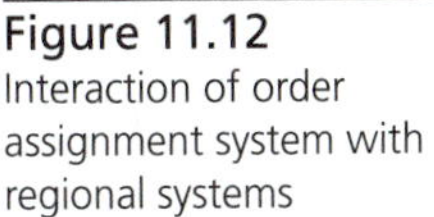

Figure 11.12
Interaction of order assignment system with regional systems

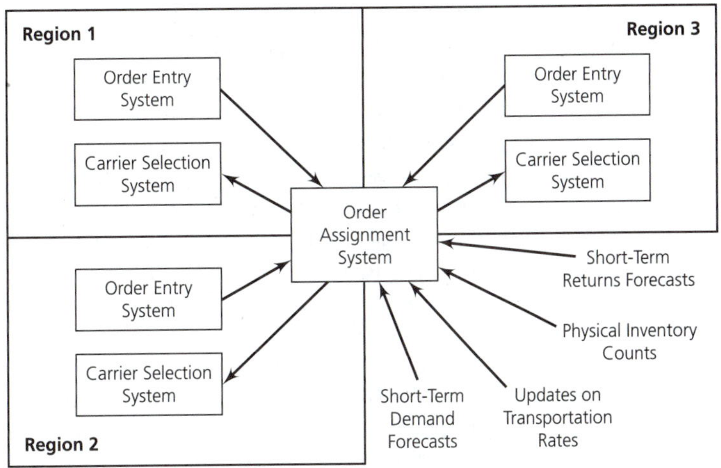

then hired consultants who were experts in building optimization modeling systems to expand the prototype model and implement an efficient modeling system based on it.

A high-level view of the system's interaction with other IT systems used by the company is given in Figure 11.12. As shown, the company maintains several regional offices around the United States, where orders for containers are placed in the order entry system. Each night, the regional offices send the latest updates on orders received to the OAS installed at corporate headquarters, which is physically located at one of the regional offices. These are orders for containers over the next 10 days, which become inputs to the order assignment optimization model. Because these orders alone do not constitute a complete picture of demand to be met over this period, the model also uses short-term demand forecasts. Other forecasting models are used to develop projected returns from the distributors and the repairers over the 10 days.

The OAS also receives periodic physical inventory counts from the depots, which are used to correct the inventory figures derived by the model from earlier physical counts. Finally, it receives periodic updates on transportation rates along the lanes used for distributing the containers. The expectation is that transportation costs used by the optimization model in OAS are close to the actual rates resulting from commitments determined by the carrier selection system.

The OAS is used on a rolling horizon basis every morning. In this mode, most of the order assignments for days 1 and 2, which were previously optimized, are treated as fixed and given, although a small number may be selected for reassignment due to unexpected changes in the order or the status of inventories. The remaining orders for days 3 through 10 are free to be assigned, with particular attention paid to orders for days 3, 4, and 5. The model is less precise about assignments for days 6 through 10, allowing some ambiguity about their depot assignment. These days are modeled primarily to add stability to the inventory decisions for days

1 through 5; for example, a depot where inventories are declining over the 10-day horizon will be used somewhat sparingly by the model over the first 5 days to avoid out-of-stock situations leading to high transportation costs.

Based on the optimal plan determined by the OAS, order assignments to depots are sent to the regional offices in the early morning. Analysts there use the carrier selection system to choose carriers for specific truckload deliveries of containers from depots to customers. This system contains information about carrier costs and availability, plus any contractual arrangements that the company may be obliged to honor. Because most orders are for one or more truckloads of containers, vehicle routing complications of less-than-truckload deliveries do not enter into the analysis.

Optimization Models. The OAS uses a multiple-period linear programming model to optimize the 10-day schedule. In this model, 0-1 decision variables assign orders to depots, but they are treated as continuous (i.e., they can take on any values between 0 and 1). Given the mathematical structure of the model, most of these variables fortuitously take on values of 0 or 1 in an optimal linear programming solution. Using a heuristic tailored to the model, the fractional values of the relatively few variables that are not at such values are rounded up to 1 or down to 0. Typically, the cost of the resulting solution is very close to the cost of the original linear programming solution, which indicates that the heuristic finds a solution that is very close to being optimal in the underlying mixed integer programming model that more accurately describes the real problem to be solved.

The structure of a single-period submodel is shown if Figure 11.13. The circular flows of the reverse logistics network of Figure 11.11 are interrupted by eliminating the flows from manufacturer to distributor and from distributor to depot. Instead, returns of containers are captured by the forecasted returns to the depots. In addition, receipts from container repairers and manufacturers for the 10-day period are treated as inflows to the depots. In creating the multiple-period model, the daily submodel of Figure 11.13 is replicated 10 times, once for each day, with inventory and transportation links connecting them.

Figure 11.14 shows typical interperiod links corresponding to inventory transfers and transportation movements requiring 2 or more days travel. The inventory flows are subject to upper-bound (physical capacity) and lower-bound (safety stock) constraints. The safety stocks were computed outside the model and reflect, for each depot, uncertainties in forecasted returns and in discrepancies between physical and computed inventories. Their purpose was to ensure with a high probability that each depot could meet its order assignments over the coming 5 days of com-

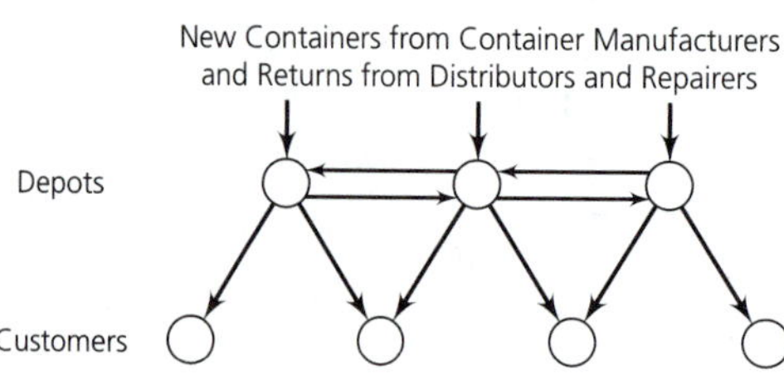

Figure 11.13
Container pool single-period network

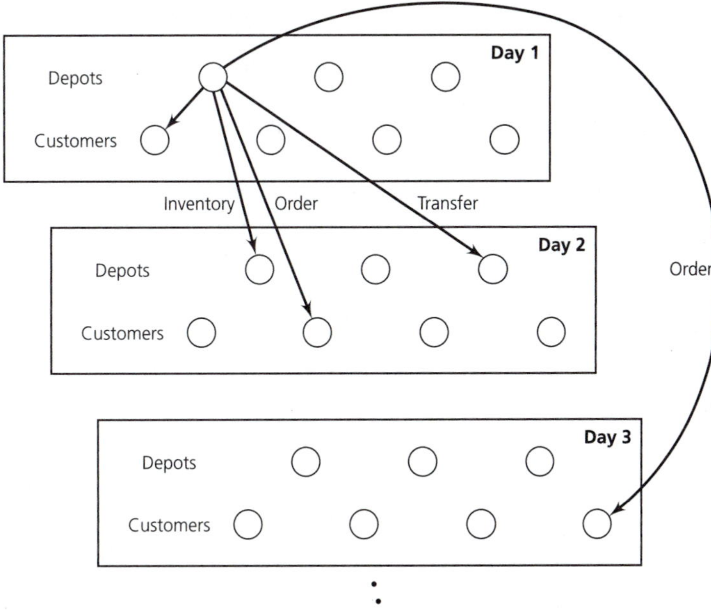

Figure 11.14
Container pool multiple-period network

pany operations. As shown, orders may be delivered the day they leave the depot or 1 or 2 days later.

Results and Conclusions. The OAS has been in use for over 5 years, during which time it has evolved through several versions. A typical run requires 20 minutes on a high-end Pentium PC. This time has remained fairly constant over the years because increases in microprocessor speeds have more than compensated for growth in the company's business and resulting size of the optimization model. Approximately 80 to 90% of the order assignments fed back to the regional offices are implemented without modification. The remainder require human intervention due to difficulties in carrier availability, changes in the timing of order delivery, or some other factor. Comparisons of early results from the model with historical order assignments not based on model results indicated a savings in avoidable operating costs of more than 10%.

Recently, the company implemented, again with the help of consultants, a strategic planning tool for evaluating depot location decisions. Thus, modeling system developments in this company followed the bottom-up route, beginning with implementation of an operational tool and then, much later, a strategic planning tool. The operational tool has also been recently extended to optimize the management of container pools in other industries, including some where less-than-truckload deliveries are needed. For these new applications, the OAS is being linked to a vehicle routing system. With this two-stage analysis, the OAS assigns orders to depots based on inventory and aggregate transportation costs; the vehicle routing system then determines optimal routes from each depot for delivering customer orders assigned to that depot.

Multiechelon Spare Parts Distribution System at IBM

Multiechelon distribution systems are needed to manage inventories for companies and organizations that have many parts or products. For retailing companies with products numbering in the tens of thousands, it is much too costly to store all products in all locations where demand for them might occur. Thus, a retailing company might store all slow-moving products in a large, central distribution center and selected slow-moving products in smaller quantities in smaller distribution centers that are close to major markets. Inventory strategies for ordering and storing these retail products will depend on their classification within an ABC scheme, seasonal factors, or promotional effects.

Multiechelon networks also play a critical role in supporting the maintenance of expensive and complex equipment such as mainframe computers or aircraft. Because the stockout of a small and relatively inexpensive part can force an expensive system out of service, inventories carried in a spare parts network may be stored at three or four levels, with occasional emergency shipments from distant stocking points, to ensure the required customer service.

We report here on the successful implementation of a service parts inventory management system, called Optimizer, at IBM.[11] Although this system was developed over 10 years ago, it is still being used to support the servicing of IBM's installed base of computers and other equipment throughout the United States. The concepts underlying Optimizer, and its execution, provide us with a successful, and rare, example of a modeling system capable of fully analyzing a complex multiechelon inventory network.

Managing Service Logistics at IBM. When the implementation project began, IBM's after-sales service business in the United States was handled by its National Service Division (NSD). The NSDs goals were to provide high-quality, after-market support to IBM's customers and to make a competitive profit. They served commercial and government customers and IBM internal accounts. Third-party service companies competed with IBM for these markets.

The NSD employed over 10,000 customer engineers (CEs), who were trained to repair and maintain every type of installed system. This large working force was necessary to provide rapid response to equipment failures. When a failure occured, a CE was dispatched to the failure site, where she would most likely require parts for replacement, diagnostics, or tools. These parts may have been dispatched to the site before or after the CE arrived, or they may have been available from inventory kept at the site. The CE also carried a limited number of parts in her car trunk or tool chest.

A distribution organization within NSD was responsible for procuring, storing, and dispatching parts. In addition to supporting the CEs, direct sales were made to dealers, third-party maintainers, and self-servicers. The distribution organization had two main functions, distribution operations, which was concerned with transportation and warehousing, and inventory planning, which was concerned with procuring and maintaining inventory across the multiechelon spare parts network. In 1990, inventory planning controlled 200,000 part numbers required to support 1000 IBM products.

The multiechelon spare parts network had four echelons. Prior to implementation of the Optimizer system, the locations in this network were as follows:

- Two automated national warehouses
- Twenty-four field distribution centers (FDCs)
- Sixty-four parts stations (PSs)
- Fifteen thousand outside locations (OLs)

The two central warehouses received parts from IBM plants and vendors and distributed them to the other locations. They also replenished the 24 FDCs and provided emergency deliveries to meet demand that the FDCs could not meet. Finally, they shipped domestically manufactured parts to non-U.S. IBM facilities and to tens of thousands of authorized dealers and external customers.

The FDCs were located in major metropolitan areas, where they provided emergency support to their assigned regions and replenished PSs and OLs assigned to them. The PSs were located in service branch offices. They were responsible only for filling emergency orders that resulted from parts and system failures. The OLs were unstaffed stocking locations and included on-site customer stocking points, CE car trunks or tool chests, and shared inventory at local branches.

Prior to development of the Optimizer system, inventory planning and control across the multiechelon network was performed by simple models embedded in IBM's parts inventory management system. These models did not take into account synergies among levels in the network. Instead, excessive inventories were stored at all levels to achieve acceptable customer service.

Optimization Model. The optimization models employed in Optimizer were extensions of the (s, S) inventory model discussed in Section 11.1; that is, whenever inventory falls to s units or less, order up to S. Such a model, called the **service allocation model,** was developed for each location at each level of the network. The model's objective was to minimize the expected cost of stocking parts assigned to the location, subject to service constraints on parts availability at that location. These were constraints on the fraction of a part's demand that was filled immediately from on-hand stock at that location. For each part, the constraint's tightness varied according to its the priority class and its criticality to overall system reliability.

The cost and service functions in the service allocation model, which depended on product demands at the location, were described as approximating functions of the means and variances of these demands and replenishment lead times. A heuristic solution method was then developed for optimizing it. Simulations showed that the heuristic methods gave reasonably accurate solutions.

The solution method for the service allocation problem was then embedded in an iterative method for optimizing inventories throughout the multiechelon network. This optimization is complicated because there were the three following types of demand for a part at a location:

1. Requirements generated by part failures in customer machines directly supported by this location

2. Emergency requirements passed from locations at lower echelons in the network
3. Replenishment requirements to restock locations at lower echelons in the network

An overview of the iterative method is depicted in Figure 11.15. The method begins at the lowest level of the network, or $E = 1$. At each step in the iterative method, a service allocation problem at echelon level E and location L is (approximately) optimized. Prior to the optimization, the demand for each part seen by location L from various customers and locations is aggregated into total demand. Subsequent to the optimization, the pass-up demand that location L creates for locations higher in the echelon is computed.

Modeling System Implementation. Once research on the inventory models had been completed and validated, a multifunctional project group was formed to design, test, and install an inventory management system (Optimizer) based on them. Because the development took place during the mid-1980s, the platform for implementation was an IBM mainframe. The project group was made up of the following teams:

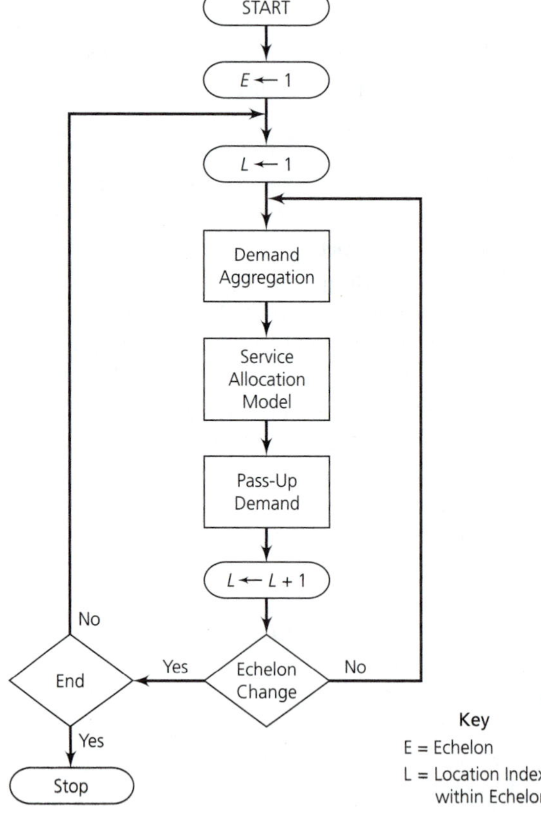

Figure 11.15 Multiechelon inventory optimization scheme. *Source:* Cohen et al. [1990, 73]

- **The user team.** Members drawn from functional areas that would be affected by the introduction of Optimizer. They attended system-design sessions, reviewed acceptance tests, and helped write design specifications.
- **The information systems team.** Programmers to develop data acquisition and reporting routines and user interfaces.
- **The model development team.** Computer scientists, operations researchers, and programmers responsible for overall system architecture and the implementation of efficient scientific programs for optimizing the multiechelon inventory models.

The work plan was organized into three overlapping phases: Preimplementation test, field implementation test, and national implementation. The prototype system developed during the preimplementation test had minimal user interfaces. Its purpose was mainly to test the validity of the models in analyzing actual inventory problems. Initially, the models required significant modification to more accurately handle critical parts and to smooth out stock replenishment plans.

The field implementation test was an extensive exercise with a limited number of users from the field. In addition, the project team implemented a measurement system for monitoring the results of the field test and comparing them with inventory performance under the previous system. The main purpose of the field test was to shake out bugs and infelicities in the system. Given the effort made in the first two phases, the national implementation, which was a full roll-out of the system, went smoothly. The system was, and still is, run on a weekly basis to update replenishment plans.

The final Optimizer system was a PL/1 application consisting of the following four major modules:

- A forecasting module to estimate the failure rates of parts, which were combined with information on the installed machine base to estimate the means and variances of the part failure probability distributions
- A data acquisition module to process over 15 gigabytes of data as inputs
- A modeling system module to optimize the multiechelon problem
- An interface module for viewing and communicating output from the modeling system

The system went on-line in 1988 and is still in operation more than 10 years later.

Results and Conclusions. After national implementation was completed, the measurement system installed during the field implementation was used to quantify benefits from the use of Optimizer. The bottom line was very impressive. The time-average value of inventory recommended by the stock policies of Optimizer was 20 to 25 percent below those determined by the existing system, a difference in excess of a half a billion dollars in inventory investment. Given this result, NSD management decided to devote part of the inventory savings to improve service and reduce operating costs. Still, Optimizer conservatively determined annual inventory investment savings of a quarter of a billion dollars.

Shortly after the introduction of Optimizer, NSD implemented supply chain network changes to decrease the number of field distribution centers, increase the number of parts stations, and increase the fill rates at parts stations and outside locations. These changes, along with tighter inventory management due to Optimizer, yielded a 10 percent improvement in parts availability at the lower echelons, while maintaining parts availability levels at higher echelons, and a reduction in operating costs of $20 million per year. The system has also been used as a what-if tool to evaluate proposed changes in service strategies and in the network configuration.

11.4 Inventory Management in Manufacturing Supply Chains

In this section, we discuss two applications in which models and modeling systems were used successfully to study manufacturing supply chains from an inventory management perspective. Both models employ inventory theory to approximately optimize inventory deployment decisions across a multiechelon supply chain. Such supply chains are more complicated than the multiechelon spare parts distribution network examined in the previous section because they involve manufacturing transformations and lead times that add uncertainty to the planning process. Moreover, manufacturing capacity constraints may restrict the creation of buffer safety stocks between manufacturing stages.

Optimizing Inventory across Hewlett Packard's Printer Supply Chains

In the late 1980s, Hewlett Packard (HP) created a corporate group to help managers integrate their supply chain activities, with an emphasis on managing inventories of parts, components, and finished products. In this subsection, we discuss a model developed by this group in the early 1990s to study inventory management strategies for the family of DeskJet printers, which were sold in markets around the world.[12] Although the optimization model addressed strategic and tactical supply chain issues, it was quite unlike the models discussed in Section 11.2 in that it focused exclusively on analyzing the complex relationships among multiechelon inventories.

An overview of a typical supply chain network for the DeskJet printer product line is given in Figure 11.16, in which we have explicitly shown key inventory stockpile locations as well as facilities. The manufacture of critical components, as well as assembly and testing of the DeskJet printers, occurred at different facilities in the Vancouver area. Supply chain coordination in Vancouver was complicated because several HP divisions were involved in these manufacturing activities. One division manufactured application-specific integrated circuits (ASICs) that were provided as

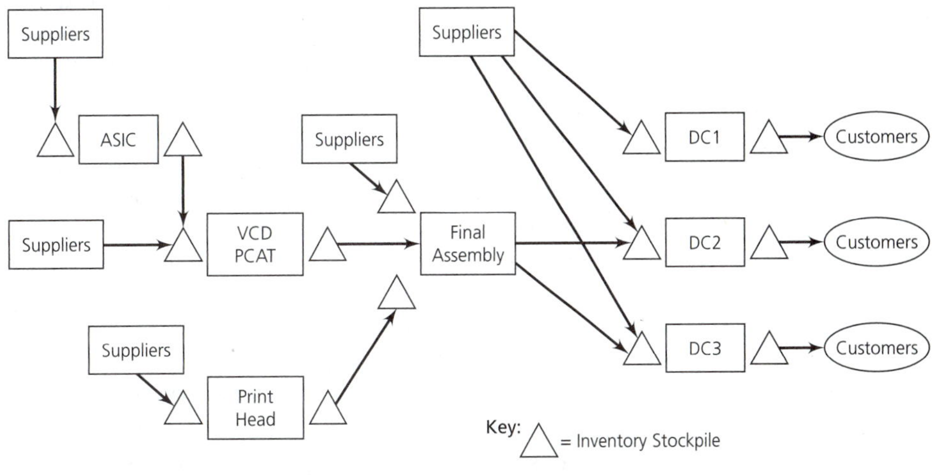

Figure 11.16
DeskJet printer supply chain network. *Source:* Lee and Billington [1993, 838]

inputs to printed circuit board assembly and testing (PCAT) in Vancouver. This stage involved the assembly and testing of other electronic components in addition to the ASICs. Completed circuit boards were passed to final assembly and testing, also in Vancouver, where they were combined with other components such as motors, printheads, and cases to produce finished products, which were then tested. This final assembly stage involved customizing the printers for different countries by incorporating appropriate power supply modules and packaging them with instructions in the local languages.

The worldwide market for printers was, and still is, highly competitive. HP's customers, who are dealers in computer peripherals, wish to carry low inventories and, at the same time, provide superior service to the end-use consumers who are their customers. As a result, HP maintained high safety stocks of the DeskJet printers at the DCs, which were reflected in high safety stock requirements for up-stream components at the factories. The need for safety stocks was pronounced due to serious uncertainties in demand, manufacturing processes, and the supply of parts from HP's suppliers. Finally, the market for printers was dynamic, with new HP and competing products, either entirely new platforms or upgrades of existing products, appearing quite frequently.

Model Requirements. Given this background, supply chain managers at HP commissioned a modeling system development project to address the following needs:

1. **Inventory and service benchmarking, planning, and control.** The managers sought an analytical tool that would rigorously determine the relationship between inventories at various levels in the supply chain and customer service,

measured in order fulfillment rate, that would be provided. This would assist them in determining appropriate investments in inventories. It would also support negotiations between manufacturing and marketing on desirable levels of customer service.

2. **What-if analyses.** Given the dynamic nature of their supply chain operations, the managers sought a tool that would allow them to explore alternate responses to changing conditions before implementing a strategy. Examples included the following:
   a. Changes in market demand due to competitive factors, product life cycle, or new product entrants
   b. Supply chain changes such as introduction of a new DC or the shutting down of an existing one
   c. Changes in production capacity due to new technologies or learning effects
3. **Evaluation of supply chain design for new products.** The managers sought a tool to evaluate the impact on inventory investment and service performance of alternate supply chain designs for new products.

Overview of the Model. The supply chain model developed for this application uses a periodic review, or (R, S) submodel, for managing inventories of each SKU at each of the stocking locations in Figure 11.16. That is, the stock level of each SKU at each location is reviewed every R periods, and stock is ordered to bring the stock up to S units when the shipment arrives. The value of these up-to stock levels is driven by target values for order fulfillment rates on finished products, which have implications to order fulfillment rates at all upstream levels of the supply chain.

In particular, the model is based on computations that combine parameters describing the supply replenishment lead times for parts needed at each stocking point with the demand felt at that point. The replenishment lead time depends on upstream expected production rates and capacities and their variances, plus the probabilities of occurrences of downtimes. The demand felt at each stocking point is computed via a mathematical representation of the demand transmission process. This representation is similar to the one employed in the modeling approach discussed above for IBM's spare-parts inventory system. Advanced constructions of mathematical inventory theory are used to compute the up-to stock levels and the implied safety stock for each inventory site in the supply chain model.

Illustrative Results and Conclusions. The model was used to analyze a number of supply chain planning problems of the types discussed above. For example, it was used to study supply chain strategies for the introduction of a new printer. The original plan for this product was for Vancouver to make the printing engine and ship it to a partner company in Japan, which would integrate it into the final product and ship it to three DCs located in Japan, the United States, and Europe. The partner company would also use the engines to manufacture a final product to be sold under its own brand name.

As computed by the inventory theory model, Figure 11.17 displays the composition of inventory costs to sustain a 98% order fulfillment rate computed by the model. It clearly indicates that the biggest opportunity for reducing inventory costs lies with reducing finished goods inventories at the DCs. Table 11.1 contains results summarizing the following alternative scenarios for designing the new supply chain:

1. **Engine buffer.** Use larger inventories of engines at Vancouver to buffer against demand uncertainties at the three DCs.
2. **Air engine.** Shorten lead time by shipping engines from Vancouver to Japan by air.
3. **Engine at Singapore.** Use HP's Singapore plant to manufacture the engines, thereby reducing expected travel time and its variance.
4. **Colocation.** Convince the Japanese partner to produce the finished product at its plant in Singapore.

Clearly, a supply chain design based on scenario 4 was the most cost effective. It not only significantly reduced inventory carrying costs but also reduced freight costs. The results of the model provided a rational basis for HP to negotiate with its

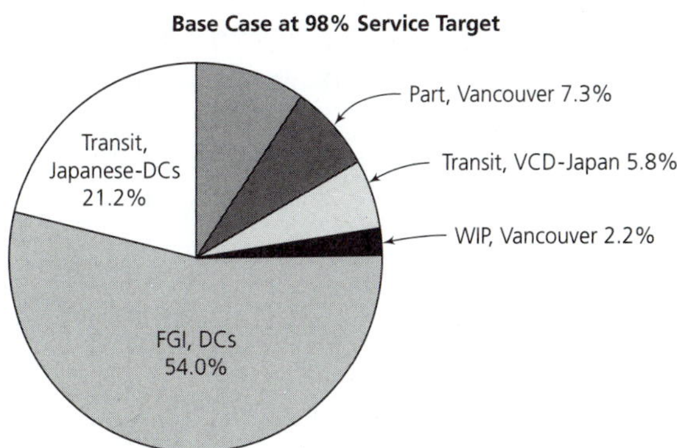

Figure 11.17
Relative inventory costs for new printer base case at 98% service target. *Source:* Lee and Billington [1993, 843]

Table 11.1 Comparing the opportunities for new printer (at 98% service goal)

Item	Base Case	Engine Buffer	Air Engine	Engine at Singapore	Co-location
Inventory (weeks supply)[a]	17.6	20.26	13.7	15.0	10.1
Inventory ($)[b]	22.0M	21.6M	19.6M	20.4M	15.0M
Inventory reduction		0.4M	2.6M	1.6M	7.0M
Savings/yr.		100K	600K	396K	1680K
Freight savings/yr. ($)		0K	−382K	120K	200K
Potential savings/yr. ($)		100K	218K	516K	1880K

Source: Lee and Killington [1993, 843]

[a] FGI, engine + pipeline.

[b] Based on 24% annually.

Japanese partner to implement the strategy suggested by scenario 4. The results of the modeling exercise also illustrate the synergy between analysis and intuition because the design corresponding to scenario 4 only emerged after considerable managerial thinking about ways to reduce total supply chain cost.

Optimal Safety Stock Placement in Kodak's Manufacturing Supply Chains

In this subsection, we report on a model for managing inventories across manufacturing supply chains where the supply chains and their planning problems are very similar to those just discussed but for which the modeling approach is quite different.[13] The model and the modeling system were originally developed for the Eastman Kodak Company where it has been used to analyze 11 products in the company's equipment division. Details are provided about its application to the internal supply chain of a digital camera.

As depicted in Figure 11.18, the key subassemblies for the digital camera are a traditional 35-mm camera, an imager, and a circuit-board assembly. In creating this figure, we distinguish between **finished products** of the entire manufacturing supply chain, which are sent to the distribution centers, and **finished goods,** which are intermediate products that are outputs from intermediate stages of production. Each rectangle represents a manufacturing stage and a triangle indicates that safety stock is

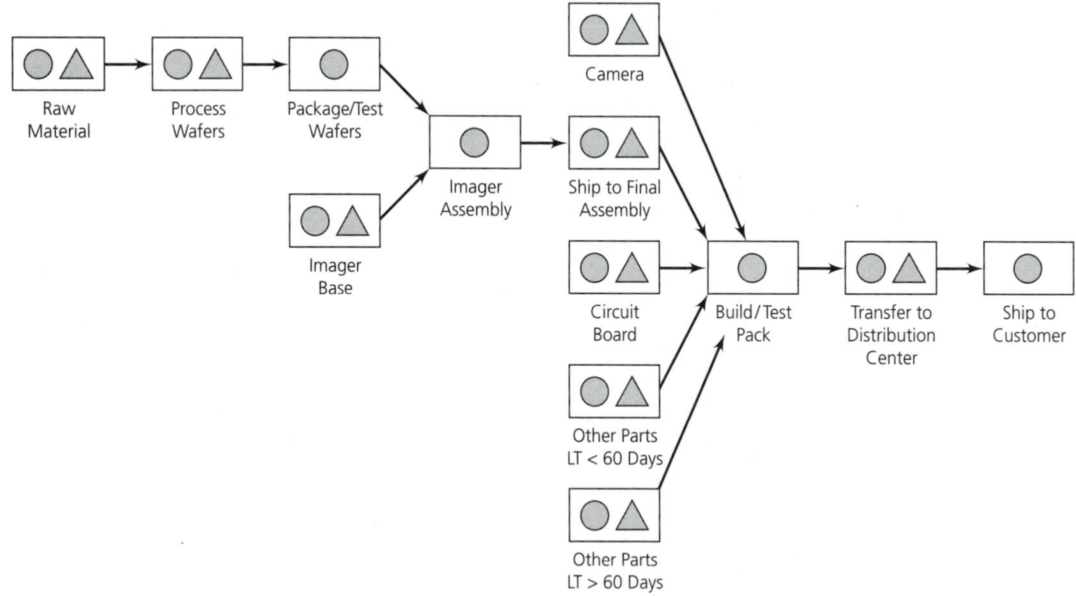

Figure 11.18
Digital camera supply chain. *Source:* Graves and Willems [2000]

held for that stage's finished goods. Each manufacturing stage is viewed as a "customer" for the finished goods produced by its immediate upstream stages.

Kodak procures the 35-mm camera from an outside vendor, and the imager and the circuit board are manufactured internally. The imager captures and digitizes the picture and sends an electronic description of it to the circuit-board assembly, which processes and stores it. The figure also depicts other parts used in the camera. To control the size of the model, approximately 100 parts were aggregated into two classes: those with short procurement lead time (less than 60 days) and those with long procurement lead time (greater than 60 days).

The digital camera is manufactured by removing the back of the 35 mm camera and replacing it with a housing that contains the imager and the circuit board. After these operations have been completed, the product is tested, packaged, and shipped to the distribution center. Final customers, who are high-end photography shops and computer superstores, receive shipments from the distribution centers.

As we have shown it, the model incorporates aggregations of certain operations. For example, the imager and circuit-board stages each contain several substages that are not explicitly modeled. Similarly, the build, test, packaging stage consists of several substages. The model was subsequently expanded to capture more details about these stages.

Overview of the Model and Modeling System. The optimization model developed for this application focuses on determining the optimal placement and sizes of safety stocks in manufacturing supply chains such as those displayed in Figure 11.18. As in the HP DeskJet printer case just discussed, it is assumed that each stage in the supply chain operates with a periodic-review, base-stock policy with a common review period. The model transforms the safety stock problem from a probabilistic one, ensuring that demand will met with a high probability of occurrence, to a deterministic one, ensuring that demand will be met with certainty. In other words, the deterministic model guarantees a 100% order fulfillment rate for all customers in the supply chain. This is accomplished by convincing managers across the supply chain to establish and accept upper bounds on demand such that, if they were exceeded, they would resort to nonstandard tactics for dealing with it. Examples are by negotiating with a customer to delay shipment of a large order, by extending manufacturing in some departments to overtime shifts, and by subcontracting. In the basic form of the model, demands for finished products, and therefore demands for the finished goods of each stage, remain constant over the planning horizon. The model has been extended to incorporate some classes of nonconstant demand.

In summary, the optimization model seeks to determine a safety stock strategy that guarantees a 100% order fulfillment rate at all stages while minimizing the total cost of holding these safety stocks. The explicit decision variables in the model are the guaranteed service times for each stage of the supply chain. The assumption of constant demand over the planning horizon allows the derivation of an analytical form of the safety stock required at each stage as a function of these decision variables. The constraints of the model impose the condition that the net replenishment time for each stage is nonnegative, which ensures integrity of the supply chain's replenishment process and ensures that the service times satisfy their guarantees.

The resulting model is a complex combinatorial optimization problem. An efficient dynamic programming algorithm was developed for models defined over a large, but limited, class of supply chain networks. An analytical engine based on it was implemented and embedded in a modeling system. The model can also be expressed as a mixed integer programming model, although this formulation has not yet been tested. These optimization models and methods were discussed in Chapter 4.

The modeling system has a graphical user interface for easy manipulation of input data. It produces supply chain displays similar to Figure 11.18. The displays change as the user explores the placement and sizing of safety stocks across the chain.[14]

Implementation and Results. As we observed in the Hewlett Packard application, and would see in most manufacturing firms, coordinated management of inventories across Kodak's supply chain required managers in functionally separate departments to cooperate in unaccustomed ways. For example, the circuit-board assembly and imager assembly departments acted as arm's-length suppliers to the assembly group that performed final assembly and testing. Distribution, which is a separate organization, took ownership of the product once it left the final assembly area.

To promote enhanced coordination among these groups, Kodak created a digital camera product flow team made up of members of the various departments and representatives from marketing. The team elected to implement and apply the model in the following three phases:

1. Optimize only those safety stocks under the direct control of the final assembly area
2. Incorporate a key supplier into the model
3. Expand the model to the entire supply chain

The decision to begin by optimizing inventories in the final assembly area was based on the high cost of the materials used in the product. The relative, but disguised, costs are given in Table 11.2, along with their production lead times.

In setting up the optimization model, the group agreed that the supply chain system should keep safety stocks guaranteeing 100% order fulfillment up to a demand for finished product that was 1.645σ above the mean, which corresponds to a demand level that was slightly more than twice its the expected value. This characterization excluded very large one-time orders for which there was advanced warning. Such orders were handled by a separate anticipatory policy. Marketing required that the maximal service time from a distribution center to a customer was 5 days. The final assembly group imposed the condition that the service time for the imager had to be zero; this caused the total safety stock cost to increase by 8.7%.

The optimal solution to the model for the phase 1 supply chain problem determined that the subassembly stages, aggregate parts stages, and the build/test/package stages in Figure 11.18 should hold safety stocks and quote zero service times. Further,

Table 11.2 Digital camera lead times and cost

Item	Production Lead Time	Cost Added
Camera	60	750
Imager	60	950
Circuit Board	40	650
Other Parts LT <60 days	60	150
Other Parts LT >60 days	150	200
Build/Test/Pack	6	250
Transfer to DC	2	50
Ship to Customer	3	0

Source: Graves and Willems [2000]

the model determined that the ship-to distribution and ship-to customer stages should quote maximal service times of 2 and 5 days, respectively. In summary, the optimal strategy was to hold inventories of components, subassemblies, and completed cameras at the manufacturing site and to hold no inventory in the distribution center, which would act as a flow-through facility that ships cameras immediately upon receipt.

The product team elected to explore suboptimal solutions constrained by organizational considerations to see if they were near the true optimum in cost. One case it explored allowed safety stocks at the distribution center as well as the manufacturing site with zero service time guarantees. The model showed that such a policy would increase safety stock costs in excess of 12%. A second case allowed safety stock at the distribution center, but not at the manufacturing site. The model determined a safety stock strategy subject to this constraint that was only 2% more costly than the optimal solution. This policy was the one implemented because it satisfied distribution's desire to hold inventory.

The success of the modeling system during phase 1 led to its application in phases 2 and 3, and to other products and product families. Inventory costs and delivery performance improved significantly as a result of using the modeling tool as shown in Table 11.3, which provides a summary of the performance of two assembly sites where the modeling system has been applied. The sales volume has remained relatively constant over the 3 years. Note that the sites changed their operating system from make to schedule to replenish to order during 1996. The modeling system was used to guide them in this transition. The significant inventory cost savings and improvement in delivery performance, due in large part to the modeling system, are a testimonial to the benefits that models can provide.

The modeling system has also been used by project teams at Kodak for related purposes, including the following:

- Identification of key vendors for whom reductions in lead times would have the greatest benefit
- Evaluation of the cost effectiveness of reductions in manufacturing lead time

Table 11.3 Inventory model results

Site	Y/E 95	Y/E 96	Y/E 97
Assembly Site A			
Worldwide FGI	\$6.7M	\$3.3M	\$3.6M
Raw material & WIP	\$5.7M	\$5.6M	\$2.9M
Delivery performance	80%	94%	97%
Manufacturing operation	MTS	RTO	RTO
Assembly Site B			
Worldwide FGI	\$4.0M	\$4.0M	\$3.2M
Raw material & WIP	\$4.5M	\$1.6M	\$2.5M
Delivery performance	Unavailable	78%	94%
Manufacturing operation	MTS	RTO	RTO

Source: Graves and Willems [2000]

MTS = make to schedule.
RTO = replenish to order.

- Comparison of investments in manufacturing lead-time reductions versus cost savings from reductions in pipeline and safety stock costs
- Quantification of the cost of service time guarantees to final customers

Finally, the modeling system has provided a standard terminology and set of assumptions for cross-functional product teams at Kodak to use in coordinating their integrated supply chain efforts.

11.5 Final Thoughts

In Section 11.1, we reviewed probabilistic models for managing inventory. The central problem attacked by these models is: For a given item, determine the quantity of safety stock that optimally hedges the costs of ordering and carrying inventory against the uncertainty that demand over the order replenishment period might cause inventory to be exhausted before replenishment stock is received, thereby incurring shortage costs due to customer dissatisfaction or lost sales. These models consider individual items in isolation from other items. Other supply chain costs and constraints are ignored.

In Section 11.2, we discussed methods for approximating inventory decisions and associated costs in deterministic optimization models for strategic and tactical planning. The methods varied by the scope of the application, as follows:

1. **Strategic supply chain models.** For snapshot models of the type often used in strategic studies, we examined constructive methods for approximating total

inventory cost (safety stock plus replenishment costs) for each product and each facility as a cost function with a decreasing marginal cost relationship to total product throughput at the facility. We argued that such functions reflect properties underlying the probabilistic models of Section 11.1.

2. **Tactical supply chain models.** We suggested the use of multiple-period optimization models that track and control inventory at the end of each period of each product (product family) at each facility. Safety stocks could be imposed on ending inventories based on computations made prior to constructing the optimization model. We also discussed methods for imposing terminal conditions on inventories to keep them from incorrectly falling to zero at the end of the multiple-period planning horizon.

In sections 11.3 and 11.4, we presented successful modeling applications for several inventory planning problems. We provided overviews of how the probabilistic inventory models reviewed in Section 11.1 could be extended, albeit in an ad hoc manner, to complex models for problems arising in the management of multiechelon distribution and manufacturing systems. One approach for manufacturing supply chains transformed the probabilistic safety stock problem into a deterministic problem by considering a bounded worse case that all participants of the supply chain agreed should be serviced with certainty. Cases with demand beyond the bound were to be considered as anomalies that would be handled as exceptions. The resulting inventory model could be formulated and optimized either as a (deterministic) dynamic programming or mixed integer programming model, which could be combined with similar mixed integer programming models for production planning and scheduling. Such extensions are an area of future research.

An important area of research is to better understand the **bull-whip effect,** which describes how variability in demand increases as one moves up the supply chain.[15] Models similar to those discussed in Section 11.4 have been applied to study this phenomenon and to control it. One of the important results found thus far is that the bullwhip effect can be reduced by providing managers at every stage of the supply chain with current information about demand for finished goods and its impact on upstream manufacturing and distribution activities.[16]

The four models discussed in Sections 11.3 and 11.4 addressed inventory management problems by taking as given the structure of the supply chain, such as the location of facilities and their interconnections, and the missions of these facilities, such as the products to be manufactured or stored there and the resources available for these activities. Clearly, the resulting inventory strategies were suboptimal from a global perspective. Thus, there is merit to an approach for integrating inventory and other supply chain decisions that allows them to be analyzed by separate models whose results are systematically combined.

This is the idea underlying the decomposition scheme depicted in Figure 11.19. A mixed integer programming model determines an optimal design and operating strategy for the company's supply chain. These decisions are passed to the inventory submodel that determines an optimal inventory policy based on them. The inventory submodel is further analyzed to provide feedback, which is labeled Sensitivity Analysis, to the mixed integer programming model about how changes in the supply

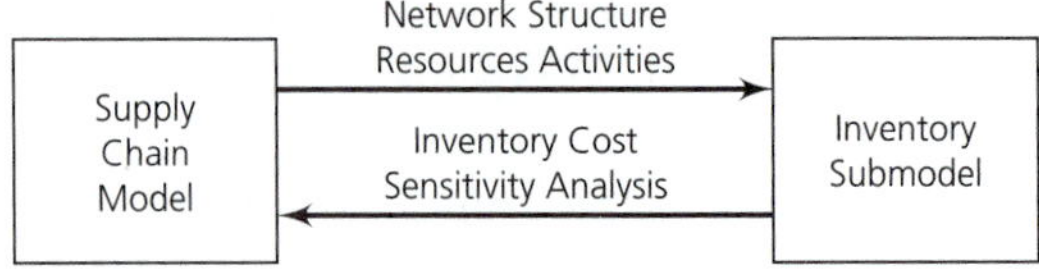

Figure 11.19
Supply chain decomposition scheme

chain and its activities would improve inventory management. The difficult step in this scheme is computation of this feedback. Recent research results suggest that such computation may be possible.[17]

Finally, we discussed in Section 11.1 how stochastic programming models extend deterministic optimization models in a way that closely parallels probabilistic inventory models. Unfortunately, stochastic programming models could not be applied to inventory management problems involving thousands or even hundreds of items. Hierarchical planning methods for overcoming this limitation is another important area of applied research.

Exercises

In addition to the following exercises, modeling exercises involving data files and discussion exercises involving white papers may be found on the Web site (www.scm-models.com).

1. Re-do Example 11.2 where the safety stock $r^* - E(D)$ is specified by the requirement that P (demand during lead time $\geq r^*) = 0.05$. Thus, according to the standardized normal distribution, r^* should lie 1.645 standard deviations above the expected demand over the lead time. What is the safety stock in this case, and what is the implied backlogging cost c_B?

2. The Giant Supermarket orders turkeys for Thanksgiving. Each turkey costs \$8 and sells for \$17. Any turkey left unsold at Thanksgiving will be sold after Thanksgiving for \$5. Based on historical data, the marketing department has computed the probability density function shown in the following table:

Demand D	250	300	350	400	450	500
$P(D)$	0.12	0.18	0.24	0.22	0.19	0.05

   a. How would you price out lost sales?

   b. What is the expected profit if Giant buys 400 turkeys?

   c. How many turkeys would you recommend that Giant buy?

3. Describe how you would use 0-1 variables to capture the safety stock cost relationship displayed in Figure 11.8.

4. Vendor-managed inventory (VMI) is a recent development that can provide benefits to both a manufacturer and its retailing or industrial customers. Under a VMI scheme, customers engage the manufacturer to manage and replenish their in-house inventories, which may reside in DCs, shop-floors, or retail stores. Discuss the possible benefits and drawbacks to a manufacturer and to its customers of VMI. In addition, discuss costs, capacities, and decisions asso-

ciated with VMI that are not standard elements of supply chain models. What data and policy information do a manufacturer and its customer need to share? Finally, sketch modeling approaches to be taken by a manufacturer to optimize decisions relating to VMI.

5. The model developed and used for analyzing optimal safety stock placement at Kodak that we reviewed in Section 11.4 eliminates uncertainty in safety stock planning or, equivalently, redefines the supply chain problem so that a 100% order fulfillment rate at all stages is guaranteed. It does this by selecting a maximal level of demand above which the supply chain will be managed by exception. Each stage of the manufacturing supply chain then determines its service time and its inventory strategy to meet the 100% fulfillment rate while minimizing total holding costs. This construction eliminates the serious and unresolved technical problem of trying to integrate a mixed integer programming model for optimizing supply chain operations with a probabilistic model for determining safety stocks. In fact, the resulting model is a pure mixed integer programming model, which can be extended in various ways to capture other planning phenomena. Discuss the extent to which you believe similar constructions can and should be used to model other supply chain problems where inventory costs are significant and uncertainties are important.

Notes

1. A model to be discussed in the following section was developed by Wilson [1934] and analyzed extensively by Hadley and Whitin [1963].
2. See the article on supply chain management in *The Economist,* June 20–26, 1998.
3. For example, Nahamias [1993] and Peterson and Silver [1985].
4. Discussion of the EOQ model and the (r, q) model is taken from Winston [1994, Chapter 17].
5. See Stenger [1994] for a discussion of uncertainties affecting inventory management decisions.
6. For a review of basic concepts from statistics and probability theory, see Winston [1994, Chapter 11].
7. This approach is suggested by Ballou [1992, 450] and Stenger [1994, 357].
8. See Stenger [1994, 357].
9. See Ballou [1992, 448]. A mixed integer programming construction is needed to describe this cost curve in an optimization model.
10. See Fleishmann et al. [1997].
11. See Cohen et al. [1990] for a discussion of this application and Federgrun [1993] for a review of modeling approaches for multiechelon systems.
12. See Lee and Billington [1993].
13. See Graves and Willems [2000].
14. The system may be downloaded from a Web site at MIT; see the book's Web site (www.scm-models.com) for more details.
15. See Lee, Padmanabhan, and Whang [1997a] and [1997b] for further information about the bullwhip effect.
16. Recent research into managerial control of the bullwhip effect can be found in Chen et al. [1999].
17. The scheme depicted in Figure 11.20 is a resource-directed decomposition method with well-known mathematical properties; see Shapiro [1979, Chapter 6]. The feedback from the submodel required by this method are effectively derivatives of the submodel's objective function. Recent research on computing such derivatives (Glasserman and Tayur [1996]) for inventory models suggest such a decomposition method could be devised.

References

R. H. Ballou, R. H. [1992], *Business Logistics Management,* 3rd ed. Englewood Cliffs, N.J.: Prentice-Hall.

Chen, F., Z. Drezner, J. K. Ryan, and D. Simchi-Levi [1999], "The Bullwhip Effect: Managerial Insights on the Impact of Forecasting and Information on Variability in the Supply Chain," in *Quantitative Models for Supply Chain Management,* edited by S. Tayur, R. Ganeshan, and M. Magazine. Norwell, Mass.: Kluwer.

*Cohen, M., Kamesam, P., Kleindorfer, P., Lee, H., Takerian, A. [1990], "IBM's Multi-Item Echelon Inventory System for Managing Service Logistics, *Interfaces,* 20, 65–82.

* *The Economist* [1998], June 20–26.

Federgrun, A. [1993], "Centralized Planning Models for Multi-Echelon Inventory Systems under Uncertainty," in *Handbook in Operations Research and Management Science: Vol. 4, Logistics of Production and Inventory,* edited by S. C. Graves, A. H. G. Rinooy Kan, and P. H. Zipkin. Amsterdam: North-Holland.

Fleishmann, M., J. M. Bloemhof-Ruwaard, R. Dekker, E. Van der Laan, J. A. E. E. Van Nunen, and L. J. Van Wassenhove [1997], "Quantitative Models for Reverse Logistics: A Review," *European Journal of Operational Research,* 103, 1–17.

Glasserman, P., and S. Tayur [1995], "Sensitivity Analysis for Base-Stock Levels in Multi-Echelon Production-inventory Systems," *Management Science,* 41, 263–281.

*Graves, S. C., and S. P. Willems [2000], "Optimizing Strategic Safety Stock Placement in Supply Chains," *Manufacturing and Service Operations Management,* 2, 68–83.

Hadley, G., and T. M. Whitin [1963], *Analysis of Inventory Systems.* Englewood Cliffs, N.J.: Prentice-Hall.

*Lee, H. L., and C. Bilington [1993], "Material Management in Decentralized Supply Chains," *Operations Research,* 41, 835–847.

Lee, H., P. Padmanabhan, and S. Whang [1997a], "The Bullwhip Effect in Supply Chains," *Sloan Management Review,* 38, 93–102.

Lee, H., P. Padmanabhan, and S. Whang [1997b], "Information Distortion in a Supply Chain: The Bullwhip Effect," *Management Science,* 38, 546–58.

Nahamias, S. [1993], *Production and Operations Analysis,* 2nd ed., Irwin.

Peterson, R., and E. Silver [1985], *Decision Systems for Inventory Management and Production Planning.* New York: Wiley.

Robeson, J. F., Copacino, W. C., and Howe, R. E. [1994], *The Logistics Handbook.* New York: The Free Press.

Shapiro, J. F. [1979], *Mathematical Programming: Structures and Algorithms.* New York: Wiley.

Stegner, A. J. [1994], "Inventory Decision Framework," Chapter 15 in Robeson, Copacino, and Howe [1994].

Wilson, R. H. [1934], "A Scientific Routine for Stock Control," *Harvard Business Review,* XIII, 116–128.

*Winston, W. L. [1994], *Operations Research: Applications and Algorithms,* 3rd ed., Pacific Grove, Calif.: Duxbury Press.

*See the credits section at the end of this book for more information.

IV The Future

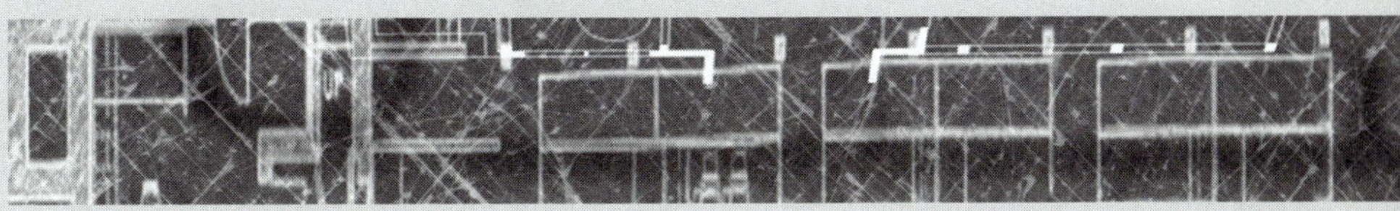

12 Organizational Adaptation to Optimization Modeling Systems

The premise of this book is that managers are increasingly interested in fact-based management of their supply chains. Accordingly, we devoted our attention to the study of data-driven optimization models that support supply chain decision making. In previous chapters, we reviewed many successful applications of modeling systems, which confirmed our contention that technical requirements for implementing such systems are not barriers to new and deeper applications. Instead, the barriers are due to human and organizational behavior that runs counter to the acceptance and effective use of data and models for supply chain management.

This chapter examines these barriers and suggests approaches for overcoming them. Companies that succeed in implementing new supply chain processes to exploit transactional and analytical information technology (IT) will achieve significant competitive management. Our discussion draws on the following four overlapping areas of research:

- Behavioral studies about how organizations actually make decisions
- Factors that render IT a valuable resource that contributes to the firm's competitive advantage
- Business process redesign (BPR), especially as it is made necessary by and seeks to exploit IT developments in improving supply chain management
- Supply chain coordination processes and incentive structures

Although scholars working in these areas have not yet recognized the emerging role of optimization systems in enhancing decision making and exploiting IT, their research implicitly identifies the need for such systems.

The term *IT* is shorthand for *IT infrastructure* within the firm and connecting the firm with its vendors and customers. Specifically, IT infrastructure refers to hardware, software for communicating and managing data, software for executing descriptive and normative modeling analyses, and, IT personnel responsible for ensuring that appropriate hardware and software are acquired, maintained, connected, and enhanced. The effective use of hardware and software for communicating and managing data over the Internet is obviously a topic of great current interest and importance.

We will also find it convenient in the discussion that follows to use the terms *organization* and *decision maker,* which organizational behaviorists employ in presenting their research into decision making. We will treat *organization, company,* and *firm* as synonyms, although not all organizations are companies. Similarly, we will treat *decision maker* and *manager* as synonyms, although one could argue that some decision makers are not managers.

In Section 12.1, we provide an overview of research into how organizations make decisions that is based heavily on the work of James March and his collaborators.[1] March has summarized this research in what he calls "a cluster of (four) contested issues about human action."[2] The contested issues speak directly to the conflict between rational, data-driven decision making and organizational politics that impedes the identification and implementation of effective decisions. These issues are examined in detail in Section 12.2 from the perspective of integrated supply chain management and the application of modeling systems. The concepts presented in Sections 12.1 and 12.2 are applied in later sections when we examine the impact of a company's IT infrastructure and its efforts at business process redesign on supply chain management.

In Section 12.3, we review factors contributing to the success of IT in providing the firm with competitive advantage. These factors are examined from the perspective of the resource-based view of the firm. We also discuss the complementarity between IT resources and human and business resources in achieving competitive advantage. The acquisition, application, and enhancement of modeling systems for supply chain management invoke conflicts between exploratory and exploitative cultures and identities in the firm. We discuss these conflicts in Section 12.4 and suggest approaches for effecting teamwork among modeling system developers, who are explorers; IT administrators, who are exploiters; and supply chain managers and analysts, who are the clients of the other two groups. Considerable IT managerial skill is needed to create and maintain teamwork among these individuals who have diverse cultural viewpoints.

Much has been written in recent years about the interplay between BPR and IT. Depending on its appropriateness and flexibility, IT is believed to serve either as an enabler or inhibitor of BPR. Although this is true for a wide range of business processes dependent on transactional IT, we argue that modeling systems *invoke* new business processes, not simply cause them to be redesigned. Typical new processes include those for creating and updating supply chain decision databases, making model runs, interpreting model results, and negotiating plans derived from these results. In Section 12.5, we discuss this aspect of BPR, with reference to the repetitive, monthly application of a modeling system for tactical planning in a firm that manufactures and distributes consumer goods. The role of incentives in promoting coordinated supply chain decision making is also discussed in Section 12.6. Although considerable theoretical research into incentive structures has been performed, little research has yet been done on structures that promote the acceptance among middle managers of integrated supply chain plans.

In Section 12.7, we examine in detail the stages of a strategic supply chain modeling study for two reasons. First, we wish to provide a road map of a typical study for managers who have never been involved in one. Second, although such a study requires a serious effort by the company, the effort is manageable and in most cases will produce important results in 4 to 6 months.

We conclude the chapter with Section 12.8 where we discuss future developments in supply chain management, modeling systems, information technology, and organizational adaptation. Organizational adaptation to modeling systems and fact-based decision making is the major source of uncertainty about the future. We expect that historians will look back on the current period as the beginning of the information revolution, which relieves the author of great responsibility in making accurate long-term predictions.

12.1 How Organizations Make Decisions

Over the past 40 years, scholars studying how individuals and organizations make decisions became divided into two camps. One camp includes economists, management scientists, and other social scientists who hold the view that individuals and organizations should and will be rational in their decision making, at least within limits set by their information gathering resources.[3] In particular, they espouse the theory of bounded rationality, which states that decision makers are rational to an extent consistent with information they have acquired about the state of the world, possible actions they may take, and the consequences of these actions.

The second camp includes organizational behaviorists concerned with understanding how decisions in organizations are actually made, rather than how they should be made according to rational principles.[4] Although organizations may attempt to make intelligent decisions leading to desirable outcomes, behaviorists have found that, because they are separated by space and time, decision makers are inconsistent in their decision-making processes. Moreover, organizations are hard pressed to overcome problems caused by ignorance, conflict, and ambiguity.

This paradox along with recent developments in IT suggests that the business world is in the midst of trying to resolve, at least for supply chain management, the following conundrum of the information revolution:

> Is the reluctance and inability of managers to engage in rational decision making diminishing or persisting as they are provided with increasingly flexible and rapid access to comprehensive data pertinent to their decisions?

Based on our experiences over the past few years discussing and implementing modeling systems in a range of companies, we are optimistic that managerial reluctance and inability to pursue rational decision making are diminishing. Of course, a firm's commitment to rational (fact-based) decision making still leaves considerable room in selecting or developing tools to support it.

In this section, we examine the behavioral view of organizational decision making without offering comments about the impact of recent IT developments, especially as they affect supply chain management. Our discussion draws heavily on the research by James March and his collaborators.[5] In the following section, we relate supply chain modeling and management to four contested issues about organizational decision, which Professor March has posited as summaries to the discussion in this section.

The Theory of Rational Choice versus the Reality of Organizational Behavior

The **theory of rational choice** for an individual decision maker is based on the following four elements:[6]

- A knowledge of alternatives—a set of alternatives for action
- A knowledge of consequences—an understanding of the consequences, possibly probabilistic, of each action
- A consistent preference ordering—allows alternative actions and their consequences to be evaluated and compared
- A decision rule—allows a single alternative to be selected based on the preference ordering

Proponents of the theory of rational choice are vague about the processes to be followed by the decision maker in acquiring knowledge of the alternatives and consequences and then applying her preference ordering and decision rule in selecting a decision. Specifically, they largely ignore methods for providing the decision maker with descriptive and normative models to assist her in selecting a decision.

Rational choice extends to multiple decision makers in an organization who can be expected to more or less agree on available alternatives and possible consequences. Moreover, they will find mechanisms for merging individual preference orderings in making group decisions. Again, the role of analytical methods in achieving consensus has been ignored.

Scholars have modified original theories of rational choice to a **theory of bounded rationality** that acknowledges limits on information available to the decision maker. Specifically, a decision maker's knowledge of alternatives and consequences is bounded by her capabilities to search for information characterizing them. The decision maker's scarce resource is attention, which she may allocate in ad hoc ways depending on her individual frames (mind-sets), behavior patterns, and the importance of the decision. Because attainment of perfect information is virtually impossible, the decision maker will tend to slack off from the pursuit of an optimal alternative, settling instead for an alternative whose consequences will achieve or exceed a prespecified goal. This approach to decision making is called **satisficing.**[7]

Organizational behaviorists concerned with understanding how decisions in organizations are actually made agree that information gathering leading to intelligence, defined as well-informed and effective decision making, will never be completely successful. From a pragmatic viewpoint, what matters is the organization's ability to employ the intelligence available to it to achieve outcomes that fulfill its desires as closely as possible. However, based on numerous field studies, behaviorists believe that problems associated with decision making are more complex and pervasive than those suggested by bounded rationality. Any assessment of organizational intelligence is linked to the complexity of the organization in which desires, actions, and outcomes are distributed across space and time. Intelligent action from one group's perspective at a given point in time may appear unintelligent to another group at another point in time. Moreover, because preferences change over time, actions that appeared intelligent at first may subsequently be viewed less favorably, and vice versa.

Furthermore, the pursuit of organizational intelligence is frustrated by the following three problems:

1. **Ignorance.** First, decision makers are often ignorant of the past because historical events have not been well documented or understood. They may also be ignorant of cause and effect that could explain the past and help develop accurate forecasts. Finally, they may be ignorant of decision options, constraints, and preferences for outcomes that could help them frame their plans.
2. **Conflict.** Decision makers separated in space, time, and responsibility have different preferences. In any decision-making situation, it is problematic whether they will agree or refuse to cooperate and exchange information.
3. **Ambiguity.** Decision makers' preferences and their identities within an organization are not well understood and change with time. Moreover, they are likely to change as the result of actions taken and outcomes realized. Thus, the pursuit of intelligent decision-making processes involves tracking a moving target of vague and sometimes rapidly changing preferences.

Finally, organizational decision making is constantly torn between **exploration** and **exploitation.** Exploration refers to processes involving search, discovery, and innovation. It requires the organization to vary and sometimes abandon its standard practices and take risks with experimental new products, technologies, markets, or processes. The organization cannot expect to be successful in a high percentage of its explorations, but they are necessary if the organization is to adapt to changing conditions. Exploitation refers to processes that refine, routinize, and perfect the organization's activities. It serves to make these activities more efficient and reliable. Exploitation efforts are much more likely to be successful than exploration efforts, but they cannot identify major redirections for the organization.

The tension between exploration and exploitation leads to balancing problems. On the one hand, excessive exploration can induce a **failure trap** in which failed experiments lead to new experiments that also fail, in large part because the organization abandons potentially successful experiments before they can prove their worth. On the other hand, excess exploitation can induce a **success trap** in which short-term success with exploitation efforts inhibits exploration efforts needed for longer-term adaptation and survival of the organization.

Uncertainty and Risk

Decision makers' attitudes about uncertainty and risk are another area where rational and behavioral theories differ. Rational theory assumes that a decision maker has an inherent aversion to risk, which can be identified by examining his preferences for risky alternatives. Once the decision maker's revealed preferences have been extracted, his utility function has been plotted, and probabilities of uncertain events have been estimated, decisions are selected so as to maximize expected utility.[8]

Organizational behaviorists believe a decision maker's attitude toward risk is not systematic to the extent that it can be characterized by an immutable utility function. Although a decision maker may make an effort to objectively understand the risks associated with particular decisions, his propensity to take risks will depend on conditions surrounding the decision and the consequences. Clearly, if the decision maker anticipates a severe organizational rebuke if an action causes failure, he will be much more risk averse than he would be if the organization is openly supportive of exploratory actions that have no guarantee of success. Another behavioral aspect of risk taking is the reliability of the organization and the actors with whom the decision maker interacts. If the organization, or the decision maker's boss, is inconsistent in its response to risk taking, this will add to the decision maker's perception of such risks.

A decision maker's attitude toward risk will also vary significantly as a function of the goal that he and the organization expects to achieve from his actions. If action leads to payoffs exceeding the goal, behaviorists have found that the decision maker will subsequently be more risk averse than he will be if the goal is not achieved. If the goal is not achieved, the decision maker may be inclined to take larger and larger risks in trying to achieve the goal.

Rule-Based Decision Making

Scholars studying organizational behavior have suggested that rule-based decision making is a realistic alternative to the rational decision making described above. In particular, rational decision making, which involves anticipatory, calculated, and consequential actions, runs counter to widely observed decision logic based on appropriateness, obligation, duty, and rules. In other words, most decisions taken in an organization are defined or dictated by accepted operating procedures, professional standards, or other mind-sets linked to the decision makers' concept of their identities.

Thus, rather than evaluating alternatives in terms of the values of their consequences, a decision maker is more likely to follow a logic of appropriateness, which depends on the following factors:

- **Identity.** Decision makers have conceptions of their personal, professional, and official identities, which may vary depending on the particular situation
- **Situation.** Situations are classified into categories with associated rules that are consistent with their identities

- **Matching.** Decision makers chose actions for specific situations that are appropriate to their identities in those situations

Adherence to rules occurs not only when routine decisions must be made, but even when unstructured situations arise. In the latter case, the decision maker will still follow identity-driven conceptions of appropriateness rather than trying to maximize expected utility.

Behaviorists have found that rules evolve slowly over time and incorporate experiential knowledge that would be difficult to extract from current data and practices. They have identified the following four major methods whereby rules are developed:

1. Decision makers may consciously select rules based on rational analysis of the actions to be taken and the possible consequences. This method is viewed as a form of contractual agreement among rational parties.
2. Rules are developed as the result of learning, or feedback from the environment, about the benefits and losses of implementing certain actions. This learning may be rationally adaptive in that better, even optimal, rules are identified and implemented over time. However, learning may be only partially rational, which introduces anomalies in the rules. It may be superstitious, causing decision makers to become trapped at local, safe optima that are distant from global optima. Competence associated with technological learning may be trapped at a minimalist or inadequate level, restricting the organization to suboptimal technologies when a greater effort to improve competence would have a much larger payoff.
3. Decision makers are prone to imitation and may accept rules merely because others have accepted them. Imitation may lead to good rules, but not always, especially during periods of rapid changes in technology when decision makers are more prone, for reasons of safety, to follow the herd.
4. The organization's collection of rules will evolve other time, and possibly improve in their overall effectiveness, but they may always be far from optimal. There is no guarantee than the collection will be as good as it could or should be unless the organization finds mechanisms that promote the identification and diffusion of intelligent rules while stifling ineffective ones.

Additional conflicts and ambiguities arise when decision makers implement rules. This is because, in most organizations, many rules are implicitly, rather than explicitly, stated and understood. Therefore, they are subject to considerable interpretation and variation. When a conflict arises between actors who disagree about the meaning or impact of a rule, some form of rational analysis is needed and may be sought to resolve it.

Deriving Meaning from the Decision Environment

Decision makers seek to develop explicit or implicit descriptions of past, present, and future situations that may affect or be affected by their decisions and seek to be aware of their rules, preferences, and identities. In other words, they seek the meaning behind the confusing world in which they live and work. This meaning is constantly evolving due to inputs to and outputs from decision making. It is encoded in **frames,** or mind-sets, that decision makers adopt to help them resolve problems.

Theories of rational decision making assume that, before making decisions, decision makers attempt to understand the possible consequences of possible actions and their preferences for them. Alternate theories of rule-based action assume that, before making decisions, decision makers attempt to understand the accompanying situations so that they can select rules that match them and are appropriate to their identities. These efforts to establish the meaning of decision making situations are often far from perfect.

Behavioral research has also shown that individuals oversimplify decision-making situations. They reduce complex situations to simple numbers, thereby ignoring underlying complexities that may be crucial to the selection of an effective decision. They also emphasize information that is close to them in time and space. Further, they tend to interpret a situation so as to confirm their prior beliefs and importance.

Theories of both rational and rule-based decision making treat decision outcomes as the major concern of decision makers. Again, behavioral studies indicate that implemented decisions are only loosely coupled to the information upon which they were based. Often, more effort is made to justify a decision after it has been made than to evaluate it before it was made. This is because the decision-making process is viewed as an occasion to reconfirm, challenge, or change relationships among individuals in the organization. Moreover, actions taken and expressed preferences occur simultaneously as the decision makers play out the consequences of the actions.

Behaviorists have gone further in positing that the meaning derived from decision making may be more important than the actual outcomes. By this, they wish to convey that decision processes enhance the identities of key individuals in the organization. In the extreme, the organization will glorify the symbols, myths, and rituals associated with decision making, while assuming that the outcomes are as good as they can be and therefore introspection and analysis can be largely ignored.

Decision-Making Ecologies

Rational theories assume decisions are made coherently by a group of decision makers at a particular point in time runs counter to the conflict and confusion associated with actual decision making across an organization or among multiple organizations. Social interactions surrounding decision making play a large role in defining the rules and expectations of the organization and intertwining them with the rules and expectations of other organizations with which it interacts. This interaction clouds the evolution of accepted organizational histories and decision rules.

Ecology is defined as the branch of sociology that studies the relationship between human groups and their physical and social environments. Organizational behaviorists have extended its meaning to "an 'ecological' vision of decision making, a vision that considers how the structure of relationships among individual units interacts with the behavior of these units to produce systemic properties not easily attributable to the individual behavior alone."[9] Recent research supports this ecological vision by identifying conflicts that result when individuals or groups with inconsistent preferences or identities attempt to make decisions. Moreover, decisions tend to be linked by their proximity in time, rather than causality. The assumptions underlying decision making also change with time as a function of the actions taken and the consequences realized.

Because rational theories may be impractical, one is tempted to view organizational decision making as a political process that allows decisions to be made without achieving consensus. Through some combination of power, negotiation, exchange, or alliance, the organization ultimately takes action. However, complications due to the political process may impede the implementation of decisions once they have been made. Ultimately, despite political infighting, the various actors will be called upon to trust one another, a viewpoint that has been supported by recent research that finds trust and reputation are more important to getting things done than cleverness in bargaining.

12.2 Contested Issues about Organizational Decision Making

James March has summarized the conflicts in organizational decision making discussed in the previous section in terms of four contested issues. We reproduce them here and comment upon them from the perspective of optimization models and modeling systems for integrated supply chain management.[10] The issues recapitulate the conceptual and observed disparities discussed in the previous section between rational theories of decision making and observations by organizational behaviorists about actual decision making. Our goal is to better understand principles for adapting the organization to the use of data and modeling systems for supply chain management. Before getting into the details, we make several comments about the context in which these issues should be examined.

In today's world, no one would argue that a wide range of supply chain decisions should be made only after decision makers have analyzed or paid attention to relevant data, which are, or should be, stored and accessed in computerized databases. We do not presume that ERP systems have already led to effective database management in most companies. Many complaints have been heard from managers about the success of ERP system implementation projects in their companies. Beyond the cost, which is sometimes enormous, the resulting information systems are often incomplete and too rigid in their specification and management of data. Nevertheless, over time, we can expect that better ERP systems and implementation practices will be developed and employed. Moreover, current Internet developments promoting the creation of virtual supply chains of diverse companies only emphasizes the need for better ERP systems and analytical tools to process and interpret data.

The immutable fact is that processes for making and implementing supply chain decisions must be data driven. Companies are finding ways to link modeling systems to their ERP systems or to work around them. By contrast, the abstract viewpoint that decision making is carried out by managers who interact with one another and the people who work for them while paying little or random attention to data is outdated. The central role to be played by data management and modeling systems must be factored into behavioral studies of the evolution of organizational decision making for supply chain management.

Supply chain management is particularly well suited to data-driven decision making. The supply chain decision database discussed in Chapter 6 is made up mainly of objective, numerical data describing purchasing, manufacturing, distribution, and transportation activities. Moreover, if a reasonable effort is made, accurate relationships expressing costs and resource utilization as a function of independent decision variables can be developed using methods of management accounting, engineering, and transportation science. Similarly, accurate forecasts of demand can be developed, at least for planning periods up to 1 or 2 years. By contrast, in other areas of business decision making such as marketing, new product development, or selection of a new CEO, managers find it more difficult or inappropriate to employ decision models characterized by numerical relationships.

It is ironic, but not surprising, that abstract theories of organizational decision making elaborated over the past 40 years should now have relevance and importance to systems engineers and modeling practitioners struggling to exploit new IT. We should not underestimate the breadth and depth of the difficulties they encounter. Nevertheless, we find that software developers and managers now display considerable determination in their efforts to use IT to improve business decision making. Theories of organizational decision making provide important concepts, as well as a rich vocabulary, for examining, understanding, and overcoming human barriers to the successful exploitation of IT for these purposes.

In the discussion below, our comments about the current state of decision making in supply chain management are based in large part on the author's impressions from daily conversations over several years with managers, consultants, and software developers. As such, the evidence presented is episodic rather than systematic. By contrast, many of the behavioral observations reviewed in the previous section are based on systematic studies. New studies are needed to understand changes in organizational decision making in the face of globalization and astonishingly dynamic developments in IT.

Choice-Based versus Rule-Based Decision Making

The first issue is whether decisions are to be viewed as *choice-based* or *rule-based.* Do decision makers pursue a logic of consequence, making choices among alternatives by evaluating their consequences in terms of prior preferences? Or do they pursue a logic of appropriateness, fulfilling identities or rules by recognizing situations and following rules that match appropriate behavior to the situations they encounter?[11]

A modeling practitioner believes that choice-based approaches to decision making are superior to rule-based approaches because they produce better decisions. The implication is that decision makers should be encouraged to develop or acquire optimization modeling systems to assist them in developing their plans. However, such an assertion runs counter to the discussion in the previous section. According to many behavioral studies, human decision makers do not generally behave in a rational manner when choosing among alternatives by evaluating their consequences in terms of prior preferences.

For supply chain management, however, a different attitude appears to be emerging. Many managers now believe that decisions regarding the design and operation of their supply chain should be fact based; that is, based on data. For this reason, most medium- and large-sized firms now employ, or are looking to acquire, data management and modeling systems to help manage their production lines and distribute their products. Despite the disappointments with ERP systems, information systems are becoming sufficiently efficient and responsive that an increasing number of managers believe that data-driven modeling systems can achieve and sustain competitive advantage in their supply chain operations.

As a result, new types of identities are emerging. These are routers, production schedulers, inventory managers, strategy analysts, and their managers who have the responsibilities of maintaining supply chain decision databases and using optimization modeling systems to identify effective plans. Their organizational self-images are closely linked to the rational, data-driven processes for which they are responsible. The rules they follow include routinely exercising modeling systems in making choice-based decisions, admittedly with human modification of the plans when the situation warrants it.

The newness of these identities leaves open the question of their likely evolution. An issue that we will reconsider in Section 12.3 is the required overlap of knowledge and skills in supply chain operations and IT required by this type of worker. Moreover, senior managers in many companies have not yet fully realized the importance of such employees to the efficient operation of their supply chains. An extreme example of such ignorance occurred recently in a company that leases containers to manufacturers. On a daily basis, the company exercises an operational modeling system to assign orders to depots so as to minimize transportation, inventory, and replacement costs. To cut costs, senior management set quotas for staff reduction that caused the only two analysts in the company responsible for running the system to be let go. Another employee, who formerly ran the system, was called in to train new personnel but, shortly thereafter, left the company. The company is now muddling through with lightly trained personnel and runs the risk of a serious degradation in the efficiency of its operations.

Choice-Based versus Rule-Based Models. The terms *choice based* and *rule based* are descriptors, but with a somewhat altered meaning, of different philosophies behind the design of modeling systems for supply chain management. In this context, we interpret choice based as representing optimization models that provide a comprehensive, systems analysis view of supply chain decision problems. In such a model, the feasible set of possible consequences is delineated by constraints on available resources, materials balances, product specifications, demand requirements, and so on. Actions correspond to decision variables that are mathematically transformed into consequences lying within the feasible set. Preferences are specified by an objective function that is used by an optimization algorithm to determine an optimal solution; if the preferences involve more than one objective function, an optimization algorithm can be used to explore the efficient frontier of solutions. Such exploration was illustrated in Section 3.6.

We interpret rule based in the modeling context as representing descriptive models that attempt to provide acceptable, feasible solutions to supply chain problems using decisions rules that transform input data describing the problem to a solution. The individual rules are myopic and must be organized into a computational scheme that attempts to find a good feasible solution. An example is a model that determines a company's supply chain plan for next year by assigning market demands to distribution centers according to simple rules and then assigns induced demand at each distribution center to plants according to another set of simple rules. Little or no attempt is made to determine a low total cost solution, to examine the opening of new distribution centers, to evaluate the shutting down of existing distribution centers, or even to ensure that the rules lead to a feasible solution that does not violate the plants' capacities. A materials requirements planning system that determines detailed production schedules for several weeks based on a predetermined master schedule of finished goods, while ignoring capacity constraints, is another example of a rule-based modeling system.

Rule-based modeling systems have the advantage of being easier to understand than optimization modeling systems. They may also be easier to implement, although developers might find it difficult to assemble myopic rules to cover a complicated range of contingencies. Otherwise, rule-based systems are generally inferior to optimization modeling systems in the quality of the solutions they provide. The supply chain plans they identify are no better than the rules used, which might be quite poor. Even if all or most of these rules are sound, they may not produce high-quality global plans because of higher-order interactions and ripple effects that are ignored. Moreover, the quality of the rules will surely decay over time as the planning problems change, but the lack of global benchmarks will make it difficult to decide when to revise them.

Clear versus Ambiguous Decision Making

The second issue is whether decision making is typified more by *clarity* and *consistency* or by *ambiguity* and *inconsistency*. Are decisions occasions in which individuals and institutions achieve coherence and reduce equivocality? Or are they occasions in which inconsistency and ambiguity are exhibited, exploited and expanded?[12]

Conflicts among decision makers' preferences are the central focus of this issue, although similar conflicts arise in decision makers' perceptions of alternative actions and their consequences. As we discussed in the previous section, behavioral research has shown that organizational preferences are often not clear and consistent. Preferences regarding solutions to a given planning problem will vary depending on the decision makers' organizational and personal identities. Moreover, their preferences are not stable and may change between the time actions are taken and when the consequences are realized.

Data-driven modeling systems appear to be best suited to situations in which the feasible set of actions is known and preferences are clear and consistent. Nevertheless, we argue that models and modeling systems can also play a central role in resolving conflicts arising when supply chain decision makers are inconsistent and ambiguous about their preferences, available actions, and possible consequences. Our arguments involve the following four perspectives on supply chain decision making and modeling:

- Ambiguity and inconsistency depend on the scope of the planning problem.
- Modeling systems can reconcile ambiguity and inconsistency.
- The supply chain decision database provides frames.
- Bounds on optimization modeling.

Ambiguity and Inconsistency Depend on the Scope of the Planning Problem. The extent of conflicts in decision makers' preferences between clarity and ambiguity, and between consistency and inconsistency, depends on the scope of the supply chain decision problem. A hierarchy of supply chain planning problems spanning operational to strategic, along with modeling systems for analyzing them, was examined in detail in Section 2.3. Operational problems lend themselves to greater clarity and consistency than strategic problems because they are more focused and involve less uncertainty. We can expect operational planning managers to agree that the objective function for an operational problem, such as scheduling production or routing vehicles, is to meet short-term orders or forecasted demand with acceptable customer service while minimizing avoidable costs.

The objective function for operational planning may become ambiguous if promised orders cannot be met. Nevertheless, under the pressure of executing the company's business, clear goals for dealing with excess sales can be defined and incorporated in a modeling system. We saw an example of this in Section 10.4 when we discussed the production scheduling system developed for Harris Corporation's semiconductor sector, which separated orders and forecasted demands into categories of decreasing importance that were sequentially scheduled. In short, by probing the ambiguities and inconsistencies regarding decision makers' preferences for operational actions, the modeling practitioner can incorporate policy constraints and decision variables in a model that provides managers with flexibility about how the model optimizes operational decisions. Again, because of time pressures, decision makers will expect the modeling system to routinely produce plans based in part on these policies, which they will review before releasing them for execution.

Time pressures do not allow decision makers with diverse responsibilities and identities to engage in extended disputes or negotiations.

As the planning horizon gets longer, the scope of decision making and the degree of uncertainty about alternatives and consequences becomes larger. Thus, we can expect greater ambiguity and inconsistency to exist in the minds of individual decision makers and groups of decision makers who have the responsibility for managing a company's entire supply chain. The form and style of applying modeling systems to supply chain planning over tactical and strategic planning horizons can, and must, reflect managers' ambiguous and inconsistent attitudes about the decision problems at hand.

Modeling Systems Can Reconcile Ambiguity and Inconsistency. Modeling systems can serve as rational arbiters for reconciling ambiguity and inconsistency among decision makers' preferences arising in longer-term planning problems. Unlike an operational modeling system whose purpose is to provide a good, implementable plan after a single optimization run, the model employed by a tactical or strategic modeling system should include options that allow the solution to be shaped to conform to differing preferences among the decision makers. Conflicts can be evaluated and, it is hoped, resolved by examining the results of multiple what-if scenarios.

Examples of model constructions for shaping a supply chain solution include the following:

- For each product family, upper and lower bounds on the number of plants that manufacture it with a conditional minimum and an absolute maximum on the quantity produced at each plant
- For each raw material, part, or family of parts, upper and lower bounds on the number of vendors that supply it with a conditional minimum and an absolute maximum on the quantity acquired at each vendor
- For prescribed sets of possible locations (e.g., New England states, all third-party sites) upper and lower bounds on the number of distribution centers that are located there
- A utility that generates the outbound network connecting distribution centers to markets according to maximal allowable service distance, possibly by product class
- User flexibility in selecting an objective function from among several choices including minimizing total supply chain cost of meeting fixed and given demand, minimizing maximal cycle time for manufacturing and distributing products to the markets, maximizing net revenues by varying product mix, and maximizing return on assets
- Transformation of any objective function to a goal constraint with specified target

Not all solution-shaping options would be employed in a single scenario run, but a robust range of options should be available. Of course, the above list is not comprehensive. The modeling practitioner will be challenged to create model structures for dealing with specific ambiguities and inconsistencies found among the decision makers' preferences. An argument can be made, however, that if the practitioner cannot readily translate an ambiguity or inconsistency into appropriate data and model structures, she should pursue the issue further with the decision maker to determine its rational aspect. Ultimately, she will either determine a satisfactory approach to modeling the issue or conclude that it is insignificant.

By examining plans suggested by optimizing several what-if scenarios, the decision makers can move toward an acceptable plan that is based more on objective, comprehensive analysis than on unfounded suppositions and superstitions. For important strategic planning exercises, a facilitator might be needed to assist decision makers in defining and prioritizing the initial scenarios, in defining follow-on scenarios as information is gleaned from the initial ones, and in interpreting results. To promote discussion, and move toward consensus, model inputs and outputs should be visually displayed as geographical maps and other graphical displays that compare and contrast plans produced by different scenarios.

We have already noted that, as the planning horizon gets longer and strategic planning issues move onto the decision agenda, the potential for ambiguity and inconsistency among decision makers increases. Fewer resources will be viewed as fixed and given; the company might elect to sell plants or even business units or to acquire another company of comparable size. Uncertainties about consequences and preferences loom much larger, and therefore conflicts regarding long-term objectives of the company can easily arise. The application of modeling systems to test scenarios as described above can reduce these conflicts and help the company identify and implement more intelligent and effective plans.

Because conflicts among decision makers will never disappear, and moreover they change over time, it is important to reapply the modeling system and associated processes on an appropriately frequent basis to review and modify past decisions as well as to select new decisions. Such exercises are also needed to deal with revealed uncertainties in the company's operations and markets and in external factors such as technology and macroeconomics. Sometimes, the strategic decision-making processes should be evoked on an emergency basis to help the company react to large, unforeseen events.

Another consideration is the importance of integrating supply chain management with demand management at the strategic planning level. As we discussed in Section 8.1, serious conflicts between supply chain and marketing managers have long been recognized.[13] The challenge for both senior managers seeking this level of integration and modeling practitioners is to convince marketing managers that descriptive and normative models of their decision problems are possible and important. Success in such efforts lies mainly in the future, although we presented examples in Sections 8.2 and 8.3 of successful applications.

The stochastic programming models discussed in Sections 3.7, 8.7, 8.8, and 11.2 are an intriguing possibility for examining and reconciling ambiguities and inconsistencies associated with the risks of an uncertain future. These models consider simultaneously multiple scenarios of an unknown future. They determine a strategy that maximizes expected discounted net revenues by determining an optimal contingency plan for each scenario and a here-and-now strategy that optimally hedges against these plans.

The first benefit of a stochastic programming model, for example, to analyze the company's expansion over the next 3 years, would be to achieve a consensus among senior managers regarding the range and form of scenarios to consider. The scenario planning methodology described in Section 8.9 would be useful in achieving such a convergence. A second benefit would be the imposition of constraints on the contingency plans of individual scenarios reflecting preferences with respect to risk. For example, constraints limiting the loss in any year in any scenario to $50 million or limiting the probability of realizing any loss in any year to 0.10 (one in ten). Another benefit would be to test the sensitivity of optimal strategies on probabilities associated with the individual scenarios.

The above discussion illustrates ways in which modeling systems for supply chain management are appropriate for supporting both exploitation and exploration of organizational intelligence. A combination of exploitation and exploration is associated with operational and short-term tactical planning when the needs and preferences associated with supply chain planning are clear and consistent. For the most part, managers must exploit their available resources in making decisions about these problems. Still, within somewhat fixed constraints, the models explore the set of feasible actions to find those that are most effective.

Greater exploration is needed for long-term tactical and strategic planning. In addition to their relevance in reconciling ambiguity and inconsistency to arrive at consensual decisions, exploratory processes can promote adaptive growth and learning in the firm. Strategic planning entails much higher levels of ambiguity and inconsistency, which must be constructively managed to enhance the prospects for survival and competitiveness of the firm. Modeling systems provide mechanisms for focusing learning during exploration to make it more constructive, including the maintenance of historical data about actions, consequences, and preferences as well as the testing and comparison of multiple scenarios of the future. In other words, modeling systems can provide a clear and consistent framework in which to track and reconcile organizational ambiguities and inconsistencies.

The Supply Chain Decision Database Provides Frames. This leads us to the third perspective on issue 2 as it relates to supply chain decision making. The supply chain decision database provides a frame for efficient and effective data gathering and intelligence monitoring, especially for tactical and strategic planning. It provides a focus for managing the attention of supply chain decision makers, from both historical and prospective viewpoints.

The supply chain decision database was examined extensively in Chapter 6. Its form is a consequence of optimization modeling of the company's supply chain, which for many applications provides a natural parsing of the data into approximately 25 file sets describing homogeneous elements of a company's supply chain. Moreover, it fosters aggregation of products, customers, and suppliers, which provides decision makers with a much clearer view of their supply chain than vast quantities of transactional data. Thus, it offers a pragmatic approach to coping with the realities of decision makers' limited information-gathering resources and capabilities.

It also allows decision makers to specify options to be explored. New products, markets, facilities, and suppliers can be readily added to the structural file sets of the supply chain; data regarding costs, capacities, transformation recipes, demand, and so on, must be added to scenario file sets to analyze such new options. Thus, data needed to evaluate new options is clearly framed. Finally, it allows decision makers to specify their preferences in the form of constraints on supply chain plans and/or goal constraints on selected objective functions.

Bounds on Optimization Modeling. The final perspective on issue 2 as it relates to supply chain decision making is the need to recognize that there are bounds on optimization modeling that are analogous to bounds on the rationality of decision makers. Individuals engaged in creating, applying, and maintaining modeling systems must be realistic in their choice of a model and a system for applying it. Forecasting and other descriptive models can never yield perfect descriptions. Optimization models can never capture all the details of the supply chain planning problems to be analyzed. Human experience and expertise in modeling and the use of modeling systems are critical in making intelligent judgments about the level of effort appropriate to the development of such systems and to their evolution as these problems change.

From the modeling practitioner's perspective, the bounds on modeling are almost always limitations of time, resources, and the attention of managers rather than limitations on the capabilities of models. Although such capabilities are definitely bounded, most companies today do not pursue supply chain modeling and modeling system approaches to anywhere near the points of diminishing returns. For example, we have participated in several strategic studies using optimization models that have identified savings in the tens of millions of dollars per year. Implemented strategies have realized a high percentage of these savings. The cost of such a study is typically 1 to 3% of the identified savings. Yet, in many cases, the company has been unable or unwilling to institutionalize use of the modeling system to track strategic plans as they evolve and to support related tactical decision making. An optimistic response to this short sightedness is to observe that we are still in the early stages of organizational adaptation to new IT for supply chain management, including the use of modeling systems.

Instrumental versus Interpretive Decision Making

> The third issue is whether decision making is an *instrumental* activity or an *interpretive* activity. Are decisions to be understood primarily in terms of the way they fit into a problem solving, adaptive calculus? Or are they to be understood primarily in terms of the way they fit into efforts to establish individual and social meaning?[14]

Our response to this issue is to suggest that instrumental and interpretive activities need to be harmonized if a company is to achieve competitive supply chain management. The supply chain decision database for a medium- or large-sized company may contain 100,000 numbers or more. It is derived from a much larger transactional database. Decision makers cannot successfully interpret the economic meaning of these numbers based solely on intuition, reports summarizing raw data, and social interactions with other decision makers. Conversely, plans suggested by modeling systems cannot and should not be implemented without managerial interpretation of their individual and social meaning.

In this subsection, we examine the harmonization of instrumental and interpretive activities from the following four perspectives:

- Instrumental versus interpretive activity in operational planning.
- Instrumental versus interpretive analysis in strategic and tactical planning.
- Coordination of managers and analysts.
- Instrumental decision making requires business process redesign.

Instrumental versus Interpretive Analysis in Operational Planning. As with earlier issues, the balance between instrumental and interpretive decision making depends on the scope of the supply chain problems being addressed. At the operational level of planning, the large number of detailed decisions to be made and the time pressure on making them dictates the extensive use of modeling systems. Still, human oversight or review of the plans suggested by the modeling systems is needed to fine-tune them to accommodate individual and social meaning.

For example, a routing system for daily deliveries might occasionally produce a route with stops at locations A, B, and C, where A and C are close together but B is quite distant from both A and C. According to the delivery windows for the three locations, such a route might actually be efficient from an optimization viewpoint. Nevertheless, the driver of the route would resent the extra travel and the implicit risk that it implies. If traffic proves unexpectedly heavy on the streets leading from A to B and from B to C, he could be late in making the delivery to location C. Being aware of the driver's concern, the router might manually revise the route to exclude the delivery to location B, perhaps by assigning it to another route with locations near B.

This example illustrates an important challenge for the modeling practitioner. As much as possible, an optimization model for operational planning should accommodate individual and social meaning in its instrumental search for a good solution. As we discussed in Section 5.2, the unified optimization methodology applied to vehicle routing divides computation into route generation and route selection. Thus, for the above example, we would reflect the driver's needs for a concentrated route in the route-generation routine by a constraint limiting the distance traveled between successive stops in a route. This distance might be a parameter controlled by the router.

Instrumental versus Interpretive Analysis in Strategic and Tactical Planning. At the other extreme, strategic supply chain planning has been largely an interpretive activity until recently, when modeling systems have begun to be applied. Interpretive activity is appropriate at the initial stage of a strategic planning exercise when senior managers interact to identify long-term actions open to the company and the consequences and uncertainties associated with these actions. After that, models and modeling systems can and should be employed to assist them in understanding the complex interactions and ripple effects among their strategic options. Of course, model results will require further interpretive activity, which in turn will require further modeling analysis, and so on. The cycle between interpretive and instrumental analysis should continue until senior managers are willing "to bet the company" on the actions they have chosen for implementation.

In many companies, tactical supply chain planning problems also remains largely an interpretive activity. Decisions about where products are made and how markets are served are based on rules accepted by plant and distribution managers as organizationally sound. The rules are rarely verified by a comprehensive supply chain model. This lack of instrumental activity is more pronounced for tactical planning than it is for strategic planning. Unlike modeling analysis of strategic planning decisions, which can be undertaken as an ad hoc activity that is not in the mainstream of running the company, routine analysis of tactical decisions using a modeling system requires an extensive organizational infrastructure.

Managerial incentives are an important source of conflict between instrumental and interpretive activity. In principle, managerial incentives should reflect overall supply chain efficiencies, but this is not yet the case in many companies. Thus, there can easily be social resistance by managers to instrumental plans developed by a model that produce metrics reflecting unfavorably or even neutrally on their performances. Some companies have attempted to tie incentives to overall supply chain performance, but to date there is little information about their form or impact. The difficulty is to link an individual manager's performance to that of an entire supply chain. This is an area requiring applied research and experimentation.

Coordination of Managers and Analysts. Instrumental supply chain decision making requires analysts dedicated to the tasks of preparing input data, generating and optimizing models, reviewing model results, and releasing plans. Occasionally, managers serve as their own analysts, but usually the roles are distinct. Most companies have not yet fully realized the importance of supply chain analysts. As a result, issues surrounding their job definitions and career paths have not yet been articulated and examined.

Supply chain analysts must also work closely with managers responsible for implementing decisions determined by a model or by management exception. In the vernacular of issue 3, decisions suggested by a model that are implemented more or less automatically constitute instrumental activities. Decisions suggested by a model that are perceived by the analyst or her manager, or flagged by the modeling system, as being irregular and requiring human intervention constitute interpretive activities. Management by exception of such decisions may invoke instrumental activities if the modeling system is used to further analyze them. Conversely, management by exception may invoke interpretive activities if the analyst or her manager solves such problems by communicating and negotiating with other analysts or managers within the company.

Harmonization of the analyst with the manager, and among analysts and managers with overlapping responsibilities, requires a collective agreement about when supply chain decision making is an instrumental activity using a modeling system and when it is an interpretive activity requiring communication and negotiation. Moreover, the company must recognize that the efficiency of its supply chain design and operations is highly dependent on the efficacy of the modeling systems it selects and deploys and on the resulting quality of the collective agreements it reaches. The company must make a conscious effort to promote a balance between exploitation using existing modeling systems and exploration of new systems as technology advances.

Instrumental Decision Making Requires Business Process Redesign. We have just argued that disdain for instrumental supply chain planning is not a viable option in today's world. The need for advanced, instrumental decision making is well understood, and initiatives are underway in many companies to acquire modeling systems. Unfortunately, the business process redesign needed to effectively employ instrumental systems is poorly understood. Too often, senior managers view supply chain planning using modeling systems as a mechanistic endeavor that requires little adaptation to be fully effective. After buying and installing a software package, they expect instant rewards.

Instrumental exercises with a modeling system fail when the company has not implemented processes for systematically gathering data, performing analyses, and interpreting and disseminating plans. Moreover, as changes occur within the company and among its customers and vendors, processes are not in place that allow supply chain managers to explore new actions, and possibly new analytical tools, to ensure that instrumental decision making evolves to meet new decision-making needs. These barriers to instrumental planning of the company's supply chain can be overcome if historical social meanings used in interpretive planning processes are consciously and deliberately transformed into new meanings that entail wider application of modeling systems in achieving fact-based planning.

Supply Chain Management as an Interacting Ecology

> The fourth issue is whether outcomes of decision processes are seen as primarily attributable to the actions of *autonomous actors* or to the systemic properties of an *interacting ecology.* Is it possible to describe decisions as resulting from intentions, identities, and interests of independent actors? Or is it necessary to emphasize the ways in which individual actors, organizations, and societies fit together?[15]

This issue speaks directly to the motivation behind supply chain management. Recognizing that their supply chain activities are designed and executed by an interacting ecology of managers that is not as efficient as it can and should be, companies are seeking modeling systems to improve performance and gain competitive advantage. Despite this interest, modeling practitioners must be prudent and realistic in their recommendations. Although proposed or extant modeling systems might be technologically capable of significantly improving supply chain management in a company, considerable determination, resources, and time will be needed to adapt the organization to effectively use such tools. This is especially true for planning problems in the large, gray area between short-term, myopic operational planning and long-term, episodic strategic planning.

Modeling and planning issues linked to hierarchical planning discussed in Chapter 2 are relevant to processes for overcoming inefficient and unresponsive behavior of the company's interacting supply chain ecology. The haphazard manner in which intertemporal decisions are made needs to be replaced by disciplined, repetitive processes for analyzing decisions using modeling systems. At the same time, because modeling systems cannot replace managerial judgment, these instrumental processes need to be combined with interpretive processes before supply chain plans are released. New working relationships between analysts and their managers are required to harmonize instrumental and interpretive decision making. New forms of matrix organizations must be devised where managers with decision-making responsibilities in focused functional areas also participate in broader supply chain planning activities.

Flexible and powerful information and modeling systems are available to support such new supply chain ecologies; the missing essentials are organizational processes for exploiting them. The optimistic view is that companies will soon develop such processes and associated learning experiences. The expectation and hope is not that modeling systems will replace human decision makers but rather that the implicit, and as yet unrealized, benefits of the information revolution to improved supply chain decision making will soon be achieved.

12.3 Information Technology as Competitive Advantage

This section examines elements of a company's IT strategy that can lead to competitive advantage. Much of our discussion relates to effective IT practices and process redesign across the full spectrum of a company's activities and in companies that only sell services. Whenever possible, we will focus on supply chain management, which, more than other areas of management, requires fact-based decision making that relies on analysis of large, numerical databases. Success with new IT approaches for supply chain management can point the way to innovations in other areas.

We begin with a brief history of IT as competitive advantage. After that, we apply the resource-based view of the firm to study how a firm can create unique, valuable IT resources. In the following subsection, we discuss specific attributes of IT resources that can be exploited in achieving competitive advantage.

Recent History of IT as Competitive Advantage

Prior to 1990, managers and scholars were generally upbeat about the contributions that IT could make to a firm's competitive advantage.[16] Although paybacks from investments in IT were difficult to measure, it was commonly believed that such investments yielded positive net returns to the company through greater efficiency and managerial expertise. Moreover, the company's organizational structure could be expected to effortlessly adapt to evolving IT developments.

During the late 1980s and well into the 1990s, scholarly and managerial opinions moved in the opposite direction. Empirical studies in several industries found no discernable link between information technology and competitive advantage.[17] As a result, scholars began to question the value of investments in IT. Clearly, computers and information systems could not be discarded, but they felt that many firms were spending too much on IT and, at the same time, not adapting to use it effectively.

As competition and globalization increased during the 1990s, and offerings from software firms expanded and improved, the notion that a company could survive without continuous improvements in IT became a dead issue. Since the mid-1990s, managers have come to accept the necessity of IT to their company's competitive advantage, but not its sufficiency. In other words, they accept that, without acquiring and exploiting appropriate IT, they will be at a competitive disadvantage, but information technology alone will not suffice to ensure them competitive advantage.[18]

The emergence of IT resources as necessary but not sufficient for competitive advantage is due to several, overlapping factors. First, companies today acquire software from development firms that are economically motivated to create and sell their systems as commodities. Thus, improvements in supply chain management and other activities due to new software systems are available to all firms that can afford to acquire and implement them. Although modest customization of these systems may be possible, it is rarely sufficient to provide the firm with competitive advantage.

Second, software and hardware must be combined with human and organizational learning and expertise to become truly effective. As we discuss below and in the following section, these developments require considerable time, resources, and a commitment to business process redesign. Third, important software and associated reengineering efforts, such as those associated with ERP systems, have often proven disappointing, in effect flattening the playing field to a mediocre level. These frustrations, along with recent concerns about Y2K problems, have inhibited the creation of effective supply chain modeling systems and supporting business processes.

Resource-Based Analysis

The resource-based view of the firm discussed in Chapter 7 provides insightful concepts for formulating strategies to achieve competitive advantage through IT.[19] According to the theory, a firm's sustained competitive advantage depends on the creation of immobile, heterogeneous resources. These are resources that are valuable, unique to the firm, and cannot be stolen, substituted for, or imitated. Specifically, valuable IT resources may survive competitive pressures if they are protected by barriers to imitation, which we now review.

Time Compression Diseconomies. Considerable passage of time is needed to train humans to competently employ new IT and for organizations to adapt to exploit it. Many supply chain modeling systems require significant training and involve an extended learning curve. And, as we discuss below, many organizations are only in the early stages of adapting to them.

Historical Uniqueness. Many resources prove valuable almost by accident of location or product. For example, a company may be the first to have manufacturing and/or distribution facilities in a geographical location near a growing market. This barrier is also called first-mover advantage; a firm that has moved first in selling to a particular market can often fend off later competitors, especially if there are significant switching costs for the firm's customers. First-mover advantage is relevant to software companies selling transactional and analytical IT systems for supply chain management. Although a company may not be totally pleased with its installed software, it may be reluctant to invest additional large sums for an uncertain improvement. The same ideas obtain for supply chain companies selling services that have an important IT component; for example, vendor-managed inventories that are administered in large part by a superior inventory management system.

Connections among Resources. This barrier to competition is particularly relevant to IT resources because such resources are not inherently valuable but only serve to render other supply chain resources valuable. An example occurred in the deployment of production planning and scheduling software in an industrial gases company. In this company, physical resources and their costs were fixed in the short and medium terms, whereas electric power and energy costs contributed as much as 60% of total operating costs, depending on the plant. Using proprietary chemical engineering and modeling software, the company was able to reduce power and energy costs by several percentage points, thereby achieving a significant competitive edge in selling its commodity products.

Causal Ambiguity. This phenomenon is an extension of the previous one to situations where valuable connections among resources in a firm's portfolio are poorly understood and therefore cannot be easily imitated. The lack of understanding may be due to cultural or social complexities not fully under the control of company managers. The point is that if such connections are not well understood, they are difficult to imitate. For example, due to his technical insights and a close working relationship with the company's routers, an IT manager in a pharmaceutical company perceives deficiencies in routes produced by a customized routing system used for daily delivery of the company's products. Further analysis reveals that the deficiencies are the result of an expansion of delivery hours from 9 A.M. to 5 P.M. to 6 A.M. to 9 P.M. and the hiring of part-time drivers, which necessitates refinement in the logic of the routing algorithms. Once implemented, the company regains its industry leadership in cost per delivery.

Attributes of IT as Possible Sources of Competitive Advantage

In the previous subsection, we discussed strategic factors that can contribute to IT as competitive advantage. In this subsection, we examine how four attributes of IT might contribute to a firm's competitive advantage from the research-based view.[20]

Access to Capital. Companies have been making large capital investments in IT for decades, although recent ERP system implementation projects costing \$50 million, or more, appear to be reaching new heights. The risks, both technological and market driven, of these projects are also large. An IT development project is exploratory in nature and therefore subject to possible failures as the result of implementation difficulties, cost overruns, completion delays, substandard performance, or hardware and software incompatibilities. Market risks refer to failure of an IT system to be sufficiently accepted or demanded by the company's customers even if it succeeds technically. We currently see many e-commerce companies failing to reach sufficient volume in the sale of their products to consumers to justify the investment in IT and physical infrastructure.

Clearly, some companies in an industry may be better positioned to make major investments in IT. It is unlikely, however, that only one firm in an industry will be able to raise the capital needed for a critical IT implementation. Moreover, through implicit and explicit learning across the industry, a successful, innovative IT development will probably be imitated by other firms at lower cost and risk. The innovator firm could try to maintain its advantage by implementing new innovations, but such efforts can quickly become counterproductive due to time compression diseconomies. In addition, the innovative company often would prefer to exploit its successful IT implementation to obtain a healthy return on its investment rather than to seek new investments. Thus, IT investments per se are necessary but not sufficient for competitive advantage.

Proprietary Technology. A firm possessing valuable proprietary technology, either through patents or secrecy, can achieve competitive advantage. Patents protecting IT are rare, and when they do exist, they usually offer little protection against imitation. Software can be recoded relatively easily and can be modified to the extent that patent violation would be difficult to establish. Hardware is generally sold as a commodity, and exotic hardware configurations are easy to imitate. Similarly, proprietary IT is difficult to keep secret due to workforce mobility, reverse engineering, and informal communication among scientists and technicians. Thus, we must look for other attributes of IT to find the means for the firm to achieve competitive advantage.

Technical IT Skills. Technical IT skills include knowledge of programming languages, experience with operating systems, experience in constructing Web sites, and an understanding of system integration issues. Until quite recently, technical IT skills were considered an unlikely source of possible competitive advantage because they were assumed to be spread homogeneously across competing firms. In other words, skilled IT human resources were assumed to be a commodity that could be acquired as needed by any firm. In addition, because the work performed by IT personnel is generally structured and well codified, an occasional departing worker could be replaced by a new one without a long break-in period.

Today's IT labor market is much less perfect for several reasons. Individuals with superior IT skills are in short supply. Even if a company can attract them with high salaries, they are liable to quickly move on to positions in other companies at still higher salaries. Moreover, many individuals with strong IT skills prefer working at high-tech firms, especially e-commerce and other firms that offer them stakes in their companies. This strategy can backfire, however, if the price of the firm's publicly traded shares drop significantly. Finally, because IT is changing so rapidly, many firms are hard pressed to codify work activities, which exacerbates the problem of replacing departed personnel. Thus, in today's labor market, any firm that can attract, retain, and retrain workers with superior IT skills should consider them as heterogeneous resources. Exploitation requires proficient IT management to ensure that the technical skills are effectively applied to managing other resources in the firm.

Many firms face difficulties staffing their IT departments to develop and support the full range of IT systems needed to manage their supply chains in a competitive manner. An increasingly attractive alternative for these firms is to outsource some of their IT needs. For example, some firms are seeking long-term arrangements with consulting companies to periodically assist senior management in making strategic supply chain studies using a modeling system. The consulting company would be responsible for updating the supply chain decision database each time a new study is initiated and for performing the study in cooperation with the firm's senior management. The Internet offers intriguing possibilities for streamlining these studies, especially for medium- and small-sized companies that cannot afford the fees associated with large, in-house consulting projects.

Managerial IT Skills. IT managers oversee IT staff activities concerned with the design, development, and exploitation of IT applications to support and enhance other business functions in the firm and those connecting the firm to its suppliers and customers. To effectively manage these activities, they must have the ability to understand and appreciate the business needs of functional managers, suppliers, and customers. They must also have interpersonal skills that promote constructive working relationships with these managers. Finally, IT managers have the important responsibility of broadly monitoring IT innovations and anticipating future IT needs of the company.

Managerial IT skills will contribute to a firm's competitive advantage because they tend to be protected by the barriers to imitation discussed in the previous subsection. In particular, managerial IT skills are often developed over long periods of time, with experience being gained by trial and error over hundred or thousands of problem-solving situations, which invoke barriers due to time compression diseconomies, and causal ambiguity. Relationships of friendship and trust leading to successful working relationships require years to develop and therefore invoke historical uniqueness.

Successful working relationships between IT managers and other functional managers are often difficult to achieve due to culture conflicts. Conflicts arise among the needs and goals of supply chain managers; modeling system developers, who are exploratory in their approach to decision making; and IT administrators, who are exploitative. This tension, and its resolution for supply chain management systems, is discussed in detail in Section 12.4. An IT manager who can overcome such conflicts to combine valuable IT resources with complementary human and business resources will contribute significantly to the firm's competitive advantage. In the next two subsections, we discuss these complementary resources.

Complementary Organizational Resources

Our discussion can be summarized by observing that the firm has the following three options for achieving competitive advantage through IT:

> (1) Reinvent IT advantages perpetually through continuous, leading-edge IT innovations; (2) move first and erect unassailable first-mover advantages; or, (3) embed (IT) in organizations in such a way as to produce valuable, sustainable resource complementarity.[21]

Of these, the first two are not practical. The long and steep learning curve associated with many IT innovations does not allow them to be continuously replaced. Moreover, before committing to a risky IT innovation for supply chain management, an IT manager may correctly choose to observe its success or failure in other companies. Because new IT hardware and off-the-shelf software are sold as commodities, it is difficult for the firm to create unassailable first-mover advantages based only on them.

Thus, the firm has little choice but to follow the third option, which has been identified by scholars over the years as the surest path to developing and applying IT for competitive advantage. The desire to fuse IT resources with "latent, difficult-to-imitate, firm-specific advantages embodied in existing (h)uman and (b)usiness resources" is the impetus behind integrated supply chain management.[22] In the paragraphs that follow, we discuss the interaction of IT with these complementary resources.

Complementary Human Resources. The need to combine technological resources with complementary human resources at a fundamental organizational level has long been recognized by scholars. Nevertheless, the business community did not become seriously introspective about synergies between IT and their organizational structure until around 1990, prompted by global competition, accelerating changes in technology, and popular business books.[23] The notion that IT makes possible and requires organizational flattening, openness, and integration finally entered the mainstream of corporate thinking about that time.

Ten years later, despite considerable but erratic progress, many managers would agree that companies are still grappling with the difficulty of deriving sustainable competitive advantage from IT. The issues discussed in Sections 12.1 and 12.2 about the tension between rational and political decision making in the firm are highly relevant to these problems. Modeling systems for supply chain management provide an important, but not yet widely appreciated, frame or structure for combining IT with human resources to achieve such competitive advantage.

The following seven human and organizational resources potentially can be combined with IT resources to achieve competitive advantage:[24]

1. *Open organization.* Because a primary purpose of IT is to facilitate the dissemination of information, it is clearly necessary and desirable that artificial barriers to such dissemination be eliminated. The implication is that firms must abandon traditional hierarchies based on "knowledge as power" in favor of open, flatter, leaner organizations where managers at all levels have access to whatever information will help them perform their tasks. Many firms have accepted in principle the need for such changes but have failed to fully realize them in practice because their impact on processes and culture, accompanied by organizational resistance, have been underestimated. Such resistance may be partly intergenerational, suggesting that many firms must wait for retirement of senior managers whose formative years were spent in firms where IT was not a pervasive factor.
2. *Organizational consensus.* We have argued several times that organizational openness requires trust and cooperation. IT innovators must seek to reduce conflict over decision making when it occurs and foster the exchange of information and ideas across functional boundaries. Approaches for soliciting, evaluating, and reconciling multiple views to achieve consensus must be actively sought and promoted.
3. *CEO commitment.* The company needs visionary support from its CEO when it seeks to explore and exploit innovations in IT. Calculated risk taking, such as the implementation and application of a supply chain modeling system, should be encouraged and rewarded. Unfortunately, the evidence suggests that, at least until recently, many CEOs find IT threatening, too often support the status quo, and exhibit a commitment to IT innovation that is shallow and uninformed. Some scholars suggest that such attitudes cannot persist; they suggest that ". . . business strategy and achieving superior performance are essentially about knowing how to compete in the Information Age. . . ."[25]
4. *Organizational flexibility.* Organizational flexibility refers largely to business process changes to exploit new IT. When considering such changes, scholars refer to three levels of flexibility. First-order change is superficial and comprises incremental modifications to existing processes but no significant change in the status quo. Second-order change involves some adoption of new processes that radically modify the status quo, but often on an ad hoc basis. Third-order change refers to shifts in organizational culture that foster an ongoing capability for change.
5. *Integration of IT and organizational strategy.* Many strategic options in supply chain management can only be fully evaluated and supported by IT innovations, including wider application of modeling systems. For example, in considering its strategic outlook, a manufacturer of paint coatings seeking to increase its net revenues and return on assets wants a modeling system that coordinates upstream production of resins with downstream production in several SKUs of diverse product lines. A rule-based approach to such decisions

can be seriously suboptimal because it will be slow to recognize changes in the markets and in internal operating efficiencies. The company must commit to a rigorous analysis of its strategy using a modeling system, and to the adoption of new business processes for ongoing use of the modeling system to reevaluate its strategy as events within and outside the company evolve.

6. *Human expertise in supply chain management.* By its very nature, human expertise in supply chain activities such as purchasing, manufacturing, transportation, or warehouse management is complementary to benefits from IT in general and modeling systems in particular. Consider, for example, an industrial chemicals company with production engineers who are highly skilled in setting up and controlling equipment to manufacture new products. In evaluating plans for a portfolio of possible new products for the coming year, which were proposed either by customers or the company's sales personnel, models can be used to advantage in deciding how to exploit these human skills.

   First, descriptive models based on historical data should be developed to forecast costs and learning curves for the new products. Second, an optimization model that maximizes net revenues from the manufacture and sale of all the company's products should be constructed and exercised to determine which new products compete successfully with existing products for scarce manufacturing resources. Although a primary purpose of the optimization model is to evaluate decisions about new products for the coming year, its planning horizon should be considerably longer to assess their longer-term profitability.

   The modeling systems can also serve to refine the intuition of the production engineers. Surprises among decisions about proposed new products that are either selected or rejected by the optimization model can be analyzed to pinpoint manufacturing resources that perhaps should be expanded or reduced. Human judgment can then be used to identify manufacturing options that expand scarce resources and new product options that better exploit current, underutilized resources.

   The skillful IT manager must seek to promote such synergy. Modeling systems must accurately reflect the major constraints and goals of supply chain managers. At the operational level of planning, they should serve to exploit the company's supply chain resources and human expertise in managing them by exploring the operational solution space. At the strategic level of planning, analysts exercising the modeling systems should widely explore the strategic solution space by considering a range of options and by running multiple scenarios.

7. *IT training.* Finally, organizational commitment to IT training is critical to the fusion of IT with the human resources discussed in the preceding paragraphs. Because much IT training is broadly available as a commodity, the company's IT training strategy must include activities that enhance specific resources and capabilities within the firm if it is to contribute to its competitive advantage. Moreover, in today's IT labor market, an important factor affecting the realization of superior IT training is the company's ability to hire IT and functional employees who have sufficient education and motivation to absorb such training.

Complementary Business Resources. Achieving and sustaining competitive advantage by fusing IT and business resources is the essence of integrated supply chain management. In earlier chapters we discussed approaches for coordinating geographically diverse, physical supply chain resources and exploiting supplier and customer relationships. Business processes supporting coordination must rely heavily on Transactional and Analytical IT. In most companies, significant business process redesign is needed to achieve effective coordination. We pursue this topic in greater depth in Section 12.5.

12.4 Exploitative versus Exploratory IT Developments

Our discussions in Chapter 2 about the differences between Transactional and Analytical IT reflect the organizational tension between exploitation and exploration of data and intelligence. ERP and other transactional data systems are exploitative; they employ software and invoke processes for simplifying and standardizing the meaning, format, and management of corporate data. If done well, such exploitation can lead to efficient and reliable communication of data across the company and between the company and its suppliers and customers. But, as we have argued above, exploitative efforts alone are limited in their ability to help supply chain managers make good decisions.

By contrast, modeling systems are exploratory; they employ analytical tools for searching complex decision spaces to discover optimal, or demonstrably good, supply chain plans. Design and validation exercises for modeling systems are also exploratory. In performing these exercises, modeling practitioners and system implementers seek an effective balance between a model's complexity and its accuracy in describing supply chain decision problems. If done well, such exploration can produce efficient and reliable tools to support managerial decision making that leads to competitive supply chain costs, while maintaining or improving customer service. But risk taking and experimentation, both in the development and the application of these systems, must be carefully managed or the company may too often suffer losses rather than reliable gains.

Conflicts between exploitative and exploratory approaches are unavoidable when developing and applying modeling systems for supply chain management. Superior IT management skills are needed to navigate the stormy waters of opposing cultures to fully reap the benefits of a modeling system. As depicted by the triangle shown in Figure 12.1, the development and use of a modeling system requires productive conversation among three groups with diverse mind-sets—supply chain managers and analysts (clients), modeling system developers (explorers), and IT administrators (exploiters).

In many instances, the supply chain managers, supply chain analysts, and IT administrators are employees of the company whose supply chain is to be analyzed by the modeling system, but the system developer is an external software company.

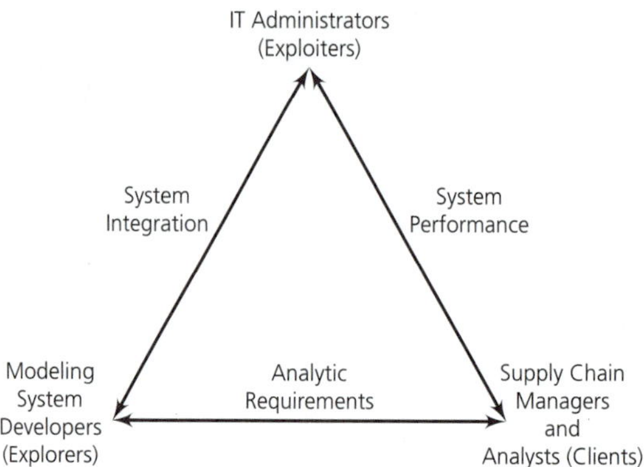

Figure 12.1
Exploration versus exploitation of modeling systems

The client company will acquire either an off-the-shelf or a customized modeling system from this software company. Today, few manufacturing and distribution companies have internal operations research groups of sufficient size and expertise to develop modeling systems. Even if a company were willing to invest in this internal capability, it would find it difficult to assemble such a group because individuals with the requisite combination of operations research and IT technical skills are in short supply.

The organizational separation of IT administrators and modeling system developers may be advantageous because it reduces tensions that would exist if the two groups resided in the same company. Of course, they must still work together. Requirements for integrating the modeling system into the company's computer network must be established at the time acquisition or development of the system is being considered. Conversations between modeling system developers and IT administrators, who will be responsible for embedding the modeling system in the company's integrated system and maintaining its integrity, are obviously important. However, such conversations cannot be allowed to inhibit those between the modeling systems developers and the managers who have the supply chain problems.

The issues involved in striking a balance between exploitation and exploration vary across the three stages in the life cycle of a modeling system: acquisition or development, use, and enhancement. We discuss each in turn in the following paragraphs.

Acquisition or Development of a Modeling System

The choice between acquiring an off-the-shelf modeling system or developing a customized modeling system may be difficult. From an IT perspective, implementation and performance risks may be significantly reduced if an off-the-shelf system can be acquired, presuming one that adequately models the given class of problems is available. It is more likely that a suitable off-the-shelf system can be found for strategic or tactical planning than for operational planning, which entails greater detail specific to the company. Assessing the suitability of an off-the-shelf system can be difficult because the supply chain managers who will apply the system, with the help of their analysts, will probably not have sufficient knowledge to evaluate the reality underlying marketing claims made by off-the-shelf software companies. To overcome this ambiguity, the company should seek independent judgment from knowledgeable modeling practitioners, either employees of the company who have backgrounds in operations research or outside consultants.

A central concern should be the extent to which a proposed modeling system uses optimization models to analyze the given class of problems or whether it uses decision rules based on historical experience. Optimization models are preferred because they provide much greater scope for exploration of the decision space. Decision rules may be easier for the manager to understand, but their use limits the scope of analysis and, in some cases, may suggest plans that are seriously flawed from an economic viewpoint.

Whether an off-the-shelf or a customized modeling system is being considered, the modeling system developers should enter into an appropriately lengthy conversation with the clients about their supply chain decision problems. The aim of the conversation is to ensure that the existing or proposed analytical capabilities of the modeling system will be suitably aligned with these problems. Achieving such an alignment is an important responsibility of the modeling system developers. It is an exploratory activity based on their modeling and modeling system experience and expertise. Such skill is very rarely found among IT administrators whose organizational and professional identities are focused on maintaining efficient and reliable systems and in keeping abreast of the latest developments in IT.

Of course, a software company may be willing to provide minor customization of its off-the-shelf system. Extensive customization is generally not offered because the software company does not want the burden of supporting multiple versions of its systems. Thus, the supply chain managers and their company may face a difficult choice between acquiring an off-the-shelf system, which has known features and performance characteristics, and a customized system, which promises to more accurately analyze the class of problems at hand but will be more risky and costly to develop. Skilled IT managers are needed to resolve this dilemma while keeping in mind that the company may find it difficult to achieve competitive advantage by deploying an off-the-shelf software commodity.

Use of a Modeling System

Effective use of a modeling system to support supply chain decision making requires a hand off from modeling system developers (explorers) to IT administrators (exploiters). This hand off must be planned in advance to ensure a rapid and orderly transition, which is easier said than done, as witnessed by difficulties experienced by companies seeking to extend their ERP systems to incorporate modeling system capabilities. Such difficulties may arise because exploiters responsible for implementing ERP systems are poorly suited to the exploratory tasks of modeling system development.

As we discuss in the following section, new business processes are needed for effective application of data and modeling systems to supply chain management. Different processes are needed depending on the scope of the modeling analysis.

Only time will reveal the stable form of these processes and the extent to which managers will come to employ modeling systems to resolve the organizational issues surrounding decision making that we examined in the Sections 12.1 and 12.2.

Enhancement of a Modeling System

Although the focus of modeling system implementation shifts from exploration to exploitation once the system has been tested and is ready to be embedded in the company's network, the IT manager must recognize that future enhancement of the modeling system by the system developers will be important. A modeling system application will lose its effectiveness over time due to changes in the company's operations, in its competitive environment, and in technology that affects the constraints and goals for managing the company's supply chain. Thus, the company must be willing and able to periodically reexplore the form and functionality of a modeling system to identify worthwhile enhancements. This again requires IT management skill in convincing IT administrators, who may wish to sustain the status quo, of the need to reopen conversations between the system developers and the supply chain managers.

12.5 Business Process Redesign and IT

Much has been written in recent years about the successes and failures of BPR. BPR began in the early 1990s as an often quick and dirty method to improve efficiency by using IT to replace people. By the mid 1990s, it was viewed by many as an oversold fad that was applied too narrowly.[26] This deficiency has been recognized and companies take a broader view of the needs and benefits of BPR, especially as it aims to exploit developments in IT.

In this subsection, we examine briefly the interplay between BPR and IT infrastructure, with an emphasis on applications of modeling systems to supply chain management. Case studies suggest that BPR is often motivated by a firm's need to improve cross-functional coordination, which is both dependent on and prompted by the company's existing or proposed IT infrastructure.[27] Thus, we have another example of integrated planning as a serious motivator for change within the firm.

Depending on its appropriateness and flexibility, IT may serve as an enabler or inhibitor of BPR. Although efficient and reliable information systems may enable improved supply chain processes, we will argue that modeling systems invoke such processes. In other words, if the firm wishes to achieve superior supply chain management, which requires analysis with modeling systems, it must create new processes that facilitate systematic use of such systems and exploit insights provided by them. We provide a detailed illustration of this below.

The IT infrastructure is made up of technical and managerial expertise leading to the communication of timely and reliable data, decision support, and connectivity within and outside the firm. For completeness, we have provided Table 12.1, which lists, from the perspective of the IT specialist, typical firmwide IT infrastructure services needed for business process redesign. The core services are those that will probably be found in most companies. The additional services may be found in companies that have more advanced capabilities.

The absence of specific references to models and Analytical IT in Table 12.1 illustrates the current focus by IT scholars and consultants on Transactional IT. One could argue that the boldface services corresponding to functional integration imply modeling system development and application, but most IT professionals have not yet realized this connection. Moreover, they have not yet recognized the importance

Table 12.1 IT infrastructure and services

Core Information Technology Infrastructure Services

1. Manage firmwide communication network services
2. **Manage groupwide or firmwide messaging services***
3. Recommend standards for at least one component of IT architecture (e.g., hardware, operating systems, data, communications)
4. Implement security, disaster planning, and business recovery services for firmwide installations and applications
5. Provide technology advice and support services
6. Manage, maintain, and support large-scale data processing facilities (e.g., mainframe operations)
7. **Manage firmwide or businesswide applications and databases***
8. Perform IS project management
9. Provide data management advice and consulting services
10. Perform IS planning for business units

Additional Information Technology Infrastructure Services

11. **Enforce IT architecture and standards***
12. Manage firmwide or business-unit workstation networks (e.g., LANs, POS)
13. Manage and negotiate with suppliers and outsourcers
14. Identify and test new technologies for business purposes
15. Develop business-unit-specific applications (usually on a chargeback or contractual basis)
16. Implement security, disaster planning, and recovery for business units
17. **Electronically provide management information (e.g., EIS)***
18. Manage business-unit-specific applications
19. **Provide firmwide or business-unit data management, including standards***
20. **Develop and manage electronic linkages to suppliers or customers***
21. **Develop a common systems development environment***
22. Provide technology education services (e.g., training)
23. Provide multimedia operations and development (e.g., videoconferencing)

Adapted from Broadbent, Weill, and St. Clair [1991]

*The boldface services are boundary crossing where they are clearly and actively integrative, supporting information flows beyond one functional area.

of living with and balancing the conflicts inherent in exploratory Analytical IT and exploitative Transactional IT.

Figure 12.2 depicts a paradigm characterizing a company's IT infrastructure in terms of **reach** and **range.**[28] Reach refers to the firm's ability to easily connect with other organizations. Developments in e-commerce are rapidly expanding this capability to a global marketplace in which all firms may easily communicate. Range refers to IT activities that the firm can carry out automatically and seamlessly with various organizations and individuals. The shaded area indicates the average reach and range of 27 firms that were surveyed in the late 1990s.[29] Developments in ERP systems are intended to extend the reach of more complex transactional activities. Internet developments are rapidly making the results of the survey obsolete by extending the reach of simple and complex transactions.

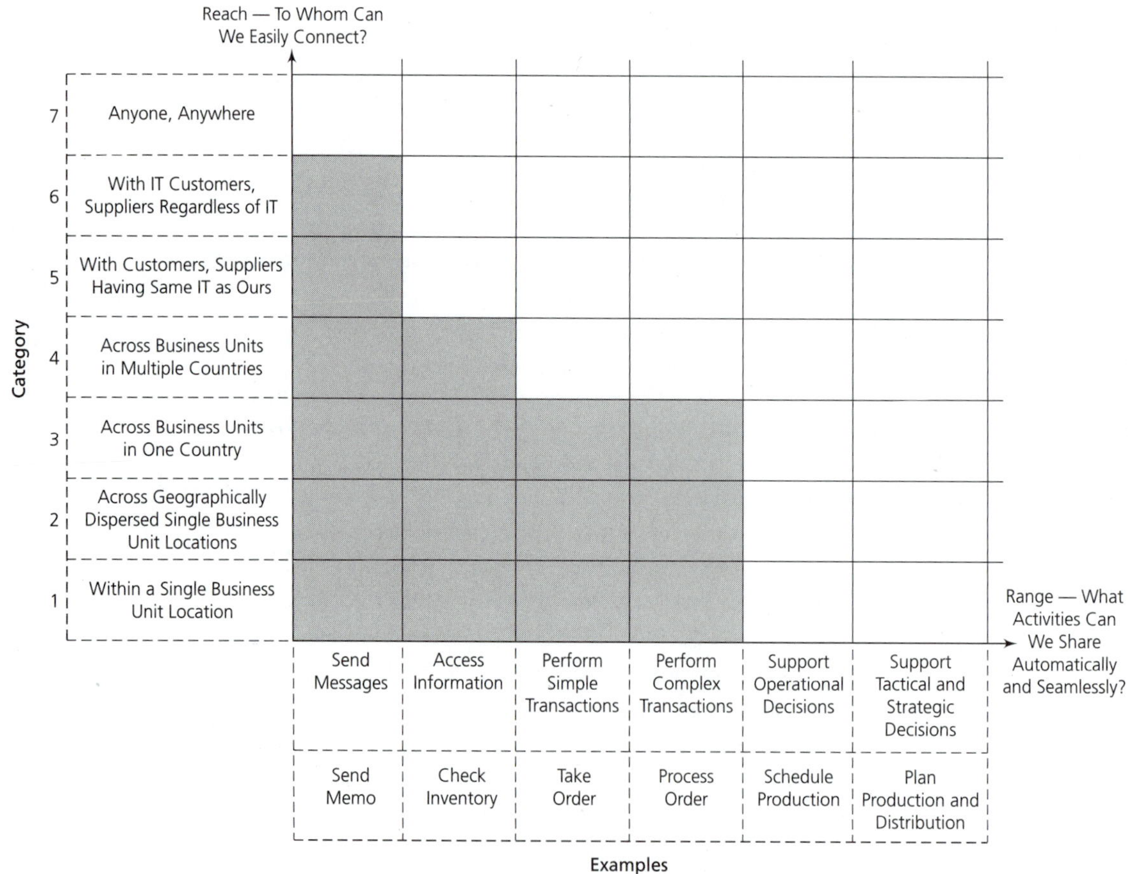

Figure 12.2
Reach and range of IT infrastructure. Adapted from Keen [1991] and Broadbent, Weill, and St. Clair [1999]

In constructing Figure 12.2, we extended the range of activities to include Analytical IT, which was ignored in earlier presentations of the reach/range paradigm. We have separated Analytical IT into "support operational decisions," which require a limited reach to category 1 and possibly 2, and "support tactical and strategic decisions," which requires a much larger range, one as far as categories 5 and 6. These Analytical IT activities emphasize the importance of creating and employing a standardized format for the supply chain decision database across the company's business units, customers, and suppliers.

Modeling Systems Invoke Business Process Redesign

Routine and repetitive modeling analysis of tactical supply chain decisions is an important but unexplored class of applications. It invokes or requires new business processes for developing and maintaining the supply chain decision database, making model runs, interpreting model results, and disseminating plans derived from these results. The requisite organizational change might better be called **business process expansion** because new data management processes, job descriptions (identities), communication protocols, and incentive schemes must be created.

We are currently working with three companies—a plumbing equipment manufacturer, a pet food manufacturer, and a beer manufacturer—where such applications are being implemented. In all three, senior management is seeking to make better decisions each month or each quarter in selecting which plants to manufacture each product line, taking into account downstream logistics costs as well as differences in manufacturing efficiencies and capacities. The companies are motivated by the promise of significant reductions in supply chain costs. They are also motivated by the promise of tighter control of supply chain operations leading to better customer service and quicker response to changing market conditions. Although the technical challenges of managing and communicating data and generating and optimizing tactical planning models are far from trivial, the more serious challenges are to foster flexible decision making and to focus organizational will in implementing new decision-making processes.

Figure 12.3 depicts the processes needed for routine tactical planning with a modeling system in a company that manufactures and distributes products. We have assumed that routine analysis is to be performed each month. At the center of the planning process is analysis using an optimization model that is performed under the direction of the company's **supply chain coordinator** with the assistance of a staff of analysts. This is a multiple-period model that is exercised once a month on a rolling horizon basis to determine specific production and distribution guidelines for the company's facilities during the coming month and beyond. The guidelines include production targets for each plant, sourcing plans for suppliers, and assignments of markets to distribution centers for sourcing of finished products.

In most companies, the position of supply chain coordinator is new and requires careful definition, especially in the authority given him to enforce guidelines. Procedures allowing production and distribution managers to negotiate exceptions to the guidelines, either before or after occurrence of the exceptions, are also required. As we discuss below, the rolling horizon analysis provides ample opportunity for the supply chain coordinator and supply chain managers to discuss and resolve contentious planning issues before the final plans for a given month must be implemented.

In selecting the supply chain coordinator, the company should seek an individual who has a broad knowledge of the company's operations and respect of her peers. The coordinator and her staff must also have close working relationships with IT personnel in developing and maintaining data acquisition systems supporting the monthly tactical planning exercise. This last requirement presumes that the company's IT department has individuals who have the requisite skills and experience in supporting supply chain data and operations.

As shown in Figure 12.3, analysis is based on three types of databases: corporate, external, and the supply chain decision databases; the latter is linked directly to the optimization modeling system. Four new processes for exploiting these data and performing the modeling analysis are needed; they are discussed in the following subsections.

Data Collection and Transformation Processes. Chapter 6 was devoted entirely to a discussion of the form and content of the supply chain decision database and how it is derived from transactional databases. Our concern here is with business processes to support its construction and maintenance. These processes are combinations of automated IT procedures for communicating and transforming data with human processes for encoding new and revised data, reviewing data, and resolving data errors and omissions. The automated IT procedures should include routines for checking data errors. Although a very high percentage of data transfer may be automated, situations will arise that require the intervention of human judgment to correct errors or update stale data. Analysts working for the supply chain coordinator will be responsible for striking a pragmatic balance between rejecting seriously flawed data and pursuing perfectly accurate data.

The division of labor between human and automated IT procedures in updating data depends on the company and the industry. It is also changing rapidly as technology evolves. For example, some companies still rely on physical inventory counts to correct or fine-tune their information, whereas others rely exclusively on electronic means. Similarly, forecasts of demand for finished products over the coming months may be produced exclusively by automated forecasting models, or they may entail some human oversight and intervention to eliminate outliers and other anomalies that the models cannot or should not accommodate.

The tactical planning cycle requires teamwork among the coordinator and his analysts at company headquarters who are responsible for creating the supply chain decision database and making model runs, managers and analysts at the company's plants and distribution centers, and managers and analysts at facilities operated by suppliers and customers. Interactions with managers and analysts outside the company, including individuals working for other business units of the same corporation, may be more difficult to achieve because their IT infrastructure might be different. This important, but not widely recognized, challenge faces companies seeking to manage virtual supply chains over the Internet of which they are a part.

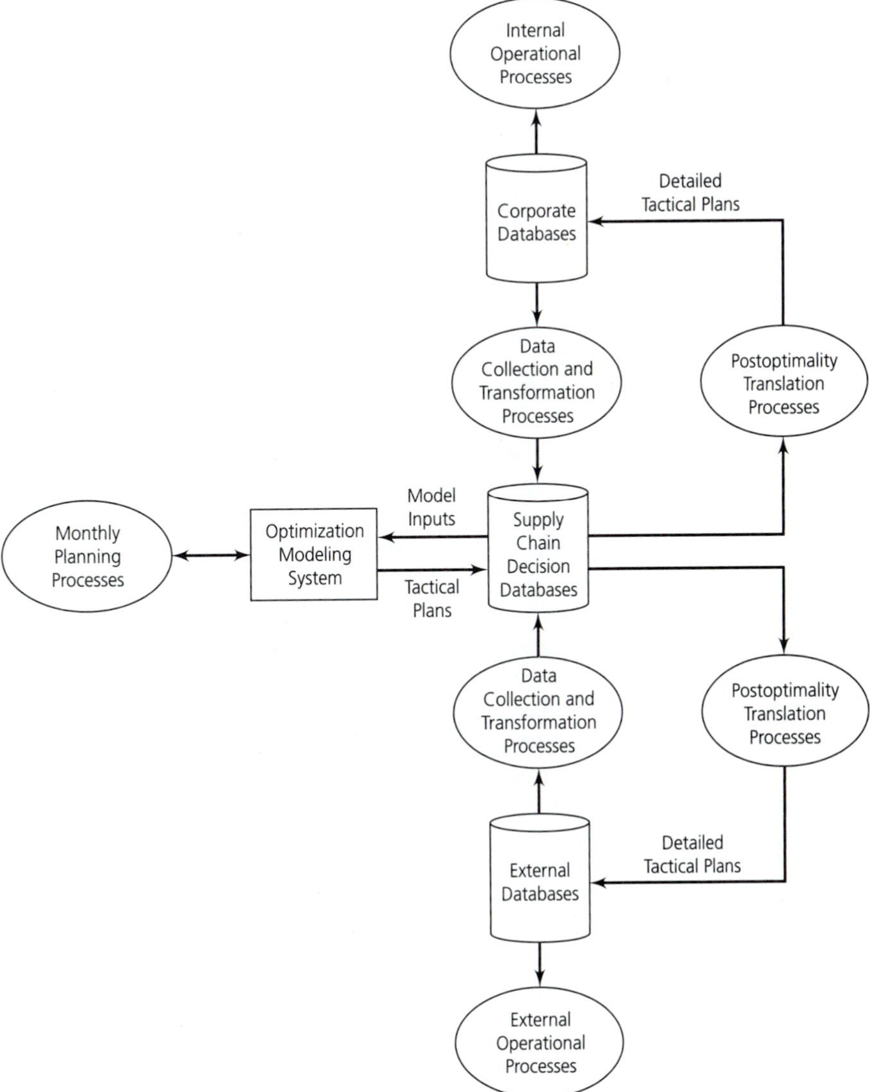

Figure 12.3
Data and process flow monthly tactical planning using an optimization modeling system

Monthly Planning Processes. We assume the planning process called the **supply chain review** is initiated at the same time every month, leaving 2 or 3 days for supply chain analysts to firm up the integrated supply chain plan for next month. The multiple-period model is generated and optimized, perhaps under several scenarios, to finalize this plan. To be concrete, we assume the model has six periods, each 1 month long. Its objective is to minimize the cost of meeting forecasted demand for finished products over the 6-month horizon. Alternatively, if some leeway in product mix is allowed, the model will seek to maximize net revenues over the 6-month horizon.

In a given month, the model that is generated and optimized is closely related to the model used the previous month. The differences are as follows:

- The submodel describing month 1 in the previous model has been dropped.
- The submodels describing months 2 through 6 become the submodels describing periods 1 through 5; the data for these submodels, especially demand forecasts and inventories, have been revised.
- A new submodel for month 6 has been generated and added to the overall model.

In optimizing this month's model, the supply chain plan for month 1 (the coming month) is considered firm. Its guidelines are communicated to supply chain managers who are expected to adhere to them. Brief negotiations of these guidelines may take place, which might require running a few scenarios with the model, but the assumption is that major issues affecting the guidelines for this month have been resolved in past months when earlier analyses were performed.

Similarly, in optimizing this month's model, the supply chain plans for month 2 are considered semifirm. The supply chain coordinator expects to make only small adjustments to them during the next supply chain review, unless unexpected, radical changes have occurred. Finally, the supply chain plans over months 3, 4, 5, and 6 are considered preliminary. The supply chain coordinator is prepared to enter into serious, and possibly lengthy, discussions and analyses with supply chain managers about these plans. Thus, the monthly supply chain planning exercise may continue to analyze disputed decisions for months 3, 4, 5, and 6 after the plans for the coming month have been finalized.

The supply chain review may be invoked at random times if an emergency occurs that requires serious adjustment in the plans. Examples are a major equipment failure at a plant and an unexpected strike at a distribution center. The model would be modified to depict the emergency conditions and optimized to determine short-run adjustments that would best serve the company over the longer run.

Postoptimality Translation Processes. The optimization model exercised during the supply chain review employs aggregations and other approximations. Results produced by the model require transformations that reverse the aggregations and other calculations to provide supply chain details that were ignored in the tactical planning model. In particular, details about products, markets, and vendors, which were treated in an aggregated manner in the tactical model, must be disaggregated for operational planning. As discussed in Section 6.1, aggregations used in constructing the tactical planning model were selected so that subsequent disaggregations would be relatively simple to carry out. For example, in a consumer product manufacturing company, a product family might consist only of SKUs corresponding to the same finished product but packaged in different sizes and different container types. Historical breakdowns by size and container type would be employed by the disaggregation program to provide details about individual SKUs implied by the aggregate plan. Similarly, a market zone might consist of several small customers in close geographic proximity to one another. Again, using historical data, programs to disaggregate an optimal tactical plan to provide details about how SKUs are shipped to individual customers would be easy to implement.

Similar postoptimality translations are needed for conveying detailed tactical plans to external databases maintained by the company's suppliers and customers. Suppliers will require detailed information about SKUs that they are expected to ship to company facilities during the month. Customers will need to be informed of details regarding deliveries by the company to their facilities during the month.

As we noted earlier when we discussed process 1, process 3 would be largely automated. The translation programs would include data-quality routines that flag possible errors or anomalies. Human invention by supply chain analysts would be required only to resolve these errors and anomalies.

Internal and External Operational Processes. The monthly planning data fed back into corporate and external databases constitute guidelines and targets used by supply chain managers in the company and in the company's suppliers and customers to develop their operational plans for the coming days and weeks. For example, a plant manager would use production targets for her plant for the coming month, along with other data describing how the plant's capacities would be employed to meet this production, as the master production schedule for an MRP system, which would develop detailed, daily production plans by manufacturing process. Similarly, the distribution manager would use product sourcing and inventory information as inputs to a BRP system that would plan daily shipments of finished products from plants to distribution centers.

12.6 Supply Chain Coordination Processes and Incentive Contracts

In the previous section, we discussed processes that a company should follow in constructing a tactical supply chain plan each month based on data and analysis using a modeling system. Execution of the plan requires processes for coordinating actions among managers and workers responsible for operating the company's supply chain. Included are individuals employed by the company as well as those employed by the company's suppliers and customers. Incentive schemes are also required to align the goals of the managers and workers with supply chain plans that are globally economic and profitable.

Our purpose in briefly reviewing current approaches to coordination processes and incentive contracts is to highlight the need for basic and applied research in designing and using these tools to improve supply chain management. Myopic managerial incentive schemes, which are the prevalent methods, are often counterproductive in achieving global efficiency. For example, because her bonus is based on inventory targets that ignore global supply chain consequences, an inventory manager might strive to maintain low, suboptimal inventory levels. Similarly, because a plant manager's bonus depends on plant output, he may decide to manufacture large quantities of marginally profitable products that ultimately will be sold below cost. Nevertheless, incentive schemes based on total supply chain cost or net revenues may provide insufficient direction and motivation for middle managers responsible for only a small portion of the supply chain's activity. We return to a discussion of these issues at the end of the section.

Selecting Coordination Processes

The following various methods, which are not mutually exclusive, have been proposed to facilitate coordination:[30]

- **Direct supervision** based on a traditional command hierarchy
- **Standardization** that employs rules, procedures, and norms
- **Goal setting** based on the dissemination of plans or that employs metrics specifying output
- **Mutual adjustment** based on joint decision making that involves teams or other forms of liaison among managers and workers
- **Prices** that lead independent managers to make optimal decisions even though they follow their own interest

These methods ensure that autonomous groups share resources, including information, with other groups and meet the goals of the company's short- and medium-term supply chain plans.

Scholars have found that the following three factors affect working relations among coordinating groups:

- Degree of interdependence
- Extent of conflict
- Extent of uncertainty

The interdependence of supply chain activities refers to the extent to which the activities and output of a group are controlled by or depend on the activities and output of another group. These activities can be described as sequential, reciprocal, or simultaneous. Sequential activities occur among stages in a production line or when shipping finished goods from plants to distribution centers. An example of a reciprocal activity is the delivery of pallets by a pallet leasing company to a food manufacture and their eventual return by food distributors to the leasing company's depots. An example of simultaneous activities is the scheduling of parts and components from many suppliers to arrive at an automotive plant to meet next week's production plan.

Conflict among interacting groups may be the result of organizational and cultural incentives or a host of other factors. For example, we observed a large cultural difference in a paper mill plant where stationery and other fine paper products were produced. The crews that manufactured mother rolls of paper had a process manufacturing mind-set, and the crews that trimmed these rolls and treated the paper in

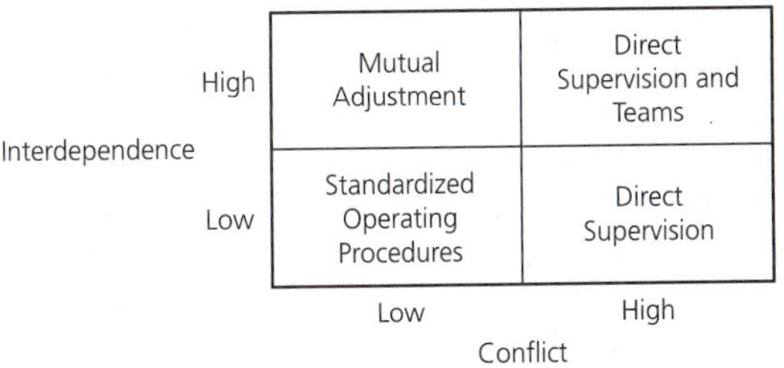

Figure 12.4
Coordination methods under different conditions of interdependence and conflict

making finished products had a job-shop mind-set. The degree of uncertainty refers to factors affecting operations such as short-term sales forecasts, production yields, and shipping times.

Assuming the degree of uncertainty is not great, Figure 12.4 depicts the options suggested in the literature for choosing one or more of the methods listed above to foster coordination.[31] When the degree of uncertainty is great, coordination requires greater use of teams or other forms of liaison among managers and workers. Of course, the company should strive to reduce conflict and uncertainty whenever and wherever possible. To a significant extent, Transactional and Analytical IT systems can serve this goal by enhancing communication and shortening the time between updating data and plans.

Principal–Agent Theories of Incentives

A principal of a firm relies on agents to do work or provide services on her behalf. The purpose of incentive contracts is to align the agents' goals with those of the principal. Many types of incentives contracts are available. They may be based on individual or group performance or some combination of the two. Some examples follow:

- **Explicit incentive pay,** such as piece-rate work or sales commissions
- **Implicit incentive pay,** based on subjective assessments of supervisors
- **Profit sharing plans,** such as employee stock ownership plans or bonuses tied to company profits
- **Gain sharing plans,** where groups of workers receive bonuses tied to the extent that common performance goals were exceeded

Of course, the possibility that an agent will be promoted to a higher-paying job is frequently used as an implicit incentive pay scheme.

For several decades, microeconomists have proposed and elaborated principal–agent theories and models as the basis for determining incentive contracts that promote efficient operations. These theories and models are consistent with theories of bounded rationality based on a decision maker's maximization of expected utility that we discussed in Section 12.1. Microeconomists refer to the possible divergence of principal and agent activities and goals as **moral hazards;** such situations occur when the agent consciously or unconsciously takes actions that are both inefficient from the principal's viewpoint and not freely observable.[32] An important purpose of incentive contracts is to mitigate these hazards.

A related problem in designing incentive contracts is the sharing of risks between the principal and the agent when agent performance is probabilistic. Specifically, this occurs when the principal can observe only a (primary) indicator of the agent's effort rather than the effort itself. Due to random events that intervene, this indicator may over- or understate the effort actually made. Thus, the principal is at risk because she might realize inferior profits due to a combination of the agent's poor effort and bad luck. Similarly, the agent's incentive pay might be less than it should be despite a superior effort because it is accompanied by bad luck in achieving the desired outcome.

Mathematical models have been developed for designing optimal incentive contracts composed of base wages pay plus incentive pay.[33] In these models, incentive pay is related to statistical analysis involving the primary indicator variable and other indicator variables that serve to reduce the unexplained variance of observed payoff. For example, the primary indicator might correspond to product sales created by the agent, and a secondary indicator might be total industry demand for that product. We omit further details of these models.

Future Research on Incentive Contracts. Developments in Transactional and Analytical IT for supply chain management have disrupted conventional thinking about incentives. In the following, we examine several areas where basic and applied research is needed to invent new forms of incentive contracts for global supply chain planning. The focus will be on incentive contracts that cover planning horizons of 1 year or shorter, which we view as long-term tactical planning down to operational planning. Our discussion assumes that new incentive contracts should be based on supply chain data and their analysis with modeling systems rather than microeconomic constructions based on functions that are difficult to measure, such as the principal's utility function or an agent's cost function for providing effort. We review research areas by posing and discussing several questions.

1. How can the principal (that is, the company, the CEO, the supply chain VP, or some other executive or committee) determine incentive contracts for supply chain managers from modeling analysis of the company's supply chain?

A comprehensive optimization model provides the principal with a rational, quantitative tool for understanding precisely the capabilities of the company's supply chain. The setting of quantitative goals and incentives for individuals or groups could follow naturally from results and insights obtained with the model. In other words, a natural component of long-term tactical planning exercises could be the computation or revision of incentive contracts for supply chain managers.

An open question is the scenario or scenarios on which to base incentive goals. For example, the principal might select a scenario that describes an idealized state of the supply chain, one in which all shipments are full truckload, all production runs are based on long-term sales forecasts, and so on. For such an analysis, the resulting supply chain goals would be unattainable standards. Alternatively, the principal might select a scenario to optimize that describes tight but attainable standards for operating the company's supply chain.

Even if we accept the principle of using integrated modeling analysis as a cornerstone in the construction of incentive contracts, we are left with the task of computing them. As we discussed above, the connection between overall supply chain performance and that of an individual supply chain manager may be weak. Some companies have dealt with this issue by determining incentive bonuses on the basis of overall company or overall supply chain performance. Such an approach may prove unsatisfying to competent managers who believe they have made more than average effort in ensuring the company's success. It seems that individual incentives can and should be derived from the details of an optimal supply chain plan that the company intends to implement for the coming year. Such incentives could be constructed from metrics derived from the plan that are specific to individual managers. This is an important area of research.

A central aspect of the microeconomic theory of incentive contracts is the derivation of schemes for sharing risk between the principal and his agents. When considering supply chain optimization models as an alternative method for incentive contracting, this requirement can be met in part by frequent use of the modeling system in a rolling horizon manner to update data, the plan, and incentive contracts. Moreover, stochastic programming models for supply chain planning are an alluring, but not yet realistic, paradigm for combining probabilistic microeconomic constructions for incentive contracts with the resource allocation capabilities of deterministic optimization models.

2. Can the hierarchy of supply chain modeling systems be employed in the computation of incentives for managers and workers in the hierarchical command structure of the company?

The hierarchy of supply chain modeling systems was discussed in Section 2.3. Informal and formal methods for integrating decisions analyzed by these systems offer the possibility of computing coherent and equitable incentive contracts for managers and workers in the chain of command. Thus, the incentive contracts of some managers would be based on their performance in making and carrying out tactical planning decisions of wide scope, whereas the incentive contracts of other managers would be based on their performance in making and carrying out operational decisions with a much narrower scope. Moreover, middle managers would serve as both principals and agents in this chain.

3. How should incentive contracts be computed for principals and agents in the separate companies of a virtual supply chain?

The computation of equitable methods for sharing reductions in cost or increases in profit is a new and unresolved problem in managing virtual supply chains for multiple companies. This problem is essentially one of incentive contracting. For some virtual supply chains, there is a dominant company that assumes the role of principal; the other companies can be treated as agents. The principal company then negotiates with the agent companies in creating incentive contracts that define and bind their activities in a productive manner. The general situation is more complicated. For some virtual supply chains, there is no dominant company. Moreover, individual companies will participate in several virtual supply chains. This issue requires considerable study.

4. In determining incentive goals for supply chain managers based on optimization models, should the principal incorporate marketing and financial decisions and constraints as well as those associated with the supply chain?

We devoted considerable discussion in earlier chapters to methods for extending supply chain models to include demand and financial management decisions, thereby optimizing after-tax net profits or some other long-term measure of company performance. In the case of a multinational corporation, the objective would be to maximize after-tax profits repatriated to the parent company. The principal must decide on the necessary and desirable scope that she wishes for the model to be used in creating incentive goals. Although a supply chain manager may have little or no control over marketing and financial decisions, his incentive contract will better reflect the principal's goals if they incorporate marketing and financial actions to be taken by the company as a whole. Of course, a model incorporating supply chain, marketing, and financial decision making raises interesting issues about coordination across major functional boundaries as well as the construction of coherent and equitable methods for computing incentive contracts. Again, this issue requires considerable study.

12.7

No Gain without Pain

Managers today face a barrage of overblown claims about the importance of new business processes and associated IT. Each fad appears with the promise that the company can make significant gains without experiencing pain. Too often, the fad quickly disappears, leaving disappointed managers in its wake. As expressed in *The Economist,*[34]

> For success in the $20-billion-a-year management consultancy business, find a fad. In recent years, total quality, culture change, core competencies, organizational flattening, benchmarking, outsourcing and downsizing have all been touted as the sole path to corporate salvation. . . . For all the hype, fad-based management usually fails to deliver. . . . (The attraction is) Instant Coffee Management: just open the jar and add water; no effort required. Worse, any manager who fails to follow the latest fad—regardless of its relevance—risks being thought unprofessional.

We contend that supply chain management, interpreted as a synonym for integrated and fact-based planning of manufacturing and distribution activities, is much more than a fad. Still, success in achieving superior supply chain management requires hard work in redesigning or refining business processes, in developing data management and modeling systems, and in adapting the organization to exploit these systems.

Stages of a Strategic Supply Chain Study

As a concrete example of the effort required to develop, validate, and exercise a modeling system, we review the typical stages of a strategic supply chain study. Our discussion is based on more than 50 such studies that we have performed over the past 20 years. Given the current state of modeling system technology, a study can be completed within 6 months or less if the company attends diligently to it. This time frame is necessary as well as desirable because it provides senior management with positive feedback from an exploratory study before interest in it has begun to wane. Our discussion assumes that an off-the-shelf modeling system, such as SLIM/2000 discussed in Section 4.4, is employed in the study.

We also assume that the study is executed by a combination of managers and analysts from within the company and outside consultants who provide the modeling system and expertise in applying it. Few companies today have the internal capability to initiate and execute a strategic study of their supply chain based on data and models. As we will suggest, however, this situation should change as companies recognize the benefits of bringing this capability in-house after completing a strategic study.

The typical study is subject to the following three layers of oversight:

- **Executive Committee.** Senior managers in the company who have authority to effect change; includes liaison from the Steering Committee
- **Steering Committee.** Key supply chain managers from the company who are highly knowledgeable about supply chain operations; headed by a senior manager from the Executive Committee who has a broad perspective of supply chain; includes individuals from Study Team
- **Study Team.** Corporate and functional managers and analysts from the company and consultants

Project management requires appropriately frequent communication up and down these three layers. The major stages of a supply chain study are discussed in the following subsections.

Stage 1—Organize Study (Duration = 1 Month). The study begins with a meeting among the members of the Steering Committee that lasts several days. Their goal is to clearly articulate the supply chain planning problems to be addressed and aligns these problems with the modeling capabilities of the consultants' preferred modeling system. In addition, definitions of product families, market zones, and supplier aggregations, where appropriate, are determined. Usually, the model identified for the study is a single-period, snapshot model.

Procedures for collecting data to populate the supply chain decision database are determined, along with a realistic division of labor between company analysts on the Study Team and the consultants. Data collection is based on templates provided by the modeling system. Some help from the company's IT department may be needed, especially if the programs to be implemented for collecting data are intended to support the company's longer-term use of the modeling system. Finally, the Steering Committee agrees on a historical period from which to create the database used in validating the model and on an initial set of scenarios to be analyzed after the validation has been completed.

Stage 2—Collect Data (Duration = 2 to 4 Months). Analysts and consultants on the Study Team fill in the templates developed in stage 1. They hold frequent meetings to discuss and resolve problems. In most companies, data collection should be completed well within the 4-month maximum. The actual elapsed time will depend on the size of the company, the number of products and facilities in its supply chain, and the extent of data standardization before the study.

This stage is the most intimidating for company managers and analysts because it involves an extensive and new exploration of the corporate database and the company's strategic options, often with uncertainty about when and how closure will be achieved. It constitutes "the pain" that the company must endure to realize "the gain" that follows. Problems due to missing or inaccurate data or to data and relationships that require statistical analysis are sure to arise. Errors simply due to faulty data handling and transformation will also arise. Finally, data must be generated to describe new options for which company analysts have little knowledge, such as plant operating costs in a new country or rates for new modes of transportation. The participation of consultants, who have successfully completed such explorations in the past, provides confidence that the current exploration will turn out well.

Stage 3—Validate Data and Model (Duration = 1 Month). The model and the data are validated by forcing supply chain activities and flows to equal what occurred during the historical validation period. The validation stage overlaps with the end of the data collection stage because initial efforts at validation will reveal areas in which data are incomplete or inaccurate. Validation is considered complete when supply chain details of the historical period are replicated to an acceptable level of accuracy. This includes both the solution simulated by the model and the breakdown of total supply chain cost into its components parts.

After validation, the model is optimized by removing all constraints forcing the solution to equal the plan of the historical period. The optimized plan illustrates how the supply chain might have been more economically operated in the past. This plan and its cost (or net revenue) can serve as benchmarks for future scenario runs, which may be subject to policy or political constraints not yet reflected in the model. Usually, the potential cost savings indicated by the optimization run is significant. As a result, most, if not all, doubts that the managers had about the value of the modeling effort disappear at this point.

Validation runs and subsequent optimization and scenario runs may be made on the consultants' computers, computers in the company where the modeling system has been installed, or both, depending on the contractual arrangement for the study. Installation of the modeling system on computers at the company during the validation stage is required if the company wishes to have the technology transferred in-house for ongoing analysis after the study has been completed. This commitment is discussed in greater detail below.

Stage 4—Analyze Scenarios (Duration = 2 to 4 Months). Initially, the Study Team runs scenarios that were specified in stage 1. New scenarios are devised as the Study Team gains insights into the strengths and weaknesses of the strategic options open to the company. Meetings are held with the Steering and the Executive Committees to review results obtained to date. Often, new strategic options and scenarios will suggest themselves as these results cause managers to expand their consciousness about the company's strategic opportunities. The number of scenarios and the time devoted to running them depend heavily on the nature of the study. It is not unusual to make 50 scenario runs, or more, in this final stage of the study.

An ambiguous issue at this stage is the extent to which demand management options are explicitly considered in the supply chain study. As we have discussed throughout the book and especially in Sections 8.1, 8.2, and 8.3, it is difficult and often inappropriate to ignore demand management options when performing a strategic supply chain study. Such integration might involve informal feedback from marketing and sales about demand scenarios, new products, and new markets. Alternatively, it might involve formal modeling of long-term marketing and sales efforts. An enlightened Executive Committee will suggest that the Steering Committee engage marketing and sales managers in the supply chain study.

Approximately 6 months after its start, the supply chain study can be considered complete. Formal completion may be necessary to bring contractual closure to the consultants' participation in the company's strategic planning exercise. At this point, the company has accomplished a great deal more than a thorough study of its supply chain strategy. With the help of the consultants, it has implemented programs for creating the supply chain decision database from transactional databases. It has also validated this database and the model. Moreover, company analysts have learned how to use the modeling system, which may have been installed in-house. The company should seek to exploit these accomplishments, especially considering the pain endured during stages 2 and 3. As we now discuss, the company has two distinct modes of exploitation; continuing strategic analysis and tactical analysis with a modified form of the model.

Stage 5a (optional)—Continue Strategic Scenario Analyses (Indefinite Duration). Upon completion of the study, the company may recognize that additional scenarios of their strategic supply chain plans need to be created and run, either immediately or after a hiatus. A straightforward approach is to internalize the strategic planning process centered about the modeling system, which entails commitment to a permanent license agreement with the modeling system provider and to ongoing involvement by managers, analysts, and information technologists in data refinement and scenario exercises. Alternatively, if the company is unwilling or unable to internalize this process, it can enter into a long-term arrangement with the external consulting company to periodically assist it.

Continuing strategic analysis might also entail the construction of a multiple-period model; for example, a model with five linked periods, each 1 year in length. The enhanced model would allow senior management to examine the timing and phasing of investments in new facilities or new products, acquisitions and mergers, entry into new markets, and so on. It would also allow the study of these options subject to trends over multiple periods in demand for the company's products.

Despite the obvious benefits of continuing the process of strategic supply chain analysis with the modeling system, many companies disband the study team after the study has been completed. They do so because they lack the organizational structure and will to sustain it or even to sustain the consulting arrangement. We expect this reluctance to diminish over the coming years as managers become more aware of the benefits and as Transactional IT systems improve in their scope and flexibility, thereby providing a stronger base from which to implement Analytical IT systems.

Stage 5b (optional)—Adapt Modeling System for Repetitive Tactical Planning (Duration Unlimited). An equally important opportunity available to the company after the strategic study has been completed is to extend the modeling system to support tactical planning, which would be performed on a routine basis, say once a month or once a quarter. The supply chain decision database and model created and validated in stages 2 and 3 can be readily extended for the purposes of tactical planning. Specially, depending on their relevance to medium-term planning, discrete options considered by the strategic model would be fixed at "yes or no" or deleted. In addition, the snapshot model would be replicated several times to describe individual months or quarters considered in tactical planning. Inventory details linking the individual periods would be added. Finally, it might be desirable to add smoothing constraints, ensuring that the tactical model will produce realistic, implementable results.

Thus far, few companies have developed tactical supply chain planning processes, with or without a model. As we discussed in Section 12.5, such a decision-making process requires significant business process redesign by the company. Given the potential benefits, we expect to see a much larger number of these applications in the not too distant future.

Summary

The review of a typical modeling study points out that improved supply chain management based on data and modeling analysis is painful, but not too painful. The heaviest burden is felt during a period of a few months when the supply chain database and implied optimization model are assembled and validated. Once this has been accomplish, the company can begin to exploit the supply chain decision database and the model to identify improved decisions about strategy and tactics.

At the strategic level, there is little reason to discontinue data-driven strategic planning once the modeling system and associated planning processes have proven valuable. The effort to extend the approach to tactical planning is admittedly much more work. Nevertheless, considering the acknowledged pain of ERP implementations in most companies, this effort is small, and the gain will be just as great. In fact, we would argue that the benefits of ERP would be significantly enhanced if the company's ERP system were integrated with tactical planning processes and systems.

12.8 Outlook for the Future of Modeling Systems and Their Applications

The growing interest in supply chain management is one manifestation of the accelerating information revolution, which, judging by the rapidity of changes in technology, is probably still in its infancy. High-tech companies are especially subject to instability and competition, but even mature companies face heightened stress and unpredictability. Globalization, mergers and acquisitions, new e-commerce markets, opportunities for enhanced business-to-business communication over the Internet, and a host of other factors have creating widespread uncertainty. The competitive response of many companies to new opportunities has become more intense, even savage. Some academics and consultants refer to it as **hypercompetition.**[35]

Of course, periods of rapid and anarchic change in capitalist markets are not new. Over 50 years ago, the economist Schumpeter suggested that such times foster **creative destruction,** which allows entrepreneurs to spawn new products and services, returning very large profits, at least in the short term.[36] They overcome competition by innovations that make rivals' positions obsolete. They may even attain monopoly power, which, according to Schumpeter, is not necessarily bad because such monopolies are transients on the path to an enhanced, richer capitalist world.

Our focus in this book has been on the role that supply chain management can play in helping companies meet the challenges of a dynamically changing world. Many of the modeling concepts underlying supply chain management are decades old. Some managagerial accounting principles even date back to the late 19th century. What is new is the availability of data to construct and optimize models supporting decision making, although information technologies enabling the management and communication of these data are still not perfected.

The following summarizes opportunities afforded by the creation and application of supply chain modeling systems:

- For operational problems, models help identify low-cost plans that meet customer service requirements.
- For tactical problems, models help identify low-cost plans that meet customer service requirements by integrating functional and locational decisions across

the supply chain; if product mix is allowed to vary, these models can help identify plans that maximize net revenue.

- For the strategic design of a supply chain network for a new product line, models help management explore trade-offs among cost or net revenue, customer service, cycle time, redundancy, and other factors of strategic importance.
- For the strategic redesign of an existing network, models help management explore options to expand or consolidate resources or markets, evaluate the economics of new technologies, or appraise new sourcing options.
- For the strategic evaluation of a merger or acquisition, models help management determine a breakeven price while evaluating potential consolidation plans for the expanded supply chain.
- For strategic, tactical, and operational planning, models help identify coherent intertemporal decisions linking overlapping planning problems.
- For studies aimed at combining supply chain and demand management, models provide important information about the average and marginal delivery costs of products to the markets.
- For studies aimed at combining supply chain and financial management, models describe interactions among strategic supply chain decisions, earnings before interest and taxes, changes in equity, and capital investments in fixed assets.
- For tactical and strategic planning processes, supply chain decision databases provide management with insights that are buried in transactional databases about costs and capacities and manufacturing, distribution, and transportation activities that are buried in extensive transactional databases.

The business world is still learning about the benefits of acquiring modeling systems to these ends.

We conclude with a forecast of advancements in business and technology that we believe will affect and be affected by modeling applications to supply chain management. There is no guarantee, of course, that the optimistic scenarios about to be described will come to pass. Still, it seems unlikely that innovative, competitive companies will pursue other scenarios that ignore the importance of data and models to effective supply chain management.

1. The interest in and commitment to fact-based, integrated decision making on the part of supply chain managers will continue to grow. Business process redesign to support and exploit such decision making will emerge as an important development over the next decade.

Managerial interest in and commitment to fact-based decision making is predicated on continuing improvements in ERP systems and their use in homogenizing and streamlining the communication and management of transactional data. Internet developments are putting pressure on ERP software companies to improve the modularity and flexibility of their packages, thereby allowing smaller companies in virtual supply chains to be plugged into large companies using the same software. These improvements will benefit all supply chain applications, not just those centered about the Internet.

Although developments in Transactional IT are evolving, ERP companies and their customers have become increasingly aware of the need for Analytical IT. Because the purposes of Transactional and Analytical IT systems are quite different, and individuals implementing them have much different viewpoints, modeling solutions offered by ERP companies and their partners have been of mixed quality. Their efforts are often marred by schemes that try to move forward from vast transactional databases to ad hoc tools that support decision making.

A better approach is to begin with an understanding and articulation of the supply chain problems to be analyzed. After that, the models and supply chain decision database needed to support decision making can be determined. The next step is to devise methods and design software that will create a decision database from the transactional databases. Then, the modeling systems and the supply chain decision database can be validated. The final step, and this is a big one, is to redesign business processes to allow the supply chain decision database to be refreshed and the modeling systems to be exercised on a repetitive basis.

In this chapter, we discussed at length many issues surrounding the adaptation of business processes to support fact-based supply chain management. For tactical and strategic planning, new processes are needed for routinely collecting data, performing modeling analysis, negotiating plans, and then implementing them. Modeling analysis can often be achieved using off-the-shelf software. New job definitions are needed for managers and analysts who carry out these activities. New managerial incentives reflecting global supply chain objectives must be devised and implemented.

New processes for operational planning are much more dependent on the details of the specific problems to be analyzed. What is the appropriate scope of these operational problems? Can they be effectively evaluated using an off-the-shelf package or should the company seek to develop a customized package? How can operational modeling systems be seamlessly integrated with transactional systems? How much time is available for each operational planning session? Solutions to these issues require business processes that harmonize exploratory practices of modeling system developers and users with exploitative practices of IT personnel. Further, implementation and maintenance of an effective customized modeling system often require application of the unified optimization methodology discussed in Chapter 5.

Many companies are grappling with these issues by investing considerable money in software, hardware, and consulting services, which, for the reasons outlined above, have often produced less than successful results. Over the next few years, a few innovator companies will implement modeling systems and develop new business processes based on using them to achieve integrated supply chain management at all levels of planning, strategic, tactical, and operational. As a result, these companies will achieve considerable competitive advantage. Their success will stimulate other companies to pursue similar advances.

2. Progress in fact-based, integrated supply chain management will stimulate similar developments in demand management and corporate financial management. Moreover, over time, these three areas of decision making will become more integrated.

In Chapter 8, we discussed extensions of supply chain models to incorporate demand management decisions, and in Chapter 9, we constructed models to illustrate integration of corporate financial decisions and constraints with supply chain decisions and constraints. In both chapters, we discussed reasons why decision making in the three areas has not yet been integrated. Yet, it is obviously suboptimal to evaluate strategic and tactical supply chain decisions without considering marketing decisions that will shift future sales to those products and geographical regions where margins will be highest. Even at the operational level, the company may have opportunities to accept or reject orders depending on their contributions to the bottom line.

Connections between net revenues from sales and the firm's shareholder value are complicated by financial decisions about capital investments in fixed assets, long-term liabilities, growth in net profits, dividends, and a host of other financial decisions. The firm's financial health, as measured by its debt-to-equity ratio, return on fixed assets, availability of cash, and other factors, has a direct but complicated impact on the value of the company's shares. Thus, it is also suboptimal to integrate supply chain and demand management decisions without considering their linkage to financial decisions.

Our presentation of models that promote integration of supply chain, demand, and financial decisions highlights the need for business process redesign with the same goals. Many companies have begun pursuing integrated planning with new supply chain processes, while leaving decision making in marketing and finance in a heavily compartmentalized state. Clearly, short-term decisions in all areas must be individually executed. Still, longer-term, strategic decisions would profit greatly by integrated planning across all areas of planning based on data, models, and managerial judgment. The challenge is to convince senior managers that such developments are not only possible but also desirable and, ultimately, necessary.

3. Business-to-business e-commerce and virtual supply chain developments will spawn new modeling concepts and new technologies for applying modeling systems.

It is still too early in the evolution of the Internet to make sweeping pronouncements about how it will affect supply chain management over the coming years. Clearly, by allowing companies to communicate rapidly and flexibly with their vendors and their customers, investments in Internet systems are already yielding large returns. Nevertheless, faster communication of data does not automatically lead to improved decision making, especially in planning how the company should manage its supply chain next week, next month, next year, and in 5 years. Modeling systems can play the same role in supporting such decisions as they can for nonvirtual supply chains in vertically integrated companies.

The point of departure in considering use of the Internet and modeling systems to achieve integrated virtual supply chain management is a study of answers to questions such as *What data should each company in a virtual supply chain share with other companies in the chain?*

Because the impetus for integrated supply chain management is fact-based decision making, we are naturally led to ask this question. For example, should a small vendor of a large manufacturing firm be required to share costs in its general ledger with the manufacturer? The answer is Probably not, but then the large manufacturer may not have accurate information to decide if it will be economic over the long term to outsource the manufacture of a part to that vendor. Many other examples of ambivalence and ambiguity in communicating and interpreting data could be cited. It may be that new theories of the firm are needed to help companies understand how to achieve new forms of cooperative alliances over the Internet.

Another question is *What new processes are needed to assist companies in a virtual supply chain to decide how decisions are made and coordinated?* A central issue in virtual supply chain management is which company or companies hold decision-making power. A large automobile manufacturer certainly has power over most of the companies in its supplier network. Up to a point, it can dictate plans to these vendors regarding production schedules, service, quality, and other factors. Such mandates can be overdone, however, as witnessed by excessive use of just-in-time inventory practices in the 1980s that inadvertently drove some small suppliers out of business.

A different situation arises when companies in the virtual supply chain are roughly of equal size. Problems of coordinated decision making can be exacerbated if these companies have significantly different organizational cultures. An open issue is how they should structure their decision-making processes, which leads us to the next question: *How are supply chain cost savings, or increases in net revenues, shared among participating companies?* This is an issue of incentives that is an elaboration of those discussed in Section 12.6 regarding the setting of global incentives within the firm. Resolution is difficult before enhanced coordination is implemented because the possible outcomes for it are not well understood.

A fourth question is *How do companies participating in multiple virtual supply chains coordinate their global decision making?* This is another instance of potential conflict among companies in a virtual supply chain that is an elaboration of conflict among business units in the same company that have customers both inside and outside the company. For a firm that supplies several downstream manufacturers or distributors, differences in arrangements may reflect IT and cultural differences. It would be disruptive for the company to implement multiple schemes for coordinated supply chain decision making in attempting to deal with such differences.

4. Success with modeling systems for supply chain management will spawn research leading to technical advances in modeling and modeling systems.

Such research is of managerial interest only to the extent that it leads to more effective modeling systems. We mention it because most implementations that have been carried out to date use models and methods for which the basic concepts were developed 10, 20, or even 40 years ago. The field of operations research will profit significantly if basic and applied research is directed at new problems arising in supply chain management. It is beyond the intended scope of the book to delve into such topics in detail. We simply list the following areas where we believe important research can be performed over the next 10 years:

- Wider and deeper application of the unified optimization methodology with particular focus on harmonization of rule-based and optimization models and methods and the use of coarse-grained parallel computing
- Improvements in mixed integer programming optimization algorithms
- Wider and deeper application of stochastic programming to problems of demand management, evaluation of real options, and investments in new technology and new products
- Flexible but rigorous methods and systems for analyzing multiobjective optimization models including software to support exploration of the efficient frontier
- Rigorous integration of mathematical programming models and methods with classical inventory theory

Exercises

In addition to the following exercises, modeling exercises involving data files and discussion exercises involving white papers may be found on the Web site (www.scm-models.com).

1. In Section 12.1, we discussed the theory of bounded rationality, which acknowledges that a decision maker has limited information upon which to make decisions. Psychological research has identified the following four simplification processes that are used by decision makers to deal with limited information:
   a. *Editing.* Decision makers tend to edit and simplify problems before entering into a choice process, using a relatively small number of cues and combining them in a simple manner.
   b. *Decomposition.* Decision makers attempt to decompose problems to reduce large problems into their component parts. The presumption is that problem elements can be defined in such a way that solving the various components of a problem individually will result in an acceptable solution to the global problem.
   c. *Heuristics.* Decision makers recognize patterns in the situations they face and apply rules of appropriate behavior to those situations.
   d. *Framing.* Decisions are framed by beliefs that define the problem to be addressed, the information that must be collected, and the dimensions that must be evaluated. Decision makers adopt paradigms to tell themselves what perspective to take on a problem, what questions to be asked, and what technologies should be used to ask the questions.[37]

   From the prospective of these four processes, discuss how modeling systems can expand the bounds of bounded rationality. In addition, address ways in which modeling systems mimic these processes.

2. In Section 12.5 we discussed the concept of the reach and range of the IT infrastructure displayed in Figure 12.2. Recall that reach refers to people with whom an individual (manager) can be easily connected and range refers to activities that can be automatically and seamlessly shared with these people. Since its creation by Peter Keen [Keen, 1991], this concept has been usefully applied by a number of IT academics and consultants. Their discussions have not included, however, the use of data and modeling systems to support managerial decision making as elements of range. Provide an explanation of this omission, including arguments about whether you agree or disagree with the assertion that the use of modeling systems should be integral to the range of IT activities.

3. It has been suggested that the following three approaches are available to the firm for exploiting IT:

   a. Adapt systems to the behavior of human beings.

   b. Change the ways in which human decision makers make decisions and employ data.

   c. Replace human beings with computers.

   Discuss the validity of this observation in the context of using IT for supply chain management. Do you think one approach can or should dominate the others?

4. Managers constantly strive to resolve the ambiguities of their business experiences and interpret these experiences to provide meaning to their jobs and life within the company. According to March,[38]

   > The instruments of meaning are myths, symbols, rituals, and stories. . . . A myth is 'any real or fictional story, recurring theme, or character type that appeals to the consciousness of a people by embodying its cultural ideals or by giving expression to deep, commonly felt emotions.' Myths are constructed to provide broad explanations of life and models for behavior.

   A myth consists of the elements of truth, beauty, and justice. Does the myth describe an important underlying truth about life? Are its plot and its descriptions of characters beautiful? Is justice triumphant at the end of the myth?

   Discuss ways in which a supply chain planning model is a *rational myth* by elaborating on the ways in which it achieves truth, beauty, and justice.

Notes

1. The main sources that we will use are March [1994] and March [1999], both of which draw on extensive research into organizational decision making and intelligence.
2. See March [1994, vii–ix] or March [1999, 14].
3. See Holmstrom and Tirole [1989].
4. A range of perspectives on managerial decision making can be found in Hickson [1995], and March [1999].
5. The reader is referred to March [1999], which contains reprints of 20 recent articles by March and his collaborators. These articles cover four

major topics: decisions in organizations, learning in organizations, risk taking in organizations, and the giving and taking of advice. Our discussion is Section 12.1 is based primarily on Chapters 1 and 2, which summarize the large body of earlier work on understanding how decision happen in organizations.

6. See March [1999, 14].
7. Satisficing is discussed by March [1994, 18–23].
8. These constructions are reviewed in Winston [1994, Chapter 13].
9. See March [1999, 29].
10. It is remarkable that March could summarize so much of his research into decision making, and that of other organizational behaviorists, in four succinct statements of contested issues about human decision making; they can be found in March [1999, 14].
11. See March [1999, 14].
12. Ibid.
13. In Table 8.1, we presented a set of frequently observed conflicts between supply chain and marketing managers.
14. See March [1999, 14].
15. Ibid.
16. See the discussion in Powell and Dent-Micallef [1997, 376–377], which contains an extensive literature on how a firm may succeed or fail in its attempts to gain competitive advantage through IT.
17. See Powell and Dent-Micallef [1997, 377].
18. Early suggestions that IT is necessary but not sufficient for a firm's competitive advantage were made by Floyd and Wooldridge [1990] and Clemons and Row [1991].
19. The relevance of the resource-based view of the firm to understanding the competitiveness of IT is discussed extensively in Mata, Fuerst, and Barney [1995] and Powell and Dent-Micallef [1997].
20. Our discussion draws on observations in Mata, Fuerst, and Barney [1995].
21. See Powell and Dent-Micallef [1997, 378].
22. See Powell and Dent-Micallef [1997, 379] and Keen [1993].
23. The biggest splash was made by Hammer and Champy [1993].
24. We draw on the discussion by Powell and Dent-Micallef [1997, 379–382].
25. See Earl and Feeney [2000, 23], who provide an interesting categorization and discussion of CEO attitudes toward IT.
26. Tom Davenport, one of the earlier proponents of BPR, states in Davenport [1996] that "re-engineering isn't dead; it is effectively over." Reasons for its initial failure and its connections to supply chain management are discussed in Burgess [1998].
27. Broadbent, Weill, and St. Clair [1999] report on four cases of business process redesign, two in oil companies and two in retailing companies, that were motivated by the need to span organizational boundaries and to reach constituencies inside and outside the firm. In fact, all four cases were centered about using IT to improve supply chain management, although the term is not employed by the authors.
28. This paradigm was invented by Keen [1991, Chapter 7]; see also Weill and Broadbent [1998] and Broadbent, Weill, and St. Clair [1999, 163–164]. It is interesting that Keen [1991, 179] anticipated e-commerce, when he states, in speaking of reach, that "(t)he ideal is to be able to connect anyone, anywhere, just as the phone system reaches across the world."
29. See Weill and Broadbent [1998, 262].
30. These coordination methods and many of the other topics covered in this section are discussed in Mehring [1998], who provides an extensive bibliography.
31. See Victor and Blackburn [1987].
32. Milgrom and Roberts [1992, 601] explain moral hazard. "Originally, an insurance term referring to the tendency of people with insurance to reduce the care they take to avoid or reduce insured losses. Now, the term refers also to *post-contractual opportunism* that arises when actions required or desired under the contract are not freely observable."
33. See Milgrom and Roberts [1992, Chapter 7].

34. See *The Economist* [1997]. The article was stimulated by Hilmer and Donaldson [1996], who seek to debunk management fads because they tend to lead managers down false trails. They also suggest on p. xiii that "(I)nstead of applauding quick fixes and standardized methods, . . . the development of management (should be) based on hard, clear thinking."
35. The book by Ilinitch, Lewin, and D'Aveni [1998] contains a collection of articles by supporters of the theory of hypercompetition. They assert that disorder, stress, and unpredictability occur naturally at inflection points during periods of change, such as the information revolution now underway. Moreover, the characteristics of this particular inflection point is unique or, at least, different from that of the industrial revolution. For example, a contingent and disenfranchised workforce has emerged in the United States. Similarly, emerging nations and smaller firms have entered markets with greater speed and less capital than in the past.
36. The original concepts about creative destruction and their central role in the growth of capitalism were given in Schumpeter [1934]; also, see Schumpeter [1950].
37. March [1994, 12–15].
38. March [1994, 208–209].

References

*Broadbent, M., P. Weill, and D. St. Clair [1999], "The Implications of Information Technology Infrastructure for Business Process Redesign," *MIS Quarterly,* 23, 159–182.

Burgess, R. [1998], "Avoiding Supply Chain Management Failure: Lessons from Business Process Re-engineering," *International Journal of Logistics Management,* 9, 15–23.

Clemons, E. and M. Row [1991], "Sustaining IT Advantage: The Role of Structural Differences," *MIS Quarterly,* 15, 275–292.

Davenport, T. [1996], "Why Re-engineering Failed: The Fad that Forgot People," *Fast Company,* Premiere Issue.

Earl, M. and D. Feeney [2000], "Opinion: How to be a CEO in the Information Age," *Sloan Management Review,* 41, 11–23.

The Economist [1997], January 25, 57.

Floyd, S., and B. Wooldridge [1990], "Path Analysis of the Relationship Between Competitive Strategy, Information Technology, and Financial Performance," *Journal of Management Information Systems,* 7, 47–64.

Hammer, M. and J. Champy [1993], *Reengineering the Corporation: A Manifesto for Business Revolution.* New York: Harper Business.

Hickson, D. J. [1995], *Management Decision Making.* Dartmouth, N.H.: Aldershot.

Hilmer, F. G. and L. Donaldson [1996], *Management Redeemed: Debunking the Fads that Undermine Our Corporations.* New York: The Free Press.

Holmstrom, B. R., and J. Tirole [1989], "The Theory of the Firm," edited by R. Schmalensee and R. D. Willig. *Handbook of Industrial Organization: Volume 1,* (pp. 61–133). Amsterdam: Elsivier.

Ilinitch, A. Y., A Y. Lewin, and R. D'Aveni, ed. [1998], *Managing in Times of Disorder: Hypercompetitive Organizational Responses,* Sage Publications.

Keen, P. G. [1991], *Shaping the Future, Business Design Through Information Technology.* Cambridge, Mass.: Harvard Business School Press.

*Keen, P. G. [1993], "Information Technology and the Management Difference: A Fusion Map," *IBM Systems Journal,* 32, 17–39.

March, J. G. [1994], *A Primer on Decision Making: How Decisions Happen.* New York: Free Press.

March, J. G. [1999], *The Pursuit of Intelligence.* Oxford, Eng.: Blackwell Publishers.

Mata, F. J., W. L. Fuerst, and J. B. Barney [1995], "Information Technology and Sustained Competitive Advantage: A Resource-Based Analysis," *MIS Quarterly,* 19, 487–505.

Mehring, J. S. [1998], *A Framework for Examining Coordination and Incentives in Supply Chains,* Working Paper 98-01-1. College of Management, University of Massachusetts, Lowell.

Milgrom, P., and J. Roberts [1992], *Economics, Organization and Management.* Englewood Cliffs, N.J.: Prentice-Hall.

Powell, T. C., and A. Dent-Metcallef [1997], "Information Technology as Competitive Advantage: The Role of Human, Business and Technology Resources," *Strategic Management Journal,* 18, 375–405.

Schumpter, J. A. [1934], *The Theory of Economic Development.* Cambridge, Mass.: Harvard University Press (original publication 1911).

Schumpter, J. A. [1950], *Capitalism, Socialism, and Democracy.* New York: Harper & Brothers.

Victor, B., and R. S. Blackburn [1987], "Interdependence: An Alternative Conceptualization," *Academy of Management Review,* 12, 486–498.

Winston, W. L. [1994], *Operations Research: Applications and Algorithms.* Pacific Grove, Calif.: Duxbury Press.

Weill, M. P., and M. Broadbent [1998], *Leveraging the New Infrastructure: How Market Leaders Capitalize on Management Information Technology.* Cambridge, Mass.: Harvard Business School Press.

*See the credits section at the end of this book for more information.

Index

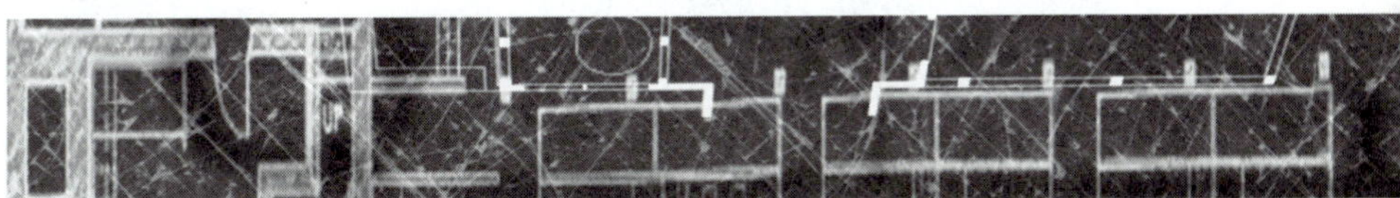

Credits

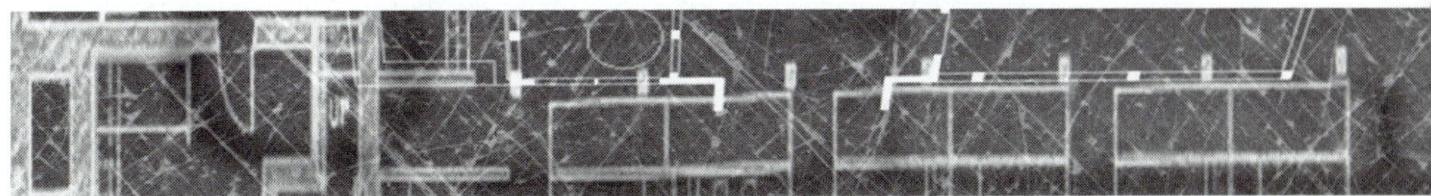

This page constitutes an extension of the copyright page. We have made every effort to trace the ownership of all copyrighted material and to secure permission from copyright holders. In the event of any question arising as to the use of any material, we will be pleased to make the necessary corrections in future printings. Thanks are due to the following authors, publishers, and agents for permission to use the material indicated.

Chapter 1

14, Fig. 1.3: Reprinted with permission of The Free Press, a Division of Simon & Schuster, Inc., from *Competitive Advantage: Creating and Sustaining Superior Performance,* by Michael E. Porter. Copyright © 1985, 1998 by Michael E. Porter.

Chapter 2

29, Fig. 2.1: Data are from Commerce Department and Macroeconomic Advisers (projections). The graph is from "The Economy Transformed, Bit by Bit," by S. Lohr in *The New York Times,* Dec. 20, 1999, p. 38. Copyright © 1999 New York Times. Reprinted by permission. **40ff, Section 2.3:** Adapted from Chapter 23 "Bottom-up vs. Top-down Approaches to Supply Chain Modeling," by J. F. Shapiro. In S. Tayur, R. Ganeshan, and M. Magazine (Eds.), *Quantitative Models for Supply Chain Management,* p. 743. Copyright © 1999 Kluwer Academic Publishers. **41, Fig. 2.2:** Adapted from Fig. 1 in Chapter 23 "Bottom-up vs. Top-down Approaches to Supply Chain Modeling," by J. F. Shapiro. In S. Tayur, R. Ganeshan, and M. Magazine (Eds.), *Quantitative Models for Supply Chain Management,* p. 743. Copyright © 1999 Kluwer Academic Publishers. **47, Table 2.1:** From Table 1 in Chapter 23 "Bottom-up vs. Top-down Approaches to Supply Chain Modeling," by J. F. Shapiro. In S. Tayur, R. Ganeshan, and M. Magazine (Eds.), *Quantitative Models for Supply Chain Management,* p. 748. Copyright © 1999 Kluwer Academic Publishers.

Chapter 7

287, Fig. 7.1: Adapted from Figure 4.2 in Chapter 4 "Logistics Strategy," by K. A. O'Laughlin and W. C. Copacino. In Robeson, Copacino and Howe (Eds.), *The Logistics Handbook,* p. 61.

Service Mark by Anderson Consulting. Copyright © 1989 Andersen Consulting. All rights reserved. **295, Fig. 7.2:** Adapted from Figure 4.2 in Chapter 4 "Logistics Strategy," by K. A. O'Laughlin and W. C. Copacino. In Robeson, Copacino and Howe (Eds.), *The Logistics Handbook,* p. 61. Service Mark by Anderson Consulting. Copyright © 1989 Andersen Consulting. All rights reserved.

Chapter 8

335, Fig. 8.4: Reprinted by permission, J. D. C. Little, "Brandaid: A Marketing-Mix Model, Parts 1 and 2," *Operations Research, 23,* 1975. Copyright © 1975 by Institute for Operations Research and the Management Sciences (INFORMS), 901 Elkridge Landing Road, Suite 400, Linthicum, Maryland 21090-2909, USA. **336, Fig. 8.5:** Reprinted by permission, J. D. C. Little, "Brandaid: A Marketing-Mix Model, Parts 1 and 2," *Operations Research, 23,* 1975. Copyright © 1975 by Institute for Operations Research and the Management Sciences (INFORMS), 901 Elkridge Landing Road, Suite 400, Linthicum, Maryland 21090-2909, USA. **348, Fig. 8.9:** Reprinted by permission, F. M. Bass, "A New Growth Model for Consumer Durables," *Management Science, 15,* pp. 215–227, 1969. Copyright © 1969 by Institute for Operations Research and the Management Sciences (INFORMS), 901 Elkridge Landing Road, Suite 400, Linthicum, Maryland 21090-2909, USA. **350, Fig. 8.10:** Reprinted with permission of The Free Press, a Division of Simon & Schuster, Inc., from *Competitive Advantage: Creating and Sustaining Superior Performance,* by Michael E. Porter. Copyright © 1985, 1998 by Michael E. Porter. **380, Fig. 8.17:** Reprinted by permission, M. L. Fisher and A. Raman, "Reducing the Cost of Demand Uncertainty Through Accurate Response to Early Sales," *Operations Research, 44,* Issue 1, Figure 1, p. 88, 1996. Copyright © 1996 by the Institute for Operations Research and the Management Sciences (INFORMS), 901 Elkridge Landing Road, Suite 400, Linthicum, Maryland 21090-2909 USA. **382, Table 8.19:** Reprinted by permission, M. L. Fisher and A. Raman, "Reducing the Cost of Demand Uncertainty Through Accurate Response to Early Sales," *Operations Research, 44,* Issue 1, p. 97, 1996. Copyright © 1996 by the Institute for Operations Research and the Management Sciences (INFORMS), 901 Elkridge Landing Road, Suite 400, Linthicum, Maryland 21090-2909 USA. **383, Table 8.20:** Adapted from "Multiple Scenario Development: Its Conceptual and Behavorial Foundation," by P. J. H. Schoemaker, 1993, *Strategic Management Journal, 14,* p. 197. Copyright (c) 1993. Reproduced by permission of John Wiley & Sons Limited. **385, Fig. 8.18:** Reprinted from *European Journal of Operational Research, 118,* J. F. Shapiro, "On the Connections Among Activity-based Costing, Mathematical Programming Models for Analyzing Strategic Decisions, and the Resource-based View of the Firm," p. 300. Copyright © 1999 with permission from Elsevier Science Publishing.

Chapter 9

404, Fig. 9.1: From "Strategic Management of Multinational Companies: Network-Based Planning Systems," by R. L. Crum, D. D. Klingman, and L. A. Travis, CSFM Research Report, 1979. **406ff, Section 9.4:** From "Optimizing Multi-national Financial Flows," Working Paper IFSRC No. 147-90, by S. R. Klimczak, T. M. Magee, and J. F. Shapiro. Copyright © Steven R. Klimczak, Timothy M. Magee, and Jeremy F. Shapiro, 1990. Supported by International Financial Services Research Center at MIT. Reprinted by permission. **410, Fig. 9.2:** From "Optimizing Multi-national Financial Flows," Working Paper IFSRC No. 147-90, by S. R. Klimczak, T. M. Magee, and J. F. Shapiro. Copyright © Steven R. Klimczak, Timothy M. Magee, and

Jeremy F. Shapiro, 1990. Supported by International Financial Services Research Center at MIT. Reprinted by permission. **411, Figs. 9.3 and 9.4:** From "Optimizing Multi-national Financial Flows," Working Paper IFSRC No. 147-90, by S. R. Klimczak, T. M. Magee, and J. F. Shapiro. Copyright © Steven R. Klimczak, Timothy M. Magee, and Jeremy F. Shapiro, 1990. Supported by International Financial Services Research Center at MIT. Reprinted by permission. **413, Tables 9.2 and 9.3:** From "Optimizing Multi-national Financial Flows," Working Paper IFSRC No. 147-90, by S. R. Klimczak, T. M. Magee, and J. F. Shapiro. Copyright © Steven R. Klimczak, Timothy M. Magee, and Jeremy F. Shapiro, 1990. Supported by International Financial Services Research Center at MIT. Reprinted by permission. **414, Tables 9.4 and 9.5:** From "Optimizing Multi-national Financial Flows," Working Paper IFSRC No. 147-90, by S. R. Klimczak, T. M. Magee, and J. F. Shapiro. Copyright © Steven R. Klimczak, Timothy M. Magee, and Jeremy F. Shapiro, 1990. Supported by International Financial Services Research Center at MIT. Reprinted by permission.

Chapter 10

434, Fig. 10.2: From Fig. 14.1 in Chapter 14 "Integrated Planning and Scheduling Systems for the Refining Industry," by R. E. Coxhead. In A. Ciriani and R. E. Leachman (Eds.), *Optimization in Industry 2,* p. 189. Copyright © 1994 John Wiley & Sons. Reproduced by permission of John Wiley & Sons Limited. **457, Fig. 10.6:** Reprinted by permission, R. C. Leachman, R. F. Benson, C. Liu, and D. J. Raar, "IMPReSS: An Automated Production Planning and Delivery Quotation System at Harris Corporation—Semiconductor Sector," *Interfaces, 26,* pp. 6–37, 1996. Copyright © 1996 by Institute for Operations Research and the Management Sciences (INFORMS), 901 Elkridge Landing Road, Suite 400, Linthicum, Maryland 21090-2909 USA. **459, Fig. 10.7:** Reprinted by permission, R. C. Leachman, R. F. Benson, C. Liu, and D. J. Raar, "IMPReSS: An Automated Production Planning and Delivery Quotation System at Harris Corporation—Semiconductor Sector," *Interfaces, 26,* pp. 6–37, 1996. Copyright © 1996 by Institute for Operations Research and the Management Sciences (INFORMS), 901 Elkridge Landing Road, Suite 400, Linthicum, Maryland 21090-2909 USA. **460, Fig. 10.8:** Reprinted by permission, R. C. Leachman, R. F. Benson, C. Liu, and D. J. Raar, "IMPReSS: An Automated Production Planning and Delivery Quotation System at Harris Corporation—Semiconductor Sector," *Interfaces, 26,* pp. 6–37, 1996. Copyright © 1996 by Institute for Operations Research and the Management Sciences (INFORMS), 901 Elkridge Landing Road, Suite 400, Linthicum, Maryland 21090-2909 USA. **462, Fig. 10.9:** Reprinted by permission, R. C. Leachman, R. F. Benson, C. Liu, and D. J. Raar, "IMPReSS: An Automated Production Planning and Delivery Quotation System at Harris Corporation—Semiconductor Sector," *Interfaces, 26,* pp. 6–37, 1996. Copyright © 1996 by Institute for Operations Research and the Management Sciences (INFORMS), 901 Elkridge Landing Road, Suite 400, Linthicum, Maryland 21090-2909 USA.

Chapter 11

478, Fig. 11.1: From Richard Schonberger in *The Economist,* June 20, 1998. Copyright © 1998 The Economist Newspaper Group, Inc. Reprinted by permission. Further reproduction prohibited. www.economist.com **486, Fig. 11.5:** From *Operations Research: Applications and Algorithms,* Third Edition, by W. L. Winston. Copyright © 1994 Brooks/Cole Thomson Learning. Reprinted by permission. **502, Fig. 11.15:** Reprinted by permission, M. Cohen, P. Kamesam,

P. Kleindorfer, H. Lee, A. Takerian, "IBM's Multi-item Echelon Inventory System for Managing Service Logistics," *Interfaces, 20,* Fig. 3, p. 73, 1990. Copyright © 1990 by Institute for Operations Research and the Management Sciences (INFORMS), 901 Elkridge Landing Road, Suite 400, Linthicum, Maryland 21090-2909 USA. **505, Fig. 11.16:** Reprinted by permission, H. L. Lee and C. Billington, "Material Management in Decentralized Supply Chains," *Operations Research, 41,* Fig. 1, p. 38, 1993. Copyright © 1993 by Institute for Operations Research and the Management Sciences (INFORMS), 901 Elkridge Landing Road, Suite 400, Linthicum, Maryland 21090-2909 USA. **507, Fig. 11.17 and Table 11.1:** Reprinted by permission., H. L. Lee and C. Billington, "Material Management in Decentralized Supply Chains," *Operations Research, 41,* 1993. Copyright © 1993 by Institute for Operations Research and the Management Sciences (INFORMS), 901 Elkridge Landing Road, Suite 400, Linthicum, Maryland 21090-2909 USA. **508, Fig. 11.18:** Reprinted by permission, S. C. Graves and S. P. Willems, "Optimizing Strategic Safety Stock Placement in Supply Chains," *Manufacturing & Service Operations Management, 2,* Fig. 4, 2000. Copyright © 2000 Institute for Operations Reserach and the Management Sciences (INFORMS), 901 Elkridge Landing Road, Suite 400, Linthicum, Maryland 21090-2909 USA. **511, Table 11.2:** Reprinted by permission, S. C. Graves and S. P. Willems, "Optimizing Strategic Safety Stock Placement in Supply Chains," *Manufacturing & Service Operations Management, 2,* Table 1, 2000. Copyright © 2000 Institute for Operations Reserach and the Management Sciences (INFORMS), 901 Elkridge Landing Road, Suite 400, Linthicum, Maryland 21090-2909 USA. **512, Table 11.3:** Reprinted by permission, S. C. Graves and S. P. Willems, "Optimizing Strategic Safety Stock Placement in Supply Chains," *Manufacturing & Service Operations Management, 2,* Table 2, 2000. Copyright © 2000 Institute for Operations Reserach and the Management Sciences (INFORMS), 901 Elkridge Landing Road, Suite 400, Linthicum, Maryland 21090-2909 USA.

Chapter 12.

551, Table 12.1: From "The Implications of Information Technology Infrastructure for Business Process Redesign," by M. Broadbent, P. Weill, and D. St. Clair, 1999, *MIS Quarterly, 23,* p. 161, Table 1. Copyright © 1999. **552, Fig. 12.2:** Adapted and reprinted by permission of Harvard Business School Press. From *Shaping the Future, Business Design Through Information Technology,* by Peter G. W. Keen. Boston, MA 1991, p. 40. Copyright © 1991 by Peter G. W. Keen; all rights reserved. Also from "The Implications of Information Technology Infrastructure for Business Process Redesign," by M. Broadbent, P. Weill, and D. St. Clair, 1999, *MIS Quarterly, 23,* p. 164. Fig. 1.